Southern Living®

ANNUAL RECIPES COOKBOOK

20TH ANNIVERSARY EDITION

Southern Living

ANNUAL RECIPES COOKBOOK
20TH ANNIVERSARY EDITION

Oxmoor House.

© 1998 by Oxmoor House, Inc.
Book Division of Southern Progress Corporation
P.O. Box 2463, Birmingham, Alabama 35201

Library of Congress Catalog Number: 97-69573
ISBN: 0-8487-1688-4

Manufactured in the United States of America
First printing 1998

WE'RE HERE FOR YOU!

We at Oxmoor House are dedicated to serving you with reliable information that expands your imagination and enriches your life. We welcome your comments and suggestions. Please write us at:

Oxmoor House, Inc.
Editor, *Southern Living® Annual Recipes Cookbook,*
20th Anniversary Edition
2100 Lakeshore Drive
Birmingham, AL 35209

To order additional publications, call 1-205-877-6560.

We Want Your
FAVORITE RECIPES!

Southern Living cooks are the best cooks of all, and we want your secrets! Please send your favorite original recipes for main dishes, desserts, and everything in between, along with any hands-on tips and a sentence about why you like each recipe. We can't guarantee we'll print them in a cookbook, but if we do, we'll send you $10 and a free copy of the cookbook. Send each recipe on a separate page with your name, address, and daytime phone number to:

Cookbook Recipes
Oxmoor House
2100 Lakeshore Drive
Birmingham, AL 35209

SYMBOLS WITHIN THIS BOOK:

QUICK! indicates that a recipe can be prepared quickly or easily.

♥ indicates a light recipe with nutritional analysis or ingredient substitutions that will reduce the amount of calories, fat, cholesterol, or sodium.

Southern Living®

Executive Editor: Kaye Mabry Adams
Foods Editors: Elle Barrett, Susan Hawthorne Nash
Associate Foods Editors: Denise Gee, Jackie Mills, R.D.
Assistant Foods Editors: Cynthia Briscoe, Donna Florio,
    Monique Hicks, Diane Hogan, Andria Scott Hurst,
    Alison Lewis, Patty M. Vann
Test Kitchens Director: Vanessa Taylor Johnson
Assistant Test Kitchens Directors: Judy Feagin, Peggy Smith
Test Kitchens Staff: Margaret Monroe, Mary Allen Perry,
    Vanessa McNeil, Vie Warshaw
Administrative Assistant: Wanda T. Stephens
Editorial Assistant: April Tanner
Senior Foods Photographer: Charles Walton IV
Photographers: Ralph Anderson, Tina Cornett,
    William Dickey, J. Savage Gibson
Senior Photo Stylist: Cindy Manning Barr
Assistant Photo Stylists: Buffy Hargett, Mary Lyn Hill
Photo Services: Tracy Duncan, Tena Payne
Production Manager: Kenner Patton
Assistant Production Manager: Bradford Kachelhofer
Editorial Contributors: Trinda Gage, Telia Johnson, Jan Moon

Oxmoor House, Inc.

Editor-in-Chief: Nancy Fitzpatrick Wyatt
Senior Editor, Editorial Services: Olivia Kindig Wells
Art Director: James Boone

Southern Living® Annual Recipes Cookbook,
20th Anniversary Edition

Senior Foods Editor: Susan Payne Stabler
Foods Editor: Janice Krahn Hanby
Copy Editor: Donna Baldone
Editorial Assistant: Stacey Geary
Production Director: Phillip Lee
Associate Production Manager: Vanessa Cobbs Richardson
Production Assistant: Faye Porter Bonner
Indexer: Mary Ann Laurens
Designer: Carol Middleton

Cover: Nanny's Famous Coconut-Pineapple Cake (page 74)
*Back Cover: (clockwise from top left) Cranberry-Cornbread
    Stuffed Cornish Hens (page 288), Antipasto Kabobs (page 20),
    Three-Cheese Soufflés (page 140), and Bow Ties, Black Beans,
    and Key Limes (page 225)*
Page 2: Curried Pumpkin Soup (page 364)
*Page 5: Summery Chicken Salad (page 319) and Honey Angel
    Biscuit (page 63)*

CONTENTS

INTRODUCTION

20TH ANNIVERSARY EDITION

We're celebrating the 20th year of publication
of the ever-popular cookbook series,
Southern Living® Annual Recipes,
with this special keepsake edition.

The *Southern Living® Annual Recipes Cookbook, 20th Anniversary Edition* showcases over 1500 of the highest-rated recipes from *Southern Living® Annual Recipes*. Never before have so many exceptional *Southern Living* recipes been gathered into one handsome volume. Plus, by popular demand, the recipes are organized into traditional food chapters to help you find your favorites.

For easy reference, we included these convenient symbols, too:

QUICK! indicates that a recipe can be prepared quickly or easily.

♥ indicates a light recipe with nutritional analysis or ingredient substitutions that will reduce the amount of calories, fat, cholesterol, or sodium.

Take a few moments to get acquainted with the chapters. Preview some of the hearty main-dish recipes that begin on page 181 or the scrumptious desserts that begin on page 117. And don't miss a whole crop of Southern vegetables and other side dishes starting on page 379.

We thank you for sharing your recipes and stories through the years, and we know you'll enjoy this unparalleled collection.

The Editors

At right: Antipasto Kabobs (page 20)

Appetizers

CHILI-CHEESE STRAWS

2 cups (8 ounces) shredded
   Monterey Jack cheese with
   peppers, softened
½ cup butter or margarine,
   softened
1 cup all-purpose flour
½ cup yellow cornmeal
1 teaspoon chili powder
½ teaspoon salt
½ teaspoon ground cumin

• **Combine** softened cheese and butter, stirring until blended. Gradually add flour and remaining ingredients, stirring until mixture is no longer crumbly and will shape into a ball.
• **Use** a cookie press fitted with a star-shaped disk to shape dough into straws, following manufacturer's instructions. Or divide dough into fourths, and roll each portion into a ¼-inch-thick rectangle on wax paper. Cut into 2- x ½-inch strips with a knife or pastry wheel. Place on ungreased baking sheets.
• **Bake** at 375° for 8 minutes or until lightly browned. Transfer to wire racks to cool. **Yield:** about 8 dozen.

PARMESAN CHEESE STRAWS

A twist on the wine and cheese theme, these elegant appetizers are great paired with your favorite vino.

⅔ cup refrigerated shredded
   Parmesan cheese *
½ cup butter or margarine,
   softened
1 cup all-purpose flour
¼ teaspoon salt
¼ teaspoon ground red pepper
¼ cup milk
Pecan halves (optional)

• **Position** knife blade in food processor bowl; add cheese and butter. Process until blended. Add flour, salt, and ground red pepper; process about 30 seconds or until mixture forms a ball, stopping often to scrape down sides.
• **Divide** dough in half; roll each portion into a ⅛-inch-thick rectangle, and cut into 2- x ½-inch strips. Or shape dough

into ¾-inch balls; flatten each ball to about ⅛-inch thickness. Place on ungreased baking sheets; brush with milk. Top with pecan halves, if desired.
• **Bake** at 350° for 7 minutes for strips and 10 minutes for rounds or until lightly browned. Transfer to wire racks to cool. **Yield:** 5 dozen straws or 3 dozen wafers.

* Substitute ⅔ cup freshly grated Parmesan cheese plus an additional ¼ cup all-purpose flour for the refrigerated shredded Parmesan cheese.

Sue-Sue Hartstern
Louisville, Kentucky

VEGETABLE CRACKERS

5½ cups all-purpose flour,
   divided
2 (0.9-ounce) envelopes spring
   vegetable soup mix *
1 teaspoon baking soda
2 tablespoons butter or margarine,
   softened
1 large egg
2 cups buttermilk
½ teaspoon salt

• **Combine** 4½ cups flour, soup mix, and soda in a large mixing bowl; add butter and egg, beating at medium speed with an electric mixer until blended. Add buttermilk, beating well.
• **Stir** in enough remaining 1 cup flour to form a soft dough. Turn dough out onto a lightly floured surface, and knead 4 or 5 times.
• **Divide** dough into fourths; roll each portion into a 10- x 12-inch rectangle (about ¹⁄₁₆ inch thick). Cut into 2-inch squares, using a pastry wheel or pizza cutter, and place on lightly greased baking sheets. Prick with a fork; sprinkle with salt.
• **Bake** at 400° for 12 to 15 minutes or until golden. Transfer to wire racks to cool completely. **Yield:** 10 dozen.

* For spring vegetable soup mix, we used Knorr.

BLUE CHEESE CRISPS

2 (4-ounce) packages crumbled
   blue cheese
½ cup butter or margarine,
   softened
1⅓ cups all-purpose flour
⅓ cup poppy seeds
¼ teaspoon ground red pepper

• **Beat** cheese and butter at medium speed with an electric mixer until creamy. Add flour, poppy seeds, and pepper; beat until blended.
• **Divide** dough in half; shape each portion into a 9-inch log. Cover and chill 2 hours.
• **Cut** each log of dough into ¼-inch-thick slices, and place on ungreased baking sheets.
• **Bake** at 350° for 13 to 15 minutes or until golden. Transfer to wire racks to cool completely. **Yield:** 6 dozen.

Shirley M. Draper
Winter Park, Florida

JALAPEÑO NUT MIX

1 cup whole natural almonds
1 cup pecan halves
1 cup dry-roasted peanuts
1 cup Brazil nuts
¼ cup butter or margarine
⅓ cup jalapeño pepper sauce
1 tablespoon hot sauce
1 tablespoon Worcestershire
   sauce
1½ teaspoons garlic powder
1½ teaspoons salt
1 teaspoon dry mustard

• **Combine** first 4 ingredients in a 15- x 10- x 1-inch jellyroll pan.
• **Bake** at 325° for 10 minutes.
• **Combine** butter and remaining 6 ingredients in a saucepan; cook over medium heat, stirring constantly, until butter melts.
• **Pour** butter mixture over nuts, stirring to coat. Bake 20 additional minutes, stirring once. Spread nuts on paper towels to cool. **Yield:** 4 cups.

PESTO-SPICED NUTS

QUICK!

2 cups pecan halves
2 cups slivered almonds
3 tablespoons olive oil
1 (0.5-ounce) envelope pesto
  sauce mix

● **Combine** pecans and almonds; set aside.
● **Combine** oil and pesto mix, stirring well. Pour over nuts; stir until evenly coated. Spread evenly in a 15- x 10- x 1-inch jellyroll pan.
● **Bake** at 350° for 13 to 15 minutes or until toasted, stirring every 5 minutes. Remove from oven; cool on paper towels. **Yield:** 4 cups.

SWEET AND SPICY PECANS

QUICK!

You can make this easy appetizer a day ahead, and store it at room temperature in an airtight container.

2 cups pecan halves
2 tablespoons butter, melted
1 tablespoon sugar
½ teaspoon ground cumin
½ teaspoon chili powder
¼ teaspoon dried crushed red
  pepper
⅛ teaspoon salt

● **Toss** pecans in butter. Combine sugar and remaining 4 ingredients; sprinkle over pecans, tossing to coat. Spread in a single layer on a baking sheet; bake at 325° for 15 minutes, stirring occasionally. Cool. **Yield:** 2 cups.

APPLE DIP

QUICK!

1 (8-ounce) package cream cheese,
  softened
⅓ cup firmly packed brown sugar
1 (7.5-ounce) package almond
  brickle chips
¼ cup sugar
1 teaspoon vanilla extract

● **Combine** cream cheese and brown sugar, mixing well; let stand 15 minutes. Stir in almond brickle chips, sugar, and vanilla. Cover and chill up to 8 hours. Serve with apple and pear wedges. **Yield:** 2½ cups.

Everette Milford
Commerce, Georgia

FIESTA DIP

QUICK!

1 (10½-ounce) package corn
  chips, crushed
¼ cup butter or margarine,
  melted
2 (16-ounce) cans refried
  beans
1 (1¼-ounce) package taco
  seasoning mix
1 (6-ounce) container frozen
  avocado dip, thawed
1 (8-ounce) carton sour cream
3 (2¼-ounce) cans sliced ripe
  olives, undrained
2 medium tomatoes, seeded and
  chopped
2 (4.5-ounce) cans chopped green
  chiles, drained
1 (8-ounce) package Monterey
  Jack cheese with peppers,
  shredded
Garnish: fresh cilantro sprigs

● **Combine** corn chips and butter; press in bottom and 1 inch up sides of a lightly greased 9-inch springform pan.
● **Bake** at 350° for 10 minutes. Cool pan on a wire rack.
● **Combine** refried beans and taco seasoning mix, stirring well; spread over prepared crust. Layer avocado dip and next 5 ingredients over refried bean mixture; cover and chill 8 hours.
● **Place** on a serving plate, and remove sides of springform pan; garnish, if desired. Serve with large corn chips. **Yield:** 18 to 20 appetizer servings.

P.T. and Joe Ross
Jackson, Mississippi

GAZPACHO DIP

3 large tomatoes, chopped
3 firm ripe avocados, chopped
4 green onions, thinly sliced
1 (4.5-ounce) can chopped green
  chiles, undrained
1 (4-ounce) can chopped ripe
  olives, undrained
3 tablespoons vegetable oil
1½ tablespoons apple cider
  vinegar
1 teaspoon salt
1 teaspoon garlic salt
¼ teaspoon pepper

● **Combine** first 5 ingredients in a large bowl. Set aside.
● **Combine** oil and remaining 4 ingredients; drizzle over tomato mixture, and toss gently.
● **Cover** and chill up to 4 hours before serving. Serve dip with tortilla or corn chips. **Yield:** 5 cups.

Note: To serve dip as a flavorful salad, spoon evenly over shredded lettuce, and top with shredded cheese and sour cream.

The Texas Experience
Richardson Woman's Club
Richardson, Texas

INDONESIAN DIP

QUICK!

⅔ cup chunky peanut butter
½ cup firmly packed light brown
  sugar
½ cup fresh lemon juice
¼ cup chili-garlic paste
1 teaspoon soy sauce

● **Combine** all ingredients; cover and chill 24 hours. Serve dip with snow peas, Belgian endive, red bell pepper strips, and blanched asparagus. **Yield:** 1½ cups.

Mrs. Paul Smith
Longboat Key, Florida

PESTO DIP

QUICK!

1 (3½-ounce) jar pesto
1 cup plain nonfat yogurt
⅓ cup chopped dried tomatoes

• **Combine** all ingredients; cover and chill. Serve with assorted raw vegetables. **Yield:** 1⅓ cups.

EGGPLANT DIP

3 cups peeled, chopped eggplant
1 medium onion, chopped
1 cup sliced fresh mushrooms
⅓ cup chopped green bell
 pepper
2 to 3 cloves garlic, pressed
⅓ cup olive oil
1 (6-ounce) can tomato paste
1 (5¾-ounce) jar chopped green
 olives
2 tablespoons red wine vinegar
1½ teaspoons sugar
1 teaspoon salt
½ teaspoon cracked black
 peppercorns
¼ teaspoon hot sauce

• **Cook** first 5 ingredients in oil in a large skillet over medium-high heat 10 minutes or until tender, stirring often. Stir in tomato paste and remaining ingredients; bring to a boil.
• **Reduce** heat, and simmer 30 to 40 minutes or to desired thickness, stirring occasionally. Serve with French bread. **Yield:** 4 cups.

Judy H. Loveless
Memphis, Tennessee

SWISS-ONION DIP

1 (10-ounce) package frozen
 chopped onion, thawed
3 cups (12 ounces) shredded Swiss
 cheese
1 cup mayonnaise or salad
 dressing
1 tablespoon coarse-grained Dijon
 mustard
⅛ teaspoon pepper

• **Drain** onion on paper towels.
• **Combine** onion, cheese, and remaining ingredients. Spoon mixture into a 1-quart baking dish.
• **Bake** at 325° for 25 minutes or until bubbly and lightly browned. Serve dip with melba toast rounds. **Yield:** 4 cups.

♥ To reduce fat and calories in the dip, substitute reduced-fat mayonnaise for regular mayonnaise.

Kathy Sellers
Nashville, Tennessee

HUMMUS

QUICK!

Slather ½ cup of this creamy bean spread inside a pita to make a sandwich. Or serve it as a dip with pita chips or fresh vegetables.

1 (15-ounce) can chickpeas,
 drained
⅓ cup lemon juice
¼ cup tahini *
2 tablespoons chopped onion
2 tablespoons chopped fresh
 parsley
1 clove garlic
1 tablespoon reduced-sodium soy
 sauce
1½ teaspoons ground cumin
¼ teaspoon ground red pepper

• **Position** knife blade in food processor; add all ingredients, and process until smooth. **Yield:** 2 cups.

Joan Ranzini
Waynesboro, Virginia

* Tahini is a thick paste made from sesame seeds. You can find tahini in the peanut butter section of most large supermarkets.

♥ Per ½-cup serving: Calories 195
Fat 9.2g Cholesterol 0mg
Sodium 385mg

CREAMY DRIED TOMATO HUMMUS
(pictured at right)

QUICK!

1 (15-ounce) can chickpeas, rinsed
 and drained *
1 cup oil-packed dried tomatoes,
 drained
1 clove garlic, chopped
½ cup mayonnaise or salad
 dressing
¼ cup freshly grated Parmesan
 cheese
2 tablespoons lemon juice
¼ teaspoon dried basil
⅛ teaspoon ground red
 pepper
Garnish: chopped oil-packed dried
 tomatoes

• **Position** knife blade in food processor bowl; add all ingredients except garnish. Process until smooth, stopping once to scrape down sides. Garnish, if desired. Serve with assorted raw vegetables and crackers. **Yield:** 2 cups.

* Chickpeas are also called garbanzo beans. Look for them in the canned vegetable section at your grocery store.

Krista Becker
Nashville, Tennessee

BLACK-EYED PEA CON QUESO

½ cup butter or margarine
1 large onion, finely chopped
2 cloves garlic, pressed
1 (16-ounce) loaf process cheese
 spread, cubed
5 jalapeño peppers, unseeded and
 chopped
2 (15.8-ounce) cans black-eyed
 peas, drained

• **Melt** butter in a Dutch oven; add onion and garlic, and cook until tender, stirring often.
• **Add** cheese, and cook over low heat, stirring constantly, until cheese melts.
• **Stir** in jalapeño pepper and peas; cook until thoroughly heated, stirring often. Serve with tortilla chips. **Yield:** 3 cups.

Creamy Dried Tomato Hummus

FLORENTINE ARTICHOKE DIP

1 (10-ounce) package frozen
    chopped spinach, thawed
2 (6-ounce) jars marinated
    artichoke hearts, undrained
3 large cloves garlic, minced
1½ (8-ounce) packages cream
    cheese, softened
1 cup grated Parmesan cheese
½ cup mayonnaise
2 tablespoons lemon juice
1½ cups fine, dry breadcrumbs

• **Drain** spinach; press between layers
of paper towels. Drain and chop artichoke hearts.
• **Combine** spinach, artichoke hearts,
garlic, and next 4 ingredients, stirring
well. Spoon into a lightly greased 11- x
7- x 1½-inch baking dish; sprinkle with
breadcrumbs.
• **Bake** at 375° for 25 minutes; serve
with assorted crackers or breadsticks.
Yield: 4 cups.

Tamora Cornwall
Charlotte, North Carolina

ONE-MINUTE SALSA

QUICK!

1 (10-ounce) can diced tomatoes
    and green chiles, undrained
1 (14½-ounce) can stewed
    tomatoes, undrained
½ to 1 teaspoon pepper
½ teaspoon garlic salt

• **Combine** all ingredients in container
of an electric blender; process 30 seconds. Serve salsa with tortilla chips.
Yield: 3 cups.

Debbie Jones
Lewisville, Texas

BLACK BEAN-CORN SALSA

3 ears fresh white corn
¾ cup water
3 medium tomatoes, peeled,
    seeded, and finely chopped
2 jalapeño peppers, seeded and
    minced
2 (15-ounce) cans black beans,
    rinsed and drained
1 cup chopped fresh cilantro
⅓ cup fresh lime juice
¼ teaspoon salt
¼ teaspoon freshly ground
    pepper
2 avocados, finely chopped

• **Cut** corn from cob, and place in a
saucepan; add water, and bring to a boil.
Cover, reduce heat, and simmer 6 to 7
minutes or until tender. Drain corn;
transfer to a large bowl.
• **Add** tomato and next 6 ingredients to
corn, stirring gently. Cover and chill.
• **Stir** avocado into corn mixture, and
serve with tortilla chips. **Yield:** 8 cups.

Note: You can double recipe, if desired.
Stop and Smell the Rosemary:
Recipes and Traditions to Remember
Junior League of Houston, Texas

ROASTED TOMATO SALSA

12 plum tomatoes
2 cloves garlic, unpeeled
1 small onion, quartered
1 medium jalapeño pepper
1½ tablespoons olive oil
1 teaspoon ground cumin
¼ teaspoon salt
3 tablespoons fresh lime
    juice
¼ cup chopped fresh cilantro

• **Toss** first 4 ingredients with olive oil;
spread vegetables evenly in a 13- x 9- x
2-inch pan. Broil 5½ inches from heat
(with electric oven door partially
opened) 10 minutes or until vegetables
are charred; cool.
• **Peel** garlic, discarding skins. Remove
and discard tomato cores. Remove
and discard stem (but not seeds) from
pepper.

• **Position** knife blade in food processor bowl; add roasted vegetables. Pulse
4 times or until coarsely chopped. Stir in
cumin and remaining ingredients. Serve
with tortilla chips. **Yield:** 3 cups.

Stanlay Webber
Winston-Salem, North Carolina

AMBROSIA SPREAD

QUICK!

1 (11-ounce) can mandarin
    oranges, drained
1 (8-ounce) container cream
    cheese with pineapple,
    softened
¼ cup flaked coconut, toasted
¼ cup slivered almonds, chopped
    and toasted

• **Reserve** 3 orange sections for garnish.
Chop remaining orange sections, and
set aside.
• **Stir** together cream cheese, coconut,
and almonds. Fold in chopped oranges.
• **Arrange** reserved orange sections on
top. Cover and chill. Serve spread with
date nut bread, banana bread, or gingersnaps. **Yield:** 1⅔ cups.

Jennifer Mungo
Columbia, South Carolina

BUTTERY CHEESE SPREAD

QUICK!

1 clove garlic
2 (8-ounce) packages cream
    cheese, softened
1 cup butter or margarine,
    softened
1 teaspoon dried oregano
¼ teaspoon dried basil
¼ teaspoon dried dillweed
¼ teaspoon dried marjoram
¼ teaspoon dried thyme
¼ teaspoon pepper

• **Position** knife blade in food processor bowl; add garlic. Process until finely
chopped. Add cream cheese and remaining ingredients; process until
smooth, stopping twice to scrape down
sides. **Yield:** about 3 cups.

Note: You can store cheese mixture, covered, in refrigerator up to 1 week or freeze up to 3 months.

Brenda H. Rohe
Charlotte, North Carolina

FETA CHEESE SPREAD

Paula's spread can be made ahead. "My husband is Greek and loves feta cheese, so I'm always looking for ways to use it," Paula says.

1 (8-ounce) package reduced-fat cream cheese, softened
2 (4-ounce) packages crumbled feta cheese
2 tablespoons skim milk
10 fresh mint leaves
1 to 2 cloves garlic
Garnishes: chopped tomato, chopped cucumber, sliced green onions

• **Position** knife blade in food processor bowl. Add cheeses, skim milk, mint, and garlic, and process until smooth. Transfer to a serving bowl. Garnish, if desired. Serve with toasted baguette slices or fresh vegetables. **Yield:** 2 cups.
Paula Covault
LaGrange, Kentucky

♥ Per 2-tablespoon serving: Calories 76
Fat 6.4g Cholesterol 24mg
Sodium 216mg

CORN AND WALNUT SPREAD

QUICK!

2 (8-ounce) packages cream cheese, softened
¼ cup fresh lime juice
1 tablespoon ground cumin
1 teaspoon salt
1 teaspoon ground black pepper
½ teaspoon ground red pepper
1 (8-ounce) can whole kernel corn, drained
1 cup chopped walnuts, toasted
1 (4.5-ounce) can chopped green chiles, drained
4 green onions, chopped

• **Combine** first 6 ingredients. Stir in corn and remaining ingredients. Cover and chill up to 8 hours. Serve with crackers, or use as a stuffing for celery or cherry tomatoes. **Yield:** 4 cups.
Carrie Easley
Dallas, Texas

BUTTERY HAM SPREAD

QUICK!

1 cup butter or margarine, softened
1 (8-ounce) package cream cheese, softened
2 (5-ounce) cans tender chunk ham, drained and flaked
2 tablespoons chopped green onions
1 tablespoon lemon juice
¼ teaspoon salt
⅛ teaspoon pepper

• **Combine** butter and cream cheese in a large mixing bowl; beat with an electric mixer until creamy. Add ham and remaining ingredients, mixing well. Serve with crackers. **Yield:** 4 cups.
Sue-Sue Hartstern
Louisville, Kentucky

CRABMEAT MOUSSE

1 envelope unflavored gelatin
3 tablespoons cold water
¼ cup mayonnaise or salad dressing
2 tablespoons fresh lime juice
2 tablespoons fresh lemon juice
1 tablespoon chopped fresh parsley
1 tablespoon chopped fresh or frozen chives
1 tablespoon prepared mustard
¼ teaspoon salt
¼ teaspoon pepper
2 cups fresh lump crabmeat
¾ cup whipping cream, whipped
2 or 3 limes, thinly sliced
2 avocados, mashed
2 tablespoons fresh lime juice
1 tablespoon chopped fresh or frozen chives

• **Sprinkle** gelatin over cold water in a small saucepan; let stand 1 minute. Cook over low heat, stirring until gelatin dissolves (about 2 minutes).
• **Combine** gelatin mixture, mayonnaise, and next 7 ingredients in a large bowl. Drain crabmeat, removing any bits of shell. Fold crabmeat and whipped cream into gelatin mixture; spoon mixture into a lightly greased 4-cup (8-inch) ring mold.
• **Cover** and chill until set.
• **Unmold** onto a serving plate, and arrange lime slices around edge.
• **Combine** avocado and 2 tablespoons lime juice; spoon into center of mousse, and sprinkle with 1 tablespoon chives. Serve with assorted crackers. **Yield:** 20 to 25 appetizer servings.
Jim and Jane Bowyer
Maitland, Florida

CURRIED CHICKEN MOUSSE

1 envelope unflavored gelatin
1 cup cold water, divided
2 teaspoons chicken-flavored bouillon granules
¼ teaspoon salt
¼ teaspoon ground red pepper
1 teaspoon curry powder
2 teaspoons minced onion
1½ cups finely chopped cooked chicken
¼ cup finely chopped celery
1 (2-ounce) jar diced pimiento, drained
1 tablespoon chopped fresh parsley
1 cup whipping cream

• **Sprinkle** gelatin over ½ cup cold water in a saucepan; let stand 1 minute. Cook over low heat, stirring until gelatin dissolves (about 2 minutes).
• **Add** bouillon granules and next 3 ingredients, stirring until granules dissolve; remove from heat. Stir in remaining ½ cup water and onion; chill until consistency of unbeaten egg white.
• **Stir** in chicken and remaining ingredients; spoon into a lightly oiled 4-cup mold. Cover and chill at least 8 hours. Unmold and serve with crackers. **Yield:** 18 to 20 appetizer servings.

BASIL-CHEESE TERRINE

1 (8-ounce) package cream cheese, softened
1 (4-ounce) package crumbled blue cheese
1 cup loosely packed torn fresh spinach
¾ cup loosely packed fresh flat-leaf parsley leaves
¼ cup loosely packed fresh basil leaves
2 cloves garlic, minced
¼ teaspoon salt
¼ cup olive oil
1 cup freshly grated Parmesan cheese
¼ cup chopped pine nuts
½ cup oil-packed dried tomatoes, sliced
Garnishes: fresh basil sprigs, cherry tomato wedges

• **Position** knife blade in food processor bowl; add cream cheese and blue cheese, and process until smooth, stopping once to scrape down sides. Spoon into a small bowl, and set aside.
• **Add** spinach and next 4 ingredients to processor bowl, and process until finely chopped, stopping once to scrape down sides. With processor running, pour oil in a slow, steady stream through food chute. Stir in Parmesan cheese and chopped pine nuts.
• **Line** a 7½- x 3- x 2-inch loafpan with plastic wrap, allowing edges to extend over sides of pan. Spread half of cheese mixture in loafpan; top with half of tomatoes. Spread with pesto mixture; top with remaining tomatoes, and spread with remaining cheese mixture. Cover with plastic wrap; chill 24 hours.
• **Let** stand at room temperature 30 minutes; invert onto a serving platter. Serve with assorted crackers and breadsticks. Garnish, if desired. **Yield:** 16 appetizer servings.

Kathy G. Mezrano
Kathy G. & Co.
Birmingham, Alabama

ALMOND-RASPBERRY BRIE

QUICK!

1 (12-ounce) wedge Brie cheese
2 tablespoons seedless red raspberry jam
1 tablespoon Chambord or other raspberry-flavored liqueur (optional)
1½ teaspoons brown sugar
3 tablespoons sliced almonds
1 tablespoon honey

• **Slice** Brie in half horizontally. Place bottom half of Brie on a microwave-safe serving plate.
• **Combine** jam and Chambord, if desired; spread on top of cheese, leaving a 1-inch margin around edge; top with remaining cheese half.
• **Sprinkle** with brown sugar and almonds, and drizzle with honey.
• **Microwave** at HIGH 1 minute or just until soft. Serve Brie immediately with wafer cookies or gingersnaps. **Yield:** 4 to 6 appetizer servings.

PARMESAN-COATED BRIE

1 large egg, lightly beaten
1 tablespoon water
½ cup Italian-seasoned breadcrumbs
¼ cup freshly grated Parmesan cheese
1 (15-ounce) round Brie cheese with herbs
¼ cup vegetable oil
Garnish: fresh rosemary sprigs

• **Combine** egg and water in a shallow dish; set aside.
• **Combine** breadcrumbs and Parmesan cheese in a shallow dish; set aside.
• **Dip** Brie in egg mixture, turning to coat all sides. Place in breadcrumb mixture, turning to coat. Repeat procedure.
• **Chill** at least 1 hour.
• **Cook** Brie in hot oil in a heavy skillet over medium heat 2 minutes on each side or until golden. Garnish, if desired. Serve with crackers or French bread. **Yield:** 4 to 6 appetizer servings.

Sue-Sue Hartstern
Louisville, Kentucky

BRIE IN BRAIDED BREAD RING

⅓ cup sliced almonds
⅓ cup sesame seeds *
1 (35.2-ounce) round Brie cheese
3 tablespoons apricot or pineapple preserves
½ cup dried cranberries
½ cup diced candied pineapple
Braided Bread Ring

• **Place** almonds and sesame seeds in shallow pans; bake at 350° for 5 to 10 minutes or until toasted, stirring occasionally (do not burn).
• **Trim** rind from top of Brie; brush preserves over top. Arrange almonds, sesame seeds, cranberries, and pineapple over preserves. Place Brie in center of Braided Bread Ring; serve with toasted French baguette slices. **Yield:** 20 appetizer servings.

Braided Bread Ring

½ (32-ounce) package frozen bread dough, thawed

• **Place** two large baking sheets on oven rack, overlapping edges so that width of baking sheets is at least 15 inches; grease and set aside.
• **Divide** dough into thirds; roll each portion into a 36-inch rope, and braid. Grease outside of a 9-inch round cakepan; place in center of prepared baking sheets. Wrap braid around cakepan, pinching ends to seal.
• **Cover** and let rise in a warm place (85°), free from drafts, 1 hour or until doubled in bulk.
• **Bake** at 375° for 18 to 20 minutes or until golden. Remove from oven, and let cool on a wire rack. **Yield:** 1 (15-inch) bread ring.

* You can substitute poppy seeds for sesame seeds; do not toast poppy seeds.

Kathy G. Mezrano
Kathy G. & Co.
Birmingham, Alabama

KAHLÚA-PECAN BRIE

QUICK!

1 (15-ounce) round Brie cheese
½ cup finely chopped pecans, toasted
2 tablespoons Kahlúa or other coffee-flavored liqueur
1½ tablespoons brown sugar

● **Remove** rind from top of cheese, cutting to within ½ inch of outside edges. Place on an oven-safe dish.
● **Combine** pecans, Kahlúa, and brown sugar; spread over top of cheese. Bake at 350° for 3 to 5 minutes or just until soft. Serve immediately with apple slices or gingersnaps. **Yield:** 8 appetizer servings.

Note: To make ahead, assemble appetizer, and chill up to 4 hours; let stand at room temperature 10 to 15 minutes before baking. You may also slice apples ahead, and chill in a zip-top plastic bag with orange or pineapple juice to cover to prevent browning.

Janis Bevers
Tulsa, Oklahoma

MARINATED CHEESE

To make these appetizers ahead, marinate the cheese overnight in the refrigerator. You can also toast the bread slices a day ahead and store at room temperature wrapped in towels. Assemble the cheese and toasted bread right before your party.

¾ pound fresh mozzarella cheese in brine *
1 (8-ounce) bottle olive oil vinaigrette
1 clove garlic, crushed
¼ teaspoon freshly ground pepper
1 French baguette, thinly sliced
Garnishes: cherry tomato slices, fresh basil leaves, fresh parsley sprigs

● **Remove** cheese from brine; discard brine. Cut cheese into ¼-inch-thick slices. Place cheese in a single layer in a shallow dish.

● **Combine** vinaigrette, garlic, and pepper; pour over cheese. Cover and chill 8 hours.
● **Place** bread slices on a baking sheet. Bake at 350° for 8 minutes or until lightly toasted, turning once.
● **Drain** cheese. Place 1 cheese slice on each bread slice. Garnish, if desired. **Yield:** 20 appetizer servings.

✱ Substitute 1 (8-ounce) package mozzarella cheese for fresh.

MANGO CHUTNEY TORTA

1 cup 1% low-fat cottage cheese
2 (8-ounce) packages cream cheese, softened
1 teaspoon curry powder
1 (9-ounce) jar mango chutney, divided
1 cup dry roasted peanuts, divided
1 cup sliced green onions, divided
1 cup golden raisins, divided
Garnishes: sliced green onions, chopped dry roasted peanuts, toasted coconut

● **Position** knife blade in food processor bowl; add cottage cheese, and process until smooth, stopping once to scrape down sides. Add cream cheese and curry; process until smooth. Set aside half of cottage cheese mixture.
● **Add** 2 tablespoons chutney and half each of peanuts, green onions, and raisins to remaining cheese mixture; pulse 3 or 4 times or until coarsely chopped.
● **Spoon** mixture into an 8½- x 4½- x 3-inch loafpan lined with plastic wrap; spread with ¼ cup chutney.
● **Pulse** reserved cheese mixture, 2 tablespoons chutney, and remaining half of peanuts, green onions, and raisins 3 or 4 times or until coarsely chopped; spoon over torta. Cover and chill 8 hours.
● **Invert** onto a serving plate; garnish, if desired. Serve with assorted crackers. **Yield:** 25 appetizer servings.

Kathy G. Mezrano
Kathy G. & Co.
Birmingham, Alabama

FIESTA CHEESECAKE

1½ cups finely crushed tortilla chips
¼ cup butter or margarine, melted
2 (8-ounce) packages cream cheese, softened
1 (3-ounce) package cream cheese, softened
2 large eggs
2½ cups (10 ounces) shredded Monterey Jack cheese with peppers
1 (4.5-ounce) can chopped green chiles, drained
¼ teaspoon ground red pepper
1 (8-ounce) carton sour cream
½ cup chopped green bell pepper
½ cup chopped yellow bell pepper
½ cup chopped red bell pepper
½ cup chopped green onions
1 medium tomato, chopped
2 tablespoons finely chopped ripe olives
2 bunches fresh cilantro or parsley (optional)

● **Combine** tortilla chips and butter; press in bottom of a lightly greased 9-inch springform pan. Bake at 325° for 15 minutes. Cool on a wire rack.
● **Beat** cream cheese at medium speed with an electric mixer 3 minutes or until fluffy; add eggs, one at a time, beating after each addition. Stir in shredded cheese, chiles, and ground red pepper.
● **Pour** mixture into prepared pan, and bake at 325° for 30 minutes. Cool 10 minutes on a wire rack. Gently run a knife around edge of pan to release sides; carefully remove sides of pan. Let cool completely on wire rack.
● **Spread** sour cream evenly over top; cover and chill.
● **Arrange** green bell pepper and next 5 ingredients on top as desired. Place on a bed of fresh cilantro or parsley, if desired. Serve with tortilla chips. **Yield:** 1 (9-inch) cheesecake or 25 appetizer servings.

Libby and Jim Collet
Dallas, Texas

Goat Cheese With Sun-Dried Tomatoes and Rosemary

GOAT CHEESE WITH SUN-DRIED TOMATOES AND ROSEMARY
(pictured at left)

6 dried tomato halves
3 cloves garlic, pressed
2 tablespoons olive oil
1 tablespoon chopped fresh
    rosemary or dried rosemary
1 French baguette, thinly sliced
Olive oil
1 (11-ounce) package goat
    cheese
Garnish: fresh rosemary sprigs

• **Cover** tomato with boiling water; let stand 5 minutes. Drain and chop. Combine tomato, garlic, oil, and rosemary; cover and chill up to 4 hours.
• **Brush** baguette rounds with additional olive oil. Place on an ungreased baking sheet, and bake at 350° for 8 minutes or until lightly toasted.
• **Just** before serving, place goat cheese on a serving plate, and top with tomato mixture. Serve with baguette rounds, and garnish, if desired. **Yield:** 8 appetizer servings.

Note: Tomatoes should not be marinated more than 4 hours.

The Lucullan Society
Lynchburg, Virginia

PEPPERED GOAT CHEESE
QUICK!

1 (3-ounce) package goat
    cheese
1 to 2 teaspoons freshly cracked
    pepper
2 to 3 teaspoons olive oil
Garnishes: fresh rosemary sprigs,
    fresh oregano sprigs

• **Roll** goat cheese in pepper to coat; drizzle with olive oil. Garnish, if desired, and serve with French baguette slices. **Yield:** 2 to 4 appetizer servings.

Bill Keller
Birmingham, Alabama

OREGANO CHEESE PUFFS

Fontina cheese contains about 45% butterfat, so it's smooth in texture and is packed with a creamy rich flavor – definitely worth a try.

¾ cup milk
3 tablespoons butter or margarine
¾ cup all-purpose flour
½ teaspoon salt
⅛ teaspoon pepper
3 large eggs
½ cup (2 ounces) shredded
    fontina cheese, divided
1½ teaspoons dried oregano

• **Bring** milk and butter to a boil in a medium saucepan. Reduce heat to low; add flour, salt, and pepper all at once, stirring vigorously until mixture leaves sides of pan and forms a smooth ball. Remove from heat, and let cool 5 to 10 minutes.
• **Add** eggs, one at a time, beating with a wooden spoon after each addition. Stir in ¼ cup cheese and oregano. Drop by level tablespoonfuls onto greased baking sheets.
• **Bake** cheese puffs at 400° for 18 minutes. Sprinkle with remaining ¼ cup cheese, and bake 2 to 3 additional minutes. Serve immediately. **Yield:** 2½ dozen.

Valerie Stutsman
Norfolk, Virginia

SPINACH-ARTICHOKE-TOMATO PUFFS

1 (10-ounce) package frozen
    chopped spinach, thawed
1 (14-ounce) can artichoke hearts,
    drained
1 (8-ounce) jar dried tomatoes in
    oil, drained
1 (3-ounce) package goat cheese
¼ teaspoon salt
¼ teaspoon pepper
1½ (17¼-ounce) packages frozen
    puff pastry sheets, thawed

• **Drain** spinach well, pressing between layers of paper towels to remove excess moisture.

• **Position** knife blade in food processor bowl; add spinach, artichoke hearts, and tomato. Pulse 5 times or until chopped, stopping often to scrape down sides. Add goat cheese, salt, and pepper; process until blended. Set aside.
• **Roll** 1 pastry sheet into a 15- x 12-inch rectangle on a surface sprinkled lightly with cornmeal. Cut into 3-inch squares.
• **Spoon** about 1 tablespoon spinach mixture in center of each square. Fold all corners toward center, slightly overlapping edges.
• **Grease** baking sheets, and sprinkle with cornmeal. Place pastries on baking sheets. Repeat procedure with remaining puff pastry and spinach mixture.
• **Bake** at 400° for 12 to 15 minutes. Serve immediately. **Yield:** 5 dozen.

Chef Jim Napolitano
Cumberland Club
Nashville, Tennessee

ST. LOUIS TOASTED RAVIOLI

2 tablespoons milk
1 large egg, lightly beaten
¾ cup dry Italian-seasoned
    breadcrumbs
½ teaspoon salt (optional)
½ (27.5-ounce) package frozen
    cheese-filled ravioli, thawed *
Vegetable oil
Grated Parmesan cheese
Spaghetti or pizza sauce

• **Combine** milk and egg. Place breadcrumbs and salt, if desired, in a shallow bowl. Dip ravioli in milk mixture; coat with breadcrumb mixture.
• **Pour** oil to depth of 2 inches into a Dutch oven; heat to 350°. Fry ravioli, a few at a time, 1 minute on each side or until golden. Drain on paper towels.
• **Sprinkle** with Parmesan cheese, and serve immediately with warm spaghetti or pizza sauce. **Yield:** about 2 dozen.

* You can substitute refrigerated fresh ravioli for frozen ravioli. Vary the flavor by using sausage, chicken, Italian, or other filling varieties.

Charlie Gitto Jr.
Charlie Gitto's
St. Louis, Missouri

HOT ARTICHOKE CROSTINI

QUICK!

Crostini is a popular Italian appetizer literally meaning "little crusts." It's simple toasted bread crowned with wonderfully gooey cheese and surprising bits of color and flavor.

1 French baguette
1 cup mayonnaise
1 cup grated Parmesan cheese
1 (14-ounce) can artichoke hearts, drained and chopped
1 (4.5-ounce) can chopped green chiles, drained
2 cloves garlic, minced
Garnishes: chopped green onions, chopped tomato, cooked and crumbled bacon

• **Cut** baguette into 36 (¼- to ½-inch) slices; place, cut side down, on an aluminum foil-lined baking sheet.
• **Bake** at 400° for 5 minutes or until lightly browned.
• **Combine** mayonnaise and next 4 ingredients; spread on bread slices.
• **Bake** at 400° for 5 minutes or until cheese melts. Garnish, if desired, and serve immediately. **Yield:** 3 dozen.

Johnnie Capone
Baton Rouge, Louisiana

ALMOND-BACON-CHEESE CROSTINI

QUICK!

1 French baguette
2 slices bacon, cooked and crumbled
1 cup (4 ounces) shredded Monterey Jack cheese
⅓ cup mayonnaise
¼ cup sliced almonds, toasted
1 tablespoon chopped green onions
¼ teaspoon salt
Garnish: toasted sliced almonds

• **Cut** baguette into 36 (¼- to ½-inch) slices; place, cut side down, on an aluminum foil-lined baking sheet.
• **Bake** at 400° for 5 minutes or until lightly browned.

• **Combine** bacon and next 5 ingredients; spread on bread slices.
• **Bake** at 400° for 5 minutes or until cheese melts. Garnish, if desired, and serve immediately. **Yield:** 3 dozen.

Valerie Stutsman
Norfolk, Virginia

MOZZARELLA CROSTINI

1 (16-ounce) loaf unsliced Italian bread
⅓ cup olive oil
1 clove garlic, finely chopped
¼ teaspoon salt
¼ teaspoon pepper
½ cup sliced green onions
5 to 7 plum tomatoes, cut into 36 slices
1½ cups (6 ounces) shredded mozzarella cheese
Garnish: sliced green onions

• **Cut** bread into 36 (¼- to ½-inch) slices; place, cut side down, on an aluminum foil-lined baking sheet.
• **Bake** at 400° for 5 minutes or until lightly browned.
• **Combine** olive oil and next 3 ingredients. Brush on bread slices. Top evenly with ½ cup sliced green onions; top each with a tomato slice. Sprinkle with cheese.
• **Bake** at 400° for 5 to 7 minutes or until cheese melts. Garnish, if desired, and serve immediately. **Yield:** 3 dozen.

Mrs. E. W. Hanley
Palm Harbor, Florida

SWISS-BLUE CHEESE CROSTINI

QUICK!

1 French baguette
4 cloves garlic, pressed
¼ cup olive oil
12 oil-packed dried tomatoes, halved
1 cup (4 ounces) shredded Swiss cheese
1 (4-ounce) package crumbled blue cheese
¼ cup chopped fresh parsley

• **Slice** bread into 24 (¼- to ½-inch) slices, and place on an aluminum foil-lined baking sheet.
• **Bake** at 400° for 5 minutes or until lightly browned.
• **Combine** garlic and oil; brush on bread slices. Top each slice with a tomato half; set aside.
• **Combine** cheeses and parsley; spoon on top of tomatoes.
• **Bake** at 400° for 5 minutes or until cheese melts. Serve immediately. **Yield:** 2 dozen.

Helen H. Maurer
Christmas, Florida

MAJORCAN MUSHROOM TAPAS

This appetizer won the $12,000, 16-day trip to Spain in the 1994 Bays English Muffin Contest.

⅓ cup finely chopped shallots
1 teaspoon minced garlic
1 to 2 tablespoons olive oil
¾ pound mixed fresh mushrooms, thinly sliced *
2 tablespoons dry sherry or Madeira
½ teaspoon salt
1 tablespoon finely chopped fresh thyme or 1 teaspoon dried thyme
5 English muffins, split and lightly toasted
12 ounces mascarpone or cream cheese, softened
Almond-Garlic Streusel
Garnish: fresh thyme

• **Cook** shallot and garlic in oil over medium-high heat, stirring constantly, until tender. Add mushrooms, sherry, and salt; cook, stirring constantly, 10 to 12 minutes or until mushrooms are tender. Stir in thyme, and cook until most of liquid evaporates.
• **Spread** muffins with cheese; top evenly with mushroom mixture. Place muffins on a baking sheet.
• **Bake** at 350° for 5 minutes or until thoroughly heated. Remove appetizers from oven, and spoon Almond-Garlic Streusel evenly over mushroom

mixture. Garnish, if desired. **Yield:** 10 appetizer servings.

* Substitute button, crimini, oyster, and/or shiitake mushrooms for mixed fresh mushrooms.

Almond-Garlic Streusel

QUICK!

1　English muffin
2½　teaspoons olive oil
3　cloves garlic, minced
¼　teaspoon freshly ground black
　　　pepper
¼　cup chopped slivered
　　　almonds

● **Place** English muffin in container of an electric blender; process until fine crumbs.
● **Combine** crumbs, olive oil, and remaining ingredients in a large skillet; cook over medium-high heat 3 to 5 minutes or until crumbs and almonds are golden. Spread on a paper plate or paper towel to cool. **Yield:** 1 cup.

OVEN-BAKED TOMATO APPETIZERS

1　French baguette
12　plum tomatoes (1¼ pounds)
2 to 3　teaspoons olive oil
½　teaspoon sugar
½　teaspoon salt
1　teaspoon dried thyme
½　cup crumbled feta cheese

● **Cut** 24 (½-inch) slices from baguette; place on a baking sheet. Bake at 400° for 8 minutes; cool.
● **Cut** tomatoes in half lengthwise; scoop out seeds and pulp, and reserve for another use. Place tomato halves, cut side up, on a rack in broiler pan; brush lightly with olive oil. Sprinkle tomato halves evenly with sugar, salt, and thyme.
● **Bake** at 350° for 30 minutes. Place tomato halves, cut side up, on bread; sprinkle with cheese. Serve immediately. **Yield:** 2 dozen.

Jim Griffith
Guntersville, Alabama

GRILLED EGGPLANT APPETIZER

2　(1-pound) eggplants, peeled and
　　　cut into ½-inch slices
½　teaspoon salt
½　cup coarsely chopped fresh
　　　basil
2　cloves garlic, minced
1　tablespoon olive oil
Vegetable cooking spray
¼　teaspoon ground red pepper
1　(22-inch) French baguette, cut
　　　into ½-inch slices
4　plum tomatoes, each cut into
　　　10 slices
⅓　cup freshly grated Parmesan
　　　cheese

● **Sprinkle** eggplant with salt, and let stand 30 minutes.
● **Combine** basil, garlic, and olive oil; set aside.
● **Rinse** eggplant slices, and pat dry.
● **Coat** food rack with cooking spray; place rack on grill over medium coals (300° to 350°). Place eggplant slices on rack in a single layer.
● **Cook,** without grill lid, 8 to 10 minutes on each side. Place half of eggplant slices in an airtight container, and sprinkle with basil mixture; top with remaining eggplant slices. Cover and chill 8 hours.
● **Position** knife blade in food processor bowl; add eggplant mixture and red pepper. Process until smooth, stopping once to scrape down sides.
● **Spread** about 1½ teaspoons eggplant mixture on each of 40 baguette slices, and top each with a tomato slice. Sprinkle evenly with cheese.
● **Broil** 5½ inches from heat (with electric oven door partially opened) 2 to 3 minutes or until cheese melts. Serve immediately. **Yield:** 40 appetizers.

♥ Per appetizer: Calories 41
Fat 0.8g　Cholesterol 1mg
Sodium 99mg

FRIED WONTON ENVELOPES

Carol always serves these with her own Guacamole Dip, but you can buy guacamole in the dairy case to save time.

1　(8-ounce) package Monterey
　　　Jack cheese with peppers,
　　　cut into 24 (1- x 1- x ½-inch)
　　　pieces
24　small wonton wrappers
Vegetable cooking spray
Vegetable oil
Guacamole Dip (optional)

● **Place** 1 cheese cube in center of each wonton wrapper. Moisten edges of wrapper with water. Fold corners of wrapper to center, enclosing filling and overlapping edges slightly.
● **Place** wontons on sheets of wax paper sprayed with cooking spray; cover wontons with additional wax paper to prevent drying out.
● **Pour** oil to depth of 3 inches into a Dutch oven; heat to 350°. Fry wontons, 3 or 4 at a time, until golden on each side, turning once. Drain on paper towels. Serve immediately with Guacamole Dip, if desired. **Yield:** 2 dozen.

Guacamole Dip

QUICK!

2　large ripe avocados, mashed
3　tablespoons fresh lime juice
½　teaspoon salt
1　tablespoon chopped fresh
　　　cilantro or ½ teaspoon dried
　　　cilantro
2　tablespoons finely chopped
　　　green onions
3　tablespoons mayonnaise or salad
　　　dressing

● **Combine** all ingredients; cover and chill. **Yield:** 1¼ cups.

Carol Barclay
Portland, Texas

ROASTED GARLIC CANAPÉS

Don't limit yourself by only using this roasted garlic mixture for fancy canapés. It's just as good served as a spread for crackers.

2 heads garlic
2 tablespoons olive oil
2 (8-ounce) packages cream cheese, softened
½ cup butter or margarine, softened
¾ teaspoon salt
Assorted fresh vegetables and toasted breads
Garnishes: assorted fresh herb sprigs, sliced citrus wedges, sliced olives

• **Cut** off pointed end of garlic heads, leaving tight outer covering intact. Place garlic heads, cut side up, on a square of aluminum foil or in a garlic roaster. Drizzle with olive oil; wrap in foil or cover with lid.
• **Bake** at 350° for 1 hour or until golden. Cool.
• **Squeeze** out pulp from each clove.
• **Position** knife blade in food processor bowl; add garlic pulp. Process until smooth, stopping once to scrape down sides. Add cream cheese; pulse 2 or 3 times, stopping once to scrape down sides.
• **Add** butter and salt; process 1 minute or until smooth, stopping once to scrape down sides. Store in the refrigerator in an airtight container up to 5 days. Pipe onto vegetables and breads. Garnish, if desired. **Yield:** 2⅔ cups.

Note: To prepare garlic ahead, roast heads as directed. Cool and separate into cloves. Freeze in an airtight container up to 3 months. The cloves will thaw in minutes.

ANTIPASTO KABOBS
(pictured on page 7)

◄QUICK!►

Choose this recipe that serves 10 if you're having company or make it to feed your family a couple of times. Even quicker – skip the skewers, and toss ingredients in a bowl, instead.

1 (9-ounce) package refrigerated cheese-filled tortellini
1 (14-ounce) can quartered artichoke hearts, drained
1 (6-ounce) can pitted ripe olives, drained
8 ounces thinly sliced pepperoni
1 (8-ounce) bottle reduced-fat Parmesan Italian dressing

• **Cook** tortellini according to package directions, omitting salt. Drain and cool.
• **Thread** tortellini and next 3 ingredients onto 25 (6-inch) wooden skewers. Place in a 13- x 9- x 2-inch dish; drizzle with dressing, turning to coat.
• **Cover** and chill at least 4 hours. Drain before serving. **Yield:** 10 to 12 appetizer servings.

CALIENTE MARINATED OLIVES

2 (3-ounce) jars pimiento-stuffed olives, drained
2 (3-ounce) jars almond-stuffed olives, drained
4 cloves garlic, minced
2 tablespoons dried crushed red pepper
2 teaspoons dried cumin
½ cup water
1 tablespoon olive oil
3 tablespoons chopped fresh cilantro

• **Combine** all ingredients except chopped cilantro in a medium saucepan; bring to a boil over medium heat. Reduce heat, and simmer 5 minutes. Remove from heat; cool.
• **Stir** in chopped cilantro. Cover and chill at least 8 hours or up to 1 week. **Yield:** 2½ cups.

Nan Jacobs
Birmingham, Alabama

MARINATED VEGETABLES

1 cup red wine vinegar
½ cup vegetable oil
½ cup olive oil
1 tablespoon salt
1 teaspoon garlic powder
1 teaspoon cracked pepper
1 teaspoon dried oregano
1 (10-ounce) package frozen brussels sprouts
2 green bell peppers
1 yellow onion
2 zucchini
4 small yellow squash
1 pound fresh broccoli
1 (5.75-ounce) can jumbo pitted ripe olives, drained
1 (6-ounce) jar jumbo pimiento-stuffed olives, drained
1 (14-ounce) can quartered artichoke hearts, drained
½ pound fresh small mushrooms
1 pint cherry tomatoes

• **Combine** first 7 ingredients in a large saucepan, and bring mixture to a boil. Remove from heat, and let cool.
• **Cook** brussels sprouts according to package directions; drain.
• **Cut** green bell peppers into thin strips. Slice onion, zucchini, and yellow squash; separate onion into rings. Cut broccoli into flowerets.
• **Place** vinegar mixture, vegetables, olives, and artichoke hearts in a large heavy-duty, zip-top plastic bag. Seal and chill 8 hours, turning vegetable mixture occasionally.
• **Add** mushrooms and cherry tomatoes, and toss gently to combine. Serve vegetables immediately. **Yield:** 20 to 25 appetizer servings.

P.T. and Joe Ross
Jackson, Mississippi

FIGS WITH PROSCIUTTO, WALNUTS, AND CREAM

1 tablespoon fresh mint
   leaves
2 tablespoons fresh lemon
   juice
¾ cup whipping cream
12 fresh figs, stemmed
12 thin slices prosciutto or
   cooked ham (4 ounces)
24 walnut halves

• **Combine** fresh mint leaves and lemon juice in a small bowl; crush mint leaves with back of a spoon. Let mixture stand at room temperature 20 minutes; remove and discard mint leaves.

• **Stir** whipping cream into lemon juice, and let stand until mixture is slightly thickened.

• **Cut** figs in half lengthwise; cut prosciutto in half.

• **Place** a walnut half on each fig half, and wrap with a slice of prosciutto. Place figs on a rack in broiler pan.

• **Broil** 5½ inches from heat (with electric oven door partially opened) 2 to 3 minutes.

• **Pour** whipping cream mixture evenly onto each serving plate; arrange wrapped fig halves on top of whipping cream mixture. **Yield:** 6 appetizer servings.

Chef Frank Stitt
Highlands Bar & Grill
Birmingham, Alabama

APPETIZER CRÈMES BRÛLÉE

Crèmes Brûlée don't have to be sweet. For these savory ones, use the basic recipe in the desserts chapter (on page 127), but omit the brown sugar topping. Serve them warm from the oven as an appetizer with a mixed green salad or as an accompaniment with steaks, roasts, or chops.

Onion Crème Brûlée: Melt 2 tablespoons butter in a skillet over low heat; add 1 cup coarsely chopped onion, and cook 45 minutes or until caramelized, stirring occasionally. Reduce sugar to 1 tablespoon in basic recipe (page 127), omit vanilla, and add 1 teaspoon salt and caramelized onion to custard mixture. Place mixture in container of an electric blender, and process until smooth. Proceed as directed in basic recipe, baking 50 minutes. **Yield:** 5 appetizer or side-dish servings.

Roasted Garlic Crème Brûlée: Cut off the flat end of 2 garlic heads, and spread apart whole cloves, leaving tight outer covering intact. Trim pointed end so head will sit flat. Place garlic heads, trimmed ends down, on a sheet of aluminum foil. Drizzle with 2 teaspoons olive oil; wrap in foil. Bake at 350° for 1 hour; cool. Squeeze out garlic pulp from each clove. Reduce sugar to 1 tablespoon in basic recipe (page 127), omit vanilla, and add 1 teaspoon salt and garlic pulp to custard mixture. Place mixture in container of an electric blender, and process until smooth. Proceed as directed in basic recipe, baking 40 minutes. **Yield:** 5 appetizer or side-dish servings.

Roquefort and Black Pepper Crème Brûlée: Reduce sugar to 1 tablespoon in basic recipe (page 127), omit vanilla, and add 1 teaspoon salt, ¼ cup Roquefort cheese, and 1 teaspoon freshly ground pepper to custard mixture in container of an electric blender, and process until smooth. Proceed as directed in basic recipe, baking 45 minutes. **Yield:** 5 appetizer or side-dish servings.

ONION BLOSSOM

Purchase more than 1 onion for this recipe because you'll need to practice the cutting technique. If you mess up, you can chop that onion for another use and start again with a new one.

1 large Vidalia or other sweet
   onion
2 tablespoons all-purpose flour
1 large egg, lightly beaten
1 cup crushed saltine crackers
Vegetable oil
½ teaspoon salt (optional)
Dark honey mustard or Ranch-style
   dressing

• **Peel** onion, leaving root end intact. Cut onion vertically into quarters, cutting to within ½ inch of root end. Cut each quarter vertically into thirds.

• **Place** onion in boiling water 1 minute; remove and place in ice water 5 minutes. Loosen "petals," if necessary. Drain onion, cut side down.

• **Place** flour in a heavy-duty, zip-top plastic bag; add onion, shaking to coat. Dip onion in egg.

• **Place** crushed saltine crackers in plastic bag; add onion, shaking to coat. Chill onion 1 hour.

• **Pour** oil to depth of 3 inches into an electric fryer or heavy saucepan, and heat to 375°.

• **Fry** onion 5 to 7 minutes or until golden; drain on paper towels. Sprinkle with salt, if desired. Serve with mustard or dressing. **Yield:** 2 appetizer servings.

Jean Scott
Floyd, Virginia

SAMOSAS

½ cup dried lentils
2 cloves garlic, minced
2 carrots, scraped and diced
1 medium onion, diced
½ teaspoon salt
1 teaspoon dried crushed red
pepper
1 to 2 teaspoons curry powder
1 teaspoon ground cumin
2 to 3 tablespoons chopped fresh
cilantro
9 egg roll wrappers
Vegetable oil
1 (9-ounce) jar mango chutney

• **Cook** lentils according to package directions, adding garlic and next 6 ingredients; drain. Stir in cilantro.
• **Cut** each wrapper into 4 squares; spoon about 1 teaspoon lentil mixture on half of each square. Moisten edges with water, and fold in half diagonally, pressing edges with a fork to seal.
• **Pour** oil to depth of 1 inch into a large skillet or Dutch oven; heat to 375°. Fry, 3 at a time, 30 seconds or until golden, turning once; drain on paper towels. Serve immediately with mango chutney. **Yield:** 3 dozen.

Dempse McMullen
Natchez, Mississippi

STUFFED JALAPEÑO PEPPERS

2 (11-ounce) cans whole pickled
jalapeño peppers, undrained
1 cup (4 ounces) shredded
Cheddar cheese
1 cup (4 ounces) shredded
mozzarella cheese
1½ cups all-purpose flour,
divided
2 large eggs
1 cup milk
½ cup cornmeal
1½ tablespoons seasoned salt
Vegetable oil

• **Drain** jalapeño peppers, reserving ¼ cup liquid; rinse peppers with cold water. Cut in half lengthwise, and remove and discard seeds. Pat peppers dry with paper towels.

• **Combine** reserved pepper liquid and cheeses. Spoon cheese mixture into pepper halves, and roll in ½ cup flour to coat. Place on baking sheets; cover and freeze 1 hour.
• **Combine** eggs and milk in a shallow dish, stirring well. Combine ½ cup flour, cornmeal, and seasoned salt in a shallow dish.
• **Roll** stuffed jalapeño peppers in remaining ½ cup flour; dip in egg mixture, and dredge in cornmeal mixture to coat. Cover and freeze stuffed peppers up to 2 days.
• **Pour** oil to depth of 3 inches into a Dutch oven; heat to 350°. Fry peppers in hot oil 3 to 4 minutes or until golden (do not overcook). Serve with sour cream or guacamole. **Yield:** 3 to 4 dozen.

Jan Bryan
Garland, Texas

HERBED CHEESE-STUFFED MUSHROOMS

¾ pound large fresh mushrooms
1 (3-ounce) package cream cheese,
softened
½ cup freshly grated Parmesan
cheese
1 tablespoon chopped fresh
parsley
1½ teaspoons chopped fresh
rosemary
1½ teaspoons chopped fresh
thyme
¼ teaspoon Worcestershire
sauce
Pinch of salt
Pinch of pepper
Pinch of ground nutmeg

• **Clean** mushrooms with damp paper towels. Remove and discard stems or reserve for another use.
• **Combine** cream cheese and remaining 8 ingredients in a small bowl, stirring well. Spoon or pipe cream cheese mixture evenly into mushroom caps, and place in a lightly greased 13- x 9- x 2-inch pan.
• **Bake** at 350° for 20 minutes. **Yield:** about 1½ dozen.

Barkley Shreve
Mobile, Alabama

CAJUN HOT PUFFS

1 (17¼-ounce) package frozen
puff pastry sheets, thawed
Cornmeal
½ pound hot smoked link sausage
40 sliced pickled jalapeño peppers,
drained (about 1 cup)

• **Roll** 1 pastry sheet into a 15- x 12-inch rectangle on a surface lightly sprinkled with cornmeal. Cut into 3-inch squares.
• **Cut** sausage into ¼-inch slices. Cut each slice in half crosswise. Place a piece of sausage and a slice jalapeño pepper in center of each square. Fold corners to center, slightly overlapping edges.
• **Place** filled pastries, seam side down, on greased baking sheets sprinkled with cornmeal. Repeat procedure with remaining pastry, sausage, and jalapeño pepper.
• **Bake** at 400° for 12 to 15 minutes. Serve immediately. **Yield:** 40 puffs.

Note: You can freeze unbaked Cajun Hot Puffs up to 3 months. Let thaw, and bake according to directions.

Chef Jim Napolitano
Cumberland Club
Nashville, Tennessee

CAJUN BLACKENED FILET MIGNON

Vegetable cooking spray
1 (1½-pound) beef tenderloin,
trimmed
2 tablespoons Cajun blackened
seasoning
1 (8-ounce) carton reduced-fat
sour cream
¼ cup prepared horseradish
1 (16-ounce) sourdough baguette,
cut into 24 slices and toasted
¼ cup sliced green onions

• **Spray** all sides of beef with cooking spray; sprinkle with seasoning, and spray again.
• **Heat** a cast-iron or ovenproof heavy skillet over medium-high heat 3 to 5 minutes; add beef, and cook 3 to 4 minutes on each side.

• **Bake** at 400° for 15 minutes or until a meat thermometer inserted in thickest portion of meat registers 145° (medium-rare). Let stand 10 minutes. Cut into 24 slices; set aside.
• **Combine** sour cream and horseradish; set horseradish sauce aside.
• **Place** a slice of tenderloin on each toasted baguette slice. Top with horseradish sauce; sprinkle evenly with green onions. **Yield:** 2 dozen canapés.

Dick and Inez Thompson
Bay St. Louis, Mississippi

FRIED BEEF PIES

¾ pound lean ground beef
2 large plum tomatoes, chopped
1 small green bell pepper, chopped
1 small onion, chopped
1 small carrot, scraped and
　　coarsely shredded
1 stalk celery, thinly sliced
¼ cup currants
1 tablespoon capers
1 teaspoon salt
1½ teaspoons pepper
48 wonton wrappers
Vegetable oil

• **Brown** ground beef in a large skillet, stirring until it crumbles; drain well, and place in a large bowl.
• **Add** tomato and next 5 ingredients to skillet; cook over medium heat, stirring constantly, 5 minutes or until vegetables are tender. Add to beef.
• **Stir** in capers, salt, and pepper.
• **Spoon** 1 tablespoon beef mixture onto half of each wonton wrapper. Moisten edges with water; fold wrapper over filling, forming a triangle, and press edges to seal.
• **Pour** oil to depth of 1 inch into a large heavy skillet or Dutch oven; heat to 375°. Fry pies in hot oil 1 to 2 minutes or until golden, turning once. Drain well on paper towels, and serve immediately. **Yield:** 4 dozen.

MARINATED PORK TENDERLOIN WITH JEZEBEL SAUCE

¼ cup lite soy sauce
¼ cup dry sherry or Madeira
2 tablespoons olive oil
1 tablespoon dry mustard
1 teaspoon ground ginger
1 teaspoon sesame oil
8 drops of hot sauce
2 cloves garlic, minced
2 (¾-pound) pork tenderloins
½ cup apple cider vinegar
3 dozen party rolls
Jezebel Sauce

• **Combine** first 8 ingredients in a shallow dish or large heavy-duty, zip-top plastic bag; add tenderloins. Cover or seal, and chill 8 hours, turning tenderloins occasionally.
• **Remove** tenderloins from marinade, reserving ½ cup marinade. Combine reserved marinade and ½ cup apple cider vinegar in a saucepan; bring to a boil, and set aside.
• **Cook** tenderloins, covered with grill lid, over medium-hot coals (350° to 400°) about 20 minutes or until a meat thermometer inserted in thickest portion registers 160°, turning occasionally and basting with marinade mixture during first 15 minutes of cooking time. Remove tenderloins from heat; slice and serve warm or chilled with party rolls and Jezebel Sauce. **Yield:** 10 to 12 appetizer servings.

Jezebel Sauce

QUICK!

1 cup apple jelly
1 cup pineapple-orange marmalade
　　or pineapple preserves
1 (6-ounce) jar prepared mustard
1 (5-ounce) jar prepared
　　horseradish
¼ teaspoon pepper

• **Beat** apple jelly in a mixing bowl at medium speed with an electric mixer until smooth. Add marmalade and remaining ingredients; beat at medium speed until blended. Cover and chill. **Yield:** 3 cups.

P.T. and Joe Ross
Jackson, Mississippi

TEXAS FIRECRACKERS

True to their name, these appetizers start with a little sizzle, and when you discover the peppers inside, they end with a "pow."

2 (22-ounce) jars pepperoncini
　　salad peppers, drained *
6 ounces Monterey Jack cheese
　　with peppers, cut into 24
　　(1½- x ¼- x ¼-inch)
　　rectangles
1 (6-ounce) skinned and boned
　　chicken breast half, cooked
　　and cut into 24 strips
24 sheets frozen phyllo pastry,
　　thawed
Butter-flavored cooking spray
48 long fresh chives (optional) **

• **Select** 24 (2-inch-long) salad peppers; set others aside for garnish. Remove and discard stems and seeds from peppers; drain well on paper towels.
• **Stuff** each pepper with 1 piece cheese and 1 chicken strip; set aside.
• **Spray** both sides of 4 phyllo sheets with cooking spray; stack. Cut in half lengthwise and then crosswise.
• **Place** 1 pepper on each phyllo stack, at 1 long end. Starting with long end, roll phyllo around pepper. Twist ends to seal. Place on a baking sheet. Repeat procedure with remaining phyllo and stuffed peppers.
• **Bake** at 375° for 20 minutes or until golden. Tie twisted ends of pastry with chives, if desired. Serve immediately. **Yield:** 2 dozen.

* Substitute 24 (2-inch) banana peppers for pepperoncini salad peppers. Roast peppers at 400° until charred (about 12 minutes). Cool completely; remove and discard stems and seeds.

** Slice green portion of green onions lengthwise; substitute for chives.

Note: Freeze unbaked Texas Firecrackers in an airtight container up to 3 months. To serve, remove from freezer and let stand at room temperature 30 minutes; bake as directed.

Carol Barclay
Portland, Texas

TORTILLA BITES

Cajun-style blackened seasoning provides the spice accent for this make-ahead appetizer.

1 pound unpeeled large fresh
   shrimp
¼ cup Cajun blackened seasoning
1 (8-ounce) package cream cheese,
   softened
½ teaspoon ground red pepper
¼ teaspoon salt
2 cloves garlic, crushed
Vegetable cooking spray
1 large red bell pepper
6 (8-inch) flour tortillas
18 large fresh spinach leaves
1 medium avocado, thinly sliced
   (optional)
Fresh Salsa

• **Peel** shrimp, and devein, if desired; cut shrimp in half lengthwise. Combine shrimp and blackened seasoning in a heavy-duty, zip-top plastic bag; seal bag, and toss to coat. Chill 1 hour.
• **Combine** cream cheese and next 3 ingredients; set aside.
• **Thread** shrimp onto skewers.
• **Coat** food rack with cooking spray; place rack on grill over medium-hot coals (350° to 400°). Place shrimp and red bell pepper on rack.
• **Cook,** covered with grill lid, about 10 minutes, turning shrimp once and red pepper occasionally.
• **Remove** shrimp from grill when done; remove shrimp from skewers, and set aside.
• **Remove** red bell pepper from grill when skin is blistered and black. Remove and discard skin and seeds, and cut pepper into thin strips. Set pepper strips aside.
• **Spread** cream cheese mixture evenly on 1 side of each tortilla. Place 3 spinach leaves on half of the cream cheese. Top spinach evenly with shrimp, red bell pepper strips, and avocado slices, if desired. Roll each tortilla tightly, starting at spinach side.
• **Cut** each tortilla crosswise into 5 portions, and secure each portion with a wooden pick. Cover and store in refrigerator. Serve with Fresh Salsa. **Yield:** 30 appetizers.

Fresh Salsa

QUICK!

1 small purple onion,
   quartered
2 jalapeño peppers, seeded and
   quartered
2 cloves garlic
¼ cup chopped fresh cilantro
2 tablespoons fresh lime juice
1 teaspoon salt
1 (14½-ounce) can diced
   tomatoes, drained

• **Position** knife blade in food processor bowl; add first 6 ingredients. Pulse 6 times or until vegetable mixture is finely chopped.
• **Combine** onion mixture and tomatoes. Cover and store in refrigerator up to 1 week. **Yield:** 2 cups.

Wendy V. Kitchens
Charlotte, North Carolina

GRILLED HONEY CHICKEN WINGS

10 chicken wings
½ cup soy sauce
¼ cup dry sherry
¼ cup honey
¼ teaspoon garlic powder
¼ teaspoon ground ginger
3 tablespoons butter

• **Cut** off wingtips, and discard; cut wings in half at joint.
• **Combine** soy sauce and remaining 5 ingredients in a small saucepan; cook over medium heat, stirring constantly, until thoroughly heated. Reserve ¼ cup marinade, and chill.
• **Pour** remaining marinade into a large heavy-duty, zip-top plastic bag; add chicken, and seal. Chill 2 hours, turning occasionally.
• **Remove** chicken from marinade, discarding marinade. Cook chicken, covered with grill lid, over medium-hot coals (350° to 400°) 20 minutes, turning once and basting with reserved ¼ cup marinade. **Yield:** 20 appetizers or 2 to 3 main-dish servings.

Sharon Chapman
Aiken, South Carolina

THAI LETTUCE FOLDS
(pictured at right)

2 tablespoons peanut oil
2 cloves garlic, minced
4 skinned and boned chicken
   breast halves, cut into ¼-inch
   cubes
⅓ cup chicken broth
2 green onions with tops, finely
   chopped
1 tablespoon chopped fresh mint
   leaves
1 tablespoon chopped fresh
   cilantro
1 tablespoon lime juice
½ teaspoon ground red pepper
¼ teaspoon ground ginger
16 Bibb lettuce leaves
½ pound fresh bean sprouts
Cucumber Dipping Sauce

• **Heat** peanut oil in a large skillet over medium-high heat 1 minute. Add garlic and chicken; cook 3 to 5 minutes, stirring constantly. Add broth, and cook over medium heat until most of liquid evaporates. Stir in green onions and next 5 ingredients.
• **Spoon** 2 tablespoons chicken mixture onto each lettuce leaf; sprinkle with bean sprouts, and fold over. Serve with Cucumber Dipping Sauce. **Yield:** 16 appetizer servings.

Cucumber Dipping Sauce

QUICK!

½ cup water
¼ cup sugar
¼ cup rice wine vinegar
1 tablespoon plum sauce
¼ teaspoon dried crushed red
   pepper
⅛ teaspoon salt
½ cup finely chopped cucumber
1 tablespoon chopped fresh
   cilantro
1 tablespoon chopped fresh mint
   leaves

• **Combine** first 6 ingredients in a small saucepan.
• **Bring** to a boil; reduce heat, and simmer 3 minutes. Remove from heat; cool.
• **Stir** in cucumber, cilantro, and mint. **Yield:** about 1 cup.

Thai Lettuce Folds

SWEET-AND-SOUR CHICKEN WINGS

16 chicken wings
2 teaspoons salt
2 large eggs, lightly beaten
1 cup cornstarch
Vegetable oil
1½ cups sugar
1 cup apple cider vinegar
½ cup ketchup
2 tablespoons soy sauce

● **Cut** off wingtips, and discard; cut wings in half at joint. Sprinkle chicken with salt; dip in egg, and dredge with cornstarch.
● **Pour** oil to depth of 2 inches into a Dutch oven; heat to 375°. Fry chicken wings, a few at a time, 8 minutes or until golden; drain on paper towels.
● **Line** a 13- x 9- x 2-inch baking dish with aluminum foil, and add chicken.
● **Combine** sugar and remaining 3 ingredients in a small saucepan; bring to a boil over medium heat, stirring constantly. Remove from heat. Reserve ½ cup mixture; pour remaining mixture over chicken.
● **Bake** at 400° for 30 minutes. Serve chicken wings with reserved ketchup mixture. **Yield:** 32 appetizers or 3 to 4 main-dish servings.

Linda Heath
Bolivar, Missouri

OYSTERS CHESAPEAKE

Rock salt
5 cloves garlic, minced
¼ cup butter or margarine, melted
2 medium onions, finely chopped
2½ cups finely chopped cooked country ham
½ cup dry white wine
2½ dozen fresh oysters in the shell
4 (¾-ounce) slices Swiss cheese, cut into 30 strips

● **Sprinkle** a thin layer of rock salt in two 15- x 10- x 1-inch jellyroll pans; set pans aside.
● **Cook** garlic in butter in a large skillet over medium heat, stirring constantly, until slightly brown. Add chopped onion, and cook until tender, stirring constantly. Stir in ham, and cook until moisture evaporates (about 5 minutes). Add wine, and simmer 5 minutes.
● **Scrub** oysters shells and open, discarding tops. Arrange shell bottoms (containing oysters) over rock salt. Spoon 1 heaping tablespoon ham mixture on each oyster; top with cheese. Bake at 400° for 10 minutes or until cheese melts. Serve immediately. **Yield:** 2½ dozen.

Roland S. Ormrod
Towson, Maryland

OYSTERS BIENVILLE

3 cups water
¾ pound unpeeled medium-size fresh shrimp
3 pounds rock salt
⅓ cup butter or margarine
⅔ cup chopped scallions or green onions
3 tablespoons finely chopped fresh parsley
2 cloves garlic, minced
⅓ cup all-purpose flour
1¼ cups milk
⅓ cup half-and-half
2 egg yolks, lightly beaten
3 tablespoons dry sherry
1 teaspoon salt
½ teaspoon ground white pepper
¼ to ½ teaspoon ground red pepper
⅔ cup chopped fresh mushrooms
3 dozen fresh oysters in the shell
¼ cup grated Parmesan cheese
¼ cup soft breadcrumbs
¼ teaspoon paprika
Garnishes: lemon wedges, fresh parsley sprigs

● **Bring** water to a boil; add shrimp, and cook 3 to 5 minutes or until shrimp turn pink. Drain well; rinse with cold water. Chill. Peel shrimp, and devein, if desired. Chop shrimp, and set aside.
● **Sprinkle** a layer of rock salt in two 15- x 10- x 1-inch jellyroll pans; set aside.
● **Melt** butter in a large skillet; add scallions, chopped parsley, and garlic. Cook over medium-high heat, stirring constantly, until tender. Add flour, stirring until smooth. Cook 1 minute, stirring constantly. Gradually add milk and half-and-half; cook over medium heat, stirring constantly, until thickened. Gradually stir about one-fourth of hot mixture into yolks; add to remaining hot mixture, stirring constantly. Stir in sherry and next 4 ingredients; cook 2 minutes, stirring constantly. Stir in shrimp.
● **Scrub** oyster shells and open, discarding tops. Arrange shell bottoms (containing oysters) over rock salt. Spoon shrimp mixture evenly over oysters. Combine cheese, breadcrumbs, and paprika; sprinkle over shrimp mixture and oysters. Bake at 350° for 15 to 20 minutes or until lightly browned. Garnish, if desired. **Yield:** 3 dozen.

Men's Gourmet
Raleigh, North Carolina

CRABMEAT-STUFFED OYSTERS

2 dozen fresh oysters in the shell *
1 pound lump crabmeat
½ cup soft breadcrumbs
⅓ cup milk
1 large egg, lightly beaten
¼ cup mayonnaise
½ teaspoon baking powder
2 teaspoons dried onion flakes
2 teaspoons chopped fresh parsley
¼ teaspoon garlic salt
¼ teaspoon ground white pepper
2 tablespoons thinly sliced green onions
1 (2-ounce) jar sliced pimiento, drained

● **Scrub** oyster shells, and open, discarding tops. Arrange shell bottoms (containing oysters) in a 15- x 10- x 1-inch jellyroll pan. Set aside.
● **Drain** crabmeat, removing any bits of shell. Combine crabmeat, breadcrumbs, and next 8 ingredients. Spoon mixture evenly over each oyster; sprinkle with green onions. Place 1 or 2 pimiento strips on each oyster. (Reserve any remaining pimiento for another use.)

● **Bake** at 400° for 15 minutes or until thoroughly heated. **Yield:** 6 appetizer servings.

✳ Substitute 2 (12-ounce) containers fresh oysters for oysters in the shell. (Reserve extra oysters for another use.) Bake according to directions in shell-shaped baking dishes found in kitchen shops.

Roland S. Ormrod
Towson, Maryland

MINIATURE CRAB CAKE SANDWICHES

QUICK!

2 cups biscuit mix
1 teaspoon dried dillweed
1 (8-ounce) carton sour cream
½ cup butter or margarine, melted
Miniature Crab Cakes

● **Combine** first 4 ingredients, stirring until blended. Turn dough out onto a lightly floured surface, and knead lightly 5 or 6 times.
● **Roll** dough to ½-inch thickness; cut with a 1-inch round cutter, and place on lightly greased baking sheets.
● **Bake** at 450° for 6 to 8 minutes or until lightly browned. Cool.
● **Split** biscuits, and place a Miniature Crab Cake in each. Serve with tartar sauce. **Yield:** 4½ dozen.

Miniature Crab Cakes

QUICK!

1 pound fresh lump crabmeat
½ cup fine, dry breadcrumbs
2 tablespoons mayonnaise
2 teaspoons Old Bay seasoning
2 tablespoons chopped fresh parsley

● **Drain** crabmeat, removing any bits of shell. Combine crabmeat, breadcrumbs, and remaining ingredients; shape into 1-inch patties, and place on lightly greased baking sheets.
● **Bake** at 400° for 8 to 10 minutes or until crab cakes are golden. Serve warm. **Yield:** 4½ dozen.

CRABMEAT HORS D'OEUVRE

QUICK!

½ cup chopped green onions
3 tablespoons mayonnaise
1½ teaspoons lime juice
¼ teaspoon Dijon mustard
Dash of ground red pepper
1 pound fresh lump crabmeat
½ to 1 bunch fresh watercress
2 to 3 tablespoons capers

● **Combine** first 5 ingredients. Drain crabmeat, removing any bits of shell. Gently fold crabmeat into mayonnaise mixture.
● **Arrange** watercress on a serving plate; top with crabmeat mixture, and sprinkle evenly with capers. Serve with assorted crackers. **Yield:** 8 appetizer servings.

Wilder Selman
New Orleans, Louisiana

HOISIN CRAB POT STICKERS

½ pound fresh lump crabmeat
5 fresh mushrooms, finely chopped
⅔ cup sliced green onions
3 tablespoons hoisin sauce
1 tablespoon dark sesame oil
1 teaspoon grated fresh ginger
1 (12-ounce) package wonton wrappers
2 tablespoons vegetable oil, divided
1 cup chicken broth, divided
Soy sauce (optional)

● **Drain** crabmeat, and remove any bits of shell. Combine crabmeat, mushrooms, and next 4 ingredients.
● **Place** 1 teaspoon crabmeat mixture in center of each wonton wrapper; moisten edges of wrappers with water. Fold wrappers in half, forming triangles; pinch edges to seal. Stand pot stickers on folded edge; press down to flatten slightly.
● **Pour** 1 tablespoon oil into a large non-stick skillet; place over medium-high heat until hot. Fry half of pot stickers in hot oil about 3 minutes or until golden

on bottom. Add ½ cup chicken broth; reduce heat to medium.
● **Cover** and cook 8 minutes until tender. Repeat procedure with remaining oil, pot stickers, and broth. Serve with soy sauce, if desired. **Yield:** 4 dozen.

LoriAnn Glen
Overland, Missouri

SHRIMP PUFFS

⅔ cup uncooked rice
1½ pounds unpeeled medium-size fresh shrimp
1 cup all-purpose flour
1½ teaspoons baking powder
1 tablespoon Creole seasoning
½ teaspoon garlic powder
2 large eggs, separated
¾ cup milk
1 tablespoon vegetable oil
1 medium onion, chopped
½ cup chopped green onions
Vegetable oil

● **Cook** rice according to package directions; set aside.
● **Peel** shrimp, and devein, if desired; chop shrimp, and set aside.
● **Combine** flour and next 3 ingredients in a large bowl. Combine egg yolks, milk, and 1 tablespoon oil, stirring well; gradually add to dry ingredients, stirring just until blended. Add rice, shrimp, and onions, stirring gently.
● **Beat** egg whites at high speed with an electric mixer until stiff peaks form, and gently fold into shrimp mixture.
● **Pour** oil to depth of 3 inches into a Dutch oven; heat to 375°. Drop shrimp mixture by heaping teaspoonfuls into hot oil; cook 3 to 4 minutes or until golden, turning once. Drain on paper towels, and serve immediately with rémoulade or tartar sauce. **Yield:** 5 dozen.

CURRIED SHRIMP BALLS

QUICK!

How easy can it get? Just 5 ingredients. Traditional goes tropical when creamy shrimp balls are rolled in toasted, curried coconut.

1 cup flaked coconut
1 teaspoon curry powder
2 (8-ounce) packages cream cheese, softened
1 (6-ounce) can shrimp, rinsed, drained, and chopped
2 tablespoons finely chopped onion

• **Combine** coconut and curry powder; place on a baking sheet, and bake at 325° for 5 minutes or until golden. Set coconut mixture aside.
• **Combine** cream cheese, shrimp, and onion; shape into 1-inch balls, and roll in coconut mixture. Cover and chill. **Yield:** 3 dozen.

Janet Filer
Arlington, Virginia

COCONUT FRIED SHRIMP

1 pound unpeeled medium-size fresh shrimp
¾ cup biscuit mix
1 tablespoon sugar
¾ cup beer
¾ cup all-purpose flour
2½ cups flaked coconut
Vegetable oil
Orange-Lime Dip

• **Peel** shrimp, leaving tails intact; devein, if desired, and set shrimp aside.
• **Combine** biscuit mix, sugar, and beer, stirring until smooth; set aside.
• **Coat** shrimp with flour; dip in beer mixture, allowing excess coating to drain. Gently roll coated shrimp in flaked coconut.
• **Pour** oil to depth of 3 inches in a large saucepan; heat to 350°.
• **Cook** shrimp, a few at a time, 1 to 2 minutes or until golden; drain on paper towels, and serve immediately with Orange-Lime Dip. **Yield:** about 3 dozen.

Orange-Lime Dip

QUICK!

1 (10-ounce) jar orange marmalade
3 tablespoons spicy brown mustard
1 tablespoon fresh lime juice

• **Combine** all ingredients in a small saucepan; cook over medium heat, stirring constantly, until marmalade melts. Cool. Cover and store in refrigerator up to 1 week. **Yield:** about 1¼ cups.

CITRUS-MARINATED SMOKED SHRIMP

Hickory or fruitwood chips
2 pounds unpeeled jumbo fresh shrimp
1 (6-ounce) can frozen orange juice concentrate, thawed and undiluted, divided
¼ cup honey
2 tablespoons water
1 tablespoon chopped fresh basil
1 tablespoon chopped fresh thyme

• **Soak** wood chips in water at least 30 minutes.
• **Peel** shrimp, and devein, if desired.
• **Combine** ¼ cup juice concentrate, honey, and remaining 3 ingredients.
• **Place** shrimp in a shallow dish or large heavy-duty, zip-top plastic bag; pour orange juice mixture over shrimp, stirring or shaking to coat. Cover or seal, and chill 1 hour.
• **Prepare** charcoal fire in smoker; let burn 15 to 20 minutes.
• **Drain** chips, and place on coals. Place water pan in smoker; add remaining orange juice concentrate to pan.
• **Remove** shrimp from marinade; pour marinade into water pan. Add water to pan to depth of fill line.
• **Thread** shrimp onto skewers, and place on upper and lower food racks. Cover with smoker lid.
• **Cook** 45 minutes to 1 hour. **Yield:** 8 appetizer servings.

Charlie Gagne
Birmingham, Alabama

VIETNAMESE EGG ROLLS

½ (3¾-ounce) package cellophane noodles
½ pound lean boneless pork
1 pound unpeeled large fresh shrimp
3 cloves garlic, pressed
1 tablespoon sesame oil
6 green onions, chopped
2 tablespoons chopped fresh cilantro
2 teaspoons grated fresh ginger
20 egg roll wrappers
Vegetable oil

• **Soak** noodles in hot water to cover 10 minutes or until soft; drain. Cut into 2-inch pieces; set aside.
• **Trim** excess fat from pork, and cut into 1-inch pieces; set aside.
• **Peel** shrimp, and devein, if desired.
• **Position** knife blade in food processor bowl, and add pork. Process until pork is coarsely chopped. Add shrimp, and process until mixture is finely chopped.
• **Cook** meat mixture and garlic in sesame oil in a wok or large skillet over medium-high heat, stirring constantly, 5 minutes or until meat crumbles and shrimp turn pink.
• **Add** noodles, green onions, cilantro, and ginger; cook 2 to 3 minutes, stirring constantly. Cool completely.
• **Spoon** ¼ cup mixture in center of each egg roll wrapper. Fold top corner of wrapper over filling, tucking tip of corner under filling; fold left and right corners over filling. Lightly brush remaining corner with water; tightly roll filled end toward remaining corner, and gently press to seal.
• **Pour** vegetable oil to depth of 2 inches into a wok or Dutch oven; heat to 375°. Fry egg rolls, a few at a time, until golden, turning once; drain. **Yield:** 20 egg rolls.

Agnes Nguyen
Birmingham, Alabama

At right: *Sweet-Tart Lemonade (page 30)*

BEVERAGES

APRICOT-ORANGE-CARROT COOLER

QUICK!

1 medium carrot, scraped and
    sliced
½ cup water
1 cup orange juice, chilled
1 (12-ounce) can apricot nectar,
    chilled

• **Combine** carrot and water in a small saucepan; bring to a boil. Cover, reduce heat, and simmer 12 minutes or until tender. Remove from heat; cool.
• **Combine** carrot, cooking liquid, orange juice, and apricot nectar in container of an electric blender; process until smooth, stopping once to scrape down sides. **Yield:** 5 cups.

GRAPEFRUIT FREEZE

1½ cups sugar
1 cup water
½ cup chopped fresh mint leaves
1 (46-ounce) can unsweetened
    grapefruit juice
Garnish: fresh mint sprigs

• **Combine** sugar and water in a medium saucepan; bring to a boil. Remove from heat. Add chopped mint; cover and let stand 5 minutes.
• **Pour** mixture through a wire-mesh strainer into an 8-cup container; discard chopped mint. Add grapefruit juice. Divide mixture into two 1-quart freezer containers; cover and freeze. Remove from freezer 2 hours before serving. Stir until slushy. Garnish, if desired. **Yield:** about 2 quarts.

Regina Axtell
Buffalo, Texas

SPARKLING STRAWBERRY TEA

QUICK!

1 (10-ounce) package frozen
    strawberries, thawed
1½ quarts boiling water
3 family-size tea bags
½ cup sugar
1 (6-ounce) can frozen lemonade
    concentrate, thawed and
    undiluted
1 (2-liter) bottle lemon-lime
    carbonated beverage,
    chilled
Garnish: fresh mint sprigs

• **Place** strawberries in container of an electric blender or food processor; process until smooth, stopping once to scrape down sides. Set strawberry puree aside.
• **Pour** boiling water over tea bags; cover and steep 5 minutes.
• **Remove** tea bags, squeezing gently. Stir in sugar, lemonade concentrate, and strawberry puree; chill.
• **Stir** in chilled lemon-lime beverage gently just before serving; serve tea over ice. Garnish, if desired. **Yield:** about 4 quarts.

Regina Axtell
Buffalo, Texas

GINGER-ALMOND TEA

QUICK!

1 cup boiling water
5 regular-size tea bags
1½ cups sugar
4 cups water
¾ cup lemon juice
1 tablespoon vanilla extract
1 teaspoon almond extract
1 (1-liter) bottle ginger ale,
    chilled

• **Pour** boiling water over tea bags; cover and steep 5 minutes.
• **Remove** tea bags, squeezing gently. Stir in sugar and next 4 ingredients; chill.
• **Stir** in ginger ale just before serving. Serve tea over ice. **Yield:** 3 quarts.

Charlene Howard
Crystal Springs, Mississippi

TROPICAL TEA-SER

QUICK!

Orange juice
2 cups boiling water
5 orange-mango zinger tea bags
1 cup sugar
2 cups pineapple juice

• **Pour** orange juice into ice cube trays; freeze until firm.
• **Pour** boiling water over tea bags; cover and steep 5 minutes.
• **Remove** tea bags from water, squeezing gently. Stir in sugar; cool.
• **Stir** in pineapple juice. Pour over flavored cubes. **Yield:** 4½ cups.

SWEET-TART LEMONADE
(pictured on previous page)

QUICK!

2 cups Sugar Syrup
1¾ to 2 cups fresh lemon juice
3 cups cold water

• **Combine** all ingredients, stirring well. Serve over ice. **Yield:** 7 cups.

Note: To prepare lemonade by the glass, combine 3 tablespoons Sugar Syrup, ¼ cup fresh lemon juice, and ¾ cup cold water; stir mixture well.

Sugar Syrup

QUICK!

Lemon juice keeps the Sugar Syrup
from forming crystals.

1 cup water
2 cups sugar
¼ teaspoon lemon juice

• **Combine** all ingredients in a small saucepan; cook over low heat until sugar dissolves. Bring to a boil; reduce heat, and simmer 1 minute. Remove from heat; cool. Store in an airtight container at room temperature up to 2 weeks. **Yield:** 2 cups.

Mint Syrup: Add 1 cup loosely packed mint leaves to saucepan, and cook as directed. Cool. Discard mint.

Ginger Syrup: Add ¼ cup chopped fresh ginger to saucepan, and cook as directed. Cool. Remove and discard ginger; use syrup immediately. Do not store.

Berry Syrup: Substitute ½ cup seedless raspberry jam or strawberry jam for ½ cup of the sugar, and cook syrup as directed. Cool.

Orange Syrup: Remove rind from 2 oranges, using a vegetable peeler; add orange rind to saucepan, and cook as directed. Cool. Remove and discard orange rind.

LEMON-LIME MARGARITAS

2 tablespoons fresh lime juice
Margarita salt
1 cup tequila
¼ cup Triple Sec or other
     orange-flavored liqueur
¼ cup fresh lime juice
¼ cup fresh lemon juice
¼ cup sugar
Crushed ice

• **Place** 2 tablespoons lime juice and margarita salt in separate saucers. Dip rims of six widemouthed glasses into lime juice, and then into salt. Set glasses aside.
• **Combine** tequila and next 4 ingredients in container of an electric blender; add enough crushed ice to bring mixture to 4-cup level. Process until frothy. Pour into prepared glasses. Serve immediately. **Yield:** 4 cups.

MANGO MARGARITAS

1 (26-ounce) jar sliced mangoes,
     undrained
Colored decorator sugar
1 (6-ounce) can frozen limeade
     concentrate, thawed and
     undiluted
1 cup gold tequila
½ cup Triple Sec or Cointreau
¼ cup Grand Marnier
Crushed ice

• **Spoon** 3 tablespoons mango liquid into a saucer; pour mangoes and remaining liquid into container of an electric blender.
• **Place** sugar in a saucer; dip rims of glasses into mango liquid, and then into sugar. Set aside.
• **Add** limeade concentrate and next 3 ingredients to blender container; process until smooth, stopping once to scrape down sides.
• **Pour** half of mixture into a small pitcher, and set aside.
• **Add** enough ice to remaining mixture in blender to bring mixture to 5-cup level; process until slushy, stopping once to scrape down sides. Pour into prepared glasses; repeat with remaining mango mixture and ice. Serve immediately. **Yield:** 2½ quarts.

Stop and Smell the Rosemary:
Recipes and Traditions to Remember
Junior League of Houston, Texas

PIÑA COLADAS

For your next party, serve Piña Coladas in fresh pineapple shells, and garnish with a fruit kabob.

1 cup chopped fresh pineapple *
2 cups pineapple juice
1 cup dark rum
1 (15-ounce) can cream of
     coconut
1 quart rum-raisin or vanilla ice
     cream, divided
2 cups crushed ice, divided
Pineapple Shells (optional)
     (see note)
Garnishes: pineapple chunks,
     maraschino cherries

• **Combine** first 4 ingredients in a bowl, stirring well.
• **Combine** 1¼ cups pineapple mixture, 1 cup ice cream, and ½ cup ice in container of an electric blender; process until smooth. Repeat procedure 3 times with remaining ingredients. Serve immediately in pineapple shells, if desired. Garnish, if desired. **Yield:** about 9 cups.

* Substitute 1 (8-ounce) can crushed pineapple, drained, for 1 cup fresh.

Note: To make Pineapple Shells, cut off green tops of pineapples; cut a thin slice from bottoms, if necessary, to stand upright. Carefully remove pulp with a sharp knife, leaving ½-inch-thick shells.
William Moreno
Richmond, Virginia

WATERMELON DAIQUIRI

4 cups peeled, seeded, and cubed
     watermelon
½ cup light rum
¼ cup fresh lime juice
¼ cup Triple Sec or other
     orange-flavored liqueur
Ice cubes

• **Freeze** watermelon in a shallow pan at least 6 hours.
• **Combine** frozen watermelon, rum, lime juice, and liqueur in container of an electric blender; process until smooth, stopping once to scrape down sides.
• **Add** enough ice cubes to bring mixture to 5-cup level; process until smooth. Repeat procedure, if necessary, until mixture measures 5 cups. **Yield:** 5 cups.
Shirley M. Draper
Winter Park, Florida

CRANBERRY SANGRÍA

QUICK!

Get the full-bodied flavor of traditional sangría with just 4 ingredients.

1 (48-ounce) bottle cranberry
     juice cocktail
3 cups port wine
1 orange, thinly sliced
1 lemon, thinly sliced

• **Combine** all ingredients; cover and chill at least 3 hours. **Yield:** 2½ quarts.
Agnes L. Stone
Ocala, Florida

Brandy Alexanders

SANGRÍA TEA

1 (10-ounce) package frozen
    raspberries, thawed
3 cups water
¾ cup sugar
1 family-size tea bag
2 cups dry red wine
1 lemon, sliced
1 lime, sliced
1 (16-ounce) bottle orange soda,
    chilled
Garnishes: lemon slices, lime slices

• **Place** raspberries in container of an electric blender or food processor; process until smooth, stopping once to scrape down sides.
• **Pour** raspberries through a fine wire-mesh strainer into a pitcher, discarding seeds. Set aside.
• **Combine** water and sugar in a saucepan; bring to a boil, stirring often. Remove from heat; add tea bag. Cover and steep 5 minutes.
• **Remove** tea bag, squeezing gently; cool tea.
• **Pour** tea into pitcher; stir in wine and lemon and lime slices. Chill.
• **Stir** in orange soda just before serving. Serve tea over ice. Garnish, if desired. **Yield:** 2 quarts.

BRANDY ALEXANDER
(pictured at left)

QUICK!

2 cups vanilla ice cream
3 to 4 tablespoons brandy
3 to 4 tablespoons white crème de
    cacao
Garnish: white chocolate shavings

• **Combine** first 3 ingredients in container of an electric blender; process until smooth, stopping once to scrape down sides.
• **Spoon** evenly into glasses. Garnish, if desired. Serve immediately. **Yield:** 2 servings.

Rebecca Salisbury Rice
Murfreesboro, Tennessee

PEACH MELBA SUNDAE SHAKE

⅔ cup fresh or frozen raspberries,
    thawed
2 tablespoons sugar
1 large peach, peeled and sliced ✱
¾ cup milk
2 cups peach ice cream, softened
Peach ice cream
Garnishes: fresh raspberries,
    fresh peach slices, fresh
    mint sprigs

• **Combine** ⅔ cup raspberries and sugar in container of an electric blender; process until smooth, stopping once to scrape down sides. Transfer to a small container, and set aside. Wash blender container.
• **Combine** sliced peach and milk in container of blender; process until smooth. Add 2 cups peach ice cream, and process until smooth, stopping once to scrape down sides.
• **Spoon** about 2 tablespoons raspberry mixture into bottom of two 16-ounce glasses; add peach mixture. Top each with a scoop of ice cream, and drizzle with remaining raspberry mixture. Garnish, if desired. **Yield:** 2 servings.

✱ You can substitute 1 cup frozen peach slices, thawed, for a fresh peach.
Mrs. Harland J. Stone
Ocala, Florida

PINEAPPLE MILK SHAKE

QUICK!

3 cups vanilla ice cream
1 (8-ounce) can crushed
    pineapple, undrained
½ cup milk

• **Combine** all ingredients in container of an electric blender; process just until smooth, stopping once to scrape down sides. **Yield:** 3 cups.

Andy and Mike Karandzieff
Crown Candy
St. Louis, Missouri

PUNCH FOR A BUNCH

8 cups water, divided
1½ cups sugar
1 (7.5-ounce) bottle frozen lemon
    juice, thawed
1 (6-ounce) can frozen orange
    juice concentrate, thawed and
    undiluted
2 (6-ounce) cans unsweetened
    pineapple juice (1½ cups)
1 (2-liter) bottle ginger ale,
    chilled

• **Combine** 2 cups water and sugar in a medium saucepan. Bring to a boil; reduce heat, and simmer 20 minutes. Cool. Stir in remaining 6 cups water and fruit juices.
• **Cover** and freeze at least 8 hours, stirring juice mixture twice during freezing process.
• **Remove** from freezer 30 minutes before serving. Break into chunks; add ginger ale, and stir until slushy. **Yield:** 5 quarts.

Lynn L. Williams
Lexington, Virginia

FRUIT JUICE PUNCH

QUICK!

3 cups pineapple juice
2 cups water
2 cups apple juice
1 (6-ounce) can frozen lemonade
    concentrate, undiluted
1 (6-ounce) can frozen orange
    juice concentrate,
    undiluted
2 teaspoons lemon instant tea
    mix
2 cups ginger ale, chilled

• **Combine** first 6 ingredients in a large bowl, stirring well; cover and chill at least 2 hours.
• **Stir** in ginger ale just before serving. **Yield:** about 2½ quarts.

Fruit Juice and Vodka Punch: Stir in 1½ cups vodka before chilling. **Yield:** 3 quarts.

Liz Randall
Spindale, North Carolina

SUNSET PUNCH

QUICK!

1 quart cranberry juice cocktail
1 quart pink lemonade
1 quart orange juice
1 quart pineapple juice
1 quart ginger ale, chilled
1 quart raspberry sherbet or
    sorbet

● **Combine** first 4 ingredients in a large bowl; chill. Stir in ginger ale; scoop sherbet into punch. Serve immediately. **Yield:** 1½ gallons.

Bernadette Colvin
Houston, Texas

MOCHA PUNCH

*This drink is so thick and rich
it could almost be dessert.*

1 (2-ounce) jar instant coffee
    granules
2 cups boiling water
1 cup sugar
1 gallon milk
½ gallon chocolate ice cream,
    softened
½ gallon vanilla ice cream,
    softened
2 cups whipping cream, whipped

● **Combine** coffee granules and boiling water, stirring until coffee dissolves. Add sugar, stirring until sugar dissolves. Cover and chill.
● **Combine** coffee mixture and milk in a large punch bowl; gently stir in ice creams. Spoon whipped cream on top. **Yield:** about 2½ gallons.

Carolyn Kornegay
Gray, Tennessee

BERRY-COLADA PUNCH

QUICK!

1 (16-ounce) package frozen
    strawberries, thawed
1 (15-ounce) can cream of
    coconut
3 cups pineapple juice, chilled
3 cups club soda, chilled
2 cups rum (optional)

● **Combine** strawberries and cream of coconut in container of an electric blender; process until smooth, stopping once to scrape down sides. Pour into a pitcher or large bowl. Stir in pineapple juice, club soda, and rum, if desired. Serve over crushed ice. **Yield:** 2½ quarts.

Judi Grigoraci
Charleston, West Virginia

CARIBBEAN PUNCH

3 cups water
1 to 1½ cups sugar
1 (12-ounce) can frozen orange
    juice concentrate, thawed and
    undiluted
1 (6-ounce) can frozen lemonade
    concentrate, thawed and
    undiluted
½ cup pineapple juice
1½ cups mashed ripe banana
    (about 3 medium)
2 cups light rum (optional)
3 (12-ounce) cans ginger ale

● **Combine** water and sugar in a large saucepan; bring mixture to a boil, stirring until sugar dissolves. Set sugar mixture aside.
● **Combine** orange juice concentrate and next 3 ingredients in container of an electric blender; process until smooth, stopping once to scrape down sides.
● **Combine** sugar mixture and orange juice mixture in a large plastic container. Add rum, if desired, and ginger ale, stirring well. Cover and freeze.
● **Remove** from freezer, and let stand at room temperature 30 minutes before serving. **Yield:** about 3½ quarts.

Joy L. Garcia
Bartlett, Tennessee

LEMON CHAMPAGNE PUNCH

1 (12-ounce) can frozen lemonade
    concentrate, thawed and
    undiluted
1 (46-ounce) can unsweetened
    pineapple juice, chilled
1 (750-milliliter) bottle Rhine
    wine
Strawberry Ice Ring
2 (750-milliliter) bottles
    champagne, chilled

● **Combine** first 3 ingredients in a punch bowl. Place Strawberry Ice Ring in bowl.
● **Stir** in champagne just before serving. **Yield:** 1 gallon.

Strawberry Ice Ring

Whole fresh strawberries

● **Fill** a 6-cup ring mold two-thirds full with water, and freeze.
● **Arrange** whole strawberries on top; freeze 30 minutes. Slowly add enough water to fill mold, and freeze.
● **Let** stand at room temperature 5 minutes or until loosened to unmold. **Yield:** 1 ring mold.

Thru the Grapevine
Junior League of Greater Elmira-Corning,
New York

FROZEN MARGARITA PUNCH

QUICK!

4 (12-ounce) cans frozen limeade
    concentrate, thawed and
    undiluted
3 quarts water
3 cups Triple Sec or other
    orange-flavored liqueur
3 cups tequila
2 (2-liter) bottles lemon-lime
    carbonated beverage, chilled

● **Combine** first 4 ingredients.
● **Cover** and freeze at least 8 hours, stirring twice during freezing process.
● **Remove** from freezer 30 minutes before serving. Break into chunks; add lemon-lime carbonated beverage, and stir until mixture is slushy. **Yield:** 2½ gallons.

PINK PUNCH

*This punch is supposed to
be slushy, so prepare it at least
8 hours before you serve it.*

3 (6-ounce) cans frozen pink
  lemonade concentrate, thawed
  and undiluted
2 (750-milliliter) bottles pink
  sparkling wine
3 (2-liter) bottles lemon-lime
  carbonated beverage, divided

• **Combine** lemonade concentrate,
wine, and 2 bottles lemon-lime beverage
in an airtight container, stirring well;
cover and freeze 8 hours or until mixture is firm.
• **Let** mixture stand at room temperature
10 minutes; place in a punch bowl.
Add remaining bottle lemon-lime beverage, stirring gently until slushy. **Yield:**
2½ gallons.

Kathy Bowes
Metairie, Louisiana

IRISH COFFEE-EGGNOG PUNCH

2 quarts refrigerated eggnog
⅓ cup firmly packed brown sugar
3 tablespoons instant coffee
  granules
½ teaspoon ground cinnamon
½ teaspoon ground nutmeg
1 cup Irish whiskey (optional) *
1 quart coffee ice cream, scooped
  into balls
Garnishes: sweetened whipped
  cream, freshly grated nutmeg

• **Combine** first 5 ingredients in a large
mixing bowl; beat at low speed with an
electric mixer until sugar dissolves.
Chill 15 minutes; stir until coffee granules dissolve. Stir in whiskey, if desired.
• **Cover** and chill at least 1 hour. Pour
into a punch bowl or individual cups,
leaving enough room for ice cream.
Spoon in ice cream. Garnish, if desired.
Yield: about 3 quarts.

* Substitute ½ teaspoon rum extract.
Paula McCollum
Springtown, Texas

AMARETTO SLUSH

QUICK!

1 (46-ounce) can pineapple
  juice
3 cups amaretto
1 (12-ounce) can frozen pink
  lemonade concentrate, thawed
  and undiluted
1 (6-ounce) can frozen pink
  lemonade concentrate, thawed
  and undiluted
⅓ cup lemon juice
1 (3-liter) bottle lemon-lime
  carbonated beverage,
  chilled

• **Combine** first 5 ingredients in a large
plastic container.
• **Cover** and freeze at least 8 hours, stirring twice during freezing process. To
serve, combine equal portions of frozen
mixture and lemon-lime beverage, stirring well. Cover and store any remaining frozen mixture in freezer. Serve
immediately. **Yield:** 6 quarts.

Elizabeth A. Crawley
New Orleans, Louisiana

PIÑA COLADA SLUSH

QUICK!

1 (46-ounce) can pineapple juice
2 (12-ounce) cans frozen
  lemonade concentrate, thawed
  and undiluted
3 cups water
2 cups light rum
1 (15-ounce) can cream of
  coconut
1 (3-liter) bottle lemon-lime
  carbonated beverage,
  chilled

• **Combine** first 5 ingredients in a large
plastic container.
• **Cover** and freeze at least 8 hours, stirring twice during freezing process. To
serve, combine equal portions of frozen
mixture and lemon-lime beverage, stirring well. Cover and store any remaining frozen mixture in freezer. Serve
immediately. **Yield:** 6 quarts.

Linda Janca
Mount Mourne, North Carolina

HOT SPICED PUNCH

QUICK!

*When brewed, this punch sends a
wonderful aroma throughout your house.*

3 (¼-inch-thick) slices fresh
  ginger
1 stick cinnamon
8 whole cloves
4 cardamom seeds
1 gallon apple cider
1 quart pineapple juice
6 lemons, peeled and sliced
6 small oranges, peeled and
  sliced

• **Place** first 4 ingredients in a cheesecloth bag; combine spice bag, cider, and
remaining ingredients in a large Dutch
oven. Bring to a boil; reduce heat, and
simmer 15 minutes, stirring occasionally. Remove and discard spice bag.
Serve punch warm. **Yield:** about 5
quarts.

Hot Spiced Rum Punch: Gently stir in
1½ cups rum before serving. **Yield:** 5½
quarts.

Ellie Wells
Lakeland, Florida

GOLDEN WASSAIL

QUICK!

1 quart unsweetened pineapple
  juice
1 quart apple cider
1 (11.5-ounce) can apricot nectar
1 cup orange juice
2 (2-inch) sticks cinnamon
1 teaspoon whole cloves
¼ teaspoon salt
¼ teaspoon ground cardamom
Garnish: cinnamon sticks

• **Combine** first 8 ingredients in a large
Dutch oven; bring to a boil over
medium-high heat, stirring occasionally.
Reduce heat, and simmer 15 minutes.
• **Remove** and discard cinnamon sticks
and cloves; garnish, if desired. Serve immediately. **Yield:** 2 quarts.

Marty Sprague
Fort Worth, Texas

CINNAMON WINTER CIDER

QUICK!

1 (12-ounce) can frozen apple
    juice concentrate, thawed and
    undiluted
1 (12-ounce) can frozen
    cranberry-apple juice
    concentrate, thawed and
    undiluted
1 (6-ounce) can frozen lemonade
    concentrate, thawed and
    undiluted
9 cups water
5 (3-inch) sticks cinnamon
6 whole cloves
1 teaspoon ground nutmeg
⅓ cup cinnamon schnapps or
    rum

• **Combine** first 7 ingredients in a Dutch oven; bring to a boil. Cover, reduce heat, and simmer 15 minutes. Remove and discard spices. Stir in schnapps; serve warm. **Yield:** 3 quarts.

Louise W. Mayer
Richmond, Virginia

SUGAR-AND-SPICE HOT CHOCOLATE

¼ cup cocoa
⅓ cup sugar
½ teaspoon ground cinnamon
¼ teaspoon ground nutmeg
⅛ teaspoon salt
½ cup hot water
3½ cups milk
1 teaspoon vanilla extract
Garnishes: whipped cream, ground
    cloves

• **Combine** first 5 ingredients in a large saucepan; stir in hot water.
• **Bring** mixture to a boil over medium heat, stirring constantly; reduce heat, and simmer 2 minutes.
• **Add** milk, and cook, stirring constantly, until mixture is thoroughly heated (do not boil). Remove from heat; add vanilla, stirring with a wire whisk until mixture is frothy. Garnish, if desired. **Yield:** 4 cups.

Charlotte Pierce Bryant
Greensburg, Kentucky

TENNESSEE HOT CHOCOLATE

For a richer, darker cup of hot chocolate, use Dutch-processed cocoa. It has a lower natural acidity, which is perfect for this recipe.

3 cups milk
¾ cup half-and-half
½ cup sugar
½ cup cocoa
⅓ to ½ cup bourbon
1 teaspoon vanilla extract
Marshmallows (optional)

• **Combine** milk and half-and-half in a medium saucepan; cook over medium heat until mixture is thoroughly heated (do not boil). Add sugar and cocoa, stirring with a wire whisk until blended. Remove from heat, and whisk in bourbon and vanilla. Pour into mugs, and top with marshmallows, if desired. **Yield:** 4½ cups.

Wylene B. Gillespie
Gallatin, Tennessee

MEXICAN COFFEE

½ cup ground dark roast coffee
1 tablespoon ground cinnamon
¼ teaspoon ground nutmeg
5 cups water
¼ cup firmly packed dark brown
    sugar
⅓ cup chocolate syrup
1 cup milk
1 teaspoon vanilla extract
Sweetened whipped cream
Garnish: ground cinnamon

• **Place** coffee in coffee filter or filter basket; add cinnamon and nutmeg. Add water to coffeemaker; brew according to manufacturer's instructions.
• **Combine** brown sugar, chocolate syrup, and milk in a large heavy saucepan. Cook over low heat, stirring constantly, until sugar dissolves. Stir in coffee and vanilla. Serve immediately with a dollop of whipped cream; garnish, if desired. **Yield:** 6½ cups.

ORANGE COFFEE

4 sugar cubes
1 large orange
¼ cup sugar
2 tablespoons butter or margarine
½ cup brandy
¼ cup Triple Sec or other
    orange-flavored liqueur
4 cups brewed coffee
Garnishes: sweetened whipped
    cream, orange zest

• **Rub** sugar cubes over surface of orange until cubes are light yellow; place cubes in a large saucepan. Cut orange in half, and squeeze juice into saucepan, discarding orange halves; add ¼ cup sugar and butter.
• **Cook** over medium-high heat until sugar dissolves, stirring often. Stir in brandy and liqueur, and bring to a boil. Remove from heat.
• **Ignite** mixture carefully with a long match, and let burn until flames die. Stir in coffee, and pour into cups. Garnish, if desired. **Yield:** about 5 cups.

Mike Singleton
Memphis, Tennessee

SPICY TOMATO WARM-UP

QUICK!

1 (46-ounce) can spicy vegetable
    juice
3 beef-flavored bouillon cubes
3 tablespoons lemon juice
1 tablespoon Worcestershire sauce
⅛ teaspoon pepper
¼ to ½ teaspoon hot sauce

• **Combine** all ingredients in a large saucepan; cook over medium heat until bouillon cubes dissolve. Serve warm. **Yield:** 5½ cups.

At right: Orange-Pecan Scones (page 45), Basic Buttermilk Biscuits (page 44), and Potato-Bacon Biscuits (page 44)

BREADS

ARTICHOKE BREAD

¼ cup butter or margarine
2 to 3 cloves garlic, pressed
2 teaspoons sesame seeds
1 (14-ounce) can artichoke hearts,
   drained and chopped
1 cup (4 ounces) shredded
   Monterey Jack cheese
1 cup grated Parmesan cheese
½ cup sour cream
1 (16-ounce) loaf unsliced French
   bread
½ cup (2 ounces) shredded
   Cheddar cheese

● **Melt** butter in a skillet over medium-high heat. Add garlic and sesame seeds; cook, stirring constantly, until lightly browned. Remove from heat. Stir in artichoke hearts and next 3 ingredients. Set aside.
● **Cut** bread in half lengthwise. Scoop out center of each half, leaving a 1-inch shell; set shells aside. Crumble removed pieces of bread, and stir into artichoke mixture. Spoon mixture evenly into shells, and sprinkle with Cheddar cheese.
● **Place** each half on a baking sheet, and cover with aluminum foil. Bake at 350° for 25 minutes; uncover and bake 5 additional minutes or until cheese melts. Cut into slices. **Yield:** 12 servings.

Karin Barro
Shreveport, Louisiana

CHEESY GARLIC-STUFFED BREAD

1 (8-ounce) package cream cheese,
   softened
1 cup (4 ounces) shredded Swiss
   cheese
1 cup fresh parsley sprigs
2 to 4 cloves garlic
1 (20-ounce) large round loaf
   bread

● **Position** knife blade in food processor bowl; add first 4 ingredients. Process until smooth, stopping once to scrape down sides; set aside.
● **Slice** off top half of bread loaf; set top aside. Hollow out bottom half of bread

loaf, leaving a 1-inch shell. Set shell aside.
● **Cut** inside bread pieces into 1-inch cubes; place on a large baking sheet.
● **Bake** at 350° for 12 minutes or until lightly browned. Set aside.
● **Spoon** cheese mixture into center of bread shell, and replace bread top. Wrap filled bread in heavy-duty aluminum foil, and place on a baking sheet.
● **Bake** at 350° for 30 minutes or until thoroughly heated. Serve with toasted bread cubes. **Yield:** about 8 servings.

Sue-Sue Hartstern
Louisville, Kentucky

DILLY GARLIC BREAD

QUICK!

½ cup butter or margarine,
   softened
2 cloves garlic, pressed
¼ cup finely chopped fresh dill
1 (16-ounce) loaf French bread,
   cut in half horizontally
¼ cup grated Parmesan
   cheese

● **Combine** first 3 ingredients, and spread mixture evenly on cut sides of bread. Sprinkle with Parmesan cheese. Place on a baking sheet.
● **Bake** at 375° for 8 minutes or until golden. Slice crosswise into 1-inch slices. Serve immediately. **Yield:** 1 loaf.

Joy Knight Allard
San Antonio, Texas

GARLIC BREAD

QUICK!

The addition of Parmesan cheese and herbs perks up this familiar favorite.

½ cup butter or margarine,
   softened
¼ cup grated Parmesan cheese
2 cloves garlic, pressed
¼ teaspoon dried marjoram
¼ teaspoon dried oregano
1 (16-ounce) loaf French bread,
   cut into 1-inch slices

● **Combine** first 5 ingredients, and spread between bread slices.
● **Reassemble** loaf, and wrap in heavy-duty aluminum foil; place on a baking sheet.
● **Bake** at 350° for 20 minutes. Open foil, and bake 5 additional minutes or until bread is crisp and golden. Serve immediately. **Yield:** 1 loaf.

Jane Krebs
Fernandina Beach, Florida

BACON-CHEESE FRENCH BREAD

QUICK!

1 (16-ounce) loaf unsliced French
   bread
5 slices bacon, cooked and
   crumbled
2 cups (8 ounces) shredded
   mozzarella cheese
¼ cup butter or margarine, melted

● **Cut** bread into 1-inch slices. Reassemble loaf, and place on a large piece of heavy-duty aluminum foil.
● **Combine** bacon and cheese; place between bread slices. Drizzle butter over loaf, and wrap in foil.
● **Bake** at 350° for 20 minutes or until thoroughly heated. **Yield:** 1 loaf.

CHEESY FRENCH BREAD

QUICK!

1 (8-ounce) package shredded
   Mexican cheese blend
¾ cup mayonnaise
1½ teaspoons dried parsley flakes
⅛ teaspoon garlic powder
1 (16-ounce) loaf French bread,
   cut in half horizontally

● **Combine** first 4 ingredients, stirring well. Spread evenly on cut sides of bread; place on a baking sheet.
● **Bake** at 350° for 15 to 20 minutes or until melted and lightly browned. Slice crosswise into 1-inch slices. Serve immediately. **Yield:** 1 loaf.

Lisa Lock
Fort Worth, Texas

MEMMIE'S SPOONBREAD

1½ cups boiling water
1 cup cornmeal
1 teaspoon salt
2 tablespoons butter or margarine
1 cup milk
2 large eggs, lightly beaten
2 teaspoons baking powder

• **Pour** water gradually over cornmeal, stirring until smooth. Add salt and butter, stirring until blended; cool 10 minutes. Gradually stir in milk and eggs. Add baking powder, stirring until blended. Pour mixture into a lightly greased 1½-quart baking dish.
• **Bake** at 375° for 40 minutes or until lightly browned. **Yield:** 4 to 6 servings.
Savannah Style
Junior League of Savannah, Georgia

VICKSBURG CORNBREAD

Johnny named this for his memories of the years when he traveled from his childhood home in Vicksburg, Mississippi, to visit his grandmother, "Ma E," just to get some of her cornbread.

2 tablespoons bacon drippings
1 cup all-purpose flour
1 cup yellow cornmeal
1 tablespoon baking powder
1 teaspoon salt
1 cup milk
1 large egg
5 ounces Gouda cheese, cut into
     cubes (optional)
¼ cup finely chopped green onions
     (optional)

• **Place** bacon drippings in a 10-inch cast-iron skillet, tilting pan to coat bottom evenly; heat in a 375° oven for 10 minutes.
• **Combine** flour and next 3 ingredients in a bowl. Combine milk and egg, stirring well. Add to flour mixture, stirring just until dry ingredients are moistened. If desired, stir in cheese and green onions.
• **Pour** hot drippings from skillet into batter; stir until blended. Pour batter into skillet.

• **Bake** at 375° for 20 minutes or until done. Immediately remove from skillet. **Yield:** 8 servings.

Note: Omit cheese and green onions when preparing cornbread for dressing.
Chef Johnny Earles
Criolla's
Destin, Florida

SOUR CREAM CORNBREAD
(pictured on page 375)

QUICK!

3 large eggs, lightly beaten
1 cup self-rising cornmeal
1 (8¾-ounce) can cream-style
     corn
1 (8-ounce) carton sour cream
¼ cup vegetable oil

• **Heat** a lightly greased 8-inch cast-iron skillet in a 400° oven 5 minutes.
• **Combine** all ingredients, stirring just until dry ingredients are moistened.
• **Remove** cast-iron skillet from oven, and spoon batter into hot skillet.
• **Bake** at 400° for 20 minutes or until golden. **Yield:** 6 servings.

Note: You can bake batter in lightly greased hot cornstick pans at 400° for 16 to 18 minutes. Yield: 16 cornsticks.
Laura Morris
Bunnell, Florida

PECAN CORNBREAD

1½ cups yellow cornmeal
1 cup unbleached flour
1 tablespoon baking powder
1 teaspoon salt
¼ cup sugar
1½ cups half-and-half
¾ cup butter or margarine, melted
2 large eggs, lightly beaten
½ cup chopped pecans

• **Combine** first 5 ingredients in a large bowl; make a well in center of mixture. Set aside.
• **Combine** half-and-half and remaining 3 ingredients. Add to dry ingredients,

stirring just until moistened. Pour into a well-greased 9- x 5- x 3-inch loafpan.
• **Bake** at 375° for 45 to 50 minutes or until golden. Remove from pan, and serve immediately or cool on a wire rack. **Yield:** 1 (9-inch) loaf.
Thelma Peedin
Princeton, North Carolina

SERRANO CHILE BLUE CORNBREAD

1¼ cups blue cornmeal
1 cup all-purpose flour
1 tablespoon baking powder
1 teaspoon salt
⅛ teaspoon baking soda
2 tablespoons sugar
2 tablespoons butter or margarine
3 to 4 serrano chiles, finely
     chopped
3 cloves garlic, minced
1 red bell pepper, finely chopped
1 green bell pepper, finely chopped
2 large eggs, lightly beaten
1 cup buttermilk
⅓ cup butter or margarine, melted
⅓ cup shortening, melted
2 tablespoons plain low-fat yogurt
1 (11-ounce) can white corn,
     drained
3 tablespoons chopped fresh
     cilantro

• **Combine** first 6 ingredients in a large bowl; make a well in center of mixture. Set aside.
• **Melt** butter in a large skillet; add serrano chiles and next 3 ingredients. Cook over medium heat, stirring constantly, 2 to 3 minutes or until vegetables are tender. Set aside.
• **Combine** eggs and next 5 ingredients; add to dry ingredients, stirring just until moistened. Stir in vegetable mixture and cilantro.
• **Place** a well-greased 10-inch cast-iron skillet in a 450° oven for 4 minutes or until hot. Remove from oven; spoon batter into skillet.
• **Bake** at 450° for 25 minutes or until cornbread is lightly browned. **Yield:** 8 to 10 servings.
Kelli Silliman
Dallas, Texas

SOUFFLÉ CORNBREAD

1 (28-ounce) package frozen
    whole kernel corn, thawed *
6 tablespoons butter or margarine,
    softened
2 large eggs, separated
½ cup whipping cream
1½ cups yellow cornmeal
1 cup all-purpose flour
1 tablespoon baking powder
1½ teaspoons salt
⅓ cup sugar
Vegetable cooking spray

• **Position** knife blade in food processor; add corn to bowl, and process 1 to 2 minutes or until juicy. Pour corn through a wire-mesh strainer into a 2-cup liquid measuring cup, discarding solids in strainer. (You'll need 1¼ cups corn liquid. If liquid doesn't readily separate from solids in processing, combine ¾ cup processed corn and ½ cup milk.)
• **Beat** butter and egg yolks in a large mixing bowl at medium speed with an electric mixer until smooth. Add corn liquid and whipping cream, stirring well. (Mixture will be lumpy.)
• **Combine** cornmeal and next 4 ingredients; add to corn mixture, stirring until blended.
• **Heat** a 10-inch cast-iron skillet in a 375° oven for 5 to 10 minutes.
• **Beat** egg whites at high speed until stiff peaks form; gently fold into cornmeal mixture.
• **Remove** skillet from oven; coat with cooking spray. Pour cornmeal mixture into skillet.
• **Bake** at 375° for 25 minutes or until golden. **Yield:** 8 servings.

* Substitute 2 (15¼-ounce) cans whole kernel corn or 5½ cups fresh corn kernels (8 to 10 ears) for frozen corn.
Chef Johnny Earles
Criolla's
Destin, Florida

SPINACH CORNBREAD

QUICK!

1 (10-ounce) package frozen
    chopped spinach, thawed
1 (6-ounce) package Mexican
    cornbread mix
1 cup chopped onion
¾ cup cottage cheese
½ cup butter or margarine,
    melted
4 large eggs, lightly beaten
½ teaspoon salt

• **Drain** spinach well, pressing between layers of paper towels. Place spinach in a bowl; add cornbread mix and remaining ingredients, stirring until blended. Pour into a lightly greased 8-inch square baking dish.
• **Bake** at 400° for 30 minutes or until lightly browned. Serve immediately. **Yield:** 9 servings.

Sandra Stewart
Northport, Alabama

GARLIC-THYME CORN STICKS

QUICK!

1¼ cups yellow cornmeal
¾ cup all-purpose flour
1 tablespoon sugar
1 tablespoon plus 1 teaspoon
    baking powder
¾ teaspoon salt
¾ teaspoon garlic powder
1 tablespoon chopped fresh
    thyme or 1 teaspoon dried
    thyme
2 large eggs, lightly beaten
1 cup milk
¼ cup vegetable oil

• **Heat** well-greased cast-iron corn stick pans in a 425° oven for 3 minutes or until hot.
• **Combine** first 7 ingredients in a large bowl; make a well in center of mixture.
• **Combine** eggs, milk, and oil; add to dry ingredients in bowl, stirring just until moistened.
• **Remove** pans from oven; spoon batter into pans, filling two-thirds full. Bake at 425° for 12 minutes or until lightly browned. **Yield:** 1½ dozen.

SAVORY CORN STICKS

2 jalapeño peppers, seeded and
    chopped
2 cloves garlic, minced
⅓ cup vegetable oil
½ cup yellow cornmeal
½ cup all-purpose flour
2 teaspoons baking powder
¾ teaspoon salt
1 tablespoon sugar
1 tablespoon chopped fresh
    cilantro or 1 teaspoon dried
    cilantro
1 large egg, lightly beaten
½ cup milk
Vegetable cooking spray

• **Cook** jalapeño peppers and garlic in oil in a saucepan over medium heat, stirring constantly, until tender; set aside.
• **Combine** cornmeal and next 5 ingredients; add jalapeño pepper mixture, egg, and milk, stirring until smooth.
• **Coat** a cast-iron breadstick or corn stick pan with cooking spray; heat in a 425° oven 3 minutes or until hot. Remove pan from oven; spoon batter into pan. Bake at 425° for 15 to 20 minutes or until lightly browned. **Yield:** 8 breadsticks or 6 corn sticks.

APRICOT-ORANGE BREAD

1 (6-ounce) package dried apricot
    halves, diced
¾ cup firmly packed brown sugar
1 cup nonfat buttermilk
½ cup fat-free egg substitute
3 tablespoons vegetable oil
1 tablespoon grated orange rind
1¼ teaspoons vanilla extract
¼ teaspoon almond extract
1½ cups all-purpose flour
¾ cup whole wheat flour
1½ teaspoons baking powder
1 teaspoon baking soda
½ teaspoon salt
Vegetable cooking spray
Garnishes: dried apricot halves,
    orange rind strips, cinnamon
    sticks, grape leaves

• **Combine** first 8 ingredients; let stand 5 minutes.

• **Combine** all-purpose flour and next 4 ingredients in a large bowl; make a well in center of mixture. Add apricot mixture to dry ingredients, stirring just until moistened.

• **Coat** a 6-cup Bundt pan or a 9- x 5- x 3-inch loafpan with cooking spray. Spoon batter into pan.

• **Bake** at 350° for 35 minutes or until a wooden pick inserted in center comes out clean. Cool in pan on a wire rack 10 minutes; remove from pan, and cool on wire rack. Garnish, if desired. **Yield:** 21 servings.

Edna Mae Sharp
Sun City Center, Florida

♥ Per serving: Calories 122
Fat 2.2g Cholesterol 0mg
Sodium 141mg

FRUITY BANANA BREAD

Vegetable cooking spray
⅓ cup margarine, softened
¾ cup sugar
½ cup fat-free egg substitute
1¾ cups all-purpose flour
2¾ teaspoons baking powder
1 cup mashed ripe banana
¾ cup coarsely chopped dried
    mixed fruit

• **Coat** an 8½- x 4½- x 3-inch loafpan with cooking spray; set aside.

• **Beat** margarine at medium speed with an electric mixer until creamy; gradually add sugar, beating well. Add egg substitute, beating until blended.

• **Combine** flour and baking powder; add to butter mixture. Beat at low speed until blended. Stir in mashed banana and dried fruit. Pour batter into prepared loafpan.

• **Bake** at 350° for 1 hour or until a wooden pick inserted in center comes out clean. Cool in pan on a wire rack 10 minutes; remove from pan, and cool completely on a wire rack. **Yield:** 1 loaf.

Hilda Marshall
Bealeton, Virginia

♥ Per ½-inch slice: Calories 149
Fat 3.8g Cholesterol 0mg
Sodium 54mg

BUTTERNUT SPICE LOAF

1 (2-pound) butternut squash
½ cup butter, softened
1½ cups sugar
2 large eggs
2 cups self-rising flour
1 teaspoon ground cinnamon
½ teaspoon ground nutmeg
½ teaspoon ground allspice
¼ teaspoon ground ginger
½ cup chopped pecans

• **Cut** squash in half lengthwise; remove seeds. Place squash, cut side down, in a shallow pan; add water to depth of ½ inch. Cover with aluminum foil, and bake at 400° for 1 hour or until tender; drain. Scoop out pulp; mash. Discard shell. Measure 1¾ cups pulp; reserve any remaining pulp for another use.

• **Beat** butter at medium speed with an electric mixer until creamy; gradually add sugar, beating well. Add eggs, one at a time, beating after each addition.

• **Combine** flour and spices; add to butter mixture alternately with squash, beginning and ending with flour mixture. Stir in pecans.

• **Spoon** batter into a greased and floured 9- x 5- x 3-inch loafpan; bake at 350° for 1 hour or until a wooden pick inserted in center comes out clean. Cool in pan on a wire rack 10 minutes. Remove from pan, and let cool completely on wire rack. **Yield:** 1 loaf.

Loretta Wuest
Cantonment, Florida

MANGO BREAD

2 cups all-purpose flour
2 teaspoons baking soda
½ teaspoon salt
1½ cups sugar
2 teaspoons ground cinnamon
3 large eggs, lightly beaten
¾ cup vegetable oil
2 cups finely chopped mango
½ cup chopped pecans or walnuts
1 tablespoon lime juice
½ cup raisins (optional)

• **Combine** first 5 ingredients, and make a well in center of mixture.

• **Combine** eggs and oil; add to dry ingredients, stirring just until moistened. Stir in mango, pecans, lime juice, and raisins, if desired.

• **Spoon** batter into two greased and floured 8½- x 4½- x 3-inch loafpans.

• **Bake** at 375° for 1 hour or until a wooden pick inserted in center comes out clean. Cool in pans on wire racks 10 minutes; remove from pans, and let cool completely on wire racks. **Yield:** 2 loaves.

Carrie Treichel
Johnson City, Tennessee

BLUEBERRY TEA BREAD

2 tablespoons sifted cake flour
2 tablespoons sugar
1 tablespoon chopped almonds
½ teaspoon ground cinnamon
½ cup butter, divided
1½ cups fresh blueberries
3 cups sifted cake flour, divided
1½ cups sugar
2 teaspoons baking powder
½ teaspoon salt
1 large egg, lightly beaten
1 cup milk
1 tablespoon vanilla extract

• **Combine** first 4 ingredients; stir in 1 teaspoon butter until crumbly. Set aside.

• **Combine** blueberries and 2 tablespoons flour; toss to coat. Set aside.

• **Combine** remaining cake flour, 1½ cups sugar, baking powder, and salt in a large bowl; cut in remaining butter with pastry blender until mixture is crumbly.

• **Combine** egg, milk, and vanilla, stirring well; add to flour mixture, stirring until dry ingredients are moistened. Add blueberry mixture, stirring gently (batter will be thin and lumpy).

• **Pour** batter into a greased and floured 9- x 5- x 3-inch loafpan, and sprinkle almond mixture evenly over batter.

• **Bake** at 350° for 1 hour and 10 minutes or until a wooden pick inserted in center comes out clean. Cool in pan on a wire rack 10 minutes; remove from pan, and let cool completely on wire rack. **Yield:** 1 loaf.

Wendy Dotson
Houston, Texas

ZUCCHINI LOAVES

You can freeze these loaves up to 1 month; drizzle with glaze after thawing.

3 large eggs, lightly beaten
1½ cups sugar
3 cups shredded zucchini
¾ cup vegetable oil
2 teaspoons vanilla extract
2 cups all-purpose flour
1 cup whole wheat flour
½ cup wheat germ
¼ cup nonfat dry milk powder
1 teaspoon baking powder
1 teaspoon baking soda
1 teaspoon salt
2 teaspoons ground cinnamon
½ teaspoon ground nutmeg
¼ teaspoon ground cloves
1 cup sifted powdered sugar
2 tablespoons milk
½ teaspoon vanilla extract
¼ cup chopped pecans, toasted

• **Combine** first 5 ingredients; stir well.
• **Combine** all-purpose flour and next 9 ingredients, stirring well. Add to zucchini mixture, stirring just until blended. Spoon batter evenly into two greased and floured 8- x 4- x 2½-inch loafpans.
• **Bake** at 350° for 45 to 50 minutes or until a wooden pick inserted in center comes out clean. Cool in pans on wire racks 10 minutes; remove from pans, and let cool completely on wire racks.
• **Combine** powdered sugar, milk, and ½ teaspoon vanilla, stirring until smooth. Drizzle evenly over loaves; sprinkle with pecans. **Yield:** 2 loaves.

Ann Birkmire
Sharon, Massachusetts

CRUNCHY BREAKFAST BREAD

1¾ cups all-purpose flour
2½ teaspoons baking powder
½ teaspoon salt
1 cup sugar
¾ cup nutlike cereal nuggets
½ cup raisins
2 tablespoons grated orange rind
1 large egg, lightly beaten
1 cup milk
¼ cup vegetable oil

• **Combine** first 7 ingredients in a large bowl; make a well in center of mixture.
• **Combine** egg, milk, and oil; add to dry ingredients, stirring just until dry ingredients are moistened.
• **Spoon** into a greased and floured 8½- x 4½- x 3-inch loafpan. Bake at 350° for 1 hour or until a wooden pick inserted in center comes out clean. Cool in pan on a wire rack 10 minutes; remove from pan, and cool on wire rack. **Yield:** 1 loaf.

Jodie McCoy
Tulsa, Oklahoma

COWBOY COFFEE CAKE

QUICK!

2 (11-ounce) cans refrigerated buttermilk biscuits
¼ cup butter or margarine, melted
⅓ cup firmly packed brown sugar
⅓ cup chopped pecans
1 teaspoon ground cinnamon

• **Arrange** biscuits in a lightly greased 9-inch round cakepan, overlapping edges.
• **Combine** butter and remaining 3 ingredients; spread evenly over biscuits.
• **Bake** at 350° for 22 minutes or until golden. Serve warm. **Yield:** 1 (9-inch) coffee cake.

James Michelinie
Louisville, Kentucky

CINNAMON-RAISIN COFFEE CAKE

1½ cups all-purpose flour
1 tablespoon baking powder
½ teaspoon salt
¾ cup sugar
¼ cup shortening
1 large egg, lightly beaten
½ cup milk
1 teaspoon vanilla extract
½ cup firmly packed brown sugar
½ cup raisins or chopped walnuts
2 tablespoons all-purpose flour
2 teaspoons ground cinnamon
2 tablespoons butter, melted

• **Combine** first 4 ingredients; cut in shortening with pastry blender until mixture is crumbly. Combine egg, milk, and vanilla; add to flour mixture, stirring until blended. Set batter aside.
• **Combine** brown sugar and next 3 ingredients; stir in butter.
• **Spoon** two-thirds of batter into a greased and floured 9-inch round cakepan; sprinkle with brown sugar mixture, and top with remaining batter. Bake at 375° for 25 minutes or until golden. **Yield:** 1 (9-inch) coffee cake.

A Taste of Oregon
Junior League of Eugene, Oregon

NUTTY ORANGE COFFEE CAKE
(pictured at right)

¾ cup sugar
½ cup chopped pecans
2 teaspoons grated orange rind
½ (8-ounce) package reduced-fat cream cheese
2 (11-ounce) cans refrigerated buttermilk biscuits
½ cup butter or margarine, melted
1 cup sifted powdered sugar
2 tablespoons fresh orange juice

• **Combine** first 3 ingredients in a small bowl; set aside.
• **Place** about ¾ teaspoon cream cheese in center of each biscuit; fold biscuit in half over cheese, pressing edges to seal.
• **Dip** biscuits in melted butter, and dredge in sugar mixture; place biscuits, curved side down, in a single layer in curves of a lightly greased 12-cup Bundt pan, spacing evenly (do not stack). Place any remaining biscuits around center tube of pan, filling in spaces, if necessary. Drizzle any remaining butter over biscuits; sprinkle with any remaining sugar mixture.
• **Bake** at 350° for 35 to 40 minutes or until done. Immediately invert onto a serving plate.
• **Combine** powdered sugar and orange juice, stirring well; drizzle over warm coffee cake. Serve immediately. **Yield:** 1 (10-inch) coffee cake.

Barbara Kennedy
Fort Pierce, Florida

Nutty Orange Coffee Cake

MAMA CLE'S SPECIAL COFFEE CAKE

½ cup butter or margarine,
　　softened
½ cup shortening
1¼ cups sugar
2 large eggs
1 (8-ounce) carton sour cream
2 cups all-purpose flour
1 teaspoon baking powder
½ teaspoon baking soda
½ teaspoon salt
1 teaspoon vanilla extract
½ cup chopped pecans
2 tablespoons sugar
1 teaspoon ground cinnamon
Sifted powdered sugar

• **Beat** butter and shortening at medium speed with an electric mixer about 2 minutes or until creamy. Gradually add 1¼ cups sugar, beating at medium speed 5 to 7 minutes. Add eggs, one at a time, beating just until yellow disappears. Add sour cream, mixing until blended.
• **Combine** flour and next 3 ingredients in a medium bowl, stirring well. Gradually add flour mixture to butter mixture, mixing until blended. Stir in vanilla. Spoon half of batter into a greased and floured 8-inch tube pan.
• **Combine** chopped pecans, 2 tablespoons sugar, and cinnamon in a small bowl, stirring well; sprinkle half of pecan mixture over batter in pan. Repeat procedure with remaining batter and pecan mixture.
• **Bake** at 350° for 55 minutes. Cool in pan on a wire rack 10 to 15 minutes; remove coffee cake from pan, and let cool completely on wire rack. Sprinkle with sifted powdered sugar. **Yield:** 1 (8-inch) coffee cake.

Carolanne Griffith-Roberts
Birmingham, Alabama

PINEAPPLE-COCONUT COFFEE CAKE

2 (15¼-ounce) cans crushed
　　pineapple, undrained
½ cup butter or margarine,
　　softened
1 cup sugar
1 cup firmly packed brown
　　sugar
2 large eggs
2½ cups all-purpose flour
1 teaspoon baking powder
1 teaspoon baking soda
¼ teaspoon salt
1 (3½-ounce) can flaked
　　coconut
1 cup chopped pecans
1 teaspoon vanilla extract
2 cups sifted powdered sugar
¼ cup flaked coconut, toasted
¼ cup chopped pecans, toasted

• **Drain** pineapple, reserving ¼ cup juice; set aside.
• **Beat** butter at medium speed with an electric mixer until creamy; gradually add 1 cup sugar and brown sugar, beating mixture well. Add eggs, one at a time, beating after each addition.
• **Combine** flour and next 3 ingredients; add to butter mixture, mixing well. Stir in pineapple, 3½-ounce can coconut, 1 cup pecans, and vanilla.
• **Spoon** batter into two greased and floured 8½- x 4½- x 3-inch loafpans.
• **Bake** at 350° for 55 minutes or until a wooden pick inserted in center comes out clean. Cool in pans on wire racks 10 minutes; remove from pans, and let cool completely on wire racks.
• **Combine** powdered sugar and reserved juice; drizzle over cakes. Sprinkle with ¼ cup coconut and ¼ cup pecans. **Yield:** 2 coffee cakes.

Ann Boyle
Duluth, Georgia

BASIC BUTTERMILK BISCUITS
(pictured on page 37)

QUICK!

⅓ cup butter or margarine
2 cups self-rising soft-wheat flour
¾ cup buttermilk
Butter or margarine, melted

• **Cut** ⅓ cup butter into flour with pastry blender until mixture is crumbly. Add buttermilk, stirring until dry ingredients are moistened.
• **Turn** dough out onto a lightly floured surface; knead 3 or 4 times.
• **Roll** dough to ¾-inch thickness; cut with a 2½-inch round cutter, and place on a baking sheet.
• **Bake** biscuits at 425° for 12 to 14 minutes. Brush with melted butter. **Yield:** 10 biscuits.

Cornmeal-Jalapeño Biscuits: Substitute 1 cup self-rising cornmeal for 1 cup self-rising flour. Add 1 cup (4 ounces) shredded Monterey Jack cheese with peppers or 1 cup (4 ounces) shredded sharp Cheddar cheese and 1 chopped jalapeño pepper. Bake as directed. **Yield:** 10 biscuits.

Potato-Bacon Biscuits: Substitute 1 cup instant potato flakes for 1 cup self-rising flour. Add 8 slices cooked and crumbled bacon and ½ cup (2 ounces) shredded Colby cheese. Bake as directed. **Yield:** 10 biscuits.

Tomato-Herb Biscuits: Substitute ⅓ cup olive oil for butter or margarine. Stir in ½ cup grated Parmesan cheese, ¼ cup chopped oil-packed dried tomatoes, 1 teaspoon dried Italian seasoning, and ¼ teaspoon pepper. Bake biscuits as directed. **Yield:** 10 biscuits.

Country Ham Biscuits: Reduce butter to ¼ cup and buttermilk to ¼ cup. Add 1 (8-ounce) carton sour cream and 1 cup finely chopped cooked country ham. Bake biscuits as directed. **Yield:** 10 biscuits.

Beer and Cheese Biscuits: Add 1 cup (4 ounces) shredded Swiss cheese and 1 teaspoon dried sage or rubbed sage to flour mixture. Substitute ¾ cup beer for buttermilk. Bake biscuits as directed. **Yield:** 10 biscuits.

Orange-Pecan Scones: Add 3 tablespoons sugar, 1 teaspoon grated orange rind, 1 teaspoon vanilla extract, and ½ cup chopped pecans. Divide dough in half; roll each portion into a 7-inch circle, and place on a lightly greased baking sheet. Cut each circle into 8 wedges. Bake as directed. **Yield:** 16 scones.

BISCUITS

QUICK!

2 cups self-rising soft wheat
    flour
⅛ teaspoon baking powder
1 tablespoon sugar
¾ cup shortening
1 cup buttermilk
1 tablespoon butter or margarine,
    melted

• **Combine** first 3 ingredients in a large bowl; cut in shortening with pastry blender until mixture is crumbly. Add buttermilk, stirring with a fork until dry ingredients are moistened. (Dough will resemble cottage cheese and be sticky.)
• **Turn** dough out onto a heavily floured surface, and knead lightly 4 or 5 times.
• **Roll** dough to ¾-inch thickness; cut with a 2½-inch round cutter. Stack two baking sheets, one on top of the other. Lightly grease top baking sheet.
• **Place** biscuits on top baking sheet, and bake at 450° for 10 to 12 minutes or until lightly browned. Brush with butter. **Yield:** 10 biscuits.

Kregg Owens
Rome, Georgia

CINNAMON-RAISIN BREAKFAST BISCUITS

1⅓ cups corn flakes cereal
2 tablespoons brown sugar
1 teaspoon ground cinnamon
2 tablespoons butter or margarine,
    melted
2½ cups biscuit mix
2 tablespoons sugar
½ cup raisins
⅓ cup buttermilk
⅓ cup tonic water
½ teaspoon vanilla extract
Frosting

• **Combine** first 3 ingredients in container of an electric blender or food processor; process until mixture resembles fine crumbs. Transfer to a small bowl; add butter, stirring until moistened. Set aside.
• **Combine** biscuit mix, 2 tablespoons sugar, and raisins in a large bowl; add

RASPBERRY-ALMOND BISCUITS

3 cups all-purpose flour
1 tablespoon baking powder
½ teaspoon baking soda
⅛ teaspoon salt
½ cup sugar
¾ cup butter or margarine, cut
    into pieces
1 cup fresh or frozen raspberries,
    thawed and well drained
½ cup chopped almonds
1½ teaspoons grated orange rind
¾ cup milk
¾ cup plain yogurt

• **Combine** first 5 ingredients in a large bowl; cut in butter with pastry blender until mixture is crumbly. Stir in raspberries, almonds, and orange rind. Add milk and yogurt, stirring with a fork until dry ingredients are moistened. (Dough will be very sticky.) Turn dough out onto a heavily floured surface, and knead lightly 5 or 6 times.
• **Roll** to ¾-inch thickness; cut with a 2½-inch round cutter. Place on a lightly greased baking sheet. Bake at 400° for 20 to 25 minutes or until lightly browned. **Yield:** 20 biscuits.

buttermilk, tonic water, and vanilla, stirring with a fork until dry ingredients are moistened.
• **Turn** dough out onto a lightly floured surface, and knead lightly 3 or 4 times. Gradually sprinkle with cereal mixture; knead just until blended.
• **Shape** into 12 balls, and place on a lightly greased baking sheet. Press each into a ½-inch-thick biscuit.
• **Bake** at 400° for 15 to 18 minutes or until browned. Transfer immediately to a wire rack, and spread with Frosting. **Yield:** 1 dozen.

Frosting

QUICK!

1½ cups sifted powdered sugar
2 tablespoons butter or margarine,
    melted
2 tablespoons sour cream
1 teaspoon vanilla extract

• **Combine** all ingredients in a small bowl. **Yield:** ⅔ cup.

Margaret Cotton
Franklin, Virginia

MIXER CHEESE BISCUITS

1 cup margarine, softened
2 cups (8 ounces) shredded extra-
    sharp Cheddar cheese
2 cups all-purpose flour
½ teaspoon salt
½ teaspoon ground red pepper
1 teaspoon lemon juice

• **Beat** margarine at medium speed with an electric mixer until creamy; gradually add cheese, beating well. Add flour, salt, and pepper; beat at low speed until blended. Add lemon juice, and beat at medium speed 20 minutes.
• **Pipe** or drop dough by level tablespoonfuls onto ungreased baking sheets.
• **Bake** at 300° for 20 minutes or until set. Transfer to wire racks to cool. **Yield:** 6 dozen.

Pass the Plate
The cookbook committee of
Christ Episcopal Church
New Bern, North Carolina

MEXICAN FIESTA SPOON BISCUITS

1 (17.3-ounce) can large
    refrigerated buttermilk
    biscuits
1 (10.8-ounce) can large
    refrigerated buttermilk
    biscuits
1 (16-ounce) jar chunky salsa
2 cups (8 ounces) shredded
    Monterey Jack cheese
1 small green bell pepper,
    chopped
½ cup sliced green onions
1 (2¼-ounce) can sliced ripe
    olives, drained

● **Cut** each biscuit into 8 pieces.
● **Combine** biscuits and salsa, tossing gently to coat. Spoon mixture into a lightly greased 13- x 9- x 2-inch baking dish. Top with shredded cheese and remaining ingredients.
● **Bake** at 350° for 45 minutes or until edges are golden and center is set; let stand 15 minutes. Cut biscuits into squares; serve with soup or salad. **Yield:** 15 servings.

LaJuan Coward
Jasper, Texas

ROSEMARY BISCUITS
QUICK!

4 cups biscuit mix
1½ teaspoons dried rosemary,
    crushed
1⅓ cups milk
¼ cup butter or margarine,
    melted

● **Combine** biscuit mix and rosemary in a large bowl. Add milk, stirring with a fork until dry ingredients are moistened. Turn dough out onto a lightly floured surface, and knead lightly 3 or 4 times.
● **Roll** dough to ½-inch thickness; cut with a 2-inch round cutter, and place on a lightly greased baking sheet.
● **Bake** at 450° for 8 minutes or until lightly browned. Brush with melted butter. **Yield:** 3 dozen.

COCONUT MUFFINS
QUICK!

2 cups all-purpose flour
2 teaspoons baking powder
1 cup sugar
½ cup frozen coconut, thawed
2 large eggs, lightly beaten
½ cup butter or margarine, melted
1 (8-ounce) carton plain low-fat
    yogurt
¼ teaspoon coconut extract

● **Combine** first 4 ingredients in a large bowl; make a well in center of mixture.
● **Combine** eggs and remaining 3 ingredients; add to dry ingredients, stirring just until moistened. Spoon into lightly greased or paper-lined muffin pans, filling three-fourths full.
● **Bake** at 375° for 25 minutes. Remove from pans immediately. **Yield:** 1 dozen.

Carol Joffrion
Shreveport, Louisiana

BANANA-NUT MUFFINS

1½ cups all-purpose flour
½ cup wheat germ
⅓ cup sugar
1 tablespoon baking powder
½ teaspoon salt
1¼ cups mashed ripe banana
    (about 3 medium)
½ cup milk
¼ cup vegetable oil
1 large egg, lightly beaten
Vegetable cooking spray
Topping

● **Combine** first 5 ingredients in a large bowl; make a well in center of mixture.
● **Combine** banana and next 3 ingredients; add to dry ingredients, stirring just until moistened.
● **Place** paper baking cups in muffin pans, and coat with cooking spray; spoon 3 tablespoons batter into each baking cup.
● **Bake** at 400° for 15 to 20 minutes or until golden. Remove from oven, and sprinkle 1 teaspoon Topping over each muffin. Return to oven, and bake 5 additional minutes. Remove from pans immediately. **Yield:** 15 muffins.

Topping
QUICK!

⅓ cup flaked coconut
⅓ cup chopped pecans
2 tablespoons honey
2 tablespoons butter or margarine,
    melted

● **Combine** all ingredients in a small bowl, and stir until blended. **Yield:** about ½ cup.

Mimi Davis
Owensboro, Kentucky

BLUEBERRY-STREUSEL MUFFINS

¼ cup slivered almonds
¼ cup firmly packed brown sugar
1 tablespoon all-purpose flour
2 tablespoons butter or margarine
½ cup regular oats, uncooked
2 cups all-purpose flour
2 teaspoons baking powder
¼ teaspoon baking soda
¼ teaspoon salt
½ cup sugar
2 teaspoons grated lemon rind
1½ cups fresh or frozen
    blueberries
1 large egg, lightly beaten
¾ cup buttermilk
¼ cup vegetable oil

● **Position** knife blade in food processor bowl; add almonds, and pulse 2 or 3 times or until chopped. Add brown sugar and 1 tablespoon flour; process 5 seconds. Add butter; pulse 5 times or until mixture is crumbly. Stir in oats; set aside.
● **Combine** 2 cups flour and next 5 ingredients in a large bowl; add blueberries, tossing gently. Make a well in center of mixture.
● **Combine** egg, buttermilk, and oil; add to flour mixture, stirring just until moistened. Spoon batter into greased muffin pans, filling two-thirds full; sprinkle with oat mixture.
● **Bake** at 400° for 15 to 20 minutes or until golden. Remove from pans immediately; cool on wire racks. **Yield:** 1 dozen.

GRANOLA MUFFINS

QUICK!

1½ cups reduced-fat biscuit mix
1 cup firmly packed brown sugar
1 teaspoon ground cinnamon
1 cup oats and honey granola
    cereal with almonds *
½ cup raisins
1 large egg, lightly beaten
¾ cup skim milk
1 tablespoon vegetable oil
Vegetable cooking spray

● **Combine** first 3 ingredients in a large bowl; stir in cereal and raisins. Make a well in center of mixture; set aside.
● **Combine** egg, milk, and oil; add to dry ingredients, stirring just until moistened. (Batter will be thin.)
● **Coat** muffin cups with cooking spray; spoon into muffin pans, filling three-fourths full.
● **Bake** at 375° for 15 to 20 minutes or until golden. **Yield:** 16 muffins.

* For oats and honey granola cereal with almonds, we used Quaker 100% Natural Oats & Honey Cereal.

Amanda E. Anglin
Magnolia, Mississippi

♥ Per muffin: Calories 140
Fat 3.3g Cholesterol 14mg
Sodium 153mg

KEY LIME MUFFINS

QUICK!

The fresh lime flavor of these muffins makes them the perfect choice to serve with a cup of tea.

2 cups all-purpose flour
1 tablespoon baking powder
½ teaspoon salt
1 cup sugar
⅓ cup milk
2 large eggs, lightly beaten
¼ cup vegetable oil
1 teaspoon grated lime rind
¼ cup Key lime juice

● **Combine** first 4 ingredients in a large bowl; make a well in center of mixture.

● **Combine** milk and remaining 4 ingredients; add to dry ingredients, stirring just until moistened. Spoon into lightly greased muffin pans, filling three-fourths full.
● **Bake** at 400° for 18 minutes or until lightly browned. Remove from pans immediately. **Yield:** 1 dozen.

Clairiece Gilbert Humphrey
Charlottesville, Virginia

POPPY SEED-LEMON MUFFINS

QUICK!

1 (18.5-ounce) package yellow
    cake mix with pudding
⅔ cup vegetable oil
⅔ cup apricot nectar
4 large eggs
⅓ cup poppy seeds
½ teaspoon grated lemon rind
2½ tablespoons fresh lemon
    juice

● **Combine** all ingredients, stirring until blended. Spoon into greased muffin pans, filling two-thirds full.
● **Bake** at 400° for 18 to 20 minutes or until done. Remove from pans immediately, and cool on wire racks. **Yield:** about 2 dozen.

Glyna Meredith Gallrein
Louisville, Kentucky

ORANGE BLOSSOM MUFFINS

QUICK!

2 cups biscuit mix
¼ cup sugar
1 large egg, lightly beaten
½ cup orange juice
2 tablespoons vegetable oil
½ cup orange marmalade
½ cup chopped pecans
3 tablespoons sugar
1 tablespoon all-purpose flour
½ teaspoon ground cinnamon
¼ teaspoon ground nutmeg

● **Combine** biscuit mix and ¼ cup sugar in a large bowl; make a well in center of mixture.

● **Combine** egg, orange juice, and oil; add to biscuit mixture, stirring just until moistened. Stir in marmalade and pecans.
● **Place** paper baking cups in muffin pans; spoon batter into cups, filling two-thirds full.
● **Combine** 3 tablespoons sugar and remaining 3 ingredients; sprinkle evenly over batter.
● **Bake** at 400° for 18 minutes. Remove from pans immediately. **Yield:** 1 dozen.

Bill and Tricia Kelly
Greenville, South Carolina

PUMPKIN-APPLE MUFFINS

QUICK!

1⅔ cups all-purpose flour
1 teaspoon baking soda
¼ teaspoon baking powder
¼ teaspoon salt
1 tablespoon pumpkin pie spice
1 cup sugar
1 cup canned pumpkin
½ cup butter or margarine, melted
2 large eggs, lightly beaten
1 Granny Smith apple, peeled and
    finely chopped
3 tablespoons sugar
1 teaspoon pumpkin pie spice

● **Combine** first 6 ingredients in a large bowl; make a well in center of mixture.
● **Combine** pumpkin, butter, and eggs, and add to dry ingredients, stirring just until moistened. Fold in chopped apple, and spoon into greased muffin pans, filling two-thirds full.
● **Combine** 3 tablespoons sugar and 1 teaspoon pumpkin pie spice; sprinkle evenly over muffins.
● **Bake** at 350° for 20 minutes. Remove from pans immediately, and cool on wire racks. **Yield:** 2 dozen.

June Silver
Morristown, Tennessee

RASPBERRY-STREUSEL MUFFINS

The streusel (German for "sprinkle") makes a delicious crown for these sweet muffins. It's a crumbly topping of flour, butter, sugar, and, in this recipe, chopped pecans.

1¾ cups all-purpose flour, divided
2 teaspoons baking powder
½ cup sugar
1 large egg, lightly beaten
½ cup milk
½ cup butter, melted
1 cup frozen unsweetened raspberries
2 tablespoons butter or margarine, melted
¼ cup chopped pecans
¼ cup firmly packed brown sugar

• **Combine** 1½ cups flour, baking powder, and sugar in a large bowl; make a well in center of mixture.
• **Combine** egg, milk, and ½ cup butter; add to dry ingredients, stirring just until moistened. Fold in raspberries. Spoon into greased muffin pans, filling two-thirds full.
• **Combine** remaining ¼ cup flour, 2 tablespoons butter, pecans, and brown sugar; sprinkle over muffins.
• **Bake** at 375° for 20 to 25 minutes. Remove from pans immediately. **Yield:** 1 dozen.

Bill and Tricia Kelly
Greenville, South Carolina

HOT BUTTERED RUM MUFFINS

½ cup butter or margarine, softened
½ cup sugar
2 large eggs
2 cups all-purpose flour
2 teaspoons baking powder
½ teaspoon salt
⅛ teaspoon ground cloves
⅛ teaspoon ground nutmeg
½ cup milk
5 tablespoons rum, divided
3 tablespoons sugar

• **Beat** butter at medium speed with an electric mixer until creamy. Add ½ cup sugar, beating well. Add eggs, one at a time, beating just until blended after each addition.
• **Combine** flour and next 4 ingredients. Combine milk and 3 tablespoons rum. Add flour mixture to butter mixture alternately with milk mixture, beginning and ending with flour mixture. Beat mixture at low speed until blended after each addition.
• **Spoon** into greased muffin pans, filling three-fourths full.
• **Bake** at 375° for 20 to 25 minutes or until golden. Remove from pans immediately; place on a wire rack.
• **Combine** remaining 2 tablespoons rum and 3 tablespoons sugar in a small saucepan; cook over low heat, stirring constantly, until sugar dissolves. Brush over warm muffins. **Yield:** 1 dozen.

Sandra Souther
Gainesville, Georgia

CHEESE MUFFINS

QUICK!

These golden pillowy muffins get top marks for ease, taste, and versatility.

2 tablespoons butter or margarine, divided
½ cup chopped onion
1½ cups biscuit mix
1 cup (4 ounces) shredded sharp process American cheese, divided
1 large egg, lightly beaten
½ cup milk
1 tablespoon sesame seeds, toasted

• **Melt** 1 tablespoon butter in a skillet over medium-high heat; add onion, and cook, stirring constantly, 3 minutes or until tender.
• **Combine** onion, biscuit mix, and ½ cup cheese in a large bowl. Combine egg and milk; add to onion mixture, stirring just until moistened.
• **Spoon** into greased muffin pans, filling half-full. Sprinkle with remaining ½ cup cheese and sesame seeds; dot with remaining 1 tablespoon butter.

• **Bake** at 400° for 13 minutes or until golden. Remove from pans immediately, and serve warm. **Yield:** 1 dozen.

Bill and Tricia Kelly
Greenville, South Carolina

DILLY CHEESE MUFFINS

QUICK!

3 cups biscuit mix
1½ cups (6 ounces) shredded Swiss cheese
1 tablespoon sugar
1 large egg
1¼ cups milk
1 tablespoon vegetable oil
1 tablespoon chopped fresh dill
½ teaspoon dry mustard
Vegetable cooking spray

• **Combine** first 3 ingredients in a large bowl; make a well in center of mixture.
• **Combine** egg and next 4 ingredients, stirring well; add to dry ingredients, stirring just until moistened.
• **Place** paper baking cups in muffin pans; coat with cooking spray. Add batter, filling two-thirds full.
• **Bake** at 350° for 25 to 28 minutes. Remove from pans immediately, and cool on wire racks. **Yield:** 1½ dozen.

Kathy Jones
Montreal, Missouri

SUNNY CORN MUFFINS

2 ears fresh corn in husks
2 tablespoons butter or margarine
¼ cup finely chopped onion
1 cup all-purpose flour
1 cup yellow cornmeal
1½ teaspoons baking powder
½ teaspoon baking soda
1 teaspoon salt
2 tablespoons sugar
1 cup buttermilk
1 large egg
¼ cup butter or margarine, melted
1 cup (4 ounces) shredded Cheddar cheese
1 (4.5-ounce) can chopped green chiles, drained
¼ cup sunflower kernels

- **Remove** husks from corn; tear husks into ½-inch strips. Soak husks in hot water 15 minutes; drain. Cut corn kernels from cobs.
- **Melt** 2 tablespoons butter in a large skillet over medium-high heat; add corn and onion, and cook until tender, stirring often. Set aside.
- **Combine** flour and next 5 ingredients in a large bowl; make a well in center of mixture.
- **Combine** buttermilk, egg, and ¼ cup melted butter; add to dry ingredients, stirring just until moistened. Stir in corn mixture, cheese, and chiles.
- **Arrange** 4 husk strips across each of 12 lightly greased muffin cups to resemble spokes; spoon batter into cups, filling each three-fourths full. Sprinkle with sunflower kernels.
- **Bake** at 375° for 18 to 20 minutes or until muffins are golden (corn husks will brown deeply). Remove immediately from pans; cool on wire racks. **Yield:** 1 dozen.

EASY CARAMEL-CHOCOLATE STICKY BUNS

1 (15-ounce) can coconut-pecan frosting
1 cup pecan halves
2 (10-ounce) cans refrigerated buttermilk biscuits
20 chocolate kisses, unwrapped

- **Spread** frosting in bottom of a lightly greased 9-inch square pan. Arrange pecan halves over frosting. Set aside.
- **Separate** biscuits; flatten each to about ¼-inch thickness. Place a chocolate kiss to 1 side of center of each biscuit. Fold biscuit in half, forming a semicircle; press edges of biscuits gently to seal. Repeat procedure with remaining biscuits and chocolate kisses. Arrange biscuits over pecans, placing flat sides down.
- **Bake** at 375° for 28 to 30 minutes or until lightly browned. Cool in pan on a wire rack 5 minutes; invert onto serving plate, and serve immediately. **Yield:** 20 servings.

Doris J. Phillips
Fayetteville, Arkansas

FRENCH BREAKFAST PUFFS

⅓ cup butter or margarine, melted
½ cup sugar
1 large egg
1½ cups all-purpose flour
1½ teaspoons baking powder
½ teaspoon salt
¼ teaspoon ground nutmeg
½ cup milk
¼ cup sugar
½ teaspoon ground cinnamon
2 tablespoons butter or margarine, melted

- **Beat** first 3 ingredients at medium speed with an electric mixer until creamy and well blended.
- **Combine** flour and next 3 ingredients; add to butter mixture alternately with milk, beginning and ending with flour mixture. Beat at low speed until blended after each addition. Spoon into greased miniature (1¾-inch) muffin pans, filling two-thirds full.
- **Bake** at 350° for 14 to 16 minutes. Remove from pans immediately.
- **Combine** ¼ cup sugar and cinnamon. Dip tops of muffins in 2 tablespoons melted butter, and then in sugar mixture. **Yield:** 28 miniature muffins.

Note: If using regular muffin pans, bake 20 to 25 minutes. Yield: 10 muffins.

Virginia Cookery, Past and Present
Olivet Episcopal Church Women
Franconia, Virginia

HAZELNUT SCONES

2 cups all-purpose flour
2 teaspoons baking powder
¼ teaspoon salt
½ cup sugar
⅓ cup butter
½ cup chopped blanched hazelnuts
2 large eggs, lightly beaten
½ cup whipping cream
1½ tablespoons Frangelico or other hazelnut-flavored liqueur
1 tablespoon sugar
18 whole hazelnuts

- **Combine** first 4 ingredients in a large bowl; cut in butter with pastry blender until mixture is crumbly. Stir in chopped hazelnuts; make a well in center of mixture, and set aside.
- **Combine** eggs, whipping cream, and liqueur; add to dry ingredients, stirring just until moistened.
- **Roll** dough to ¾-inch thickness on a lightly floured surface. Cut with a 2½-inch daisy-shaped cutter, and place on baking sheets. Sprinkle tops evenly with 1 tablespoon sugar, and place a hazelnut in each center.
- **Bake** at 350° for 15 minutes. Serve with Lemon Honey (see recipe on page 354), butter, and strawberry jam. **Yield:** 1½ dozen.

Sharon McCullar
Victoria Room
Shreveport, Louisiana

CRANBERRY SCONES

2½ cups all-purpose flour
2 teaspoons baking powder
½ teaspoon salt
½ cup sugar
½ teaspoon ground cloves
¼ cup butter or margarine
1 cup whipping cream
¾ cup fresh or frozen cranberries, thawed, coarsely chopped

- **Combine** first 5 ingredients; cut in butter with pastry blender until mixture is crumbly.
- **Reserve** 1 tablespoon whipping cream; add remaining whipping cream and chopped cranberries to dry ingredients, stirring just until dry ingredients are moistened.
- **Turn** dough out onto a lightly floured surface; knead 5 or 6 times. Shape into an 8-inch circle. Cut into 8 wedges, and place on a lightly greased baking sheet. Prick wedges with a fork 3 or 4 times, and brush with reserved 1 tablespoon whipping cream.
- **Bake** at 425° for 18 minutes or until lightly browned. Serve warm with whipped cream, if desired. **Yield:** 8 scones.

Mary Bonney
Sterling, Virginia

QUICK CALAS

Pronounced "kah-LAHS," these fried rice cakes, similar to beignets, are named from an African word for rice. They've been popular in New Orleans for more than a century.

2 cups cooked long-grain rice
2 cups biscuit mix
2 tablespoons sugar
1 teaspoon ground cinnamon
1 teaspoon ground nutmeg
2 large eggs, lightly beaten
½ cup evaporated milk
1 teaspoon vanilla extract
Vegetable oil
Sifted powdered sugar

• **Combine** first 5 ingredients in a bowl. Combine eggs, milk, and vanilla; add to dry ingredients, stirring well. Cover and chill 1 hour.
• **Pour** oil to depth of 2 inches into a Dutch oven or electric fryer; heat to 350°. Drop batter by tablespoonfuls into hot oil. Fry calas, a few at a time, 2 minutes or until golden, turning once. Drain on paper towels. Sprinkle with powdered sugar; serve warm. **Yield:** about 4 dozen.

ACORN SQUASH PUPPIES

1 (1¾-pound) acorn squash
2 cups self-rising cornmeal
¼ cup all-purpose flour
1 large egg, lightly beaten
½ cup milk
½ cup finely chopped onion
Vegetable oil

• **Cut** acorn squash in half crosswise; remove and discard seeds. Place squash, cut side down, in a shallow baking dish or pan. Add water to dish to depth of ½ inch.
• **Bake** at 375° for 45 minutes or until tender. Drain and cool slightly.
• **Scoop** out pulp, discarding shells. Place pulp in container of an electric blender or food processor; process until smooth. Measure 1¼ cups squash puree; set aside. (Reserve any remaining puree for another use.)

• **Combine** cornmeal and flour in a large bowl; make a well in center of mixture. Set aside.
• **Combine** squash puree, egg, milk, and onion. Add to dry ingredients, stirring just until moistened.
• **Pour** oil to depth of 2 inches into a Dutch oven; heat to 360°. Drop by tablespoonfuls into hot oil. Cook 2 minutes or until golden, turning once. Drain on paper towels. **Yield:** 2 dozen.

Mary Horton
Moulton, Alabama

BAKED HUSH PUPPIES

QUICK!

1 cup yellow cornmeal
1 cup all-purpose flour
1 tablespoon baking powder
1 teaspoon salt
1 teaspoon sugar
⅛ teaspoon ground red pepper
2 large eggs, lightly beaten
¾ cup milk
½ cup finely chopped onion
¼ cup vegetable oil
Vegetable cooking spray

• **Combine** first 6 ingredients in a large bowl; make a well in center of mixture. Set aside.
• **Combine** eggs and next 3 ingredients, stirring well; add to dry ingredients, stirring just until moistened.
• **Coat** miniature muffin pans with cooking spray. Spoon about 1 tablespoon batter into each muffin cup, filling about three-fourths full.
• **Bake** at 425° for 15 minutes or until golden. Remove from pans, and serve immediately. **Yield:** 3 dozen.

Millie Givens
Savannah, Georgia

❤ Per hush puppy: Calories 55
Fat 2.4g Cholesterol 13mg
Sodium 71mg

CORN-JALAPEÑO FRITTERS
(pictured at right)

2 cups milk, divided
1 cup quick-cooking yellow grits
3 tablespoons butter or margarine, softened
1 teaspoon baking powder
1 teaspoon salt
2 large eggs, lightly beaten
¼ cup finely chopped red bell pepper
½ cup finely chopped green onions
1 to 2 teaspoons seeded, minced jalapeño pepper
2 tablespoons finely chopped fresh basil
1 cup fresh corn, cut from cob (about 2 ears)
¼ cup all-purpose flour
2 tablespoons olive oil, divided
Garnish: sour cream, green onion fan

• **Combine** ½ cup milk and grits; set aside.
• **Heat** remaining 1½ cups milk in a medium saucepan over medium-high heat until boiling. Add grits mixture, stirring constantly with a wire whisk. Cook 2 minutes or until thickened.
• **Remove** from heat, and pour into a large bowl; cool slightly. Add butter and next 9 ingredients, stirring well.
• **Heat** 1 tablespoon olive oil in a large nonstick skillet or griddle over medium heat until hot.
• **Pour** 1 tablespoon batter for each fritter into hot skillet, and cook fritters until tops are covered with bubbles and edges look cooked; turn and cook other side. Repeat procedure with remaining olive oil and batter. Garnish, if desired. **Yield:** 2 dozen.

Helen H. Maurer
Christmas, Florida

Corn-Jalapeño Fritters

ITALIAN CHEESE BREADSTICKS

QUICK!

1 (11-ounce) can refrigerated
    breadsticks
2 teaspoons dried Italian
    seasoning
1½ teaspoons garlic powder
¾ cup (3 ounces) shredded
    mozzarella cheese

• **Twist** breadsticks, and place on a baking sheet. Sprinkle with Italian seasoning and garlic powder.
• **Bake** at 350° for 10 to 13 minutes; sprinkle with cheese, and bake 5 additional minutes or until cheese melts and breadsticks are golden. Serve with spaghetti sauce and Ranch-style salad dressing for dipping. **Yield:** 6 servings.

Jennifer Cobble
Birmingham, Alabama

SEASONED BREADSTICKS

QUICK!

1 (11-ounce) can refrigerated
    breadsticks
Olive oil
1 teaspoon chili powder
½ teaspoon ground cumin

• **Unroll** dough onto a large cutting board; cut dough crosswise into thirds. Separate dough into 24 pieces; stretch each piece to 11 inches, and place ¼ inch apart on cutting board. Brush dough lightly with olive oil.
• **Combine** chili powder and cumin; sprinkle evenly over dough. Twist ends of dough pieces in opposite directions 3 or 4 times. Place breadsticks 1 inch apart on ungreased baking sheets, pressing ends securely.
• **Bake** at 350° for 12 to 14 minutes or until golden. Transfer to wire racks to cool. **Yield:** 2 dozen.

Caryn Hogan
Birmingham, Alabama

QUICK ROLLS

QUICK!

2¼ cups biscuit mix, divided
1 (8-ounce) carton sour cream
½ cup butter, melted

• **Combine** 2 cups biscuit mix, sour cream, and butter, stirring well.
• **Sprinkle** remaining ¼ cup biscuit mix over work surface. Drop dough by level tablespoonfuls onto biscuit mix, and roll into balls. Place 3 balls into each of 12 greased muffin cups.
• **Bake** at 350° for 15 to 20 minutes or until rolls are golden. **Yield:** 1 dozen.

Carolyn W. Olah
Crawfordville, Florida

CRÊPES

French for "pancake," the paper-thin crêpe is one of the most versatile recipes to cross the Atlantic. This savory recipe is perfect for a filling of chicken or vegetables.

1 cup all-purpose flour
¼ teaspoon salt
1¼ cups milk
2 large eggs
⅔ cup butter, melted and divided

• **Beat** first 3 ingredients at medium speed with an electric mixer until smooth. Add eggs, beating well; stir in 2 tablespoons melted butter. Cover and chill at least 1 hour.
• **Brush** bottom of a 6-inch nonstick skillet with melted butter; place over medium heat until hot.
• **Pour** 2 tablespoons batter into pan; quickly tilt in all directions so batter covers bottom of pan. Cook 1 minute or until crêpe can be shaken loose from pan. Turn crêpe over, and cook about 30 seconds. Place crêpe on a dish towel to cool. Repeat procedure with remaining batter. **Yield:** 16 (6-inch) crêpes.

Note: You can make crêpes ahead by stacking them between sheets of wax paper and placing in an airtight container. Store in the refrigerator up to 2 days or freeze up to 3 months.

EASY PANCAKES

QUICK!

1 (5.5-ounce) package or 1¼ cups
    biscuit mix *
1 large egg, beaten
⅔ cup milk
1 tablespoon vegetable oil

• **Place** biscuit mix in a medium bowl; make a well in center. Combine egg, milk, and oil, stirring well; add to biscuit mix, stirring just until dry ingredients are moistened.
• **Pour** about ¼ cup batter for each pancake onto a hot, lightly greased griddle. Cook pancakes until tops are covered with bubbles and edges of pancakes look cooked; turn and cook other side. **Yield:** 8 pancakes.

* You can substitute 1 (7-ounce) package bran muffin mix for biscuit mix.

GINGERBREAD PANCAKES

1 cup all-purpose flour
2 teaspoons baking powder
½ teaspoon salt
1 tablespoon sugar
1 tablespoon ground cinnamon
½ teaspoon ground ginger
¼ teaspoon ground allspice
⅛ teaspoon ground nutmeg
⅛ teaspoon ground cloves
1 large egg, lightly beaten
1 cup buttermilk
3 tablespoons butter or margarine,
    melted
1 tablespoon molasses
Orange Marmalade Syrup

• **Combine** first 9 ingredients in a large bowl; make a well in center of mixture.
• **Combine** egg and remaining 3 ingredients; add to dry ingredients, stirring just until moistened.
• **Spoon** about 2 tablespoons batter for each pancake onto a hot, lightly greased griddle.
• **Cook** until tops are covered with bubbles and edges look cooked; turn and cook other side. Serve pancakes with warm Orange Marmalade Syrup. **Yield:** 10 pancakes.

Orange Marmalade Syrup

QUICK!

⅔ cup maple syrup
⅓ cup orange marmalade

● **Combine** ingredients in a small saucepan, and bring to a boil, stirring constantly. **Yield:** 1 cup.

Joel Allard
San Antonio, Texas

HONEY-BUTTERED PEANUT BUTTER WAFFLES

QUICK!

⅓ cup chunky peanut butter
1 cup pancake mix
2 tablespoons sugar
1 (5-ounce) can evaporated milk
½ cup water
1 large egg
Honey Butter

● **Place** peanut butter in a 1-quart glass bowl. Microwave at HIGH 20 to 30 seconds.
● **Add** pancake mix and next 4 ingredients; beat at medium speed with an electric mixer just until smooth.
● **Bake** in a preheated, oiled waffle iron until golden. Serve with Honey Butter. **Yield:** 8 (4-inch) waffles.

Honey Butter

QUICK!

¼ cup butter, softened
2 tablespoons honey

● **Combine** butter and honey, stirring until blended. **Yield:** ⅓ cup.

Valerie Stutsman
Norfolk, Virginia

BELGIAN WAFFLES

4 large eggs, separated
3 tablespoons butter, melted
½ teaspoon vanilla extract
1 cup all-purpose flour
½ teaspoon salt
1 cup milk
Sweetened whipped cream
Sliced fresh strawberries

● **Beat** egg yolks at medium speed with an electric mixer until thick and pale. Add butter and vanilla, beating until blended. Set aside.
● **Combine** flour and salt. Add flour mixture and milk to egg mixture, beating until smooth. Set aside.
● **Beat** egg whites until stiff peaks form; fold into batter.
● **Bake** in a preheated, oiled Belgian waffle iron until golden. Serve with sweetened whipped cream and strawberries. **Yield:** 8 (4-inch) waffles.

Jane Maloy
Wilmington, North Carolina

ALMOND SUNBURST

1 (16-ounce) package hot roll mix
Vegetable cooking spray
Cornmeal
Fruit Filling
Glaze
Garnish: toasted sliced almonds

● **Prepare** roll mix according to directions up to point of shaping dough.
● **Coat** a 12-inch pizza pan with cooking spray; sprinkle with cornmeal.
● **Turn** dough out onto a floured surface; knead 4 or 5 times. Roll into a 15- x 10-inch rectangle; sprinkle with Fruit Filling to within 1 inch from edge.
● **Roll** up, jellyroll fashion, starting at long side; moisten edge with water, and pinch seam to seal. Place, seam side down, on prepared pan. Shape into a ring; moisten ends with water, and pinch together to seal.
● **Make** cuts in dough at 1-inch intervals, using kitchen shears, cutting from outside edge to, but not through, inside edge. Gently turn each slice on its side, slightly overlapping slices.

● **Cover** and let rise in a warm place (85°), free from drafts, 30 minutes or until doubled in bulk.
● **Bake** at 350° for 25 minutes or until golden. Remove to a wire rack; cool 15 minutes. Drizzle with Glaze. Garnish, if desired. **Yield:** 1 coffee cake.

Fruit Filling

QUICK!

½ cup raisins *
½ cup chopped dried apricot halves *
½ cup dried cherries *
½ cup chopped almonds
⅓ cup firmly packed brown sugar
2 teaspoons ground cinnamon
2 teaspoons grated orange rind
1 teaspoon grated lemon rind

● **Combine** all ingredients, stirring well. **Yield:** 2 cups.

* You can substitute 1 (6-ounce) package dried tropical fruit medley for the raisins, apricots, and cherries.

Glaze

QUICK!

1 cup sifted powdered sugar
2 tablespoons milk
1 teaspoon almond extract

● **Combine** all ingredients, stirring until smooth. **Yield:** ⅓ cup.

Greek Sunburst: Combine 1 (10-ounce) package frozen chopped spinach, thawed and well drained, 1 (4-ounce) package crumbled basil-tomato feta cheese, and ¼ teaspoon salt. Spread mixture over dough. Shape and let rise as directed. Sprinkle with 3 tablespoons grated Parmesan cheese, and bake as directed.

Pizza Sunburst: Spread ½ cup pizza sauce over dough. Brown ½ pound ground pork sausage in a small skillet, stirring until it crumbles; drain. Sprinkle sausage and 1 cup (4 ounces) shredded Cheddar cheese over pizza sauce. Shape dough, and let rise as directed. Sprinkle with 2 tablespoons grated Parmesan cheese, and bake as directed.

YEAST GINGERBREAD MEN

1 (¼-ounce) envelope active dry
   yeast
¼ cup warm water (105° to 115°)
¾ cup milk
½ cup sugar
⅓ cup butter or margarine
1 teaspoon salt
1 large egg
3 cups all-purpose flour, divided
1 cup graham cracker crumbs
½ teaspoon ground cinnamon
½ teaspoon ground cloves
½ teaspoon ground ginger
¼ cup currants or raisins
1 large egg, beaten

• **Combine** yeast and warm water in a 1-cup liquid measuring cup; let stand 5 minutes.
• **Combine** milk and next 3 ingredients in a small saucepan; heat until butter melts, stirring occasionally. Cool to 105° to 115°.
• **Combine** yeast mixture, milk mixture, 1 egg, 1 cup flour, graham cracker crumbs, and next 3 ingredients in a mixing bowl; beat at medium speed with an electric mixer until smooth. Gradually stir in remaining 2 cups flour.
• **Cover** and let rise in a warm place (85°), free from drafts, 1 hour or until doubled in bulk.
• **Punch** dough down, and divide into 6 portions; set 5 portions aside. Form three-fourths of 1 portion of dough into an oblong shape about 5 inches long; place on a lightly greased baking sheet. Cut a lengthwise slit halfway through bottom to form legs. Divide remaining one-fourth of that portion into 3 equal parts. Shape 1 part into a head and remaining 2 parts into arms; gently press each to attach to body. Gently push currants into dough for eyes and buttons. Repeat procedure with remaining dough.
• **Cover** and let rise in a warm place, free from drafts, 40 minutes. Gently brush each with beaten egg.
• **Bake** at 350° for 15 minutes or until golden. Cool on wire racks. **Yield:** 6 gingerbread men.

Louise Smith
Columbus, Georgia

EASTER EGG BREAD

Margie bakes enough loaves to give to her immediate family. If you start baking about a week ahead, you can do it, too.

2 cups sugar
1½ cups milk
1 cup butter or margarine
3 (¼-ounce) envelopes active dry
   yeast
1 tablespoon all-purpose flour
1 teaspoon sugar
⅓ cup warm water (105°
   to 115°)
6 large eggs, lightly beaten
9 cups all-purpose flour
2 hard-cooked eggs, unshelled and
   dyed
1 large egg, lightly beaten
1 teaspoon sesame seeds

• **Combine** first 3 ingredients in a large saucepan; cook over medium heat until butter melts. Cool milk mixture to 105° to 115°.
• **Combine** yeast and next 3 ingredients in a large bowl; let stand 5 minutes. Stir in 6 lightly beaten eggs. Gradually add 9 cups flour alternately with milk mixture, stirring well.
• **Turn** dough out onto a well-floured surface, and knead until dough is smooth and elastic (about 5 minutes). Place dough in a well-greased bowl, turning to grease top.
• **Cover** and let rise in a warm place (85°), free from drafts, 1 hour.
• **Punch** dough down, and divide in half; divide each half into 3 portions. Shape each portion into a 2½-foot rope. Pinch 3 ropes together at 1 end to seal; braid ropes. Place braid on a lightly greased baking sheet, and shape into a circle. Place 1 hard-cooked egg where braids meet, shaping dough around egg. Repeat procedure with remaining 3 ropes of dough.
• **Cover** and let rise in a warm place, free from drafts, 30 minutes.
• **Brush** bread with 1 beaten egg, and sprinkle with sesame seeds.
• **Bake** at 350° for 30 minutes or until golden. **Yield:** 2 loaves.

Margie Spanos
Birmingham, Alabama

CHALLAH

Challah is a traditional Jewish yeast bread that's rich with eggs and light in texture. Though it can be formed in many shapes, the bread is most often braided.

1 (¼-ounce) envelope active dry
   yeast
1 teaspoon sugar
½ cup warm water (105° to 115°)
½ cup vegetable oil
½ cup warm water (105° to 115°)
¼ cup sugar
2 large eggs
2 teaspoons salt
4 to 4½ cups all-purpose flour
Vegetable cooking spray
1 egg white
1 teaspoon water
1 teaspoon sesame seeds or poppy
   seeds

• **Combine** yeast, 1 teaspoon sugar, and ½ cup warm water in a 1-cup liquid measuring cup; let stand 5 minutes.
• **Combine** oil and next 4 ingredients in a large mixing bowl; beat at medium speed with an electric mixer until blended. Add yeast mixture and 2 cups flour; beat until smooth. Gradually stir in enough remaining flour to make a soft dough. (Dough will be sticky.) Cover and let rest 10 minutes.
• **Turn** dough out onto a well-floured surface; knead 5 minutes. Place in a well-greased bowl, turning to grease top.
• **Cover** and let rise in a warm place (85°), free from drafts, 1 to 1½ hours or until doubled in bulk.
• **Punch** dough down; turn out onto a well-floured surface, and knead several times. Divide into thirds. Shape each third into a 14-inch rope. Place ropes on a greased baking sheet (do not stretch); pinch ends together at one end to seal. Braid ropes; pinch loose ends to seal. Spray with cooking spray.
• **Cover** and let rise in a warm place, free from drafts, 30 to 40 minutes or until doubled in bulk.
• **Beat** egg white and 1 teaspoon water; gently brush over bread. Sprinkle with sesame seeds. Bake at 375° for 30 to 35 minutes or until golden. **Yield:** 1 loaf.

Sally Wolfish
Dallas, Texas

PANDORO

This classic Italian bread is traditionally baked in a tall, star-shaped pan. If you can't find one, use an 8-inch springform pan instead.

"Sponge"
1 teaspoon active dry yeast
1 tablespoon warm water (105° to 115°)
6½ cups bread flour, divided
¼ cup sugar
2 large eggs
¼ cup butter or margarine, softened and cut into pieces
4 large eggs
2 egg yolks
1 cup sugar
1 teaspoon salt
2 teaspoons vanilla extract
1½ tablespoons grated lemon rind
1¼ cups butter or margarine, softened and cut into pieces
½ cup chopped candied citron
¼ to ½ cup bread flour
Butter-flavored cooking spray

● **Prepare** "Sponge" according to recipe, and set aside.
● **Combine** yeast and warm water in a 1-cup liquid measuring cup; let stand 5 minutes.
● **Add** yeast mixture, 2½ cups flour, ¼ cup sugar, and 2 eggs to "Sponge"; stir vigorously with a wooden spoon until blended. Gradually stir in ¼ cup softened butter.
● **Cover** and let rise in a warm place (85°), free from drafts, 45 minutes or until dough is doubled in bulk.
● **Add** 4 eggs and next 5 ingredients; beat at medium speed with an electric mixer until smooth. Gradually add 2 cups flour, beating until blended. Stir in remaining 2 cups flour with a wooden spoon. Gradually stir in 1¼ cups butter and citron.
● **Turn** dough out onto a heavily floured surface, and knead until smooth and elastic (about 5 minutes), adding an additional ¼ to ½ cup flour, if necessary. Place in a well-greased bowl, turning to grease top.

● **Cover** and let rise in a warm place, free from drafts, 1½ hours or until doubled in bulk.
● **Punch** dough down, and divide in half; place in two Pandoro pans or 2 (8-inch) springform pans coated with cooking spray.
● **Cover** and let rise in a warm place, free from drafts, 1½ hours or until doubled in bulk.
● **Bake** at 350° for 30 minutes. Cover with aluminum foil, reduce oven temperature to 300°, and bake 20 additional minutes.
● **Remove** from pans, and cool on wire racks. **Yield:** 2 loaves.

"Sponge"

2 (¼-ounce) envelopes active dry yeast
½ cup warm water (105° to 115°)
1 large egg
2 tablespoons sugar
¾ cup bread flour

● **Combine** yeast and warm water in a 1-cup liquid measuring cup; let stand 5 minutes.
● **Combine** yeast mixture, egg, sugar, and flour in a large mixing bowl; beat at medium speed with an electric mixer until smooth.
● **Cover** "Sponge," and let rise in a warm place (85°), free from drafts, 30 minutes or until doubled in bulk. **Yield:** about 1½ cups.

Jim and Sandra Kolka
Marietta, Georgia

PANETTONE

Panettone is a sweet yeast bread that's studded with currants and citron, and baked in a tall cylindrical shape. The bread originated in Milan, Italy, and is traditionally served at Christmastime.

2 (¼-ounce) envelopes active dry yeast
1 cup warm water (105° to 115°)
½ cup butter, softened
½ cup sugar
2 large eggs, beaten
3 egg yolks, beaten
2 teaspoons salt
2 teaspoons grated lemon rind
1 teaspoon vanilla extract
5 to 6 cups bread flour, divided
1 cup chopped candied citron
1 cup currants
2 tablespoons butter, melted

● **Combine** yeast and warm water in a 2-cup liquid measuring cup; let stand 5 minutes.
● **Combine** yeast mixture, ½ cup butter, and next 6 ingredients in a large bowl, stirring with a wooden spoon until blended. Gradually stir in 3 cups flour, mixing well. Stir in citron and currants. Gradually stir in enough remaining 3 cups flour to make a soft dough.
● **Turn** dough out onto a lightly floured surface, and knead until smooth and elastic (about 2 minutes). Place in a well-greased bowl, turning to grease top.
● **Cover** and let rise in a warm place (85°), free from drafts, 1½ hours or until doubled in bulk.
● **Punch** dough down, and place in a greased 2-quart soufflé dish; brush with melted butter. Cover and let rise in a warm place, free from drafts, 1 hour or until almost doubled in bulk. Using a sharp knife, gently cut a deep X in top of bread.
● **Bake** on lower rack of oven at 350° for 8 minutes. Reduce oven temperature to 325°, and bake 1 hour or until bread sounds hollow when tapped. (Cover loosely with aluminum foil after 45 minutes to prevent excessive browning, if necessary.) Remove from dish immediately; cool on a wire rack. **Yield:** 1 loaf.

Jim and Sandra Kolka
Marietta, Georgia

MANDELKRANTZ

Christine Kenyon inherited this breakfast bread recipe from her great-grandmother, who immigrated from Sweden. Cardamom creates the distinctive aroma you'll enjoy as the bread bakes.

2 (¼-ounce) envelopes active dry yeast
1 teaspoon sugar
¼ cup warm water (105° to 115°)
2 cups milk, divided
¾ cup shortening
1 cup sugar
1 teaspoon salt
¼ teaspoon ground cardamom
3 large eggs, lightly beaten
6 to 7 cups soft wheat flour, divided
⅓ cup butter or margarine, softened
1 teaspoon almond extract
¾ cup sugar, divided
¾ cup chopped walnuts, divided

• **Combine** yeast, 1 teaspoon sugar, and warm water in a 1-cup liquid measuring cup; let stand 5 minutes.
• **Combine** 1 cup milk, shortening, and next 3 ingredients in a Dutch oven; cook over low heat until shortening dissolves. Remove from heat. Add yeast mixture, remaining 1 cup milk, eggs, and 4 cups flour, stirring well with a wooden spoon. Stir in enough remaining flour to make a soft dough.
• **Cover** and let rise in a warm place (85°), free from drafts, 1 hour or until doubled in bulk.
• **Punch** dough down; turn dough out onto a lightly floured surface, and knead 4 to 5 minutes. Divide dough into thirds. Roll 1 portion of dough into a 12- x 8-inch rectangle.
• **Combine** butter and almond extract; spread one-third of mixture over dough to within ½ inch of sides. Sprinkle with ¼ cup sugar and ¼ cup walnuts. Roll up dough, jellyroll fashion, starting at long side. Press firmly to eliminate air pockets; fold ends under.
• **Place** dough, seam side down, in a well-greased 9- x 5- x 3-inch loafpan. Repeat procedure with remaining 2 portions of dough.

• **Cover** and let dough rise in a warm place, free from drafts, 45 minutes or until doubled in bulk.
• **Bake** at 350° for 30 to 35 minutes. Cover with aluminum foil to prevent excessive browning, if necessary. Remove bread from pans immediately; cool slightly on wire racks before slicing. **Yield:** 3 loaves.

Christine Kenyon
Lawrenceville, Georgia

HONEY-OAT BREAD

QUICK!

¾ cup plus 2 tablespoons water
¼ cup vegetable oil
¼ cup honey
¼ cup fat-free egg substitute
1¼ cups whole wheat flour
1 cup bread flour
½ cup unprocessed oat bran
¾ teaspoon salt
1 tablespoon active dry yeast

• **Combine** all ingredients in bread machine according to manufacturer's instructions. Process in regular bake cycle. Remove from baking pan, and cool on a wire rack. **Yield:** 1 loaf.

QUICK WHOLE WHEAT BREAD

2¼ cups water
½ cup butter or margarine
4 cups bread flour, divided
2 cups whole wheat flour
2½ teaspoons salt
2 teaspoons sugar
1 (¼-ounce) envelope rapid-rise yeast

• **Combine** water and butter in a saucepan; heat until butter melts, stirring occasionally. Cool to 120° to 130°.
• **Combine** 3 cups bread flour, whole wheat flour, and remaining 3 ingredients in a large mixing bowl; stir well. Gradually add liquid mixture to flour mixture, beating at high speed with an electric mixer. Beat 2 additional minutes at medium speed. Gradually stir in

enough remaining flour to make a soft dough. Cover bowl, and let dough rest 10 minutes.
• **Punch** dough down; turn out onto a lightly floured surface, and knead lightly 4 or 5 times. Divide dough in half, shaping each into a loaf. Place each loaf in a greased 8½- x 4½- x 3-inch loafpan.
• **Cover** and let rise in a warm place (85°), free from drafts, 45 minutes or until doubled in bulk.
• **Bake** at 350° for 45 minutes or until loaves sound hollow when tapped. Remove from pans immediately; cool on wire racks. **Yield:** 2 loaves.

ANISE-WHOLE WHEAT BREAD

2 (¼-ounce) envelopes active dry yeast
2 cups warm water (105° to 115°)
3 cups all-purpose flour, divided
1½ cups whole wheat flour
2¼ teaspoons salt
3 tablespoons butter or margarine, softened
3 tablespoons honey
1 tablespoon anise seeds, crushed and divided

• **Combine** yeast and warm water in a 2-cup liquid measuring cup; let stand 5 minutes.
• **Combine** yeast mixture, 1½ cups all-purpose flour, whole wheat flour, and next 3 ingredients in a large mixing bowl. Beat at low speed with an electric mixer until blended; beat at medium speed 2 minutes. Stir in remaining 1½ cups all-purpose flour.
• **Cover** and let rise in a warm place (85°), free from drafts, 50 minutes or until doubled in bulk.
• **Lightly** butter a 2-quart soufflé dish; sprinkle with 2 teaspoons anise seeds. Set aside.
• **Vigorously** stir dough 30 seconds; pour into prepared soufflé dish, and sprinkle with remaining seeds.
• **Bake** at 375° for 50 to 55 minutes or until lightly browned. Remove from soufflé dish, and let cool completely on a wire rack. **Yield:** 1 loaf.

Mary Belle Purvis
Greeneville, Tennessee

RAISIN-WHOLE WHEAT BREAD

1½ cups raisins
2 (¼-ounce) envelopes active dry yeast
1¾ cups warm water (105° to 115°)
3 tablespoons honey
2 tablespoons vegetable oil
2 teaspoons salt
3 cups whole wheat flour
2¼ to 2½ cups unbleached flour, divided

• **Place** raisins in a small saucepan; cover with water. Bring to a boil; cover, remove from heat, and let stand 15 minutes. Drain and pat dry. Set aside.
• **Combine** yeast and 1¾ cups warm water in a 2-cup liquid measuring cup; let stand 5 minutes.
• **Combine** yeast mixture, honey, oil, and salt in a large bowl. Gradually add whole wheat flour, mixing until blended. Gradually stir in 2¼ cups unbleached flour, stirring to make a soft dough. Stir in raisins.
• **Turn** dough out onto a lightly floured surface, and knead until smooth and elastic (about 8 minutes), adding enough remaining ¼ cup unbleached flour to prevent dough from sticking to hands. Place in a well-greased bowl, turning to grease top.
• **Cover** and let rise in a warm place (85°), free from drafts, 1 hour or until doubled in bulk.
• **Punch** dough down; turn out onto a lightly floured surface, and knead lightly 8 to 10 times. Divide dough in half. Shape each portion into a loaf. Place into two well-greased 8½- x 4½- x 3-inch loafpans.
• **Cover** and let rise in a warm place, free from drafts, 30 minutes or until doubled in bulk.
• **Bake** at 350° for 35 to 40 minutes or until loaves sound hollow when tapped. Remove from pans immediately; cool on wire racks. **Yield:** 2 loaves.

Dr. Harold Cannon
Birmingham, Alabama

ROASTED RED BELL PEPPER BREAD

Serve this flavorful bread with soup, toast it for a snack, or slice it for sandwiches.

2 red bell peppers
1 (¼-ounce) envelope active dry yeast
1 teaspoon sugar
1⅓ cups warm water (105° to 115°)
2 tablespoons olive oil
3½ to 4½ cups bread flour, divided
1½ teaspoons salt
1 tablespoon cracked pepper
2 tablespoons chopped fresh rosemary
1 cup (4 ounces) shredded provolone cheese
1 cup grated Parmesan cheese

• **Place** red bell peppers on a baking sheet; broil 5½ inches from heat (with electric oven door partially opened) about 5 minutes on each side or until blackened. Place peppers in a heavy-duty, zip-top plastic bag; seal and let stand 10 minutes to loosen skins. Peel peppers; remove and discard seeds. Chop peppers, and set aside.
• **Combine** yeast, sugar, and warm water in a 2-cup liquid measuring cup; let stand 5 minutes. Stir in olive oil. Set aside.
• **Combine** 3½ cups flour, roasted pepper, salt, and remaining 4 ingredients in a large bowl; gradually add yeast mixture, stirring until blended.
• **Turn** dough out onto a well-floured surface, and knead until smooth and elastic (about 10 minutes), adding remaining 1 cup flour as needed to prevent sticking. Place in a well-greased bowl, turning to grease top.
• **Cover** and let rise in a warm place (85°), free from drafts, 1 hour or until doubled in bulk.
• **Punch** dough down, and divide in half; shape each portion into a 12-inch loaf. Place loaves on a lightly greased large baking sheet. Let rise in a warm place, free from drafts, 45 minutes or until doubled in bulk.
• **Bake** at 450° for 25 minutes or until loaves sound hollow when tapped, covering with aluminum foil after 15 minutes to prevent excessive browning. Remove from baking sheet immediately; cool on wire racks. **Yield:** 2 loaves.

Rublelene Singleton
Scotts Hill, Tennessee

OLIVE-DILL CASSEROLE BREAD

2 (¼-ounce) envelopes active dry yeast
2 cups warm water (105° to 115°)
¼ cup minced fresh dill or 1½ tablespoons dried dillweed
2 tablespoons sugar
3 tablespoons chopped pimiento-stuffed olives
2 tablespoons butter or margarine, melted
2 teaspoons salt
4½ cups all-purpose flour, divided
1 teaspoon dillseeds

• **Combine** yeast and warm water in a 1-quart liquid measuring cup; let stand 5 minutes.
• **Combine** yeast mixture, minced dill, and next 4 ingredients in a large mixing bowl. Add 2 cups flour, beating at medium speed with an electric mixer until mixture is smooth. Gradually stir in enough remaining flour to make a soft dough.
• **Place** dough in a well-greased bowl, turning to grease top.
• **Cover** and let rise in a warm place (85°), free from drafts, 45 minutes or until doubled in bulk. (Dough may be light and bubbly.)
• **Punch** dough down, and vigorously stir with a wooden spoon 30 seconds. Turn out into a lightly greased 2-quart round casserole. Sprinkle top of dough with dillseeds.
• **Bake** at 375° for 55 to 60 minutes, covering top of bread with aluminum foil to prevent excessive browning, if necessary. Remove bread from casserole, and let cool on a wire rack. **Yield:** 1 loaf.

Note: You can freeze baked bread up to 3 months.

Mary Belle Purvis
Greeneville, Tennessee

PEANUT LOVER'S BREAD

1 (¼-ounce) envelope active dry
  yeast
¼ cup warm water (105°
  to 115°)
¾ cup buttermilk
3 cups all-purpose flour, divided
¾ teaspoon baking powder
¼ teaspoon baking soda
¾ teaspoon salt
¼ cup sugar
¼ cup peanut oil
¼ cup butter or margarine,
  softened
Peanut Filling
Butter-flavored cooking spray

• **Combine** yeast and warm water in a
1-cup liquid measuring cup; let stand 5
minutes.
• **Heat** buttermilk in a small saucepan;
cool to 105° to 115°.
• **Combine** 2 cups flour, baking powder,
and next 4 ingredients in a large bowl.
Add yeast mixture and buttermilk; beat
at medium speed with an electric mixer
1 to 2 minutes. Stir in remaining 1 cup
flour. Place dough in a well-greased
bowl, turning to grease top. Cover and
chill 8 hours.
• **Punch** dough down; turn out onto a
floured surface, and knead until smooth
and elastic (about 5 minutes).
• **Roll** dough into a 16- x 12-inch rectangle; spread with butter. Sprinkle with
Peanut Filling, lightly pressing filling
into dough.
• **Cut** into 3 (4- x 16-inch) pieces; fold
each portion lengthwise in half over filling, pinching seams together to form
ropes. Place ropes, seam side down, on
a greased baking sheet (do not stretch);
pinch rope ends together at 1 end to
seal. Braid ropes; pinch loose ends to
seal, and tuck under. Lightly spray braid
with cooking spray.
• **Cover** and let rise in a warm place
(85°), free from drafts, 45 to 60 minutes
or until doubled in bulk. Bake at 375°
for 20 to 25 minutes or until golden.
Yield: 1 loaf.

Peanut Filling

QUICK!

¾ cup finely chopped unsalted
  peanuts
⅓ cup crushed French fried onions
3 tablespoons real bacon bits
2 teaspoons poppy seeds
2 tablespoons grated Parmesan
  cheese
¼ teaspoon garlic powder
1 egg white, lightly beaten

• **Combine** all ingredients, stirring well.
Yield: 1¼ cups.

June Kilgore
Dothan, Alabama

WALNUT BREAD

2 (¼-ounce) envelopes active dry
  yeast
¼ cup warm water (105° to 115°)
1½ cups milk
2 tablespoons olive oil
2 tablespoons honey
2 teaspoons salt
2 cups unbleached flour, divided
2 cups whole wheat flour
1 cup rye flour
1 cup coarsely chopped walnuts

• **Combine** yeast and warm water in a
1-cup liquid measuring cup; let stand 5
minutes.
• **Combine** yeast mixture, milk, and
next 3 ingredients in a large mixing
bowl; beat at medium speed with an
electric mixer until well blended.
• **Combine** 1½ cups unbleached flour,
wheat flour, rye flour, and walnuts; gradually add to yeast mixture, beating after
each addition.
• **Turn** dough out onto a lightly floured
surface; knead in remaining ½ cup unbleached flour, and continue kneading
until smooth and elastic (about 5 minutes). Place in a well-greased bowl,
turning to grease top.
• **Cover** and let rise in a warm place
(85°), free from drafts, 1 hour or until
doubled in bulk.
• **Punch** dough down; divide in half.
Shape each portion into a 6-inch ball;
place on a lightly greased baking sheet.

• **Cover** and let rise in a warm place,
free from drafts, 45 minutes or until
doubled in bulk.
• **Using** a sharp knife, gently make a ¼-
inch-deep cut in the shape of an X in the
top of each loaf; bake at 375° for 20 to
25 minutes or until loaves sound hollow
when tapped. Remove to wire racks to
cool. **Yield:** 2 loaves.

Dr. Harold Cannon
Birmingham, Alabama

OATMEAL BREAD

1 (12-ounce) can evaporated milk
½ cup water
2 tablespoons shortening
2 cups regular oats, uncooked
⅓ cup firmly packed brown sugar
1½ teaspoons salt
1 (¼-ounce) envelope active dry
  yeast
½ cup warm water (105° to 115°)
3¾ to 4¼ cups all-purpose flour
2 teaspoons regular oats, uncooked

• **Combine** first 3 ingredients in a
saucepan; bring to a boil. Pour mixture
over 2 cups oats; stir in sugar and salt.
Cool to 105° to 115°.
• **Combine** yeast and warm water in a
1-cup liquid measuring cup; let stand 5
minutes.
• **Combine** yeast mixture and oat mixture in a large mixing bowl. Stir in
enough flour to make a soft dough.
• **Turn** dough out onto a floured surface, and knead until smooth and elastic
(about 5 minutes). Place in a well-
greased bowl, turning to grease top.
• **Cover** and let rise in a warm place
(85°), free from drafts, 1 hour or until
doubled in bulk.
• **Punch** dough down, and divide in half.
Shape each portion into a loaf, and
place into two well-greased 8½- x 4½- x
3-inch loafpans. Cover and let rise in a
warm place, free from drafts, 30 minutes or until doubled in bulk. Sprinkle
with 2 teaspoons oats. Bake at 350° for
35 minutes or until loaves sound hollow
when tapped. Remove from pans, and
cool on wire racks. **Yield:** 2 loaves.

Betty Czebotar
Baltimore, Maryland

SAFFRON BREAD

Saffron is the world's most expensive spice. To be economical, substitute 2 teaspoons turmeric for ¼ teaspoon saffron in this recipe. We liked both versions.

2½ cups warm milk (105° to 115°), divided
2 (¼-ounce) envelopes active dry yeast
8 cups all-purpose flour, divided
1½ cups sugar
¼ teaspoon salt
¼ teaspoon ground saffron
¾ cup butter, melted
1 large egg, lightly beaten
1 cup slivered almonds
1 cup golden raisins
2 tablespoons butter, melted
2 teaspoons sugar
Slivered almonds (optional)

• **Combine** ½ cup warm milk and yeast in a 1-cup liquid measuring cup; let stand 5 minutes.
• **Combine** remaining 2 cups warm milk, 1 cup flour, sugar, and next 4 ingredients; add almonds and raisins. Stir in yeast mixture.
• **Add** remaining 7 cups flour, 1 cup at a time, stirring after each addition until smooth. Place dough in a large well-greased bowl, turning to grease top.
• **Cover** and let rise in a warm place (85°), free from drafts, 2 hours or until doubled in bulk.
• **Turn** dough out onto a well-floured surface, and knead 5 minutes or until smooth.
• **Divide** dough in half. Divide each half into 3 portions. Shape each portion into an 18-inch rope. Pinch loose ends of ropes at 1 end to seal; braid ropes. Repeat procedure with remaining half of dough. Place braids on greased baking sheets.
• **Cover** and let rise in a warm place, free from drafts, 30 minutes or until doubled in bulk.
• **Brush** braids with 2 tablespoons melted butter; sprinkle with 2 teaspoons sugar and additional slivered almonds, if desired.
• **Bake** at 400° for 25 to 30 minutes, covering bread with aluminum foil after 20 minutes to prevent excessive browning. **Yield:** 2 loaves.

Note: For a variation, shape dough into S-shaped rolls. Bake at 400° for 10 to 13 minutes. Yield: 3 dozen.

Kathy Seaberg
St. Petersburg, Florida

PARMESAN BREAD

1 (¼-ounce) envelope active dry yeast
1 cup warm water (105° to 115°)
3 cups all-purpose flour, divided
¼ cup butter or margarine, melted
1 large egg, beaten
2 tablespoons sugar
2 teaspoons dried onion flakes
1 teaspoon salt
1 teaspoon dried Italian seasoning
½ teaspoon garlic salt
⅔ cup grated Parmesan cheese, divided
1 tablespoon butter or margarine, melted

• **Combine** yeast and warm water in a 2-cup liquid measuring cup; let stand 5 minutes.
• **Combine** yeast mixture, 2 cups flour, ¼ cup butter, and next 6 ingredients in a large mixing bowl. Beat at medium speed with an electric mixer 2 minutes. Gradually stir in ⅓ cup Parmesan cheese and remaining 1 cup flour to make a soft dough.
• **Cover** and let rise in a warm place (85°), free from drafts, 1 hour or until doubled in bulk.
• **Punch** dough down, and place in a greased 2-quart casserole. Brush with 1 tablespoon melted butter; sprinkle with remaining ⅓ cup Parmesan cheese.
• **Cover** and let rise in a warm place, free from drafts, 45 minutes or until doubled in bulk.
• **Bake** at 350° for 30 minutes or until golden. Let bread cool in casserole on a wire rack 10 minutes. Remove bread from casserole, and let cool on wire rack. **Yield:** 1 loaf.

Velma McGregor
Gretna, Virginia

MINI SWISS CHEESE LOAVES

Fill Mini Swiss Cheese Loaves with turkey or chicken for lunch or serve them as a savory bread with dinner.

1 (¼-ounce) envelope active dry yeast
¼ cup warm water (105° to 115°)
2⅓ cups all-purpose flour, divided
2 tablespoons sugar
1 teaspoon salt
¼ teaspoon baking soda
1 (8-ounce) carton plain nonfat yogurt
1 large egg
1 cup (4 ounces) shredded reduced-fat Swiss cheese *
Vegetable cooking spray
2 teaspoons sesame seeds, toasted

• **Combine** yeast and warm water in a 1-cup liquid measuring cup; let stand 5 minutes.
• **Combine** yeast mixture, 1 cup flour, sugar, and next 4 ingredients in a large mixing bowl.
• **Beat** batter at low speed with an electric mixer 30 seconds or until blended. Beat at high speed 2 minutes, scraping bowl occasionally.
• **Stir** in remaining 1⅓ cups flour and cheese, mixing well.
• **Divide** batter evenly among 8 (5- x 3- x 2-inch) loafpans coated with cooking spray; sprinkle evenly with sesame seeds.
• **Cover** and let rise in a warm place (85°), free from drafts, 1 hour. (Batter may not double in bulk.)
• **Bake** at 350° for 25 minutes or until golden. Remove loaves from pans; serve warm or cool on a wire rack. **Yield:** 8 loaves.

* For reduced-fat Swiss cheese, we used Alpine Lace.

Shannon Arrington
Woodland, Alabama

♥ Per loaf: Calories 226
Fat 4.9g Cholesterol 38mg
Sodium 380mg

French Bread

FRENCH BREAD
(pictured at left)

Crusty French Bread served with seasoned olive oil can double easily as an appetizer – not just the bread for the meal.

2 (¼-ounce) envelopes rapid-rise yeast
2 tablespoons sugar
2½ cups warm water (105° to 115°)
1 tablespoon salt
1 tablespoon butter, softened
6½ to 7 cups all-purpose flour, divided
1 egg white
1 tablespoon cold water

• **Combine** first 3 ingredients in a 1-quart liquid measuring cup; let stand 5 minutes.
• **Combine** yeast mixture, salt, and butter in a large bowl. Gradually stir in enough flour to make a soft dough. Place in a well-greased bowl, turning to grease top.
• **Cover** and let rise in a warm place (85°), free from drafts, 40 minutes or until doubled in bulk.
• **Punch** dough down; turn out onto a lightly floured surface. Knead lightly 5 times. Divide dough in half. Roll 1 portion into a 15- x 10-inch rectangle. Roll up dough, starting at long side, pressing firmly to eliminate air pockets. Pinch ends to seal; turn under.
• **Place** dough, seam side down, on a greased baking sheet sprinkled with cornmeal. Repeat procedure with remaining dough.
• **Cover** and let rise in a warm place, free from drafts, 30 minutes or until doubled in bulk. Make 4 or 5 (¼-inch-deep) cuts on top of each loaf with a sharp knife.
• **Bake** at 400° for 25 minutes.
• **Combine** egg white and water; brush over loaves, and bake 5 additional minutes. **Yield:** 2 loaves.

Nancy P. Mumpower
Bristol, Virginia

DRIED TOMATO FOCACCIA

10 pieces dried tomatoes (about ⅓ cup)
½ cup boiling water
1 cup milk
2 tablespoons butter or margarine
3½ to 4 cups bread flour, divided
2 (¼-ounce) envelopes active dry yeast
2 tablespoons sugar
2 teaspoons salt
1 large egg
3 tablespoons dried chives *
¼ cup olive oil
¼ teaspoon dried oregano *
¼ teaspoon dried rosemary *

• **Combine** tomatoes and boiling water in a saucepan; let stand 30 minutes.
• **Remove** tomatoes, reserving liquid; finely chop tomatoes, using kitchen shears, and set aside.
• **Add** milk and butter to reserved tomato liquid, and heat until mixture reaches 120° to 130°.
• **Combine** 1½ cups flour, yeast, sugar, and salt in a large mixing bowl. Gradually add liquid mixture to flour mixture, beating at low speed with an electric mixer until blended. Add egg, and beat 3 minutes at medium speed. Stir in tomato, chives, and enough remaining flour to make a soft dough.
• **Turn** dough out onto a floured surface, and knead 5 minutes. Place in a well-greased bowl, turning to grease top. Cover and let rise in a warm place (85°), free from drafts, 1 hour or until doubled in bulk.
• **Combine** olive oil, oregano, and rosemary; set aside.
• **Punch** dough down. For round loaves, divide dough in half; shape each portion into a 10-inch round. For sandwich buns, divide dough into 12 balls, and shape each portion into a 3-inch round. Place on lightly greased baking sheets; flatten dough slightly, and brush with half of olive oil mixture. Cover and let rest 10 minutes.
• **Bake** at 350° for 15 minutes. Brush with remaining olive oil mixture, and bake 5 to 10 additional minutes or until lightly browned and bread sounds hollow when tapped. Cool on wire racks. **Yield:** 2 (10-inch) loaves or 12 sandwich buns.

* You can substitute ¼ cup chopped fresh chives, ¾ teaspoon chopped fresh oregano, and ¼ teaspoon chopped fresh rosemary for the dried herbs.

Eva Royal
Evening Shade, Arkansas

ONION FOCACCIA

3 (¼-ounce) envelopes active dry yeast
2 cups warm water (105° to 115°)
3 tablespoons olive oil
2 teaspoons salt
6 cups unbleached flour, divided
1 large purple onion, chopped
1 tablespoon olive oil

• **Combine** yeast and warm water in a 2-cup liquid measuring cup; let stand 5 minutes.
• **Combine** yeast mixture, olive oil, and salt in a large bowl. Stir in 5 cups unbleached flour to make a stiff dough.
• **Turn** out onto a lightly floured surface, and knead in enough remaining 1 cup flour to make a firm dough. Place in a well-greased bowl, turning to grease top.
• **Cover** and let rise in a warm place (85°), free from drafts, 45 minutes or until doubled in bulk.
• **Cook** onion in olive oil in a large skillet over medium-high heat, stirring constantly, until tender. Set aside.
• **Punch** dough down, and divide in half. Roll each portion into a 12-inch circle, and place in a lightly greased 12-inch pizza pan.
• **Arrange** onion evenly on each round; gently press into dough. Cover and let rise in a warm place, free from drafts, 20 minutes. Using fingertips, press small indentations into dough; let rise 10 additional minutes.
• **Bake** at 400° for 20 to 25 minutes or until golden. Remove loaves to wire racks to cool.
• **Serve** with antipasto meats, olive oil for dipping, and mustards. Yield: 2 loaves.

Dr. Harold Cannon
Birmingham, Alabama

SKILLET PIZZA CRUSTS

3 (¼-ounce) envelopes active dry
    yeast
1 teaspoon sugar
¾ cup warm water (105° to 115°)
3 cups all-purpose flour
1 teaspoon salt
½ cup warm water (105° to 115°)
2 tablespoons olive oil
Vegetable cooking spray

● **Combine** first 3 ingredients in a 2-cup liquid measuring cup; let stand 5 minutes.
● **Combine** yeast mixture, flour, and next 3 ingredients in a large bowl, stirring until well blended.
● **Turn** dough out onto a lightly floured surface, and knead 5 minutes. Place dough in a bowl coated with cooking spray, turning to coat top. Cover and let rise in a warm place (85°), free from drafts, 30 minutes or until dough is doubled in bulk.
● **Punch** dough down; knead lightly 4 or 5 times. Divide into 6 equal portions; roll each portion into an 8-inch circle.
● **Cook** each round on 1 side in a non-stick 8-inch skillet coated with cooking spray over medium heat about 2 minutes or until dough rounds are lightly browned. Cool on a wire rack. Freeze in an airtight container up to 6 months. **Yield:** 6 (8-inch) pizza crusts.

Kathy Piques
Knoxville, Tennessee

♥ Per crust: Calories 286
Fat 5.9g Cholesterol 0mg
Sodium 392mg

PARMESAN PIZZA CRUST

2 (¼-ounce) envelopes active dry
    yeast
2 cups warm water (105° to 115°)
6 to 7 cups all-purpose flour,
    divided
2 teaspoons salt
2 teaspoons sugar
½ cup grated Parmesan cheese
½ cup vegetable oil
Vegetable cooking spray
Cornmeal
Olive oil

● **Combine** yeast and water in a 2-cup liquid measuring cup; let stand 5 minutes. Combine yeast mixture, 3 cups flour, salt, and next 3 ingredients in a large mixing bowl; beat at low speed with an electric mixer until blended. Stir in enough remaining flour to make a medium-stiff dough.
● **Cover** and let rise in a warm place (85°), free from drafts, 45 minutes or until dough is doubled in bulk.
● **Turn** dough out onto a lightly floured surface, and knead 4 or 5 times. Coat two 12-inch pizza pans with cooking spray; sprinkle with cornmeal. Divide dough in half, and pat each portion evenly into a pan; brush with olive oil, and prick with a fork.
● **Bake** at 425° for 10 minutes. Add desired sauce and toppings, and bake 15 to 20 additional minutes; sprinkle with desired cheeses, and bake 5 additional minutes. **Yield:** 2 (12-inch) pizzas.

Variation: For a double-crust pizza, pat half of dough in bottom and up sides of a 14-inch deep-dish pizza pan; set remaining half of dough aside. Bake at 425° for 10 minutes; add desired sauce, toppings, and cheese. Roll out remaining dough, and place over toppings. Fold edges together, and seal. Bake at 425° for 20 to 25 minutes or until golden. **Yield:** 1 (14-inch) double-crust pizza.

Note: To freeze, divide risen dough in half before kneading, wrap in plastic wrap, and place in heavy-duty, zip-top plastic bags; freeze up to 3 months. Thaw overnight in refrigerator.

Debbie Huffman
Woodland, Mississippi

ARMENIAN THIN BREAD

1 (¼-ounce) envelope active dry
    yeast
1 cup warm water (105° to
    115°)
3¼ to 3¾ cups all-purpose flour,
    divided
1½ teaspoons salt
1 teaspoon sugar
¼ cup butter or margarine,
    melted

● **Combine** yeast and warm water in a 2-cup liquid measuring cup; let stand 5 minutes.
● **Combine** yeast mixture, 2 cups flour, salt, sugar, and butter in a large mixing bowl; beat at medium speed with an electric mixer until smooth. Stir in enough remaining flour to make a stiff dough.
● **Turn** dough out onto a floured surface, and knead until smooth and elastic (about 8 minutes).
● **Place** in a well-greased bowl, turning to grease top. Cover and let rise in a warm place (85°), free from drafts, 1 hour or until doubled in bulk.
● **Punch** dough down, and divide into fourths; roll and stretch each portion of dough into a 14- x 10-inch rectangle. Place dough rectangles on ungreased baking sheets.
● **Bake** at 350° for 15 to 20 minutes or until bread is lightly browned. Break bread into pieces before serving. **Yield:** 4 bread sheets.

Southern Accent
Junior League of Pine Bluff, Arkansas

HONEY ANGEL BISCUITS

1 (¼-ounce) envelope active dry
   yeast
2 tablespoons warm water (105°
   to 115°)
5 cups all-purpose flour
1 tablespoon baking powder
1 teaspoon baking soda
1 teaspoon salt
1 cup shortening
2 cups buttermilk
3 tablespoons honey
Honey Butter

• **Combine** yeast and warm water in a 1-cup liquid measuring cup; let stand 5 minutes.
• **Combine** flour, baking powder, baking soda, and salt in a large bowl; cut in shortening with pastry blender until mixture is crumbly.
• **Combine** yeast mixture, buttermilk, and honey, and add to dry ingredients, stirring just until dry ingredients are moistened.
• **Turn** dough out onto a lightly floured surface, and knead 1 minute.
• **Roll** dough to ½-inch thickness. Cut with a 2-inch round cutter, and place on ungreased baking sheets.
• **Bake** at 400° for 10 minutes or until golden. Serve with Honey Butter. **Yield:** 4 dozen.

Ruth Shirley
Dallas, Texas

Honey Butter

QUICK!

¼ cup honey
½ cup butter or margarine,
   softened

• **Combine** honey and butter in a small bowl, stirring mixture until blended. **Yield:** ⅔ cup.

Note: You can store unbaked dough in the refrigerator in an airtight container up to 1 week.

BASIL BISCUITS

1 (¼-ounce) envelope active dry
   yeast
2 tablespoons warm water (105°
   to 115°)
1 cup buttermilk
2½ cups all-purpose flour
1½ teaspoons baking powder
½ teaspoon baking soda
¼ teaspoon salt
2 tablespoons sugar
½ cup shortening
¼ cup finely chopped fresh basil
2 tablespoons finely chopped
   oil-packed dried tomatoes,
   drained

• **Combine** yeast and warm water in a 2-cup liquid measuring cup, and let stand 5 minutes. Stir in buttermilk, and set aside.
• **Combine** flour and next 4 ingredients in a large bowl; cut in shortening with pastry blender until mixture is crumbly. Add buttermilk mixture, basil, and tomato, stirring with a fork until dry ingredients are moistened. (Dough will resemble cottage cheese and be sticky.)
• **Turn** dough out onto a heavily floured surface, and knead lightly 4 or 5 times.
• **Roll** to ½-inch thickness; cut with a 2½-inch round cutter. Place on a lightly greased baking sheet. Cover and let rise in a warm place (85°), free from drafts, 30 minutes.
• **Bake** at 450° for 10 to 12 minutes or until browned. **Yield:** 1 dozen.

SWEET POTATO ANGEL BISCUITS

3 large sweet potatoes *
3 (¼-ounce) envelopes active dry
   yeast
¾ cup warm water (105° to 115°)
7½ cups all-purpose flour
1 tablespoon baking powder
1 tablespoon salt
1½ cups sugar
1½ cups shortening

• **Wash** sweet potatoes; bake at 375° for 1 hour or until done. Let potatoes cool to touch; peel and mash. Set aside 3 cups mashed sweet potato, and keep warm. Reserve any remaining mashed sweet potato for another use.
• **Combine** yeast and warm water in a 2-cup liquid measuring cup; let stand 5 minutes.
• **Combine** flour and next 3 ingredients in a large bowl; cut in shortening with pastry blender until mixture is crumbly. Add yeast mixture and mashed sweet potato, stirring until dry ingredients are moistened.
• **Turn** dough out onto a lightly floured surface; knead 5 minutes. Place dough in a lightly greased bowl, turning to grease top; cover and chill 8 hours.
• **Roll** dough to ½-inch thickness, and cut with a 2-inch round cutter. Place biscuits on ungreased baking sheets; cover and let rise in a warm place (85°), free from drafts, 20 minutes or until doubled in bulk.
• **Bake** at 400° for 10 to 12 minutes or until lightly browned. **Yield:** 7 dozen.

✱ You can substitute 3 cups canned, mashed sweet potatoes for fresh.

Note: You can freeze unbaked biscuits up to 1 month. To serve, let thaw 30 minutes; cover and let rise in a warm place (85°), free from drafts, 20 minutes or until doubled in bulk. Bake as directed.

Therese Reid
Rhodesdale, Maryland

HOT CROSS BUNS

4¼ to 4¾ cups all-purpose flour,
     divided
⅔ cup sugar
1 (¼-ounce) envelope rapid-rise
     yeast
1 teaspoon salt
1 teaspoon ground nutmeg
¼ teaspoon ground cinnamon
1 cup milk
¼ cup water
⅓ cup unsalted butter, cut up
2 large eggs
⅔ cup currants
⅓ cup chopped mixed candied
     fruit
1 tablespoon all-purpose flour
1 egg white, slightly beaten
1 cup sifted powdered sugar
1 to 1½ tablespoons milk
½ teaspoon vanilla extract

● **Combine** 2½ cups flour, sugar, yeast, salt, nutmeg, and cinnamon in a large mixing bowl, stirring well. Set aside.
● **Combine** 1 cup milk, water, and butter in a saucepan; cook over medium heat, stirring constantly, just until butter melts. Cool to 120° to 130°.
● **Add** milk mixture to flour mixture; beat at low speed with an electric mixer until dry ingredients are moistened. Add 2 eggs; beat at medium speed 3 minutes. Gradually stir in enough remaining flour to make a soft dough.
● **Turn** dough out onto a well-floured surface; knead until smooth and elastic (about 8 minutes). Place in a well-greased bowl, turning to grease top.
● **Cover** and let rise in a warm place (85°), free from drafts, 1 hour (dough may not quite double in bulk).
● **Punch** dough down, and turn out onto a floured surface. Combine currants, candied fruit, and 1 tablespoon flour in a bowl, stirring to coat. Knead about one-fourth of fruit mixture at a time into dough until all fruit mixture is evenly dispersed.
● **Divide** dough into 15 equal portions; shape each portion into a ball. Place balls in a greased 13- x 9- x 2-inch pan; cover and let rise in a warm place, free from drafts, 1 hour or until doubled in bulk. Gently brush tops with beaten egg white.

● **Bake** at 375° for 16 minutes or until buns are deep golden and sound hollow when tapped. Cool 10 minutes in pan on a wire rack.
● **Combine** sifted powdered sugar, 1 to 1½ tablespoons milk, and vanilla; pipe evenly on top of warm buns, forming a cross. **Yield:** 15 buns.

Velma Kestner
Berwind, West Virginia

OATMEAL-CINNAMON
PECAN ROLLS

1 (¼-ounce) envelope active dry
     yeast
¼ cup warm water (105° to 115°)
1 cup milk
1 cup sugar, divided
1 teaspoon salt
⅓ cup butter
2 large eggs
4 to 4½ cups all-purpose flour
1 cup quick-cooking oats,
     uncooked
⅓ cup butter, melted
⅓ cup dark corn syrup
1¼ cups firmly packed brown
     sugar, divided
¾ cup chopped pecans, toasted
2 tablespoons butter or margarine,
     softened
2 teaspoons ground cinnamon

● **Combine** yeast and warm water in a 1-cup liquid measuring cup; let stand 5 minutes.
● **Combine** milk, ½ cup sugar, salt, and ⅓ cup butter in a saucepan; cook over low heat until butter melts, stirring occasionally. Cool to 105° to 115°.
● **Combine** yeast mixture, milk mixture, eggs, and 1 cup flour in a mixing bowl; beat at medium speed with an electric mixer until well blended. Gradually stir in oats and enough remaining flour to make a soft dough.
● **Turn** dough out onto a well-floured surface, and knead until dough is smooth and elastic (about 10 minutes). Place dough in a well-greased bowl, turning to grease top.
● **Cover** and let rise in a warm place (85°), free from drafts, 1 hour or until doubled in bulk.

● **Punch** dough down; cover and let rest 10 minutes.
● **Combine** ⅓ cup melted butter, corn syrup, and ¾ cup brown sugar, stirring until blended. Spoon evenly into two 9-inch square pans. Sprinkle with pecans.
● **Divide** dough in half. Roll each portion into a 12-inch square. Spread each with 1 tablespoon softened butter, leaving a ½-inch border.
● **Combine** cinnamon, remaining ½ cup sugar, and remaining ½ cup brown sugar; sprinkle over dough.
● **Roll** up dough, jellyroll fashion, pressing firmly to eliminate air pockets; pinch seams to seal. Cut each roll into 12 (1-inch) slices, and place in prepared pans.
● **Cover** and let rise in a warm place, free from drafts, 45 minutes or until doubled in bulk.
● **Bake** at 375° for 20 minutes or until golden. Invert onto plates. **Yield:** 2 dozen.

Donna Campbell
Huntsville, Alabama

OLD-FASHIONED
CINNAMON ROLLS

⅓ cup skim milk
⅓ cup reduced-calorie margarine
¼ cup firmly packed brown sugar
1 teaspoon salt
1 (¼-ounce) envelope active dry
     yeast
½ cup warm water (105° to 115°)
½ cup fat-free egg substitute
3½ cups bread flour, divided
¾ cup quick-cooking oats,
     uncooked
Vegetable cooking spray
¼ cup reduced-calorie margarine,
     softened and divided
¾ cup firmly packed brown sugar
¼ cup raisins
2 teaspoons ground cinnamon
1 cup sifted powdered sugar
2 tablespoons water

● **Combine** first 4 ingredients in a saucepan; heat until margarine melts. Cool to 105° to 115°.
● **Combine** yeast and warm water in a 1-cup liquid measuring cup; let stand 5 minutes.

• **Combine** milk mixture, yeast mixture, egg substitute, 1 cup flour, and oats, stirring well. Gradually stir in enough remaining flour to make a soft dough.

• **Turn** dough out onto a lightly floured surface; knead until smooth and elastic (about 8 minutes). Place dough in a large bowl coated with cooking spray, turning to coat top.

• **Cover** and let rise in a warm place (85°), free from drafts, 1 hour or until doubled in bulk.

• **Punch** dough down; cover and let rest 10 minutes. Divide dough in half, and roll each portion into a 12-inch square. Spread each square of dough with 2 tablespoons margarine.

• **Combine** ¾ cup brown sugar, raisins, and cinnamon; sprinkle mixture over each square. Roll up jellyroll fashion; pinch seam to seal (do not seal ends). Cut each roll into 1-inch slices, and place in two 8-inch square pans coated with cooking spray.

• **Cover** and let rise in a warm place, free from drafts, about 30 minutes or until almost doubled in bulk.

• **Bake** at 375° for 15 to 20 minutes or until golden.

• **Combine** powdered sugar and 2 tablespoons water; drizzle over warm rolls. **Yield:** 2 dozen.

♥ Per roll: Calories 169
Fat 3.4g Cholesterol 0mg
Sodium 154mg

SWEET POTATO ROLLS

2 (¼-ounce) packages active dry
   yeast
1½ cups warm water (105° to
   115°)
3 cups whole wheat flour
3 cups all-purpose flour
⅓ cup firmly packed brown sugar
1¼ teaspoons salt
½ cup butter or margarine,
   softened
2 large eggs
1 (16-ounce) can cut sweet
   potatoes, drained

• **Combine** yeast and warm water in container of an electric blender, and process 30 seconds. Let yeast mixture stand 5 minutes.

• **Combine** flours in a large bowl. Add 1 cup flour mixture, sugar, and remaining 4 ingredients to yeast mixture in blender; process until smooth.

• **Gradually** stir yeast mixture into remaining flour mixture to make a soft dough.

• **Turn** dough out onto a heavily floured surface, and knead until smooth and elastic (about 5 minutes). Place in a well-greased bowl, turning to grease top. Cover and let rise in a warm place (85°), free from drafts, 1 hour or until doubled in bulk.

• **Punch** dough down, and divide in half; shape each portion into a ball. Roll each portion of dough into a 16-inch circle on a floured surface, and cut into 16 wedges. Roll up wedges, beginning at wide end, and place, point side down, on a greased baking sheet. Cover and let rise in a warm place, free from drafts, 30 minutes or until doubled in bulk.

• **Bake** at 350° for 15 minutes or until golden. **Yield:** 32 rolls.

Note: You can make dough ahead. Knead, place in a greased bowl, and cover securely with plastic wrap. Chill at least 6 hours. Punch dough down; proceed as directed.

Sue Ewing's Supper Club
Richmond, Virginia

CENTERPIECE ROLLS

1 large egg, lightly beaten
1 tablespoon water
1 (25-ounce) package frozen roll
   dough, thawed
Toppings: poppy seeds, caraway
   seeds, dillseeds, dried basil,
   dried thyme, dried marjoram,
   cornmeal, oats

• **Combine** egg and water. Brush top of each unbaked roll with egg mixture, and sprinkle with desired toppings.

• **Arrange** all but 5 unbaked rolls in a cluster with sides touching on a greased baking sheet. Knead remaining 5 rolls together; divide in half. Form each half into a rope long enough to go around the cluster. Twist ropes together; wrap around cluster, pressing edges to seal.

• **Let** rise in a warm place (85°), free from drafts, 1 hour or until dough is doubled in bulk.

• **Bake** at 350° for 15 minutes or until lightly browned. **Yield:** 1 loaf.

Note: You can bake rolls individually or in clusters of 2 or 3. Bake at 350° for 12 minutes or until lightly browned.

Greg Dowling
Birmingham, Alabama

WHOLESOME
WHOLE WHEAT ROLLS

2½ cups milk, divided
2 (¼-ounce) envelopes active dry
   yeast
½ cup honey
½ cup shortening
2 teaspoons salt
3 cups whole wheat flour
2 large eggs
3½ to 4 cups all-purpose flour
Melted butter or margarine

• **Heat** milk to 110° to 115°. Combine yeast and ½ cup milk in a 1-cup liquid measuring cup; let stand 5 minutes.

• **Combine** remaining 2 cups milk, honey, shortening, salt, and wheat flour in a mixing bowl; beat at medium speed with an electric mixer until smooth. Add yeast mixture and eggs; mix well. Gradually stir in enough all-purpose flour to make a stiff dough. Place in a well-greased bowl, turning to grease top.

• **Cover** and let rise in a warm place (85°), free from drafts, 1 hour or until doubled in bulk.

• **Punch** dough down; turn out onto a well-floured surface, and knead 4 or 5 times. Roll to ½-inch thickness; cut with a 2½-inch round cutter. Place on a lightly greased baking sheet.

• **Cover** and let rise in a warm place, free from drafts, about 30 minutes or until doubled in bulk.

• **Bake** at 400° for 12 to 15 minutes or until browned. Brush rolls with melted butter. **Yield:** 2 dozen.

Heidi Huffman
Woodland, Mississippi

BUTTER CRESCENT ROLLS

2 (¼-ounce) envelopes active dry
   yeast
¾ cup warm water (105°
   to 115°)
½ cup sugar
1½ teaspoons salt
½ cup butter, melted
2 large eggs, lightly beaten
4 cups all-purpose flour, divided
¼ cup butter, softened

• **Combine** yeast and warm water in a 2-cup liquid measuring cup; let stand 5 minutes.
• **Combine** yeast mixture, sugar, and next 3 ingredients in a large bowl; add 2 cups flour, stirring well. Gradually stir in remaining 2 cups flour to make a soft dough.
• **Turn** dough out onto a well-floured surface, and knead 3 or 4 times. Place dough in a well-greased bowl, turning to grease top.
• **Cover** and let rise in a warm place (85°), free from drafts, 1 hour or until doubled in bulk.
• **Punch** dough down, and divide into thirds; shape each portion into a ball. Roll each ball into a 12-inch circle on a lightly floured surface; spread with softened butter. Cut each circle into 12 wedges. Roll up each wedge, starting with wide end; place rolls, point side down, on greased baking sheets.
• **Cover** and let rise in a warm place, free from drafts, 20 minutes or until doubled in bulk.
• **Bake** at 375° for 12 minutes or until golden. Brush rolls with additional melted butter, if desired. **Yield:** 3 dozen.

Marlene Compston
Owasso, Oklahoma

MAKE-AHEAD YEAST ROLLS

QUICK!

Carole says this recipe "turns out the same way, no matter what mood you're in or what the weather is." We didn't even need to butter the tops. The baked rolls freeze well.

2 (¼-ounce) envelopes active dry
   yeast
1¼ cups warm water (105° to
   115°), divided
4½ to 5 cups all-purpose flour,
   divided
3 large eggs, lightly beaten
½ cup shortening, melted
½ cup sugar
2 teaspoons salt

• **Combine** yeast and ¼ cup warm water in a 2-cup liquid measuring cup; let stand 5 minutes.
• **Combine** yeast mixture, remaining 1 cup warm water, 2 cups flour, eggs, and remaining 3 ingredients in a large bowl; beat with a wooden spoon 2 minutes. Gradually stir in enough remaining flour to make a soft dough.
• **Cover** and let rise in a warm place (85°), free from drafts, 1 hour.
• **Punch** dough down; cover and chill at least 8 hours.
• **Punch** dough down; turn dough out onto a lightly floured surface, and knead 3 or 4 times. Divide dough in half; shape each portion into 16 (2-inch) balls. Place dough balls in two lightly greased 9-inch square pans.
• **Cover** and let rise in a warm place, free from drafts, 1½ hours or until doubled in bulk.
• **Bake** at 375° for 12 minutes or until golden. **Yield:** 32 rolls.

Note: This is an excellent, supple dough. You can make these rolls into a variety of shapes. Your yield will vary depending on how you shape the rolls.

Carole Miller Radford
Lincolnton, Georgia

OVERNIGHT YEAST ROLLS

QUICK!

2 (¼-ounce) envelopes active dry
   yeast
1 cup warm water (105° to 115°)
1 cup shortening
1 cup sugar
1 teaspoon salt
1 cup boiling water
2 large eggs
6 cups all-purpose flour

• **Combine** yeast and warm water in a 2-cup liquid measuring cup; let stand 5 minutes.
• **Place** shortening, sugar, and salt in a large mixing bowl. Add boiling water, and beat at medium speed with an electric mixer until smooth. Add eggs and yeast mixture, beating at low speed until blended; gradually beat in flour. Cover and chill 8 hours.
• **Shape** dough into 1-inch balls, and place 3 dough balls in each lightly greased muffin cup.
• **Cover** and let rise in a warm place (85°), free from drafts, 45 minutes or until doubled in bulk.
• **Bake** at 400° for 12 minutes or until lightly browned. **Yield:** 3 dozen.

Orange Rolls: Divide chilled dough in half; roll each portion into a 12- x 10-inch rectangle. Combine 2½ cups sifted powdered sugar, ¼ cup melted butter, 2 teaspoons grated orange rind, and 3 tablespoons fresh orange juice; spread mixture evenly over dough rectangles. Roll up, jellyroll fashion, starting with long side, pressing edges of dough to seal. Cut logs into 1-inch slices, and place in a lightly greased 13- x 9- x 2-inch pan. Let rise, and bake as directed. Cool slightly. Combine 2 cups sifted powdered sugar, ½ teaspoon grated orange rind, and 2 to 3 tablespoons orange juice, stirring well. Drizzle over warm rolls. **Yield:** 2 dozen.

Christine H. Morrow
Bossier City, Louisiana

QUICK YEAST ROLLS

You can have these wonderful yeast rolls ready in about an hour.

2 (¼-ounce) envelopes active dry yeast
½ cup warm milk (105° to 115°)
1 cup milk
2 tablespoons sugar
2 tablespoons vegetable oil
1 teaspoon salt
1 large egg, lightly beaten
4 cups all-purpose flour, divided

● **Combine** yeast and ½ cup warm milk in a 2-cup liquid measuring cup; let stand 5 minutes.
● **Combine** yeast mixture, 1 cup milk, and next 4 ingredients in a large bowl. Gradually add 1 cup flour, stirring until smooth. Gradually stir in enough remaining 3 cups flour to make a soft dough. Place in a well-greased bowl, turning to grease top.
● **Cover** and let rise in a warm place (85°), free from drafts, 15 minutes.
● **Punch** dough down; cover and let rise in a warm place, free from drafts, 15 minutes.
● **Turn** dough out onto a floured surface; knead 3 or 4 times. Divide dough into 24 pieces; shape into balls. Place in two greased 9-inch square pans. Cover and let rise in a warm place, free from drafts, 15 minutes.
● **Bake** at 400° for 15 minutes or until golden. **Yield:** 2 dozen.

60-MINUTE ROLLS

2 (¼-ounce) envelopes active dry yeast
½ cup warm water (105° to 115°)
1¼ cups milk
3 tablespoons sugar
2 tablespoons butter
1½ teaspoons salt
4½ to 5 cups all-purpose flour

● **Combine** yeast and warm water in a 1-cup liquid measuring cup; let stand 5 minutes.

● **Combine** milk and next 3 ingredients in a heavy saucepan; cook over medium heat, stirring constantly, just until butter melts. Pour into a large bowl; cool to 105° to 115°. Stir in yeast mixture; gradually stir in enough flour to make a soft dough.
● **Turn** dough out onto a well-floured surface; knead until smooth and elastic (about 5 minutes). Place in a well-greased bowl, turning to grease top.
● **Cover** and let stand in a warm place (85°), free from drafts, 15 minutes.
● **Divide** dough in half; shape each portion into 12 balls, and place in two greased 9-inch square pans. Cover and let rise in a warm place, free from drafts, 15 minutes.
● **Bake** at 425° for 10 to 12 minutes. **Yield:** 2 dozen.

Barbara Wagner
Gainesville, Florida

CROISSANTS

1 cup butter, softened
2 (¼-ounce) envelopes active dry yeast
3 tablespoons sugar, divided
½ cup warm water (105° to 115°)
⅔ cup milk
4 to 4½ cups all-purpose flour, divided
¼ cup vegetable oil
2 teaspoons salt
2 large eggs

● **Spread** butter into a 10- x 8-inch rectangle on a sheet of wax paper; cover and chill.
● **Combine** yeast, 1 tablespoon sugar, and warm water in a 2-cup liquid measuring cup; let stand 5 minutes.
● **Heat** milk to 105° to 115°. Combine yeast mixture, warm milk, remaining 2 tablespoons sugar, 2 cups flour, vegetable oil, salt, and eggs in a large mixing bowl. Beat at medium speed with an electric mixer until smooth. Gradually stir in enough remaining flour to make a soft dough.
● **Turn** dough out onto a lightly floured surface; knead until smooth and elastic (about 10 minutes). Place dough in a well-greased bowl, turning to grease top.

● **Cover** and let rise in a warm place (85°), free from drafts, 1 hour or until doubled in bulk.
● **Punch** dough down. Cover with plastic wrap, and chill 1 hour.
● **Punch** dough down; turn out onto a lightly floured surface, and roll into a 24- x 10-inch rectangle. Place chilled butter rectangle in center of dough rectangle; gently fold dough over butter. Pinch edges to seal.
● **Roll** dough into an 18- x 10-inch rectangle; fold into thirds, beginning with short side. Cover and chill 1 hour.
● **Repeat** rolling and folding procedure twice, chilling dough 30 minutes each time. Wrap dough in aluminum foil, and chill 8 hours.
● **Divide** dough into 4 equal portions. Roll 1 portion into a 12-inch circle on a lightly floured surface, and cut into 6 wedges (keep remaining dough chilled). Roll up each wedge tightly, beginning at wide end. Place, point side down, on greased baking sheets, curving into crescent shapes.
● **Cover** and let rise in a warm place, free from drafts, 30 minutes or until doubled in bulk.
● **Bake** at 425° for 8 minutes or until golden. Cool slightly on baking sheets; transfer to wire racks to cool. Repeat procedure with remaining dough portions. **Yield:** 2 dozen.

Chocolate-Filled Croissants: Place 2 or 3 tiny rectangles of a milk chocolate candy bar on wide end of each wedge; roll up, and proceed as directed.

Strawberry or Apricot Croissants: Spread 1 teaspoon strawberry or apricot preserves over each wedge, leaving a ¼-inch border; roll up, and proceed as directed.

Cinnamon-Sugar Croissants: Sprinkle wedges with a mixture of ground cinnamon and sugar; roll up, and proceed as directed. Combine sifted powdered sugar and milk, stirring until smooth. Drizzle over croissants after baking.

MORRISON HOUSE BRIOCHE

Don't limit this buttery bread just to breakfast. It's also delicious as a sandwich or dinner roll.

4⅓ cups all-purpose flour
2 tablespoons sugar
½ (¼-ounce) envelope active dry yeast (1½ teaspoons)
¼ cup warm water (105° to 115°)
2 teaspoons salt
8 large eggs
1¼ cups unsalted butter, chilled and cut into pieces
1 large egg, lightly beaten

• **Combine** flour and sugar in a large mixing bowl. Make a well in center of mixture; add yeast and warm water in center. Let stand 5 minutes.
• **Beat** at low speed with an electric mixer until blended; add salt and 8 eggs, one at a time, beating until blended after each addition. Gradually add butter, beating well (small bits of butter will be visible). Cover and chill at least 8 hours (dough will be sticky).
• **Divide** dough into 12 portions; pinch off a 1-inch ball of dough from each portion, and set aside.
• **Roll** larger pieces into balls on a lightly floured surface; place in well-greased individual brioche molds or muffin pan. Place molds or muffin pan on a baking sheet.
• **Make** a well in center of each ball. Shape remaining dough pieces into balls, and place in wells.
• **Brush** brioche with beaten egg; let stand 30 minutes.
• **Bake** at 350° for 30 minutes. Cool in molds or pans 10 minutes; remove from molds or pan. **Yield:** 1 dozen.

Morrison House
Alexandria, Virginia

FRENCH MARKET BEIGNETS

1 (¼-ounce) envelope active dry yeast
1 cup warm water (105° to 115°)
¾ cup evaporated milk
¼ cup sugar
1 teaspoon salt
1 large egg, lightly beaten
4 to 4½ cups all-purpose flour
Vegetable oil
Sifted powdered sugar

• **Combine** yeast and warm water in a 2-cup liquid measuring cup; let stand 5 minutes.
• **Combine** yeast mixture, evaporated milk, and next 3 ingredients. Gradually stir in enough flour to make a soft dough. Cover and chill 8 hours.
• **Turn** dough out onto a well-floured surface; knead 5 or 6 times. Roll dough into a 15- x 12½-inch rectangle; cut into 2½-inch squares.
• **Pour** oil to depth of 3 to 4 inches into a Dutch oven; heat to 375°. Fry 3 or 4 beignets at a time, 1 minute on each side or until golden. Drain; sprinkle with powdered sugar. **Yield:** 2½ dozen.

HONEY PUFFS

2 (¼-ounce) envelopes active dry yeast
1 cup warm water (105° to 115°)
2 cups warm milk (105° to 115°)
¼ cup sugar
1 teaspoon salt
1 large egg
4 cups all-purpose flour
Vegetable oil
Honey
Ground cinnamon

• **Combine** yeast and warm water in a 2-cup liquid measuring cup; let stand 5 minutes.
• **Combine** yeast mixture, warm milk, and next 3 ingredients; stir with a wooden spoon until well blended.
• **Add** flour, 1 cup at a time, stirring until smooth after each addition.
• **Cover** and let rise in a warm place (85°), free from drafts, 1 hour or until doubled in bulk.

• **Pour** oil to depth of 4 inches into a Dutch oven; heat to 375°. Drop dough by tablespoonfuls into hot oil, and fry until golden, turning once. Drain on paper towels; keep warm. Repeat procedure with remaining dough.
• **Drizzle** with honey, and sprinkle with cinnamon; serve immediately. **Yield:** 4 dozen.

Jean Voan
Shepherd, Texas

OVERNIGHT REFRIGERATOR PANCAKES

QUICK!

1 (¼-ounce) envelope active dry yeast
¼ cup warm water (105° to 115°)
4 cups all-purpose flour
2 tablespoons baking powder
2 teaspoons baking soda
1 teaspoon salt
2 teaspoons sugar
6 large eggs
4 cups buttermilk
¼ cup vegetable oil

• **Combine** yeast and warm water in a 1-cup liquid measuring cup; let stand 5 minutes.
• **Combine** flour and next 4 ingredients in a large bowl; make a well in center. Combine eggs, buttermilk, and oil; add to flour mixture, stirring just until dry ingredients are moistened. Stir in yeast mixture. Cover and chill 8 hours.
• **Remove** from refrigerator; stir well.
• **Preheat** griddle to 350°; lightly grease griddle. Pour about ¼ cup batter for each pancake onto hot griddle. Cook pancakes until tops are covered with bubbles and edges look cooked; turn and cook other side. **Yield:** 2½ dozen.

Note: You can store pancake batter in refrigerator up to 1 week.

Dolores Thielermeir
Maynard, Arkansas

At right: *Orange Butter Cake (page 70)*

CAKES

BUTTERMILK-LEMON PUDDING CAKE WITH BLUEBERRY SAUCE

⅔ cup sugar
¼ cup all-purpose flour
1½ cups buttermilk
½ cup fresh lemon juice
¼ cup butter or margarine, melted
3 large eggs, separated
1 tablespoon grated lemon rind
¼ cup sugar
Powdered sugar
Blueberry Sauce
Garnish: lemon rind curls

• **Combine** ⅔ cup sugar and flour in a large bowl; stir in buttermilk, lemon juice, butter, egg yolks, and lemon rind. Set aside.
• **Beat** egg whites at high speed with an electric mixer until foamy. Gradually add ¼ cup sugar, 1 tablespoon at a time, beating until stiff peaks form and sugar dissolves (2 to 4 minutes).
• **Fold** egg white mixture into batter; pour into a greased 9- x 5- x 3-inch loafpan, and place loafpan in a 13- x 9- x 2-inch baking pan. Add hot water to baking pan to depth of 1½ inches.
• **Bake** at 350° for 1 hour and 10 minutes, shielding with aluminum foil after 40 minutes to prevent excessive browning. Carefully remove loafpan; cool on a wire rack 15 minutes. Dust with powdered sugar. Serve over warm Blueberry Sauce, and garnish, if desired. **Yield:** 6 to 8 servings.

Blueberry Sauce

◀QUICK!▶

¼ cup sugar
2 teaspoons cornstarch
¼ cup water
2 tablespoons lemon juice
¼ teaspoon ground cinnamon
2 cups fresh or frozen blueberries

• **Combine** all ingredients in a medium saucepan; cook over medium-low heat, stirring constantly, until mixture boils and thickens. **Yield:** 1 cup.

Linda Magers
Clemmons, North Carolina

ORANGE BUTTER CAKE
(pictured on page 69)

2 cups all-purpose flour
1 cup graham cracker crumbs
1 cup firmly packed light brown sugar
½ cup sugar
1 teaspoon baking powder
1 teaspoon baking soda
¼ teaspoon salt
1 teaspoon ground cinnamon
1 cup butter, softened
1 tablespoon grated orange rind
1 cup fresh orange juice
3 large eggs, lightly beaten
Tropical Cheese Spread (optional)

• **Combine** first 12 ingredients in a large mixing bowl; beat at low speed with an electric mixer until blended. Beat at high speed 3 minutes. Pour batter into two greased and floured 8½- x 4½- x 3-inch loafpans.
• **Bake** at 350° for 45 minutes or until a wooden pick inserted in center comes out clean. Cool in pans on wire racks 10 minutes; remove from pans, and let cool completely on wire racks. Frost with Tropical Cheese Spread, if desired. **Yield:** 2 loaves.

Tropical Cheese Spread

◀QUICK!▶

1 cup chopped dried mixed fruit
¾ cup water
2 tablespoons Grand Marnier or other orange-flavored liqueur
2 (8-ounce) packages cream cheese, softened
½ cup orange marmalade

• **Combine** first 3 ingredients in a small saucepan; bring to a boil over medium heat. Cover, reduce heat, and simmer 8 minutes or until fruit is soft. Drain well.
• **Beat** cream cheese at medium speed with electric mixer until creamy; add marmalade, and beat until blended. Fold in fruit. **Yield:** 3½ cups.

Dorsella Utter
Louisville, Kentucky

ACORN SQUASH CAKE

¼ cup butter, softened
¾ cup firmly packed light brown sugar
1 large egg
1 cup cooked mashed acorn squash
½ teaspoon vanilla extract
2 cups all-purpose flour
2 teaspoons baking soda
½ teaspoon salt
1 teaspoon ground cinnamon
1 cup chopped pecans
Streusel Topping

• **Beat** butter and sugar at medium speed with an electric mixer until creamy. Add egg, beating well. Stir in squash and vanilla.
• **Combine** flour and next 3 ingredients; gradually add to squash mixture, beating at low speed after each addition. Stir in pecans. Pour batter into a greased 9-inch square pan, and sprinkle with Streusel Topping.
• **Bake** at 350° for 40 minutes. Cool cake in pan on a wire rack. **Yield:** 9 servings.

Streusel Topping

◀QUICK!▶

½ cup firmly packed light brown sugar
⅓ cup all-purpose flour
½ teaspoon ground cinnamon
¼ cup butter, softened
½ cup chopped pecans

• **Combine** all ingredients in a bowl. **Yield:** 1½ cups.

Valerie Stutsman
Norfolk, Virginia

CHEATER'S CARROT CAKE

QUICK!

1 (8.25-ounce) package yellow
    cake mix
1 (8-ounce) can crushed
    pineapple, undrained
1 cup shredded carrot
⅓ cup mayonnaise
2 large eggs, lightly beaten
1 (2-ounce) package pecan pieces
1 teaspoon ground cinnamon
½ (12-ounce) container cream
    cheese frosting

• **Combine** first 7 ingredients in a large bowl, stirring until blended. Pour into a greased and floured 9-inch square pan.
• **Bake** at 350° for 30 minutes or until a wooden pick inserted in center comes out clean. Cool completely in pan on a wire rack. Spread frosting on top of cake. **Yield:** 1 (9-inch) cake.

Bill Jackson
Alpine, Alabama

FROSTED CARROT CAKE

1½ cups all-purpose flour
⅔ cup whole wheat flour
2 teaspoons baking soda
2 teaspoons ground cinnamon
¼ teaspoon salt
1 cup firmly packed brown sugar
¾ cup fat-free egg substitute
¾ cup nonfat buttermilk
1 (8-ounce) can crushed pineapple
    in juice, drained
2 cups grated carrots
⅓ cup raisins
3 tablespoons vegetable oil
2 teaspoons vanilla extract
Vegetable cooking spray
Orange-Cream Cheese Frosting

• **Combine** first 5 ingredients; set aside.
• **Combine** brown sugar and next 7 ingredients in a large mixing bowl; add dry ingredients, and beat at medium speed with an electric mixer until well blended. Pour batter into a 13- x 9- x 2-inch pan coated with cooking spray.
• **Bake** at 350° for 30 to 35 minutes or until a wooden pick inserted in center comes out clean. Cool cake completely in pan on a wire rack. Spread Orange-Cream Cheese Frosting over top of cake. Cover and chill. **Yield:** 18 servings.

♥ Per serving: Calories 208
Fat 4.8g Cholesterol 8mg
Sodium 306mg

Orange-Cream Cheese Frosting

QUICK!

½ cup 1% low-fat cottage cheese
2 teaspoons vanilla extract
1 (8-ounce) package light cream
    cheese, softened
1 teaspoon grated orange rind
1 cup sifted powdered sugar

• **Position** knife blade in food processor bowl; add cottage cheese. Process about 1 minute or until smooth. Add vanilla, cream cheese, and orange rind, and process until smooth. Add powdered sugar, and pulse 3 to 5 times or until mixture is smooth. **Yield:** 1½ cups.

NO-MOLASSES GINGERBREAD

QUICK!

1 teaspoon baking soda
½ cup cane syrup
½ cup butter, softened
½ cup sugar
2 large eggs, lightly beaten
1½ cups all-purpose flour
1 teaspoon ground cinnamon
½ teaspoon ground ginger
¼ teaspoon ground cloves
¼ teaspoon salt
½ cup water

• **Combine** soda and syrup; set aside.
• **Beat** butter with an electric mixer until creamy. Gradually add sugar, beating well. Add eggs, one at a time, beating after each addition. Stir in syrup mixture.
• **Combine** flour and next 4 ingredients; add to butter mixture alternately with water, beginning and ending with flour mixture. Mix after each addition.
• **Pour** batter into a greased and floured 9-inch square pan. Bake at 350° for 30 minutes or until a wooden pick inserted in center comes out clean. Cool in pan

on a wire rack at least 10 minutes before serving. **Yield:** 9 to 12 servings.

Louise Smith
Columbus, Georgia

PUMPKIN GINGERBREAD WITH CARAMEL SAUCE

2¼ cups all-purpose flour
½ cup sugar
⅔ cup butter or margarine
¾ cup chopped pecans
¾ cup buttermilk
½ cup canned pumpkin
½ cup molasses
1 large egg
1½ teaspoons ground ginger
1 teaspoon baking soda
½ teaspoon ground cinnamon
¼ teaspoon salt
¼ teaspoon ground cloves
Caramel Sauce
Vanilla ice cream

• **Combine** flour and sugar; cut in butter with pastry blender until mixture is crumbly. Stir in pecans. Press 1¼ cups mixture in bottom of an ungreased 9-inch square pan; set aside.
• **Combine** remaining crumb mixture, buttermilk, and next 8 ingredients; beat at low speed with an electric mixer until blended. Pour over crumb mixture; bake at 350° for 40 minutes or until a wooden pick inserted in center comes out clean. Cool in pan on a wire rack. Cut into squares; serve with Caramel Sauce and ice cream. **Yield:** 12 servings.

Caramel Sauce

QUICK!

½ cup butter or margarine
1¼ cups firmly packed brown sugar
2 tablespoons light corn syrup
½ cup whipping cream

• **Melt** butter in a small heavy saucepan over low heat; add sugar and corn syrup. Bring to a boil; cook, stirring constantly, 1 minute or until sugar dissolves. Gradually add cream; return to a boil. Set aside. **Yield:** 2 cups.

Linda Magers
Clemmons, North Carolina

KAHLÚA GINGERBREAD WITH KEY LIME CURD

½ cup butter or margarine,
    softened
¾ cup sugar
⅓ cup firmly packed dark brown
    sugar
1 large egg
2 cups all-purpose flour
1½ teaspoons baking soda
1½ teaspoons ground ginger
1 teaspoon ground cinnamon
1 teaspoon ground cloves
½ teaspoon salt
1 cup molasses
⅔ cup hot water
⅓ cup Kahlúa or other coffee-
    flavored liqueur
2 tablespoons brewed coffee
Key Lime Curd
Whipped cream
Garnishes: fresh mint sprig, Key
    lime rind

• **Beat** butter at medium speed with an electric mixer until creamy; gradually add sugars, beating well. Add egg, beating until blended.
• **Add** flour and next 9 ingredients; beat at medium speed until smooth. Pour into a greased and floured 13- x 9- x 2-inch pan.
• **Bake** at 325° for 35 minutes or until a wooden pick inserted in center comes out clean. Cut into triangles; serve warm or at room temperature with Key Lime Curd and whipped cream. Garnish, if desired. **Yield:** 12 servings.

Key Lime Curd

2 cups sugar
1 cup butter or margarine,
    cut up
⅔ cup fresh Key lime juice
1 tablespoon grated Key lime rind
    (optional)
4 large eggs, lightly beaten

• **Combine** first 3 ingredients, and lime rind, if desired, in a large heavy saucepan; cook over medium heat, stirring constantly, until butter melts. Gradually stir one-fourth of hot mixture into eggs; add to remaining hot mixture, stirring constantly.

• **Cook** over low heat, stirring constantly, 10 minutes or until lime mixture thickens and coats a spoon. Remove from heat; cool. Cover and chill at least 2 hours. **Yield:** 3 cups.

Stop and Smell the Rosemary:
Recipes and Traditions to Remember
Junior League of Houston, Texas

GINGERY GINGERBREAD

½ cup butter, softened
½ cup sugar
1 large egg
1 cup molasses
½ cup finely grated fresh ginger
2½ cups all-purpose flour
1½ teaspoons baking soda
½ teaspoon baking powder
1 teaspoon ground cinnamon
1 teaspoon ground ginger
½ teaspoon ground cloves
1 cup hot water
Vanilla ice cream

• **Beat** butter at medium speed with an electric mixer until creamy; gradually add sugar, beating well. Add egg and molasses, beating until blended. Add fresh ginger, beating until blended.
• **Combine** flour and next 5 ingredients; add to butter mixture alternately with hot water, beginning and ending with flour mixture. Beat at low speed until blended after each addition; beat 1 additional minute or until very smooth. Pour into a greased 13- x 9- x 2-inch pan.
• **Bake** at 350° for 40 minutes or until a wooden pick inserted in center comes out clean. Cool in pan on a wire rack 10 minutes; remove from pan, and let cool completely on wire rack.
• **Cut** into squares; serve with vanilla ice cream. **Yield:** 12 servings.

Milton Hurst
Birmingham, Alabama

GRANDMA'S CHOCOLATE CAKE
QUICK!

2 cups all-purpose flour
2 cups sugar
¼ cup cocoa
1 teaspoon ground cinnamon
1 cup butter or margarine
1 cup water
1 teaspoon baking soda
2 large eggs
½ cup buttermilk
1 teaspoon vanilla extract
1 (12-ounce) package miniature
    chocolate-covered peppermint
    patties, unwrapped
Chocolate Frosting

• **Combine** first 4 ingredients, and set aside.
• **Combine** butter and water in a large saucepan; bring to a boil.
• **Remove** from heat; stir in soda. Add flour mixture, stirring well.
• **Stir** in eggs, buttermilk, and vanilla.
• **Spoon** batter into a greased and floured 13- x 9- x 2-inch pan.
• **Bake** at 350° for 30 minutes. Top with candy; bake 2 additional minutes. Gently spread melted candy over warm cake. Spread Chocolate Frosting over top. Cut into squares. **Yield:** 15 servings.

Chocolate Frosting
QUICK!

½ cup butter or margarine
⅓ cup milk
1 (16-ounce) package powdered
    sugar, sifted
¼ cup cocoa
1 teaspoon vanilla extract

• **Combine** butter and milk in a large saucepan. Bring mixture to a boil, and remove from heat.
• **Combine** powdered sugar and cocoa; add to butter mixture. Add vanilla, stirring until smooth. **Yield:** 2 cups.

Carol Boker
Memphis, Tennessee

QUICK CHOCOLATE COLA CAKE

QUICK!

1 (18.25-ounce) package devil's
  food cake mix without
  pudding
1 (3.9-ounce) package chocolate
  instant pudding mix
4 large eggs
½ cup vegetable oil
1 (10-ounce) bottle cola-flavored
  carbonated beverage
  (1¼ cups)
Chocolate-Cola Frosting

• **Combine** cake mix, pudding mix,
eggs, and oil in a large mixing bowl; beat
at low speed with an electric mixer until
blended. Set aside.
• **Bring** cola to a boil in a small
saucepan over medium heat. With mixer
on low speed, gradually pour hot cola
into cake batter. Increase speed to
medium; beat 2 minutes.
• **Pour** batter into a greased and floured
13- x 9- x 2-inch baking pan.
• **Bake** at 350° for 30 minutes or until a
wooden pick inserted in center comes
out clean. Cool in pan on a wire rack 10
minutes.
• **Spread** warm Chocolate-Cola Frosting over top of warm cake; let cake cool
completely in pan on wire rack. **Yield:**
15 servings.

Chocolate-Cola Frosting

QUICK!

½ cup butter or margarine
¼ cup plus 2 tablespoons
  cola-flavored carbonated
  beverage
3 tablespoons cocoa
1 (16-ounce) package powdered
  sugar, sifted
1 teaspoon vanilla extract
1 cup chopped pecans, toasted

• **Combine** first 3 ingredients in a large
saucepan; cook over medium heat, stirring constantly, until butter melts. (Do
not boil.) Remove from heat; add powdered sugar and vanilla, stirring until
smooth. Stir in chopped pecans. **Yield:**
about 2¼ cups.

Meredith Bennett
Joiner, Arkansas

PEANUT BUTTER-FUDGE CAKE

QUICK!

*Whether you serve it as an after-school
snack or for dessert, this recipe is sure
to be a favorite of kids of all ages.*

2 cups all-purpose flour
1 teaspoon baking soda
2 cups sugar
1 cup butter or margarine
¼ cup cocoa
1 cup water
½ cup buttermilk
2 large eggs, lightly beaten
1 teaspoon vanilla extract
1½ cups creamy peanut butter
Chocolate Frosting

• **Combine** first 3 ingredients in a large
bowl; set aside.
• **Melt** butter in a heavy saucepan over
medium heat; stir in cocoa. Add water,
buttermilk, and eggs, stirring well.
• **Cook,** stirring constantly, until mixture boils. Remove from heat; add to
flour mixture, stirring until smooth. Stir
in vanilla. Pour batter into a greased and
floured 13- x 9- x 2-inch pan.
• **Bake** at 350° for 20 to 25 minutes or
until a wooden pick inserted in center
comes out clean. Cool in pan on a wire
rack 10 minutes. Carefully spread
peanut butter over warm cake. Cool
completely.
• **Spread** Chocolate Frosting over
peanut butter; cut into squares. **Yield:**
20 to 25 servings.

Chocolate Frosting

QUICK!

1 (16-ounce) package powdered
  sugar, sifted
¼ cup cocoa
½ cup butter or margarine
⅓ cup buttermilk
1 teaspoon vanilla extract

• **Place** sugar in a bowl; set aside.
• **Bring** cocoa, butter, and buttermilk to
a boil in a small saucepan over medium
heat, stirring constantly. Pour hot mixture over sugar, stirring until smooth.
Stir in vanilla. **Yield:** 2½ cups.

Marian T. Talley
Huntsville, Alabama

MAPLE NUT CAKE

1 cup shortening
½ cup firmly packed brown sugar
1 cup maple syrup
2 large eggs
2½ cups all-purpose flour
2 teaspoons baking powder
½ teaspoon baking soda
½ teaspoon salt
2 teaspoons ground nutmeg
½ cup hot water
½ cup sherry
1 cup chopped pecans, toasted
Maple Frosting
12 to 15 pecan halves

• **Beat** shortening at medium speed
with an electric mixer until fluffy; gradually add brown sugar, beating well. Add
maple syrup and eggs, beating until
blended.
• **Combine** flour and next 4 ingredients
in a bowl; add to shortening mixture alternately with hot water and sherry, beginning and ending with flour mixture.
Beat at low speed until blended after
each addition. Stir in 1 cup chopped
pecans. Pour batter into a greased and
floured 13- x 9- x 2-inch pan.
• **Bake** at 350° for 30 minutes or until a
wooden pick inserted in center comes
out clean. Cool cake completely in pan
on a wire rack.
• **Spread** Maple Frosting on top of cake;
place a pecan half on each serving.
Yield: 12 to 15 servings.

Maple Frosting

QUICK!

¼ cup butter or margarine,
  softened
2¼ cups sifted powdered sugar,
  divided
2 to 3 tablespoons milk
½ teaspoon maple extract

• **Beat** butter at medium speed with an
electric mixer until creamy; gradually
add 1 cup powdered sugar, beating well.
Add remaining 1¼ cups powdered
sugar and milk, beating until mixture is
spreading consistency. Stir in flavoring.
Yield: 1 cup.

Sara Beebee
Kennesaw, Georgia

BEERQUICK SUGAR CAKE

QUICK!

4 cups biscuit mix
½ cup instant potato flakes
¼ cup sugar
¼ cup instant nonfat dry milk
    powder
2 large eggs, lightly beaten
1 (12-ounce) can beer, at room
    temperature
3 tablespoons vegetable oil
1 cup butter or margarine,
    melted
2 cups firmly packed brown sugar
1¼ teaspoons ground cinnamon

• **Combine** first 4 ingredients in a large bowl, and make a well in center of dry ingredients.
• **Combine** eggs, beer, and oil; add to dry ingredients, stirring just until dry ingredients are moistened.
• **Spoon** batter into a greased 15- x 10- x 1-inch jellyroll pan; let stand 10 minutes.
• **Combine** butter, brown sugar, and cinnamon; spread half of butter mixture on top of cake.
• **Bake** at 350° for 15 minutes. Remove cake from oven; spread with remaining butter mixture. Bake 10 additional minutes. Serve immediately. **Yield:** 15 to 18 servings.

Laura Greene Knapp
Cary, North Carolina

MORAVIAN SUGAR CAKE

2 (¼-ounce) envelopes active dry
    yeast
½ teaspoon sugar
½ cup warm water (105° to 115°)
1 cup butter or margarine, melted
    and divided
¾ cup water
½ cup sugar
¼ cup instant potato flakes
2 tablespoons instant nonfat dry
    milk powder
½ teaspoon salt
2 large eggs
3 cups all-purpose flour
1 cup firmly packed brown
    sugar
1 teaspoon ground cinnamon

• **Combine** first 3 ingredients in a 1-cup liquid measuring cup, and let stand 5 minutes.
• **Combine** yeast mixture, ½ cup melted butter, ¾ cup water, and next 5 ingredients in a large mixing bowl. Add 1 cup flour; beat at low speed with an electric mixer 2 minutes. Stir in enough remaining 2 cups flour to make a soft dough.
• **Cover** and let rise in a warm place (85°), free from drafts, 45 minutes or until doubled in bulk.
• **Punch** dough down; spread in a greased 15- x 10- x 1-inch jellyroll pan. Cover and let rise in a warm place (85°), free from drafts, 30 minutes.
• **Make** shallow indentations in dough at 1-inch intervals, using the handle of a wooden spoon. Drizzle with remaining ½ cup butter.
• **Combine** brown sugar and cinnamon; sprinkle over dough.
• **Bake** at 375° for 12 to 15 minutes. Cut into squares. **Yield:** 15 servings.

Eddie McGee
King, North Carolina

NANNY'S FAMOUS COCONUT-PINEAPPLE CAKE
(pictured on cover)

Jeannie won first prize in the dessert category of the Southern Living *Celebrated Holiday Recipe Contest with this cake. It beat out more than 500 other sweets. Have a taste of our Dessert of the Year.*

1 (15¼-ounce) can crushed
    pineapple in juice,
    undrained
1½ cups butter or margarine,
    softened
3 cups sugar
5 large eggs
½ cup lemon-lime soft drink *
3 cups cake flour, sifted
1 teaspoon lemon extract
1 teaspoon vanilla extract
Pineapple Filling
Cream Cheese Frosting
1 (6-ounce) package frozen
    shredded coconut, thawed
Garnish: fresh mint sprig

• **Grease** bottom and sides of three 9-inch round cakepans; line bottoms with wax paper. Grease and flour wax paper.
• **Drain** pineapple, reserving ¾ cup juice. Remove ¼ cup reserved pineapple juice for Cream Cheese Frosting, and reserve crushed pineapple for Pineapple Filling.
• **Beat** butter at medium speed with an electric mixer until creamy; gradually add sugar, beating well. Add eggs, one at a time, beating until blended after each addition.
• **Combine** ½ cup reserved pineapple juice and soft drink. Add flour to butter mixture alternately with juice mixture, beginning and ending with flour. Beat at low speed until blended after each addition. Stir in flavorings. Pour batter into prepared cakepans.
• **Bake** at 350° for 25 to 30 minutes or until a wooden pick inserted in center comes out clean. Remove from pans immediately; cool on wire racks.
• **Spread** ¾ cup Pineapple Filling between each cake layer, and spread remaining filling on top of cake, spreading to within ½ inch of edges on all layers. Spread Cream Cheese Frosting on sides of cake, and pipe border around top, if desired. Sprinkle coconut on sides and border, and garnish, if desired. **Yield:** 1 (3-layer) cake.

* For lemon-lime soft drink, we used 7-Up. Its specific level of carbonation makes the layers rise beautifully.

Pineapple Filling

QUICK!

2 cups sugar
¼ cup cornstarch
1 cup reserved drained crushed
    pineapple
1 cup water

• **Stir** together sugar and cornstarch in a saucepan. Stir in pineapple and water.
• **Cook** over low heat, stirring occasionally, 15 minutes or until very thick. Cool. **Yield:** 3 cups.

Cream Cheese Frosting

QUICK!

½ cup butter, softened
1 (3-ounce) package cream cheese, softened
1 (16-ounce) package powdered sugar, sifted
1 teaspoon vanilla extract
3 to 4 tablespoons reserved pineapple juice

• **Beat** butter and cream cheese at medium speed with an electric mixer until blended. Gradually add powdered sugar, vanilla, and enough pineapple juice to make frosting a good spreading consistency, mixing well. **Yield:** 2 cups.

Erma Jean (Jeannie) Reese
Warrenton, Georgia

LANE CAKE

1 cup unsalted butter, softened
2 cups sugar
3½ cups all-purpose flour
1 tablespoon baking powder
¼ teaspoon salt
1 cup milk
8 egg whites
Lane Cake Filling

• **Beat** butter in a large mixing bowl at medium speed with an electric mixer until creamy; gradually add sugar, beating well.
• **Combine** flour, baking powder, and salt; add to butter mixture alternately with milk, beginning and ending with flour mixture. Beat at low speed after each addition until blended.
• **Beat** egg whites at high speed until stiff peaks form. Stir one-third of egg whites into batter; gently fold in remaining egg whites. Spoon into three greased and floured 9-inch round cakepans.
• **Bake** at 325° for 25 minutes or until a wooden pick inserted in center comes out clean. Cool in pans on wire racks 10 minutes; remove from pans, and let cool completely on wire racks.
• **Spread** Lane Cake Filling between layers, and on top and sides of cake. **Yield:** 1 (3-layer) cake.

Lane Cake Filling

12 egg yolks
1½ cups sugar
¾ cup unsalted butter, melted
1½ teaspoons vanilla extract
½ cup bourbon
1½ cups finely chopped pecans
1½ cups finely chopped raisins
1½ cups flaked coconut

• **Beat** egg yolks at medium speed with an electric mixer 3 minutes; gradually add sugar, beating until blended. Beat 3 minutes. Gradually add butter; beat at low speed until blended.
• **Pour** mixture into top of a double boiler; bring water to a boil. Cook, stirring constantly, 20 minutes or until mixture thickens and candy thermometer registers 185°. Remove from heat; stir in vanilla and remaining ingredients. Cool slightly. **Yield:** 5 cups.

Chefs Edna Lewis and Scott Peacock
Atlanta, Georgia

LUSCIOUS LEMON CAKE

8 egg yolks
¾ cup butter or margarine, softened
1¼ cups sugar
2½ cups sifted cake flour
1 tablespoon baking powder
¼ teaspoon salt
¾ cup milk
1 teaspoon grated lemon rind
1 teaspoon fresh lemon juice
1 teaspoon vanilla extract
Lemon Frosting
Garnishes: lemon wedges, fresh mint leaves

• **Beat** egg yolks at high speed with an electric mixer 4 minutes or until thick and pale. Set aside.
• **Beat** butter at medium speed with an electric mixer until creamy; gradually add sugar, beating well. Add egg yolks, beating well.
• **Combine** flour, baking powder, and salt; add to butter mixture alternately with milk, beginning and ending with flour mixture. Mix after each addition. Stir in lemon rind, juice, and vanilla.

• **Spoon** batter into three greased and floured 8-inch round cakepans. Bake at 375° for 18 to 20 minutes or until a wooden pick inserted in center comes out clean. Cool in pans on wire racks 10 minutes; remove from pans, and cool completely on wire racks.
• **Spoon** about 1 cup Lemon Frosting into a decorating bag fitted with a large tip, and set aside. Spread remaining Lemon Frosting between layers and on top and sides of cake. Pipe 8 rosettes around top edge of cake, and garnish, if desired. Chill until serving time. **Yield:** 1 (3-layer) cake.

Lemon Frosting

QUICK!

1 cup butter or margarine, softened
2 teaspoons grated lemon rind
⅓ cup fresh lemon juice
8 cups sifted powdered sugar
1 to 2 tablespoons half-and-half (optional)

• **Beat** butter at medium speed with an electric mixer until creamy; stir in lemon rind and juice. (Mixture will appear curdled.) Gradually add sugar; beat at high speed 4 minutes or until spreading consistency. Gradually add half-and-half, if necessary. **Yield:** 4 cups.

Shelby W. Adkins
Penhook, Virginia

Peaches-and-Cream Cake

PEACHES-AND-CREAM CAKE
(pictured at left)

"When I started candying flowers 15 years ago, I thought it was the most wonderful thing in the world. They make a dessert special," says Marion.

1   cup unsalted butter, softened
2   cups sugar
6   large eggs
3   cups soft wheat flour
1   teaspoon baking powder
½   teaspoon baking soda
1   teaspoon salt
1   cup buttermilk
2   teaspoons vanilla extract
1 to 2   teaspoons sugar
1   cup chopped pecans, toasted
¾   cup sugar
4   egg whites
⅛   teaspoon cream of tartar
Pinch of salt
Peach Filling
Butter Whip Frosting
Candied and plain pansies

● **Beat** butter in a large mixing bowl at medium speed with an electric mixer until creamy; gradually add 2 cups sugar, beating well. Add eggs, one at a time, beating until blended after each addition.
● **Combine** flour and next 3 ingredients; add to butter mixture alternately with buttermilk, beginning and ending with flour mixture. Beat at low speed until blended after each addition. Stir in vanilla.
● **Pour** batter into two greased and floured 10-inch round cakepans or springform pans.
● **Bake** at 325° for 30 to 35 minutes or until a wooden pick inserted in center comes out clean. Cool in pans on wire racks 10 minutes; remove cake layers from pans, and let cool completely on wire racks.
● **Grease** a 10-inch springform pan; line bottom of pan with aluminum foil. Grease foil; sprinkle foil and sides of pan with 1 to 2 teaspoons sugar. Set aside.
● **Position** knife blade in food processor bowl; add pecans and ¾ cup sugar. Process until pecans are ground,

stopping once to scrape down sides; set aside.
● **Combine** egg whites, cream of tartar, and pinch of salt; beat at high speed with an electric mixer until soft peaks form. Fold in pecan mixture, and spread in prepared pan.
● **Bake** at 250° for 1 hour and 30 minutes to 1 hour and 45 minutes or until thoroughly dry. Cool completely in pan on a wire rack, and carefully remove from pan.
● **Place** 1 cake layer on a cake plate; spread cake layer with half of Peach Filling. Spread 1 cup Butter Whip Frosting over filling, and top with meringue layer.
● **Spread** remaining filling over meringue layer, and spread 1½ cups frosting over filling; top with remaining cake layer. Spread top and sides of cake with remaining frosting, as desired. Chill 2 to 3 hours; decorate with pansies. **Yield:** 1 (10-inch) cake.

Note: To make candied pansies, sprinkle 2 envelopes unflavored gelatin over 2 cups warm water; stir with a wire whisk until gelatin dissolves. Dip pansies into gelatin mixture, shaking to remove excess; sprinkle all sides of pansies with superfine sugar, covering completely. Place pansies on baking sheets; let stand 30 minutes or until dry and firm.

Peach Filling

1¾   cups dried peaches
1½   cups water
¼   cup sugar
2   tablespoons light corn
      syrup

● **Combine** dried peaches and water in a medium saucepan, and bring to a boil. Cover, remove from heat, and let stand 30 minutes or until peaches are soft.
● **Add** sugar and syrup; bring to a boil. Reduce heat, and simmer 30 minutes or until most of liquid evaporates; remove from heat.
● **Position** knife blade in food processor bowl; add peach mixture. Process until mixture is smooth, stopping once to scrape down sides; cool. **Yield:** 2 cups.

Butter Whip Frosting

QUICK!

To enhance the peach flavor of this spectacular cake, this classic buttercream frosting boasts two flavorings – vanilla and almond.

1¼   cups unsalted butter,
        softened
2   (16-ounce) packages powdered
      sugar, sifted
2   teaspoons vanilla extract
¼   teaspoon almond extract
1½   cups whipping cream

● **Combine** butter, 1 cup powdered sugar, and flavorings; beat at medium speed with an electric mixer until blended.
● **Add** remaining powdered sugar to butter mixture alternately with whipping cream, beating well after each addition. Beat at high speed until mixture is smooth and spreading consistency. **Yield:** about 6 cups.

Marion Sullivan
Charleston, South Carolina

ITALIAN CREAM CAKE

This cake is sure to win raves from your family – as it did in our Test Kitchens.

½ cup butter or margarine, softened
½ cup shortening
2 cups sugar
5 large eggs, separated
1 tablespoon vanilla extract
2 cups all-purpose flour
1 teaspoon baking soda
1 cup buttermilk
1 cup flaked coconut
Nutty Cream Cheese Frosting
Garnishes: toasted pecan halves, chopped pecans

• **Beat** butter and shortening in a large mixing bowl at medium speed with an electric mixer until creamy; gradually add sugar, beating well. Add egg yolks, one at a time, beating until blended after each addition. Add vanilla; beat until blended.
• **Combine** flour and soda; add to butter mixture alternately with buttermilk, beginning and ending with flour mixture. Beat at low speed until blended after each addition. Stir in coconut.
• **Beat** egg whites until stiff peaks form; fold into batter. Pour batter into three greased and floured 9-inch round cakepans.
• **Bake** at 350° for 25 minutes or until a wooden pick inserted in center comes out clean. Cool in pans on wire racks 10 minutes; remove from pans, and let cool completely on wire racks.
• **Spread** Nutty Cream Cheese Frosting between layers and on top and sides of cake. Garnish, if desired. **Yield:** 1 (3-layer) cake.

Nutty Cream Cheese Frosting

QUICK!

1 cup chopped pecans
1 (8-ounce) package cream cheese, softened
½ cup butter or margarine, softened
1 tablespoon vanilla extract
1 (16-ounce) package powdered sugar, sifted

• **Place** pecans in a shallow pan; bake at 350° for 5 to 10 minutes or until toasted, stirring occasionally. Cool.
• **Beat** cream cheese, butter, and vanilla at medium speed with an electric mixer until creamy. Add sugar, beating at low speed until blended. Beat at high speed until smooth; stir in pecans. **Yield:** about 4 cups.

Donna Willcut
Pryor, Oklahoma

WHIPPED CREAM CAKE

This petite cake is perfect for luncheons, anniversary dinners, teas, or birthday parties. Plan on it serving 6 to 8. And if you want a decorator look without the trouble of a homemade cake, follow the baking and assembling directions here, using 1 (18.25-ounce) package white cake mix and 2 (16-ounce) containers vanilla ready-to-spread frosting.

1 cup whipping cream
2 large eggs
1 cup sugar
1 teaspoon vanilla extract
1½ cups sifted cake flour
2 teaspoons baking powder
¼ teaspoon salt
Buttercream Frosting

• **Grease** three 6- x 2-inch round cakepans; line with wax paper. Grease and flour wax paper; set aside.
• **Beat** whipping cream with a wire whisk until foamy; set aside.
• **Beat** eggs with a wire whisk until foamy; stir in sugar and vanilla extract. Gradually stir whipping cream into egg mixture.
• **Combine** flour, baking powder, and salt; fold into whipping cream mixture. Pour batter into prepared pans.
• **Bake** at 350° for 18 minutes or until a wooden pick inserted in center comes out clean. Cool in pans on wire racks 10 minutes; remove from pans, and let cool completely on wire racks.
• **Spread** 2½ cups Buttercream Frosting between layers and on top and sides of cake.
• **Spoon** about 1 cup frosting into a decorating or heavy-duty, zip-top plastic

bag fitted with a No. 5 round tip; pipe curly lines over top and sides of cake. Do not overlap lines.
• **Spoon** remaining frosting into a decorating or heavy-duty, zip-top plastic bag fitted with a No. 2B large basketweave tip; pipe a ruffle around base of cake. **Yield:** 1 (3-layer) cake.

Note: If you have only one 6- x 2-inch round cakepan, bake layers one at a time. Cover the remaining batter and set aside while each layer bakes. Wash, dry, and prepare pan again before baking each remaining layer.

Buttercream Frosting

QUICK!

1½ cups butter
1 (16-ounce) package powdered sugar, sifted
2 tablespoons milk
1 teaspoon vanilla extract

• **Beat** butter at medium speed with an electric mixer until creamy; gradually add sugar, beating until light and fluffy. Add milk and vanilla, beating to spreading consistency. **Yield:** about 4 cups.

Helen Walker
Edmond, Oklahoma

CAMEO CAKE

1½ cups butter
¾ cup water
1 (4-ounce) bar white chocolate, broken into pieces *
1½ cups buttermilk
4 large eggs, lightly beaten
1½ teaspoons vanilla extract
3½ cups all-purpose flour, divided
1 cup chopped pecans, toasted
2¼ cups sugar
1½ teaspoons baking soda
White Chocolate-Cream Cheese Frosting
Garnishes: crystallized violas with leaves, shaved white chocolate, or toasted chopped pecans

• **Combine** butter and water in a medium saucepan; bring to a boil over medium heat, stirring occasionally.

Remove from heat. Add white chocolate, stirring until chocolate melts. Stir in buttermilk, eggs, and vanilla; set aside.

• **Combine** ½ cup flour and 1 cup pecans, stirring to coat; set aside.

• **Combine** remaining 3 cups flour, sugar, and soda in a large bowl; gradually stir in white chocolate mixture. Fold in pecan mixture. (Batter will be thin.) Pour into three greased and floured 9-inch round cakepans.

• **Bake** at 350° for 20 to 25 minutes or until a wooden pick inserted in center comes out clean. Cool in pans on wire racks 10 minutes; remove from pans, and let cool completely on wire racks.

• **Spread** White Chocolate-Cream Cheese Frosting between layers and on top and sides of cake. Store cake in refrigerator. Garnish, if desired. **Yield:** 1 (3-layer) cake.

White Chocolate- Cream Cheese Frosting

QUICK!

1 (4-ounce) bar white chocolate *
1 (8-ounce) package cream cheese, softened
1 (3-ounce) package cream cheese, softened
⅓ cup butter or margarine, softened
6½ cups sifted powdered sugar
1½ teaspoons vanilla extract

• **Melt** white chocolate in a heavy saucepan over low heat, stirring constantly. Remove from heat; cool 10 minutes, stirring occasionally.

• **Beat** cream cheese and butter at medium speed with an electric mixer until creamy. Gradually add white chocolate, beating constantly until blended. Gradually add powdered sugar, beating until smooth. Stir in vanilla. **Yield:** about 5 cups.

* For white chocolate, we used Ghirardelli Classic White Confection.

CHOCOLATE CHIFFON CAKE WITH COFFEE BUTTERCREAM

Make-ahead tip: Bake and freeze the cake layers up to 3 months ahead. Assemble a few hours before serving.

6 (1-ounce) squares bittersweet chocolate, chopped
¾ cup water
1 cup butter, softened
2 cups sugar
4 large eggs
2 teaspoons vanilla extract
2½ cups sifted cake flour
2 teaspoons baking soda
⅛ teaspoon salt
1½ cups sour cream
Coffee Buttercream
Chocolate-covered coffee beans

• **Combine** chocolate and water in a heavy saucepan; cook over low heat, stirring constantly, until melted.

• **Beat** butter at medium speed with an electric mixer until creamy; gradually add sugar, beating well. Add eggs, one at a time, beating after each addition. Add chocolate mixture and vanilla; beat 1 minute or just until combined.

• **Combine** flour, soda, and salt; add to chocolate mixture alternately with sour cream, beginning and ending with flour mixture. Mix at low speed just until blended after each addition. Pour batter into three greased and floured 9-inch round cakepans.

• **Bake** at 350° for 25 to 30 minutes or until a wooden pick inserted in center comes out clean. Cool in pans on wire racks 10 minutes; remove from pans, and let cool completely on wire racks.

• **Spread** Coffee Buttercream between layers and on top and sides of cake. Arrange coffee beans on top of cake. **Yield:** 1 (3-layer) cake.

Coffee Buttercream

QUICK!

4 to 5 tablespoons instant coffee granules
3 tablespoons hot water
1 cup butter, softened
6 cups sifted powdered sugar

• **Dissolve** coffee granules in water.

• **Beat** butter at medium speed with an electric mixer until creamy; gradually add coffee mixture and sugar, beating until blended. **Yield:** 2½ cups.

*Susan Curtin
Birmingham, Alabama*

APPLESAUCE CAKE

¾ cup shortening
2 cups sugar
3 large eggs
3 cups all-purpose flour
1½ teaspoons baking soda
½ teaspoon salt
1 teaspoon ground cinnamon
½ teaspoon ground cloves
¼ teaspoon ground nutmeg
1½ cups applesauce
1 cup raisins
1 cup chopped walnuts or pecans

• **Beat** shortening at medium speed with an electric mixer 2 minutes or until fluffy. Gradually add sugar, beating 5 to 7 minutes. Add eggs, one at a time, beating just until yellow disappears.

• **Combine** flour and next 5 ingredients; add to shortening mixture alternately with applesauce, beginning and ending with flour mixture. Beat at low speed just until blended after each addition. Stir in raisins and chopped nuts.

• **Pour** batter into a greased and floured 12-cup Bundt pan.

• **Bake** at 350° for 1 hour or until a wooden pick inserted in center comes out clean, shielding with aluminum foil after 45 minutes to prevent excessive browning.

• **Cool** cake in pan on a wire rack 10 to 15 minutes; remove from pan, and let cool completely on wire rack. **Yield:** 1 (10-inch) cake.

*Virginia Cookery, Past and Present
Olivet Episcopal Church Women
Franconia, Virginia*

APPLE-WALNUT CAKE

1 **cup butter or margarine,**
    softened
2 **cups sugar**
2 **large eggs**
1 **tablespoon vanilla extract**
2 **cups sifted cake flour**
1 **teaspoon baking powder**
¼ **teaspoon salt**
1 **(8-ounce) carton sour cream**
1 **cup peeled, finely chopped**
    apple
1 **cup finely chopped walnuts**
2 **tablespoons brown sugar**
½ **teaspoon ground cinnamon**
Cream Cheese Glaze

• **Beat** butter at medium speed with an electric mixer until creamy; gradually add 2 cups sugar, beating well. Add eggs, one at a time, beating after each addition. Stir in vanilla.
• **Combine** flour, baking powder, and salt. Add flour mixture to butter mixture alternately with sour cream, beginning and ending with flour mixture. Mix at low speed just until blended after each addition. Pour half of batter into a greased and floured 12-cup Bundt pan.
• **Combine** apple and next 3 ingredients; spoon over batter in pan, leaving a ½-inch border around center and outer edges. Add remaining batter.
• **Bake** at 350° for 50 to 55 minutes or until a wooden pick inserted in center comes out clean. Cool in pan on a wire rack 10 minutes. Remove from pan; cool completely on wire rack.
• **Drizzle** with Cream Cheese Glaze. Store cake in refrigerator. **Yield:** 1 (10-inch) cake.

Cream Cheese Glaze

QUICK!

1 **(3-ounce) package cream cheese,**
    softened
2 to 2½ **teaspoons milk**
1 **teaspoon vanilla extract**
Dash of salt
1½ **cups sifted powdered sugar**

• **Beat** cream cheese in a small mixing bowl at medium speed with an electric mixer until creamy. Add milk, vanilla,

and salt, and beat until smooth. Gradually add powdered sugar, beating until smooth. **Yield:** 1 cup.

Louise W. Mayer
Richmond, Virginia

ORANGE CAKE
(pictured on opposite page)

½ **cup butter, softened**
2 **cups sugar**
7 **large eggs, separated**
3 **cups sifted cake flour**
1 **tablespoon baking powder**
¼ **teaspoon salt**
½ **cup fresh orange juice**
½ **cup water**
1 **teaspoon vanilla extract**
Orange Glaze
Candied Orange Zest

• **Beat** butter at medium speed with an electric mixer about 2 minutes or until creamy. Gradually add sugar, beating 5 to 7 minutes.
• **Beat** egg yolks lightly; add to butter mixture, beating until well blended.
• **Combine** flour, baking powder, and salt; add to butter mixture alternately with orange juice and water, beginning and ending with flour mixture. Beat at low speed with an electric mixer until blended after each addition. Stir in vanilla.
• **Beat** egg whites at high speed with an electric mixer until foamy; reduce speed to medium, and beat until stiff peaks form. Fold egg white into batter; spoon batter into a greased and floured 12-cup Bundt pan or 10-inch tube pan.
• **Bake** at 350° for 40 minutes or until a wooden pick inserted in center comes out clean. Immediately place pan on a double layer of damp cloth towels; press towels around sides of pan, and let stand 10 to 15 minutes. Remove cake from pan, and let cool completely on a wire rack.
• **Spoon** Orange Glaze over cake; top with Candied Orange Zest. **Yield:** 1 (10-inch) cake.

Orange Glaze

2 **large oranges**
2 **cups sugar**
1 **tablespoon cornstarch**
⅓ **cup lemon juice**
8 **egg yolks, lightly beaten**
½ **cup butter, softened**

• **Squeeze** juice from oranges, and pour through a wire-mesh strainer into a 1-cup liquid measuring cup, straining out any seeds. Measure 1 cup orange juice; reserve remaining orange juice for another use.
• **Combine** sugar and cornstarch in a small saucepan; add lemon juice and 1 cup orange juice, stirring well with a wire whisk. Cook over low heat, stirring constantly, until sugar dissolves (about 10 minutes).
• **Stir** about one-fourth of hot mixture into yolks; add to remaining hot mixture, stirring constantly. Cook over low heat, stirring constantly, 10 minutes or until mixture is thickened. Remove from heat; add softened butter, stirring until well blended. Cool; cover and chill. **Yield:** 3½ cups.

Candied Orange Zest

2 **large oranges**
1 **cup water**
½ **cup sugar**
Sugar (optional)

• **Remove** zest (orange part only) from oranges, using a zester, being careful not to remove white pith. Cut zest into 2-inch strips.
• **Combine** water and ½ cup sugar in a small saucepan; Bring to a boil over medium heat. Reduce heat to low; stir in rind, and cook 15 to 20 minutes or until candy thermometer registers 220°.
• **Remove** zest strips from syrup with a slotted spoon, and spread in a single layer on wax paper to cool.
• **Sprinkle** with additional sugar, if desired. **Yield:** 1 cup.

Sissy Nash and Kathy Nash Cary
Louisville, Kentucky

Orange Cake

CHOCOLATE-SPICE POTATO CAKE

1 cup butter or margarine,
  softened
2 cups sugar
4 large eggs
2 cups all-purpose flour
2 teaspoons baking powder
1 teaspoon ground cinnamon
1 teaspoon ground cloves
1 teaspoon ground nutmeg
¼ cup cocoa
½ cup milk
⅔ cup instant potato flakes
1 cup (6 ounces) semisweet
  chocolate morsels
1 cup chopped pecans

• **Beat** butter at medium speed with an electric mixer about 2 minutes or until creamy; gradually add sugar, beating 5 to 7 minutes. Add eggs, one at a time, beating just until yellow disappears.
• **Combine** flour and next 5 ingredients; add to butter mixture alternately with milk, beginning and ending with flour mixture. Set batter aside.
• **Prepare** potato flakes according to package directions. Add mashed potato to batter, and beat until blended. Stir in chocolate morsels and pecans. Pour batter into a greased and floured 10-inch tube pan.
• **Bake** at 350° for 1 hour and 20 minutes or until a wooden pick inserted in center comes out clean. Cool in pan on a wire rack 10 minutes; remove from pan, and let cool completely on wire rack. **Yield:** 1 (10-inch) cake.

Anna Rucker
Norfolk, Virginia

CANDY BAR CAKE

3 (2.15-ounce) chocolate-coated
  caramel and creamy nougat
  bars, chopped *
1 cup butter, softened and
  divided
2 cups sugar
4 large eggs
1 teaspoon vanilla extract
3 cups all-purpose flour
½ teaspoon baking soda
1 cup buttermilk
1 cup chopped pecans

• **Combine** candy bars and ½ cup butter in a heavy saucepan; cook over medium heat, stirring constantly, until candy bars melt. Set aside.
• **Beat** remaining ½ cup butter at medium speed with an electric mixer about 2 minutes or until creamy. Gradually add sugar, beating at medium speed 5 to 7 minutes. Add eggs, one at a time, beating just until yellow disappears. Stir in vanilla.
• **Combine** flour and soda; add to butter mixture alternately with buttermilk, beginning and ending with flour mixture. Mix at low speed just until blended after each addition. Stir in candy bar mixture and pecans.
• **Pour** batter into a greased and floured 10-inch tube pan. Bake at 325° for 1 hour and 25 minutes or until a wooden pick inserted in center of cake comes out clean. Cool in pan 15 minutes on a wire rack. Remove from pan, and let cool completely on wire rack. **Yield:** 1 (10-inch) cake.

* For the chocolate-coated caramel and creamy nougat bars, we used Milky Way candy bars.

Marie Bilbo
Meadville, Mississippi

GRANDMOTHER'S FRUITCAKE

Bake a bit of history. Grandmother's Fruitcake has been in Catherine's family for 150 years.

4 cups all-purpose flour, divided
1 pound chopped dates
1 pound candied citron
1 pound chopped pecans
1 pound dried figs, coarsely
  chopped
1 (15-ounce) package raisins
1 (10-ounce) package currants
1 cup butter or margarine,
  softened
2 cups sugar
12 large eggs, lightly beaten
1 cup milk
¾ cup light corn syrup
2 teaspoons baking soda
1 teaspoon baking powder
2 teaspoons ground nutmeg
2 teaspoons ground cinnamon
2 teaspoons ground allspice
1 cup brandy
30 pecan halves (optional)
Brandy
6 red candied cherry halves
  (optional)

• **Make** a liner for a 10-inch tube pan by drawing an 18-inch circle on brown paper (not recycled). Cut out circle; set pan in center, and draw around base of pan and inside tube. Remove pan, and fold circle into eighths, with lines on the outside.
• **Cut** off pointed tip of triangle along line. Unfold paper; cut along folds to the outside line. Place liner in pan; grease and set aside. Repeat procedure for second tube pan.
• **Combine** ½ cup flour, dates, and next 5 ingredients in a large bowl, tossing gently to coat. Set aside.
• **Beat** butter in a large mixing bowl at medium speed with an electric mixer until creamy; gradually add sugar, beating mixture well. Add eggs, beating until blended after each addition. Add milk and corn syrup, mixing well.
• **Combine** remaining 3½ cups flour, baking soda, and next 4 ingredients; add to butter mixture alternately with 1 cup brandy, beginning and ending with flour mixture. Mix at low speed after

each addition until blended. Pour over fruit mixture; stir well. Spoon batter evenly into prepared pans. Place pecan halves in flower designs on top of batter, if desired.

● **Bake** at 350° for 1 hour or until a wooden pick inserted in center comes out clean. Remove from oven; cool completely in pans on wire racks.

● **Remove** cakes from pans; peel paper from cakes, and discard. Wrap cakes in brandy-soaked cheesecloth; store in airtight containers in a cool place. Pour a small amount of brandy over cakes each week for at least 1 month. Before serving, place cherry halves in center of pecan flowers, if desired. **Yield:** 2 (5-pound) cakes.

Catherine Maddux
Memphis, Tennessee

NO-BAKE FRUITCAKE

For gifts, cut each loaf lengthwise into fourths. Wrap in plastic wrap; then in decorative paper. Tie ends with ribbon.

1 (16-ounce) package round buttery crackers
1 pound red and green candied cherries
1 pound candied pineapple, chopped
1 (15-ounce) package golden raisins
4 cups chopped pecans, toasted
1 cup chopped walnuts, toasted
1 (7-ounce) can flaked coconut
1 (12-ounce) can evaporated milk
1 pound large marshmallows

● **Line** three 9- x 5- x 3-inch loafpans with heavy-duty plastic wrap; set aside. Place 1 stack crackers in a large heavy-duty, zip-top plastic bag; finely crush crackers, using a meat mallet or rolling pin. Place cracker crumbs in a large bowl. Repeat procedure with remaining crackers.

● **Add** cherries and next 5 ingredients to crumbs, tossing gently to coat.

● **Combine** evaporated milk and marshmallows in a heavy saucepan; cook over medium heat, stirring constantly, until marshmallows melt. Pour over fruit mixture, and stir well. Spoon mixture evenly into prepared pans, pressing firmly.

● **Cover** and store in refrigerator 3 days. Remove from pans; wrap in heavy-duty plastic wrap, and then aluminum foil. Store in the refrigerator. **Yield:** 3 (2½-pound) cakes.

Lois Edwards
Sparta, North Carolina

CHOCOLATE FRUITCAKES

1 cup butter or margarine
6 (1-ounce) squares semisweet chocolate
1¼ cups sugar
3 large eggs
1 cup all-purpose flour
¼ teaspoon salt
1 cup red candied cherries, cut in half
1 cup green candied pineapple, cut into ½-inch wedges
¾ cup walnut halves
¾ cup pecan halves
Garnishes: red candied cherries, smilax leaves

● **Melt** butter and chocolate in a heavy saucepan over low heat, stirring often. Remove from heat; cool 15 minutes.

● **Stir** in sugar. Add eggs, one at a time, stirring well after each addition. Add flour and salt, stirring until blended. Stir in cherries and next 3 ingredients. Spoon mixture into four greased and floured 5- x 3- x 2-inch loafpans.

● **Bake** at 350° for 35 minutes or until a wooden pick inserted in center comes out clean. Cool in pans on wire racks 10 minutes; remove from pans, and cool on wire racks.

● **Wrap** in heavy-duty plastic wrap; chill 8 hours before cutting. Garnish, if desired. **Yield:** 4 (12-ounce) loaves.

Note: To make a less rich chocolate fruitcake, reduce butter to ½ cup and chocolate to 4 (1-ounce) squares.

Leslie Coles Walker
Chesapeake, Virginia

SMOOTHEST SOUTHERN POUND CAKE

1 cup butter or margarine, softened
3 cups sugar
3 cups sifted cake flour
¼ teaspoon baking soda
6 large eggs
1 (8-ounce) carton sour cream
1 teaspoon vanilla extract

● **Beat** butter at medium speed with an electric mixer (not a handheld one) about 2 minutes or until creamy. Gradually add sugar, beating at medium speed 5 to 7 minutes. Combine cake flour and baking soda, and add to butter mixture 1 cup at a time. (Batter will be extremely thick.)

● **Separate** eggs; add yolks to batter, and mix well. Stir in sour cream and vanilla.

● **Beat** egg whites until stiff, and fold into batter.

● **Spoon** into a greased and floured 12-cup Bundt or 10-inch tube pan. Bake at 300° for 2 hours or until a wooden pick inserted in center comes out clean. (You may also spoon batter into two 9- x 5- x 3-inch loafpans; bake at 300° for 1½ hours or until a wooden pick inserted in center comes out clean.) Cool in pan on a wire rack 10 to 15 minutes. Remove from pan; cool completely on wire rack. **Yield:** 1 (10-inch) cake or 2 loaves.

Note: Standard Mixing Method: If you are using a handheld mixer or prefer a conventional pound cake method, here's the procedure we suggest.

● **Beat** butter at medium speed with an electric mixer about 2 minutes or until creamy. Gradually add 3 cups sugar, beating at medium speed 5 to 7 minutes. Add eggs, one at time, beating just until yellow disappears.

● **Combine** cake flour and baking soda; add to butter mixture alternately with sour cream, beginning and ending with flour mixture. Mix at lowest speed just until mixture is blended after each addition. Stir in vanilla. Bake as directed.

Chip Smith
Houston, Texas
and Paul Frederick
Huntsville, Alabama

POUND CAKE

Vegetable cooking spray
All-purpose flour
½ cup corn oil margarine, softened
⅔ cup sugar
⅓ cup fat-free egg substitute
2½ cups sifted cake flour
½ teaspoon baking powder
¼ teaspoon baking soda
¼ teaspoon salt
1 (8-ounce) carton low-fat vanilla yogurt
1 tablespoon vanilla extract
¾ teaspoon almond extract

• **Coat** bottom of a 9- x 5- x 3-inch loafpan with cooking spray; dust with flour, and set aside.
• **Beat** margarine at medium speed with an electric mixer until creamy. Gradually add sugar; beat well. Add egg substitute; beat until blended.
• **Combine** flour and next 3 ingredients; add to margarine mixture alternately with yogurt, beginning and ending with flour mixture. Mix just until blended after each addition. Stir in flavorings.
• **Spoon** batter into prepared pan. Bake at 350° for 1 hour and 5 minutes or until a wooden pick inserted in center comes out clean. Cool in pan on a wire rack 10 minutes; remove cake from pan, and let cool completely on wire rack. **Yield:** 18 servings.

Mrs. Abner Belcher
Americus, Georgia

♥ Per serving: Calories 143
Fat 5.3g Cholesterol 1mg
Sodium 66mg

AZTEC POUND CAKE

1 cup butter, softened
1 tablespoon grated orange rind
2 cups sugar
6 large eggs, separated
2 cups all-purpose flour
1 cup yellow cornmeal
½ teaspoon baking soda
¼ teaspoon salt
1 (8-ounce) carton sour cream
1 teaspoon vanilla extract

• **Beat** butter and orange rind at medium speed with an electric mixer about 2 minutes or until creamy; gradually add sugar, beating well. Add egg yolks, one at a time, beating just until yellow disappears.
• **Combine** flour, cornmeal, soda, and salt; add to butter mixture alternately with sour cream, beginning and ending with flour mixture. Beat at low speed just until blended after each addition. Stir in vanilla.
• **Beat** egg whites at high speed until stiff peaks form; fold into batter. Pour batter into two greased and floured 8½- x 4½- x 3-inch loafpans.
• **Bake** at 325° for 1 hour and 5 minutes or until a wooden pick inserted in center comes out clean.
• **Cool** cakes in pans on a wire rack 10 minutes; remove from pans, and let cool completely on wire rack. **Yield:** 2 loaves.

Joy Knight Allard
San Antonio, Texas

BROWN SUGAR-RUM POUND CAKE

1½ cups butter, softened
1 (16-ounce) package light brown sugar
1 cup sugar
5 large eggs
¾ cup milk
¼ cup dark rum
2 teaspoons vanilla extract
3 cups all-purpose flour
1 teaspoon baking powder
¼ teaspoon salt
1 cup chopped pecans
Sweetened whipped cream (optional)

• **Beat** butter at medium speed with an electric mixer about 2 minutes or until creamy. Gradually add sugars, beating 5 to 7 minutes. Add eggs, one at a time, beating just until yellow disappears.
• **Combine** milk, rum, and vanilla, and set aside.
• **Combine** flour, baking powder, and salt; add to butter mixture alternately with milk mixture, beginning and ending with flour mixture. Beat at low speed just until blended after each addition. Fold in chopped pecans. Pour batter into a greased and floured 13-cup Bundt pan.
• **Bake** at 325° for 1 hour and 20 minutes or until a wooden pick inserted in center comes out clean.
• **Cool** in pan on a wire rack 10 to 15 minutes; remove from pan, and let cool completely on wire rack. Serve with sweetened whipped cream, if desired. **Yield:** 1 (10-inch) cake.

Denise Allen
Birmingham, Alabama

BLACK WALNUT POUND CAKE

1 cup butter, softened
½ cup shortening
3 cups sugar
5 large eggs
3 cups all-purpose flour
½ teaspoon baking powder
1 cup milk
½ cup black walnuts, chopped
½ teaspoon vanilla extract

• **Beat** butter and shortening at medium speed with an electric mixer about 2 minutes or until creamy. Gradually add sugar, beating at medium speed 5 to 7 minutes. Add eggs, one at a time, beating just until yellow disappears.
• **Combine** flour and baking powder; add to butter mixture alternately with milk, beginning and ending with flour mixture. Mix at low speed just until blended after each addition. Stir in walnuts and vanilla. Pour batter into a greased and floured 10-inch tube pan.
• **Bake** at 325° for 1 hour and 30 minutes or until a wooden pick inserted in center comes out clean. Cool in pan on a wire rack 10 to 15 minutes; remove from pan, and let cool completely on wire rack. **Yield:** 1 (10-inch) cake.

Note: You can freeze baked cake up to 3 months. Thaw and, if desired, reheat to serve.

BETTY'S BUTTERNUT POUND CAKE WITH CARAMEL SAUCE

1 cup butter or margarine, softened
½ cup shortening
3 cups sugar
5 large eggs
1 (5-ounce) can evaporated milk
3¼ cups all-purpose flour
¼ teaspoon salt
2 tablespoons vanilla, butter, and nut flavoring
Caramel Sauce

• **Beat** butter and shortening at medium speed with an electric mixer about 2 minutes or until creamy. Gradually add sugar, beating at medium speed 5 to 7 minutes. Add eggs, one at a time, beating just until yellow disappears.
• **Add** enough water to evaporated milk to measure 1 cup.
• **Combine** flour and salt; add to butter mixture alternately with milk mixture, beginning and ending with flour mixture. Mix at low speed just until blended after each addition. Stir in flavoring. Pour into a greased and floured 10-inch tube pan.
• **Bake** at 325° for 1 hour and 25 minutes or until a wooden pick inserted in center comes out clean. Cool in pan on a wire rack 10 to 15 minutes; remove from pan, and cool completely on wire rack. Serve with warm Caramel Sauce. **Yield:** 1 (10-inch) cake.

Note: You can bake cake in two 8½- x 4½- x 3-inch loafpans at 325° for 1 hour and 15 minutes or until a wooden pick inserted in center comes out clean.

Caramel Sauce

QUICK!

1 cup firmly packed brown sugar
1 cup whipping cream
1 cup half-and-half
3 tablespoons butter or margarine

• **Combine** all ingredients in a small heavy saucepan, and cook over low heat 45 minutes or until mixture is thickened, stirring occasionally. **Yield:** about 2 cups.

CHEESY POUND CAKE

Traditional pound cake takes on added flavor with a surprise ingredient – Cheddar cheese.

1½ cups butter, softened
1 (8-ounce) package cream cheese, softened
3 cups sugar
6 large eggs
3 cups all-purpose flour
Dash of salt
2 cups (8 ounces) finely shredded sharp Cheddar cheese
1 tablespoon vanilla extract
Apple butter (optional)

• **Beat** butter and cream cheese in a large mixing bowl at medium speed with an electric mixer about 2 minutes or until creamy. Gradually add sugar, beating at medium speed 5 to 7 minutes. Add eggs, one at a time, beating just until yellow disappears.
• **Combine** flour and salt; gradually add to butter mixture, beating at low speed just until blended after each addition. Stir in Cheddar cheese and vanilla. Pour batter into a greased and floured 10-inch tube pan.
• **Bake** at 325° for 1 hour and 45 minutes or until a wooden pick inserted in center comes out clean.
• **Cool** cake in pan on a wire rack 10 to 15 minutes; remove from pan, and let cool completely on wire rack. Serve with apple butter, if desired. **Yield:** 1 (10-inch) cake.

LaDonna Funderburk
Moultrie, Georgia

CHOCOLATE POUND CAKE

1 cup butter or margarine, softened
1 cup shortening
3 cups sugar
5 large eggs
3 cups all-purpose flour
½ teaspoon baking powder
½ teaspoon salt
¼ cup cocoa
1 cup milk
1 tablespoon vanilla extract

• **Beat** butter and shortening in a large mixing bowl at medium speed with an electric mixer about 2 minutes or until creamy. Gradually add sugar, beating at medium speed 5 to 7 minutes. Add eggs, one at a time, beating just until yellow disappears.
• **Combine** flour and next 3 ingredients; add to butter mixture alternately with milk, beginning and ending with flour mixture. Mix at low speed just until blended after each addition. Stir in vanilla. Pour batter into a greased and floured 10-inch tube pan.
• **Bake** at 325° for 1 hour and 30 minutes or until a wooden pick inserted in center of cake comes out clean. Cool in pan on a wire rack 10 to 15 minutes; remove cake from pan, and let cool completely on wire rack. **Yield:** 1 (10-inch) cake.

Louise Floyd
West Selma, Alabama

CHOCOLATE CHIP POUND CAKE

1 (18.25-ounce) yellow cake mix with pudding
1 (3.9-ounce) package chocolate instant pudding mix
½ cup sugar
¾ cup vegetable oil
¾ cup water
4 large eggs
1 (8-ounce) carton sour cream
1 cup (6 ounces) semisweet chocolate morsels
Sifted powdered sugar

• **Combine** first 3 ingredients in a large mixing bowl, stirring with a wire whisk to remove large lumps. Add oil and next 3 ingredients, stirring until smooth. Stir in chocolate morsels. Pour batter into a greased and floured 12-cup Bundt pan.
• **Bake** at 350° for 1 hour or until a wooden pick inserted in center comes out clean.
• **Cool** cake in pan on a wire rack 10 minutes; remove from pan, and let cool completely on wire rack.
• **Sprinkle** with sifted powdered sugar. **Yield:** 1 (10-inch) cake.

Becky DeWare
The Woodlands, Texas

Cute-As-A-Button
Cherry Pound Cake

CUTE-AS-A-BUTTON CHERRY POUND CAKE
(pictured at left)

This pound cake takes about 2 hours to bake, and the results are well worth the effort.

1 cup butter or margarine, softened
½ cup shortening
3 cups sugar
6 large eggs
1 (6-ounce) jar red maraschino cherries, drained and chopped
½ teaspoon almond extract
½ teaspoon vanilla extract
3¾ cups all-purpose flour
¼ teaspoon salt
¾ cup milk
Cream Cheese Frosting
Garnish: 1 (4-ounce) package melt-away mints *

● **Beat** butter and shortening at medium speed with an electric mixer about 2 minutes or until creamy. Gradually add sugar, beating at medium speed 5 to 7 minutes. Add eggs, one at a time, beating just until yellow disappears. Stir in cherries and flavorings.
● **Combine** flour and salt; add to the butter mixture alternately with milk, beginning and ending with the flour mixture. Mix at low speed just until blended after each addition. Pour batter into a greased and floured 10-inch tube pan.
● **Bake** at 300° for 1 hour and 45 minutes to 2 hours or until a wooden pick inserted in center comes out clean. Cool in pan on a wire rack 10 minutes; remove from pan, and let cool completely on wire rack.
● **Frost** top and sides of cake with Cream Cheese Frosting. Garnish, if desired. **Yield:** 1 (10-inch) cake.

* For melt-away mints, we used Smooth 'n Melty Petite Mints by Guittard Chocolate Company.

Cream Cheese Frosting
QUICK!

1 (8-ounce) package cream cheese, softened
½ cup butter, softened
1 (16-ounce) package powdered sugar, sifted
1 teaspoon vanilla extract

● **Combine** cream cheese and butter, beating until creamy. Add sugar and vanilla; beat until light and fluffy. **Yield:** 3 cups.

Carolyn McDaniel
York, South Carolina

BANANA POUND CAKE

1 cup shortening
½ cup butter, softened
3 cups sugar
5 large eggs
3 ripe bananas, mashed
3 tablespoons milk
2 teaspoons vanilla extract
3 cups all-purpose flour
1 teaspoon baking powder
½ teaspoon salt

● **Beat** shortening and butter at medium speed with an electric mixer about 2 minutes or until creamy. Gradually add sugar, beating at medium speed 5 to 7 minutes. Add eggs, one at a time, beating just until yellow disappears.
● **Combine** banana, milk, and vanilla.
● **Combine** flour, baking powder, and salt; add to shortening mixture alternately with banana mixture, beginning and ending with flour mixture. Beat at low speed just until blended after each addition. Pour batter into a greased and floured 10-inch tube pan.
● **Bake** at 350° for 1 hour and 20 minutes or until a wooden pick inserted in center comes out clean.
● **Cool** cake in pan on a wire rack 10 to 15 minutes; remove from pan, and let cool completely on wire rack. **Yield:** 1 (10-inch) cake.

Janet Bean
Charlotte, North Carolina

EGGNOG-PECAN POUND CAKE

1 cup butter or margarine, softened
½ cup vegetable oil
3 cups sugar
6 large eggs
3 cups all-purpose flour
1 teaspoon baking powder
1 tablespoon ground mace
1½ cups refrigerated eggnog
1 teaspoon vanilla extract
1 teaspoon lemon extract
2 cups coarsely chopped pecans

● **Beat** butter and vegetable oil at medium speed with an electric mixer about 2 minutes. Gradually add sugar, beating at medium speed 5 to 7 minutes. Add eggs, one at a time, beating just until yellow disappears.
● **Combine** flour, baking powder, and mace; add to butter mixture alternately with eggnog, beginning and ending with flour mixture. Mix at low speed just until blended after each addition. Stir in flavorings; fold in chopped pecans. Pour batter into a greased and floured 10-inch tube pan.
● **Bake** at 350° for 1 hour and 15 minutes or until a wooden pick inserted in center comes out clean; cover cake loosely with aluminum foil after 45 minutes to prevent excessive browning. Cool cake in pan on a wire rack 10 to 15 minutes; remove from pan, and let cool completely on wire rack. **Yield:** 1 (10-inch) cake.

Sharon Griffin Squire
Little Rock, Arkansas

IRISH CREAM AND COFFEE POUND CAKE

1½ cups butter or margarine, softened
3 cups sugar
6 large eggs
1½ tablespoons instant coffee granules
¼ cup hot water
½ cup Irish cream liqueur
4 cups all-purpose flour
1 teaspoon vanilla extract
1 teaspoon almond extract
Irish Cream Glaze
2 to 3 tablespoons sliced almonds, toasted

• **Beat** butter at medium speed with an electric mixer about 2 minutes or until creamy. Gradually add sugar, beating 5 to 7 minutes. Add eggs, one at time, beating just until yellow disappears.
• **Dissolve** coffee granules in hot water; stir in liqueur.
• **Add** flour to butter mixture alternately with coffee mixture, beginning and ending with flour mixture. Mix at low speed just until blended after each addition. Stir in flavorings.
• **Pour** batter into a greased and floured 13-cup Bundt pan. Bake at 300° for 1 hour and 40 minutes or until a wooden pick inserted in center comes out clean. Cool in pan on a wire rack 10 to 15 minutes; remove from pan, and let cool 30 minutes on wire rack. Brush with glaze; sprinkle with almonds. Cool completely. **Yield:** 1 (10-inch) cake.

Irish Cream Glaze

QUICK!

1 teaspoon instant coffee granules
2 tablespoons hot water
1½ tablespoons Irish cream liqueur
⅔ cup sifted powdered sugar

• **Dissolve** coffee granules in hot water; add liqueur and powdered sugar, stirring until blended. **Yield:** about ½ cup.

Note: You can freeze glazed cake up to 1 month.

H. W. Asbell
Tallahassee, Florida

LEMONY POUND CAKE

1 cup vegetable oil
2½ cups sugar
1 cup buttermilk
4 egg whites
1 large egg, lightly beaten
1 teaspoon vanilla extract
1 teaspoon butter flavoring
½ teaspoon lemon extract
3 cups all-purpose flour
¼ teaspoon baking soda
¼ teaspoon salt

• **Beat** oil and sugar at medium speed with an electric mixer 2 minutes.
• **Combine** buttermilk and next 5 ingredients, stirring until blended.
• **Combine** flour, soda, and salt; add to oil mixture alternately with buttermilk mixture, beginning and ending with flour mixture. Beat at low speed just until blended after each addition. Pour batter into a greased and floured 10-inch tube pan.
• **Bake** at 325° for 1 hour or until a wooden pick inserted in center comes out clean.
• **Cool** cake in pan on a wire rack 10 to 15 minutes; remove from pan, and let cool completely on wire rack. **Yield:** 1 (10-inch) cake.

Pretty and Pink Pound Cake Loaf: Prepare batter; divide into thirds. Spread 1 portion into a greased and floured 9- x 5- x 3-inch loafpan. Stir ¼ cup seedless raspberry jam and, if desired, 2 drops of red liquid food coloring into second portion; spread gently over first layer. Spoon remaining batter over top. Bake at 325° for 1 hour and 35 minutes or until a wooden pick inserted in center comes out clean. **Yield:** 1 loaf.

Joseph L. Whitten
Odenville, Alabama

ORANGE-PECAN POUND CAKE

1 cup butter or margarine, softened
1 cup sugar
3 large eggs
1½ teaspoons grated orange rind
½ teaspoon grated lemon rind
¼ teaspoon orange extract
½ cup finely chopped pecans
2 cups all-purpose flour, divided
½ teaspoon baking powder
⅛ teaspoon salt
⅓ cup milk
Garnishes: orange and lemon rind strips, pecan halves

• **Beat** butter at medium speed with an electric mixer about 2 minutes or until creamy. Gradually add sugar, beating at medium speed 5 to 7 minutes. Add eggs, one at a time, beating just until yellow disappears. Stir in grated rinds and orange extract.
• **Combine** pecans and ¼ cup flour; set aside. Combine remaining 1¾ cups flour, baking powder, and salt; add to butter mixture alternately with milk, beginning and ending with flour mixture. Mix at low speed just until blended after each addition; stir in floured pecans.
• **Pour** batter into a greased and floured 9- x 5- x 3-inch loafpan. Bake at 325° for 1 hour and 5 minutes or until a wooden pick inserted in center comes out clean. Cool in pan on a wire rack 10 to 15 minutes; remove from pan, and let cool completely on wire rack. Garnish, if desired. **Yield:** 1 loaf.

Gayle Nicholas Scott
Chesapeake, Virginia

TRIPLE-MINT ICE CREAM ANGEL DESSERT

1 (10-inch) angel food cake
4 cups chocolate-mint ice cream, softened and divided
2 cups pink peppermint ice cream, softened
Whipped Cream Frosting
Chocolate-Mint Sauce

• **Split** cake horizontally into 4 equal layers. Place bottom cake layer on a serving plate; spread top of layer with half of chocolate-mint ice cream to within ½ inch from edge. Top with second cake layer; cover and freeze 45 minutes or until firm. Spread second cake layer with pink peppermint ice cream. Add third cake layer; cover and freeze 45 minutes or until firm. Spread third layer with remaining chocolate-mint ice cream, and top with remaining cake layer; cover and freeze until firm.
• **Spread** Whipped Cream Frosting on top and sides of cake. Cover and freeze until firm or up to 12 hours, if desired; let stand at room temperature 15 to 20 minutes before serving. Serve with Chocolate-Mint Sauce. **Yield:** 1 (10-inch) cake.

Whipped Cream Frosting

QUICK!

3 cups whipping cream
3 tablespoons powdered sugar
1½ teaspoons vanilla extract

• **Beat** whipping cream at low speed with an electric mixer until thickened; add sugar and vanilla, beating until firm peaks form. **Yield:** 6 cups.

Chocolate-Mint Sauce

QUICK!

¾ cup half-and-half
1 (10-ounce) package mint chocolate morsels
1½ cups miniature marshmallows
¼ teaspoon salt
1 teaspoon vanilla extract

• **Heat** half-and-half in a small heavy saucepan over low heat. Stir in chocolate morsels, marshmallows, and salt; cook, stirring constantly, until chocolate morsels and marshmallows melt. Remove from heat; stir in vanilla. **Yield:** 1½ cups.

Note: Dip knife in hot water to make cutting cake easier.

Jan Carlton
Virginia Beach, Virginia

ANGEL CAKE SURPRISE

1 (10-inch) angel food cake
½ cup semisweet chocolate morsels
3 cups whipping cream, divided
1 tablespoon Chambord or other raspberry-flavored liqueur *
¼ cup sifted powdered sugar
Garnishes: grated semisweet chocolate, fresh raspberries

• **Slice** off top one-third of cake; set aside. Using a sharp knife, hollow out center of remaining cake, leaving a 1-inch shell; reserve cake pieces for another use. Place cake shell on serving plate, and set aside.
• **Melt** chocolate morsels in a small heavy saucepan over low heat until smooth, stirring often; remove from heat, and let cool.
• **Beat** 1 cup whipping cream until firm peaks form; fold in liqueur and melted chocolate. Spoon into cake shell; place top one-third of cake over filling, pressing firmly.
• **Beat** remaining 2 cups whipping cream until foamy; add powdered sugar, beating until firm peaks form. Spread sweetened whipped cream over top and sides of cake; cover and chill up to 8 hours. Garnish, if desired. Yield: 1 (10-inch) cake.

* Substitute 1 tablespoon Cointreau or other orange-flavored liqueur for Chambord, if desired.

Louise Jackson
Shreveport, Louisiana

ORANGE ANGEL FOOD CAKE

One taste of this updated standby proves that fat-free desserts can be terrific.

1 cup sugar
½ cup water
2 tablespoons orange liqueur
½ teaspoon lemon juice
15 orange sections
10 egg whites
1 teaspoon cream of tartar
¼ teaspoon salt
1½ cups sugar
¾ cup all-purpose flour
1 teaspoon vanilla extract
1 (18-ounce) jar orange marmalade
½ cup sifted powdered sugar

• **Combine** first 4 ingredients in a heavy saucepan; cook over medium-high heat, stirring constantly, 5 minutes or until a candy thermometer registers 200°. Remove from heat.
• **Dip** orange sections, one at a time, into syrup, and place on parchment paper until cool.
• **Beat** egg whites, cream of tartar, and salt at high speed with an electric mixer until foamy. Gradually add 1½ cups sugar, 2 tablespoons at a time, beating until stiff peaks form and sugar dissolves (2 to 4 minutes). Gradually fold in flour, ¼ cup at a time; fold in vanilla.
• **Line** a 15- x 10- x 1-inch jellyroll pan with parchment paper; spread marmalade over paper. Pour batter over marmalade.
• **Bake** at 325° for 25 minutes; cool in pan on a wire rack. Sprinkle with powdered sugar. Invert onto a large cutting board or baking sheet; peel off parchment paper, and cut cake into circles with a 2½-inch round cutter. Serve with orange sections. **Yield:** 5 servings.

Sara Quattlebaum
Columbia, South Carolina

♥ Per serving: Calories 287
Fat 0.2g   Cholesterol 0mg
Sodium 79mg

CHOCOLATE CAKE ROLLS

Vegetable cooking spray
4 large eggs
½ cup water
1 (18.25- or 18.5-ounce) package
    Swiss chocolate, devil's food,
    or fudge cake mix
2 to 4 tablespoons cocoa

• **Coat** two 15- x 10- x 1-inch jellyroll pans with cooking spray; line with wax paper, and coat with cooking spray. Set aside.

• **Beat** eggs in a large mixing bowl at medium-high speed with an electric mixer 5 minutes. Add water, beating at low speed until blended. Gradually add cake mix, beating at low speed until moistened. Beat at medium-high speed 2 minutes. Divide batter in half, and spread batter evenly into prepared pans. (Layers will be thin.)

• **Bake** each cake at 350° on the middle rack in separate ovens for 13 minutes or until cake springs back when lightly touched in the center. (If you don't have a double oven, bake one pan at a time, setting one pan aside.)

• **Sift** 1 to 2 tablespoons cocoa in a 15- x 10-inch rectangle on a cloth towel; repeat with second towel. When cakes are done, immediately loosen from sides of pans, and turn each out onto a prepared towel. Peel off wax paper. Starting at narrow end, roll up each cake and towel together; place cakes, seam side down, on wire racks. Cool cakes completely. Use cake rolls for Chocolate-Cranberry Roulage, Chocolate-Orange Roulage, or Mint-Chocolate Roulage. **Yield:** 2 cake rolls.

CHOCOLATE-ORANGE ROULAGE

2 cups whipping cream
5 to 6 tablespoons Grand Marnier
    or other orange-flavored
    liqueur, divided *
1 tablespoon finely grated
    orange rind
Chocolate Cake Rolls (see recipe
    at left)
Cocoa
Chocolate-Orange Sauce
Garnish: orange rind curls

• **Beat** whipping cream at medium-high speed with an electric mixer until soft peaks form. Fold in 2 to 3 tablespoons Grand Marnier and orange rind; set aside.

• **Unroll** cake rolls; brush each lightly with remaining 2 to 3 tablespoons Grand Marnier. Spread each cake with half of whipped cream mixture. Reroll cakes without towels; place, seam side down, on a baking sheet. Cover and freeze at least 1 hour or up to 3 months.

• **Dust** cakes with cocoa, and cut into slices. Serve with Chocolate-Orange Sauce. Garnish if desired. **Yield:** 2 filled cake rolls (5 to 6 servings each).

* Substitute 5 to 6 tablespoons frozen orange juice concentrate, thawed and undiluted, for liqueur.

Chocolate-Orange Sauce

QUICK!

¾ cup half-and-half
2 cups (12 ounces) semisweet
    chocolate morsels
1½ cups miniature marshmallows
¼ teaspoon salt
¼ cup Grand Marnier or other
    orange-flavored liqueur *

• **Heat** half-and-half in a heavy saucepan over low heat. Stir in chocolate morsels, marshmallows, and salt. Cook over low heat, stirring constantly, until chocolate and marshmallows melt. Remove from heat; stir in Grand Marnier. Cool. **Yield:** 2 cups.

* Substitute ¼ cup frozen orange juice concentrate, thawed and undiluted, for liqueur.

CHOCOLATE-CRANBERRY ROULAGE
(pictured at right)

1 (12-ounce) carton cranberry-
    orange crushed fruit
¾ cup cranberry juice cocktail
2 tablespoons powdered sugar
1½ tablespoons cornstarch
4 to 5 tablespoons crème de cassis
    or other black currant-flavored
    liqueur, divided *
2 cups whipping cream
Chocolate Cake Rolls (see recipe
    at far left)
Cocoa
Garnishes: fresh cranberries, fresh
    mint sprigs

• **Combine** first 4 ingredients in container of an electric blender or food processor; process until smooth, stopping several times to scrape down sides.

• **Pour** mixture into a small saucepan; bring to a boil over medium heat, stirring constantly. Boil 1 minute, stirring constantly. Stir in 2 tablespoons crème de cassis. Cool.

• **Beat** whipping cream at medium-high speed with an electric mixer until soft peaks form. Fold in ⅔ cup cranberry mixture; cover and chill the remaining cranberry mixture for garnish.

• **Unroll** cake rolls; brush each lightly with remaining 2 to 3 tablespoons crème de cassis. Spread each cake with half of whipped cream mixture. Reroll cakes without towels; place, seam side down, on a baking sheet. Cover and freeze cakes at least 1 hour or up to 3 months.

• **Dust** cakes with cocoa, and cut into 1- to 2-inch slices. Spoon remaining cranberry mixture evenly onto dessert plates. Top each with a cake slice. Garnish, if desired. **Yield:** 2 filled cake rolls (5 to 6 servings each).

* Substitute 4 to 5 tablespoons cranberry juice cocktail for crème de cassis.

Chocolate-Cranberry Roulage

MINT-CHOCOLATE ROULAGE

2 cups whipping cream
5 to 6 tablespoons green crème de menthe, divided *
Chocolate Cake Rolls (see recipe on page 90)
Cocoa
Chocolate-Mint Sauce
Garnishes: whipped cream, fresh mint sprigs

• **Beat** 2 cups whipping cream at medium-high speed with an electric mixer until soft peaks form. Fold in 2 to 3 tablespoons crème de menthe; set aside.
• **Unroll** cake rolls; brush lightly with remaining 2 to 3 tablespoons crème de menthe. Spread each cake with half of whipped cream mixture. Reroll cakes without towels; place, seam side down, on a baking sheet. Cover and freeze at least 1 hour or up to 3 months.
• **Dust** cakes with cocoa, and cut into slices. Serve with Chocolate-Mint Sauce. Garnish, if desired. **Yield:** 2 filled cake rolls (5 to 6 servings each).

* Substitute 1½ teaspoons mint extract and 5 drops of green liquid food coloring for crème de menthe in the whipped cream. Omit brushing cake rolls with crème de menthe.

Chocolate-Mint Sauce
QUICK!

¾ cup half-and-half
1 (10-ounce) package mint chocolate morsels
1½ cups miniature marshmallows
¼ teaspoon salt
1 teaspoon vanilla extract

• **Heat** half-and-half in a small heavy saucepan over low heat. Stir in chocolate morsels, marshmallows, and salt; cook, stirring constantly, until chocolate morsels and marshmallows melt. Remove from heat, and stir in vanilla. Cool. **Yield:** 2 cups.

EASY PUMPKIN SWIRL

3 large eggs
1 cup sugar
⅔ cup canned pumpkin
¾ cup biscuit mix
2 teaspoons ground cinnamon
1 teaspoon pumpkin pie spice
1 cup chopped pecans
2 to 3 tablespoons powdered sugar
1 (8-ounce) package cream cheese, softened
⅓ cup butter or margarine, softened
1 cup sifted powdered sugar
1 teaspoon vanilla extract

• **Grease** bottom and sides of a 15- x 10- x 1-inch jellyroll pan; line with wax paper, and grease wax paper. Set aside.
• **Beat** eggs at high speed with an electric mixer until thick and pale. Gradually add 1 cup sugar, beating until soft peaks form and sugar dissolves (2 to 4 minutes). Fold in pumpkin.
• **Combine** biscuit mix and spices; fold into pumpkin mixture, and spread evenly into prepared pan. Sprinkle with chopped pecans. Bake at 375° for 13 to 15 minutes.
• **Sift** 2 to 3 tablespoons powdered sugar in a 15- x 10-inch rectangle on a cloth towel. When cake is done, immediately loosen from sides of pan, and turn out onto sugared towel. Carefully peel off wax paper. Starting at narrow end, roll up cake and towel together, and cool cake completely on a wire rack, seam side down.
• **Beat** cream cheese and butter at medium speed with an electric mixer until creamy; add 1 cup powdered sugar and vanilla, beating well. Unroll cake; spread with cream cheese mixture, and reroll without towel. Place on a serving plate, seam side down; cover and chill at least 2 hours. **Yield:** 1 filled cake roll (5 to 6 servings).

Ernestine Jones
Gore Springs, Mississippi

PINEAPPLE UPSIDE-DOWN CAKE ROLL

1 (20-ounce) can crushed pineapple in juice, undrained
1 (2.25-ounce) package sliced almonds, toasted
¼ cup butter or margarine
¾ cup firmly packed brown sugar
3 large eggs
1 cup sugar
¼ cup warm water
1 teaspoon vanilla extract
1 cup all-purpose flour
1 teaspoon baking powder
¼ teaspoon salt
¼ cup sifted powdered sugar, divided
Gingered Crème Chantilly

• **Drain** pineapple, pressing between layers of paper towels; set aside.
• **Reserve** 1 tablespoon sliced almonds; chop remaining almonds, and set aside.
• **Melt** butter in a small saucepan over medium-low heat. Add brown sugar, and cook, stirring constantly, 1 minute or until blended; stir in pineapple. Spread evenly in a lightly greased 15- x 10- x 1-inch jellyroll pan; sprinkle with chopped almonds. Set aside.
• **Beat** eggs in a large mixing bowl at medium-high speed with an electric mixer 3 minutes; gradually add 1 cup sugar, beating well after each addition. Add warm water and vanilla; beat 5 minutes or until thick and creamy.
• **Combine** flour, baking powder, and salt; sprinkle over batter, and fold into batter. Pour evenly over pineapple mixture, spreading to edges of pan.
• **Bake** at 375° for 13 minutes or until cake springs back when lightly touched in center. Cool in pan on a wire rack 5 minutes; loosen from sides of pan with a knife.
• **Sift** 3 tablespoons powdered sugar in a 15- x 10-inch rectangle on a cloth towel; turn cake out onto sugar. Starting at narrow end, roll up cake (without towel), and place, seam side down, on wire rack to cool completely.
• **Transfer** to a serving platter; sprinkle lightly with remaining 1 tablespoon powdered sugar. Top with reserved sliced almonds; serve with Gingered

Crème Chantilly. **Yield:** 1 filled cake roll (5 to 6 servings).

Gingered Crème Chantilly

QUICK!

You'll find crystallized ginger on your grocer's spice rack.

1 cup whipping cream
2 tablespoons powdered sugar
3 tablespoons minced crystallized ginger

● **Beat** whipping cream until foamy; gradually add powdered sugar, beating until soft peaks form. Fold in ginger. **Yield:** 2 cups.

Corile W. Wilhelm
Terra Alta, West Virginia

TOFFEE-PECAN ROULAGE

Vegetable cooking spray
4 large eggs
½ cup water
1 (18.25- or 18.5-ounce) package yellow cake mix
¼ cup almond brickle chips
¼ cup finely chopped pecans, toasted
2 to 4 tablespoons powdered sugar
2 cups whipping cream
2 tablespoons powdered sugar
4 to 6 tablespoons praline liqueur, divided *
Powdered sugar
Praline Sauce
Garnishes: whipped cream, toasted pecan halves

● **Coat** two 15- x 10- x 1-inch jellyroll pans with cooking spray. Line with wax paper; coat with cooking spray.
● **Beat** eggs in a mixing bowl at medium-high speed with an electric mixer 5 minutes. Add water, beating at low speed until blended. Gradually add cake mix, beating at low speed until moistened. Beat at medium-high speed 2 minutes. Fold in brickle chips and chopped pecans. Divide batter in half, and spread evenly into prepared pans. (Layers will be thin.)

● **Bake** each cake at 350° on the middle rack in separate ovens for 13 minutes or until cake springs back when lightly touched in the center. (If you don't have a double oven, bake one pan at a time, setting one pan aside.)
● **Sift** 1 to 2 tablespoons powdered sugar in a 15- x 10-inch rectangle on a cloth towel; repeat with second towel. When cakes are done, immediately loosen from sides of pans, and turn each out onto a sugared towel. Peel off wax paper. Starting at narrow end, roll up each cake and towel together; place, seam side down, on wire racks to cool completely.
● **Beat** whipping cream at medium-high speed with an electric mixer until foamy; gradually add 2 tablespoons powdered sugar, beating until soft peaks form. Fold in 2 to 3 tablespoons praline liqueur.
● **Unroll** cakes; brush each lightly, using remaining 2 to 3 tablespoons liqueur. Spread each cake with half of whipped cream mixture. Reroll cakes without towels; place, seam side down, on a baking sheet. Cover and freeze at least 1 hour or up to 3 months.
● **Dust** cakes with additional powdered sugar. Cut into 1- to 2-inch slices; spoon warm Praline Sauce evenly onto dessert plates. Top each with a cake slice. Garnish, if desired. **Yield:** 2 filled cake rolls (5 to 6 servings each).

✳ Substitute 2 tablespoons vanilla extract for praline liqueur. Use 1 tablespoon in whipped cream, and brush cakes with a mixture of 1 tablespoon vanilla plus 2 teaspoons water.

Praline Sauce

QUICK!

1 cup firmly packed brown sugar
½ cup half-and-half
½ cup butter or margarine
½ cup finely chopped pecans, toasted
½ teaspoon vanilla extract

● **Combine** first 3 ingredients; bring to a boil over medium heat, stirring constantly. Boil 1 minute, stirring constantly. Remove from heat; stir in pecans and vanilla. **Yield:** about 2 cups.

CHOCOLATE-ALMOND PETITS FOURS

¾ cup butter or margarine, softened
2 (8-ounce) cans almond paste
1½ cups sugar
8 large eggs
1½ cups all-purpose flour
1 (12-ounce) can apricot filling
Chocolate Ganache
6 ounces white chocolate, melted (optional)

● **Grease** bottom and sides of two 15- x 10- x 1-inch jellyroll pans, and line with wax paper; grease and flour wax paper. Set aside.
● **Beat** butter and almond paste at medium speed with an electric mixer until creamy. Gradually add sugar, beating well. Add eggs, one at a time, beating after each addition. Stir in flour.
● **Spread** batter evenly into prepared pans. Bake at 400° for 8 to 10 minutes. Cool in pans on wire racks.
● **Turn** cake out onto a flat surface; remove wax paper, and spread with apricot filling. Top with remaining cake, and cut with a 1½-inch round cutter.
● **Place** small cakes on a wire rack in a large shallow pan. Using a squeeze bottle, coat top and sides with warm Chocolate Ganache. (Spoon up excess frosting that drips through rack; reheat and refill bottle, and use to continue frosting cakes.) Chill cakes 10 minutes. Pipe dots on frosted cakes with white chocolate, if desired. **Yield:** 3½ dozen.

Chocolate Ganache

QUICK!

1½ cups whipping cream
24 (1-ounce) squares semisweet chocolate, chopped

● **Heat** whipping cream in a heavy saucepan over low heat. Add chocolate, stirring until smooth. (Mixture thickens as it cools; reheat over low heat, if necessary.) **Yield:** 3 cups.

Note: Freeze Chocolate-Almond Petits Fours up to 3 months.

Shannon Stansell-Boykin
Birmingham, Alabama

Chocolate-Raspberry Shortcake

CHOCOLATE-RASPBERRY SHORTCAKE
(pictured at left)

½ cup butter or margarine,
   softened
1¼ cups sugar
2 large eggs, separated
1¼ cups sifted cake flour
2 teaspoons baking powder
¼ teaspoon salt
⅓ cup cocoa
⅔ cup milk
1 teaspoon vanilla extract
2 tablespoons seedless raspberry
   jam
2 tablespoons Chambord or
   other raspberry-flavored
   liqueur
2 cups whipping cream
¼ cup sifted powdered sugar
3 cups fresh raspberries
Garnish: fresh mint sprigs

• **Grease** two 9-inch round cakepans; line with wax paper, and grease wax paper. Set aside.
• **Beat** butter at medium speed with an electric mixer 2 minutes or until creamy; gradually add sugar, beating well. Add egg yolks, one at a time, beating until blended after each addition.
• **Combine** flour and next 3 ingredients; add to butter mixture alternately with milk, beginning and ending with flour mixture. Beat at low speed until blended after each addition. Stir in vanilla.
• **Beat** egg whites at high speed with an electric mixer until stiff peaks form; gently fold into batter. Pour batter into prepared pans.
• **Bake** at 350° for 18 minutes or until a wooden pick inserted in center comes out clean. Cool in pans on wire racks 10 minutes. Remove from pans; cool completely on wire racks.
• **Cook** jam in a small saucepan over low heat until melted; stir in liqueur. Set jam mixture aside.
• **Beat** whipping cream at medium speed with an electric mixer until foamy; gradually add powdered sugar, beating until soft peaks form.
• **Place** 1 cake layer on a serving plate; brush with half of jam mixture. Arrange half of raspberries over jam. Spread half of whipped cream over raspberries.

• **Top** with remaining cake layer, and brush with remaining jam mixture. Spread remaining whipped cream over jam mixture; arrange remaining raspberries on top of shortcake. Garnish, if desired. **Yield:** 10 servings.

Mattie Scott
Birmingham, Alabama

PEAR SHORTCAKES

2 cups apple juice, divided
6 firm ripe pears, peeled and
   chopped
1 cup sugar
3 tablespoons lemon juice
½ teaspoon ground nutmeg
¼ teaspoon ground cinnamon
⅛ teaspoon ground cloves
1½ tablespoons cornstarch
½ cup slivered almonds,
   toasted
2 teaspoons grated lemon rind
8 Orange-Pecan Scones (see
   recipe on page 45)
1 cup whipping cream, whipped

• **Combine** 1¾ cups apple juice, chopped pears, and next 5 ingredients in a large saucepan; bring to a boil. Cook 10 to 12 minutes or until pear is tender. Remove pear from liquid, reserving liquid. Set pear aside. Bring liquid to a boil; reduce heat, and cook until liquid is reduced to 1 cup.
• **Combine** remaining ¼ cup apple juice and cornstarch; stir into reduced mixture. Bring to a boil, stirring constantly. Boil 1 minute, stirring constantly. Remove from heat. Stir in pear, almonds, and lemon rind; cool.
• **Split** scones; place bottom half on serving plates, and top with pear mixture, half of whipped cream, and remaining scone halves. Dollop each with remaining whipped cream. **Yield:** 8 servings.

ORANGE-STRAWBERRY SHORTCAKE

2 pints fresh strawberries, sliced
2 (11-ounce) cans mandarin
   oranges, drained
½ cup sugar
1½ tablespoons Triple Sec or
   other orange-flavored liqueur
2 cups biscuit mix
1 tablespoon sugar
1½ teaspoons ground cinnamon
⅔ cup milk
2 cups whipping cream
½ cup sifted powdered sugar
¼ cup sour cream

• **Combine** first 4 ingredients, stirring until sugar dissolves. Cover and chill 2 hours.
• **Combine** biscuit mix and next 3 ingredients; stir with a fork until dry ingredients are moistened. Turn out onto a lightly floured surface; knead 4 or 5 times. Place on a lightly greased baking sheet; press into a 7- x ¾-inch round.
• **Bake** at 425° for 15 minutes or until done. Carefully remove from pan; cool on a wire rack.
• **Beat** whipping cream until foamy; gradually add powdered sugar, beating until soft peaks form. Add sour cream, and beat until stiff peaks form.
• **Split** biscuit round in half horizontally. Place bottom half on a serving dish. Drain fruit, reserving 2 tablespoons liquid. Spoon two-thirds of fruit on bottom round; drizzle with reserved liquid. Spoon half of whipped cream mixture over fruit. Add top biscuit round. Top with remaining fruit and whipped cream mixture. **Yield:** 8 servings.

Joyce Ogletree
Newnan, Georgia

LEMON CHEESECAKE

¾ cup graham cracker crumbs
2 tablespoons sugar
1 tablespoon ground cinnamon
1 tablespoon butter or margarine,
     softened
5 (8-ounce) packages cream
     cheese, softened
1⅔ cups sugar
5 large eggs
⅛ teaspoon salt
1½ teaspoons vanilla extract
¼ cup lemon juice

● **Combine** first 3 ingredients; stir well, and set aside.
● **Grease** bottom and sides of a 10-inch springform pan with butter. Add crumb mixture; tilt pan to coat sides and bottom. Chill.
● **Beat** cream cheese at medium speed with an electric mixer until creamy; gradually add 1⅔ cups sugar, beating well at high speed. Add eggs, one at a time, beating well after each addition. Stir in salt, vanilla, and lemon juice; pour mixture into prepared crust.
● **Bake** at 300° for 1 hour and 20 minutes. (Center may be soft but will set when chilled.) Cool in pan on a wire rack; cover and chill 8 hours. **Yield:** 1 (10-inch) cheesecake.

Dale Safrit
Columbus, Ohio

LEMON DELIGHT CHEESECAKE

1 cup graham cracker crumbs
3 tablespoons sugar
2 tablespoons margarine,
     melted
3 (8-ounce) packages fat-free
     cream cheese, softened
¾ cup sugar
2 tablespoons all-purpose flour
3 tablespoons lemon juice
¾ cup fat-free egg substitute
1 (8-ounce) carton lemon nonfat
     yogurt
Garnishes: lemon slices, fresh
     mint sprigs

● **Combine** first 3 ingredients; press in bottom of a 9-inch springform pan.

● **Combine** cream cheese, ¾ cup sugar, and flour; beat at medium speed with an electric mixer until fluffy. Gradually add lemon juice and egg substitute, beating well. Add yogurt, beating well; pour into prepared pan. Cover loosely with aluminum foil.
● **Bake** at 350° for 1 hour or until set. Remove from oven, and immediately run a knife around edge of pan to release sides. Cool cheesecake completely in pan on a wire rack. Cover and chill at least 8 hours.
● **Remove** sides of pan. Garnish, if desired. **Yield:** 6 servings.

Note: For a crisper crust, prebake crust at 350° for 6 to 8 minutes.

Lynette Granade
Mobile, Alabama

♥ Per serving: Calories 402
Fat 6.6g Cholesterol 22mg
Sodium 894mg

CHEESECAKE WITH
RASPBERRY-LEMON SAUCE

Vegetable cooking spray
¾ cup graham cracker crumbs,
     divided
3 (8-ounce) packages nonfat
     cream cheese, softened
1½ cups sugar, divided
1 cup fat-free egg substitute
1 tablespoon grated lemon rind
1 teaspoon vanilla extract
4 egg whites
⅓ cup nonfat sour cream
1 (12-ounce) package frozen
     unsweetened raspberries,
     thawed
1 teaspoon grated lemon rind
1½ teaspoons fresh lemon juice

● **Coat** bottom and sides of a 9-inch springform pan with cooking spray; sprinkle with ½ cup graham cracker crumbs, and set aside.
● **Beat** cream cheese at medium speed with an electric mixer until creamy. Gradually add ¾ cup sugar, beating well. Add egg substitute, 1 tablespoon lemon rind, and vanilla, beating until blended.

● **Beat** egg whites at high speed until soft peaks form; gently fold into cream cheese mixture. Pour batter into prepared pan.
● **Bake** at 350° for 45 minutes or until lightly browned.
● **Combine** ¼ cup sugar and sour cream; spread over cheesecake, and sprinkle with remaining ¼ cup graham cracker crumbs.
● **Bake** at 450° for 5 minutes. Remove from oven; let cool completely. Gently run a knife around edge of pan to release sides; cover and chill at least 4 hours.
● **Combine** raspberries and remaining ½ cup sugar in a small saucepan; cook over medium-low heat, stirring constantly, until sugar dissolves. Pour mixture through a wire-mesh strainer into a bowl, discarding solids. Stir in 1 teaspoon grated lemon rind and lemon juice. Serve sauce with cheesecake. **Yield:** 8 servings.

Sandi Pichon
Slidell, Louisiana

♥ Per serving: Calories 308
Fat 1.4g Cholesterol 15mg
Sodium 542mg

KEY LIME CHEESECAKE
WITH STRAWBERRY-BUTTER
SAUCE

2 cups graham cracker crumbs
¼ cup sugar
½ cup butter or margarine,
     melted
3 (8-ounce) packages cream
     cheese, softened
1¼ cups sugar
6 large eggs, separated
1 (8-ounce) carton sour cream
1½ teaspoons grated lime
     rind
½ cup Key lime juice
Strawberry-Butter Sauce

● **Combine** first 3 ingredients in a small bowl, stirring well. Firmly press mixture in bottom and 1 inch up sides of a buttered 9-inch springform pan.
● **Bake** crust at 350° for 8 minutes; let cool in pan on a wire rack.

• **Beat** cream cheese at medium speed with an electric mixer until creamy; gradually add 1¼ cups sugar, beating well. Add egg yolks, one at a time, beating after each addition. Stir in sour cream, lime rind, and lime juice.

• **Beat** egg whites at high speed until stiff peaks form; fold into cream cheese mixture. Pour batter into prepared crust.

• **Bake** at 350° for 1 hour and 5 minutes; turn oven off. Partially open oven door; let cheesecake cool in oven 15 minutes. Remove from oven, and immediately run a knife around edge of pan to release sides.

• **Cool** completely in pan on a wire rack; cover and chill 8 hours. Serve with Strawberry-Butter Sauce. **Yield:** 1 (9-inch) cheesecake.

Strawberry-Butter Sauce

QUICK!

1¼ cups fresh strawberries, hulled
¼ cup butter or margarine, melted
½ cup sifted powdered sugar
1½ teaspoons grated lime rind

• **Position** knife blade in food processor bowl; add strawberries. Process until smooth, stopping once to scrape down sides. Stir in butter and remaining ingredients. **Yield:** 1 cup.

Nita and Harold Norman
Coral Gables, Florida

PIÑA COLADA CHEESECAKE

1⅔ cups fine dry breadcrumbs
¼ cup sugar
½ cup butter or margarine, melted
4 (8-ounce) packages cream cheese, softened
¾ cup sugar
4 large eggs
1 (15¼-ounce) can crushed pineapple, drained
1 (15-ounce) can cream of coconut
1 (8-ounce) carton sour cream
2 tablespoons cornstarch
1 teaspoon vanilla extract
1 teaspoon rum flavoring
1 teaspoon lemon juice
Topping

• **Combine** breadcrumbs, ¼ cup sugar, and butter; press in bottom and 1 inch up sides of a 10-inch springform pan. Bake at 350° for 10 to 12 minutes. Cool on a wire rack.

• **Beat** cream cheese in a large mixing bowl at medium speed with an electric mixer until creamy. Gradually add ¾ cup sugar, beating well. Add eggs, one at a time, beating after each addition. Stir in pineapple and next 6 ingredients; spoon into crust.

• **Bake** at 350° for 1 hour and 20 minutes; turn oven off. Sprinkle topping over cheesecake; return to oven. Leave in oven with door closed 1 hour; cool to room temperature on a wire rack. Cover and chill. **Yield:** 1 (10-inch) cheesecake.

Topping

QUICK!

¼ cup butter or margarine
½ cup flaked coconut
½ cup finely chopped almonds
¼ cup sugar

• **Melt** butter in a small saucepan over medium heat; add coconut and remaining ingredients, and cook until coconut and almonds are golden, stirring often. **Yield:** about 1 cup.

PUMPKIN CHEESECAKE

Try a twist on traditional pumpkin pie at your next holiday get-together. A crisp gingersnap crust cradles a rich pumpkin filling, while clouds of sweetened whipped cream blanket the top.

1¼ cups gingersnap crumbs (25 to 30 cookies)
3 tablespoons butter or margarine, melted
3 (8-ounce) packages cream cheese, softened
1¼ cups sugar, divided
1 tablespoon vanilla extract
6 large eggs, separated
2 (16.25-ounce) cans pumpkin pie mix
2 large eggs, lightly beaten
1 cup whipping cream
1 tablespoon powdered sugar

• **Combine** cookie crumbs and butter; press in bottom and 1 inch up sides of a lightly greased 12-inch springform pan. Set aside.

• **Beat** cream cheese at medium speed with an electric mixer until smooth; add 1 cup sugar and vanilla, beating until creamy. Stir in 6 egg yolks. Pour 2½ cups mixture into prepared crust; set aside.

• **Add** pumpkin pie mix and 2 eggs to remaining cream cheese mixture, stirring well; set aside.

• **Beat** egg whites at high speed until foamy. Add remaining ¼ cup sugar, 1 tablespoon at a time, beating until stiff peaks form and sugar dissolves (2 to 4 minutes). Fold into pumpkin mixture; pour over cream cheese mixture in crust.

• **Bake** at 300° for 1½ hours. Turn oven off, and gently run a knife around edge of pan to release sides. Let stand in oven with door partially open for 1½ hours. Remove sides of pan; cover and chill cheesecake.

• **Beat** whipping cream and powdered sugar at high speed until soft peaks form; spread on sides of cheesecake. **Yield:** 1 (12-inch) cheesecake.

Sudi Swirles and Jan Hryharrow
Durham, North Carolina

PEANUT BUTTER CHEESECAKE

1½ cups salted pretzel crumbs
⅓ cup butter or margarine, melted
5 (8-ounce) packages cream cheese, softened
1½ cups sugar
¾ cup creamy peanut butter
3 large eggs
2 teaspoons vanilla extract
1 (8-ounce) carton sour cream
3 tablespoons creamy peanut butter
½ cup sugar

● **Combine** pretzel crumbs and butter; firmly press in bottom and 1 inch up sides of a 10-inch springform pan.
● **Bake** at 350° for 5 minutes. Set prepared pan aside.
● **Beat** cream cheese in a mixing bowl at medium speed with an electric mixer until creamy; gradually add 1½ cups sugar, beating well. Add ¾ cup peanut butter, and beat well. Add eggs, one at a time, beating after each addition. Stir in vanilla. Pour into prepared pan.
● **Bake** at 350° for 40 minutes; turn oven off, and partially open door. Leave cheesecake in oven 30 minutes.
● **Combine** sour cream, 3 tablespoons peanut butter, and ½ cup sugar, stirring until sugar dissolves. Spread sour cream mixture over warm cheesecake. Cool completely in pan on a wire rack.
● **Cover** and chill 8 hours. **Yield:** 1 (10-inch) cheesecake.

Jill Goldblatt
Pelham, Alabama

CHOCOLATE-ALMOND CHEESECAKE

1½ cups chocolate wafer crumbs
1 cup slivered almonds, toasted and chopped
⅓ cup sugar
⅓ cup butter or margarine, softened
3 (8-ounce) packages cream cheese, softened
1 cup sugar
¼ cup amaretto
1 teaspoon almond extract
1 teaspoon vanilla extract
4 large eggs
1 (16-ounce) carton sour cream
1 tablespoon sugar
1 teaspoon vanilla extract
½ cup slivered almonds, toasted

● **Combine** first 4 ingredients; firmly press in bottom and 1 inch up sides of a 9-inch springform pan. Set aside.
● **Beat** cream cheese in a large mixing bowl at medium speed with an electric mixer until creamy; gradually add 1 cup sugar, beating well. Add liqueur, almond extract, and 1 teaspoon vanilla; beat well. Add eggs, one at a time, beating after each addition.
● **Pour** into prepared crust. Bake at 375° for 50 minutes; remove from oven, and let stand 5 minutes (center will be soft). Combine sour cream, 1 tablespoon sugar, and 1 teaspoon vanilla; spread evenly on top of cheesecake. Bake at 500° for 5 minutes. Let cool in pan on a wire rack. Cover and chill 8 hours.
● **To** serve, remove sides of pan, and press ½ cup slivered almonds around top edge of cheesecake. **Yield:** 1 (9-inch) cheesecake.

Sharon Kay Johnston
Fort Worth, Texas

WHITE CHOCOLATE CHEESECAKE

Much easier than traditional cheesecake, this one does not use eggs. Simply mix the ingredients, pour them over a crust of pound cake crumbs, and bake for just 30 minutes.

1¼ cups pound cake crumbs
3 (4-ounce) bars white chocolate *
3 (8-ounce) packages cream cheese, softened
1 cup sugar
1 (16-ounce) carton sour cream
1 tablespoon apricot brandy (optional)
1 teaspoon vanilla extract
Garnishes: sliced strawberries, sliced kiwifruit, fresh mint sprigs

● **Press** crumbs in bottom of a lightly greased 9-inch springform pan.
● **Bake** at 350° for 5 minutes. Cool on a wire rack.
● **Melt** white chocolate in a heavy saucepan over low heat, stirring constantly. Cool.
● **Beat** cream cheese at medium speed with an electric mixer 3 minutes or until creamy; add sugar, and beat 5 minutes. Add chocolate; beat 5 minutes. Add sour cream, brandy, if desired, and vanilla, mixing until blended. Pour into prepared pan.
● **Bake** at 350° for 30 to 35 minutes. Cool 10 minutes in pan on a wire rack. Gently run a knife around edge of pan to release sides. Let cool completely in pan on wire rack. Cover and chill 8 hours. Remove cake from pan, and garnish, if desired. **Yield:** 1 (9-inch) cheesecake.

* For white chocolate, we used Ghirardelli Classic White Confection.

Margot Hahn
Washington, D.C.

CHOCOLATE-MINT BAKED ALASKA CHEESECAKE

1 cup chocolate wafer crumbs
2 tablespoons sugar
3 tablespoons butter or margarine, melted
1 cup mint chocolate morsels
3 (8-ounce) packages cream cheese, softened
⅔ cup sugar
3 large eggs
1 teaspoon vanilla extract
3 egg whites
1 (7-ounce) jar marshmallow cream

• **Combine** first 3 ingredients; press in bottom of a 9-inch springform pan.
• **Bake** at 350° for 10 minutes. Set prepared pan aside.
• **Melt** chocolate morsels in a small heavy saucepan over low heat, stirring constantly. Set aside.
• **Beat** cream cheese at medium speed with an electric mixer until creamy; gradually add ⅔ cup sugar, beating well. Add eggs, one at a time, beating after each addition. Stir in melted chocolate and vanilla. Pour into prepared pan.
• **Bake** at 350° for 50 minutes.
• **Remove** from oven; gently run a knife around edge of pan to release sides, and cool completely in pan on a wire rack.
• **Cover** and chill 8 hours.
• **Beat** egg whites at high speed with an electric mixer until soft peaks form. Gradually add marshmallow cream, beating until stiff peaks form. Remove sides of pan from cheesecake. Place cheesecake on a baking sheet. Carefully spread egg white mixture over top and sides of cake.
• **Bake** at 325° for 25 to 30 minutes or until golden. Serve immediately. **Yield:** 1 (9-inch) cheesecake.

Erma Jackson
Huntsville, Alabama

FROZEN PEPPERMINT CHEESECAKE

1½ cups chocolate wafer crumbs
¼ cup sugar
¼ cup butter or margarine, melted
1 (8-ounce) package cream cheese, softened
1 (14-ounce) can sweetened condensed milk
1 cup crushed hard peppermint candy
3 drops of red liquid food coloring
2 cups whipping cream, whipped
Garnishes: whipped cream, crushed hard peppermint candy

• **Combine** first 3 ingredients; firmly press in bottom and 1 inch up sides of a 9-inch springform pan. Chill.
• **Beat** cream cheese at high speed with an electric mixer until creamy. Add condensed milk, 1 cup crushed candy, and food coloring; beat well.
• **Fold** in whipped cream. Pour into pan. Freeze until firm. Garnish, if desired. **Yield:** 1 (9-inch) cheesecake.

Rublelene Singleton
Scotts Hill, Tennessee

CHOCOLATE-MINT TORTE

Vegetable cooking spray
1 (18.25-ounce) package 97% fat-free devil's food cake mix
3 egg whites
1¾ cups water
1 (2.6-ounce) package whipped topping mix
⅔ cup skim milk
2 tablespoons green crème de menthe

• **Coat** a 15- x 10- x 1-inch jellyroll pan with cooking spray; line with wax paper, and coat with cooking spray.
• **Combine** cake mix, egg whites, and water in a large mixing bowl; beat at high speed with an electric mixer 2 minutes. Pour batter into prepared pan.
• **Bake** at 350° for 18 to 20 minutes or until a wooden pick inserted in center comes out clean.
• **Cool** in pan on a wire rack 10 minutes. Invert onto wire rack.

• **Carefully** remove wax paper (cake will be very tender); cool completely. Cut cake crosswise into thirds.
• **Combine** 2 envelopes whipped topping mix, milk, and liqueur; beat at high speed with an electric mixer 4 minutes or until stiff peaks form.
• **Spread** topping between layers, reserving ½ cup. Pipe or dollop topping on top of cake. Chill at least 2 hours or freeze, if desired. **Yield:** 12 servings.

♥ Per serving: Calories 204
Fat 3g Cholesterol 0mg
Sodium 319mg

TRIPLE CHOCOLATE TORTE

½ cup sugar
¼ cup cocoa
3 tablespoons all-purpose flour
¼ teaspoon baking powder
1 (4-ounce) bar bittersweet chocolate, finely chopped
½ cup boiling water
2 egg yolks
2 tablespoons chocolate-flavored liqueur
4 egg whites
½ cup sugar
Sifted powdered sugar

• **Combine** first 4 ingredients; add chocolate and water, stirring until smooth. Stir in egg yolks and liqueur.
• **Beat** egg whites at high speed with an electric mixer until foamy. Add ½ cup sugar, 1 tablespoon at a time, beating until stiff peaks form and sugar dissolves (2 to 4 minutes).
• **Stir** one-third of egg whites into mixture; fold in remaining whites. Pour into a greased 8-inch springform pan.
• **Bake** at 375° for 28 minutes or until a wooden pick inserted in center comes out clean. Cool in pan on a wire rack 10 minutes; remove sides of pan, and cool (will be cracked on top). Sprinkle with sugar. **Yield:** 10 servings.

Sharon O'Dell
St. George Island, Florida

♥ Per serving: Calories 171
Fat 4.7g Cholesterol 44mg
Sodium 37mg

LUCY'S APRICOT PRALINE TORTE

1 (16-ounce) loaf pound cake
1 cup apricot preserves
Praline Buttercream
Sifted powdered sugar

• Cut cake horizontally into 3 layers.
• Melt preserves in a saucepan over low heat. Spread half of preserves over bottom layer of cake. Spread half of Praline Buttercream over preserves; place second cake layer on top of buttercream. Repeat procedure with remaining preserves and buttercream; top with remaining cake layer. Sprinkle with powdered sugar. **Yield:** 10 to 12 servings.

Praline Buttercream

½ cup unsalted butter, softened
2½ cups sifted powdered sugar
2 to 3 tablespoons whipping cream
½ cup Praline Powder
1 teaspoon vanilla extract

• Beat butter in a small mixing bowl at medium speed with an electric mixer until creamy; gradually add sugar, beating mixture well. Beat in whipping cream, and fold in Praline Powder and vanilla. **Yield:** 2 cups.

Praline Powder

2 tablespoons butter
¼ cup sugar
¾ cup almonds, chopped and toasted

• Cook butter and sugar in a small saucepan over medium heat until sugar melts and turns a light caramel color (mixture will separate), stirring occasionally. Remove from heat, and stir in almonds.
• Pour onto a greased aluminum foil-lined baking sheet, and cool. Break into chunks.
• Position knife blade in food processor bowl; add chunks of praline mixture, and process until finely crushed. **Yield:** 1 cup.

The Texas Experience
Richardson Woman's Club
Richardson, Texas

CARAMEL-SWEET POTATO TORTE

6 large eggs, separated
1⅓ cups mashed cooked sweet potato
¾ teaspoon ground cinnamon
½ teaspoon ground nutmeg
¼ teaspoon ground cloves
1½ teaspoons vanilla extract
¾ cup chopped pecans
¾ cup chopped dates
¾ cup crushed round buttery crackers
½ teaspoon cream of tartar
¾ cup sugar
Caramel Whipped Cream Filling
Garnish: pecan halves

• Line three 8-inch round cakepans with wax paper; grease and flour wax paper.
• Beat egg yolks, sweet potato, and next 4 ingredients at medium speed with an electric mixer until smooth. Stir in pecans, dates, and cracker crumbs.
• Beat egg whites and cream of tartar at high speed until foamy. Add sugar, 2 tablespoons at a time, beating until soft peaks form and sugar dissolves. Fold into yolk mixture.
• Bake at 350° for 25 minutes or until a wooden pick inserted in center comes out clean.
• Cool in pans on wire racks 10 minutes. Remove from pans, peeling off wax paper; cool on wire racks.
• Spread filling between layers and on top of cake. Garnish, if desired. Cover and chill 3 to 4 hours. **Yield:** 10 servings.

Caramel Whipped Cream Filling

2 tablespoons butter
1 tablespoon all-purpose flour
⅔ cup firmly packed brown sugar
⅓ cup light corn syrup
2 tablespoons half-and-half
1½ cups whipping cream

• Melt butter in a heavy saucepan over low heat; whisk in flour until smooth. Cook 1 minute, whisking constantly. Stir in brown sugar and corn syrup; cook 5 minutes, whisking constantly.
• Remove from heat; cool 15 minutes. Gradually whisk in half-and-half.
• Beat cream until soft peaks form; fold into mixture. **Yield:** about 4 cups.

CHOCOLATE-ALMOND TORTE

3 shortbread finger cookies, crushed *
1 cup sugar
⅓ cup walnut pieces
3 tablespoons slivered almonds
1 (8-ounce) package semisweet chocolate squares, chopped
½ cup butter, cut into pieces
1 tablespoon amaretto
4 large eggs
1 cup whipping cream
2 tablespoons powdered sugar

• Press crushed cookies evenly in bottom of a buttered 8-inch springform pan; set aside.
• Position knife blade in food processor bowl, and add 1 cup sugar, walnuts, and almonds; process until ground, stopping once to scrape down sides. Transfer mixture to a bowl; set aside.
• Combine chocolate and butter in a 1-quart liquid measuring cup; microwave at MEDIUM (50% power) 3 to 4 minutes or until melted, stirring after each minute. Let mixture stand 15 minutes.
• Stir liqueur into nut mixture. Add eggs, one at a time, stirring just until blended after each addition. Stir in chocolate mixture. Pour over crushed cookies in pan.
• Bake at 325° for 35 to 40 minutes or until set; cool completely. Remove sides from pan.
• Beat whipping cream and powdered sugar until soft peaks form, and serve with torte. **Yield:** 6 to 8 servings.

* For shortbread finger cookies, we used Walker Shortbread Fingers.

Note: You can chill torte. Remove from refrigerator 30 minutes before serving.

Liz Lorber
Atlanta, Georgia

At right: *Candy Bar Brownies (page 112)*

COOKIES AND CANDIES

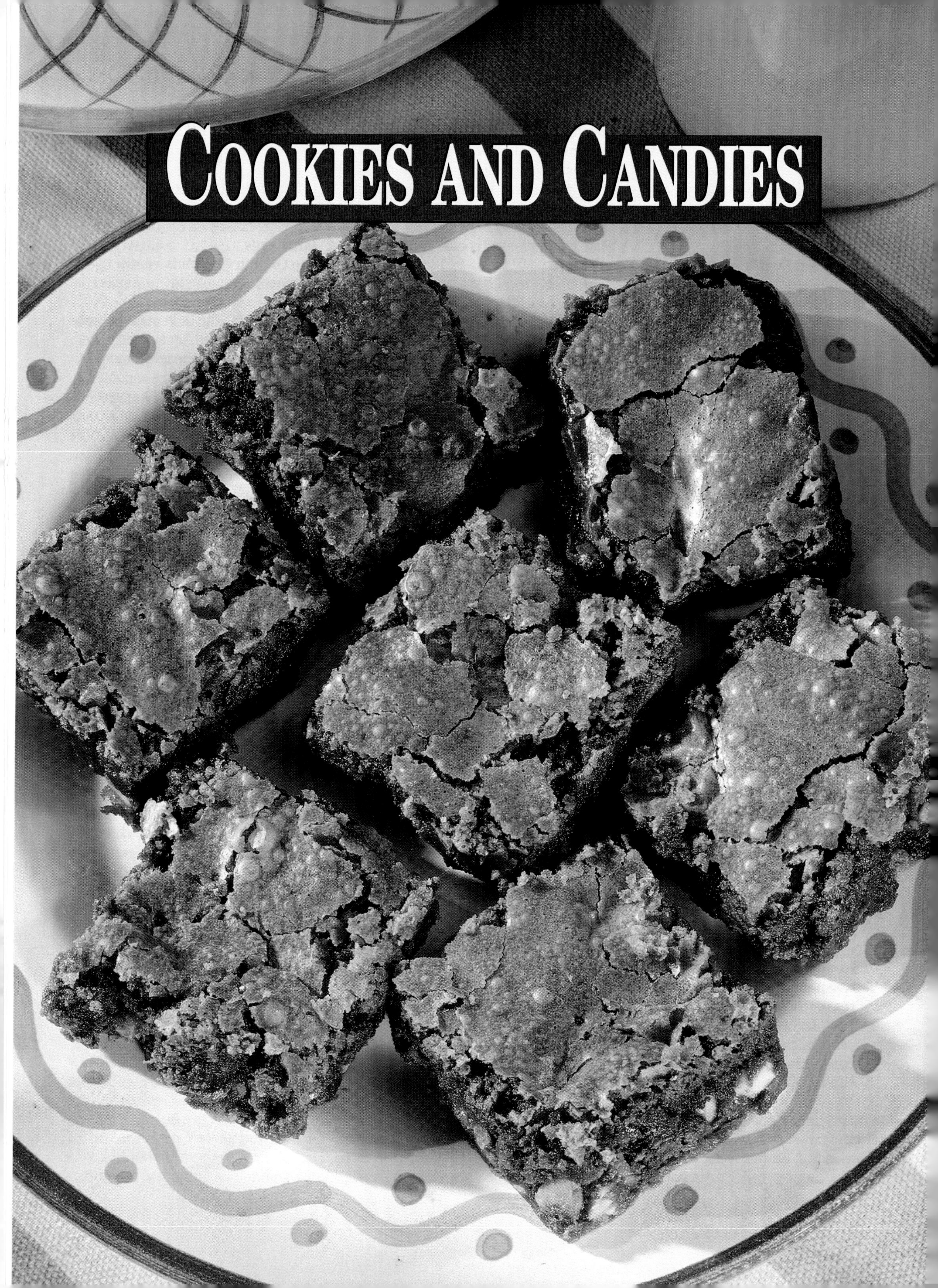

COOKIES AND CANDIES

ALABAMA FUDGE-PECAN CHEWIES

Make these treats up to 2 days before serving or bake them ahead and freeze. Store them in the freezer up to 3 months.

1 (14-ounce) can sweetened condensed milk
2 cups (12 ounces) semisweet chocolate morsels
¼ cup butter or margarine
1 cup all-purpose flour
½ cup chopped pecans
1 teaspoon vanilla extract
60 pecan halves

• **Combine** first 3 ingredients in a heavy saucepan; cook over medium-low heat, stirring constantly, until chocolate and butter melt. Remove from heat.
• **Stir** in flour, chopped pecans, and vanilla.
• **Drop** by teaspoonfuls onto ungreased cookie sheets. Press a pecan half into the center of each cookie.
• **Bake** at 350° for 7 minutes. (Do not overbake.) Transfer cookies to wire racks to cool. **Yield:** 5 dozen.

Jane Boswell
Birmingham, Alabama

RICH DATE-NUT CHOCOLATE CHIP COOKIES

½ cup butter or margarine, softened
¾ cup firmly packed brown sugar
1 large egg
1 tablespoon vanilla extract
¾ cup chopped dates
1 cup all-purpose flour
½ teaspoon baking soda
¼ teaspoon baking powder
¼ teaspoon salt
2 cups (12 ounces) semisweet chocolate morsels
¾ cup coarsely chopped walnuts
½ cup flaked coconut

• **Beat** butter at medium speed with an electric mixer until fluffy; gradually add brown sugar, beating well. Add egg and vanilla, mixing well. Stir in dates; let

stand 5 minutes. Beat at high speed 3 minutes.
• **Combine** flour and next 3 ingredients; gradually add to butter mixture, mixing well. Gently stir in morsels, walnuts, and coconut.
• **Drop** dough by level tablespoonfuls onto lightly greased cookie sheets.
• **Bake** at 350° for 10 to 12 minutes or until lightly browned. Transfer to wire racks to cool. **Yield:** 3 dozen.

Beverly Garver
Anderson, South Carolina

CHUNKY MACADAMIA NUT-WHITE CHOCOLATE COOKIES

½ cup butter or margarine, softened
¾ cup firmly packed brown sugar
2 tablespoons sugar
1 large egg
1½ teaspoons vanilla extract
2 cups all-purpose flour
¾ teaspoon baking soda
½ teaspoon baking powder
⅛ teaspoon salt
1 cup (6 ounces) vanilla-milk morsels or 1 (6-ounce) package white chocolate-flavored baking bars, cut into chunks
2 (3.5-ounce) jars macadamia nuts, coarsely chopped

• **Beat** butter at medium speed with an electric mixer until fluffy; gradually add sugars, beating well. Add egg and vanilla, mixing well.
• **Combine** flour and next 3 ingredients; gradually add to butter mixture, mixing well. Stir in morsels and nuts.
• **Drop** by rounded teaspoonfuls onto lightly greased cookie sheets.
• **Bake** at 350° for 8 to 10 minutes or until lightly browned. Transfer to wire racks to cool. **Yield:** 5 dozen.

Elizabeth S. Evins
Atlanta, Georgia

DOUBLE-CHOCOLATE COOKIES

QUICK!

1 (18.25-ounce) package devil's food cake mix with pudding
½ cup vegetable oil
2 large eggs
1 cup (6 ounces) semisweet chocolate morsels

• **Combine** first 3 ingredients, and beat at medium speed with an electric mixer until blended. Stir in chocolate morsels.
• **Drop** dough by rounded teaspoonfuls about 2 inches apart onto ungreased cookie sheets.
• **Bake** at 350° for 10 minutes. Cool cookies on cookie sheets 5 minutes; transfer to wire racks to cool completely. **Yield:** 3 dozen.

Marie Davis
Charlotte, North Carolina

ORANGE CRINKLES

QUICK!

To celebrate Halloween, add pumpkin faces to these bright orange cookies, using brown decorating frosting and assorted candies.

1 (18.25-ounce) package orange cake mix
½ cup vegetable oil
2 large eggs
2 teaspoons grated orange rind

• **Combine** all ingredients in a large bowl, stirring mixture well.
• **Drop** dough by rounded teaspoonfuls 2 inches apart onto ungreased cookie sheets.
• **Bake** at 350° for 12 minutes or until lightly browned. Cool on cookie sheets 1 minute; transfer to wire racks to cool completely. **Yield:** 3 dozen.

Marie Davis
Charlotte, North Carolina

CATS' TONGUES

These crisp, slightly sweet cookies are long and thin and resemble their name in shape.

¼ cup unsalted butter, softened
⅓ cup sugar
2 egg whites
⅛ teaspoon vanilla extract
⅓ cup all-purpose flour
Pinch of salt

● **Beat** butter at medium speed with an electric mixer until creamy; gradually add sugar, beating well. Add egg whites and vanilla, beating just until blended.
● **Combine** flour and salt; gradually add to butter mixture, beating just until blended after each addition.
● **Drop** by level teaspoonfuls onto greased cookie sheets; pull a knife through batter until each cookie is about 5 inches long (1 end will be wider).
● **Bake** at 425° for 4 to 5 minutes or until edges are lightly browned. Immediately remove from cookie sheets, and let cool on wire racks. **Yield:** 2½ dozen.

Note: If cookies harden on cookie sheets, return them to oven briefly to soften.

Chefs Edna Lewis and Scott Peacock
Atlanta, Georgia

BASIC BUTTER COOKIE DOUGH

1 cup butter or margarine, softened
½ cup firmly packed brown sugar
½ cup sugar
1 large egg
3½ cups all-purpose flour
2 teaspoons baking powder
½ teaspoon salt
2 tablespoons milk
2 teaspoons vanilla extract

● **Beat** butter in a large mixing bowl at medium speed with an electric mixer until creamy. Gradually add sugars, beating well. Add egg, beating well.
● **Combine** flour, baking powder, and salt; add to butter mixture alternately with milk, beginning and ending with flour mixture. Beat at low speed after each addition until mixture is blended. Stir in vanilla.
● **Divide** dough into 2 equal portions; wrap each portion in plastic wrap to prevent drying out. Chill. Proceed with cookie instructions of choice. **Yield:** 2¼ pounds.

Note: You can freeze this cookie dough, but cookies made from thawed dough may be drier than if baked immediately.
Ellender Mills
Raleigh, North Carolina

SPICE THINS

½ teaspoon ground ginger
½ teaspoon ground cinnamon
¼ teaspoon ground nutmeg
½ Basic Butter Cookie Dough recipe (see recipe at left)
2 (2-ounce) squares vanilla-flavored candy coating, melted
Ground cinnamon

● **Stir** or knead first 3 ingredients into Basic Butter Cookie Dough.
● **Shape** dough into 1-inch balls, and place on lightly greased cookie sheets. Dip a flat-bottom glass into flour, and flatten balls to ¼-inch thickness.
● **Bake** at 350° for 10 minutes or until lightly browned. Transfer to wire racks to cool.
● **Drizzle** candy coating over cookies; sprinkle with cinnamon. **Yield:** 2½ dozen.

PEANUT BUTTER SHORTBREAD

⅔ cup creamy peanut butter
½ Basic Butter Cookie Dough recipe (see recipe at left)
36 milk chocolate kisses, unwrapped

● **Knead** peanut butter into Basic Butter Cookie Dough until smooth and well blended.
● **Shape** dough into 1-inch balls, and place on lightly greased cookie sheets.
Make an indentation in center of each ball with thumb or spoon handle.
● **Bake** at 350° for 12 minutes or until lightly browned. Immediately press chocolate kiss in center of each cookie. Remove to wire racks to cool. **Yield:** 3 dozen.

SCOTTISH SHORTBREAD

Agnes, a native of Scotland, shares her mother's recipe for Scottish Shortbread.

1 cup butter, softened
1 cup margarine, softened
1 cup sifted powdered sugar
4 cups all-purpose flour
½ teaspoon baking powder
¼ teaspoon salt

● **Beat** butter and margarine at medium speed with an electric mixer until creamy; gradually add powdered sugar, beating well.
● **Combine** flour, baking powder, and salt; add to butter mixture. Mix at low speed until well blended.
● **Turn** dough out onto a well-floured surface; knead 10 times.
● **Shape** on a large cookie sheet into a 15- x 10-inch rectangle. Pierce dough with a fork at 2-inch intervals.
● **Bake** at 300° for 1 hour or until short-bread is golden. Cut immediately into 2½- x 1-inch pieces. Cool on cookie sheet 10 minutes; transfer to a wire rack to cool completely. **Yield:** 5 dozen.
Agnes Hunter Dauphinée
Trussville, Alabama

JAVA SHORTBREAD COOKIES

1 cup butter or margarine, softened
2 teaspoons instant coffee granules
½ cup sifted powdered sugar
2 cups all-purpose flour
3 ounces vanilla-flavored candy coating, melted
½ cup chopped pecans

• **Beat** butter and coffee granules in a mixing bowl at medium speed with an electric mixer until creamy; gradually add powdered sugar, beating well. Stir in flour.
• **Shape** dough into 3-inch logs; place on an ungreased cookie sheet.
• **Bake** at 350° for 8 minutes or until lightly browned. Transfer to wire racks to cool.
• **Dip** both ends of cookies into candy coating, and then into chopped pecans. Place on wax paper until set. **Yield:** 2½ dozen.

Wendy V. Kitchens
Charlotte, North Carolina

FINIKIA

Pronounced fin-EE-key-ah, these cookies are similar to shortbread.

1 cup sugar
1 cup vegetable oil
1 cup orange juice
½ cup butter, softened
1 tablespoon ground cinnamon
4 teaspoons baking powder
1 teaspoon baking soda
6 to 6½ cups all-purpose flour
Honey Syrup
3 cups ground walnuts

• **Combine** first 5 ingredients in a large mixing bowl, and beat at medium speed with an electric mixer until well blended. Gradually add baking powder, baking soda, and enough flour to make a medium dough (dough should not stick to your hands).
• **Turn** dough out onto a lightly floured surface, and knead several times.

• **Shape** dough into 1¼-inch balls, and flatten each into a 3- x 1-inch oval. Place on ungreased cookie sheets.
• **Bake** at 350° for 20 minutes or until lightly browned. Transfer to wire racks to cool.
• **Dip** cookies into hot Honey Syrup with a slotted spoon; roll in ground walnuts, and place on wire racks to cool. **Yield:** 4¼ dozen.

Honey Syrup

QUICK!

2 cups sugar
1 cup water
1 cup honey
2 tablespoons lemon juice

• **Combine** sugar and water in a saucepan, and bring to a boil over medium heat. Reduce heat, and simmer 10 minutes.
• **Add** honey and lemon juice, stirring well; return to a boil. Reduce heat, and simmer 5 minutes. **Yield:** 2¾ cups.

Mary Pappas
Richmond, Virginia

LEMON CRISPS

QUICK!

1 (18.25-ounce) package lemon cake mix with pudding
1 cup crisp rice cereal
½ cup butter or margarine, melted
1 large egg

• **Combine** all ingredients, stirring mixture well.
• **Shape** dough into 1-inch balls; place about 2 inches apart on ungreased cookie sheets.
• **Bake** at 350° for 9 minutes or until edges are golden. Cool on cookie sheets 1 minute; transfer to wire racks to cool completely. **Yield:** 4 dozen.

Marie Davis
Charlotte, North Carolina

GINGER COOKIES

Eloise has been making 1,500 of these delicious cookies each Christmas for almost 50 years. "I am confident that I have made at least 50,000 of these," she reports. Her cookies are so popular that the neighborhood kids call her the "Ginger Cookie Lady."

1½ cups shortening
2 cups sugar
2 large eggs
½ cup molasses
4 cups all-purpose flour
2 teaspoons baking soda
1 teaspoon ground cinnamon
1 teaspoon ground cloves
1 teaspoon ground ginger
Sugar

• **Combine** first 9 ingredients in a large mixing bowl; beat at medium speed with an electric mixer until blended.
• **Shape** into 1-inch balls, and roll in additional sugar. Place on greased cookie sheets, and flatten slightly with a flat-bottomed glass.
• **Bake** at 375° for 8 to 10 minutes. Transfer to wire racks to cool. **Yield:** 7 dozen.

Eloise Pope
Milton, West Virginia

COFFEE NUGGETS

Make-ahead tip: Bake and freeze cookies up to 3 months in advance or store in an airtight container at room temperature a couple of days before serving.

2 tablespoons instant coffee granules
1 cup butter or margarine, softened
⅓ cup sifted powdered sugar
2 cups all-purpose flour
1 cup finely chopped pecans
2 teaspoons vanilla extract
Sifted powdered sugar

• **Crush** coffee granules into a fine powder, using a mortar and pestle or back of a spoon; set coffee powder aside.

• **Beat** butter at medium speed with an electric mixer until creamy; gradually add ⅓ cup powdered sugar, beating well. Add coffee powder, flour, pecans, and vanilla, mixing until blended. Cover and chill at least 1 hour.
• **Shape** dough into 1-inch balls; place on ungreased cookie sheets.
• **Bake** at 350° for 12 minutes or until lightly browned. Transfer to wire racks; cool 10 minutes. Roll in additional powdered sugar; cool completely on wire racks. Roll in powdered sugar again, if desired. **Yield:** 3½ dozen.

Katharine Reinke
Baltimore, Maryland

DOUBLE-CHOCOLATE SUGAR COOKIES

2 cups (12 ounces) semisweet chocolate morsels, divided
1 cup butter or margarine, softened
1 cup sugar
1 large egg
2 tablespoons milk
1 teaspoon vanilla extract
3 cups all-purpose flour
1 teaspoon baking powder
½ teaspoon baking soda
½ teaspoon salt
½ cup sugar

• **Melt** 1 cup semisweet chocolate morsels in a heavy saucepan over low heat. Set aside.
• **Beat** butter at medium speed with an electric mixer until fluffy; gradually add 1 cup sugar, beating well. Add egg, milk, and vanilla, mixing well. Add melted morsels, mixing until blended.
• **Combine** flour and next 3 ingredients; gradually add to butter mixture, mixing well. Stir in remaining 1 cup chocolate morsels.
• **Shape** dough into balls, 1 tablespoon at a time; roll balls in ½ cup sugar. Place on lightly greased cookie sheets.
• **Bake** at 400° for 8 to 10 minutes. (Cookies will be soft and will firm up as they cool.) Transfer to wire racks to cool. **Yield:** 4½ dozen.

Jill D. Abell
Snellville, Georgia

FUDGE PUDDLES

½ cup butter or margarine, softened
½ cup creamy peanut butter
½ cup sugar
½ cup firmly packed brown sugar
1 large egg
½ teaspoon vanilla extract
1¼ cups all-purpose flour
¾ teaspoon baking soda
½ teaspoon salt
Fudge Filling
2 tablespoons chopped peanuts

• **Beat** butter and peanut butter in a large mixing bowl at medium speed with an electric mixer until creamy; gradually add sugars, beating well. Add egg and vanilla, mixing well.
• **Combine** flour, baking soda, and salt; add to butter mixture, mixing well. Cover and chill 1 hour.
• **Shape** dough into 48 (1-inch) balls. Place in lightly greased miniature (1¾-inch) muffin pans. Bake at 325° for 12 to 14 minutes or until lightly browned. Cool in pans on wire racks 5 minutes. Carefully remove cookies from pans, and let cool completely on wire racks.
• **Spoon** warm Fudge Filling into a heavy-duty, zip-top plastic bag; seal. Snip a tiny hole in one corner of bag; pipe a small amount of filling in center of each cookie. Sprinkle with peanuts. Cool. Filled cookies may be frozen up to 8 months. **Yield:** 4 dozen.

Fudge Filling
QUICK!

1 (14-ounce) can sweetened condensed milk
1 cup milk chocolate morsels
1 cup (6 ounces) semisweet chocolate morsels
1 teaspoon vanilla extract

• **Combine** all ingredients in a heavy saucepan; cook over low heat until chocolate morsels melt, stirring often. **Yield:** 2 cups.

Note: Heat any remaining Fudge Filling over low heat; serve over pound cake.

Barbara Ritchie
Waynesboro, Virginia

CARAMEL-FILLED CHOCOLATE COOKIES

1 cup butter or margarine, softened
1 cup sugar
1 cup firmly packed brown sugar
2 large eggs
2¼ cups all-purpose flour
¾ cup cocoa
1 teaspoon baking soda
2 teaspoons vanilla extract
1 cup finely chopped pecans, divided
1 tablespoon sugar
1 (8-ounce) package chewy caramels in milk chocolate

• **Beat** butter at medium speed with an electric mixer until creamy. Gradually add sugars, beating well. Add eggs, beating well.
• **Combine** flour, cocoa, and soda; add to butter mixture, mixing well. Stir in vanilla and ½ cup chopped pecans. Cover and chill 1 hour.
• **Combine** remaining ½ cup pecans and 1 tablespoon sugar; set aside. Divide dough into 2 portions; work with 1 portion at a time, keeping remaining portion chilled. Gently press 1 tablespoon cookie dough around each candy, forming a ball. Dip 1 side of cookie in pecan mixture. Place, pecan side up, 2 inches apart on ungreased cookie sheets. Bake at 375° for 8 minutes. (Cookies will look soft.) Let cool 1 minute on cookie sheets. Transfer to wire racks to cool. **Yield:** about 3 dozen.

Krista Kiger
Winston-Salem, North Carolina

CRISPY OATMEAL-TOFFEE LIZZIES

1 cup butter-flavored shortening
1 cup sugar
1 cup firmly packed brown sugar
2 large eggs
1 tablespoon milk
1 teaspoon vanilla extract
2 cups all-purpose flour
1 teaspoon baking soda
1 teaspoon salt
2 cups quick-cooking oats, uncooked
2 cups (12 ounces) semisweet chocolate morsels
¾ cup almond brickle chips
½ cup chopped pecans

• **Beat** shortening in a large mixing bowl at medium speed with an electric mixer until fluffy; gradually add sugars, beating mixture well. Add eggs, one at time, beating until blended after each addition. Add milk and vanilla, beating until blended.
• **Combine** flour, baking soda, and salt; gradually add to shortening mixture, beating at low speed until blended. Stir in oats and remaining ingredients; cover and chill 1 hour.
• **Shape** dough into 1¼-inch balls; place 2 inches apart on lightly greased cookie sheets. Flatten cookies to ¼-inch thickness with a flat-bottomed glass dipped in flour.
• **Bake** at 350° for 12 minutes or until cookies begin to brown around edges. Transfer to wire racks to cool. **Yield:** 6 dozen.

Sandra Russell
Gainesville, Florida

PEANUT BLOSSOM COOKIES

QUICK!

1 (14-ounce) can sweetened condensed milk
¾ cup creamy peanut butter
1 teaspoon vanilla extract
2 cups biscuit mix
⅓ cup sugar
1 (9-ounce) package milk chocolate kisses, unwrapped

• **Combine** milk and peanut butter, stirring until smooth; stir in vanilla. Add biscuit mix, stirring well.
• **Shape** dough into 1-inch balls; roll balls in sugar, and place on ungreased cookie sheets. Make an indentation in center of each ball of dough with thumb or spoon handle.
• **Bake** at 375° for 8 to 10 minutes or until lightly browned. Remove cookies from oven, and press a chocolate kiss in center of each cookie. Transfer cookies to wire racks to cool completely. **Yield:** 4 dozen.

Ann Elsie Schmetzer
Madisonville, Kentucky

PEANUT BUTTER AND CHOCOLATE CHUNK COOKIES

½ cup butter or margarine, softened
¾ cup sugar
⅔ cup firmly packed brown sugar
2 egg whites
1¼ cups chunky peanut butter
1½ teaspoons vanilla extract
1 cup all-purpose flour
½ teaspoon baking soda
¼ teaspoon salt
5 (2.1-ounce) chocolate-covered crispy peanut-buttery candy bars, cut into ½-inch pieces *

• **Beat** butter at medium speed with an electric mixer until creamy; gradually add sugars, beating well. Add egg whites, beating well. Stir in peanut butter and vanilla. Set aside.
• **Combine** flour, soda, and salt; gradually add to butter mixture, mixing well. Stir in candy.
• **Shape** dough into 48 (1½-inch) balls, and place 2 inches apart on lightly greased cookie sheets.
• **Bake** at 350° for 11 minutes or until browned. Cool 3 minutes on cookie sheets; transfer to wire racks to cool completely. **Yield:** 4 dozen.

* For chocolate-covered crispy peanut-buttery candy bars, we used Butterfinger candy bars.

Linda Magers
Clemmons, North Carolina

SNOWBALL SURPRISES

1 cup butter or margarine, softened
½ cup sugar
1 teaspoon vanilla extract
2 cups all-purpose flour
1 cup finely chopped pecans
10 chocolate-coated peppermint mini patties, quartered
Sifted powdered sugar

• **Beat** butter at medium speed with an electric mixer until creamy; gradually add ½ cup sugar, beating well. Stir in vanilla. Gradually stir in flour and pecans, mixing well; cover and chill at least 1 hour.
• **Press** 1 tablespoon dough around each candy piece, forming a ball. Place on ungreased cookie sheets; bake at 350° for 12 minutes. (Cookies will not brown.) Let cool 5 minutes on cookie sheets, and roll in powdered sugar. Transfer to wire racks to cool. **Yield:** 40 cookies.

Note: You can freeze cookies in an airtight container up to 1 month.

Nellie H. Leech
Lexington, Virginia

CHOCOLATE-GINGERBREAD COOKIES

To gild these cookies, lightly brush edible gold luster dust onto the cookies, using a small, dry paintbrush.

½ cup butter or margarine, softened
¾ cup sugar
1 large egg
½ cup molasses
3 cups all-purpose flour
2 tablespoons cocoa
1 teaspoon baking soda
1 teaspoon ground cinnamon
½ teaspoon salt
½ teaspoon baking powder
Garnish: edible gold luster dust

• **Beat** butter in a large mixing bowl at medium speed with an electric mixer until creamy; gradually add sugar, beating well. Add egg and molasses, beating well.

- **Combine** flour and next 5 ingredients. Gradually add to butter mixture, beating until blended.
- **Divide** dough in half; wrap each portion of dough in plastic wrap, and chill 1 hour.
- **Roll** each portion of dough to ⅛-inch thickness on a lightly floured surface. Cut into desired sizes with 1½- to 2½-inch star-shaped cookie cutters; place on lightly greased cookie sheets.
- **Bake** at 350° for 5 to 7 minutes. Transfer cookies to wire racks to cool. Garnish, if desired. **Yield:** about 5 dozen.

Note: Edible gold luster dust adds shine to baked goods. You can find the gold luster dust at most cooking and baking specialty stores.

APRICOT KOLACHES

1 (12-ounce) jar apricot preserves
½ cup finely chopped walnuts or pecans
¼ teaspoon ground cinnamon
¼ teaspoon ground nutmeg
¼ teaspoon ground cloves
1 cup butter or margarine, softened
1 (8-ounce) package cream cheese, softened
2 tablespoons sugar
2 cups all-purpose flour
1 large egg, lightly beaten
1 tablespoon water
Sifted powdered sugar

- **Combine** first 5 ingredients in a small bowl; set filling aside.
- **Beat** butter and cream cheese at medium speed with an electric mixer until creamy; add sugar, beating well. Add flour, mixing at low speed until well blended. Divide dough into thirds.
- **Roll** each portion to ⅛-inch thickness on a lightly floured surface, and cut with a 3-inch round cutter. Spoon ½ teaspoon filling in center of each round. Combine egg and water; brush on edges. Fold opposite sides to center, slightly overlapping edges; pinch to seal. Place on lightly greased cookie sheets.

- **Bake** at 350° for 12 minutes or until golden. Transfer to wire racks to cool. Sprinkle with powdered sugar. **Yield:** 5 dozen.

JoAnn Ritmiller
Baltimore, Maryland

COCONUT SHORTBREAD COOKIES

¾ cup butter or margarine, softened
⅓ cup sugar
1½ teaspoons vanilla extract
1¾ cups all-purpose flour
½ teaspoon baking powder
¼ teaspoon salt
1 cup flaked coconut
1 cup (6 ounces) semisweet chocolate morsels
2 teaspoons shortening
Flaked coconut, toasted

- **Beat** butter at medium speed with an electric mixer until creamy; gradually add sugar, beating well. Stir in vanilla.
- **Combine** flour, baking powder, and salt; gradually add to butter mixture, mixing well. Stir in 1 cup coconut. Cover and chill 1 hour.
- **Roll** dough to ¼-inch thickness on a lightly floured surface. Cut dough into desired shapes with 2-inch cookie cutters, and place on lightly greased cookie sheets.
- **Bake** at 300° for 25 to 30 minutes or until edges are lightly browned. Remove cookies to wire racks to cool.
- **Melt** chocolate morsels and shortening in a small heavy saucepan over medium-low heat. Dip edges of cookies in chocolate mixture; dip in toasted coconut. Place on cookie sheets lined with wax paper. Chill 10 minutes. **Yield:** 2 dozen.

Note: You can freeze cookies up to 6 months.

Evelyn I. Randall
Spartanburg, South Carolina

SNOW FLURRIES

½ cup butter or margarine, softened
½ cup shortening
1 cup sugar
2 large eggs
1 tablespoon grated lemon rind
1 teaspoon vanilla extract
½ teaspoon almond extract
3½ cups all-purpose flour
½ teaspoon baking powder
½ teaspoon salt
⅓ cup raspberry jam
1 cup sifted powdered sugar

- **Beat** butter and shortening at medium speed with an electric mixer until soft and creamy; gradually add 1 cup sugar, beating well. Add eggs, lemon rind, and flavorings, mixing well.
- **Combine** flour, baking powder, and salt; gradually add to butter mixture, mixing well. Cover and chill 1 hour. Divide dough in half; store 1 portion in refrigerator.
- **Roll** remaining portion of dough to ⅛-inch thickness on a lightly floured surface. Cut with a 2½-inch star-shaped cutter, and place on ungreased cookie sheets.
- **Bake** at 375° for 7 to 8 minutes or until lightly browned; cool 2 minutes on cookie sheets. Transfer to wire racks to cool. Repeat procedure with remaining portion of dough.
- **Just** before serving, spread center of half of cookies with about ¼ teaspoon raspberry jam. Place a second cookie on top, alternating points of stars of top and bottom cookies. Sprinkle generously with powdered sugar. **Yield:** 5 dozen.

Edith Askins
Greenville, Texas

ITALIAN CINNAMON STICKS

¾ **cup sugar**
½ **cup walnuts, ground**
1 **teaspoon ground cinnamon**
1 **cup butter or margarine,**
    softened
1 **(8-ounce) package cream cheese,**
    softened
2½ **cups all-purpose flour**
1 **large egg, lightly beaten**

- **Combine** first 3 ingredients; set aside.
- **Beat** butter and cream cheese at medium speed with an electric mixer until creamy; gradually add flour, mixing until well blended.
- **Shape** dough into a ball; wrap in plastic wrap, and chill 30 minutes.
- **Divide** dough in half; place 1 portion between two sheets of lightly floured wax paper, and roll into a 10-inch square (about ⅛ inch thick). Brush with egg; sprinkle with half of sugar mixture. Cut into 5- x ½-inch strips; twist strips, and place on ungreased baking sheets. Repeat procedure with remaining dough, egg, and sugar mixture.
- **Bake** at 350° for 10 to 12 minutes or until golden. Transfer to wire racks to cool. **Yield:** about 6½ dozen.

Ellie Wells
Lakeland, Florida

PEPPERMINT ROUNDS

1 **cup butter or margarine,**
    softened
½ **cup sugar**
1 **large egg**
1 **teaspoon vanilla extract**
2½ **cups all-purpose flour**
½ **teaspoon salt**
1 **cup regular oats, uncooked**
⅓ **cup hard peppermint candy,**
    crushed
Powdered sugar
Frosting

- **Beat** butter at medium speed with an electric mixer until creamy; gradually add sugar, beating well. Add egg and vanilla, beating well.
- **Combine** flour and salt; add to butter mixture. Stir in oats and peppermint

candy. Cover and chill 1 hour. Divide dough in half.
- **Roll** each portion to ⅛-inch thickness on a surface dusted with powdered sugar. Cut with a 2½-inch cookie cutter; place on greased and foil-lined cookie sheets.
- **Bake** at 350° for 8 minutes; transfer to wire racks to cool.
- **Spread** cookies with white frosting. Before frosting sets, drizzle lines of pink frosting across top of each cookie. Carefully draw a wooden pick through lines of frosting for a scalloped pattern. **Yield:** 4 dozen.

Frosting

QUICK!

4 **cups sifted powdered sugar**
¼ to ½ **cup half-and-half**
Dash of salt
1 **teaspoon peppermint extract**
Red liquid food coloring

- **Combine** first 4 ingredients, stirring until smooth. (Add additional half-and-half for desired consistency.)
- **Remove** ¼ cup frosting, and stir in 1 or 2 drops of red food coloring for pink frosting. **Yield:** 1½ cups.

Out of Our League
Junior League of Greensboro,
North Carolina

LEMON THYME COOKIES

1 **cup butter or margarine,**
    softened
1½ **cups sugar**
2 **large eggs**
2½ **cups all-purpose flour**
2 **teaspoons cream of tartar**
½ **teaspoon salt**
½ **cup chopped fresh lemon thyme**

- **Beat** butter at medium speed with an electric mixer until creamy; gradually add sugar, beating well. Add eggs, one at a time, beating until blended after each addition.
- **Combine** flour, cream of tartar, and salt; gradually add to butter mixture. Beat at low speed until blended after each addition. Stir in lemon thyme.

- **Shape** dough into 2 (10-inch) rolls; wrap each in wax paper, and chill at least 2 hours.
- **Unwrap** dough; cut each roll into ½-inch-thick slices, and place on lightly greased cookie sheets.
- **Bake** at 350° for 10 minutes. Transfer to wire racks to cool. **Yield:** 3½ dozen.

MEMORY BOOK COOKIES
(pictured at right)

1 **cup butter or margarine,**
    softened
2 **cups firmly packed brown sugar**
2 **large eggs**
1 **teaspoon vanilla extract**
3½ **cups all-purpose flour**
1 **teaspoon baking soda**
½ **teaspoon salt**
1 **cup chopped pecans**

- **Beat** butter at medium speed with an electric mixer until creamy; gradually add sugar, beating well. Add eggs and vanilla; mix well.
- **Combine** flour, soda, and salt; gradually add to butter mixture, mixing well. Stir in pecans.
- **Shape** dough into two 16-inch rolls; wrap in wax paper, and chill at least 4 hours.
- **Unwrap** and cut into ⅓-inch slices; place on ungreased cookie sheets.
- **Bake** at 375° for 6 to 8 minutes. Transfer to wire racks to cool. **Yield:** 8 dozen.

Note: You can freeze dough up to 3 months. Slice dough while frozen, and bake as directed.

Kitty Cromer
Anderson, South Carolina

Memory Book Cookies

CHOCOLATE CHIP-CINNAMON BISCOTTI

⅓ cup butter or margarine, softened
½ cup firmly packed brown sugar
½ cup sugar
1 tablespoon instant coffee or espresso granules
2 large eggs
2 cups all-purpose flour
1½ teaspoons baking powder
⅛ teaspoon salt
½ teaspoon ground cinnamon
1 cup chopped walnuts or pecans
1 cup semisweet chocolate mini-morsels
2 (2-ounce) squares vanilla-flavored candy coating, melted

• **Combine** first 4 ingredients in a large mixing bowl; beat at medium speed with an electric mixer until light and creamy. Add eggs, one at a time, beating until blended.
• **Combine** flour and next 3 ingredients; add to butter mixture, stirring until blended. Fold in nuts and chocolate morsels. Divide dough in half.
• **Shape** each portion of dough into a 10- x 2-inch log on a lightly greased cookie sheet.
• **Bake** at 350° for 25 minutes or until firm. Let cool on cookie sheet 5 minutes. Transfer logs to wire racks to cool completely.
• **Cut** each log diagonally into ½-inch-thick slices with a serrated knife, using a gentle sawing motion. Place slices on ungreased cookie sheets.
• **Bake** at 350° for 10 minutes; turn cookies over, and bake 10 additional minutes. Transfer to wire racks to cool.
• **Dip** 1 side of each cookie into candy coating; chill until set. **Yield:** 2½ dozen.

Carol Y. Chastain
San Antonio, Texas

CHOCOLATE-HAZELNUT BISCOTTI

For the same number of calories as a rice cake, you can have a slice of biscotto.

2 large eggs
⅔ cup sugar
1 tablespoon Frangelico or other hazelnut-flavored liqueur
2 cups sifted cake flour
1½ teaspoons baking powder
¼ teaspoon salt
1½ tablespoons cocoa
⅔ cup hazelnuts, chopped and toasted
Vegetable cooking spray

• **Beat** eggs at medium speed with an electric mixer until foamy. Gradually add sugar, beating at high speed until mixture is thick and pale. Add liqueur, beating until blended. Combine flour and next 3 ingredients; fold into egg mixture. Fold in nuts. Cover and chill 30 minutes.
• **Coat** a cookie sheet with cooking spray. Divide dough into 3 portions, and spoon portions 2 inches apart onto cookie sheet.
• **Shape** each portion of dough into an 8- x 1½-inch strip. Cover and chill 30 minutes; reshape dough, if necessary.
• **Bake** at 375° for 20 minutes or until lightly browned. Transfer to wire racks to cool. Cut diagonally into ½-inch-thick slices. Lay slices flat on cookie sheet. Bake at 375° for 5 minutes; turn slices over, and bake 5 additional minutes. Transfer to wire racks to cool. **Yield:** 3½ dozen.

Andy Lorber
Atlanta, Georgia

♥ Per cookie: Calories 50
Fat 1.7g Cholesterol 11mg
Sodium 17mg

FRUITCAKE BISCOTTI

Here's a fresh look at tradition – the flavors of fruitcake in a crunchy cookie. But don't worry about that old stigma. These are so good, there's no chance they'll still be hanging around after the New Year.

½ cup butter or margarine, softened
2 cups sugar
4 large eggs
1½ teaspoons grated lemon rind
½ teaspoon vanilla extract
¼ teaspoon almond extract
5 cups all-purpose flour
2 teaspoons baking soda
1 teaspoon baking powder
½ teaspoon salt
¾ cup whole blanched or slivered almonds, coarsely chopped
¾ cup dried cranberries
¾ cup dried tart cherries
½ cup candied orange rind

• **Beat** butter at medium speed with an electric mixer until creamy; gradually add sugar, beating well. Add eggs, one at a time, beating after each addition. Add rind and flavorings, mixing well.
• **Combine** flour and next 3 ingredients in a bowl; add to butter mixture, beating just until dry ingredients are moistened.
• **Turn** dough out onto a lightly floured surface; lightly flour hands, and knead in almonds, cranberries, cherries, and orange rind. Divide dough in half.
• **Shape** each portion into a 14- x 2-inch log on a lightly greased cookie sheet. Flatten logs slightly.
• **Bake** at 325° for 30 to 35 minutes or until golden. Cool on cookie sheet 5 minutes. Transfer to a wire rack to cool.
• **Cut** each log diagonally into ½-inch-thick slices with a serrated knife, using a gentle sawing motion. Place slices on ungreased cookie sheets.
• **Bake** at 325° for 10 minutes; turn cookies over, and bake 10 additional minutes. Transfer to wire racks to cool. **Yield:** 3½ dozen.

Note: If you can't find dried cranberries and cherries, substitute raisins, dates, or chopped dried apricots.

Cindy Briscoe
Birmingham, Alabama

RAISIN BARS

1 cup all-purpose flour
¼ cup sugar
⅓ cup butter or margarine
2 large eggs
1 cup sugar
2 tablespoons all-purpose flour
½ teaspoon baking powder
¼ teaspoon salt
1 tablespoon grated orange rind
2 tablespoons orange juice
¾ cup raisins, chopped
½ cup flaked coconut
2 teaspoons orange juice
2 teaspoons lemon juice
1½ teaspoons butter or
    margarine, softened
1 cup sifted powdered sugar

• **Combine** 1 cup flour and ¼ cup sugar; cut in ⅓ cup butter with pastry blender until mixture is crumbly. Press mixture in bottom of a lightly greased 9-inch square pan.
• **Bake** at 350° for 15 minutes.
• **Combine** eggs and next 8 ingredients, stirring until blended. Pour over crust.
• **Bake** at 350° for 20 to 25 minutes.
• **Combine** 2 teaspoons orange juice, lemon juice, and 1½ teaspoons butter in a small bowl; beat at medium speed with an electric mixer until smooth. Gradually add powdered sugar, beating until smooth. Pour mixture over hot layer. Cool in pan on a wire rack. Cut into bars. Freeze in an airtight container up to 3 months, if desired. **Yield:** about 3 dozen.

Three Rivers Cookbook I
Child Health Association
Sewickley, Pennsylvania

GOOEY TURTLE BARS

QUICK!

½ cup butter, melted
1½ cups vanilla wafer crumbs
2 cups (12 ounces) semisweet
    chocolate morsels
1 cup pecan pieces
1 (12-ounce) jar caramel topping

• **Combine** butter and wafer crumbs in a 13- x 9- x 2-inch baking pan; press in bottom of pan. Sprinkle with chocolate morsels and pecans.
• **Remove** lid from caramel topping; microwave at HIGH 1 to 1½ minutes or until hot, stirring after 30 seconds. Drizzle over pecans.
• **Bake** at 350° for 12 to 15 minutes or until morsels melt; cool in pan on a wire rack. Chill at least 30 minutes; cut into squares. **Yield:** 2 dozen.

PEANUT BUTTER-JAM BARS

½ cup butter or margarine,
    softened
½ cup sugar
½ cup firmly packed brown
    sugar
½ cup chunky peanut butter
1 large egg
1 teaspoon vanilla extract
1¼ cups all-purpose flour
¾ teaspoon baking soda
½ teaspoon baking powder
2 cups peanut butter morsels,
    divided
1 cup strawberry jam

• **Beat** butter at medium speed with an electric mixer until creamy; gradually add sugars, beating well. Add peanut butter, egg, and vanilla, mixing well.
• **Combine** flour, soda, and baking powder; gradually add to butter mixture, mixing well. Reserve 1 cup dough.
• **Stir** 1 cup peanut butter morsels into remaining dough; press in bottom of a 13- x 9- x 2-inch pan. Spread jam evenly over dough. Crumble reserved dough over jam, and sprinkle with remaining peanut butter morsels.
• **Bake** at 325° for 40 minutes or until golden. Cool completely in pan on a wire rack, and cut into bars. Cookies may be frozen up to 3 months. **Yield:** about 3 dozen.

Patty Flowers
Midland, Texas

MISSISSIPPI MUD

2 cups sugar
1½ cups all-purpose flour
½ cup cocoa
2 teaspoons baking powder
½ teaspoon salt
1 cup butter or margarine, melted
4 large eggs, lightly beaten
1 cup chopped pecans, divided
3 cups miniature marshmallows
Chocolate Frosting

• **Combine** first 5 ingredients in a large bowl. Add butter and eggs, stirring until smooth. Stir in ½ cup pecans. Pour mixture into a greased and floured 13- x 9- x 2-inch pan.
• **Bake** at 350° for 25 to 30 minutes or until a wooden pick inserted in center comes out clean. Immediately sprinkle marshmallows over top; return to oven, and bake 1 additional minute. Remove from oven; spread marshmallows on top. Let stand 5 minutes.
• **Spread** Chocolate Frosting evenly over marshmallows, and sprinkle with remaining ½ cup pecans. Cool completely in pan on a wire rack, and cut into squares. **Yield:** 2 dozen.

Chocolate Frosting

QUICK!

1 (16-ounce) package powdered
    sugar, sifted
⅓ cup cocoa
½ cup butter or margarine, melted
⅓ cup evaporated milk
1 teaspoon vanilla extract

• **Combine** all ingredients in a large mixing bowl; beat at medium speed with an electric mixer until dry ingredients are moistened. Beat mixture at high speed until spreading consistency. **Yield:** 2½ cups.

Note: If marshmallows do not spread easily after 1 minute in oven, do not bake longer. Let stand 1 to 2 minutes to soften.

Dee Elkins
Little Rock, Arkansas

GERMAN CHOCOLATE CHESS SQUARES

1 (18.25-ounce) package German chocolate cake mix with pudding
1 large egg, lightly beaten
½ cup butter or margarine, melted
1 cup chopped pecans
1 (8-ounce) package cream cheese, softened
2 large eggs
1 (16-ounce) package powdered sugar, sifted

• **Combine** first 4 ingredients in a large bowl, stirring until dry ingredients are moistened. Press in bottom of a greased 13- x 9- x 2-inch pan; set aside.
• **Combine** cream cheese, 2 eggs, and 1 cup sifted powdered sugar; beat at medium speed with an electric mixer until blended. Gradually add remaining powdered sugar, beating well. Pour over chocolate layer, spreading evenly.
• **Bake** at 350° for 40 minutes. Cool in pan on a wire rack, and cut into squares. **Yield:** 4 dozen.

Barbara Sutton
Portsmouth, Virginia

RICH BROWNIES

QUICK!

1 (10¼-ounce) package fudge brownie mix
½ cup miniature marshmallows
½ cup semisweet chocolate morsels
½ cup chopped pecans

• **Prepare** brownie mix according to package directions, folding marshmallows, chocolate morsels, and pecans into batter. Spread batter evenly in a greased 8-inch square pan.
• **Bake** at 350° for 24 minutes or until done. Cool in pan on a wire rack; cut into squares. **Yield:** 16 brownies.

TRIPLE DECKER BROWNIES

1½ cups quick-cooking oats, toasted
1 cup all-purpose flour
1 cup firmly packed brown sugar
½ teaspoon baking soda
¼ teaspoon salt
¾ cup butter or margarine, melted
2 (1-ounce) squares unsweetened chocolate
½ cup butter or margarine
1½ cups sugar
2 large eggs
1⅓ cups all-purpose flour
½ teaspoon baking powder
¼ teaspoon salt
½ cup milk
1 teaspoon vanilla extract
1 cup chopped pecans
Chocolate Frosting

• **Combine** first 5 ingredients in a large bowl; add ¾ cup melted butter, stirring well. Press mixture in bottom of two greased 8-inch square pans. Bake at 350° for 10 minutes.
• **Melt** chocolate and ½ cup butter in a large heavy saucepan over low heat; remove from heat. Add 1½ cups sugar and eggs, mixing well.
• **Combine** 1⅓ cups flour, baking powder, and ¼ teaspoon salt; add to chocolate mixture alternately with milk. Stir in vanilla and pecans. Spread over crust, and bake at 350° for 20 to 25 minutes. Cool in pans on wire racks. Spread with Chocolate Frosting. Cut into 2-inch squares. **Yield:** 32 brownies.

Chocolate Frosting

QUICK!

2 (1-ounce) squares unsweetened chocolate
¼ cup butter or margarine
3 cups sifted powdered sugar
2 teaspoons vanilla extract
3 to 4 tablespoons hot water

• **Melt** chocolate and butter in a heavy saucepan over low heat; remove from heat. Stir in powdered sugar, vanilla, and 1 tablespoon water. Stir in additional water until desired spreading consistency. **Yield:** 1½ cups.

NO-BAKE BROWNIES

QUICK!

2 cups (12 ounces) semisweet chocolate morsels
1 (12-ounce) can evaporated milk, divided
3 cups vanilla wafer crumbs
2 cups miniature marshmallows
1 cup chopped pecans
1 cup sifted powdered sugar
½ teaspoon salt

• **Combine** chocolate morsels and 1 cup evaporated milk in a heavy saucepan; cook over low heat until morsels melt, stirring occasionally. Set chocolate mixture aside.
• **Combine** wafer crumbs and remaining 4 ingredients in a large bowl; stir until blended. Reserve ½ cup chocolate mixture. Stir remaining chocolate mixture into crumb mixture. Press in a well-greased 9-inch square pan.
• **Combine** reserved ½ cup chocolate mixture and 2 teaspoons evaporated milk; spread over crumb mixture. (Reserve remaining evaporated milk for another use.) Cover and chill. Cut into squares. **Yield:** 3 dozen.

Jane Tutwiler
Birmingham, Alabama

CANDY BAR BROWNIES
(pictured on page 101)

4 large eggs, lightly beaten
2 cups sugar
¾ cup butter or margarine, melted
2 teaspoons vanilla extract
1½ cups all-purpose flour
½ teaspoon baking powder
¼ teaspoon salt
⅓ cup cocoa
4 (2.07-ounce) chocolate-coated caramel-peanut nougat bars, coarsely chopped *
3 (1.55-ounce) milk chocolate bars, finely chopped

• **Combine** first 4 ingredients in a large bowl; stir well.
• **Combine** flour and next 3 ingredients; stir into sugar mixture. Fold in chopped nougat bars.

- **Spoon** into a greased and floured 13- x 9- x 2-inch pan; sprinkle with chopped milk chocolate bars. Bake at 350° for 30 to 35 minutes. Cool in pan on a wire rack; cut into squares. **Yield:** 2½ dozen.

✻ For chocolate-coated caramel-peanut nougat bars, we used Snickers.

Mardee Johnson
Winston-Salem, North Carolina

MACADAMIA-FUDGE DESIGNER BROWNIES

2½ cups sugar
1½ cups butter or margarine
5 (1-ounce) squares unsweetened chocolate
6 large eggs, lightly beaten
2 cups all-purpose flour
1 cup coarsely chopped macadamia nuts or almonds
Fudge Frosting
Garnish: chopped macadamia nuts

- **Combine** sugar, butter, and chocolate in a large saucepan; cook over low heat until chocolate melts, stirring often. Remove from heat; cool 10 minutes.
- **Stir** in eggs, flour, and nuts. Pour mixture into a greased and floured 13- x 9- x 2-inch pan.
- **Bake** at 350° for 30 to 35 minutes. Cool in pan on a wire rack.
- **Pour** Fudge Frosting over top; chill 15 minutes, and cut into squares. Garnish, if desired. **Yield:** 4 dozen.

Fudge Frosting

QUICK!

1 cup whipping cream
12 (1-ounce) squares semisweet chocolate

- **Heat** whipping cream in a medium saucepan over medium heat; add chocolate, stirring until smooth. Remove from heat, and cool to room temperature. **Yield:** 2½ cups.

Daisy Cook
Tyler, Texas

RASPBERRY BROWNIES

QUICK!

½ cup butter or margarine, softened
1 cup sugar
2 large eggs
2 (1-ounce) squares unsweetened chocolate, melted
¾ cup all-purpose flour
1 cup chopped walnuts
⅓ cup raspberry jam

- **Beat** butter at medium speed with an electric mixer until soft and creamy; gradually add sugar, beating well. Add eggs and melted chocolate, mixing well. Add flour, mixing well; stir in walnuts.
- **Spoon** half of batter into a greased and floured 9-inch square pan. Spread jam over batter; top with remaining batter. Bake at 350° for about 28 to 30 minutes. **Yield:** 3 dozen brownies.

Mrs. Harland J. Stone
Ocala, Florida

TURTLE CANDIES

2 cups (12 ounces) semisweet chocolate morsels
64 pecan halves (about 1¼ cups)
28 caramels, unwrapped
2 tablespoons whipping cream

- **Microwave** chocolate morsels in a glass bowl at HIGH for 1½ minutes, stirring after 1 minute. Stir until smooth; cool until slightly thickened.
- **Drop** chocolate by tablespoonfuls onto a wax paper-lined baking sheet, shaping into 16 (1½-inch) circles. Reserve remaining chocolate. Arrange 4 pecans over each circle of chocolate, and chill until firm.
- **Place** caramels and whipping cream in a glass bowl. Microwave at HIGH 2 minutes or until caramels melt; stir after 1 minute. Let stand 4 minutes or until slightly thickened. Spoon caramel mixture evenly over pecans.
- **Microwave** remaining chocolate at HIGH 1 minute, stirring after 30 seconds; quickly spread chocolate over caramel mixture. Chill until firm. **Yield:** 16 candies.

PEANUT CLUSTERS

QUICK!

2 cups peanut butter morsels or butterscotch morsels
1 cup (6 ounces) semisweet chocolate morsels
1 (12-ounce) can salted peanuts

- **Combine** peanut butter morsels and chocolate morsels in a heavy saucepan; cook over low heat until morsels melt, stirring often. Remove from heat; add peanuts, stirring to coat.
- **Drop** by rounded teaspoonfuls onto wax paper. Cool completely, and store in an airtight container at room temperature. **Yield:** about 4 dozen.

Judy Hughes
Indian Harbour Beach, Florida

MICROWAVE TOFFEE

QUICK!

½ cup finely chopped pecans
½ cup butter or margarine
1 cup sugar
1 teaspoon salt
¼ cup water
¾ cup semisweet chocolate morsels
¼ cup finely chopped pecans

- **Sprinkle** ½ cup pecans in a 9-inch circle on a greased cookie sheet; set aside.
- **Coat** top 2 inches of a 2½-quart glass bowl with butter; place remaining butter in bowl. Add sugar, salt, and water (do not stir.) Microwave at HIGH 11 minutes or until mixture just begins to turn light brown; pour over pecans. Sprinkle with morsels; let stand 1 minute. Spread morsels over sugar mixture, and sprinkle with ¼ cup chopped pecans. Cover and chill until firm. Break into bite-size pieces. **Yield:** 1 pound.

Jan Ramsey
Quitaque, Texas

Chocolate Pralines;
Basic Pralines;
Orange Pralines

BASIC PRALINES
(pictured at left)

Vegetable cooking spray
1½ cups sugar
¾ cup firmly packed brown
    sugar
¼ cup plus 2 tablespoons
    butter
½ cup milk
1½ cups chopped pecans

• **Lightly** coat a few sheets of wax paper with cooking spray; set aside.
• **Combine** 1½ cups sugar and remaining ingredients in a heavy 3-quart saucepan. Bring to a boil over medium heat, stirring constantly. Boil, uncovered, stirring constantly, 1 to 2 minutes or until a candy thermometer registers 220°. (You may need to lower the heat with a thinner saucepan, and rely on a candy thermometer instead of a timer.)
• **Remove** from heat, and beat with a wooden spoon 4 to 6 minutes or just until mixture begins to thicken. Working rapidly, drop by tablespoonfuls onto prepared wax paper; let stand until firm. **Yield:** 2½ dozen.

Orange Pralines: Add 2½ to 3 tablespoons Cointreau or other orange-flavored liqueur before cooking.

Café au Lait Pralines: Add 1½ tablespoons instant coffee granules before cooking.

Mocha Pralines: Add 1½ to 2 tablespoons instant coffee granules and ½ cup semisweet chocolate morsels before cooking.

Chocolate-Peanut Butter Pralines: Add ½ cup semisweet chocolate morsels and ¼ cup creamy peanut butter before cooking.

Peanut Butter Pralines: Add 2 tablespoons creamy peanut butter before cooking, and stir 1 teaspoon vanilla into cooked mixture before beating.

Chocolate-Mint Pralines: Add 5 (½-ounce) chocolate-covered peppermint patties before cooking.

Hot Spicy Pralines: Add ½ teaspoon ground red pepper before cooking.

Bourbon Pralines: Add 3 tablespoons bourbon before cooking.

Chocolate Pralines: Add 2 (1-ounce) squares unsweetened chocolate before cooking.

Vanilla Pralines: Stir 1 teaspoon vanilla extract into cooked mixture before beating.

Joe Cahn
New Orleans School of Cooking and
General Store in Jax Brewery
New Orleans, Louisiana

BITTERSWEET TRUFFLES

½ cup butter or margarine
¾ cup cocoa
1 (14-ounce) can sweetened
    condensed milk
1 teaspoon vanilla extract
Cocoa

• **Melt** butter in a heavy saucepan over low heat; stir in ¾ cup cocoa. Stir in milk until smooth. Cook over medium heat, stirring constantly, until thickened and smooth (about 3 minutes). Remove from heat; stir in vanilla. Pour into a greased 8-inch square pan.
• **Cover** and chill 3 hours or until firm.
• **Shape** mixture into 1¼-inch balls; roll in additional cocoa. Place balls in miniature paper baking cups. Store in an airtight container in the refrigerator up to 1 week. **Yield:** 3 dozen.

Rublelene Singleton
Scotts Hill, Tennessee

ORANGE-PECAN TRUFFLES

8 (1-ounce) squares semisweet
    chocolate
⅓ cup butter or margarine
½ cup orange marmalade
½ cup chopped pecans, toasted
2 tablespoons orange-flavored
    liqueur *
1 cup finely chopped pecans

• **Combine** chocolate squares and butter in top of a double boiler; bring water to a boil. Reduce heat to low; cook until chocolate melts, stirring occasionally.
• **Remove** from heat; stir in marmalade, ½ cup chopped pecans, and liqueur. Cool slightly; cover and chill until firm (at least 2 hours).
• **Shape** truffle mixture into ¾-inch balls, and roll in 1 cup finely chopped pecans. (Truffle mixture tends to stick to hands.) Place truffles in paper or foil bonbon cups.
• **Store** candy in airtight containers in refrigerator up to 3 weeks or freeze up to 12 months. Serve cold. **Yield:** 3 dozen.

* You can substitute 2 tablespoons of orange juice for liqueur.

Louise W. Mayer
Richmond, Virginia

MICROWAVE CHOCOLATE FUDGE

QUICK!

3 cups semisweet chocolate
      morsels
1 (14-ounce) can sweetened
      condensed milk
¼ cup butter or margarine, cut
      into pieces
1 cup chopped walnuts

● **Combine** first 3 ingredients in a 2-
quart glass bowl. Microwave at MED-
IUM (50% power) 4 to 5 minutes, stirring
at 1½-minute intervals.
● **Stir** in chopped walnuts, and pour
mixture into a buttered 8-inch square
dish. Cover and chill at least 2 hours.
Cut into squares. **Yield:** 2 pounds.

Suzan L. Wiener
Spring Hill, Florida

DIAMOND FUDGE

QUICK!

1 cup (6 ounces) semisweet
      chocolate morsels
1 cup creamy peanut butter
½ cup butter or margarine
1 cup sifted powdered sugar

● **Combine** first 3 ingredients in a
saucepan; cook over low heat, stirring
constantly, just until mixture is smooth.
Remove from heat. Add powdered
sugar, stirring until smooth.
● **Spoon** into a buttered 8-inch square
pan; cover and chill until firm. Let stand
at room temperature about 10 minutes
before cutting into squares. Store in refrigerator. **Yield:** 1½ pounds.

A Centennial Sampler
The American Association of University
Women of Elkins, West Virginia

FOUR-CHIPS FUDGE

¾ cup butter or margarine
1 (14-ounce) can sweetened
      condensed milk
3 tablespoons milk
2 cups (12 ounces) semisweet
      chocolate morsels
1 (11½-ounce) package milk
      chocolate morsels
1 (10-ounce) package peanut
      butter-flavored morsels
1 cup butterscotch-flavored
      morsels
1 (7-ounce) jar marshmallow
      cream
1½ teaspoons vanilla extract
½ to 1 teaspoon almond extract
1 pound walnuts, coarsely chopped

● **Melt** butter in a heavy Dutch oven
over low heat; stir in condensed milk
and milk. Add all morsels; cook, stirring
constantly, until smooth. Remove from
heat; stir in marshmallow cream and flavorings. Stir in walnuts.
● **Spoon** into a buttered 15- x 10- x 1-
inch jellyroll pan; spread evenly. Cover
and chill; cut into squares. Store in an
airtight container in the refrigerator.
Yield: 5 pounds.

Annie Grace
Walkertown, North Carolina

MINT FUDGE

2 cups sugar
⅓ cup cocoa
Pinch of salt
⅔ cup milk
2 tablespoons light corn syrup
¼ cup butter or margarine
¼ teaspoon peppermint extract
1 cup sifted powdered sugar
3 to 4 teaspoons milk
3 drops of peppermint extract
1 or 2 drops of green liquid food
      coloring

● **Combine** first 5 ingredients in a heavy
3-quart saucepan; bring mixture to a
boil over medium heat, stirring constantly. Cover and boil 3 minutes.
● **Remove** lid, and cook until sugar mixture reaches soft ball stage or candy

thermometer registers 234°. Remove
from heat; cool 10 minutes.
● **Add** butter and ¼ teaspoon peppermint extract; beat until mixture thickens and begins to lose its gloss.
● **Pour** mixture into a buttered 8-inch
square pan or dish. Cool and cut into
squares.
● **Place** squares at least ½-inch apart on
a wax-paper lined baking sheet; set
aside.
● **Combine** powdered sugar and remaining 3 ingredients, stirring until
blended.
● **Place** mixture in a heavy-duty, zip-top
plastic bag; seal. Snip a tiny hole in one
corner of bag; drizzle over fudge. **Yield:**
1¼ pounds.

WHITE CHOCOLATE-COFFEE
FUDGE

2 cups sugar
⅔ cup evaporated milk
½ cup butter or margarine
12 large marshmallows
1 tablespoon instant coffee
      granules
Pinch of salt
1 (6-ounce) package white
      chocolate-flavored baking bar,
      chopped
1 cup chopped pecans or walnuts
1 teaspoon vanilla extract

● **Combine** first 6 ingredients in a large
saucepan. Cook over medium-low heat,
stirring constantly, until mixture comes
to a boil.
● **Cover**, reduce heat, and simmer 5
minutes; remove from heat.
● **Add** baking bar and remaining ingredients; stir until chocolate melts. Spoon
into a buttered 8-inch square pan,
spreading evenly. Cool and cut into
squares. **Yield:** 2 pounds.

At right: *Berry Napoleon (page 121)*

DESSERTS

ORANGE BAKED APPLES WITH COOKIE CRUMBS

6 medium cooking apples (about 2¼ pounds)
¼ cup unsweetened apple juice
1 tablespoon lemon juice
1 (4-inch) stick cinnamon, broken in half
⅓ cup orange marmalade
6 small gingersnaps, crushed

● **Core** apples, starting at stem end, to, but not through, opposite end. Peel top third of each apple.
● **Place** apples in an 11- x 7- x 1½-inch baking dish; add apple juice, lemon juice, and cinnamon stick to baking dish. Cover.
● **Bake** at 350° for 30 minutes. Uncover and spoon marmalade evenly into center of each apple; sprinkle with crushed gingersnaps. Bake 10 additional minutes or until apples are tender. **Yield:** 6 servings.

Beth Workman
Greensboro, North Carolina

CHAMPAGNE ORANGES

½ cup sugar
½ cup orange marmalade
1½ cups champagne *
8 large navel oranges, peeled and sectioned
½ cup slivered almonds, toasted

● **Combine** sugar and orange marmalade in a small saucepan; cook over medium heat until sugar dissolves, stirring often. Remove from heat, and let cool slightly.
● **Combine** sugar mixture, champagne, and orange sections, stirring gently. Cover and chill 8 hours. To serve, spoon orange sections into individual compotes or dessert dishes, and sprinkle evenly with toasted almonds. **Yield:** 8 servings.

* Substitute 1½ cups sparkling white grape juice for champagne.

Louise Bainter
Grove, Oklahoma

GINGER-ORANGE BAKED FRUIT

6 cups pitted prunes, cut in half
6 cups frozen sliced peaches, thawed and drained
1½ cups raisins
3 cups orange juice
1 (18-ounce) jar orange marmalade
1 tablespoon ground ginger
1 (3½-ounce) can flaked coconut, toasted

● **Layer** first 3 ingredients in a lightly greased 13- x 9- x 2-inch baking dish.
● **Combine** orange juice, marmalade, and ginger; pour over fruit.
● **Bake**, uncovered, at 350° for 45 to 50 minutes or until bubbly; sprinkle with coconut. Serve with a slotted spoon. If desired, bake fruit as directed, omitting coconut; spoon into individual compotes, and sprinkle with coconut. **Yield:** 18 to 20 servings.

Joel Allard
San Antonio, Texas

MIXED FRUIT COMPOTE

½ cup dried pitted prunes
½ cup dried apricot halves
1 cup apple juice
1 (2-inch) stick cinnamon
1 tablespoon grated orange rind
1 navel orange, peeled, sectioned, and chopped
1 grapefruit, peeled, sectioned, and chopped
1 Granny Smith apple, peeled, cored, and chopped
1 banana, sliced
⅓ cup orange juice
1 to 2 tablespoons brown sugar
3 tablespoons chopped walnuts, toasted

● **Combine** prunes and apricots in a small bowl; set aside.
● **Combine** apple juice and cinnamon stick in a small saucepan; cook over medium heat until hot, and pour over fruit mixture. Cover and let stand 8 hours.

● **Remove** and discard cinnamon stick; add orange rind and next 6 ingredients, tossing gently. Sprinkle with walnuts. **Yield:** 6 to 8 servings.

Dairy Hollow House
Eureka Springs, Arkansas

HONEYED PEACHES 'N' CREAM

The subtle tang and nutty hint of the luxuriously thick sauce adds flattering flavor notes to this ginger-spiced dessert.

¼ cup Chambord or other raspberry-flavored liqueur
2 tablespoons honey
1 teaspoon lemon juice
½ teaspoon ground ginger
4 cups sliced fresh or frozen peaches, thawed
Crème Fraîche Sauce or vanilla ice cream
2 tablespoons slivered almonds, toasted (optional)

● **Combine** first 4 ingredients in a bowl; add peaches, tossing gently. Cover and chill 2 hours.
● **Spoon** mixture into individual dessert dishes; top with Crème Fraîche Sauce or vanilla ice cream. Sprinkle with almonds, if desired, and serve immediately. **Yield:** 6 servings.

Crème Fraîche Sauce
QUICK!

⅓ cup sour cream
⅓ cup whipping cream
2 tablespoons powdered sugar

● **Combine** all ingredients; cover and chill 8 hours. **Yield:** ⅔ cup.

Louise Jackson
Shreveport, Louisiana

CARAMEL PEACHES

*Four simple ingredients and
one baking dish make this caramelized
peach dessert a must-try recipe. Fresh
peaches are our first choice, but
when they're not in season,
substitute frozen peach slices.*

6 large peaches, peeled and sliced *
3 tablespoons sugar
¼ cup butter or margarine, cut
   into small pieces
1 cup whipping cream

● **Place** peaches in a lightly greased 11-
x 7- x 1½-inch baking dish; sprinkle
with sugar, and dot with butter.
● **Bake** at 400° for 25 to 30 minutes or
until tender and liquid is slightly thickened, stirring once. Stir in whipping
cream; bake 15 additional minutes, stirring every 5 minutes. Cool on a wire
rack 15 minutes; serve warm. **Yield:** 4 to
6 servings.

* You can substitute 6 cups frozen
sliced peaches, thawed, for fresh.

PEACH MELBA MERINGUES WITH BUTTERMILK CUSTARD SAUCE

4 egg whites
¼ teaspoon cream of tartar
1 cup sugar
Buttermilk Custard Sauce
5 cups sliced fresh peaches
1 cup fresh raspberries
Raspberry Sauce

● **Beat** egg whites and cream of tartar at
high speed with an electric mixer until
foamy. Add sugar, 1 tablespoon at a
time, beating until stiff peaks form and
sugar dissolves (2 to 4 minutes).
● **Drop** mixture, ½ cup at a time, onto a
baking sheet lined with parchment
paper; shape with a spoon to resemble
shallow bowls.
● **Bake** at 250° for 1 hour. Turn oven off,
and let stand in oven 1½ hours. Remove
from oven, and cool completely; remove
from paper.
● **Pour** Buttermilk Custard Sauce evenly
onto serving plates; top with meringue

shells. Spoon peaches and raspberries
into shells.
● **Place** ¼ cup Raspberry Sauce in a
heavy-duty, zip-top plastic bag; seal.
Snip a tiny hole in one corner of bag;
squeeze small circles of sauce onto Buttermilk Custard Sauce around shells.
Pull a wooden pick through circles in
several directions to make a design.
● **Drizzle** remaining sauce over fruit;
serve immediately. **Yield:** 8 servings.

♥ Per serving: Calories 344
Fat 3.8g   Cholesterol 113mg
Sodium 127mg

Buttermilk Custard Sauce

QUICK!

3 cups buttermilk
¾ cup sugar
1 tablespoon cornstarch
4 egg yolks, lightly beaten
1 teaspoon vanilla extract

● **Combine** first 4 ingredients in a heavy
saucepan, whisking until blended. Bring
to a boil over medium heat, whisking
constantly; cook 1 minute, whisking
constantly. Remove from heat; stir in
vanilla. Cover and chill. **Yield:** 3 cups.

Raspberry Sauce

QUICK!

1 (12-ounce) package frozen
   unsweetened raspberries,
   thawed and undrained
2 tablespoons sugar
2 tablespoons Framboise or other
   raspberry-flavored liqueur
1 teaspoon cornstarch
1 tablespoon cold water

● **Combine** first 3 ingredients in container of an electric blender; process
until smooth, stopping once to scrape
down sides. Pour through a wire-mesh
strainer into a small saucepan, pressing
with back of a spoon; discard seeds.
● **Combine** cornstarch and water; stir
until smooth. Stir into raspberry mixture in pan. Bring to a boil over medium
heat; boil 1 minute, stirring constantly.
Yield: 1 cup.

*Susan H. Clark
Greer, South Carolina*

PEAR-BLUE CHEESE GRATIN

¼ cup sugar
1 tablespoon all-purpose flour
1 teaspoon cornstarch
1 large egg
1 egg yolk
1 cup half-and-half
2 tablespoons butter or
   margarine
½ teaspoon vanilla extract
2 tablespoons cream cheese,
   softened
3 tablespoons crumbled blue
   cheese, softened
1 (8½-ounce) can pear halves,
   drained
2 to 3 tablespoons sifted powdered
   sugar
¼ cup walnuts, chopped
¼ cup gingersnap crumbs

● **Combine** first 3 ingredients in a small
bowl; set aside. Beat egg and egg yolk in
a small mixing bowl at high speed with
an electric mixer until thick and pale;
add sugar mixture, beating until
blended. Set aside.
● **Cook** half-and-half in a small saucepan over medium heat until hot (do not
boil). Gradually stir about one-fourth of
hot liquid into egg mixture; add to remaining hot mixture, stirring constantly
with a wire whisk. Cook over low heat,
stirring constantly, until thickened. Remove from heat; stir 1 minute. Transfer
to a bowl; stir in butter and vanilla.
Cover and chill at least 2 hours or
overnight.
● **Combine** cream cheese and blue
cheese; beat at medium speed with an
electric mixer until smooth. Fold into
chilled mixture; spoon evenly into four
lightly greased 4-inch gratin dishes or
10-ounce custard cups. Place an in-
verted pear half in each; sprinkle with
powdered sugar. Place gratins in a 9-
inch square pan; broil 5½ inches from
heat (with electric oven door partially
opened) 1½ minutes or until lightly
browned. Combine walnuts and gingersnap crumbs; sprinkle evenly over
gratins. Broil 30 to 40 additional seconds. Serve warm. **Yield:** 4 servings.

Pear en Croûte

PEARS EN CROÛTE
(pictured at left)

2 (15-ounce) packages
    refrigerated piecrusts
5 or 6 firm ripe pears, unpeeled
    (about 2 pounds)
1 egg yolk
1 tablespoon water
Caramel Sauce
Garnish: fresh mint leaves

• **Unfold** piecrusts, one at a time; place on a lightly floured surface, and roll each into a 10-inch square. Cut each square into 1-inch strips. Starting at bottom of pear, carefully begin wrapping with 1 pastry strip, overlapping strip ¼ inch as you cover pear. Continue wrapping by moistening ends of strips with water and joining to previous strip until pear is completely covered. Repeat procedure with remaining pears and pastry strips.
• **Place** pears on a baking sheet. Combine egg yolk and water; brush evenly on pastry. Bake at 350° for 1 hour or until tender.
• **Spoon** 2 to 3 tablespoons Caramel Sauce onto each dessert plate; top with a pear. Garnish, if desired. **Yield:** 5 or 6 servings.

Note: To make ahead, wrap pears in pastry; cover tightly with plastic wrap, and chill 8 hours. Remove plastic wrap; brush with egg yolk mixture, and bake as directed.

Caramel Sauce
QUICK!

1 (12-ounce) jar caramel ice cream
    topping
1 (14-ounce) can sweetened
    condensed milk
¼ cup Cointreau or other orange-
    flavored liqueur
2 tablespoons lemon juice

• **Combine** caramel topping and milk in top of a double boiler; bring water to a boil. Reduce heat to low; cook, stirring constantly, until smooth. Stir in Cointreau and lemon juice. **Yield:** 2½ cups.
Jane Micol Schatzman
Winston-Salem, North Carolina

BERRY NAPOLEONS
(pictured on page 117)

Edged with a pool of Strawberry Sauce or served plain, Berry Napoleons are the perfect finish to a summer meal.

Vegetable cooking spray
1½ cups quick-cooking oats,
    uncooked
½ cup butter or margarine,
    melted
¾ cup sugar
1 teaspoon all-purpose flour
1 teaspoon baking powder
1 large egg, lightly beaten
½ cup chopped pecans
1 teaspoon vanilla extract
¾ cup semisweet chocolate
    morsels
1½ tablespoons Chambord or
    other raspberry-flavored
    liqueur
1 tablespoon butter or margarine
2 cups whipping cream
¼ cup sifted powdered sugar
1 pint fresh blackberries or
    raspberries
Garnish: fresh berries
Strawberry Sauce (optional)

• **Cover** baking sheets with aluminum foil, and coat with cooking spray. Set aside.
• **Combine** oats and ½ cup melted butter in a bowl; stir in ¾ cup sugar, flour, and baking powder. Add egg, pecans, and vanilla, stirring until blended.
• **Drop** mixture by rounded teaspoonfuls 2 inches apart into 36 mounds onto prepared cookie sheets.
• **Bake** at 325° for 12 minutes or until lightly browned. Allow to cool completely on cookie sheets. Remove from foil, and place cookies on wax paper.
• **Combine** chocolate morsels, liqueur, and 1 tablespoon butter in a small saucepan; cook over low heat, stirring constantly, until chocolate morsels and butter melt.
• **Spoon** mixture into a heavy-duty, zip-top plastic bag; seal. Snip a tiny hole in one corner of bag, and gently squeeze bag to drizzle chocolate over cooled cookies. Let cookies stand until chocolate is firm.

• **Beat** whipping cream until foamy; gradually add powdered sugar, beating until soft peaks form. Set aside ¾ cup whipped cream.
• **Place** 1 cookie on each serving plate. Pipe or dollop ½-inch layer of whipped cream onto each cookie; top with berries. Top each with a second cookie, and repeat procedure. Top with remaining cookies. Pipe or dollop with reserved ¾ cup whipped cream; top each with a berry. If desired, spoon about 1 tablespoon Strawberry Sauce around 1 side of napoleon. Garnish, if desired. **Yield:** 12 servings.

Strawberry Sauce
QUICK!

1 (10-ounce) package frozen
    strawberries
1 tablespoon cornstarch

• **Puree** strawberries in blender.
• **Pour** mixture through a wire-mesh strainer into a small saucepan, pressing with back of a spoon. Discard seeds.
• **Add** cornstarch to juice. Bring mixture to a boil over medium heat, stirring constantly. Boil 1 minute. Cool before serving. **Yield:** 1 cup.

Mrs. Carl W. Terry
Huntsville, Alabama

PEANUT BUTTER AND CHOCOLATE NAPOLEONS

1 cup creamy peanut butter
1 (8-ounce) package cream cheese, softened
½ cup sugar
1 teaspoon vanilla extract
½ cup whipping cream, whipped
24 chocolate wafers
3 (1-ounce) squares semisweet chocolate, melted
¼ cup milk
Chocolate Sauce

• **Combine** first 4 ingredients in a large mixing bowl; beat at medium speed with an electric mixer until blended. Fold in whipped cream. Reserve ½ cup peanut butter mixture.
• **Pipe** or spoon one-fourth of remaining peanut butter mixture evenly onto 6 chocolate wafers. Top each with a second chocolate wafer; pipe or spoon another one-fourth of peanut butter mixture evenly onto the wafers. Repeat procedure with a third wafer and another one-fourth of peanut butter mixture, and top with remaining wafers. Pipe or dollop with remaining one-fourth of peanut butter mixture; chill.
• **Spoon** melted chocolate into a heavy-duty, zip-top plastic bag; seal. Snip a tiny hole in one corner of bag. Pipe chocolate to form an overlapping leaf design onto six dessert plates. Chill plates until chocolate is firm. For each chocolate garnish, pipe remaining melted chocolate onto wax paper in overlapping leaf designs; chill until chocolate is firm.
• **Combine** ½ cup reserved peanut butter mixture and milk.
• **Spoon** peanut butter mixture and Chocolate Sauce inside piped design on prepared plates. Use a wooden pick to spread sauces to edges of the leaves. Arrange napoleons on plates. Top each napoleon with a chocolate garnish. Serve immediately. **Yield:** 6 servings.

Chocolate Sauce

QUICK!

½ cup whipping cream
2 tablespoons sugar
3 (1-ounce) squares semisweet chocolate
½ teaspoon vanilla extract

• **Combine** whipping cream and sugar in a small saucepan over low heat. Add chocolate, and cook, stirring constantly, until chocolate melts. Remove from heat, and stir in vanilla. **Yield:** ¾ cup.

HELLO DOLLY DESSERT

2 cups graham cracker crumbs
¼ cup sugar
2 tablespoons ground cinnamon
½ cup butter or margarine, melted
2½ cups chopped pecans
2 cups (12-ounces) semisweet chocolate morsels
2 (6-ounce) packages white chocolate, finely chopped *
1 (14-ounce) package flaked coconut
1 (14-ounce) can sweetened condensed milk

• **Combine** first 3 ingredients; stir in butter. Press in bottom and 1 inch up sides of a 10-inch springform pan.
• **Layer** with chopped pecans, chocolate morsels, white chocolate, and coconut; press down firmly. Pour condensed milk evenly over coconut.
• **Bake** at 350° for 40 to 45 minutes. Cool 10 minutes in pan on a wire rack. Run a knife around edge to release sides; remove sides of pan. Cool completely on wire rack. Slice and reheat before serving. **Yield:** 12 to 15 servings.
Concho Confetti Cafe and Catering
San Angelo, Texas

* For white chocolate, we used Nestle's Baking Bars and Baker's Premium White Chocolate. We tried white chocolate morsels, but the layers didn't stay together.

CARAMEL FONDUE

QUICK!

3 (14-ounce) packages caramels, unwrapped
⅓ to ½ cup milk
1 (8-ounce) container cream cheese

• **Combine** caramels, ⅓ cup milk, and cream cheese in a Dutch oven; cook over low heat, stirring constantly, until mixture is smooth. Add additional milk if mixture is too thick for dipping. Spoon into a fondue pot or chafing dish. Serve with fruit or cake. **Yield:** 4 cups.
Carolyn Look
El Paso, Texas

CHOCOLATE PLUNGE

QUICK!

2 cups light corn syrup
1½ cups whipping cream
3 (12-ounce) packages semisweet chocolate morsels

• **Combine** corn syrup and whipping cream in a heavy saucepan; bring mixture to a boil.
• **Remove** from heat; add chocolate morsels, stirring until smooth. Spoon into a fondue pot or chafing dish. Serve with fruit or cake. **Yield:** 7 cups.
Mary Pappas
Richmond, Virginia

WHITE CHOCOLATE FONDUE

QUICK!

1 pound vanilla-flavored candy coating
½ cup half-and-half
2 tablespoons brandy

• **Melt** coating in a heavy saucepan over low heat, stirring constantly. Gradually add half-and-half, stirring constantly until blended. Stir in brandy.
• **Serve** at room temperature with fresh strawberries. **Yield:** 2 cups.
Ann Ruff
Bellaire, Texas

CHOCOLATE POTS DE CRÈME

QUICK!

Luscious Chocolate Pots de Crème boast just 4 ingredients and require only a saucepan and a few utensils to make.

1 cup (6 ounces) semisweet
  chocolate morsels
1 cup whipping cream
½ cup half-and-half
2 egg yolks

• **Combine** first 3 ingredients in a heavy saucepan; cook over low heat, stirring constantly, until chocolate melts.
• **Beat** egg yolks until thick and pale. Gradually stir about one-fourth of hot mixture into yolks; add to remaining hot mixture, stirring constantly.
• **Cook** over low heat, stirring constantly, 2 minutes or until mixture thickens slightly. Spoon into individual pots de crème cups or custard cups. Cover and chill. **Yield:** 4 to 6 servings.

Mrs. C. M. Conklin II
Dallas, Texas

CHOCOLATE-ALMOND SILK PUDDING

QUICK!

4 cups skim milk
½ cup amaretto
1½ cups sugar
½ cup cocoa
½ cup cornstarch
1½ teaspoons vanilla extract

• **Combine** milk and liqueur in a heavy saucepan; cook over medium heat until hot (do not boil).
• **Sift** sugar, cocoa, and cornstarch together in a large heavy saucepan; add hot milk mixture, whisking until smooth. Bring to a boil over medium heat; boil 1 minute. Stir in vanilla.
• **Pour** into 10 custard cups; cover with wax paper, and chill. **Yield:** 5 cups.

Sandi Pichon
Slidell, Louisiana

❤ Per ½-cup serving: Calories 210
Fat 0.7g Cholesterol 4mg
Sodium 59mg

FUDGY CHOCOLATE PUDDING

2 (4-ounce) bars dark sweet
  chocolate bars
⅔ cup strongly brewed coffee
1 cup sugar
1 cup butter
4 large eggs
½ cup whipping cream
1 tablespoon powdered sugar

• **Combine** chocolate and coffee in top of a double boiler; bring water to a boil. Reduce heat to low; cook until chocolate melts, stirring occasionally. Gradually whisk in 1 cup sugar. Add butter, 1 tablespoon at a time, whisking until butter melts.
• **Whisk** eggs until thick and pale. Gradually stir about one-fourth of hot mixture into eggs; add to remaining hot mixture, whisking constantly. Pour into six 6-ounce greased custard cups, and place cups in a 13- x 9- x 2-inch pan. Add hot water to pan to depth of 1 inch. Cover pan with aluminum foil.
• **Bake** at 350° for 45 minutes or until set. Remove from pan; cool on a wire rack. Cover and chill at least 8 hours.
• **Beat** whipping cream at high speed with an electric mixer until foamy; gradually add powdered sugar, beating until soft peaks form. Pipe or dollop onto pudding. **Yield:** 6 servings.

W. N. Cottrell II
New Orleans, Louisiana

LEMON-PEAR PUDDING

3 large pears, peeled and thinly
  sliced
¼ cup sugar
¼ cup fresh lemon juice
1 cup self-rising flour
¾ cup firmly packed brown sugar
1 teaspoon grated lemon rind
½ cup butter or margarine
Whipped cream

• **Combine** first 3 ingredients; place in a greased 8-inch square baking dish.
• **Combine** flour, brown sugar, and lemon rind; cut in butter with pastry blender until mixture is crumbly, and sprinkle evenly over pear mixture.

• **Bake** at 400° for 30 to 35 minutes. Serve warm with whipped cream. **Yield:** 6 servings.

Wylene B. Gillespie
Gallatin, Tennessee

BUTTERMILK BREAD PUDDING WITH BUTTER-RUM SAUCE

QUICK!

1 (16-ounce) loaf unsliced French
  bread
¼ cup butter or margarine
1 quart buttermilk
1 cup raisins
2 large eggs, lightly beaten
1⅓ cups firmly packed light brown
  sugar
1 tablespoon vanilla extract
Butter-Rum Sauce

• **Tear** bread into 1-inch pieces; reserve 7½ cups. Reserve remaining bread for another use.
• **Melt** butter in a 13- x 9- x 2-inch pan in 350° oven.
• **Combine** 7½ cups bread pieces, buttermilk, and raisins in a bowl; set aside.
• **Combine** eggs, brown sugar, and vanilla, whisking well.
• **Add** egg mixture to bread mixture, stirring gently. Pour into pan of melted butter.
• **Bake** at 350° for 1 hour. Serve warm or cold with Butter-Rum Sauce. **Yield:** 10 to 12 servings.

Butter-Rum Sauce

QUICK!

½ cup butter or margarine,
  softened
½ cup sugar
1 egg yolk
¼ cup water
3 tablespoons rum

• **Combine** first 4 ingredients in a small saucepan, stirring well.
• **Cook** over medium heat until sugar dissolves and sauce begins to thicken (about 10 minutes). Gently stir in rum. **Yield:** ¾ cup.

Marie Davis
Charlotte, North Carolina

DURFEE'S BREAD PUDDING

1 (16-ounce) loaf French bread
½ cup raisins
6 large eggs, lightly beaten
4 cups milk
1½ cups sugar
2 tablespoons butter or margarine, melted
½ teaspoon almond extract
¼ teaspoon vanilla extract
⅓ cup slivered almonds, toasted

• **Cut** bread into 1¼-inch-thick slices; place in a single layer in a lightly greased 13- x 9- x 2-inch baking dish. Sprinkle with raisins.
• **Combine** eggs and next 5 ingredients in a large bowl, stirring until blended. Pour egg mixture over bread, and let stand 30 minutes.
• **Sprinkle** almonds over egg mixture; place dish in a large pan. Add hot water to pan to depth of 1 inch.
• **Bake** at 350° for 45 minutes or until a knife inserted in center comes out clean, shielding with aluminum foil after 30 minutes to prevent excessive browning. Serve warm with whipped cream. **Yield:** 12 to 15 servings.

Odile Besseau and Durfee Bedsole
The Taylor House
Marshall, Texas

BREAD PUDDING WITH WHISKEY SAUCE

1 (16-ounce) loaf French bread
3 cups milk
1 cup cream sherry
3 large eggs, beaten
2 cups sugar
2 tablespoons butter, melted
2 tablespoons vanilla extract
1 cup raisins
2 tablespoons butter or margarine, melted
½ cup honey
Whiskey Sauce

• **Break** bread into small chunks, and place in a large bowl. Add milk and sherry; let stand 10 minutes. Stir until thoroughly mixed.

• **Combine** eggs, sugar, 2 tablespoons butter, and vanilla; add to bread mixture, stirring well. Stir in raisins.
• **Spoon** mixture into a lightly greased 11- x 7- x 1½-inch baking dish. Combine 2 tablespoons butter and honey; pour over pudding. Bake at 350° for 45 minutes or until set. Serve with warm Whiskey Sauce. **Yield:** 10 to 12 servings.

Whiskey Sauce

QUICK!

1 cup sugar
1 cup milk
½ cup butter
2 tablespoons cornstarch
¼ cup cold water
½ cup bourbon

• **Combine** sugar, milk, and butter in a heavy saucepan; cook over low heat until sugar dissolves and butter melts.
• **Combine** cornstarch and water; add to butter mixture. Add bourbon, and bring to a boil over medium heat; cook 1 minute. **Yield:** 2¾ cups.

Julie and Cliff Collins
French Quarter
New Orleans, Louisiana

CREOLE BREAD PUDDING SOUFFLÉ

½ cup butter or margarine, softened
1 cup sugar
5 large eggs
2 cups whipping cream
1 tablespoon vanilla extract
⅛ teaspoon ground cinnamon
¼ cup raisins
12 (1-inch-thick) slices French bread
1 tablespoon butter or margarine
1½ tablespoons sugar
6 large eggs, separated
½ cup sugar
½ cup sifted powdered sugar
Whiskey Sauce

• **Beat** ½ cup butter at medium speed with an electric mixer until creamy; gradually add 1 cup sugar, beating well. Add eggs, one at a time, beating after

each addition. Gradually add cream, mixing well. Stir in vanilla, cinnamon, and raisins. Pour mixture into a lightly greased 13- x 9- x 2-inch pan.
• **Arrange** bread slices in pan over cream mixture; let stand 10 minutes. Turn bread slices over; let stand 10 minutes. Cover pan with aluminum foil; place in a larger shallow pan. Pour hot water to depth of 1 inch into larger pan. Bake at 350° for 40 minutes. Remove foil, and bake 10 additional minutes. Place 2½ cups baked bread mixture in a large bowl; set aside. Reserve remainder for another use. (For a quick dessert, reheat remainder, and serve with leftover Whiskey Sauce.)
• **Grease** a 1½-quart soufflé dish with 1 tablespoon butter; coat bottom and sides of dish with 1½ tablespoons sugar, and set aside.
• **Combine** egg yolks and ½ cup sugar in top of a double boiler; place over simmering water, and beat at high speed with an electric mixer 4 minutes or until mixture thickens. Add yolk mixture to bread mixture in bowl, and beat at medium speed until smooth. Set aside.
• **Beat** egg whites at high speed with an electric mixer until foamy. Gradually add powdered sugar, beating until stiff peaks form; fold into bread mixture. Pour into prepared soufflé dish. Bake at 375° for 40 minutes; serve with warm Whiskey Sauce. **Yield:** 6 to 8 servings.

Whiskey Sauce

QUICK!

1 cup sugar
1 cup whipping cream
⅛ teaspoon ground cinnamon
1 tablespoon butter or margarine
1½ teaspoons cornstarch
¼ cup cold water
1 tablespoon bourbon

• **Combine** first 4 ingredients in a heavy saucepan. Cook over medium heat until sugar dissolves, stirring often.
• **Combine** cornstarch and water; stir into cream mixture, and bring to a boil, stirring constantly. Boil 1 minute, stirring constantly. Remove from heat, and stir in bourbon. **Yield:** 1⅔ cups.

Commander's Palace
New Orleans, Louisiana

TIRAMISÙ

Tiramisù literally means "pick me up" in Italian. Try it with mascarpone or with our reduced-fat substitute.

1 (3-ounce) package vanilla
  pudding mix
2 cups skim milk
1 cup mascarpone cheese *
2¾ cups reduced-fat frozen
  whipped topping, thawed and
  divided
1 loaf angel food cake
1½ teaspoons instant coffee
  granules
½ cup hot water
¼ cup brandy
¼ cup Kahlúa or other coffee-
  flavored liqueur
Garnish: cocoa

• **Combine** pudding mix and milk in a saucepan; bring to a boil over medium heat, stirring constantly. Remove from heat; pour pudding into a mixing bowl, and cool.
• **Add** mascarpone cheese to pudding; beat at low speed with an electric mixer until smooth. Fold in 1¾ cups whipped topping, and set aside.
• **Slice** cake in half horizontally. Cut each layer vertically into 16 equal rectangles, and set aside.
• **Dissolve** coffee granules in hot water; stir in brandy and Kahlúa. Brush over tops and bottoms of cake pieces.
• **Line** bottom and sides of a 3-quart trifle bowl or soufflé dish with half of cake pieces; cover with half of pudding mixture. Repeat procedure with remaining cake pieces and pudding mixture. Cover and chill 8 hours.
• **Spread** remaining 1 cup whipped topping over Tiramisù, and garnish, if desired. Cover and chill. **Yield:** 12 servings.

* Mascarpone cheese is a soft, buttery Italian cheese made from fresh cream. You can find it in the gourmet section at large supermarkets.

♥ Substitute 1 (8-ounce) package reduced-fat cream cheese, 3 tablespoons reduced-fat sour cream, and 2 tablespoons skim milk for mascarpone. With this substitution, you'll save 5.4 fat grams and 46 calories per serving.

Lucy Susan Barrett
Birmingham, Alabama

♥ Per serving: Calories 257
Fat 11.1g Cholesterol 18mg
Sodium 174mg

SWEET POTATO FLAN

2 medium sweet potatoes
  (1¾ pounds) *
¾ cup sugar
2 (14-ounce) cans sweetened
  condensed milk
2 cups milk
10 large eggs
1 teaspoon ground cinnamon
½ teaspoon ground allspice
¼ teaspoon ground cloves
1 teaspoon vanilla extract
Garnish: toasted coconut

• **Pierce** sweet potatoes several times with a fork; place on a baking sheet.
• **Bake** at 375° for 1 hour or until done; cool to touch. Peel sweet potatoes, and mash. Set aside 1 cup mashed sweet potato; reserve any remaining sweet potato for another use.
• **Sprinkle** sugar in a 10-inch round cakepan; place over medium heat, and cook, shaking pan constantly, until sugar melts and turns a light golden brown. Cool. (Caramelized sugar may crack slightly as it cools.)
• **Combine** ½ cup mashed sweet potato, 1 can sweetened condensed milk, 1 cup milk and half of next 5 ingredients in container of an electric blender; process until smooth, stopping once to scrape down sides. Pour sweet potato mixture into a large bowl.
• **Repeat** procedure; add sweet potato mixture to bowl, stirring well with a wire whisk.
• **Pour** mixture over caramelized sugar in cakepan; cover with aluminum foil, and place cakepan in a larger shallow pan. Add hot water to larger pan to depth of ½ inch.
• **Bake** at 325° for 1 hour and 15 minutes or until a knife inserted in center comes out clean. Remove pan from water, and uncover; cool on a wire rack 30 minutes.
• **Cover** and chill at least 8 hours.
• **Run** a knife around edge of flan to loosen; invert onto a serving plate. Garnish, if desired. **Yield:** 1 (10-inch) flan.

* Substitute 1 cup canned mashed sweet potatoes for fresh.

W. N. Cottrell
New Orleans, Louisiana

FLAN DE QUESO

½ cup sugar
1 (14-ounce) can sweetened
  condensed milk
1 (8-ounce) package cream cheese,
  cubed and softened
4 large eggs
3 slices white bread, torn
1 cup water
⅔ cup evaporated milk
3 tablespoons butter or margarine,
  melted
1 teaspoon vanilla extract

• **Sprinkle** sugar in a 9-inch round cakepan; place over medium heat, and cook, shaking pan occasionally, until sugar melts and turns a light golden brown. Cool. (Caramelized sugar may crack slightly as it cools.)
• **Combine** condensed milk and remaining 7 ingredients in container of an electric blender; process until smooth, stopping once to scrape down sides. Pour over caramelized sugar.
• **Place** cakepan in a larger shallow pan. Add hot water to larger pan to depth of 1 inch.
• **Bake**, uncovered, at 350° for 55 minutes or until a knife inserted in center of flan comes out clean.
• **Remove** cakepan from water; cool on a wire rack at least 30 minutes.
• **Run** a knife around edge of flan to loosen; invert flan onto a serving plate. Cool. **Yield:** 6 servings.

Note: You can also caramelize sugar on a gas cooktop, stirring to speed caramelization.

Myrna M. Ruiz
Marietta, Georgia

Basic Crèmes Brûlée

BASIC CRÈME BRÛLÉE
(pictured at left)

2 cups whipping cream
5 egg yolks
½ cup sugar
1 tablespoon vanilla extract
½ cup firmly packed light brown
    sugar
Garnishes: fresh raspberries,
    fresh mint sprigs

• **Combine** first 4 ingredients; stir with a wire whisk until sugar dissolves and mixture is smooth. Pour evenly into 5 (5- x 1-inch) round individual baking dishes; place dishes in a large roasting pan or a 15- x 10- x 1-inch jellyroll pan. Add hot water to pan to depth of ½ inch.
• **Bake** at 275° for 45 to 50 minutes or until almost set. Cool custards in water in pan on a wire rack. Remove from pan; cover and chill at least 8 hours.
• **Sprinkle** brown sugar evenly over each custard; place custards in pan.
• **Broil** 5½ inches from heat (with electric oven door partially opened) until sugar melts. Let stand 5 minutes to allow sugar to harden. Garnish, if desired. **Yield:** 5 servings.

Berry Crème Brûlée: Place 8 to 10 fresh blackberries or raspberries in each baking dish; pour custard mixture over berries. Proceed as directed in basic recipe, baking 45 minutes.

Chocolate Crème Brûlée: Combine 4 (1-ounce) squares semisweet chocolate and ½ cup whipping cream from basic recipe in a small heavy saucepan; cook over low heat, stirring constantly, until chocolate melts. Add remaining 1½ cups whipping cream; reduce vanilla to 1 teaspoon. Proceed as directed in basic recipe, baking 55 minutes. For a Chocolate-Raspberry version, place 8 to 10 fresh raspberries in each baking dish, add custard, and increase baking time to 1 hour and 5 minutes.

Double Raspberry Crème Brûlée: Reduce vanilla to 1 teaspoon; add 1 additional egg yolk and 1½ tablespoons Framboise or other raspberry-flavored liqueur to custard mixture. Place 8 to 10 fresh raspberries in each baking dish; pour custard mixture over berries. Proceed as directed in basic brûlée recipe, baking 55 minutes.

Ginger Crème Brûlée: Reduce vanilla to 1 teaspoon; add 2 tablespoons grated fresh ginger to custard mixture. Proceed as directed in basic brûlée recipe, baking 1 hour and 5 minutes.

Orange Crème Brûlée: Reduce vanilla to 1 teaspoon; add 1 additional egg yolk, 2 tablespoons grated orange rind, and 2 tablespoons Grand Marnier or other orange-flavored liqueur to custard mixture. Proceed as directed in basic brûlée recipe, baking 1 hour.

Peppermint Crème Brûlée: Reduce vanilla to 1 teaspoon; add 1 additional egg yolk and 3 tablespoons peppermint schnapps. Proceed as directed in basic recipe, baking 50 minutes. Substitute 5 hard peppermint candies, crushed, for brown sugar; broil as directed.

White Chocolate-Macadamia Nut Crème Brûlée: Combine 4 ounces white chocolate and ½ cup whipping cream from basic brûlée recipe in a heavy saucepan; cook over low heat, stirring constantly, until chocolate melts. Add remaining 1½ cups whipping cream; reduce vanilla to 1 teaspoon. Proceed as directed in basic brûlée recipe. Place 1 tablespoon chopped macadamia nuts, toasted, in each baking dish; pour custard over nuts. Bake as directed 1 hour and 10 minutes.

GOAT CHEESE CUSTARD

1 large egg
⅓ cup sugar
1 teaspoon cornstarch
1½ teaspoons lemon juice
1 teaspoon vanilla extract
3 (5.3-ounce) containers creamy
    goat cheese
¼ cup milk
1 (16-ounce) package frozen
    strawberries, thawed
¼ cup amaretto
2 tablespoons sugar

• **Combine** first 5 ingredients in a large bowl, whisking until smooth.
• **Whisk** goat cheese and milk until smooth; add to egg mixture, whisking until smooth.
• **Pour** into four lightly greased 6-ounce custard cups, and place cups in a 9-inch square pan. Add hot water to pan to depth of 1 inch.
• **Bake** at 375° for 10 minutes; reduce oven temperature to 325°, and bake 35 additional minutes or until almost set. Transfer to a wire rack to cool. Cover and chill 8 hours.
• **Combine** strawberries, liqueur, and 2 tablespoons sugar in container of an electric blender or food processor; process until smooth, stopping once to scrape down sides. Pour through a wire-mesh strainer into a bowl, pressing with back of a spoon; discard seeds. Cover and chill.
• **Spoon** ¼ cup strawberry sauce on each serving plate; unmold custards onto plates. **Yield:** 4 servings.

Note: Serve leftover strawberry sauce over ice cream.

CHOCOLATE TRUFFLE MOUSSE WITH RASPBERRY SAUCE

8 (1-ounce) squares semisweet
    chocolate
¼ cup light corn syrup
¼ cup butter or margarine
2 egg yolks, lightly beaten
1 cup whipping cream, divided
2 tablespoons powdered sugar
½ teaspoon vanilla extract
Garnish: chocolate curls
Raspberry Sauce

• **Combine** first 3 ingredients in a heavy saucepan; cook over low heat, stirring constantly, until chocolate melts.
• **Combine** yolks and ¼ cup cream. Gradually stir about ½ cup chocolate mixture into yolk mixture; add to remaining chocolate mixture, stirring constantly. Cook over medium-low heat 1 minute or until a thermometer registers 160°. Remove from heat; cool to room temperature.
• **Beat** remaining ¾ cup whipping cream until foamy; gradually add powdered sugar, beating until soft peaks form. Stir in vanilla.
• **Stir** ½ cup whipped cream mixture into chocolate mixture; fold in remaining cream mixture. Spoon into four stemmed glasses; cover and chill at least 8 hours. Garnish, if desired. Serve with Raspberry Sauce. **Yield:** 4 servings.

Raspberry Sauce

QUICK!

1 (10-ounce) package frozen
    raspberries, thawed
2 teaspoons cornstarch
⅓ cup light corn syrup

• **Place** raspberries in container of an electric blender; process 1 minute or until smooth, stopping once to scrape down sides. Pour mixture through a wire-mesh strainer into a small saucepan, discarding seeds. Add cornstarch, stirring well; stir in corn syrup.
• **Cook** over medium heat, stirring constantly, until mixture boils. Boil 1 minute, stirring constantly. Remove from heat; cool. **Yield:** 1⅓ cups.

Nancy Williams
Starkville, Mississippi

PEPPERMINT CANDY MOUSSE

8 ounces hard peppermint candies
    (about 2 cups)
½ cup half-and-half
1 envelope unflavored gelatin
1 tablespoon cold water
1½ cups whipping cream
Chocolate sauce

• **Place** candies in a heavy-duty, zip-top plastic bag; seal bag, and crush until the consistency of powder, using a meat mallet or rolling pin.
• **Combine** powdered candies and half-and-half in a small saucepan. Cook mixture over low heat, stirring constantly, about 10 minutes or until candy dissolves. (Remove and discard any undissolved candy.) Set warm peppermint mixture aside.
• **Sprinkle** gelatin over 1 tablespoon cold water in a large bowl; let stand 1 minute. Add warm peppermint mixture, stirring until gelatin dissolves (about 2 minutes). Cool.
• **Beat** whipping cream until soft peaks form. Gently fold into peppermint mixture. Pour mixture into a lightly oiled 4-cup mold.
• **Cover** and chill at least 8 hours. Unmold onto a serving plate. Serve with Chocolate Sauce. **Yield:** 6 to 8 servings.

Rublelene Singleton
Scotts Hill, Tennessee

VANILLA SOUFFLÉS WITH VANILLA CRÈME SAUCE

This top-rated dessert is one of our most requested recipes.

Vegetable cooking spray
Sugar
1½ tablespoons butter or
    margarine
1½ tablespoons all-purpose
    flour
6 tablespoons half-and-half
2 tablespoons sugar
2 large eggs, separated
1 tablespoon vanilla extract
1 tablespoon sugar
Sifted powdered sugar
Vanilla Crème Sauce

• **Coat** the bottom and sides of two 6-ounce baking dishes with cooking spray; sprinkle with sugar. Set aside.
• **Melt** butter in a small saucepan over medium heat; add flour, stirring until mixture is smooth. Cook 1 minute, stirring constantly.
• **Add** half-and-half, stirring constantly; stir in 2 tablespoons sugar. Cook over medium heat, stirring constantly, until thickened. Remove from heat; set aside.
• **Beat** egg yolks until thick and pale. Gradually stir about half of hot mixture into egg yolks; add to remaining hot mixture, stirring constantly. Cook over medium heat 2 minutes; stir in vanilla. Cool 15 to 20 minutes.
• **Beat** egg whites at high speed with an electric mixer until foamy. Gradually add 1 tablespoon sugar, beating until soft peaks form. Gradually fold egg whites into half-and-half mixture. Spoon into prepared baking dishes.
• **Bake** at 350° for 25 minutes or until puffed and set. Sprinkle with powdered sugar, and serve immediately with Vanilla Crème Sauce. **Yield:** 2 servings.

Vanilla Crème Sauce

QUICK!

½ cup sugar
1 teaspoon cornstarch
½ teaspoon vanilla extract
1 cup whipping cream
4 egg yolks

• **Combine** first 3 ingredients in a heavy saucepan; gradually stir in whipping cream. Cook over low heat, stirring constantly, until sugar dissolves. Set aside.
• **Beat** egg yolks until thick and pale. Gradually stir about half of hot whipping cream mixture into yolks; add to remaining hot mixture, stirring constantly. Cook over medium heat, stirring constantly, until thickened.
• **Pour** through a wire-mesh strainer into a small bowl, discarding lumps. Cover and store in refrigerator up to 3 days. Serve with Vanilla Soufflés, fresh fruit, pound cake, or ice cream. **Yield:** 1½ cups.

LEMON SOUFFLÉ

We used Wilton meringue powder in this soufflé. Look for it in crafts stores, cake-decorating supply stores, or at Wal-Mart.

1 tablespoon butter or margarine
2 tablespoons sugar
2 envelopes unflavored gelatin
½ cup cold water
1 teaspoon sugar
1 tablespoon grated lemon rind
¾ cup lemon juice
⅓ cup meringue powder
1½ cups sugar, divided
1 cup water
2 cups whipping cream
1 (2-ounce) package slivered
    almonds, toasted and
    chopped
Garnish: Candied Lemon Peel

• **Cut** a piece of wax paper long enough to fit around a 2-quart soufflé dish, allowing a 1-inch overlap; fold paper lengthwise into thirds. Lightly butter one side of paper and soufflé dish. Wrap paper around outside of dish, buttered side against dish, allowing it to extend 3 inches above rim; secure with tape. Sprinkle sides of dish with 2 tablespoons sugar.
• **Sprinkle** gelatin over cold water in a saucepan; let stand 1 minute. Add 1 teaspoon sugar; cook over low heat, stirring until gelatin dissolves. Stir in lemon rind and juice. Set aside.
• **Combine** meringue powder, 1 cup sugar, and water in a large bowl. Beat at high speed with an electric mixer 5 minutes. Gradually add remaining ½ cup sugar, and beat at high speed 5 minutes or until stiff peaks form. Fold in gelatin mixture.
• **Beat** whipping cream until soft peaks form. Fold into gelatin mixture.
• **Pour** into prepared dish, and chill 8 hours.
• **Remove** collar, gently pat chopped almonds around sides of soufflé. Garnish, if desired. **Yield:** 8 to 10 servings.

Candied Lemon Peel

1 large lemon
2 tablespoons light corn syrup
1 tablespoon sugar

• **Peel** lemon, and cut rind into ¼-inch-wide strips. Reserve peeled lemon for another use.
• **Combine** lemon rind and corn syrup in a small saucepan, and bring to a boil over medium heat; reduce heat, and cook 3 to 4 minutes.
• **Toss** lemon rind with sugar to coat; spread on wax paper to dry. **Yield:** about ⅓ cup.

Barbara Crowe
Birmingham, Alabama

SOUFFLÉ AU CHOCOLAT COINTREAU

Bill prefers to whip egg whites by hand, but this recipe works just fine using a mixer, too. You can cut this recipe in half to serve 6.

Butter or margarine
2 tablespoons sugar
¼ cup butter or margarine
2 cups (12 ounces) semisweet
    chocolate morsels
¼ cup Cointreau or other orange-
    flavored liqueur
12 large eggs, separated
1½ cups sifted powdered sugar
1 teaspoon ground cinnamon
1 teaspoon cream of tartar
Powdered sugar
Chocolate Cream
Garnish: orange rind strips

• **Cut** a piece of aluminum foil long enough to fit around a 2¾-quart soufflé dish or straight-sided casserole, allowing a 1-inch overlap; starting from one long side, fold foil into thirds. Lightly butter one side of foil and dish. Wrap foil around outside of dish, buttered side against dish, allowing it to extend 3 inches above rim to form a collar; secure with string or masking tape. Add 2 tablespoons sugar, tilting prepared dish to coat sides. Set aside.
• **Combine** ¼ cup butter and chocolate morsels in top of a double boiler; bring water to a boil. Reduce heat to low; cook until chocolate and butter melt, stirring often. Remove from water; cool 5 minutes. Stir in Cointreau. Set aside.
• **Beat** egg yolks; gradually add powdered sugar, beating until mixture is thick and pale. Stir in chocolate mixture and cinnamon. Set aside.
• **Beat** egg whites and cream of tartar in a large mixing bowl at high speed with an electric mixer until stiff peaks form. Gently stir 1½ cups egg white mixture into chocolate mixture.
• **Fold** remaining egg white mixture into chocolate mixture. Pour into prepared soufflé dish.
• **Bake** at 375° for 50 to 55 minutes. Sprinkle with powdered sugar, and remove collar. Serve immediately with Chocolate Cream. Garnish, if desired. **Yield:** 12 servings.

Chocolate Cream

QUICK!

1 cup whipping cream
1 tablespoon sifted powdered
    sugar
1½ teaspoons cocoa

• **Beat** all ingredients at medium speed with an electric mixer until soft peaks form. **Yield:** 2 cups.

Bill Gilchrist
Birmingham, Alabama

WATERMELON GRANITA

Granita is an Italian fruity, icy dessert. We consider it a snow cone for adults.

4 cups cubed watermelon,
    seeded
½ cup sugar
2 tablespoons lemon juice

• **Combine** all ingredients in container of an electric blender or food processor; process until smooth and sugar dissolves, stopping once to scrape down sides.
• **Pour** into an 8-inch square pan. Cover and freeze 2 hours or until almost firm, stirring occasionally.
• **Remove** from freezer 5 minutes before serving; stir, if necessary. Serve immediately. **Yield:** 4 to 6 servings.

Donna Presley
Perrytown, Arkansas

MIMOSA ICE

¾ cup sugar
1 (750-milliliter) bottle
    champagne or sparkling wine
1½ cups water
¾ teaspoon grated fresh lemon
    rind
¼ cup orange juice

● **Combine** all ingredients, stirring until sugar dissolves.
● **Pour** mixture into an 8-inch square pan, and freeze just until firm.
● **Break** mixture into chunks; place in a large mixing bowl. Beat at low speed with an electric mixer until smooth.
● **Return** mixture to pan, and freeze until firm. Let mixture stand at room temperature 10 minutes before serving. **Yield:** 5¼ cups.

PINK GRAPEFRUIT AND TARRAGON SORBET

Serve this herbal refresher as a light dessert for a casual dinner or before the entrée when you are entertaining formally.

2 cups sugar
1 cup water
2 (8-inch) sprigs fresh tarragon,
    coarsely chopped
4 cups pink grapefruit juice

● **Combine** sugar and water in a heavy saucepan; cook over medium heat, stirring constantly, until sugar dissolves. Add tarragon, and bring to a boil. Remove from heat; stir in grapefruit juice. Cover and chill at least 2 hours.
● **Pour** mixture through a wire-mesh strainer into an 8-inch square pan, discarding tarragon.
● **Freeze** until firm, stirring occasionally with a wire whisk.
● **Let** sorbet stand at room temperature about 5 minutes before serving. **Yield:** 6½ cups.

Bacchanalia
Atlanta, Georgia

♥ Per ½-cup serving: Calories 149
Fat 0g   Cholesterol 0mg
Sodium 1mg

STRAWBERRY-CHAMPAGNE SORBET

½ cup sugar
½ cup water
1 (10-ounce) package frozen
    strawberries, thawed and
    undrained
1½ cups champagne
2 tablespoons lemon juice
Fresh whole strawberries
    (optional)

● **Combine** sugar and water in a heavy saucepan; cook over medium heat, stirring constantly, until sugar dissolves. Remove sugar syrup from heat; cool.
● **Place** thawed strawberries in container of an electric blender or food processor; process until smooth. Pour through a wire-mesh strainer into an 8-inch square pan, pressing with back of a spoon against the sides of the strainer to squeeze out juice. Discard pulp and seeds. Stir sugar syrup, champagne, and lemon juice into strawberry puree. Cover and freeze at least 4 hours.
● **Position** knife blade in food processor bowl; add frozen mixture, and process until smooth. Return to pan, and freeze until firm. Repeat processing procedure, and return mixture to pan; freeze until firm.
● **Spoon** into glasses; serve with fresh strawberries, if desired. **Yield:** 3 cups.

♥ Per ½-cup serving: Calories 127
Fat 0g   Cholesterol 0mg
Sodium 4mg

ORANGE SHERBET WITH BLACKBERRY SAUCE

2 cups orange juice
¾ cup sugar
½ cup orange marmalade
1 cup half-and-half
1 cup sour cream
Blackberry Sauce

● **Combine** first 3 ingredients in a bowl, stirring until sugar dissolves. Stir in half-and-half and sour cream. Pour into a 9- x 5- x 3-inch loafpan. Freeze 2 hours or until almost firm.

● **Remove** from freezer, and place in a medium mixing bowl. Beat at medium speed with an electric mixer 1 to 2 minutes or until mixture is fluffy but not thawed.
● **Return** to loafpan; freeze 2 hours or until firm. Serve with Blackberry Sauce. **Yield:** 6 cups.

Blackberry Sauce

QUICK!

1 pint fresh blackberries *
¼ cup sugar
1 tablespoon crème de cassis
    (optional)

● **Position** knife blade in food processor bowl; add blackberries. Process 30 seconds or until smooth, stopping once to scrape down sides.
● **Pour** through a fine wire-mesh strainer into a small bowl, pressing with back of a spoon. Discard seeds.
● **Add** sugar and crème de cassis, if desired, stirring until sugar dissolves. Cover and chill. **Yield:** ¾ cup.

* Substitute 1 (12-ounce) package frozen blackberries, thawed, for fresh.

Louise Bodziony
Gladstone, Missouri

VANILLA CUSTARD ICE CREAM

2 cups milk
1 vanilla bean, split
8 egg yolks
¾ cup sugar
½ teaspoon salt
¼ cup (2 ounces) vanilla extract
2 cups whipping cream
Garnishes: crumbled pralines, fresh
    mint sprigs

● **Cook** milk in a heavy saucepan over medium heat just until bubbles appear, stirring often; remove saucepan from heat. Add vanilla bean to milk; cover and let stand 20 minutes. Remove and discard vanilla bean.
● **Combine** egg yolks and next 3 ingredients in a large bowl; whisk until mixture is thick and pale. Gradually whisk in warm milk; return mixture to saucepan.

- **Cook** over very low heat, stirring constantly, 5 to 7 minutes or until mixture coats a spoon. Remove from heat, and pour through a wire-mesh strainer into a large bowl. Let mixture cool, stirring occasionally.
- **Stir** in whipping cream; cover and chill at least 1 hour.
- **Pour** chilled mixture into container of a 1-gallon hand-turned or electric ice cream freezer, and freeze according to manufacturer's instructions. Garnish, if desired. **Yield:** 2 quarts.

Chefs Edna Lewis and Scott Peacock
Atlanta, Georgia

BUTTER CRISP ICE CREAM

2 cups finely crushed corn flakes
   cereal
2 cups chopped pecans
1 cup firmly packed brown
   sugar
½ cup butter or margarine,
   melted
4 envelopes unflavored gelatin
2 cups sugar
¼ teaspoon salt
6 cups milk, divided
6 large eggs, lightly beaten
1 quart whipping cream
2 tablespoons vanilla extract

- **Combine** first 3 ingredients; stir in butter. Spoon mixture into an ungreased 15- x 10- x 1-inch jellyroll pan. Bake at 350° for 25 minutes, stirring occasionally; cool. Set aside.
- **Combine** gelatin, 2 cups sugar, and salt in a large saucepan; stir in 2 cups milk. Let stand 1 minute. Cook over low heat, stirring until gelatin dissolves (about 5 minutes).
- **Gradually** stir a small amount of hot milk mixture into eggs; add to remaining hot milk mixture, stirring constantly. Cook over medium heat until thermometer registers 160° (about 3 to 5 minutes), stirring often. Add remaining 4 cups milk, whipping cream, and vanilla.
- **Pour** mixture into freezer container of a 5-quart hand-turned or electric freezer. Freeze mixture according to manufacturer's instructions.

- **Spoon** ice cream into a large airtight container, and stir in reserved corn flakes mixture. Cover and freeze. **Yield:** 1 gallon.

Erma Jackson
Huntsville, Alabama

FROZEN ALMOND CRUNCH

Crunchy bits of caramelized almonds flavor this frozen delight.

⅔ cup sliced almonds
½ cup sugar
½ cup butter or margarine
1 tablespoon all-purpose flour
2 tablespoons milk
½ gallon vanilla ice cream,
   softened
Dark Chocolate Sauce

- **Combine** first 5 ingredients in a heavy saucepan; bring to a boil over medium heat, stirring constantly. Remove from heat, and set aside.
- **Line** a 15- x 10- x 1-inch jellyroll pan with aluminum foil; spread almond mixture in pan in a thin layer.
- **Bake** at 350° for 7 minutes or until golden (do not overbake). Cool; remove from foil, and crumble.
- **Sprinkle** half of almond mixture in bottom of a 10-inch springform pan. Spoon ice cream evenly on top; sprinkle with remaining almond mixture, gently pressing down slightly with back of a spoon.
- **Cover** and freeze 8 hours or until firm. Serve with Dark Chocolate Sauce. **Yield:** 12 servings.

Dark Chocolate Sauce
QUICK!

½ cup butter
4 (1-ounce) squares unsweetened
   chocolate
1½ cups sugar
½ cup cocoa
Pinch of salt
1 cup milk
1 teaspoon vanilla extract *

- **Melt** butter and chocolate in a heavy saucepan over low heat, stirring often.

- **Combine** sugar, cocoa, and salt; stir sugar mixture and milk into chocolate mixture.
- **Bring** just to a boil over medium heat, stirring constantly; remove from heat, and stir in vanilla. Cool, stirring occasionally. Store sauce in the refrigerator up to 1 week. **Yield:** 3 cups.

* Substitute 1 to 2 tablespoons Kahlúa for flavoring.

Note: Sauce thickens when chilled. To serve, microwave at HIGH, stirring at 30-second intervals, until sauce is drizzling consistency.

Peggy W. Feist
Eatonton, Georgia

CARAMEL ICE CREAM
DESSERT

1⅓ cups all-purpose flour
⅔ cup quick-cooking oats,
   uncooked
⅔ cup firmly packed brown sugar
⅔ cup chopped pecans or walnuts
⅔ cup butter or margarine, melted
1 cup firmly packed brown sugar
½ cup butter or margarine
¼ cup evaporated milk
½ gallon vanilla ice cream,
   softened

- **Combine** first 4 ingredients, and stir in melted butter; press firmly in a lightly greased 15- x 10- x 1-inch jellyroll pan.
- **Bake** at 350° for 12 minutes or until lightly browned; remove cookie to wire rack. Cool and crumble.
- **Combine** 1 cup brown sugar, ½ cup butter, and evaporated milk in a heavy saucepan. Bring to a boil over medium heat, stirring constantly; boil 3 minutes. Cool caramel sauce.
- **Sprinkle** half of crumbs into bottom of a lightly greased 10-inch springform pan. Drizzle with half of caramel sauce. Spread ice cream over sauce. Drizzle with remaining caramel sauce; sprinkle with remaining crumbs.
- **Cover** and freeze until firm. **Yield:** 12 servings.

Becky Haney
Winston-Salem, North Carolina

CINNAMON ICE CREAM SOMBREROS

4 cups milk
1 teaspoon vanilla extract
¼ cup ground cinnamon
1⅓ cups sugar
12 egg yolks
1 cup whipping cream
1 (8-ounce) package semisweet chocolate
8 ounces premium white chocolate baking squares
Chocolate Sauce
Cornmeal Sombreros
Garnish: fresh strawberry fans

• **Combine** first 3 ingredients in a saucepan; bring to a boil over medium heat, stirring occasionally. Remove from heat; cover and let stand 15 minutes.
• **Combine** sugar and egg yolks in a large mixing bowl; beat at high speed with an electric mixer 3 minutes or until thick and pale. Gradually stir about one-fourth of hot mixture into yolks; add to remaining hot mixture, stirring constantly. Cook over low heat until mixture reaches 185° (about 3 minutes). Remove from heat; set saucepan in ice. Stir in whipping cream; cover and chill.
• **Pour** mixture into freezer container of a 1-gallon hand-turned or electric freezer. Freeze according to manufacturer's instructions. Spoon ice cream into a 13- x 9- x 2-inch pan; cover and freeze 8 hours.
• **One** hour before assembling, scoop ice cream into 10 balls, and place on a baking sheet. Cover with plastic wrap, and immediately return to freezer.
• **Melt** semisweet chocolate in a small saucepan over low heat, stirring until smooth. Place a 14- x 10-inch piece of wax paper on a cloth towel, and spread melted chocolate evenly into a 12- x 8-inch rectangle. Make "waves" of chocolate by loosely gathering towel crosswise under wax paper. Let chocolate harden; peel off wax paper. Break or cut chocolate into 3- x 2-inch pieces, and freeze until ready to serve. Repeat procedure with white chocolate.
• **To** serve, spoon warm Chocolate Sauce onto dessert plates. Place Cornmeal Sombreros on sauce, and fill with ice cream balls. (Reserve remaining sombreros for another use.) Position chocolate pieces around ice cream. Garnish, if desired. **Yield:** 10 servings.

Chocolate Sauce

QUICK!

1 cup whipping cream
2½ cups semisweet chocolate morsels
¼ cup butter or margarine
2 tablespoons sugar
1 teaspoon vanilla extract

• **Place** whipping cream in a saucepan; bring to a boil over medium heat. Remove from heat; add chocolate morsels and remaining ingredients, stirring until smooth. Cover and chill. Just before serving, cook over low heat until warm. **Yield:** 2½ cups.

Cornmeal Sombreros

¾ cup all-purpose flour
⅓ cup yellow cornmeal
3 tablespoons sugar
1 teaspoon salt
¾ cup milk
½ cup water
3 large eggs
1 tablespoon butter or margarine, melted
Vegetable cooking spray
8 cups vegetable oil

• **Combine** first 4 ingredients in container of an electric blender; process 1 minute. Add milk and next 3 ingredients; process 25 seconds, stopping once to scrape down sides. Transfer batter to a bowl; cover and chill at least 1 hour or overnight.
• **Coat** bottom of a 5-inch crêpe pan or small nonstick skillet with cooking spray; place over medium heat just until hot, not smoking. Pour 3 tablespoons batter into pan, and quickly tilt pan in all directions so batter covers pan in a thin film. Cook about 1 minute or until crêpe can be shaken loose from pan. Flip crêpe, and cook about 30 seconds.
• **Place** crêpes on a towel to cool. Stack between layers of wax paper to prevent sticking. Repeat until all batter is used. Freeze crêpes, if desired. (Thaw crêpes before frying.)
• **Pour** oil into a Dutch oven; heat to 375°. Spray a tortilla or "bird's nest" frying basket with cooking spray. Arrange 1 crêpe in bottom basket; place smaller basket on top, and secure with clip. Completely immerse basket in hot oil; fry crêpe until golden (about 1 minute). Remove from oil, and unclip frying basket. Gently turn out sombrero onto paper towels. Repeat procedure with remaining crêpes. **Yield:** 15 sombreros.

Libby and Jim Collet
Dallas, Texas

FRENCH TOAST BANANA SPLITS
(pictured at right)

3 large eggs
½ cup whipping cream
½ cup Frangelico
1½ to 2 teaspoons ground cinnamon
1 teaspoon vanilla extract
½ cup sugar
2 large bananas, sliced
2 teaspoons unsalted butter
6 croissants
1 (5-ounce) jar hot fudge topping
1 quart vanilla ice cream
½ cup chopped hazelnuts, toasted

• **Whisk** together eggs and whipping cream. Stir in liqueur, cinnamon, and vanilla. Pour into a shallow dish.
• **Place** sugar in a separate shallow dish; dredge banana in sugar.
• **Melt** butter in a nonstick skillet over medium heat; add banana, and cook until lightly browned, turning once. Remove from skillet, and keep warm.
• **Cut** croissants in half horizontally; dip in egg mixture, coating well. Cook in skillet over medium heat, 3 or 4 halves at a time, until lightly browned, turning once. Place on individual serving plates.
• **Remove** lid from hot fudge topping; microwave topping at HIGH 1 minute, stirring after 30 seconds.
• **Top** croissants with ice cream; drizzle with topping. Spoon bananas over top, and sprinkle with toasted hazelnuts. Serve immediately. **Yield:** 6 servings.

Caroline Kennedy
Lighthouse Point, Florida

French Toast Banana Splits

LOLLAPALOOZA

This crazy, mixed-up name perfectly describes this fudge sundae that begins with an awesome brownie.

¼ cup butter or margarine
1 cup (6 ounces) semisweet
   chocolate morsels
¾ cup sugar
⅔ cup all-purpose flour
¼ teaspoon baking powder
¼ teaspoon salt
2 large eggs, lightly beaten
½ teaspoon vanilla extract
½ cup chopped pecans
½ cup semisweet chocolate
   morsels
Ice cream
Easy Hot Fudge Sauce

• **Combine** butter and 1 cup chocolate morsels in a heavy saucepan. Cook over low heat, stirring constantly, until chocolate and butter melt. Remove from heat.
• **Add** sugar and next 5 ingredients, stirring until blended. Stir in pecans and ½ cup chocolate morsels.
• **Spread** mixture into a lightly greased 8-inch square pan.
• **Bake** at 350° for 30 minutes or until center is set. Cool in pan on a wire rack.
• **Cut** into squares, and serve with ice cream and warm Easy Hot Fudge Sauce. **Yield:** 16 servings.

Easy Hot Fudge Sauce

QUICK!

2 cups (12 ounces) semisweet
   chocolate morsels
1 (12-ounce) can evaporated milk
1 cup sugar
1 tablespoon butter or margarine
1 teaspoon vanilla extract

• **Combine** first 3 ingredients in a heavy saucepan.
• **Cook** over medium heat, stirring constantly, until chocolate melts and mixture comes to a boil.
• **Add** butter and vanilla, stirring until butter melts. **Yield:** 3 cups.

Cheryl Welch
Everyday Gourmet
Jackson, Mississippi

MINT-CHOCOLATE CHIP ICE CREAM SQUARES

3 cups cream-filled chocolate
   sandwich cookie crumbs
   (about 30 cookies, crushed)
¼ cup butter or margarine, melted
½ gallon mint-chocolate chip ice
   cream, slightly softened
1 (5-ounce) can evaporated milk
½ cup sugar
1½ (1-ounce) squares
   unsweetened chocolate
1 tablespoon butter or margarine
1 (12-ounce) carton frozen
   whipped topping, thawed
1 cup chopped pecans, toasted
Garnish: fresh mint sprigs

• **Combine** cookie crumbs and ¼ cup butter. Press in bottom of a lightly greased 13- x 9- x 2-inch pan; freeze.
• **Spread** ice cream evenly over crust; freeze until firm.
• **Combine** evaporated milk and next 3 ingredients in a small heavy saucepan. Bring to a boil over low heat, stirring constantly with a wire whisk. Cook, stirring constantly, 3 to 4 minutes or until thickened. Cool to room temperature.
• **Spread** chocolate mixture over ice cream; top with whipped topping, and sprinkle with pecans. Cover and freeze until firm. To serve, let stand at room temperature 10 minutes, and cut into squares. Garnish, if desired. **Yield:** 15 servings.

CARAMEL-TOFFEE BOMBE

1⅓ cups gingersnap cookie crumbs
   (about 20 cookies)
¼ cup butter or margarine, melted
1 quart vanilla ice cream, softened
4 (1.4-ounce) English toffee-
   flavored candy bars, crushed
Praline Sauce

• **Line** a 2-quart bowl with heavy-duty plastic wrap. Set aside.
• **Combine** cookie crumbs and butter; press mixture into prepared bowl. Combine ice cream and crushed candy, and spoon into bowl. Cover and freeze at least 8 hours.

• **To** serve, let bowl stand at room temperature 5 minutes; invert onto a serving plate. Carefully remove bowl and plastic wrap. Cut into wedges, and serve immediately with warm Praline Sauce. **Yield:** 10 to 12 servings.

Praline Sauce

QUICK!

½ cup firmly packed brown sugar
½ cup half-and-half
¼ cup butter or margarine
¼ cup slivered almonds, toasted
   and chopped
1 teaspoon vanilla extract

• **Combine** first 3 ingredients in a small saucepan; bring mixture to a boil over medium heat, stirring occasionally. Boil 2 minutes, stirring occasionally. Remove from heat; stir in almonds and vanilla. **Yield:** 1 cup.

Paula McCollum
Springtown, Texas

BANANAS GLACÉ

QUICK!

⅓ cup light rum
⅓ cup apricot preserves
2 tablespoons butter or margarine
2 large firm bananas
Vanilla ice cream
Garnishes: dried apricot halves,
   fresh mint leaves

• **Combine** first 3 ingredients in a small skillet; cook over medium heat until butter melts, stirring often.
• **Peel** bananas, and cut in half lengthwise. Cut each half into 6 pieces; add to skillet.
• **Cook** over low heat until thoroughly heated, stirring occasionally. Serve banana mixture immediately over vanilla ice cream; garnish, if desired. **Yield:** 4 servings.

Rita W. Cook
Corpus Christi, Texas

At right: Macadamia Nut French Toast (page 147)

EGGS AND CHEESE

GREEN EGGS AND HAM

Guacamole-stuffed eggs are topped with country ham in this recipe.

6 ounces thinly sliced country ham
12 large hard-cooked eggs
1 ripe avocado, mashed
2 tablespoons finely chopped onion
1 clove garlic, minced
2 tablespoons mayonnaise or salad dressing
1½ to 2 tablespoons fresh lime juice
1 teaspoon hot sauce
1 small tomato, peeled, seeded, and finely chopped

● **Cook** ham in a nonstick skillet over medium heat 5 minutes or until browned, turning once. Drain and finely chop.
● **Cut** eggs in half lengthwise, and carefully remove yolks. Mash yolks with a fork; add avocado and next 5 ingredients, stirring well. Fold in tomato, and spoon into egg whites. Top with ham. **Yield:** 2 dozen.

HERB-SOUR CREAM STUFFED EGGS

QUICK!

8 large hard-cooked eggs
⅓ to ½ cup sour cream
2 to 3 tablespoons finely chopped fresh chives or 2 to 3 teaspoons freeze-dried chives
1 to 2 tablespoons finely chopped fresh dill or 1 to 2 teaspoons dried dillweed
2 teaspoons white wine vinegar
¼ teaspoon salt
⅛ teaspoon ground white pepper
Garnish: fresh parsley sprigs

● **Cut** eggs in half lengthwise, and carefully remove yolks. Mash yolks; add sour cream and next 5 ingredients, stirring until smooth. Spoon or pipe into egg whites. Garnish, if desired. **Yield:** 16 servings.

SWEET DEVILED EGGS

QUICK!

8 large hard-cooked eggs
1 tablespoon sugar
2 tablespoons prepared mustard
2 tablespoons half-and-half
1 tablespoon white vinegar
½ teaspoon salt
Paprika
Garnish: fresh parsley sprigs

● **Cut** eggs in half lengthwise, and carefully remove yolks. Mash yolks; add sugar and next 4 ingredients, stirring until smooth. Spoon or pipe into egg whites. Sprinkle with paprika, and garnish, if desired. **Yield:** 16 servings.

Note: Can't find an egg-dyeing kit? Just mix 1 cup water, ¼ cup white vinegar, and a few drops of liquid food coloring for a homemade version.

Adelyne Smith
Dunnville, Kentucky

VEGETABLE-EGG SAUTÉ

3 tablespoons butter or margarine
2 medium onions, sliced
3 green bell peppers, thinly sliced
2 medium tomatoes, thinly sliced
½ cup chopped fresh parsley
¾ teaspoon salt
½ teaspoon pepper
6 large eggs
½ cup (2 ounces) shredded Muenster cheese

● **Melt** butter in a 12-inch cast-iron skillet over medium-high heat; add onion, and cook 7 minutes, stirring often. Add bell pepper, tomato, and parsley; cook 7 minutes, stirring constantly. Drain. Stir in salt and pepper.
● **Make** 6 shallow wells in vegetables with back of a spoon; break an egg into each well.
● **Cook** 6 minutes or until set. Sprinkle evenly with cheese; cover and cook 1 to 2 additional minutes or until cheese melts. Serve on toast or English muffins. **Yield:** 6 servings.

Note: For firmer eggs, cook 6 minutes; then broil 5½ inches from heat (with electric oven door partially opened) 2 additional minutes. Sprinkle with cheese; broil 1 additional minute.

Martha Smith Vaughn
Tarrant, Alabama

CHEESE-CHIVE SCRAMBLED EGGS

QUICK!

6 large eggs, lightly beaten
2 tablespoons water
¼ teaspoon seasoned salt
Dash of pepper
2 tablespoons butter or margarine
3 ounces reduced-fat cream cheese, cut into ¼-inch cubes and softened
1 tablespoon frozen chopped chives, thawed

● **Combine** first 4 ingredients.
● **Melt** butter in a large nonstick skillet over medium heat; tilt pan to coat bottom. Add egg mixture to pan; top with cream cheese and chives.
● **Cook**, without stirring, until mixture begins to set on bottom. Draw a spatula across bottom of pan to form large curds. Continue cooking until eggs are thickened but still moist; do not stir constantly. **Yield:** 4 to 6 servings.

Linda Sutton
Winston-Salem, North Carolina

CRABMEAT BRUNCH SCRAMBLE

QUICK!

¼ cup butter or margarine
1 (6-ounce) package ready-to-serve frozen crabmeat, thawed and drained
2 tablespoons sliced green onions
8 large eggs, lightly beaten
½ cup reduced-fat sour cream
2 tablespoons grated Parmesan cheese
½ teaspoon salt
⅛ teaspoon pepper
3 English muffins, split, toasted, and buttered

- **Melt** butter in a large skillet; add crabmeat and green onions. Cook over medium-high heat, stirring constantly, until green onions are tender; set aside.
- **Combine** eggs and next 4 ingredients. Add to crabmeat mixture.
- **Cook**, without stirring, over medium heat until mixture begins to set on bottom. Draw a spatula across bottom of pan to form large curds. Continue cooking until eggs are thickened but still moist; do not stir constantly.
- **Serve** immediately over English muffin halves. **Yield:** 6 servings.

Tricia Chaffin
Little Rock, Arkansas

FEATHERBED EGGS

Vegetable cooking spray
¾ cup crumbled Cornbread
1½ cups (6 ounces) shredded extra-sharp Cheddar cheese
6 large eggs, lightly beaten
1½ cups milk
1 teaspoon hot sauce
1 teaspoon Pickapeppa sauce
¼ teaspoon freshly ground pepper
¼ teaspoon seasoned salt

- **Coat** six 6-ounce ramekins or custard cups with cooking spray. Place about 2 tablespoons bread in bottom of each ramekin. Top each with ¼ cup cheese.
- **Combine** eggs and remaining ingredients; pour ½ cup into each ramekin. Bake at 375° for 20 to 25 minutes or until golden. **Yield:** 6 servings.

Cornbread

QUICK!

¼ cup butter or margarine
1 cup yellow cornmeal
1 cup all-purpose flour
1 tablespoon baking powder
¼ teaspoon baking soda
¼ teaspoon salt
2 tablespoons sugar
1¼ cups buttermilk
1 large egg, lightly beaten
¼ cup corn oil

- **Melt** butter in an 8-inch cast-iron skillet in a 375° oven for 5 minutes.

- **Combine** cornmeal and next 5 ingredients; make a well in center of mixture.
- **Combine** buttermilk, egg, and oil; add to dry ingredients, stirring just until dry ingredients are moistened.
- **Remove** skillet from oven. Pour batter into skillet. Bake at 375° for 25 minutes or until golden. **Yield:** about 6 cups crumbled cornbread or 6 servings.

Dairy Hollow House
Eureka Springs, Arkansas

EGGS CREOLE

3¾ cups water
¾ cup regular grits, uncooked
1 cup diced hot smoked sausage
¼ cup (1 ounce) shredded Cheddar cheese
2 tablespoons butter or margarine
¼ teaspoon salt
¼ cup all-purpose flour
1 large egg, beaten
1 tablespoon milk
¾ cup Italian-seasoned breadcrumbs
Vegetable oil
Poached Eggs
Creole Sauce

- **Bring** water to a boil in a large saucepan; gradually stir in grits, and return to a boil. Cover, reduce heat, and simmer 10 minutes or until done, stirring occasionally. Remove from heat; stir in sausage and next 3 ingredients.
- **Spoon** mixture into a lightly greased 13- x 9- x 2-inch pan, pressing firmly and smoothing surface. Cover and chill 24 hours.
- **Turn** grits out onto wax paper. Cut out 12 rounds with a 2½-inch round cutter, and reserving remaining grits for another use.
- **Sprinkle** rounds with flour. Combine egg and milk; dip rounds into egg mixture, and dredge in breadcrumbs.
- **Pour** oil to depth of 1 inch into a large heavy skillet. Fry grits rounds in hot oil over medium-high heat 1 to 2 minutes on each side or until lightly browned. Drain on paper towels. Place 2 rounds on each plate; top each with 2 poached eggs and Creole Sauce. Serve immediately. **Yield:** 6 servings.

Poached Eggs

QUICK!

You can poach these eggs ahead, if need be. Just slip them into simmering water for a minute or two to reheat them.

12 large eggs

- **Lightly** grease a large saucepan; add water to depth of 2 inches. Bring water to a boil; reduce heat and maintain at a light simmer.
- **Break** eggs, one at a time, into a saucer; slip eggs, one at a time, into water, holding saucer close to surface of water. Simmer 5 minutes or until cooked. Remove eggs with a slotted spoon, and trim edges, if desired. **Yield:** 12 eggs.

Creole Sauce

QUICK!

1 medium onion, cut into thin strips
1 medium-size green bell pepper, cut into thin strips
2 stalks celery, cut into thin strips
2 cloves garlic, sliced
1 bay leaf
2 tablespoons butter or margarine, melted
2 teaspoons paprika
2 medium tomatoes, diced
1 cup tomato juice
1½ tablespoons Worcestershire sauce
1 to 1½ tablespoons hot sauce
1½ tablespoons cornstarch
½ cup cold water

- **Cook** first 5 ingredients in butter in a large skillet over medium-high heat, stirring constantly, until vegetables are crisp-tender. Stir in paprika and next 4 ingredients; simmer 5 minutes or until mixture is reduced by one-fourth.
- **Combine** cornstarch and water, stirring well. Stir into sauce; bring to a boil, stirring constantly. Boil 1 minute, stirring constantly. Remove from heat. Remove and discard bay leaf. Serve warm. **Yield:** 3¾ cups.

Commander's Palace
New Orleans, Louisiana

*Lump Crab
Hash With Three-
Pepper Hollandaise;
Morrison House
Brioche, page 68*

LUMP CRAB HASH WITH THREE-PEPPER HOLLANDAISE
(pictured at left)

This recipe gets its title from the blend of pink, green, and white peppercorns in the hollandaise sauce. If you don't have a peppercorn blend, substitute black pepper.

1 large red potato, peeled and cubed
1 medium-size sweet potato, peeled and cubed
1 large red bell pepper
1 pound fresh jumbo lump crabmeat
2 tablespoons butter
1 cup chopped purple onion
1 large tomato, peeled, seeded, and chopped
2 green onions, chopped
¾ teaspoon salt
¾ teaspoon pepper
8 poached eggs
Three-Pepper Hollandaise

● **Cook** potato in boiling water to cover 4 to 5 minutes or until almost tender; drain and set aside.
● **Place** bell pepper on an aluminum foil-lined baking sheet.
● **Broil** pepper 5½ inches from heat (with electric oven door partially opened) about 5 minutes on each side or until pepper looks blistered.
● **Place** pepper in a plastic bag; seal and let stand 10 minutes to loosen skin. Peel pepper; remove and discard seeds. Coarsely chop pepper, and set aside.
● **Drain** crabmeat, removing any bits of shell; set aside.
● **Melt** butter in a skillet or Dutch oven over medium-high heat; add potato and 1 cup onion, and cook, stirring constantly, until onion is tender.
● **Add** crabmeat, bell pepper, tomato, and next 3 ingredients; cook until thoroughly heated. Spoon hash onto individual serving plates; place poached eggs onto hash, and top with Three-Pepper Hollandaise. **Yield:** 4 servings.

Three-Pepper Hollandaise
QUICK!

3 egg yolks, lightly beaten
⅓ cup dry white wine
1 tablespoon lemon juice
1 teaspoon Worcestershire sauce
1 teaspoon freshly ground mixed peppercorns
1 cup butter, melted

● **Combine** first 5 ingredients in top of a double boiler; bring water to a boil. Reduce heat to low; cook, stirring constantly with a wire whisk, 4 minutes or until a thermometer registers 160°. Remove from heat immediately.
● **Add** butter in a thin stream, whisking until blended. **Yield:** 1 cup.

Chef Ken Vedrinski
Woodlands Resort and Inn
Summerville, South Carolina

BELL PEPPER FRITTATA

3 cloves garlic, minced
1 large purple onion, sliced
2 red bell peppers, cut into thin strips
1 yellow bell pepper, cut into thin strips
3 tablespoons olive oil, divided
2 yellow squash, thinly sliced
2 zucchini, thinly sliced
½ pound fresh mushrooms, sliced
6 large eggs
¼ cup whipping cream
2½ to 3 teaspoons salt
2 teaspoons freshly ground pepper
8 slices sandwich bread, cubed
1 (8-ounce) package cream cheese, cubed
2 cups (8 ounces) shredded Swiss cheese

● **Cook** first 4 ingredients in 1 tablespoon oil in a large skillet until tender. Drain and pat dry; set aside.
● **Cook** squash and zucchini in 1 tablespoon oil in skillet until tender. Drain and pat dry; set aside.
● **Cook** mushrooms in remaining 1 tablespoon oil in skillet until tender. Drain and pat dry; set aside.

● **Whisk** together eggs and next 3 ingredients in a large bowl; stir in vegetables, half of bread cubes, cream cheese, and Swiss cheese. Press remaining bread cubes in bottom of a lightly greased 10-inch springform pan, and place on a baking sheet. Pour vegetable mixture into pan.
● **Bake** at 325° for 1 hour, covering with aluminum foil after 45 minutes to prevent excessive browning. Serve warm. **Yield:** 8 servings.

Yvonne M. Greer
Mauldin, South Carolina

POTATO-BACON FRITTATA

3 tablespoons butter or margarine
2 cups frozen potatoes with onions and peppers *
6 large eggs
2 tablespoons milk
¼ teaspoon salt
¼ teaspoon pepper
1 cup (4 ounces) shredded Cheddar cheese
6 slices bacon, cooked and crumbled
Garnish: diced fresh tomato or picante sauce

● **Melt** butter in a 10-inch nonstick skillet over medium heat; add frozen potatoes, and cook 10 minutes or until browned.
● **Combine** eggs and next 3 ingredients, stirring with a wire whisk; pour over potatoes. As mixture starts to cook, gently lift edges of frittata with a spatula, and tilt pan so uncooked portion flows underneath. If center remains uncooked, carefully turn frittata over, and cook 5 minutes or until center is done.
● **Place** frittata on serving platter, and sprinkle with shredded cheese. Cover with aluminum foil; let stand 5 minutes.
● **Sprinkle** with crumbled bacon; garnish, if desired. Serve immediately. **Yield:** 6 servings.

* For potatoes with onions and peppers, we used Potatoes O'Brien.

Judi Grigoraci
Charleston, West Virginia

FRESH VEGETABLE FRITTATA

1 large red bell pepper, chopped
1 cup sliced fresh mushrooms
1½ cups (6 ounces) shredded
    Swiss cheese, divided
¼ pound asparagus, cut into
    1-inch pieces
7 large eggs, lightly beaten
½ cup mayonnaise
½ teaspoon salt
2 tablespoons chopped fresh basil

• **Layer** pepper, mushrooms, and half of cheese in a lightly greased 9½-inch deep-dish pieplate. Top with asparagus and remaining cheese.
• **Combine** eggs and remaining 3 ingredients; pour evenly over cheese. Bake at 375° for 35 minutes or until a knife inserted in center comes out clean. Let stand 5 minutes. Serve warm or at room temperature. **Yield:** 8 servings.

Martha Johnston
Birmingham, Alabama

GOLDEN CHEESE-SHIITAKE OMELET

2 ounces fresh shiitake mushrooms
2 tablespoons butter, divided
1 small onion, finely chopped
⅔ cup cottage cheese
4 large eggs, lightly beaten
¼ teaspoon salt
¼ teaspoon freshly ground pepper

• **Remove** stems from mushrooms; discard. Cut caps into thin slices.
• **Melt** 1 tablespoon butter in a nonstick skillet over medium heat. Add mushrooms and onion; cook, stirring constantly, until tender. Transfer to a bowl, and stir in cottage cheese. Wipe skillet.
• **Combine** eggs, salt, and pepper; beat with a fork. Melt remaining butter, rotating pan to coat bottom. Add egg mixture. As mixture starts to cook, gently lift edges with a spatula, and tilt pan so uncooked portion flows underneath.
• **Spoon** mushroom mixture evenly onto half of omelet; fold omelet in half. Serve immediately. **Yield:** 2 servings.

Mariet Van den Munckh of Vedder
Dublin, Georgia

DILL-CHEESE-HAM OMELET

QUICK!

6 large eggs, lightly beaten
¼ cup milk
¼ teaspoon curry powder
½ teaspoon dried dillweed
2 teaspoons Worcestershire sauce
Vegetable cooking spray
½ cup chopped green onions
½ cup chopped cooked ham
½ cup (2 ounces) shredded
    Cheddar cheese
¼ cup (1 ounce) shredded Havarti
    cheese

• **Combine** first 5 ingredients; set aside.
• **Coat** a 10-inch omelet pan or nonstick skillet with cooking spray; add green onions, and cook over medium heat until tender.
• **Add** egg mixture. As mixture starts to cook, gently lift edges with a spatula, and tilt pan so uncooked portion flows underneath. Top with ham and cheeses.
• **Cover** and cook 3 minutes or until set. Fold in half; serve immediately. **Yield:** 4 servings.

Tom Maze
Petersburg, Virginia

SHRIMP AND CHEESE OMELET

QUICK!

2 large eggs
1 tablespoon water
1 tablespoon butter or margarine
3 tablespoons shredded Monterey
    Jack cheese
¼ cup coarsely chopped cooked
    shrimp
1 tablespoon sliced green
    onions
2 teaspoons chopped fresh
    parsley

• **Whisk** together eggs and 1 tablespoon water; set aside.
• **Heat** an 8-inch omelet pan or nonstick skillet over medium heat. Add butter, and rotate pan to coat. Add egg mixture. As mixture starts to cook, gently lift edges with a spatula, and tilt pan so uncooked portion of egg mixture flows underneath.

• **Sprinkle** half of omelet with cheese and next 3 ingredients; fold in half. Serve immediately. **Yield:** 1 serving.

♥ To reduce fat and cholesterol, substitute ½ cup fat-free egg substitute and 1 egg white, vegetable cooking spray, and reduced-fat Monterey Jack cheese for eggs, butter, and cheese, respectively.

THREE-CHEESE SOUFFLÉS
(pictured at right)

The subtle blend of Parmesan,
Cheddar, and cream cheeses makes this
a soufflé you won't soon forget.

2 tablespoons grated Parmesan
    cheese
4 large eggs, separated
1 cup (4 ounces) shredded sharp
    Cheddar cheese
1 (3-ounce) package cream cheese,
    cubed
⅓ cup half-and-half
¼ cup grated Parmesan cheese
½ teaspoon onion salt
½ teaspoon dry mustard
¼ teaspoon ground red pepper

• **Sprinkle** 2 tablespoons Parmesan cheese evenly into five buttered individual soufflé dishes or 6-ounce custard cups. Set aside.
• **Beat** egg whites at high speed with an electric mixer until stiff.
• **Combine** egg yolks, Cheddar cheese, and remaining 6 ingredients in container of an electric blender; process 30 seconds or until smooth. Process at high speed 10 to 15 seconds; pour into a bowl. Gently fold in egg whites; pour into prepared dishes. Seal in aluminum foil, and freeze up to 1 week.
• **Unwrap** soufflés, and place in an 8-inch square pan. Add hot water to pan to depth of 1 inch.
• **Bake** at 400° for 10 minutes; reduce oven temperature to 350°, and bake 20 to 25 additional minutes or until puffed and golden. Serve immediately. **Yield:** 5 servings.

Note: If not freezing soufflés, bake as directed at 350° for 20 to 25 minutes.

Three-Cheese Soufflés

CHILE-CHEESE SOUFFLÉS

¼ cup butter or margarine
¼ cup all-purpose flour
1¾ cups milk
¾ cup (3 ounces) shredded sharp
     Cheddar cheese
¾ cup (3 ounces) shredded
     Monterey Jack cheese
1 (4.5-ounce) can chopped green
     chiles, drained
1 teaspoon salt
6 large eggs, separated

• **Melt** butter in a heavy saucepan over low heat; add flour, whisking until smooth. Cook 1 minute, whisking constantly. Gradually add milk, and cook over medium heat, whisking constantly, until thickened and bubbly.
• **Add** cheeses, chiles, and salt, stirring until cheeses melt.
• **Beat** egg yolks at medium speed with an electric mixer until thick and pale. Gradually stir about one-fourth of hot mixture into yolks; add to remaining hot mixture, stirring constantly. Bring to a boil; remove from heat.
• **Beat** egg whites at high speed until stiff but not dry; gently fold into cheese mixture. Pour into nine buttered individual soufflé dishes or 6-ounce custard cups. Seal in aluminum foil, and freeze up to 1 week.
• **Unwrap** soufflés, and place in a 13- x 9- x 2-inch pan. Add hot water to pan to depth of 1 inch.
• **Bake** at 400° for 10 minutes; reduce oven temperature to 350°, and bake 25 additional minutes or until puffed and golden. Serve immediately. **Yield:** 9 servings.

Note: If not freezing soufflés, bake as directed at 350° for 25 minutes.

QUICHE CASSEROLE

QUICK!

6 slices whole wheat bread, torn
¼ teaspoon garlic powder
1 (26-ounce) carton frozen quiche
     filling with ham, thawed
1 medium-size red bell pepper, cut
     into rings

• **Place** bread evenly in a lightly greased 11- x 7- x 1½-inch baking dish; set aside.
• **Stir** garlic powder into quiche filling; pour over bread.
• **Bake** at 400° for 20 minutes; top with pepper rings, and bake 5 additional minutes. Let casserole stand 5 minutes before serving. **Yield:** 4 to 6 servings.

SUNDAY EGG CASSEROLE

2 tablespoons butter or margarine
4 tablespoons dry sherry, divided
1 pound fresh mushrooms, sliced
1 (10¾-ounce) can cream of
     chicken soup, undiluted
1 (8-ounce) carton sour cream
2 tablespoons all-purpose flour
½ teaspoon salt
½ teaspoon pepper
1 tablespoon finely chopped onion
1 (2-ounce) jar chopped pimiento,
     drained
1 (10-ounce) package frozen
     English peas, thawed and
     drained
14 hard-cooked eggs, cut
     lengthwise into 4 wedges
1 (8-ounce) can sliced water
     chestnuts, drained
1 cup fresh breadcrumbs (2 slices
     bread)
1 tablespoon butter or margarine,
     melted

• **Melt** 2 tablespoons butter in a large skillet; add 2 tablespoons sherry and mushrooms, and cook over medium heat 5 minutes or until mushrooms are tender. Drain well; set aside.
• **Combine** remaining 2 tablespoons sherry, soup, and next 6 ingredients in a medium saucepan. Cook 2 minutes or until mixture is bubbly; stir in mushrooms and peas.

• **Arrange** egg wedges and water chestnuts in bottom of a lightly greased 13- x 9- x 2-inch baking dish. Pour soup mixture evenly over top.
• **Combine** breadcrumbs and melted butter. Sprinkle over soup mixture.
• **Bake** at 375° for 20 minutes or until top is golden. **Yield:** 6 to 8 servings.

Brenda Russell
Signal Mountain, Tennessee

EGGS BAKED IN
MUSHROOM SAUCE

1 pound fresh mushrooms, sliced
¼ cup butter or margarine,
     melted
3 tablespoons all-purpose flour
2 cups whipping cream
1 egg yolk, lightly beaten
1 teaspoon beef-flavored bouillon
     granules
1 tablespoon grated onion
2 tablespoons chopped fresh
     parsley
¼ teaspoon salt
¼ teaspoon pepper
⅛ teaspoon dried thyme
8 large eggs
Grated Parmesan cheese
4 English muffins, halved and
     toasted

• **Cook** mushrooms in melted butter in a large saucepan over medium heat 5 minutes, stirring constantly; remove mushrooms with a slotted spoon, and set aside. Add flour to drippings in saucepan, stirring until smooth. Cook, stirring constantly, 1 minute.
• **Combine** whipping cream and next 3 ingredients. Gradually add to flour mixture; cook over medium heat, stirring constantly, until mixture is thickened and bubbly. Stir in reserved mushrooms, parsley, and next 3 ingredients.
• **Pour** into a lightly greased 13- x 9- x 2-inch baking dish. Make 8 indentations in mushroom mixture, and break an egg into each. Sprinkle each with Parmesan cheese, and bake at 350° for 7 to 8 minutes. Serve over English muffin halves. **Yield:** 8 servings.

Sally B. Harris
Tarboro, North Carolina

LAYERED VEGETABLE CHEESECAKE

1⅓ cups dry breadcrumbs
⅓ cup butter or margarine,
    melted
2 (8-ounce) packages Neufchâtel
    cheese, softened
2 large eggs
⅓ cup all-purpose flour
1 (8-ounce) carton sour cream
¼ cup minced onion
¼ teaspoon salt
¼ teaspoon ground white pepper
¾ cup shredded carrot
¾ cup diced green bell pepper
¾ cup diced red bell pepper
Cucumber-Dill Sauce
Garnishes: cucumber slices, fresh
    dill sprigs

• **Combine** breadcrumbs and butter; press in bottom and 1 inch up sides of a 9-inch springform pan. Set aside.
• **Beat** cheese at high speed with an electric mixer until fluffy. Add eggs, one at a time, beating well after each addition. Add flour and next 4 ingredients; beat until blended.
• **Pour** about one-fourth of cheese mixture into prepared pan; sprinkle with carrot. Top with one-third remaining cheese mixture; sprinkle with green bell pepper. Top with half of remaining cheese mixture; top with red bell pepper. Top with remaining cheese mixture.
• **Bake** at 300° for 1 hour or until set. Turn oven off, and partially open oven door; leave cheesecake in oven 1 hour. Remove from oven; cool completely in pan on a wire rack. Cover and chill. Serve with Cucumber-Dill Sauce. Garnish, if desired. **Yield:** 6 to 8 servings.

Cucumber-Dill Sauce

QUICK!

1 (8-ounce) carton plain yogurt
⅓ cup mayonnaise or salad
    dressing
½ cup chopped unpeeled
    cucumber
¼ teaspoon salt
¼ teaspoon dried dillweed

• **Combine** all ingredients, stirring well. Cover and chill. **Yield:** 1½ cups.

GARLICKY HAM AND SPINACH GRITS

1 head garlic
2 to 3 teaspoons olive oil
4 ounces thinly sliced country
    ham, cut into ¼-inch strips
1 tablespoon peanut or
    vegetable oil
3 cups chicken broth
1 cup quick-cooking grits
½ cup butter or margarine
¼ teaspoon salt
¼ teaspoon pepper
1 cup milk
4 large eggs
1 cup (4 ounces) shredded Swiss
    cheese
1 (10-ounce) package frozen
    chopped spinach, thawed and
    well drained
¼ cup grated Parmesan cheese

• **Cut** off flat end of garlic head, and spread apart whole cloves, leaving tight outer covering intact. Trim pointed end so head will sit flat. Place garlic head, trimmed end down, in a garlic roaster or on a sheet of aluminum foil.
• **Drizzle** with olive oil; cover with lid or wrap in aluminum foil.
• **Bake** at 350° for 1 hour or until golden. Cool.
• **Squeeze** out pulp from each clove.
• **Position** knife blade in food processor bowl, and add garlic pulp. Process until smooth, stopping often to scrape down sides. Set aside.
• **Cook** ham in peanut oil in a skillet over medium-high heat, stirring constantly, until browned. Drain on paper towels, and set aside.
• **Bring** broth to a boil in a large saucepan; stir in grits. Cook over medium heat 3 to 5 minutes or until thick, stirring often. Remove from heat.
• **Stir** in garlic puree, butter, salt, and pepper.
• **Combine** milk and eggs; add to grits mixture, stirring well. Fold in ham, Swiss cheese, and spinach.
• **Grease** an 11- x 7- x 1½-inch baking dish or eight 10-ounce custard cups. Sprinkle bottom and sides of baking dish or cups with Parmesan cheese, coating well. Spoon grits mixture evenly into baking dish or cups.

• **Bake** at 350° for 45 minutes (35 minutes for cups) or until puffed and firm. Serve immediately. **Yield:** 8 servings.

Note: To freeze Garlicky Ham and Spinach Grits, prepare as directed, but do not bake. Cover unbaked grits with aluminum foil, and freeze. To serve, thaw in refrigerator; remove from refrigerator, and let stand 30 minutes. Bake as directed.

CHRISTMAS MORNING STRATA

1 pound ground pork sausage
2 teaspoons prepared mustard
6 slices white sandwich bread,
    crusts removed
2 cups (8 ounces) shredded Swiss
    cheese
1½ cups milk
3 large eggs, lightly beaten
½ teaspoon Worcestershire
    sauce
⅛ teaspoon salt
⅛ teaspoon pepper
⅛ teaspoon ground nutmeg

• **Brown** sausage in a skillet over medium heat, stirring until it crumbles; drain well. Stir in mustard.
• **Fit** bread in a greased 11- x 7- x 1½-inch baking dish; top with sausage mixture and cheese.
• **Combine** milk and remaining 5 ingredients; pour over bread mixture. Cover and chill 8 hours.
• **Bake**, uncovered, at 350° for 50 minutes or until set. **Yield:** 6 servings.

Karen Belle
Lovettsville, Virginia

HAM AND EGGS CRESCENT PIZZA

1 (8-ounce) can refrigerated
   crescent rolls
¼ cup chopped onion
1 tablespoon butter or margarine,
   melted
1 cup finely chopped cooked
   ham
1 cup (4 ounces) shredded Swiss
   cheese
4 large eggs, lightly beaten
½ cup milk
½ teaspoon salt
¼ teaspoon pepper
1 tablespoon chopped fresh or
   frozen chives

• **Unroll** crescent rolls, and place in an ungreased 13- x 9- x 2-inch pan. Press crescent rolls ½ inch up sides to form a crust; seal perforations. Bake on lower rack of oven at 375° for 5 minutes, and set aside.
• **Cook** onion in butter in a small skillet over medium heat, stirring constantly, until crisp-tender; stir in ham, and spoon evenly over dough. Sprinkle with cheese.
• **Combine** eggs and next 3 ingredients; pour over cheese. Sprinkle with chives.
• **Bake** at 350° for 25 to 30 minutes or until set. Serve immediately. **Yield:** 6 to 8 servings.

Mrs. Ezra Sanders
Obion, Tennessee

JALAPEÑO CHEESE PIE

This is a good recipe for the flavor-timid. The heat of the peppers is soothingly coated with cheese. Stir in chicken or sausage for an easy brunch dish.

1 (11.5-ounce) jar whole jalapeño
   peppers, drained
4 cups (16 ounces) shredded
   Cheddar cheese
6 large eggs, lightly beaten

• **Cut** peppers in half lengthwise; remove and discard seeds. Rinse with cold water; drain on paper towels. Mince peppers.

• **Sprinkle** half of cheese in a lightly greased 11- x 7- x 1½-inch pan; top with peppers and remaining cheese. Pour eggs over top.
• **Bake** at 350° for 30 to 40 minutes or until lightly browned and set. Cool 5 to 10 minutes, and cut into squares. **Yield:** 12 servings.

Adapted from
Cooking Texas Style
Candy and Sandra Marquez
San Antonio, Texas

SPINACH PIE WITH MUENSTER CRUST

3 (10-ounce) packages frozen
   chopped spinach, thawed
2 (6-ounce) packages Muenster
   cheese slices
1 small onion, finely chopped
1 cup reduced-fat cottage cheese
3 large eggs, lightly beaten
⅓ cup grated Parmesan cheese
½ teaspoon salt
¼ teaspoon pepper
Garnish: pimiento strips

• **Drain** spinach well, pressing between layers of paper towels, and set spinach aside.
• **Cut** 2 or 3 cheese slices into small triangles, and reserve for top of pie. Cover bottom and sides of a lightly greased 9-inch pieplate with remaining Muenster slices, overlapping cheese as needed.
• **Combine** spinach, onion, and next 5 ingredients; spoon into cheese-lined pieplate.
• **Bake** at 350° for 45 minutes or until set. Top with reserved cheese triangles. Cool 10 minutes before serving. Garnish, if desired. **Yield:** 6 to 8 servings.

Michelle Stockhaus
Lorton, Virginia

SPINACH PIE PARMA

2 cups garlic-onion croutons,
   crushed
¼ cup butter or margarine,
   melted
1 pound fresh spinach, torn *
¼ cup water
3 large eggs, lightly beaten
1 cup small-curd cottage cheese
¼ cup freshly grated Parmesan
   cheese
¼ cup chopped onion
2 tablespoons sour cream
2 or 3 cloves garlic, pressed
½ teaspoon salt
⅛ teaspoon ground red pepper
4 ounces Monterey Jack cheese,
   cut into ¼-inch cubes
2 tablespoons freshly grated
   Parmesan cheese

• **Combine** croutons and butter, stirring well; press into bottom of an 8-inch square baking dish.
• **Combine** spinach and ¼ cup water in a skillet; cover and cook over medium heat 4 minutes or until wilted. Drain well on paper towels.
• **Combine** spinach, eggs, and next 7 ingredients, stirring well; stir in Monterey Jack cheese, and spoon over prepared crust.
• **Bake** at 350° for 35 minutes or until knife inserted in center comes out clean. Sprinkle with 2 tablespoons Parmesan cheese, and let stand 5 minutes. **Yield:** 6 servings.

* Substitute 1 (10-ounce) package frozen chopped spinach, thawed and well drained, for fresh.

TORTILLA PIE

QUICK!

1 (16-ounce) can refried beans
1 teaspoon chili powder
½ teaspoon ground cumin
8 (8-inch) flour tortillas
½ (16-ounce) jar chunky salsa
2 (4-ounce) cartons guacamole
1 (8-ounce) package shredded
    Mexican cheese blend
Garnishes: fresh cilantro sprigs,
    sour cream

• **Combine** first 3 ingredients in a small bowl, stirring well; set aside.
• **Place** 1 tortilla in a lightly greased 9-inch round cakepan; spread with half of bean mixture, and top with another tortilla. Spread with half of salsa, and top with another tortilla. Spread with half of guacamole, and top with another tortilla. Sprinkle with half of cheese, and top with another tortilla.
• **Repeat** layers with remaining ingredients, ending with cheese; cover with aluminum foil.
• **Bake** at 350° for 20 minutes or until thoroughly heated. Cut pie into wedges; garnish, if desired. **Yield:** 6 servings.

CREAM CHEESE QUICHE

½ (15-ounce) package
    refrigerated piecrusts
1 tablespoon butter or margarine
¼ cup chopped onion
1 (8-ounce) package cream cheese,
    cubed
¾ cup milk
4 large eggs, lightly beaten
1 cup finely chopped cooked ham
1 (2-ounce) jar diced pimiento,
    undrained
¼ teaspoon dried dillweed
⅛ teaspoon pepper

• **Fit** piecrust into a 9-inch quiche dish according to package directions; prick bottom and sides with a fork.
• **Bake** piecrust at 425° for 12 minutes; set aside.
• **Melt** butter in a small saucepan over medium-high heat; add onion, and cook until tender. Add cream cheese and

milk; cook over low heat, whisking until cream cheese melts. Gradually whisk about one-fourth of hot mixture into eggs; add to remaining hot mixture, whisking constantly. Whisk in ham and remaining 3 ingredients; pour mixture into prepared crust.
• **Bake** at 350° for 35 to 40 minutes or until set. **Yield:** 6 to 8 servings.

MEXICALI QUICHE WITH AVOCADO TOPPING

6 (6-inch) corn tortillas
½ pound ground hot pork
    sausage
¼ cup finely chopped onion
1 tablespoon chili powder
1 teaspoon ground cumin
3 large eggs, lightly beaten
1 (4.5-ounce) can chopped green
    chiles, undrained and divided
1½ cups half-and-half
½ teaspoon salt
⅛ teaspoon pepper
1½ cups (6 ounces) shredded
    Monterey Jack cheese, divided
Avocado Topping

• **Pour** water to depth of 2 inches into a large skillet. Bring to a boil; remove from heat.
• **Dip** each tortilla in water to soften; drain on paper towels. Place tortillas in six lightly greased 10-ounce custard cups; set aside.
• **Cook** sausage and next 3 ingredients in skillet over medium heat until meat is browned, stirring until it crumbles; drain and set aside.
• **Combine** eggs, half of green chiles, half-and-half, salt, and pepper in a large bowl; stir in sausage mixture.
• **Spoon** half of egg mixture evenly into tortilla shells; sprinkle with half of cheese. Pour remaining egg mixture evenly over cheese.
• **Bake** at 350° for 20 minutes. Sprinkle with remaining half of cheese, and bake 5 additional minutes.
• **Remove** from oven, and let stand 5 minutes. Remove from custard cups, and sprinkle with remaining green chiles. Serve with Avocado Topping. **Yield:** 6 servings.

Avocado Topping

QUICK!

1 avocado, mashed
1 tomato, peeled, seeded, and
    chopped
1 clove garlic, minced
1 to 2 tablespoons lime juice

• **Combine** all ingredients in a small bowl. **Yield:** 1½ cups.

Note: To make quiche in a 9-inch deep-dish pieplate, soften 8 corn tortillas in boiling water as directed; place in lightly greased pieplate, overlapping and extending tortillas about ½ inch over edge. Spoon half of egg mixture into shell; sprinkle with half of cheese, and spoon remaining egg mixture over cheese. Bake at 350° for 30 minutes. Sprinkle with remaining cheese; bake 5 additional minutes. Remove from oven; let stand 5 minutes. Sprinkle with remaining green chiles. Serve with Avocado Topping. Yield: 6 servings.

TEX-MEX EGG BURRITOS

QUICK!

1 pound ground hot pork sausage
12 large eggs, lightly beaten
1 (4.5-ounce) can chopped green
    chiles, drained
8 (8-inch) flour tortillas, warmed
Picante sauce
Shredded Cheddar cheese
Sliced jalapeño peppers (optional)

• **Brown** sausage in a large skillet, stirring until it crumbles; drain. Add eggs and chiles to sausage.
• **Cook**, without stirring, over medium heat until mixture begins to set on bottom. Draw a spatula across bottom of pan to form large curds. Continue cooking until eggs are thickened but still moist; do not stir constantly.
• **Spoon** egg mixture evenly down center of tortillas; top each with picante sauce, cheese, and jalapeño peppers, if desired. Fold opposite sides over filling. Serve immediately. **Yield:** 8 servings.

Georgana McNeil
Houston, Texas

ROASTED CHILES RELLENOS WITH TOMATILLO SAUCE

8 Anaheim chile peppers *
10 tomatillos, husked
1 small onion, sliced
2 cloves garlic, minced
¼ teaspoon salt
¼ teaspoon pepper
¼ teaspoon ground cumin
2 tablespoons chopped fresh
    cilantro
¾ cup canned black beans,
    drained and rinsed
1 cup (4 ounces) shredded
    reduced-fat Monterey Jack
    cheese
1 egg white
¼ cup fat-free egg substitute
¾ cup all-purpose flour
1 teaspoon vegetable oil
Vegetable cooking spray

• **Place** chile peppers, tomatillos, and onion on food rack of grill.
• **Cook,** covered with grill lid, over hot coals (400° to 500°) about 5 minutes on each side or until chile peppers look blistered, and tomatillos and onion slices are lightly browned.
• **Place** peppers immediately into a heavy-duty, zip-top plastic bag; seal and chill at least 8 hours.
• **Place** grilled vegetables in an airtight container; cover and chill at least 8 hours.
• **Peel** peppers, and remove and discard seeds; set aside.
• **Combine** tomatillos, onion, garlic, and next 3 ingredients in container of an electric blender. Process until smooth, stopping once to scrape down sides. Stir in cilantro; set tomatillo sauce aside.
• **Combine** black beans and cheese; spoon into peppers (some peppers may split). Set aside.
• **Beat** egg white at high speed with an electric mixer until stiff peaks form; gradually beat in egg substitute. Set aside.
• **Coat** stuffed peppers with flour; dip into egg white mixture, and lightly re-coat peppers with flour.
• **Add** oil to a large nonstick skillet coated with cooking spray. Cook chiles in hot oil on both sides until lightly

browned. Serve immediately with tomatillo sauce. **Yield:** 4 servings.

* Instead of grilling 8 Anaheim chile peppers, substitute 3 (4.5-ounce) cans whole green chiles, drained.

❤ Per serving: Calories 311
Fat 8.3g Cholesterol 19mg
Sodium 523mg

SOUTHERN-STYLE CHILES RELLENOS

We enjoyed the Southern flair of this batch. How can you go wrong with cheese grits and country ham?

8 large poblano or Anaheim chile
    peppers
Creamy Grits
3 large eggs, lightly beaten
½ cup whipping cream
1 cup all-purpose flour
1 cup yellow cornmeal
½ teaspoon salt
Peanut oil
Country Ham Sauce
Garnishes: shredded Cheddar
    cheese, sliced green onions

• **Place** peppers on an aluminum foil-lined baking sheet.
• **Broil** 5½ inches from heat (with electric oven door partially opened) about 5 minutes on each side or until peppers look blistered.
• **Place** peppers in a bowl or heavy-duty, zip-top plastic bag; cover bowl with plastic wrap or seal bag. Let stand 10 minutes to loosen skins.
• **Peel** peppers; carefully cut peppers lengthwise on 1 side, leaving stems attached. Remove seeds.
• **Spoon** Creamy Grits into a large heavy-duty, zip-top plastic bag; seal. Snip a hole in one corner of bag; squeeze grits into peppers. Secure stuffed peppers with wooden picks, if desired. Cover and chill until firm.
• **Combine** eggs and whipping cream, stirring well.
• **Combine** flour, cornmeal, and salt in a shallow dish; carefully dredge stuffed peppers in cornmeal mixture, and dip in

egg mixture. Dredge again in cornmeal mixture.
• **Pour** peanut oil to depth of 1 inch into a large cast-iron or heavy skillet, and heat to 375°. Fry peppers, two at a time, cut side up, 2 minutes, turning once. Drain on paper towels, and remove wooden picks.
• **Serve** with Country Ham Sauce; garnish, if desired. **Yield:** 4 servings.

Creamy Grits

QUICK!

3 (10¾-ounce) cans condensed
    chicken broth, undiluted
½ cup whipping cream
1 cup quick-cooking grits,
    uncooked
2 cups (8 ounces) shredded sharp
    Cheddar cheese

• **Combine** chicken broth and whipping cream in a large saucepan; bring to a boil. Stir in grits, and return to a boil. Cover, reduce heat, and simmer 5 to 7 minutes. Stir in cheese. Cool 10 minutes. **Yield:** 4 cups.

Country Ham Sauce

QUICK!

¼ cup butter or margarine
¼ cup all-purpose flour
1 (10¾-ounce) can condensed
    chicken broth
¾ cup whipping cream
¼ cup water
¼ cup chopped country ham
1 teaspoon freshly ground
    pepper

• **Melt** butter in a heavy saucepan over low heat; add flour, stirring until smooth. Cook, stirring constantly, 3 to 5 minutes or until lightly browned.
• **Add** broth, whipping cream, and water gradually; cook over medium heat, stirring constantly with a wire whisk, until thickened and bubbly. Stir in ham and pepper. **Yield:** 2½ cups.

Terry L. Ward
Helena, Alabama

CRÊPES CON QUESO

1 cup all-purpose flour
½ cup yellow cornmeal
1 tablespoon chili powder
1 teaspoon salt
1 cup chicken broth
3 large eggs
Vegetable cooking spray
Crêpe Filling
1 cup (4 ounces) shredded
    Cheddar cheese
Garnish: fresh cilantro sprigs

● **Position** knife blade in food processor; add first 6 ingredients. Process until smooth. Cover and chill at least 2 hours.
● **Coat** an 8-inch nonstick skillet with cooking spray; place over medium heat until hot. Pour ⅓ cup batter into pan; quickly tilt pan in all directions so batter covers bottom of pan. Cook 1 minute or until crêpe can be shaken loose from pan. Turn crêpe over; cook about 30 seconds. Place on a towel to cool. Repeat with remaining batter.
● **Spoon** about ½ cup Crêpe Filling on half of each crêpe; roll up, and place, seam side down, in a lightly greased 13- x 9- x 2-inch baking dish. Sprinkle crêpes evenly with cheese.
● **Bake** at 300° for 5 minutes. Garnish, if desired. **Yield:** 4 servings.

Crêpe Filling

QUICK!

1 tablespoon butter or margarine
1 large onion, coarsely chopped
1 green bell pepper, coarsely
    chopped
1 red bell pepper, coarsely
    chopped
1 bunch green onions, sliced
4 cloves garlic, minced
2 (4.5-ounce) cans chopped green
    chiles, drained
1½ cups whipping cream
1 cup (4 ounces) shredded Swiss
    cheese
2½ cups shredded cooked
    chicken
2 teaspoons Cajun poultry
    seasoning blend *
¼ teaspoon salt
¼ teaspoon pepper

● **Melt** butter in a large skillet over medium heat; add chopped onion and next 4 ingredients, and cook, stirring constantly, 5 minutes or until tender.
● **Stir** in chiles and whipping cream; bring to a boil. Reduce heat, and simmer 15 minutes.
● **Stir** in cheese and remaining ingredients; cook 3 minutes. **Yield:** 4 cups.

* For Cajun poultry seasoning blend, we used Chef Paul Prudhomme's Poultry Magic.

Odile Besseau and Durfee Bedsole
The Taylor House
Marshall, Texas

THREE CHEESE-STUFFED FRENCH TOAST

8 (2-inch-thick) slices French
    bread
¾ cup (3 ounces) shredded
    mozzarella cheese
½ (8-ounce) package cream
    cheese, softened
1 tablespoon ricotta cheese
3 tablespoons apricot jam
2 large eggs, lightly beaten
½ cup milk
1 cup corn flake crumbs
2 tablespoons butter or margarine
1 (12-ounce) bottle apricot syrup
¼ cup butter or margarine
2 tablespoons sugar
2 teaspoons ground ginger
16 peach slices
Sifted powdered sugar

● **Starting** from 1 side, split each bread slice, leaving opposite side of bread attached (so that when open, bread looks like butterfly wings). Using a fork, hollow out a shallow pocket on the inside of each slice, discarding crumbs; set aside.
● **Combine** cheeses; stir in apricot jam. Spoon about 2 tablespoons cheese mixture into each bread slice, and place slices in a 13- x 9- x 2-inch baking dish. Cover and chill 8 hours.
● **Combine** eggs and milk; dip bread in mixture, and dredge in corn flake crumbs. Melt 2 tablespoons butter in a large skillet over medium heat; cook bread 2 minutes on each side or until golden. Place in a lightly greased 13- x 9- x 2-inch baking dish. Bake at 400° for 15 minutes.
● **Cook** syrup in a saucepan over low heat until thoroughly heated; remove from heat, and keep warm.
● **Combine** ¼ cup butter, sugar, and ginger in a large skillet over medium heat; add peaches, and cook 3 minutes, stirring gently.
● **Arrange** French toast on individual plates; top each serving evenly with peach slices, and sprinkle with powdered sugar. Serve with syrup. **Yield:** 8 servings.

Seven Sisters Inn
Ocala, Florida

MACADAMIA NUT FRENCH TOAST
(pictured on page 135)

4 large eggs, lightly beaten
¼ cup sugar
¼ teaspoon ground nutmeg
⅔ cup orange juice
⅓ cup milk
½ teaspoon vanilla extract
1 (16-ounce) loaf Italian bread,
    cut into 1-inch slices
⅔ cup butter or margarine, melted
½ cup macadamia nuts, chopped
    and toasted
Garnishes: powdered sugar, ground
    nutmeg
Maple syrup

● **Combine** first 6 ingredients in a bowl, stirring well.
● **Fit** bread slices in a single layer in a lightly greased 13- x 9- x 2-inch baking dish. Pour egg mixture over bread slices; cover and chill at least 8 hours, turning bread once.
● **Pour** butter in a 15- x 10- x 1-inch jelly-roll pan; place bread slices in a single layer in pan.
● **Bake** at 400° for 10 minutes, and sprinkle evenly with nuts. Bake 10 additional minutes. Garnish, if desired. Serve immediately with maple syrup. **Yield:** 6 servings.

Michelle Ettenger
Alpharetta, Georgia

EGGNOG FRENCH TOAST

QUICK!

1½ cups refrigerated eggnog
½ teaspoon freshly grated nutmeg
8 (1-inch-thick) slices French bread
2 tablespoons butter or margarine
Rum Syrup

• **Combine** eggnog and nutmeg in a shallow dish. Place bread slices in dish, turning to coat.
• **Melt** butter in a large skillet. Remove bread slices from eggnog mixture, allowing excess to drain. Cook in skillet 3 minutes on each side or until golden. Serve immediately with Rum Syrup. **Yield:** 4 servings.

Rum Syrup

QUICK!

1 cup pure maple syrup
2 tablespoons butter or margarine
2 tablespoons light rum or
  ½ teaspoon rum extract

• **Combine** all ingredients in a saucepan; cook over low heat until heated, stirring often. **Yield:** 1¼ cups.

*Hugh Montgomery
Birmingham, Alabama*

STUFFED FRENCH TOAST

Texans Gail Drago and Ann Ruff discovered this wonderful recipe when researching their book, Texas Historic Inns Cookbook.

1 (8-ounce) package cream cheese, softened
¼ cup crushed pineapple
½ cup chopped pecans, toasted
1 (16-ounce) loaf French bread
4 large eggs
1 cup whipping cream
1 teaspoon ground ginger
½ teaspoon vanilla extract
1 (12-ounce) jar apricot preserves
½ cup orange juice

• **Beat** cream cheese and pineapple at medium speed with an electric mixer

until mixture is light and fluffy; stir in pecans.
• **Cut** bread into 12 (1½-inch-thick) slices; cut a pocket through top crust of each slice. Stuff each slice evenly with cream cheese mixture.
• **Combine** eggs and next 3 ingredients, stirring well with a wire whisk. Dip bread slices in egg mixture, coating all sides.
• **Cook** on a lightly greased griddle over medium-high heat 3 minutes on each side or until golden.
• **Combine** preserves and orange juice in a saucepan; cook over low heat, stirring constantly, until preserves are melted. Serve with hot French toast. **Yield:** 6 servings.

*Annie's Bed and Breakfast
Big Sandy, Texas*

BRUNCH POPOVER PANCAKE

4 large eggs, lightly beaten
1 cup milk
1 cup all-purpose flour
¼ teaspoon salt
⅓ cup butter or margarine, melted
3 tablespoons orange marmalade
3 tablespoons butter or margarine
1 tablespoon lemon juice
1 (16-ounce) package frozen sliced peaches, thawed and drained
1 cup frozen blueberries, thawed

• **Place** a well-greased 12-inch cast-iron skillet in a 425° oven for 5 minutes.
• **Combine** first 5 ingredients, stirring with a wire whisk until blended.
• **Remove** skillet from oven. Pour batter into hot skillet.
• **Bake** at 425° for 20 to 25 minutes. (This pancake resembles a giant popover and will fall quickly after removing from oven.)
• **Combine** marmalade, 3 tablespoons butter, and lemon juice in a saucepan; bring to a boil. Add peaches, and cook over medium heat 2 to 3 minutes, stirring constantly.
• **Spoon** mixture on top of baked pancake. Sprinkle with blueberries. **Yield:** 4 servings.

*Bunny Campbell
Gainesville, Florida*

ARKANSAS GERMAN-BAKED PANCAKE

Innkeeper Crescent Dragonwagon published this recipe and hundreds more in her book, The Dairy Hollow House Cookbook.

3 large eggs
¾ cup milk
½ teaspoon vanilla extract
¾ cup all-purpose flour
½ teaspoon salt
1½ tablespoons butter or margarine
Apple Filling
Sifted powdered sugar
Whipped cream

• **Heat** a 12-inch cast-iron skillet in a 450° oven for 5 minutes.
• **Combine** first 3 ingredients in a mixing bowl; beat at medium speed with an electric mixer until smooth. Add flour and salt; beat 5 minutes.
• **Melt** butter in skillet; pour batter into hot skillet.
• **Bake** at 450° for 15 minutes; reduce oven temperature to 350°, and bake 8 additional minutes or until puffed and browned. Remove from oven; spoon warm Apple Filling over pancake (pancake will deflate). Sprinkle with powdered sugar, and dollop with whipped cream. Cut into wedges, and serve immediately. **Yield:** 4 servings.

Apple Filling

QUICK!

¼ cup butter or margarine
4 large Granny Smith apples, cored and sliced
¼ cup honey

• **Melt** butter in a large skillet over medium-high heat; add apple, and cook, stirring constantly, 12 minutes or until tender. Stir in honey; cook just until thoroughly heated. **Yield:** 4 servings.

*Dairy Hollow House
Eureka Springs, Arkansas*

At right: *Crab-Stuffed Lobster Tail (page 168) and Blue Cheese-Walnut Stuffed Fillet (page 187)*

FISH AND SHELLFISH

BARBECUED FISH TACOS

QUICK!

4 (8-inch) flour tortillas
1 pound amberjack or other lean,
   mild fish fillet
¼ teaspoon salt
¼ teaspoon pepper
¼ cup sweet barbecue sauce
Vegetable cooking spray
Sour cream
Sliced green onions
Lime wedges

• **Wrap** tortillas in aluminum foil.
• **Bake** at 350° for 10 minutes or until thoroughly heated.
• **Sprinkle** fish with salt and pepper; lightly brush each side with barbecue sauce. Place fish in a grill basket coated with cooking spray.
• **Cook**, covered with grill lid, over medium coals (300° to 350°) 5 minutes on each side or until fish flakes easily when tested with a fork. Remove fish from basket; flake gently with a fork.
• **Spoon** fish evenly down center of tortillas; top with sour cream and green onions. Squeeze lime wedges over tortillas; fold opposite sides over filling. **Yield:** 4 servings.

HONG KONG-STYLE SEA BASS

QUICK!

1 (2-inch) piece fresh ginger
3 green onions
½ cup vegetable oil, divided
4 cloves garlic, crushed
1 pound fresh spinach, washed and
   trimmed
4 (6-ounce) sea bass or grouper
   fillets
¼ cup sesame oil
⅓ cup reduced-sodium soy
   sauce
⅓ cup dry sherry
⅓ cup water
2 teaspoons sugar

• **Peel** ginger, and cut into thin strips. Cut green onions into 2-inch thin strips; set ginger and green onions aside.
• **Pour** ¼ cup vegetable oil into a large skillet; place over high heat until hot.

Add garlic, and cook 5 to 7 seconds, stirring constantly; remove and discard garlic. Add spinach to skillet; cook, stirring constantly, until lightly wilted. Spoon spinach onto individual serving plates, and keep warm.
• **Place** fish in a steamer basket or bamboo steamer over boiling water; cover and steam 8 minutes or until fish flakes easily when tested with a fork. Place fish on spinach; top with ginger and green onions.
• **Combine** remaining ¼ cup vegetable oil and sesame oil in skillet; place skillet over high heat until hot. Drizzle oil evenly over fish.
• **Bring** soy sauce and remaining 3 ingredients to a boil in skillet. Drizzle half of mixture over fish; serve fish immediately with remaining mixture. **Yield:** 4 servings.

Chef Chris McDonald
Atlanta Fish Market
Atlanta, Georgia

CATFISH LOUISIANA

Shrimp Topping
2 large eggs, lightly beaten
½ cup milk
½ cup buttermilk
¼ teaspoon hot sauce
1 tablespoon seasoned salt,
   divided
1½ cups all-purpose flour
4 (6-ounce) farm-raised catfish
   fillets
1 cup vegetable oil
Garnishes: chopped fresh parsley,
   chopped green onions
Hot cooked rice

• **Prepare** Shrimp Topping; set aside, and keep warm.
• **Combine** eggs and next 3 ingredients; add 1½ teaspoons seasoned salt, and set aside.
• **Combine** flour and remaining 1½ teaspoons seasoned salt in a shallow dish. Dredge each fillet in flour mixture; dip in egg mixture, and dredge again in flour mixture.
• **Pour** oil into a large heavy skillet. Fry half of fillets in hot oil over medium-high heat 5 minutes on each side or until

golden. Remove from skillet, and drain on paper towels. Repeat procedure with remaining fillets. Immediately spoon warm Shrimp Topping over catfish, and garnish, if desired. Serve with rice. **Yield:** 4 servings.

Shrimp Topping

¼ pound unpeeled small fresh
   shrimp
3 tablespoons vegetable oil,
   divided
2 tablespoons all-purpose flour
¼ cup chopped celery
¼ cup chopped green bell
   pepper
¼ cup chopped onion
1 clove garlic, minced
1 cup hot water
¼ cup dry white wine
1 teaspoon chicken-flavored
   bouillon granules
¼ teaspoon seasoned salt
¼ teaspoon paprika
½ teaspoon hot sauce

• **Peel** and devein shrimp; set aside.
• **Combine** 2 tablespoons oil and flour in a small heavy skillet, stirring with a wire whisk; cook over medium heat, stirring constantly, until roux is caramel-colored (about 6 minutes). Set mixture aside.
• **Cook** celery, green bell pepper, and onion in remaining 1 tablespoon oil in a heavy saucepan over medium-high heat 1 minute, stirring constantly. Add shrimp and garlic; cook 1 minute, stirring constantly. Stir in water and remaining 5 ingredients. Gradually add reserved flour mixture, stirring until smooth, and cook until thoroughly heated. **Yield:** 1⅓ cups.

Hub City Diner
Lafayette, Louisiana

CATFISH CAKES

Those of you who are landlocked may find fresh crab a bit pricey for everyday consumption, so take a look at this recipe. It offers an affordable and delicious alternative.

1½ pounds farm-raised catfish
   fillets *
1 large egg, lightly beaten
2 tablespoons mayonnaise or salad
   dressing
1 tablespoon prepared mustard
1 tablespoon butter or margarine,
   melted
1 teaspoon chopped fresh parsley
¾ teaspoon salt
½ teaspoon dry mustard
½ teaspoon ground black pepper
¼ teaspoon garlic salt
⅛ teaspoon ground red pepper
¾ cup crushed corn flakes cereal
Vegetable oil
Garnishes: lemon wedges, fresh
   flat-leaf parsley sprigs
Tartar sauce or cocktail sauce

• **Arrange** catfish in a lightly greased 13- x 9- x 2-inch baking dish; cover with aluminum foil, and bake at 400° for 20 minutes or until fish flakes easily when tested with a fork. Drain and flake fish; set aside.
• **Combine** egg and next 9 ingredients in a large bowl. Stir in fish.
• **Shape** into 8 (2½-inch) patties; coat with crushed cereal. Place patties on paper towels; chill 1 hour.
• **Pour** oil to depth of ½ inch into a large skillet. Fry patties in hot oil over medium heat about 2 minutes on each side or until golden. Drain well on paper towels. Garnish, if desired. Serve with tartar sauce or cocktail sauce. **Yield:** 4 servings.

❋ Substitute 1½ pounds trout for farm-raised catfish.

Decca Hodge
Bonham, Texas

BAKED CATFISH

QUICK!

¼ cup yellow cornmeal
¼ cup all-purpose flour
¼ cup grated Parmesan cheese
1 teaspoon paprika
½ teaspoon salt
½ teaspoon ground black pepper
⅛ teaspoon ground red pepper
1 egg white
2 tablespoons skim milk
4 (4-ounce) catfish fillets
Butter-flavored cooking spray
½ teaspoon sesame seeds
Lemon wedges

• **Combine** first 7 ingredients; set aside.
• **Whisk** together egg white and milk. Dip fillets in milk mixture, and dredge in cornmeal mixture.
• **Place** fillets on an aluminum foil-lined baking sheet coated with cooking spray.
• **Sprinkle** with sesame seeds, and coat each fillet with cooking spray.
• **Bake** at 350° for 30 minutes or until fish flakes easily when tested with a fork. Serve with lemon wedges. **Yield:** 4 servings.

Wanda Bishop
Little Rock, Arkansas

❤ Per serving: Calories 196
Fat 5.9g   Cholesterol 55mg
Sodium 460mg

GRILLED CATFISH WITH RELISH

3 ears fresh corn
1 large tomato, chopped
2 or 3 green onions, chopped
½ cup Italian salad dressing
6 (6-ounce) catfish fillets
Vegetable cooking spray
⅓ cup lemon juice
3 tablespoons butter or margarine,
   melted
1 tablespoon lemon-pepper
   seasoning

• **Remove** husks and silks from corn, and cut corn from cob. Cook in a small amount of boiling water 8 to 10 minutes; drain and cool. Combine corn, tomato,

green onions, and salad dressing; cover corn relish, and chill 2 hours.
• **Place** fish in a fish basket coated with cooking spray. Combine lemon juice, butter, and seasoning; brush fillets with lemon mixture.
• **Place** fish basket on grill, and close cover of grill. (Because of the shape of the fish basket, the grill will not close completely.) Cook fish over medium coals (300° to 350°) 7 to 9 minutes on each side or until fish flakes easily when tested with a fork, basting often with remaining lemon mixture. Serve with chilled corn relish. **Yield:** 6 servings.

BURK'S FARM-RAISED CATFISH FRY

6 (¾- to 1-pound) farm-raised
   catfish fillets
1 cup buttermilk
1½ to 2 tablespoons salt
1 tablespoon pepper
1½ cups self-rising cornmeal
½ cup self-rising flour
1½ to 2 quarts peanut oil

• **Make** shallow diagonal cuts 2 inches apart in thickest portion of sides of fish. Place in a large shallow dish.
• **Combine** buttermilk, salt, and pepper; pour over fish. Cover and marinate in refrigerator at least 8 hours, turning fish fillets occasionally.
• **Remove** fish from marinade, discarding marinade.
• **Combine** cornmeal and flour. Dredge fish in cornmeal mixture, coating fillets completely.
• **Pour** peanut oil to depth of 1½ inches into a large deep skillet; heat oil to 370°. Fry fish, two at a time, about 6 minutes or until golden. Drain well on paper towels. Repeat procedure with remaining fish. Serve immediately. **Yield:** 6 servings.

Bessie Burk
Rome, Georgia

OVEN-FRIED CATFISH

QUICK!

Try this recipe using any type of whitefish fillets.

¾ cup crushed corn flakes cereal
¾ teaspoon celery salt
¼ teaspoon onion powder
¼ teaspoon paprika
Dash of pepper
Vegetable cooking spray
4 (6-ounce) skinless farm-raised catfish fillets, halved

• **Combine** first 5 ingredients; set aside. Spray all sides of fish with cooking spray, and coat with corn flake mixture. Arrange fillets in a single layer on a baking sheet coated with cooking spray. Spray tops of fillets with cooking spray.
• **Bake** at 350° for 30 minutes or until fish flakes easily when tested with a fork. **Yield:** 4 servings.

Note: After trying Chef Chris Dupont's Molasses Catfish at his Cafe Dupont in Springville, Alabama, we adapted his creamy molasses sauce recipe to serve with this Oven-Fried Catfish. For a special touch, add 2 tablespoons chopped toasted pecans to the corn flake mixture in the recipe above, and proceed as directed. While the fish bakes, combine ¾ cup dry white wine and ¼ cup molasses. Cook 15 minutes or until mixture reduces to ⅓ cup. Stir in 2 tablespoons whipping cream. Spoon sauce evenly over catfish fillets. This sauce will add 5 fat grams and 100 calories to the nutritional analysis (below) of each serving, but it's worth the indulgence.

Edith Askins
Greenville, Texas

❤ Per serving: Calories 247
Fat 8.7g Cholesterol 77mg
Sodium 673mg

GRAND LAGOON STUFFED FLOUNDER

Crabmeat Stuffing
6 (1-pound) whole flounder, dressed
⅓ cup butter or margarine, melted
3 tablespoons lemon juice

• **Spoon** Crabmeat Stuffing evenly into each fish cavity. Place fish in a lightly greased 15- x 10- x 1-inch jellyroll pan.
• **Combine** butter and lemon juice; drizzle over fish.
• **Bake** at 350° for 25 minutes or until fish flakes easily when tested with a fork. **Yield:** 6 servings.

Crabmeat Stuffing

1 green bell pepper, finely chopped
½ cup finely chopped onion
2½ tablespoons finely chopped celery
½ (16-ounce) package saltine crackers, crushed
½ pound fresh crabmeat, drained and flaked
1½ teaspoons salt
1½ teaspoons pepper
2 large eggs
1 cup mayonnaise or salad dressing
¼ cup Worcestershire sauce
¼ cup prepared mustard
2 tablespoons lemon juice

• **Combine** first 7 ingredients in a large bowl; set aside.
• **Combine** eggs and remaining 4 ingredients; stir into crabmeat mixture. **Yield:** 5 cups.

Note: Use any leftover Crabmeat Stuffing to stuff peeled and butterflied jumbo shrimp (baked as directed for flounder) or shaped into croquettes and browned in hot oil.

Bay Leaves
Junior Service League of
Panama City, Florida

OVEN-FRIED FISH

QUICK!

The key to a crispy coating when oven-frying is to bake the fish at a high temperature. A fifty-fifty combination of cornmeal and fine, dry breadcrumbs enhances the crunchiness of the coating.

¼ cup cornmeal
¼ cup fine, dry breadcrumbs
½ teaspoon salt
½ teaspoon paprika
¼ teaspoon dried dillweed
⅛ teaspoon pepper
1 pound fish fillets, cut into 1-inch strips *
⅓ cup milk
3 tablespoons butter or margarine, melted
Garnishes: lemon halves tied in cheesecloth, fresh flat-leaf parsley sprigs

• **Combine** first 6 ingredients in a shallow dish. Dip fillets in milk, and dredge in cornmeal mixture. Place in a lightly greased 13- x 9- x 2-inch pan, and drizzle with butter.
• **Bake** fillets at 450° for 10 minutes or until fish flakes easily when tested with a fork. Garnish, if desired. **Yield:** 4 to 6 servings.

* For fish fillets, we used grouper and orange roughy.

Louise Ellis
Talbott, Tennessee

MONTEGO BAY GRILLED FISH WITH CARIBBEAN SALSA

3 tablespoons chopped fresh
     cilantro
1 roasted jalapeño pepper,
     chopped (see note)
2 tablespoons fresh lime juice
1 tablespoon minced garlic
1 tablespoon minced fresh
     ginger
Vegetable cooking spray
4 grouper or amberjack fillets
     (about 1½ pounds)
Caribbean Salsa

• **Combine** first 5 ingredients; set aside.
• **Coat** a grill tray with cooking spray, and place on grill rack. Heat, covered with grill lid, over hot coals (400° to 500°) 10 minutes. Place fish on grill tray.
• **Cook**, covered with grill lid, 10 minutes. Turn fish, and spread with cilantro mixture. Cook, covered with grill lid, 10 minutes or until fish flakes easily when tested with a fork. Serve with Caribbean Salsa. **Yield:** 4 servings.

Caribbean Salsa

1 large ripe banana, chopped
½ cup finely chopped red bell
     pepper
½ cup finely chopped green bell
     pepper
½ cup chopped fresh cilantro
3 green onions, finely chopped
1 roasted jalapeño pepper,
     chopped (see note)
1 tablespoon minced fresh
     ginger
2 tablespoons brown sugar
3 tablespoons fresh lime juice
1 tablespoon olive oil
¼ teaspoon salt
⅛ teaspoon pepper

• **Combine** all ingredients, tossing gently to coat; cover and chill 2 hours. **Yield:** 2½ cups.

Note: To roast jalapeños, place on an aluminum foil-lined baking sheet. Broil 5½ inches from heat (with electric oven door partially opened) about 5 minutes on each side or until blistered. Place in a heavy-duty, zip-top plastic bag; seal and let stand 10 minutes to loosen skins. Peel peppers, and remove and discard seeds.

GARLIC-BASIL MARINATED GROUPER

QUICK!

5 pounds grouper fillets
Garlic-Basil Marinade
Vegetable cooking spray
Garnish: fresh parsley sprigs

• **Arrange** fish in a large shallow dish; pour Garlic-Basil Marinade over fish. Cover and chill 1 hour.
• **Remove** fish from marinade, discarding marinade. Arrange fish in a grill basket coated with cooking spray.
• **Cook**, covered with grill lid, over medium coals (300° to 350°) 9 minutes on each side or until fish flakes easily when tested with a fork. Garnish, if desired, and serve immediately. **Yield:** 10 servings.

Garlic-Basil Marinade

QUICK!

¾ cup olive oil
½ cup tomato sauce
¼ cup balsamic vinegar
4 cloves garlic, crushed
¼ cup chopped fresh basil
1 teaspoon salt
1 teaspoon ground red pepper

• **Combine** all ingredients in a small bowl. **Yield:** 1⅔ cups.

Jim and Jane Bowyers
Maitland, Florida

HOT SPICY GROUPER

QUICK!

4 (4-ounce) grouper or snapper
     fillets
¼ cup lemon juice
2 tablespoons water
2 tablespoons hot sauce
1 tablespoon vegetable oil
2 teaspoons grated fresh ginger
½ teaspoon salt
Vegetable cooking spray
1 tablespoon sesame seeds,
     toasted
1 tablespoon chopped fresh
     parsley

• **Place** grouper in a shallow dish; set aside.
• **Combine** lemon juice and next 5 ingredients; divide marinade in half.
• **Cover** and chill 1 portion. Pour remaining portion over fish, turning to coat. Cover with aluminum foil. Chill 1 hour, turning fish occasionally.
• **Remove** fish from marinade, discarding marinade.
• **Arrange** fish in a single layer in a grill basket coated with cooking spray. Cook, covered with grill lid, over hot coals (400° to 500°) 5 minutes on each side or until fish flakes easily when tested with a fork, basting with reserved marinade.
• **Transfer** fish to a serving plate; sprinkle with sesame seeds and parsley. **Yield:** 4 servings.

Penny Caughfield
Cocoa, Florida

♥ Per serving: Calories 155
    Fat 5.9g   Cholesterol 42mg
    Sodium 393mg

*Pan-Fried Grouper
With Vanilla
Wine Sauce*

PAN-FRIED GROUPER WITH VANILLA WINE SAUCE

(pictured at left)

1   cup boiling water
1   fish-flavored bouillon cube
1   cup dry white wine
2   tablespoons chopped onion
1   vanilla bean, cut in half
      lengthwise and divided
⅓   cup all-purpose flour
¼   teaspoon salt
¼   teaspoon pepper
1   (2½-pound) grouper fillet
¼   cup butter or margarine,
      divided
2   tablespoons all-purpose flour
⅓   cup whipping cream
⅛   teaspoon salt
Garnish: fresh chives

• **Combine** first 4 ingredients and half of vanilla bean in a saucepan; bring to a boil, stirring until bouillon cube dissolves. Boil 10 minutes or until mixture is reduced to ¾ cup. Pour mixture through a wire-mesh strainer into a 1-cup liquid measuring cup, discarding solids, and set broth mixture aside.
• **Position** knife blade in food processor bowl; add remaining half of vanilla bean. Process until finely chopped. Add ⅓ cup flour, ¼ teaspoon salt, and pepper; process 10 seconds.
• **Cut** fillet into 6 equal portions. Coat each portion evenly with flour mixture; shake off excess.
• **Melt** 2 tablespoons butter in a heavy skillet; add fish, and cook 3 minutes on each side or until fish flakes easily when tested with a fork. Remove fish to a serving platter, and keep warm.
• **Melt** remaining 2 tablespoons butter in a heavy saucepan over low heat; add 2 tablespoons flour, stirring until smooth. Cook 1 minute, stirring constantly. Gradually add reserved reduced broth mixture; cook over medium heat, stirring constantly, until mixture is thickened.
• **Stir** in whipping cream and ⅛ teaspoon salt; cook over medium heat until thoroughly heated.
• **Pour** sauce over grouper. Garnish, if desired. **Yield:** 6 servings.

Kim McCully
Knoxville, Tennessee

WINE-HERB HALIBUT STEAK

▶**QUICK!**

3   tablespoons butter or
      margarine
4   (1-inch-thick) halibut steaks
½   cup dry white wine
1   tablespoon lemon juice
¼   teaspoon dried basil
¼   teaspoon dried oregano
¼   teaspoon salt
¼   teaspoon pepper
¼   teaspoon paprika

• **Melt** butter in a large skillet over medium heat. Arrange halibut steaks in a single layer, and cook 3 to 4 minutes on each side.
• **Add** wine and lemon juice; sprinkle basil and remaining 4 ingredients over steaks. Cover, reduce heat, and simmer 8 to 10 minutes or until fish flakes easily when tested with a fork. Serve with pan drippings. **Yield:** 4 servings.

Carrie Treichel
Johnson City, Tennessee

MIDDLE EASTERN MAHIMAHI

▶**QUICK!**

1   tablespoon butter or margarine
1   cup sliced green onions
½   cup finely chopped yellow bell
      pepper
2   teaspoons minced garlic
1½ cups currant jelly
¼   cup water
1   teaspoon ground cinnamon
1   teaspoon ground cumin
½   teaspoon ground red pepper
½   teaspoon lemon juice
2   bay leaves
6   mahimahi steaks (3 pounds)
1½ cups finely chopped tomato
1   teaspoon paprika
½   teaspoon seasoned salt

• **Melt** butter in a medium skillet over medium-high heat; add green onions and next 9 ingredients, and cook 2 minutes, stirring occasionally. Remove from heat; set aside.
• **Place** fish steaks in a lightly greased 13- x 9- x 2-inch baking dish; pour green onion mixture evenly over fish steaks.

Top with chopped tomato, and sprinkle evenly with paprika and seasoned salt.
• **Bake** at 425° for 20 to 30 minutes or until fish flakes easily when tested with a fork. Remove and discard bay leaves. Serve fish steaks immediately. **Yield:** 6 servings.

Marion Hall
Knoxville, Tennessee

QUICK FISH FILLETS

▶**QUICK!**

This quick and easy recipe results in fantastic fish from the oven or microwave.

1   pound orange roughy fillets
¼   cup fine, dry breadcrumbs
1   teaspoon chopped fresh
      parsley
½   teaspoon paprika
¼   cup plain yogurt
1   teaspoon prepared mustard
Vegetable cooking spray
Lemon wedges

• **Cut** orange roughy into serving-size pieces.
• **Combine** breadcrumbs, parsley, and paprika in a shallow dish.
• **Combine** yogurt and mustard. Dip fillets in yogurt mixture, and dredge in breadcrumb mixture; place in a 9-inch square baking dish coated with cooking spray.
• **Bake** at 450° for 20 minutes or microwave, covered with a paper towel, at HIGH 4 minutes or until fish flakes easily when tested with a fork. Serve with lemon wedges. **Yield:** 2 servings.

Laura Morris
Bunnell, Florida

PESTO-CRUSTED ORANGE ROUGHY

QUICK!

Try this flavorful herbed crust on any mild-flavored fish like cod, catfish, snapper, or grouper.

2 tablespoons pesto
½ cup fine, dry breadcrumbs
¼ teaspoon pepper
4 (4-ounce) orange roughy
   fillets
Vegetable cooking spray

• **Combine** pesto, breadcrumbs, and pepper in a shallow dish. Dredge fillets in breadcrumb mixture, and place in an 11- x 7- x 1½-inch baking dish coated with cooking spray. Coat fillets with cooking spray.
• **Bake** at 400° for 15 minutes or until fish flakes easily when tested with a fork. **Yield:** 4 servings.

♥ Per serving: Calories 190
Fat 7g Cholesterol 24mg
Sodium 274mg

STEAMED ORANGE ROUGHY WITH HERBS

QUICK!

This unbelievably simple recipe has so much flavor you won't need to reach for the salt shaker.

½ cup fresh parsley sprigs
½ cup fresh chives
½ cup fresh thyme sprigs
½ cup fresh rosemary sprigs
2 (8-ounce) orange roughy
   fillets *
Fresh lemon slices

• **Arrange** half of herbs in bottom of a steaming basket. Top with fillets and remaining herbs.
• **Cover** and steam fillets 7 minutes or until fish flakes easily when tested with a fork. Serve with lemon slices. **Yield:** 4 servings.

* Substitute any mild-flavored fish for orange roughy in this recipe. Try cod, grouper, snapper, or farm-raised catfish. And don't limit yourself to the herbs we suggest; use any fresh herb you have available.

♥ Per serving: Calories 79
Fat 0.8g Cholesterol 23mg
Sodium 72mg

FILLETS TOMATILLO

QUICK!

1 cup finely chopped fresh
   tomatillo (4 large tomatillos)
¼ cup finely chopped onion
¼ cup finely chopped celery
2 tablespoons chopped green bell
   pepper
1 clove garlic, minced
2 teaspoons olive oil
¼ cup clam juice or chicken
   broth
2 tablespoons canned chopped
   green chiles
2 tablespoons lime juice
½ teaspoon chopped fresh
   cilantro
½ teaspoon ground cumin
¼ teaspoon dried oregano
⅛ teaspoon salt
⅛ teaspoon ground red pepper
4 (4-ounce) orange roughy
   fillets
Vegetable cooking spray

• **Cook** first 5 ingredients in olive oil in a medium skillet over medium-high heat 5 minutes, stirring constantly.
• **Add** clam juice and next 7 ingredients; cover, reduce heat, and cook 15 minutes, stirring occasionally. Set aside, and keep warm.
• **Arrange** fish in a grill basket coated with cooking spray. Cook, covered with grill lid, over medium-hot coals (350° to 400°) 7 to 8 minutes on each side or until fish flakes easily with a fork. Serve fillets with tomatillo mixture. **Yield:** 4 servings.

Ginny Munsterman
Garland, Texas

♥ Per serving: Calories 124
Fat 3.7g Cholesterol 23mg
Sodium 193mg

GRILLED SALMON STEAKS

QUICK!

2 tablespoons mayonnaise
½ teaspoon chopped fresh dill or
  ⅛ teaspoon dried dillweed
2 (1-inch-thick) salmon steaks
Garnishes: lemon halves, fresh dill
   sprigs

• **Combine** mayonnaise and dill; spread on both sides of salmon.
• **Cook**, covered with grill lid, over medium-hot coals (350° to 400°) 5 to 6 minutes on each side or to desired degree of doneness. Garnish, if desired. **Yield:** 2 servings.

Susan Nash
Birmingham, Alabama
and
Julia Rutland
Cordova, Tennessee

GRILLED HERBED SALMON STEAKS

QUICK!

8 (¾-inch-thick) salmon steaks
¾ cup dry white vermouth or dry
   white wine
¾ cup olive oil
1½ tablespoons lemon juice
1 tablespoon chopped fresh thyme
   or 1 teaspoon dried thyme
1 tablespoon chopped fresh
   marjoram or 1 teaspoon dried
   marjoram
1 tablespoon chopped fresh sage
   or 1 teaspoon rubbed sage
1 tablespoon chopped fresh
   parsley
¾ teaspoon salt
⅛ teaspoon freshly ground pepper
Garnish: fresh thyme sprigs

• **Place** salmon in two shallow dishes. Combine vermouth and next 8 ingredients; reserve ⅓ cup marinade. Pour remaining marinade over salmon; cover and chill 1 hour.
• **Remove** salmon from marinade, discarding marinade. Cook salmon, covered with grill lid, over medium-hot coals (350° to 400°) 5 to 6 minutes on

each side or until salmon flakes easily when tested with a fork, brushing often with reserved marinade. Garnish, if desired. **Yield:** 8 servings.

Note: You can broil salmon steaks 5½ inches from heat (with electric oven door partially opened) 6 to 8 minutes on each side or until fish flakes easily when tested with a fork, brushing often with reserved marinade.

The Lucullan Society
Lynchburg, Virginia

MINT-MARINATED SALMON STEAKS

Cut into the salmon steaks near the center to test for doneness. Grilling time for the steaks may vary, depending upon weather conditions.

½ cup dry white wine
¼ cup olive oil
2 cloves garlic, minced
½ teaspoon salt
¼ teaspoon pepper
1 tablespoon lemon juice
¼ cup chopped fresh mint
4 (¾-inch-thick) salmon steaks
Vegetable cooking spray

• **Combine** first 7 ingredients, stirring until blended.
• **Place** salmon steaks in a large shallow dish, and pour wine mixture over salmon. Cover and chill 2 hours, turning salmon occasionally.
• **Remove** salmon from marinade, discarding marinade.
• **Coat** grill rack or fish basket with cooking spray, and place salmon on rack or in basket.
• **Cook** salmon, covered with grill lid, over medium coals (300° to 350°) 10 minutes on each side or until done. Remove from heat; cover and chill. **Yield:** 4 servings.

SALMON FILLETS WITH SWEET CORN RELISH

QUICK!

2 tablespoons vegetable oil
2 pounds salmon fillets, cut into 8 portions
¼ teaspoon salt
Sweet Corn Relish

• **Brush** oil on skinless side of salmon; sprinkle with salt. Cook over medium-hot coals (350° to 400°) 7 minutes on each side or until fish flakes easily when tested with a fork. Serve with Sweet Corn Relish. **Yield:** 8 servings.

Sweet Corn Relish

4 or 5 ears fresh yellow corn
1 cup chopped cabbage
⅓ cup chopped onion
⅓ cup chopped green bell pepper
⅓ cup chopped red bell pepper
¼ cup sugar
1½ teaspoons dry mustard
¾ teaspoon celery seeds
¾ teaspoon mustard seeds
¾ teaspoon ground turmeric
½ to ¾ teaspoon salt
1 cup white vinegar
¼ cup water

• **Remove** and discard husks and silks from corn. Cook corn 5 minutes in boiling water to cover; drain. Cut kernels from cob.
• **Combine** corn, cabbage, and remaining ingredients in a large saucepan; bring to a boil. Cover, reduce heat, and simmer 20 minutes. Cover and chill. **Yield:** 3 cups.

Wolf Trap Farm Park
for the Performing Arts
Vienna, Virginia

GRILLED SALMON QUESADILLA WITH CUCUMBER SALSA

1 (8-ounce) salmon fillet
4 (8- to 10-inch) flour tortillas
1 cup (4 ounces) shredded Monterey Jack cheese
2 ounces goat cheese, crumbled
2 jalapeño peppers, seeded and sliced
Cucumber Salsa

• **Cook** salmon, covered with grill lid, over medium-hot coals (350° to 400°) 5 to 6 minutes on each side or until done. Cool; flake with a fork.
• **Spoon** flaked salmon evenly over half of each tortilla. Top evenly with cheeses and pepper slices. Fold tortillas in half.
• **Cook** tortillas in a large nonstick skillet over high heat 1 minute on each side or until tortillas are slightly browned and cheese melts. Cut each quesadilla into 3 triangles, and serve with chilled Cucumber Salsa. **Yield:** 4 servings.

Cucumber Salsa

1 large cucumber, chopped
1 clove garlic, minced
1 tablespoon finely chopped poblano chile pepper
1 tablespoon finely chopped purple onion
1 tablespoon finely chopped red bell pepper
1 tablespoon finely chopped yellow bell pepper
1 tablespoon finely chopped fresh cilantro
1 teaspoon olive oil
¼ teaspoon salt
⅛ teaspoon pepper

• **Combine** all ingredients; cover and chill. **Yield:** 1¼ cups.

Tom Nickoloff
La Paz Restaurante Cantinas
Atlanta, Georgia

SALMON IN PARCHMENT

Serve this dish with rice or couscous to soak up the flavorful cooking liquid.

⅓ cup dry white wine
⅓ cup fresh lime juice
2 tablespoons chopped fresh dill
6 (4-ounce) salmon steaks
4 carrots
2 leeks
1 red bell pepper
Vegetable cooking spray
½ teaspoon salt
¼ teaspoon pepper
6 slices lime
12 fresh dill sprigs, divided

● **Combine** first 3 ingredients in a shallow dish; add salmon. Cover and chill 30 minutes.
● **Slice** carrots diagonally; thinly slice white part of leeks, and separate into rings. Thinly slice red pepper.
● **Combine** carrot, leek, and red pepper in a saucepan; add water to depth of 1 inch. Bring to a boil; boil 1 minute. Drain vegetables, and plunge into ice water to stop the cooking process; drain.
● **Cut** six 18- x 12-inch pieces of parchment paper; fold each piece in half to make a 12- x 9-inch rectangle. Trim into half heart-shaped pieces. Coat one side of each piece of parchment with cooking spray; arrange three-fourths of vegetable mixture evenly on coated sides of parchment, leaving a 1-inch border.
● **Remove** salmon from marinade, reserving marinade. Place fish over vegetables; pour 2 tablespoons reserved marinade over each steak, and sprinkle with salt and pepper. Top each with a lime slice. Place remaining vegetables on fish; top each with 1 dill sprig.
● **Bring** opposite sides of parchment together; fold edges over twice to seal, and fold pointed ends underneath packet. Place on baking sheets.
● **Bake** at 425° for 10 to 12 minutes. Cut opening in packets; top with remaining dill sprigs. **Yield:** 6 servings.

Patricia A. Chapman
Huntsville, Alabama

♥ Per serving: Calories 225
Fat 8.5g Cholesterol 62mg
Sodium 273mg

SALMON BAKE WITH PECAN-CRUNCH COATING

This pecan coating also works well on firm fish like grouper and amberjack.

4 (4- to 6-ounce) salmon fillets
⅛ teaspoon salt
⅛ teaspoon pepper
2 tablespoons Dijon mustard
2 tablespoons butter, melted
1½ tablespoons honey
¼ cup soft breadcrumbs
¼ cup finely chopped pecans
2 teaspoons chopped fresh parsley
Garnishes: fresh parsley sprigs, lemon slices

● **Sprinkle** salmon with salt and pepper. Place fillets, skin side down, in a lightly greased 13- x 9- x 2-inch pan.
● **Combine** mustard, butter, and honey; brush on fillets.
● **Combine** breadcrumbs, pecans, and chopped parsley; spoon mixture evenly on top of each fillet.
● **Bake** at 450° for 10 minutes or until fish flakes easily. Garnish, if desired. **Yield:** 4 servings.

Helen H. Maurer
Christmas, Florida

SESAME-CRUSTED SALMON WITH GINGER VINAIGRETTE

1 large English cucumber, peeled and coarsely chopped
½ cup rice wine vinegar
⅛ teaspoon salt
2 tablespoons sugar
¼ cup water
¼ cup low-sodium soy sauce
2 tablespoons rice wine vinegar
1 tablespoon honey
1 teaspoon hot sauce
½ teaspoon ground coriander
½ teaspoon dark sesame oil
4 (4-ounce) salmon fillets
1 tablespoon sesame seeds, toasted
1 large English cucumber, thinly sliced
Ginger Vinaigrette
Garnish: fresh mint sprigs

● **Position** knife blade in food processor bowl; add chopped English cucumber. Process until smooth, stopping once to scrape down sides.
● **Line** a large wire-mesh strainer with cheesecloth or a coffee filter; pour pureed cucumber through strainer into a bowl, discarding pulp.
● **Stir** ½ cup vinegar and salt into cucumber liquid; set aside.
● **Combine** sugar and water in a saucepan; bring to a boil over medium heat, stirring often. Stir into cucumber liquid mixture; set aside.
● **Combine** soy sauce and next 5 ingredients in a small bowl; brush over salmon. Place salmon in a lightly greased 13- x 9- x 2-inch pan; sprinkle with sesame seeds.
● **Bake** fillets at 450° for 10 to 12 minutes or until fish flakes easily when tested with a fork.
● **Arrange** salmon fillets and sliced cucumber in four bowls. Spoon cucumber liquid mixture evenly into each dish. Drizzle with a small amount of Ginger Vinaigrette. Garnish, if desired. **Yield:** 4 servings.

♥ Per serving: Calories 395
Fat 23.1g Cholesterol 63mg
Sodium 744mg

Ginger Vinaigrette

QUICK!

1 (1½-inch-long) piece fresh ginger, peeled
1 clove garlic
2 tablespoons rice wine vinegar
1 tablespoon low-sodium soy sauce
1 tablespoon honey
⅛ teaspoon dried crushed red pepper
¼ cup peanut oil
½ teaspoon dark sesame oil

● **Position** knife blade in food processor bowl; add ginger and garlic. Process until smooth.
● **Add** vinegar and next 3 ingredients; process 30 seconds. Slowly pour peanut oil and sesame oil through food chute with processor running, blending just until smooth. **Yield:** 1½ cup.

Bacchanalia
Atlanta, Georgia

SALMON SCALOPPINE WITH VEGETABLE CONFETTI AND PERNOD SAUCE

⅓ cup all-purpose flour
¼ teaspoon salt
¼ teaspoon pepper
1 pound salmon fillet, cut diagonally into ½-inch strips
1 leek
¼ cup butter or margarine, divided
1 carrot, scraped and cut into 2-inch thin strips
¼ cup dry white wine
¼ cup chicken broth
½ cup whipping cream
¼ teaspoon salt
⅓ cup finely chopped tomato
1½ tablespoons Pernod *

• **Combine** first 3 ingredients; dredge salmon strips in flour mixture. Set aside.
• **Wash** leek. Remove root, tough outer leaves, and dark green leaves. Cut white part of leek into thin 2-inch strips.
• **Melt** 2 tablespoons butter in a large skillet. Add leek and carrot, and cook over medium heat, stirring constantly, 2 minutes or until crisp-tender. Remove vegetables from skillet; set aside.
• **Melt** remaining 2 tablespoons butter in skillet; add salmon, and cook 2 minutes on each side. Remove from skillet, and place in a 250° oven to keep warm.
• **Add** wine and chicken broth to skillet; cook over high heat 5 minutes or until reduced to about ¼ cup.
• **Stir** in whipping cream and salt. Cook over medium-high heat 4 minutes or until sauce is thickened. Add chopped tomato and Pernod; cook 1 minute.
• **Place** salmon on serving plates; drizzle with sauce, and top with vegetables. **Yield:** 2 main-dish servings or 4 appetizer servings.

* Pernod is a yellowish, licorice-flavored liqueur.

Jean Cooper
Washington, D.C.

SMOKED SALMON

Hickory or fruitwood chips
2 teaspoons onion powder
¼ teaspoon salt
¼ teaspoon pepper
1 (1½-pound) salmon fillet with skin

• **Soak** wood chips in water at least 30 minutes.
• **Combine** onion powder, salt, and pepper; rub fillet with mixture. Cover and chill 30 minutes.
• **Prepare** charcoal fire in smoker; let burn 15 to 20 minutes.
• **Drain** chips, and place on coals. Place water pan in smoker; add water to pan to depth of fill line.
• **Place** fillet, skin side down, on upper food rack; cover with smoker lid.
• **Cook** 1½ hours or until fish flakes easily. **Yield:** 4 servings.

Sylvia D. Ellis
San Antonio, Texas

CARIBBEAN BANANA FISH

¼ teaspoon coriander seeds
¼ teaspoon lemon pepper
¼ teaspoon ground nutmeg
¼ teaspoon ground allspice
¼ teaspoon salt
¼ teaspoon pepper
Vegetable cooking spray
4 (4-ounce) red snapper fillets, skinned
¼ cup all-purpose flour
2 bananas, peeled and sliced
4 small green onions, chopped
¼ cup sweetened coconut milk
¼ cup rum

• **Crush** coriander seeds, using a mortar and pestle; add lemon pepper and next 4 ingredients, stirring well. Set aside.
• **Coat** a large nonstick skillet with cooking spray, and place over medium heat until hot.
• **Dredge** snapper fillets in flour, and arrange in hot skillet. Sprinkle half of spice mixture over fillets, and cook over medium-high heat until lightly browned. Turn fillets; sprinkle with remaining spice mixture, and cook until browned.

• **Place** banana slices over fillets, and sprinkle with chopped green onions. Add coconut milk, and cook until fish flakes easily when tested with a fork.
• **Add** rum to skillet; cover and let stand 5 minutes. **Yield:** 4 servings.

Teresa Smith
Miami, Florida

♥ Per serving: Calories 286
Fat 7.1g Cholesterol 42mg
Sodium 224mg

SNAPPER FINGERS WITH BANANA SALSA

1½ cups crushed potato chips
¼ cup grated Parmesan cheese
1 teaspoon ground thyme
1 pound snapper or grouper fillets, cut into strips
¼ cup milk
Banana Salsa
Garnish: fresh parsley sprigs

• **Combine** first 3 ingredients in a shallow dish; dip fish in milk, and dredge in potato chip mixture. Place fish in a single layer on a greased baking sheet.
• **Bake** at 500° for 8 to 10 minutes. Serve fish with Banana Salsa. Garnish, if desired. **Yield:** 8 servings.

Banana Salsa

2 medium-size ripe bananas, chopped
½ cup chopped green bell pepper
½ cup chopped red bell pepper
3 green onions, chopped
1 tablespoon chopped fresh cilantro
2 tablespoons light brown sugar
3 tablespoons fresh lime juice
1 tablespoon vegetable oil
¼ teaspoon salt
¼ teaspoon pepper
1 small jalapeño pepper, seeded and chopped (optional)

• **Combine** first 10 ingredients. Add jalapeño pepper, if desired. Cover and chill at least 3 hours. **Yield:** 8 servings.

Nita and Harold Norman
Coral Gables, Florida

YELLOWTAIL SNAPPER WITH JULIENNE VEGETABLES

½ cup Dijon mustard
2 egg yolks
4 (6- to 8-ounce) yellowtail
   snapper fillets
1½ cups coarsely chopped
   cashews
1 tablespoon unsalted butter
1 tablespoon olive oil
Julienne Vegetables
2 tablespoons chopped shallots
½ cup orange juice
1 tablespoon fresh lime juice
¼ cup unsalted butter, melted
1 tablespoon chopped fresh
   parsley
Garnishes: lime and lemon wedges,
   fresh basil, edible flowers

• **Combine** mustard and egg yolks; brush over skinless side of fillets. Dredge coated sides in nuts; chill 10 minutes.
• **Heat** 1 tablespoon butter and oil in a large nonstick skillet; place fillets, nut side down, in skillet. Cook over medium heat 5 to 8 minutes. Carefully turn; cook 5 to 8 minutes or until fish flakes easily.
• **Arrange** Julienne Vegetables on a large platter; place fillets, nut side up, on top of vegetables. Keep warm.
• **Wipe** skillet with a paper towel; add shallot, and cook over medium heat, stirring constantly, until tender. Add juices, and bring to a boil. Cook until mixture is reduced to about 3 tablespoons. Whisk in ¼ cup melted butter, 1 teaspoon at a time. Stir in parsley. Pour over fillets; garnish, if desired. Serve immediately. **Yield:** 4 to 6 servings.

Julienne Vegetables

1 clove garlic, minced
2 tablespoons olive oil
1 sweet potato, peeled and cut
   into very thin strips
1 large carrot, scraped and cut
   into very thin strips
1 small jicama, peeled and cut into
   very thin strips
3 leeks (bulb ends only), cut into
   very thin strips
½ teaspoon salt
¼ teaspoon pepper

• **Cook** garlic in olive oil in a large skillet over medium heat, stirring constantly, until golden. Add vegetables, and cook, stirring constantly, 3 to 5 minutes or until vegetables are crisp-tender. Sprinkle with salt and pepper. **Yield:** 4 to 6 servings.

PEPPERED SNAPPER WITH CREAMY DILL SAUCE

QUICK!

4 (4-ounce) snapper fillets
2 teaspoons olive oil, divided
2 tablespoons coarsely ground
   pepper
Vegetable cooking spray
2 cups hot cooked rice (cooked
   without salt or fat)
Creamy Dill Sauce

• **Brush** snapper on both sides with 1 teaspoon olive oil; sprinkle with pepper, and gently press into fish. Cover and let stand 15 minutes.
• **Coat** a large nonstick skillet with cooking spray; add remaining 1 teaspoon olive oil, and place over medium heat. Cook fillets 3 to 5 minutes on each side or until fish flakes easily when tested with a fork. Remove from heat; keep warm.
• **Spoon** rice evenly onto serving plates; top each with a fillet. Spoon warm Creamy Dill Sauce evenly over fillets. Serve immediately. **Yield:** 4 servings.

♥ Per serving: Calories 389
Fat 11.9g Cholesterol 72mg
Sodium 1825mg

Creamy Dill Sauce

QUICK!

1 (10-ounce) container
   refrigerated reduced-calorie
   Alfredo sauce
2 tablespoons dry white wine
1 teaspoon dried dillweed

• **Combine** all ingredients in a small heavy saucepan, and stir well. Cook over medium heat, stirring constantly, until mixture is thoroughly heated. **Yield:** 1 cup.

SWORDFISH STIR-FRY

QUICK!

If you can't find cellophane noodles, substitute a package of low-fat ramen noodles minus the seasoning packet. Substitute shrimp or chicken breasts for the swordfish.

1 (4-ounce) package cellophane
   noodles
1 tablespoon cornstarch
½ cup fat-free chicken broth
3 tablespoons fresh lime juice
1 tablespoon fish sauce
1 tablespoon sugar
1 teaspoon chili puree with garlic
Vegetable cooking spray
½ pound boneless swordfish fillet,
   cut into 1-inch pieces
1 teaspoon canola oil
½ red bell pepper, thinly sliced
2 cloves garlic, pressed
1 tablespoon minced fresh ginger
1 large cucumber, peeled, seeded,
   and sliced
⅓ cup chopped green onions
¼ cup chopped fresh cilantro

• **Cook** cellophane noodles according to package directions; drain and set aside.
• **Combine** cornstarch and next 5 ingredients; set aside.
• **Coat** a large nonstick skillet with cooking spray, and place over medium-high heat until hot; add fish, and stir-fry 2 to 3 minutes or until tender. Remove fish from skillet; set aside.
• **Pour** oil into skillet; add bell pepper, garlic, and ginger, and stir-fry 1 minute. Add cucumber, and stir-fry 30 additional seconds.
• **Stir** in broth mixture; bring to a boil. Boil 1 minute. Return fish to skillet; add green onions and cilantro, stirring until coated. Serve over noodles. **Yield:** 2 servings.

Chloe Dowling
Birmingham, Alabama

♥ Per serving: Calories 457
Fat 8.7g Cholesterol 44mg
Sodium 757mg

SWORDFISH WITH CASHEW AND CRACKED PEPPER CRUST

QUICK!

1½ cups cashews
2 tablespoons cracked pepper
4 (8-ounce) swordfish steaks
2 tablespoons olive oil
Garnish: fresh basil sprigs

• **Position** knife blade in food processor bowl; add cashews, and process until ground, stopping once to scrape down sides. Combine cashews and pepper in a shallow dish; coat both sides of swordfish with mixture.
• **Pour** oil into a large skillet; place over medium heat until hot. Add swordfish, and cook 10 minutes on each side or until fish flakes easily when tested with a fork. Garnish, if desired. Serve with hot cooked grits, green beans, mushrooms, and bell pepper strips. **Yield:** 4 servings.

Chef Chris McDonald
Atlanta Fish Market
Atlanta, Georgia

ORANGE-GINGER MARINATED SWORDFISH STEAKS

QUICK!

10 (8-ounce) swordfish steaks
    (about 1 inch thick)
1½ cups tomato-based barbecue
    sauce
1 cup white wine
2 tablespoons grated orange rind
1 cup orange juice
¼ cup soy sauce
2 tablespoons finely chopped fresh
   ginger
4 cloves garlic, minced
Vegetable cooking spray
Garnishes: fresh parsley sprigs,
   orange slices

• **Arrange** fish in a large shallow dish. Combine barbecue sauce and next 6 ingredients; pour marinade over fish. Cover and chill at least 2 hours or up to 24 hours, turning occasionally.
• **Remove** fish from marinade, discarding marinade. Place fish in grill baskets coated with cooking spray.

• **Cook,** covered with grill lid, over medium coals (300° to 350°) 10 minutes on each side. Garnish, if desired, and serve immediately. **Yield:** 10 servings.

Abby and Bill Myers
Jacksonville, Florida

GRILLED TROUT

You can substitute any fresh herb for the tarragon in this recipe.

¼ cup olive oil
¼ cup fresh tarragon
¼ cup lemon juice
½ teaspoon salt
2 (2-pound) dressed trout
4 sprigs fresh tarragon
1 lemon, sliced
Vegetable cooking spray

• **Combine** olive oil and tarragon in a small saucepan. Cook over very low heat 20 minutes; pour mixture through a wire-mesh strainer, discarding solids.
• **Combine** oil mixture, lemon juice, and salt, whisking to blend. Brush half of mixture inside each trout. Place 2 sprigs tarragon and 2 lemon slices inside each trout.
• **Place** trout in a large baking dish. Pour remaining oil mixture over trout. Cover and chill 2 hours.
• **Place** trout in a grill basket coated with cooking spray. Cook, covered with grill lid, over hot coals (400° to 500°) 5 minutes on each side or until fish flakes easily when tested with a fork. **Yield:** 4 servings.

♥ Per serving: Calories 233
Fat 11.6g   Cholesterol 83mg
Sodium 185mg

Baked Trout: Prepare trout as directed, and bake at 350° for 30 minutes or until fish flakes easily when tested with a fork. Do not turn trout during baking.

CLASSIC TROUT AMANDINE

QUICK!

A perfect marriage – delicate trout with buttery almonds and a rich sauce.

2 cups milk
2 teaspoons salt, divided
2 dashes of hot sauce
6 trout fillets
¾ cup all-purpose flour
½ teaspoon pepper
1¼ cups butter or margarine,
     divided
1 tablespoon olive oil
½ cup sliced almonds
2 tablespoons lemon juice
2 teaspoons Worcestershire sauce
¼ cup chopped fresh parsley

• **Combine** milk, 1 teaspoon salt, and hot sauce in a 13- x 9- x 2-inch dish; add fillets, turning to coat. Cover and chill 2 hours. Drain, discarding marinade.
• **Combine** flour and pepper in a shallow dish.
• **Melt** ¼ cup butter in a large skillet over medium heat; add oil. Dredge fillets in flour mixture; add to skillet, and cook 2 minutes on each side or until fish flakes easily when tested with a fork. Remove to a serving platter; keep warm.
• **Combine** remaining 1 cup butter and almonds in a saucepan; cook over medium heat until almonds are lightly browned. Add remaining 1 teaspoon salt, lemon juice, and Worcestershire sauce; cook 2 minutes. Remove from heat; stir in parsley. Pour almond mixture over fillets, and serve immediately. **Yield:** 6 servings.

Debbie Slatter
Kenner, Louisiana

STUFFED RAINBOW TROUT

¼ cup butter or margarine
½ cup finely chopped onion
½ cup finely chopped celery
¼ cup chopped fresh parsley
1 clove garlic, minced
½ teaspoon salt
¼ teaspoon dried tarragon
⅛ teaspoon lemon pepper
3 cups Italian bread cubes
1 large egg, lightly beaten
1 tablespoon dry white wine
4 (8- to 10-ounce) whole farm-
   raised trout, dressed
½ teaspoon salt
1 tablespoon lemon juice
1 tablespoon soy sauce
½ cup all-purpose flour
2 slices bacon, cut in half
Garnishes: lemon slices, fresh
   parsley sprigs

• **Melt** butter in a large skillet over medium heat; add onion and celery, and cook, stirring constantly, until tender. Remove from heat; stir in parsley and next 4 ingredients. Add bread cubes; toss gently. Combine egg and white wine; stir into bread mixture. Spread evenly in an 11- x 7- x 1½-inch baking dish; set aside.
• **Rinse** trout; pat dry. Sprinkle inside of fish evenly with ½ teaspoon salt. Combine lemon juice and soy sauce; brush inside of fish, reserving remaining lemon juice mixture. Dredge fish in flour. Place over stuffing, overlapping slightly. Drizzle with reserved lemon juice mixture. Place bacon over trout. Cover and bake at 350° for 45 minutes. Uncover and bake 15 additional minutes. Garnish, if desired, and serve immediately. **Yield:** 4 servings.

The Colonel's Lady
Gatlinburg, Tennessee

TROUT FILLETS WITH CAPERS

QUICK!

If you're watching your sodium intake, capers are not for you. But their pungency adds loads of flavor and no fat.

½ cup all-purpose flour
¼ teaspoon salt
½ teaspoon pepper
1 teaspoon paprika
4 (6-ounce) trout fillets
1 tablespoon olive oil
¼ cup fresh lemon juice
¼ cup capers, undrained

• **Combine** first 4 ingredients in a shallow dish; dredge fillets in mixture.
• **Pour** olive oil in a large nonstick skillet; place over medium heat. Add fillets, and cook 3 minutes; turn fillets, and cook 1 additional minute. Add lemon juice and capers; cover and remove from heat. Let stand 3 to 5 minutes or until fish flakes easily when tested with a fork.
• **Transfer** fillets to a serving platter; spoon sauce over fillets, and serve immediately. **Yield:** 4 servings.

Carrie Easley
Dallas, Texas

♥ Per serving: Calories 297
Fat 9.4g Cholesterol 97mg
Sodium 863mg

SEARED TUNA STEAKS ON MIXED GREENS WITH LEMON-BASIL VINAIGRETTE

This recipe works with shrimp, too.

4 (4-ounce) tuna steaks
1 tablespoon reduced-sodium
   Cajun seasoning
Vegetable cooking spray
8 cups mixed salad greens
Lemon-Basil Vinaigrette
Garnish: finely chopped red bell
   pepper

• **Sprinkle** tuna steaks evenly with Cajun seasoning.
• **Coat** grill rack with cooking spray; place on grill over medium-hot coals (350° to 400°). Place tuna on rack.
• **Cook**, covered with grill lid, 5 minutes on each side or to desired degree of doneness.
• **Cover** and chill at least 8 hours.
• **Combine** salad greens and half of Lemon-Basil Vinaigrette, tossing gently; arrange on four plates. Top each with a tuna steak, and drizzle evenly with remaining vinaigrette. Garnish, if desired. **Yield:** 4 servings.

♥ Per serving: Calories 189
Fat 5.1g Cholesterol 51mg
Sodium 59mg

Lemon-Basil Vinaigrette

QUICK!

2 lemons, peeled, sectioned, and
   finely chopped
2 tablespoons white wine vinegar
1 tablespoon vegetable oil
1 tablespoon fresh basil leaves,
   finely chopped
¼ teaspoon cracked black
   pepper
¼ teaspoon hot sauce

• **Combine** all ingredients in a jar. Cover tightly; shake vigorously. **Yield:** ½ cup.

Sally Koch
Metairie, Louisiana

TUNA STEAKS WITH TARRAGON BUTTER

QUICK!

2 tablespoons butter or margarine, softened
¼ teaspoon lemon juice
½ teaspoon minced fresh tarragon or ¼ teaspoon dried tarragon
2 (½-pound) tuna steaks (about ¾ inch thick)
¼ teaspoon salt
¼ teaspoon freshly ground pepper
1 tablespoon olive oil

• **Combine** first 3 ingredients in a bowl; shape into a 1-inch-thick log; cover and chill until firm.
• **Sprinkle** tuna with salt and pepper on all sides. Heat olive oil in a nonstick skillet over medium heat; cook tuna 5 minutes on each side or to desired degree of doneness. Slice tarragon butter, and serve with tuna. **Yield:** 2 servings.

BROILED TUNA WITH ROSEMARY

QUICK!

4 (4-ounce) tuna steaks
½ cup dry white wine
1 tablespoon lemon juice
1½ teaspoons fresh rosemary
½ teaspoon garlic powder
½ teaspoon dried oregano
¼ teaspoon salt
⅛ teaspoon pepper
Vegetable cooking spray
Garnish: fresh rosemary sprigs

• **Place** tuna steaks in a large heavy-duty, zip-top plastic bag. Combine wine and next 6 ingredients; pour over steaks. Seal bag, and chill 1½ hours, turning bag occasionally.
• **Remove** steaks, discarding marinade. Place steaks on a rack coated with cooking spray; place rack in broiler pan. Broil 4 to 5 inches from heat (with electric oven door partially opened) 3 to 4 minutes on each side or until done. Garnish, if desired. **Yield:** 4 servings.

♥ Per serving: Calories 165
Fat 5.5g Cholesterol 42mg
Sodium 88mg

GRILLED FLORIDA TUNA

QUICK!

½ cup mayonnaise or salad dressing
1 tablespoon lime juice
1 clove garlic, pressed
½ teaspoon ground red pepper
½ teaspoon ground cumin
4 (½-inch-thick) tuna steaks (about 1 pound)

• **Combine** first 5 ingredients. Brush on steaks. Cook, covered with grill lid, over medium coals (300° to 350°) 5 to 7 minutes on each side to desired degree of doneness. **Yield:** 4 servings.

INLAND GRILLED TUNA

QUICK!

¼ cup soy sauce
1 tablespoon maple syrup
1 tablespoon prepared horseradish
4 (6-ounce) tuna steaks
Vegetable cooking spray

• **Combine** first 3 ingredients in a shallow dish; add tuna, turning to coat. Cover tuna, and chill 1 hour, turning occasionally.
• **Remove** tuna from marinade; discard marinade. Coat grill rack with cooking spray.
• **Place** tuna on rack over medium-hot coals (350° to 400°); cook tuna, covered with grill lid, 2 minutes on each side or to desired degree of doneness. **Yield:** 4 servings.

Joel Knox
Inland Seafood Company
Atlanta, Georgia

YELLOWFIN TUNA WITH CORN, PEPPER, AND TOMATO SALSA

Spice up sweet peppers, corn, tomatoes, and tuna with a Scotch bonnet pepper. It may look like a tiny bell pepper, but zowee, it packs a powerful punch.

1 red bell pepper
1 yellow bell pepper
4 ears fresh corn
2 large tomatoes, seeded and chopped
1 Scotch bonnet pepper, seeded and chopped *
2 tablespoons ground cumin
½ teaspoon salt
¼ teaspoon ground white pepper
Hickory chips
4 tuna steaks (about 2 pounds)
1 tablespoon olive oil
2 to 3 teaspoons cracked black pepper
½ to 1 teaspoon dried thyme
Garnishes: mixed salad greens, whole chile peppers

• **Place** bell peppers on a baking sheet; bake at 425° for 5 minutes. Cool. Remove and discard seeds; chop peppers.
• **Cut** corn from cob. Cook in boiling water to cover 3 minutes. Drain; cool.
• **Combine** chopped bell pepper, corn, tomato, and next 4 ingredients. Cover and chill.
• **Soak** hickory chips in water 30 minutes. Prepare charcoal fire on one side of grill; let burn until coals are white. Drain hickory chips, and place on hot coals.
• **Brush** tuna steaks with oil; sprinkle with black pepper and thyme.
• **Cook** tuna steaks, without grill lid, directly over hot coals 2 minutes on each side. Transfer tuna steaks to opposite side of grill, and cook indirectly, covered with grill lid, 5 to 7 minutes or to desired degree of doneness.
• **Spoon** salsa onto serving plates, and top with tuna steaks. Garnish, if desired. Serve immediately. **Yield:** 4 servings.

* Substitute your favorite hot chile pepper or skip the pepper altogether.

Chef Mark Rodriguez
Jordan's Grove
Maitland, Florida

CREAMED CHIPPED TUNA

QUICK!

Instead of the usual jar of dried beef, open a can of tuna for this convenient entrée.

4 frozen puff pastry shells *
3 tablespoons butter or margarine
¼ cup finely chopped onion
3 tablespoons all-purpose flour
2 cups milk
2 (6-ounce) cans solid white tuna
     in spring water, drained and
     flaked
2 hard-cooked eggs, sliced
1 cup (4 ounces) shredded Swiss
     cheese
½ cup frozen English peas,
     thawed
¼ teaspoon salt
½ teaspoon freshly ground
     pepper
1 tablespoon finely chopped fresh
     parsley

• **Bake** pastry shells according to package directions; set aside.
• **Melt** butter in a heavy saucepan over low heat; add onion, and cook, stirring constantly, 2 minutes or until onion is tender.
• **Stir** in flour; cook 1 minute, stirring constantly. Gradually add milk, stirring constantly with a wire whisk. Cook, stirring constantly, until mixture is thickened and bubbly.
• **Stir** in tuna and next 5 ingredients, and cook, stirring constantly, until cheese melts.
• **Spoon** tuna mixture over pastry shells; sprinkle with parsley. **Yield:** 4 servings.

* Substitute 4 slices toast, cut in half, for pastry shells.

Carol Richard
Birmingham, Alabama

SMOKED FISH HASH

4 cups finely chopped peeled
     potato
2½ cups flaked smoked fish
     (about ¾ pound)
6 slices bacon, cooked and
     crumbled
2 tablespoons chopped onion
2 tablespoons chopped fresh
     parsley
⅛ teaspoon pepper
⅓ cup vegetable oil
½ cup water
Paprika

• **Combine** first 6 ingredients; set aside.
• **Heat** oil in a heavy nonstick skillet; stir in potato mixture. Add water; cover, reduce heat, and simmer 7 minutes. Uncover and cook 8 to 10 minutes or until browned, stirring occasionally.
• **Spoon** into a serving dish; sprinkle with paprika. Serve immediately. **Yield:** 6 servings.

Frank Lawlor
Sebastian, Florida

FISH-STUFFED POTATOES

6 medium baking potatoes
½ cup butter or margarine,
     melted
1 (5-ounce) can evaporated milk
2 teaspoons salt
½ teaspoon black pepper
¼ teaspoon ground red pepper
2 cups flaked smoked fish (about
     ½ pound)
1 cup (4 ounces) shredded
     Cheddar cheese
3 tablespoons finely chopped
     greens onions or chives
Paprika

• **Scrub** potatoes. Wrap each potato in aluminum foil; bake at 400° for 1 hour or until done. Cut potatoes in half lengthwise; carefully scoop out pulp, leaving ¼-inch shells intact.
• **Combine** potato pulp, butter, and next 4 ingredients. Stir in flaked fish, cheese, and green onions. Stuff shells with potato mixture, and sprinkle evenly with paprika.

• Place stuffed shells on a baking sheet. Bake at 350° for 10 minutes or until thoroughly heated. **Yield:** 6 servings.

Frank Lawlor
Sebastian, Florida

CRAB-STUFFED POTATOES

6 large baking potatoes
Vegetable oil
½ cup butter or margarine,
     softened
½ cup sour cream
1 cup (4 ounces) shredded
     Cheddar cheese
½ teaspoon salt
½ teaspoon Old Bay seasoning
¼ teaspoon pepper
½ pound fresh lump crabmeat *
¼ cup finely sliced green
     onions
2 tablespoons fine, dry
     breadcrumbs
¼ teaspoon paprika
¼ teaspoon Old Bay seasoning

• **Wash** potatoes, and rub skins with vegetable oil. Prick each potato several times with a fork. Bake at 400° for 1 hour or until potatoes are done. Let potatoes cool.
• **Cut** a 1-inch lengthwise strip from top of each potato. Carefully scoop out potato pulp, leaving a ¼-inch shell intact; mash pulp.
• **Combine** potato pulp, butter, and next 5 ingredients. Drain crabmeat, removing any bits of shell. Gently stir crabmeat and green onions into potato pulp mixture. Stuff shells with potato mixture; place on a baking sheet. Sprinkle with breadcrumbs, paprika, and ¼ teaspoon Old Bay seasoning. Bake stuffed potatoes at 425° for 15 minutes. **Yield:** 6 servings.

* You can substitute one 6-ounce can lump crabmeat, drained, for ½ pound fresh lump crabmeat.

Sandra Rhodes Potter
Cambridge, Maryland

CRABMEAT KAREN

1 cup finely chopped fresh
    mushrooms
¾ cup finely chopped green
    onions
1 large egg, lightly beaten
¼ cup whipping cream
½ teaspoon salt
¼ teaspoon ground white
    pepper
¼ teaspoon ground red pepper
1 pound fresh lump crabmeat
1 cup soft breadcrumbs
White Wine Sauce
3 (17¼-ounce) packages frozen
    puff pastry sheets, thawed
2 large eggs, lightly beaten
Garnishes: cherry tomatoes, fresh
    parsley sprigs

• **Combine** first 7 ingredients. Drain crabmeat, removing any bits of shell. Add crabmeat and breadcrumbs to mushroom mixture, tossing gently. Set aside.
• **Begin** preparing White Wine Sauce. While it is simmering, roll puff pastry to ⅛-inch thickness. Cut 12 "crabs" from pastry with a 7- x 4-inch crab-shaped cookie cutter, if available. If not, make separate paper pattern pieces, cutting the body portion about 7 x 4 inches. Cut two patterns for the claws, one about 5 x 2 inches and the other about 2 x 1 inches.
• **Placing** pattern pieces separately on the pastry, cut 12 body portions and 24 of each claw section with pastry wheel or knife. Spoon reserved crabmeat mixture evenly onto six body portions, leaving a ½-inch border on all sides. Brush edges with beaten eggs; top with remaining six body portions, pinching edges to seal. Place on a baking sheet, brushing with beaten eggs; set aside.
• **Attach** 1 longer claw section to each shorter claw section, pressing edges to seal. Brush edges of 12 "claws" with beaten eggs; top with remaining claws, pressing edges to seal. Place on a baking sheet; brush with beaten eggs. Bake "crabs" and "claws" at 375° for 20 minutes or until golden.
• **Spoon** 3 tablespoons White Wine Sauce into center of each plate. Place a warm "crab" in the center; arrange a "claw" on each side. Garnish, if desired. Serve immediately. **Yield:** 6 servings.

White Wine Sauce

¼ cup chopped shallots
½ cup dry white wine
2 teaspoons fish-flavored bouillon
    granules
2 cups boiling water
½ bunch fresh parsley
3 bay leaves
1 sprig fresh thyme
1 stalk celery, cut into pieces
2 black peppercorns
½ cup whipping cream
1½ tablespoons cornstarch
1 tablespoon water
⅛ teaspoon salt
⅛ teaspoon ground white
    pepper

• **Combine** shallot and wine in a small saucepan; bring to a boil. Reduce heat, and simmer 5 minutes or until reduced by one-third.
• **Dissolve** bouillon in boiling water; set aside.
• **Cut** a 14-inch square of cheesecloth; place parsley and next 3 ingredients in center. Tie with string. Add to wine mixture with bouillon and peppercorns. Bring to a boil, reduce heat, and simmer, uncovered, 20 minutes.
• **Pour** liquid through a large wire-mesh strainer into a bowl, reserving broth. Discard vegetables and herbs.
• **Combine** broth and whipping cream in saucepan; bring to a boil, reduce heat, and simmer, uncovered, 10 minutes. Combine cornstarch and water, stirring until smooth. Gradually stir into whipping cream mixture; cook 1 minute, stirring constantly. Stir in salt and white pepper. **Yield:** 1¼ cups.

Note: Check gourmet kitchen shops for a crab-shaped cookie cutter.

Arnaud's
New Orleans, Louisiana

CRAB IMPERIAL

1 pound fresh lump crabmeat
¼ cup butter or margarine
3 tablespoons all-purpose flour
1½ cups half-and-half
2 teaspoons chopped fresh
    parsley
1½ teaspoons dry mustard
¾ teaspoon salt
1 tablespoon lemon juice
2 teaspoons prepared horseradish
1 teaspoon Worcestershire
    sauce
1 cup soft breadcrumbs
2 tablespoons butter or margarine,
    melted

• **Drain** crabmeat, removing any bits of shell; set aside.
• **Melt** ¼ cup butter in a large heavy saucepan over low heat; add flour, stirring until mixture is smooth. Cook 1 minute, stirring constantly. Gradually add half-and-half; cook over medium heat, stirring constantly, until thickened and bubbly.
• **Stir** in parsley and next 5 ingredients; add crabmeat, stirring gently. Spoon into greased baking shells.
• **Combine** breadcrumbs and 2 tablespoons butter; sprinkle evenly over crabmeat mixture.
• **Bake** at 350° for 30 minutes or until bubbly. **Yield:** 6 servings.

Jane Maloy
Wilmington, North Carolina

CHESAPEAKE BAY CRAB CAKES

1 pound lump crabmeat
1 large egg
4 saltine crackers, crushed
1½ teaspoons dried parsley flakes
¾ teaspoon Old Bay seasoning
½ teaspoon Worcestershire sauce
3 or 4 drops of hot sauce
⅛ teaspoon freshly ground pepper
3 tablespoons mayonnaise or salad dressing
3 tablespoons mayonnaise or salad dressing
½ teaspoon Old Bay seasoning
Paprika
Tartar Sauce

• **Drain** crabmeat, removing any bits of shell.
• **Combine** egg and next 7 ingredients; stir in crabmeat.
• **Shape** into 6 (3-inch) patties. Place on a lightly greased baking sheet.
• **Combine** 3 tablespoons mayonnaise and ½ teaspoon Old Bay seasoning; spread evenly on crab cakes. Sprinkle with paprika.
• **Bake** at 350° for 20 minutes or until golden. (Do not overbake.) Serve with Tartar Sauce. **Yield:** 6 servings.

Tartar Sauce

QUICK!

1 cup mayonnaise or salad dressing
1 teaspoon Dijon mustard
1½ tablespoons finely chopped fresh parsley
1½ tablespoons chopped capers
1 hard-cooked egg, finely chopped
1 tablespoon sweet pickle relish
1 tablespoon chopped fresh chives

• **Combine** all ingredients; cover and chill. **Yield:** 1 cup.

Susan Smith
Easton, Maryland

GULF COAST CRAB CAKES
(pictured at right)

1 tablespoon butter or margarine
1 clove garlic, minced
1 tablespoon finely chopped red bell pepper
2 teaspoons finely chopped onion
1½ teaspoons finely chopped green bell pepper
1½ teaspoons finely chopped yellow bell pepper
1½ tablespoons all-purpose flour
⅓ cup whipping cream
1 pound fresh lump crabmeat
1¼ cups soft breadcrumbs, divided
½ finely chopped serrano chile pepper
1 egg yolk
2 teaspoons chopped fresh chives
1 teaspoon dry mustard
1 teaspoon stone-ground mustard
1 teaspoon lemon juice
½ teaspoon salt
¼ teaspoon pepper
¼ cup butter or margarine, divided
Vegetable oil
1 corn tortilla, cut into thin strips
Lime-Saffron Sauce
Mango Slaw
Garnish: fresh cilantro sprigs

• **Melt** 1 tablespoon butter in a large skillet over medium heat; add garlic and next 4 ingredients, and cook 3 minutes, stirring often. Stir in flour; cook 3 minutes, stirring constantly. Gradually add whipping cream, and cook, stirring constantly, until thickened. Remove from heat.
• **Drain** crabmeat, removing any bits of shell. Stir crabmeat, ¼ cup breadcrumbs, chile pepper, and next 7 ingredients into red pepper mixture. Cover and chill 3 to 4 hours.
• **Shape** crabmeat mixture into 10 (2-inch) patties; dredge in remaining 1 cup breadcrumbs.
• **Melt** 2 tablespoons butter in a large skillet over medium heat; add half of patties, and cook until golden, turning once. Drain on paper towels. Repeat procedure with remaining 2 tablespoons butter and patties. Set aside.

• **Wipe** skillet with paper towels.
• **Pour** oil to depth of 1 inch into skillet. Fry tortilla strips in hot oil over medium-high heat until golden. Drain on paper towels. Set aside.
• **Spoon** Lime-Saffron Sauce onto plates, and arrange crab cakes and Mango Slaw on sauce. Top with tortilla strips, and garnish, if desired. **Yield:** 5 servings.

Lime-Saffron Sauce

1 cup dry white wine
Pinch of saffron
½ teaspoon butter or margarine
1 small shallot, finely chopped
3 tablespoons lime juice
2 tablespoons whipping cream
½ cup butter, cut into pieces
¼ teaspoon salt

• **Combine** wine and saffron in a saucepan; bring to a boil. Remove from heat; let stand 30 minutes.
• **Melt** ½ teaspoon butter in a large skillet over medium heat; add shallot, and cook, stirring constantly, until tender. Add wine mixture and lime juice; cook over medium heat until mixture is reduced to ¼ cup.
• **Stir** in whipping cream, and cook until mixture is reduced to ¼ cup. Remove from heat; add ½ cup butter and salt, stirring until butter melts. **Yield:** about ¾ cup.

Mango Slaw

1 cup finely shredded red cabbage
1 cup peeled, chopped mango
1 medium tomato, chopped
1 serrano chile pepper, finely chopped
1 green onion, chopped
⅓ cup chopped fresh cilantro
3 tablespoons lime juice
1 teaspoon olive oil
⅛ teaspoon salt
⅛ teaspoon pepper

• **Combine** all ingredients; cover and chill at least 2 hours. Serve with a slotted spoon. **Yield:** 3 cups.

Chef Bruce Auden
BIGA
San Antonio, Texas

Gulf Coast Crab Cakes

CRAB-STUFFED LOBSTER TAILS

(pictured on page 149)

Have lobsters steamed at your supermarket to save time.

2   quarts water
2   tablespoons salt
2   (1½- to 1¾-pound) live lobsters
½   pound fresh lump crabmeat
1   clove garlic, minced
1   tablespoon chopped fresh
      parsley
2   tablespoons freshly grated
      Parmesan cheese
2   tablespoons fine, dry
      breadcrumbs
¼   teaspoon salt
¼   teaspoon Old Bay seasoning
¼   teaspoon pepper
2   tablespoons butter, melted
1   teaspoon lemon juice
Garlic-Butter Sauce
Garnishes: lemon halves, fresh
      flat-leaf parsley sprigs

• **Combine** water and 2 tablespoons salt in a large Dutch oven; bring to a boil. Plunge lobsters, head first, into boiling water; return to a boil. Cover, reduce heat, and simmer 10 minutes; drain and let cool.
• **Break** off large claws and legs. Crack claw and leg shells, using a seafood or nut cracker; remove meat, and set aside. Break off tail. Cut top side of tail shell lengthwise, using kitchen shears. Cut through center of meat and remove vein. Leave meat in shell. Rinse and set aside.
• **Drain** crabmeat, removing any bits of shell. Combine crabmeat, garlic, and next 8 ingredients; toss gently. Spoon mixture into lobster tail. Place on a baking sheet.
• **Bake** at 400° for 12 minutes or until thoroughly heated. Serve with Garlic-Butter Sauce and claw and leg meat. Garnish, if desired. **Yield:** 2 servings.

Garlic-Butter Sauce

QUICK!

½   cup butter
2   tablespoons whipping cream
2   tablespoons lemon juice
1   clove garlic, minced

• **Melt** butter in a saucepan over low heat; add whipping cream, and cook 1 minute, stirring constantly. Stir in lemon juice and garlic. **Yield:** ⅔ cup.

CRAWFISH ÉTOUFFÉE

Seafood markets sell frozen, peeled crawfish tails harvested in Louisiana or China. You can substitute peeled shrimp, but the color won't be as intense.

½   cup butter or margarine
1   large onion, chopped
¼   cup finely chopped celery
¼   cup chopped green bell pepper
2   cloves garlic, minced
1   pound peeled crawfish tails
1   teaspoon salt
½   teaspoon ground black pepper
½   teaspoon onion powder
¼   teaspoon ground white pepper
½   teaspoon hot sauce
1½ tablespoons all-purpose flour
¾   cup water
½   cup finely chopped green onions
¼   cup finely chopped fresh parsley
Hot cooked rice

• **Melt** butter in a large skillet over medium heat. Add onion and next 3 ingredients, and cook 5 minutes, stirring constantly.
• **Stir** in crawfish and next 5 ingredients; cook 5 minutes. Stir in flour; cook 2 minutes, stirring constantly.
• **Stir** in water gradually; cook over low heat 20 minutes, stirring occasionally.
• **Stir** in green onions and parsley; cook 3 minutes. Serve over rice. **Yield:** 4 to 6 servings.

Jude Theriot
Lake Charles, Louisiana

PAN-FRIED GRITS WITH CREAMED OYSTERS

3   cups whipping cream
¼   teaspoon salt
⅛   teaspoon pepper
2   medium leeks
2   (10-ounce) containers Standard
      oysters, undrained
1   clove garlic, minced
1   shallot, finely chopped
3   tablespoons butter or margarine,
      melted
8   shiitake mushroom caps, thinly
      sliced
Pan-Fried Grits
Garnish: thin strips fresh spinach
      leaves

• **Combine** first 3 ingredients in a heavy saucepan; bring to a boil over medium heat. Reduce heat to low, and simmer, uncovered, 35 to 40 minutes or until whipping cream mixture is reduced to 1½ cups, stirring occasionally. Cover and set aside.
• **Wash** leeks, and cut white part into thin strips; set aside. Reserve green tops for another use.
• **Drain** oysters, reserving ½ cup liquid; set aside.
• **Cook** garlic and shallot in butter in a large skillet over medium-high heat, stirring constantly, until tender.
• **Add** leeks and mushrooms, and cook 2 to 3 minutes or until vegetables are tender, stirring often. Add oysters and reserved liquid, and cook 3 to 5 minutes or until oysters begin to curl. Add reserved whipping cream mixture, and cook until thoroughly heated, stirring occasionally.
• **To** serve, place 2 triangles of Pan-Fried Grits on each plate; top with oyster mixture. Garnish, if desired. **Yield:** 6 servings.

Pan-Fried Grits

8   cups water
2   teaspoons salt
¼   cup butter or margarine
2   cups quick-cooking yellow grits,
      uncooked
2   large eggs, divided
⅓ to ½ cup butter or margarine,
      divided

- **Combine** first 3 ingredients in a Dutch oven; bring to a boil. Stir in grits; bring to a boil over medium heat. Reduce heat, and cook 4 to 5 minutes, stirring occasionally.
- **Beat** 1 egg with a fork. Gradually stir about one-fourth of hot mixture into beaten egg; add to remaining hot mixture, stirring constantly.
- **Pour** grits mixture into a buttered 15- x 10- x 1-inch jellyroll pan; cover and chill 8 hours. Cut chilled grits into 6 (5-inch) squares, and cut each square into 2 triangles.
- **Beat** remaining egg in a shallow dish. Dip each grits triangle in beaten egg. Melt half of remaining butter in a large skillet. Add as many grits triangles as will fit, and cook on each side until golden. Repeat procedure with remaining grits triangles and butter. **Yield:** 12 triangles.

Jeff Tuttle
Pawleys Island, South Carolina

SCALLOPED OYSTERS

QUICK!

1   quart oysters, undrained
5   cups crushed round buttery
      crackers, divided
½   teaspoon salt
½   teaspoon ground red pepper
2   teaspoons Worcestershire sauce
2   cups half-and-half
¼   cup unsalted butter, cut into
      pieces

- **Drain** oysters, reserving 3 tablespoons liquid.
- **Place** half of cracker crumbs in a greased 13- x 9- x 2-inch baking dish. Arrange oysters over crumbs; sprinkle with salt, pepper, and Worcestershire sauce. Top with remaining crumbs; drizzle with reserved oyster liquid and half-and-half. Top with butter.
- **Bake** at 400° for 30 minutes. **Yield:** 8 servings.

Sissy Nash and Kathy Nash Cary
Louisville, Kentucky

WILD RICE AND OYSTERS

6   cups chicken broth
2   (6-ounce) packages wild rice
½   cup butter or margarine, melted
      and divided
2   quarts oysters, drained
1   pound fresh mushrooms, sliced
½   cup chopped celery
½   cup chopped onion
½   cup all-purpose flour
1   cup chicken broth
1   cup whipping cream
1 to 1½   tablespoons curry
      powder
1   teaspoon onion powder
1   teaspoon dried thyme
½   teaspoon salt
¼   teaspoon pepper
¼   teaspoon hot sauce
½   cup chopped fresh parsley

- **Bring** 6 cups chicken broth to a boil in a large saucepan. Add rice; cover tightly, and simmer 50 to 60 minutes. (Drain rice after cooking if all chicken broth is not absorbed; discard broth.) Toss rice with 2 tablespoons melted butter. Set aside.
- **Cook** oysters, mushrooms, celery, and onion in 2 tablespoons butter in a large skillet over medium heat until edges of oysters begin to curl, stirring occasionally. Drain well, and set aside.
- **Pour** remaining 4 tablespoons butter into a large heavy saucepan or Dutch oven; add flour, stirring until smooth. Cook over low heat 1 minute, stirring constantly. Gradually add 1 cup chicken broth and whipping cream; cook over medium heat, stirring constantly, until mixture is thickened and bubbly. Stir in curry powder and next 5 ingredients. Add wild rice and oyster mixtures, stirring well.
- **Spoon** mixture into a lightly greased 3½-quart casserole. Bake, uncovered, at 350° for 30 minutes or until bubbly. Sprinkle with parsley. **Yield:** 10 to 12 servings.

Kreis Beall
The Inn at Blackberry Farm
Walland, Tennessee

SEARED SCALLOPS WITH TOMATO-MANGO SALSA

QUICK!

Scallops should smell sweet, not fishy. They cook very quickly and will become tough and chewy if overcooked.

1   medium tomato, finely chopped
¾   cup finely chopped mango
3   tablespoons finely chopped
      purple onion
2   tablespoons finely chopped fresh
      basil
2   tablespoons red wine vinegar
1   tablespoon capers
1   tablespoon olive oil
12   sea scallops
¼   teaspoon salt
¼   teaspoon pepper
¼   avocado, sliced
Garnish: fresh basil sprigs

- **Combine** first 6 ingredients. Cover and chill salsa at least 30 minutes.
- **Heat** olive oil in a skillet over medium-high heat until hot. Add scallops; cook 3 minutes or until scallops are white, turning once. Remove scallops from skillet; sprinkle with salt and pepper.
- **Arrange** scallops, salsa, and avocado slices evenly on plates. Garnish, if desired. **Yield:** 2 servings.

Note: You can thread scallops on skewers and grill. Cook, covered with grill lid, over hot coals (400° to 500°) 3 to 5 minutes on each side or until scallops are white.

Joe R. Farralt
Muskogee, Oklahoma

♥ Per serving: Calories 246
Fat 11.2g   Cholesterol 30mg
Sodium 782mg

Grilled Orange Scallops With Cilantro-Lime Vinaigrette

GRILLED ORANGE SCALLOPS WITH CILANTRO-LIME VINAIGRETTE
(pictured at left)

1 cup orange juice
3 tablespoons chopped fresh basil
18 sea scallops *
1 head Bibb lettuce
4 cups mixed baby lettuces
Cilantro-Lime Vinaigrette
30 yellow pear-shaped cherry
     tomatoes
30 pear-shaped cherry tomatoes
2 cucumbers, cut into thin strips
Garnishes: fresh basil sprigs, thin
     orange rind strips

• **Combine** orange juice and basil in a dish; add scallops, tossing to coat.
• **Cover** and chill about 1 hour. Uncover and drain, discarding marinade.
• **Cook** scallops, covered with grill lid, over hot coals (400° to 500°) 3 to 5 minutes on each side or until scallops are white.
• **Place** lettuces in a bowl; drizzle with Cilantro-Lime Vinaigrette, and toss gently to combine.
• **Arrange** lettuces on individual plates, and top with scallops, tomatoes, and cucumber. Garnish, if desired. Serve immediately. **Yield:** 6 servings.

* Substitute 30 large shrimp, peeled with tails intact, for sea scallops.

Note: Cook scallops directly on grill rack, but if your rack openings are too large, cook them in a grill basket or threaded on skewers.

♥ Per serving: Calories 324
Fat 11g Cholesterol 52mg
Sodium 272mg

Cilantro-Lime Vinaigrette
QUICK!

¼ cup sugar
¼ cup extra-virgin olive oil
2 tablespoons lime juice
2 tablespoons rice wine vinegar
1 clove garlic, minced
1 shallot, minced
1½ teaspoons fresh cilantro, finely
     chopped

• **Combine** all ingredients in a jar. Cover jar tightly, and shake vigorously. **Yield:** ¾ cup.

Penny Caughfield
Cocoa, Florida

SCALLOPS IN VERMOUTH-CREAM SAUCE
QUICK!

1 pound sea scallops
2 tablespoons all-purpose flour
2 tablespoons butter or margarine
¼ cup dry vermouth
½ cup whipping cream
¼ teaspoon salt
⅛ teaspoon pepper

• **Coat** scallops with flour. Melt butter in a large skillet over medium heat; add scallops. Cook 3 to 4 minutes or until scallops are white, stirring occasionally. Remove scallops from skillet.
• **Add** vermouth to skillet, stirring to loosen particles that cling to bottom. Bring to a boil; cook 3 minutes or until reduced by half. Stir in whipping cream, salt, and pepper; reduce heat to low. Add scallops; cook just until thoroughly heated. **Yield:** 2 main-dish servings or 4 appetizer servings.

Elaine C. Heintz
Staunton, Virginia

STUFFED SHRIMP WITH HOLLANDAISE SAUCE

24 unpeeled jumbo fresh shrimp
¼ cup butter, divided
1 medium onion, finely chopped
½ red bell pepper, finely chopped
½ green bell pepper, finely
     chopped
2 cloves garlic, minced
½ cup fine, dry breadcrumbs
2 tablespoons Cajun seasoning
1 large egg, lightly beaten
⅓ cup mayonnaise
1 pound frozen crawfish tails,
     thawed and chopped
2 tablespoons lemon juice
2 tablespoons dry white wine
Hollandaise Sauce

• **Peel** shrimp, leaving tails intact; devein shrimp, if desired. Butterfly shrimp by making a deep slit down back of each from large end to tail, cutting to, but not through, inside curve of shrimp. Set aside.
• **Melt** 2 tablespoons butter in a large saucepan; add onion and next 3 ingredients. Cook over medium-high heat until vegetables are tender, stirring often. Stir in breadcrumbs and seasoning; set aside.
• **Combine** egg, mayonnaise, and crawfish; stir into onion mixture.
• **Stuff** slit in each shrimp with about 3 tablespoons crawfish mixture; arrange on an aluminum foil-lined 15- x 10- x 1-inch jellyroll pan.
• **Melt** remaining 2 tablespoons butter in a small saucepan; add lemon juice and wine. Drizzle over shrimp.
• **Bake** shrimp at 400° for 20 minutes. Serve with Hollandaise Sauce. **Yield:** 6 to 8 servings.

Hollandaise Sauce

1 cup fat-free egg substitute
½ teaspoon salt
¼ cup lemon juice
1 cup butter, softened and
     divided
1 teaspoon grated lemon rind

• **Combine** egg substitute and salt in a heavy saucepan; cook over medium heat, stirring constantly with a wire whisk. Gradually add lemon juice, beating constantly with a wire whisk.
• **Remove** from heat; add ½ cup butter, 2 tablespoons at a time, beating well after each addition. (The butter should not simply melt; it should be worked into the sauce mixture with whisk.)
• **Pour** mixture into container of an electric blender. With blender on high, drop remaining ½ cup butter, 2 tablespoons at a time, into blender. Blend mixture until smooth; stir in lemon rind.
• **Return** to saucepan to keep warm, and place pan in larger pan filled with hot water. **Yield:** 2 cups.

Dick and Inez Thompson
Bay St. Louis, Mississippi

PHYLLO PIZZA

8 sheets frozen phyllo pastry,
    thawed
Butter-flavored cooking spray *
10 unpeeled large fresh shrimp
1 tablespoon olive oil
1 tablespoon lemon juice
¼ teaspoon salt
⅛ teaspoon pepper
1 (8-ounce) package cream cheese,
    softened
1 (4-ounce) package feta cheese
1 teaspoon dried tarragon
3 cherry tomatoes, cut into
    wedges
½ small green bell pepper, cut into
    thin strips
½ small red bell pepper, cut into
    thin strips
¼ cup sliced ripe olives
2 tablespoons butter, melted
1 teaspoon minced garlic

• **Place** 1 phyllo sheet in a 15- x 10- x 1-inch jellyroll pan coated with cooking spray; keep remaining phyllo sheets covered with a slightly damp towel until ready to use. Coat phyllo sheet in pan with cooking spray. Layer remaining phyllo sheets on first sheet, spraying each with cooking spray. Roll phyllo edges toward center, forming a 15- x 7-inch rectangle. Spray edges of phyllo with cooking spray, and prick bottom of crust with a fork.
• **Bake** phyllo at 400° for 5 minutes. Remove from oven, and gently press down center; bake 5 additional minutes, and let cool.
• **Peel** shrimp, and devein, if desired; slice shrimp in half lengthwise. Cook shrimp in olive oil in a skillet over medium heat 1 minute, stirring constantly. Add lemon juice, salt, and pepper. Set aside.
• **Combine** cheeses; spread on phyllo crust, and sprinkle with tarragon. Top with shrimp, tomato, bell pepper strips, and olives. Combine butter and garlic; drizzle over pizza.
• **Bake** at 400° for 10 minutes. Serve hot. **Yield:** 4 to 6 servings.

* Substitute ⅔ cup melted butter for cooking spray brushed on phyllo pastry sheets.

SHRIMP ENCHILADAS IN TOMATILLO SAUCE

Green chile sauce makes a spicy substitution for the tomatillo sauce in this recipe.

1 pound unpeeled large fresh
    shrimp
1 large onion, finely chopped
2 teaspoons olive oil
1 tablespoon all-purpose flour
1½ cups reduced-sodium chicken
    broth
1 (12-ounce) can tomatillo
    sauce
1 teaspoon ground cumin
½ teaspoon dried oregano
8 corn tortillas
1½ cups (6 ounces) shredded
    reduced-fat Monterey Jack
    cheese
½ cup nonfat sour cream

• **Peel** shrimp, and devein, if desired. Set shrimp aside.
• **Cook** onion in olive oil in a large nonstick skillet over medium-high heat, stirring constantly, until onion is tender. Add flour, stirring until smooth; cook 1 minute.
• **Stir** in chicken broth and next 3 ingredients; cook 15 minutes or until mixture is thickened.
• **Add** shrimp; cook 5 minutes or until shrimp turn pink. Remove from heat, and cool slightly.
• **Dip** corn tortillas in shrimp mixture; place on a flat surface. Place 3 or 4 shrimp in center of each tortilla, using a slotted spoon; sprinkle each with about 1 tablespoon cheese, and roll tightly.
• **Place** tortillas, seam side down, in a lightly greased 11- x 7- x 1½-inch baking dish. Pour remaining shrimp mixture over top, and sprinkle with remaining cheese.
• **Cover** and bake at 350° for 15 minutes. Uncover and bake 10 minutes or until cheese melts. Serve with sour cream. **Yield:** 4 servings.

Karl Harvey
Baton Rouge, Louisiana

♥ Per serving: Calories 360
Fat 13.3g Cholesterol 114mg
Sodium 438mg

QUESADILLAS WITH SHRIMP AND BRIE

1 medium-size purple onion,
    sliced
2 tablespoons vegetable oil,
    divided
6 (6-inch) flour tortillas
1 (15-ounce) Brie cheese
½ pound cooked shrimp, peeled,
    deveined, and coarsely
    chopped
Papaya Salsa

• **Cook** onion in 1 tablespoon oil in a skillet over medium-high heat, stirring constantly, until tender. Set aside.
• **Heat** tortillas according to package directions.
• **Trim** rind from Brie, and discard; thinly slice Brie. Place Brie slices on half of each tortilla. Top evenly with onion and shrimp; fold in half, and set aside.
• **Brush** skillet with remaining 1 tablespoon oil; cook 2 quesadillas at a time over medium heat about 1 minute or until lightly browned, turning once.
• **Cut** each into 4 wedges; serve with Papaya Salsa. **Yield:** 6 servings.

Papaya Salsa

1 ripe papaya, chopped
1 small ripe avocado, chopped
3 scallions, chopped
½ red bell pepper, finely
    chopped
½ jalapeño pepper, seeded and
    finely chopped
2 tablespoons chopped fresh
    cilantro
Juice of 1 lime

• **Combine** all ingredients; cover and chill. **Yield:** 2½ cups.

Jean Cooper
Washington, D.C.

SHRIMP WITH GIN AND GINGER

QUICK!

1½ pounds unpeeled large fresh
    shrimp (about 28)
3 tablespoons butter or margarine
2 cloves garlic, minced
2 tablespoons minced fresh ginger
⅓ cup gin
2 small carrots, cut into thin
    strips
2 small stalks celery, cut into thin
    strips
1 leek, cut into thin strips
4 fresh snow pea pods, cut into
    thin strips
¼ teaspoon salt
½ cup whipping cream

• **Peel** shrimp, and devein, if desired.
Set aside.
• **Melt** butter in a skillet over medium
heat; add shrimp, and cook, stirring constantly, until shrimp turn pink (about 2
to 3 minutes). Remove shrimp, reserving drippings in skillet; set aside, and
keep warm.
• **Cook** garlic and ginger in reserved
drippings over medium heat 1 minute,
stirring constantly.
• **Add** gin, stirring to loosen browned
particles that cling to bottom. Stir in carrot and remaining 5 ingredients; cook
over medium heat 5 minutes.
• **Stir** in shrimp; serve immediately.
Yield: 4 servings.

Kathy Ruiz
Houston, Texas

CREAMED SHRIMP ON
PECAN-CORNMEAL ROUNDS

1 pound unpeeled medium-size
    fresh shrimp
¼ cup butter or margarine
½ cup chopped onion
½ cup chopped red or green bell
    pepper
1 (10¾-ounce) can cream of
    mushroom soup, undiluted
½ cup water
¼ teaspoon ground black pepper
⅛ teaspoon ground red pepper
Pecan-Cornmeal Rounds
Garnish: fresh parsley sprigs

• **Peel** shrimp, and devein, if desired; set
aside.
• **Melt** butter in a heavy skillet over
medium-high heat; add onion and
chopped pepper. Cook 2 minutes or
until vegetables are crisp-tender. Stir in
soup and next 3 ingredients. Bring to a
boil, stirring constantly. Add shrimp; reduce heat, and simmer 10 minutes or
until shrimp turn pink.
• **Place** a plain Pecan-Cornmeal Round
on each serving plate; top with shrimp
mixture and a pecan-topped round. Garnish, if desired. **Yield:** 4 servings.

Pat Gindrup
Conroe, Texas

Pecan-Cornmeal Rounds

¾ cup plus 2 tablespoons butter,
    softened
1½ cups all-purpose flour
½ cup yellow cornmeal
2 tablespoons sugar
¾ teaspoon salt
1 egg, lightly beaten
¾ cup chopped pecans
4 pecan halves

• **Beat** butter at medium speed with an
electric mixer until creamy. Add flour
and next 4 ingredients; mix at low speed
until blended. Stir in chopped pecans.
Wrap dough in plastic wrap; chill 1 hour.
• **Turn** dough out onto a lightly floured
surface. Roll to ½-inch thickness. Cut
into 8 shapes with a 3-inch daisy-shaped
or round cutter. Place on a lightly
greased baking sheet. Press a pecan half
in center of half the rounds.
• **Bake** at 350° for 20 minutes or until
rounds are lightly browned; remove
from pan, and cool on wire racks. **Yield:**
8 rounds.

Edith Askins
Greenville, Texas

SHRIMP AND PEPPER
SOFT TACOS

¾ pound unpeeled medium-size
    fresh shrimp
2 cloves garlic, minced
1 tablespoon olive oil
½ teaspoon ground cumin
1 large onion, chopped
2 tomatoes, chopped
1 Anaheim chile pepper, seeded
    and minced
1 jalapeño pepper, seeded and
    minced
¼ cup chopped fresh cilantro
¼ teaspoon salt
4 (8-inch) flour tortillas
Fresh lime wedges
Shredded Monterey Jack cheese
    with peppers
Sour cream

• **Peel** shrimp, and devein, if desired.
• **Cook** garlic in oil in a large skillet over
medium heat, stirring constantly, until
tender; add shrimp and cumin, and cook
about 1 minute, stirring constantly. Remove shrimp, and set aside.
• **Add** onion to skillet; cook, stirring
constantly, until tender. Add shrimp,
tomato, and peppers; cook until thoroughly heated. Remove from heat, and
stir in cilantro and salt.
• **Spoon** ¾ cup shrimp mixture in center of each tortilla; squeeze lime wedges
over shrimp mixture, and top with
cheese and sour cream. Fold tortillas in
half. **Yield:** 4 servings.

Julia Hardie Kaczvinsky
Ruston, Louisiana

*Classic Charleston
Breakfast Shrimp*

CLASSIC CHARLESTON BREAKFAST SHRIMP
(pictured at left)

1 pound unpeeled medium-size
   fresh shrimp
2 tablespoons lemon juice
¼ teaspoon salt
⅛ teaspoon ground red
   pepper
¼ cup finely chopped onion
⅓ cup finely chopped green bell
   pepper
3 tablespoons melted bacon
   drippings
2 tablespoons all-purpose flour
¾ cup Shrimp Stock or chicken
   broth
Creamy Grits
Garnishes: green bell pepper strips,
   fresh lemon slices

• **Peel** and devein shrimp. Combine shrimp, lemon juice, salt, and red pepper in a small bowl; set aside.
• **Cook** onion and green bell pepper in bacon drippings in a large skillet over medium-high heat about 10 minutes, stirring constantly. Sprinkle flour over vegetables; cook, stirring constantly, about 2 minutes or until flour begins to brown. Add shrimp and Shrimp Stock; cook, stirring constantly, 2 to 3 minutes or until shrimp turn pink and gravy is smooth. Add water or additional stock, if gravy is too thick. Serve immediately over Creamy Grits. Garnish, if desired. **Yield:** 2 servings.

Note: If you make the Shrimp Stock, use the fresh shrimp left over from the stock to make Classic Charleston Breakfast Shrimp.

Shrimp Stock

2 pounds unpeeled medium-size
   fresh shrimp with heads
3 quarts water
1 large carrot
2 stalks celery, quartered
1 medium onion, quartered
½ cup fresh thyme sprigs
½ cup fresh parsley sprigs
½ cup fresh basil leaves
½ cup fresh oregano sprigs
1 tablespoon dried savory

• **Remove** heads, and peel shrimp; place heads and shells in a large Dutch oven. Reserve shrimp for another use. Add water and remaining ingredients; bring to a boil. Reduce heat, and simmer, uncovered, 45 minutes.
• **Pour** mixture through a wire-mesh strainer into a container, discarding solids. Reserve desired amount of stock, and freeze remaining stock for another use. **Yield:** 8 cups.

Creamy Grits

2 cups water
2 tablespoons butter or margarine
½ cup regular or stone-ground
   grits, uncooked
1 cup half-and-half or whipping
   cream, divided

• **Bring** water and butter to a boil in a heavy saucepan. Stir in grits; return to a boil over medium heat. Reduce heat, and cook 10 minutes or until thickened, stirring occasionally. Stir in ½ cup half-and-half; simmer 10 minutes, stirring occasionally. Add remaining ½ cup half-and-half; simmer 10 minutes, stirring occasionally. **Yield:** 2 servings.
Adapted from Hoppin' John's
Lowcountry Cooking
(Bantam)

SPICY SHRIMP AND SAUSAGE OVER CREAMY GRITS WITH TASSO GRAVY

1½ pounds Italian sausage
1½ pounds unpeeled medium-size
   fresh shrimp
2 tablespoons unsalted butter
Tasso Gravy
¼ cup whipping cream
Creamy Grits
¼ cup chopped fresh parsley

• **Prick** sausage several times with a fork; place on a rack in broiler pan. Bake at 350° for 20 minutes, turning after 10 minutes; set aside.
• **Peel** and devein shrimp; cook in butter in a large skillet 3 to 5 minutes or until shrimp turn pink. Add sausage and 2½ cups Tasso Gravy; cook over medium heat 1 to 2 minutes. Stir in whipping cream; cook until thoroughly heated. If mixture is too thick, thin with water or chicken broth.
• **Spoon** about 1 cup Creamy Grits into each shallow bowl; spoon shrimp-sausage mixture over grits. Sprinkle with parsley; serve with remaining Tasso Gravy. **Yield:** 8 to 10 servings.

Tasso Gravy

¼ cup butter
½ cup all-purpose flour
3 (10½-ounce) cans condensed
   chicken broth, undiluted
3 ounces tasso, chopped (about
   ¾ cup) *

• **Melt** butter in a heavy saucepan over low heat; add flour, stirring until smooth. Cook over low heat, stirring constantly, 3 to 5 minutes or until lightly browned. Gradually add broth to mixture; cook over medium heat, stirring constantly with a whisk, until thickened. Bring to a boil; reduce heat, and simmer 10 to 15 minutes, stirring occasionally. Stir in tasso. **Yield:** 3¾ cups.

* Tasso is cured pork or beef that has been seasoned with Cajun spices and smoked. You can substitute 3 ounces smoked, boneless pork loin, cubed, and ½ teaspoon hot sauce for tasso.

Creamy Grits

6 (10½-ounce) cans condensed
   chicken broth, undiluted
2½ cups coarsely ground regular
   white grits, uncooked
1 cup whipping cream
½ teaspoon ground white pepper

• **Bring** chicken broth to a boil in a large heavy Dutch oven; stir in grits. Bring mixture to a boil. Cover, reduce heat, and simmer 25 minutes or until broth is absorbed and grits are soft, stirring often. Stir in whipping cream and pepper; cook 20 minutes over low heat, stirring often. **Yield:** about 10 cups.
Chef Donald Barickman
Magnolias
Uptown/Down South Restaurant
Charleston, South Carolina

VIC'S OVEN SHRIMP

QUICK!

1 pound butter
1 pound margarine
4 lemons, thinly sliced
¾ cup Worcestershire sauce
¼ cup pepper
2 teaspoons salt
1 teaspoon dried rosemary
1 teaspoon hot sauce
10 pounds unpeeled medium-size
    fresh shrimp

• **Combine** first 8 ingredients in a large saucepan, and bring to a boil. Remove from heat.
• **Place** shrimp in a large roasting pan. Pour butter mixture over shrimp, stirring to coat.
• **Bake** at 400° for 20 to 25 minutes, stirring occasionally. Serve shrimp and pan juices with French bread. **Yield:** 12 servings.

One of a Kind
Junior League of Mobile, Alabama

SHRIMP C'EST BON

QUICK!

3 pounds unpeeled large fresh
    shrimp
1 (16-ounce) loaf French bread,
    cut in half lengthwise
1 cup butter
2 onions, chopped
1½ teaspoons minced garlic
1 teaspoon Creole seasoning

• **Peel** shrimp, and devein, if desired. Set aside.
• **Place** French bread halves on a baking sheet, cut side up. Bake at 350° for 5 minutes or until bread is lightly browned. Cut each bread half into 3 pieces, and set aside.
• **Melt** butter in a Dutch oven. Add onion, garlic, and seasoning. Cook over medium heat until onion is tender. Add shrimp.
• **Cover** and cook 8 minutes or until shrimp turn pink. Serve over bread. **Yield:** 6 servings.

Justin Boswell
Lafayette, Louisiana

STIR-FRY SHRIMP

QUICK!

1 tablespoon cornstarch
⅓ cup fresh lime juice
⅓ cup dry sherry
3 tablespoons hoisin sauce
1 tablespoon chili puree with garlic
2 teaspoons dark sesame oil
2 pounds unpeeled medium-size
    fresh shrimp
2 teaspoons canola oil
4 cloves garlic, minced
2 tablespoons minced fresh ginger
3 carrots, scraped and thinly sliced
1 red bell pepper, thinly sliced
½ pound fresh snow pea pods
¼ pound fresh bean sprouts
2 bunches green onions, sliced
3 cups hot cooked rice

• **Combine** first 6 ingredients; set aside.
• **Peel** shrimp, and devein, if desired; set aside.
• **Pour** oil into a large nonstick skillet; place over high heat until hot. Add garlic and next 4 ingredients; stir-fry 3 minutes. Add shrimp and sprouts; stir-fry 3 minutes or until shrimp turn pink.
• **Add** green onions and lime juice mixture; bring to a boil. Boil 1 minute or until thickened. Serve immediately over rice. **Yield:** 4 servings.

♥ Per serving: Calories 472
Fat 7.5   Cholesterol 172mg
Sodium 540mg

CAJUN SHRIMP STIR-FRY

QUICK!

4 slices bacon
2 teaspoons cornstarch
½ teaspoon fish-flavored bouillon
    granules
⅓ cup cold water
1½ pounds unpeeled medium-size
    fresh shrimp
2 teaspoons Creole seasoning
1 small green bell pepper, cut into
    1-inch pieces
½ cup diced celery
1 (14½-ounce) can Cajun-style
    stewed tomatoes, undrained
Hot cooked rice

• **Cook** bacon in a large wok or skillet until crisp; remove bacon, reserving 3 tablespoons drippings. Crumble bacon, and set aside.
• **Combine** cornstarch, bouillon granules, and water; set aside.
• **Peel** shrimp, and devein, if desired. Pat shrimp dry, and sprinkle with Creole seasoning.
• **Pour** 2 tablespoons reserved bacon drippings around top of preheated wok or skillet, coating sides; heat at medium-high (375°) for 1 minute. Add shrimp; stir-fry 2 minutes or until shrimp turn pink. Remove shrimp, and set aside.
• **Pour** remaining 1 tablespoon drippings into wok; add green bell pepper and celery, and stir-fry 2 minutes. Add tomatoes; stir-fry 2 minutes. Return shrimp to wok, and add cornstarch mixture; bring to a boil. Cook 1 minute, stirring constantly. Sprinkle with reserved bacon, and serve over rice. **Yield:** 4 servings.

ANGEL HAIR PASTA WITH SHRIMP AND ASPARAGUS

8 unpeeled jumbo fresh shrimp
4 ounces angel hair pasta,
    uncooked
¼ cup olive oil
2 tablespoons minced garlic
1 teaspoon chopped shallot
6 stalks asparagus, cut into 2-inch
    pieces
¼ cup peeled, seeded, and diced
    tomato
½ cup sliced shiitake mushrooms *
¼ teaspoon salt
⅛ teaspoon dried crushed red
    pepper
½ cup dry white wine
1 tablespoon chopped fresh basil
1 tablespoon chopped fresh
    oregano
1 tablespoon chopped fresh
    thyme
1 tablespoon chopped fresh
    parsley
¼ cup freshly grated Parmesan
    cheese

• **Peel** shrimp, and devein, if desired; set aside.

• **Cook** pasta according to package directions; drain and set aside.
• **Heat** a 9-inch skillet over high heat 1 minute; add oil, and heat 10 seconds. Add shrimp, garlic, and shallot; cook, stirring constantly, 2 to 3 minutes or until shrimp turn pink. Add asparagus and next 4 ingredients; stir in wine, scraping bottom of skillet to loosen any particles, if necessary. Add pasta, basil, and remaining ingredients; toss gently. Serve immediately. **Yield:** 2 servings.

✱ You can substitute ½ cup sliced fresh mushrooms for shiitake mushrooms.

Efrem Cutler
Dunwoody, Georgia

HERBED SHRIMP AND PASTA

QUICK!

1 pound unpeeled medium-size fresh shrimp
4 ounces angel hair pasta, uncooked
½ cup butter
2 cloves garlic, minced
1 cup half-and-half
¼ cup chopped fresh parsley
1 teaspoon chopped fresh dill or ½ teaspoon dried dillweed
¼ teaspoon salt
⅛ teaspoon pepper

• **Peel** shrimp, and devein, if desired; set aside.
• **Cook** pasta according to package directions. Drain and set aside.
• **Melt** butter in a heavy skillet over medium-high heat; add shrimp and garlic. Cook, stirring constantly, 3 to 5 minutes, or until shrimp turn pink; remove shrimp, and set aside, reserving garlic and butter in skillet.
• **Add** half-and-half to skillet; bring to a boil, stirring constantly. Reduce heat to low, and simmer about 15 minutes or until thickened, stirring occasionally.
• **Add** shrimp, parsley, and seasonings; stir until blended. Serve over angel hair pasta with steamed or sautéed red, green, and yellow bell pepper strips. **Yield:** 2 to 3 servings.

Martha S. Richardson
Deer Park, Texas

SHRIMP SCAMPI

QUICK!

1 pound unpeeled medium-size fresh shrimp
8 ounces angel hair pasta, uncooked
½ cup butter or margarine
4 cloves garlic, minced
⅓ cup dry white wine
¼ teaspoon freshly ground pepper
¾ cup grated Romano cheese
1 tablespoon chopped fresh parsley

• **Peel** shrimp, and devein, if desired; set aside.
• **Cook** pasta according to package directions; drain. Place on a large serving platter, and set aside.
• **Melt** butter in a large skillet over medium heat. Add garlic and shrimp, and cook, stirring constantly, 3 to 5 minutes or until shrimp turn pink; add wine and pepper. Bring to a boil; cook 30 seconds, stirring constantly.
• **Pour** shrimp mixture over pasta; sprinkle with cheese and parsley, and toss gently. Serve immediately. **Yield:** 4 servings.

Bunny Campbell
Gainesville, Florida

LEMON SHRIMP AND PASTA

QUICK!

Look for fish sauce in the Asian section of your grocery store.

1½ pounds unpeeled medium-size fresh shrimp
6 stalks lemon grass, thinly sliced (white part only)
1 tablespoon peanut oil
1 cup coconut milk
1½ teaspoons fish sauce
¼ cup thinly sliced green onions
1 tablespoon chopped fresh cilantro
Hot cooked angel hair pasta

• **Peel** shrimp, and devein, if desired; set aside.
• **Cook** lemon grass in oil in a skillet over medium heat 1 minute, stirring occasionally. Add coconut milk; cook over low heat until reduced by half, stirring occasionally.
• **Add** shrimp; cook 5 minutes or until shrimp turn pink. Stir in fish sauce, green onions, and cilantro; serve immediately with pasta. **Yield:** 5 to 6 servings.

SHRIMP FETTUCCINE

2 pounds unpeeled large fresh shrimp
1 (16-ounce) package fettuccine
¾ cup butter or margarine
½ cup chopped green bell pepper
¼ cup chopped onion
2 stalks celery, chopped
1 teaspoon all-purpose flour
¼ cup chopped fresh parsley
1 (8-ounce) loaf process cheese spread, cubed
1 cup half-and-half
1 cup grated Parmesan cheese

• **Peel** shrimp, and devein, if desired; set aside.
• **Cook** pasta according to package directions; drain and keep warm.
• **Melt** butter in a heavy skillet; add bell pepper, onion, and celery, and cook 3 minutes or until tender, stirring often. Add flour, stirring until blended.
• **Stir** in shrimp and parsley; reduce heat, and cook 10 to 15 minutes or until shrimp turn pink, stirring often. Remove from heat; add cheese spread and half-and-half, stirring until cheese spread melts.
• **Combine** pasta and shrimp mixture, stirring gently; serve immediately or spoon into a lightly greased 13- x 9- x 2-inch baking dish. Sprinkle with Parmesan cheese.
• **Bake** at 350° for 15 minutes or until Parmesan cheese melts. Serve immediately. **Yield:** 8 servings.

CREAMY SHRIMP AND NOODLES

1 pound unpeeled medium-size
   fresh shrimp
6 ounces fettuccine, uncooked
2 tablespoons butter or margarine
1 small red bell pepper, cut into
   strips
1¼ cups milk
2 (0.6-ounce) envelopes cream of
   chicken-flavored instant soup
   mix
½ cup frozen English peas
3 tablespoons grated Parmesan
   cheese
¼ teaspoon garlic powder

• **Peel** shrimp, and devein, if desired; set aside.
• **Cook** fettuccine according to package directions; drain and set aside.
• **Melt** butter in a large skillet over medium-high heat; add shrimp and red bell pepper. Cook 3 minutes, stirring constantly.
• **Combine** milk and soup mix; add to shrimp mixture. Stir in peas, cheese, and garlic powder. Bring to a boil; reduce heat and simmer 5 minutes or until thickened, stirring often. Toss with fettuccine. Serve immediately. **Yield:** 3 to 4 servings.

Carolyne M. Carnevale
Ormond Beach, Florida

SHRIMP CREOLE

¼ cup vegetable oil or bacon
   drippings
¼ cup all-purpose flour
1½ cups chopped onion
1 cup chopped green onions
1 cup chopped celery
1 cup chopped green bell pepper
2 cloves garlic, minced
1 (16-ounce) can chopped
   tomatoes, undrained
1 (8-ounce) can tomato sauce
1 (6-ounce) can tomato paste
1 cup water
1½ teaspoons salt
1 teaspoon black pepper
½ teaspoon ground red pepper
2 or 3 bay leaves
1 tablespoon lemon juice
1 tablespoon Worcestershire sauce
⅛ teaspoon hot sauce
5 pounds unpeeled jumbo fresh
   shrimp
½ cup finely chopped fresh
   parsley
Saffron Rice
Garnish: fresh parsley sprigs

• **Combine** oil and flour in a cast-iron skillet; cook over medium heat, stirring constantly, until roux is chocolate-colored (about 15 minutes). Stir in onion and next 4 ingredients; cook 15 minutes, stirring often.
• **Transfer** roux mixture to a large Dutch oven; add tomatoes and next 10 ingredients. Bring to a boil; cover, reduce heat, and simmer 1 hour, stirring occasionally.
• **Peel** and devein shrimp; add shrimp to tomato mixture, and simmer 10 to 15 minutes or until shrimp turn pink. Remove and discard bay leaves. Sprinkle with finely chopped parsley; serve over Saffron Rice. Garnish, if desired. **Yield:** 14 servings.

Saffron Rice

7 cups water
2 tablespoons butter or margarine
2 (10-ounce) packages saffron
   yellow rice mix

• **Bring** water and butter to a boil in a large saucepan; stir in yellow rice mix.

Cover, reduce heat, and simmer 20 minutes or until water is absorbed and rice is tender. **Yield:** 8 cups.

Note: Make Shrimp Creole 1 day in advance, and store in the refrigerator. To serve, reheat over medium heat, stirring occasionally (do not boil).

Ethel Banta
Natchez, Mississippi

TANGY HONEYED SHRIMP

1½ pounds unpeeled large fresh
   shrimp
3 tablespoons peanut oil
2 teaspoons minced garlic
1 teaspoon minced fresh ginger
1 (10½-ounce) can condensed
   chicken broth, undiluted
1 tablespoon cornstarch
2 tablespoons honey
2 tablespoons ketchup
1 tablespoon white vinegar
1 tablespoon rice wine or dry
   sherry
1 tablespoon soy sauce
⅛ teaspoon dried crushed red
   pepper
1 tablespoon sesame oil
2 green onions, cut into 1-inch
   pieces and shredded
1 teaspoon chopped fresh cilantro
Rice Timbales
Garnish: fresh cilantro sprigs

• **Using** a small knife, cut back of shrimp along vein line under running water; remove shell and vein, keeping tail intact. Drain on paper towels.
• **Pour** peanut oil around top of a preheated wok, coating sides; heat at high (400°) for 1 minute. Add drained shrimp, garlic, and ginger. Cook, stirring constantly, about 8 minutes or until shrimp turn pink.
• **Combine** broth and next 7 ingredients, stirring until smooth. Add to shrimp mixture, stirring constantly.
• **Bring** mixture to a boil; cook 1 minute. Stir in sesame oil, green onions, and chopped cilantro; cook until thoroughly heated. Serve immediately with Rice Timbales. Garnish, if desired. **Yield:** 3 to 4 servings.

Rice Timbales

2 cups water
½ teaspoon salt
1 cup long-grain rice, uncooked

● **Combine** water and salt in a heavy saucepan; bring to a boil. Gradually add rice, stirring constantly. Cover, reduce heat, and simmer 20 minutes or until water is absorbed and rice is tender.
● **Press** hot rice into four oiled 6-ounce custard cups. Immediately invert onto serving plates. Keep warm. **Yield:** 4 servings.

SEAFOOD RISOTTO

1 pound unpeeled medium-size
   fresh shrimp
½ pound fresh sea scallops
1 pound fresh squid ✳
1 pound fresh unshelled mussels
1 pound fresh unshelled clams
6 cloves garlic, minced
¼ cup olive oil
½ cup dry white wine
¼ cup lemon juice
4 sprigs fresh thyme, finely
   chopped
4 sprigs fresh oregano, finely
   chopped
Risotto
Lettuce leaves
2½ tablespoons Gremolata
½ teaspoon finely ground sea
   salt
½ teaspoon freshly ground
   pepper

● **Peel** shrimp, and devein, if desired; set aside. Cut sea scallops in half crosswise; set aside.
● **Rinse** squid under cold water. Cut into ½-inch slices, and set aside.
● **Remove** "beards" from mussels. Scrub mussels and clams thoroughly with a brush to remove grit; set aside.
● **Cook** garlic in olive oil in a large skillet over medium heat 2 to 3 minutes, stirring constantly. Add shrimp and scallops; cook, stirring constantly, 2 to 3 minutes or until shrimp turn pink. Remove shrimp and scallops with a slotted spoon; set aside.
● **Cook** squid in skillet over medium heat 2 to 3 minutes, stirring constantly; remove with a slotted spoon, and set aside.
● **Add** mussels, clams, wine, and next 3 ingredients to skillet. Bring to a boil over high heat. Cover and cook, shaking pan often, 3 to 5 minutes or until shells open. Remove and discard unopened shells.
● **Add** shrimp, scallops, and squid. Cook over medium heat until thoroughly heated.
● **Remove** seafood with a slotted spoon, reserving liquid. Stir liquid into cooked Risotto. Place Risotto on a lettuce-lined serving plate, and top with seafood mixture. Sprinkle with 2½ tablespoons Gremolata, salt, and pepper, and serve immediately. **Yield:** 12 servings.

✳ Substitute 1 pound sea scallops or shrimp.

Risotto

⅓ cup olive oil
¼ cup butter or margarine
1 large onion, chopped
4 cups Arborio rice (short grain),
   uncooked
1 cup dry white wine
2 pounds Roma tomatoes, peeled,
   seeded, and chopped
8 cups hot chicken broth
2½ tablespoons Gremolata

● **Heat** olive oil and butter in a Dutch oven over medium heat. Add onion; cook 2 to 3 minutes, stirring constantly. Add rice, stirring to coat well. Stir in wine, and cook until wine is absorbed. Stir in tomato; cook 2 minutes, stirring constantly. Reduce heat to medium-low.
● **Add** about 1 cup hot chicken broth; cook, stirring constantly, until liquid is absorbed. Repeat procedure, using remaining chicken broth, adding 1 cup at a time allowing liquid to be absorbed after each addition, stirring constantly. (This process will take about 1 hour.)
● **Stir** Gremolata into rice mixture. **Yield:** 12 servings.

Gremolata

6 cloves garlic, minced
½ cup finely chopped fresh
   flat-leaf parsley
¼ cup grated lemon rind

● **Combine** all ingredients in a small bowl. **Yield:** ⅓ cup.

Liz Lorber
Atlanta, Georgia

MISS HANNAH'S CASSEROLE

5 cups water
1½ pounds unpeeled medium-size
   fresh shrimp
3¼ cups water
½ teaspoon salt
1 cup regular grits, uncooked
2 large eggs, lightly beaten
¼ cup milk
2 cloves garlic, minced
1½ cups (6 ounces) shredded
   Cheddar cheese, divided
Garnish: chopped fresh parsley

● **Bring** 5 cups water to a boil; add shrimp, and cook 3 to 5 minutes or until shrimp turn pink. Drain well; rinse with cold water. Peel shrimp, and devein, if desired; set aside.
● **Bring** 3¼ cups water and salt to a boil in a medium saucepan; stir in grits. Cover, reduce heat, and simmer 10 minutes. Remove from heat.
● **Combine** eggs and milk; gradually stir into grits. Stir in shrimp, garlic, and 1 cup cheese.
● **Spoon** into a lightly greased 11- x 7- x 1½-inch baking dish. Sprinkle with remaining ½ cup cheese. Bake at 350° for 30 minutes. Let stand 5 minutes. Garnish, if desired. **Yield:** 6 servings.

The Gullah House Restaurant
St. Helena Island, South Carolina

SHRIMP AND RICE CASSEROLE

6 cups water
2 pounds unpeeled medium-size
    fresh shrimp
2 tablespoons butter or margarine
1 cup chopped celery
1 cup chopped onion
1 cup long-grain rice, cooked
1 cup milk
1 (10¾-ounce) can cream of
    mushroom soup, undiluted
1 (8-ounce) can whole water
    chestnuts, drained and
    chopped
½ cup mayonnaise or salad
    dressing
1 teaspoon dried parsley flakes
¼ teaspoon salt
½ teaspoon pepper
Chopped fresh parsley (optional)

• **Bring** water to a boil; add shrimp, and cook 3 to 5 minutes or until shrimp turn pink. Drain well; rinse with cold water. Peel shrimp, and devein, if desired.
• **Melt** butter in a large skillet over medium-high heat; add celery and onion, and cook, stirring constantly, until tender. Stir in shrimp, cooked rice, and next 7 ingredients. Spoon mixture into a lightly greased 2-quart casserole.
• **Bake** at 350° for 30 minutes or until bubbly. Sprinkle with parsley, if desired. **Yield:** 6 servings.

Lona B. Shealy
Leesville, South Carolina

SPICY SHRIMP CASSEROLE

2 pounds unpeeled medium-size
    fresh shrimp
3 cups cooked long-grain-and-wild
    rice mix
1 cup (4 ounces) shredded
    longhorn Cheddar cheese
1 (10¾-ounce) can cream of
    mushroom soup, undiluted
1 tablespoon butter or margarine
½ cup chopped green onions
2 teaspoons Worcestershire sauce
½ teaspoon dry mustard
½ teaspoon freshly ground
    pepper
¼ cup milk
1 teaspoon Cajun seasoning
Garnishes: green onions, peeled
    cooked shrimp

• **Peel** shrimp, and devein, if desired.
• **Combine** rice, shrimp, cheese, and soup in a bowl.
• **Melt** butter in a large skillet over medium-high heat, and add chopped green onions; cook, stirring constantly, until tender.
• **Stir** cooked green onions, Worcestershire sauce, and next 4 ingredients into rice mixture. Spoon mixture into a lightly greased 11- x 7- x 1½-inch or 2-quart baking dish.
• **Bake** at 375° for 45 minutes. Garnish, if desired. **Yield:** 6 servings.

Judy Grimes
Brandon, Mississippi

PAELLA CASSEROLE

½ pound chorizo or Italian link
    sausage, sliced
1 (2½- to 3-pound) broiler-fryer,
    cut up
1 medium onion, chopped
1 medium-size green bell pepper,
    seeded and chopped
1 medium-size red bell pepper,
    chopped
2 cloves garlic, minced
2 medium tomatoes, chopped
1 (10-ounce) package yellow
    saffron rice mix, uncooked
3½ cups water
1 pound unpeeled medium-size
    fresh shrimp
1 (10-ounce) package frozen
    English peas, thawed

• **Brown** sausage in a large Dutch oven over medium heat. Remove sausage, reserving drippings in Dutch oven; set sausage aside.
• **Add** chicken pieces to reserved drippings, and cook until browned, turning once. Remove chicken, reserving drippings in Dutch oven; set chicken aside.
• **Cook** onion, peppers, and garlic in drippings. Cook, stirring constantly, until tender. Stir in tomato.
• **Add** rice mix and 3½ cups water; bring to a boil. Stir in sausage.
• **Spoon** mixture into a lightly greased 4-quart paella pan or baking dish. Arrange chicken pieces on top.
• **Cover** casserole, and bake at 375° for 30 minutes.
• **Peel** shrimp, and devein, if desired; set aside.
• **Remove** casserole from oven; top with shrimp and peas. Cover and bake at 375° for 30 additional minutes or until chicken is done. **Yield:** 8 servings.

Barbara Dryden
Pollock, Louisiana

At right: *Beef With Tomatoes and Artichokes (page 187), Mock Caesar Salad (page 303), and Creamy Fettuccine (page 218)*

MEATS

PERFECT PRIME RIB

1 (4- to 6-pound) boneless beef rib roast
1 tablespoon Worcestershire sauce
1 teaspoon garlic powder
3 tablespoons cracked pepper
2 (4-pound) packages rock salt
½ cup water

• **Brush** roast with Worcestershire sauce; sprinkle with garlic powder. Rub pepper on all sides of roast.
• **Pour** rock salt to depth of ½ inch in a disposable aluminum foil roasting pan; place roast in center of pan. Add remaining rock salt, covering roast. Sprinkle with water.
• **Bake** at 500° for 12 minutes per pound or until meat thermometer inserted in thickest portion registers 145° (medium-rare) or to desired degree of doneness. Crack salt with a hammer; remove roast, and brush away rock salt. **Yield:** 8 servings.

Lyn Mulhearn Delcaro
Starkville, Mississippi

BRISKET

1 (5-pound) beef brisket
½ teaspoon salt
½ teaspoon pepper
1 pound carrots, scraped and cut into chunks
4 pounds small new potatoes
2 cups water
¼ cup Worcestershire sauce
1 (1-ounce) envelope onion soup mix

• **Trim** fat from brisket; place brisket in a large Dutch oven. Sprinkle with salt and pepper. Add carrot and next 3 ingredients; sprinkle with soup mix.
• **Cover** and bake at 350° for 4 hours. **Yield:** 8 servings.

Stephanie Fierman
Birmingham, Alabama

HEAVENLY SMOKED BRISKET

½ cup firmly packed dark brown sugar
2 tablespoons Cajun seasoning
2 tablespoons salt
1 tablespoon lemon-pepper seasoning
2 tablespoons Worcestershire sauce
1 (5- to 6-pound) beef brisket, untrimmed
Hickory wood chunks

• **Combine** first 5 ingredients in a small bowl. Place brisket in a large shallow dish. Spread sugar mixture evenly on both sides of brisket. Cover and chill at least 8 hours.
• **Soak** wood chunks in water 1 hour.
• **Prepare** charcoal fire in smoker; let burn 15 to 20 minutes.
• **Drain** wood chunks, and place on coals. Place water pan in smoker; add water to pan to depth of fill line.
• **Remove** brisket from marinade, and place on lower food rack. Pour remaining marinade over meat. Cover with smoker lid.
• **Cook** 5 hours or until thermometer inserted in thickest portion registers 170°. **Yield:** 12 servings.

Sam D. Morrison, Jr.
Alexandria, Louisiana

RANCHO RAMILLETE FLAUTAS

1 (5-pound) beef brisket
1 medium onion, unpeeled
1 head garlic, unpeeled
2 teaspoons salt
⅔ cup sour cream
¼ cup whipping cream
20 (8-inch) flour tortillas
1 cup vegetable oil
1 head leaf lettuce, shredded
8 ounces fresh mozzarella or Monterey Jack cheese, shredded
1 bunch radishes, shredded
2 plum tomatoes, cut in half and sliced
Picante sauce
Garnish: waffle-cut radish slices

• **Trim** fat from brisket; place brisket in a large Dutch oven, and add water to cover. Add onion, garlic, and salt, and bring mixture to a boil. Cover, reduce heat, and simmer 4 to 5 hours or until brisket is tender, adding additional water as needed.
• **Remove** brisket from Dutch oven, and chill until cool. Shred brisket with a fork; set aside.
• **Combine** sour cream and whipping cream; chill.
• **Cover** tortillas with damp paper towels, and microwave at HIGH 1 minute. Keep warm.
• **Spoon** ½ cup shredded brisket down center of each tortilla; roll up tortillas, and place, seam side down, in an ungreased 13- x 9- x 2-inch baking dish. Cover and keep warm.
• **Pour** oil into a 12-inch skillet, and place over medium-high heat until hot. Place filled tortillas, seam side down, in hot oil, and cook until golden on both sides, turning once. Drain well on paper towels.
• **Serve** warm with sour cream mixture, lettuce and next 4 ingredients. Garnish, if desired. **Yield:** 6 to 8 servings.

Note: Freeze any remaining brisket in an airtight container up to 2 weeks.

Stop and Smell the Rosemary:
Recipes and Traditions to Remember
Junior League of Houston, Texas

CORNED BEEF AND CABBAGE

1 (4-pound) corned beef brisket
3 tablespoons pickling spice
2 cups water
6 small round red potatoes (about 2 pounds)
1 cabbage, cut into 6 wedges
¾ cup sour cream
2 tablespoons prepared horseradish

• **Combine** beef brisket, pickling spice, and 2 cups water in a 6-quart pressure cooker.
• **Cover** with lid, and seal securely; place pressure control over vent tube.

Cook over high heat until pressure control rocks back and forth quickly. Reduce heat until pressure control rocks occasionally; cook 50 minutes.

• **Remove** from heat, run cold water over cooker to reduce pressure. Carefully remove lid.

• **Remove** corned beef to a serving platter, and keep warm. Add potatoes and cabbage to cooker. Cook as directed 5 minutes. Arrange potatoes and cabbage around corned beef.

• **Combine** sour cream and horseradish; serve with corned beef, potatoes, and cabbage. **Yield:** 6 servings.

Barbara Rutyna
Louisville, Kentucky

EASY OVEN ROAST

1 (3- to 3½-pound) chuck roast
2 tablespoons steak sauce
2 tablespoons onion soup mix
1 (10¾-ounce) can golden
   mushroom soup, undiluted

• **Place** roast on a large sheet of heavy-duty aluminum foil; brush with steak sauce, and sprinkle with soup mix. Spoon mushroom soup on top; wrap loosely with foil. Place in a 13- x 9- x 2-inch pan. Bake at 350° for 2 hours. **Yield:** 6 servings.

Edith Amburn
Mount Airy, North Carolina

COUNTRY-STYLE POT ROAST AND GRAVY

1 (4- to 5-pound) boneless chuck
   roast
1 tablespoon vegetable oil
1 (1-ounce) envelope onion soup
   mix
2 cups water
4 potatoes, peeled and cut into
   1-inch cubes
4 carrots, scraped and cut into
   1-inch slices
2 tablespoons all-purpose flour
½ cup water
¼ teaspoon salt
¼ teaspoon pepper

• **Brown** roast in hot oil in a Dutch oven. Add soup mix and 2 cups water; bring to a boil. Cover, reduce heat, and simmer 2 hours.

• **Add** vegetables; return to a boil. Cover, reduce heat, and simmer 30 minutes. Remove roast and vegetables to a serving platter; keep warm.

• **Remove** and discard fat from pan drippings; return 1 cup drippings to Dutch oven.

• **Combine** flour and ½ cup water, stirring until smooth. Add to drippings in Dutch oven, stirring constantly. Bring to a boil over medium heat, stirring constantly, until thickened. Stir in salt and pepper. Serve with roast. **Yield:** 8 to 10 servings.

Ethel C. Jernegan
Savannah, Georgia

MUSHROOM POT ROAST

1 (2- to 3-pound) boneless chuck
   roast
1 teaspoon salt
½ teaspoon freshly ground
   pepper
2 tablespoons all-purpose flour
2 tablespoons vegetable oil
½ cup dry sherry
¼ cup water
¼ cup ketchup
½ teaspoon dried marjoram
½ teaspoon dried rosemary
½ teaspoon dried thyme
¼ teaspoon dry mustard
2 cloves garlic, minced
1 bay leaf
1 medium onion, thinly sliced
½ pound fresh mushrooms, thinly
   sliced
¼ cup water
2 tablespoons all-purpose flour

• **Sprinkle** roast with salt, pepper, and 2 tablespoons flour. Brown on all sides in hot oil in a large Dutch oven.

• **Combine** dry sherry, ¼ cup water, and next 7 ingredients; pour over roast. Add onion; bring to a boil over medium heat. Cover, reduce heat, and simmer 1½ hours.

• **Add** mushrooms; cover and simmer 1 additional hour or until roast is tender.

• **Remove** roast, reserving liquid in pan. Remove and discard bay leaf.

• **Combine** ¼ cup water and 2 tablespoons flour, stirring until smooth. Add flour mixture to liquid in pan, stirring constantly. Bring to a boil over medium heat; boil, stirring constantly, until gravy thickens. Serve gravy with roast. **Yield:** 4 servings.

Note: A pressure cooker will cook this roast in about 40 minutes. Prepare roast as directed, adding all ingredients to cooker. Close lid, and follow manufacturer's directions.

Georgie O'Neill-Massa
Welaka, Florida

CHUCK ROAST BARBECUE

1 (2- to 2½-pound) boneless chuck
   roast, trimmed
2 medium onions, chopped
¾ cup cola-flavored beverage
¼ cup Worcestershire sauce
1 tablespoon apple cider vinegar
2 cloves garlic, minced
1 teaspoon beef-flavored bouillon
   granules
½ teaspoon dry mustard
½ teaspoon chili powder
¼ teaspoon ground red pepper
½ cup ketchup
2 teaspoons butter or margarine
6 hamburger buns

• **Combine** roast and onion in a 4-quart electric slow cooker.

• **Combine** cola and next 7 ingredients; reserve ½ cup cola mixture in refrigerator. Pour remaining cola mixture over roast and onion.

• **Cook**, covered, on HIGH 6 hours or until roast is very tender; drain and shred roast. Keep warm.

• **Combine** reserved ½ cup cola mixture, ketchup, and butter in a small saucepan; cook over medium heat, stirring constantly, just until thoroughly heated. Pour over shredded roast, stirring gently. Spoon onto buns, and serve with potato chips and pickle spears. **Yield:** 6 servings.

Lee Stearns
Mobile, Alabama

SPICY NEW YORK STRIP ROAST

1 (1¾-pound) New York strip
   steak (about 3 inches
   thick)
1 teaspoon dried thyme
1 teaspoon dried oregano
1 teaspoon dried rosemary
¼ teaspoon salt
¼ teaspoon freshly ground black
   pepper
¼ teaspoon ground red
   pepper
1 tablespoon olive oil

• **Trim** excess fat from steak.
• **Combine** thyme and next 5 ingredients in a small bowl; crush with back of a spoon. Pat mixture evenly on both sides of steak. Chill.
• **Heat** olive oil in a heavy cast-iron or ovenproof skillet over medium-high heat; add steak, and cook 3 minutes on each side.
• **Bake** at 450° for 20 to 25 minutes or to desired degree of doneness. Remove from oven; cover with aluminum foil, and let stand 10 minutes. To serve, cut steak into thin slices. **Yield:** 4 to 6 servings.

Margot Hahn
Washington, D.C.

EYE-OF-ROUND ROAST WITH FRUITED ONION MARMALADE

1 (2- to 3-pound) eye-of-round
   roast
1 teaspoon salt
½ teaspoon pepper
½ cup all-purpose flour
2 tablespoons vegetable oil
2 to 3 cloves garlic, sliced
1 (14½-ounce) can beef broth
1 (12-ounce) bottle dark beer
Fruited Onion Marmalade

• **Sprinkle** roast with salt and pepper; dredge in flour.
• **Cook** roast in hot oil in a Dutch oven over medium heat until browned on all sides.
• **Add** garlic, broth, and beer; bring to a boil. Cover, reduce heat, and simmer

1½ hours or until tender. Serve with Fruited Onion Marmalade. **Yield:** 6 to 8 servings.

Fruited Onion Marmalade

1 tablespoon butter or margarine
1 tablespoon light brown sugar
2 onions, sliced
1 (8-ounce) package chopped
   dried fruit
1 cup beef broth
1½ teaspoons apple cider
   vinegar
¼ teaspoon ground ginger

• **Cook** butter and brown sugar in a large skillet over medium-low heat, stirring constantly, until sugar dissolves. Stir in sliced onion, and cook 20 minutes or until onion is tender, stirring mixture occasionally.
• **Stir** in chopped dried fruit and remaining ingredients.
• **Cover,** reduce heat, and simmer 20 minutes or until fruit is tender. **Yield:** about 2 cups.

MUSTARD GREENS-STUFFED TENDERLOIN
(pictured at right)

1 (16-ounce) package frozen
   chopped mustard greens
3 tablespoons butter or margarine,
   divided
1 cup thinly sliced green
   onions
¾ pound country ham slices
1 cup soft breadcrumbs
¼ teaspoon ground red pepper
1 (3- to 4-pound) trimmed beef
   tenderloin
¼ teaspoon ground black
   pepper
2 to 3 tablespoons cracked black
   pepper
1 tablespoon all-purpose flour
1 cup beef broth
½ cup dry red wine
¼ teaspoon ground black pepper
Garnish: fresh mustard greens

• **Cook** greens according to package directions; drain. Press between layers of

paper towels to remove excess moisture; transfer to a large bowl.
• **Melt** 1 tablespoon butter in a skillet; add green onions, and cook until tender, stirring often. Add to greens.
• **Melt** remaining 2 tablespoons butter in skillet; add ham, and cook over medium-high heat 4 minutes, turning once. Remove ham from skillet, reserving drippings in skillet; chop ham. Stir ham, breadcrumbs, and red pepper into greens.
• **Preheat** oven to 500°.
• **Make** a lengthwise cut down center of tenderloin, cutting to, but not through, bottom. Starting from center cut, slice horizontally toward 1 side, stopping ½ inch from edge. Repeat on opposite side. Unfold meat so that it's flat. Place between two pieces of heavy-duty plastic wrap. Flatten to ½-inch thickness, using a meat mallet or rolling pin.
• **Sprinkle** ¼ teaspoon ground black pepper over tenderloin; spread with greens mixture. Roll up, jellyroll fashion, starting with a long side; secure with heavy string at 4-inch intervals.
• **Press** cracked pepper on tenderloin, and place seam side down on a lightly greased rack in a roasting pan. Place tenderloin in oven, and reduce oven temperature to 350°.
• **Bake** 40 minutes or until meat thermometer inserted in thickest portion registers 145° (medium-rare) to 160° (medium). Cover loosely with aluminum foil, and let stand 15 minutes.
• **Stir** flour into reserved ham drippings in skillet; cook over medium-low heat, stirring constantly, 4 to 5 minutes or until caramel-colored.
• **Add** broth and wine gradually, and cook over medium-low heat, stirring constantly, until gravy is thickened and bubbly. Stir in ¼ teaspoon ground black pepper.
• **Slice** tenderloin, and garnish, if desired. Serve with gravy. **Yield:** 8 to 10 servings.

Mustard Greens-Stuffed Tenderloin

PAN-ROASTED FILLET OF BEEF WITH BLUE CHEESE SAUCE

Though not for the calorie conscious, a splurge of creamy, pungent Blue Cheese Sauce is a great way to add pizzazz to your favorite steak.

1 (2-pound) trimmed beef
    tenderloin
½ teaspoon salt
½ teaspoon freshly ground
    pepper
1 tablespoon vegetable oil
Vegetable cooking spray
Blue Cheese Sauce

• **Sprinkle** tenderloin with salt and pepper; rub with oil. Cover and chill up to 8 hours.
• **Brown** tenderloin in a hot cast-iron skillet coated with cooking spray about 1 minute on each side. Transfer tenderloin to a rack coated with cooking spray, reserving drippings in skillet; place rack in broiler pan. (Set skillet aside to make sauce.)
• **Bake** at 450° for 18 minutes or until a meat thermometer inserted in thickest portion registers 145° (medium-rare) or 160° (medium).
• **Remove** tenderloin from oven, and let stand 5 minutes. Cut tenderloin into 4 equal portions.
• **Spoon** warm Blue Cheese Sauce evenly onto four serving plates, and top each with a portion of tenderloin. **Yield:** 4 servings.

Blue Cheese Sauce

3 tablespoons unsalted butter,
    softened
2 ounces crumbled blue cheese
2 cups beef broth
1 carrot, scraped and coarsely
    chopped
1 stalk celery, coarsely chopped
3 cloves garlic, chopped
3 tablespoons Madeira or port
    wine
⅓ cup half-and-half

• **Combine** butter and crumbled blue cheese; shape into 4 portions, and chill until firm.

• **Combine** beef broth, carrot, and celery in a small saucepan. Bring to a boil; reduce heat, and simmer 5 to 7 minutes or until broth is reduced to ½ cup. Remove and discard vegetables; set broth aside.
• **Cook** garlic and Madeira in a skillet over medium heat 2 minutes. Add broth, and cook 3 to 5 minutes or until mixture is reduced to ½ cup. Gradually stir in half-and-half, and cook 5 minutes or until sauce is light brown. Remove sauce from heat; set aside up to 1 hour, if desired. Just before serving, reheat sauce over low heat.
• **Add** blue cheese mixture to warm sauce, 1 portion at a time, stirring until sauce is smooth. Pour sauce through a wire-mesh strainer into a small bowl, pressing with back of a spoon. **Yield:** about 1 cup.

CHUTNEYED BEEF TENDERLOIN

4 cups low-sodium beef broth
1 carrot, scraped and chopped
1 onion, quartered
1 stalk celery, chopped
1 (8-ounce) jar chutney, finely
    chopped
1 teaspoon salt
½ teaspoon coarsely ground
    pepper
1 tablespoon butter or margarine,
    softened
1 (5- to 6-pound) beef tenderloin,
    trimmed
Wine Reduction Sauce
3 tablespoons butter
½ teaspoon chopped fresh
    thyme or ¼ teaspoon dried
    thyme

• **Combine** first 4 ingredients in a saucepan; bring to a boil over medium heat. Reduce heat, and simmer, uncovered, 40 minutes or until mixture is reduced to about 1½ cups. Pour mixture through a wire-mesh strainer into a bowl, reserving vegetables; set broth aside.
• **Position** knife blade in food processor bowl; add vegetables. Process until smooth. Set aside.

• **Combine** chutney and next 3 ingredients, stirring until smooth. Spread half of chutney mixture over all surfaces of tenderloin. Place tenderloin on a rack in a shallow roasting pan.
• **Bake** at 450° for 20 minutes. Remove from oven, and spread remaining half of chutney mixture on tenderloin. Bake 10 to 20 additional minutes or until a meat thermometer inserted in thickest portion registers 145° (medium-rare) or 160° (medium). Remove meat from pan, and let stand 15 minutes before slicing.
• **Remove** rack from pan.
• **Add** reserved broth to pan, and place pan over burners. Bring broth mixture to a boil over medium heat, stirring to loosen browned particles that cling to bottom. Pour broth mixture into a saucepan; add vegetable mixture and Wine Reduction Sauce.
• **Bring** sauce mixture to a boil; reduce heat, and simmer 5 minutes, stirring often. Whisk in 3 tablespoons butter, 1 tablespoon at a time. Stir in thyme. Serve sauce with tenderloin. **Yield:** 12 servings.

Wine Reduction Sauce

1 (750-milliliter) bottle Cabernet
    Sauvignon
3 cloves shallots, minced
1 bay leaf
3 or 4 sprigs fresh thyme

• **Combine** all ingredients in a large saucepan. Bring mixture to a boil over medium heat; reduce heat, and simmer, uncovered, until liquid is reduced to about 1 cup (about 40 minutes).
• **Pour** sauce mixture through a wire-mesh strainer into a measuring cup, pressing with back of a spoon. Discard solids. **Yield:** 1 cup.

Jan Downs
Shreveport, Louisiana

BARBECUED BEEF TENDERLOIN

Mesquite or hickory chips
1 (3½- to 4-pound) beef
       tenderloin, trimmed
½ teaspoon salt
½ teaspoon pepper
1 cup Barbecue Sauce

● **Soak** mesquite chips in water 30 minutes.
● **Prepare** charcoal fire in smoker; let burn 20 minutes. Place mesquite chips on coals. Place water pan in smoker; add water to pan to depth of fill line.
● **Sprinkle** tenderloin with salt and pepper. Place on food rack. Cover with smoker lid. Cook 30 minutes.
● **Baste** tenderloin with 1 cup Barbecue Sauce. Cover and cook 1½ to 2 hours or until a meat thermometer inserted in thickest portion registers 145° (medium-rare) or 160° (medium). Serve with additional Barbecue Sauce. **Yield:** 12 servings.

Barbecue Sauce

QUICK!

2 (16-ounce) cans tomato sauce
1¼ cups ketchup
½ cup steak sauce
¼ cup lemon juice
¼ cup honey

● **Combine** all ingredients in a large saucepan.
● **Bring** to a boil; reduce heat, and simmer 30 minutes, stirring occasionally. Store remaining sauce in refrigerator up to 1 week or freeze up to 1 month. **Yield:** 5 cups.

King Ranch
Kingsville, Texas

BLUE CHEESE-WALNUT STUFFED FILLETS
(pictured on page 149)

QUICK!

Lightly toasting the walnuts brings out their fragrance, enhances their subtle flavor, and makes them crisper. Be sure the walnuts you use are plump and meaty; shriveled nutmeats are past their prime.

¼ cup crumbled blue cheese
2 tablespoons finely chopped
       walnuts, toasted
2 teaspoons half-and-half
2 (1-inch-thick) beef tenderloin
       steaks (6 ounces each)
2 tablespoons butter or
       margarine
1 clove garlic, minced
3 green onions, finely chopped
⅓ cup Madeira

● **Combine** first 3 ingredients. Cut a pocket into side of each steak. Spoon blue cheese mixture evenly into steak pockets. Set aside.
● **Melt** butter in a medium skillet over medium-high heat; add garlic and green onions, and cook, stirring constantly, until tender. Remove garlic mixture, reserving butter in skillet; set garlic mixture aside.
● **Cook** steaks in skillet over medium-high heat 7 minutes on each side or to desired degree of doneness. Remove steaks, reserving drippings in skillet. Add wine to drippings, and cook 1 to 2 minutes or until reduced by half. Stir in garlic mixture; spoon over steaks. **Yield:** 2 servings.

Wanda Sanders Randall
Birmingham, Alabama

BEEF WITH TOMATOES AND ARTICHOKES
(pictured on page 181)

QUICK!

2 (1¼-inch-thick) beef tenderloin
       steaks (filet mignon)
Marinade
½ cup oil-packed dried tomatoes,
       undrained
1½ tablespoons finely chopped
       green onions
1 clove garlic, finely chopped
1 (14-ounce) can artichoke hearts,
       drained and quartered
¼ teaspoon dried basil

● **Place** steaks in an 8-inch square dish. Drizzle Marinade evenly over steaks; cover and chill 8 hours, turning steaks several times. Drain steaks, discarding Marinade.
● **Cook** steaks, without grill lid, over medium-hot coals (350° to 400°) 4 to 5 minutes on each side or to desired degree of doneness. Set steaks aside, and keep warm.
● **Drain** tomatoes, reserving 1 tablespoon oil from tomatoes in a large skillet. Chop tomatoes; set aside.
● **Cook** green onions and garlic in reserved oil in skillet over medium-high heat 2 minutes, stirring constantly. Add tomato, artichoke hearts, and basil; cook 5 minutes, stirring often. Thinly slice steaks, and serve with tomato mixture. **Yield:** 2 servings.

Marinade

QUICK!

1 tablespoon olive oil
2 teaspoons red wine vinegar
1 tablespoon finely chopped
       onion
1 clove garlic, minced
½ teaspoon mustard
¼ teaspoon dried basil
¼ teaspoon dried rosemary
⅛ teaspoon salt
⅛ teaspoon pepper

● **Combine** all ingredients in a small bowl. **Yield:** 3 tablespoons.

GINGERED TENDERLOIN STEAK

QUICK!

For its full flavor, look for ginger that has smooth skin. Wrinkled skin means it's dry and less flavorful.

¼ teaspoon salt
1 teaspoon pepper
1 tablespoon minced fresh ginger
2 cloves garlic, minced
2 (8-ounce) beef tenderloin steaks (1½ inches thick)
1 tablespoon butter
1 tablespoon vegetable oil
⅓ cup dry white wine
1 jalapeño pepper, seeded and minced

• **Combine** first 4 ingredients; rub on all sides of steaks. Cover and chill 2 hours.
• **Melt** butter and oil in a heavy skillet over medium-high heat; add steaks, and cook 4 minutes on each side or to desired degree of doneness. Remove steaks from skillet, and keep warm.
• **Add** wine and jalapeño pepper to skillet; cook 2 minutes, stirring constantly. Pour over steaks. **Yield:** 2 servings.

MESQUITE-GINGER BEEF WITH FRESH FRUIT RELISH

QUICK!

3 tablespoons balsamic vinegar
2 teaspoons ground red pepper
2 teaspoons mesquite-flavored barbecue seasoning
2 teaspoons brown sugar
2 teaspoons minced fresh ginger
2 cloves garlic, minced
3 tablespoons sesame oil
4 (1¼-inch-thick) beef tenderloin steaks (4 to 6 ounces each)
1 tablespoon canola oil
Fresh Fruit Relish
Garnish: fresh watercress sprigs

• **Combine** first 7 ingredients in a shallow dish or heavy-duty, zip-top plastic bag; add steaks. Cover or seal, and chill 1½ hours, turning steaks occasionally.

• **Remove** steaks from marinade, discarding marinade.
• **Pour** canola oil into a heavy nonstick skillet; place over medium heat until hot. Add steaks, and cook 4 to 6 minutes on each side or to desired degree of doneness. Serve with Fresh Fruit Relish. Garnish, if desired. **Yield:** 4 servings.

Fresh Fruit Relish

QUICK!

1 cup finely chopped mango
½ cup finely chopped fresh pineapple
¼ cup chopped red bell pepper
¼ cup finely chopped green bell pepper
3 tablespoons thinly sliced green onions
3 tablespoons chopped fresh watercress
¼ teaspoon dry mustard
2 teaspoons balsamic vinegar
2 teaspoons fresh lime juice

• **Combine** all ingredients; cover and chill. Serve with a slotted spoon. **Yield:** 2 cups.

Mary Louise Lever
Rome, Georgia

FILET MIGNON WITH MUSHROOM SAUCE

4 (4-ounce) beef tenderloin steaks
¼ teaspoon salt
¼ teaspoon freshly ground pepper
½ teaspoon dried thyme
Vegetable cooking spray
2 shallots, finely chopped
1 cup sliced fresh mushrooms
½ cup Red Wine Garlic Sauce
¼ cup fat-free beef broth
¼ teaspoon salt

• **Sprinkle** steaks with ¼ teaspoon salt, pepper, and thyme. Place steaks on a rack coated with cooking spray; place rack in broiler pan.
• **Broil** steaks 5½ inches from heat (with electric oven door partially opened) 2 to 3 minutes on each side or to desired degree of doneness. Remove

steaks from oven, and wrap in aluminum foil to keep warm; set aside.
• **Cook** shallot in a large skillet coated with cooking spray over medium heat, stirring constantly, until tender. Stir in mushrooms, and cook 1 to 2 minutes. Add Red Wine Garlic Sauce, beef broth, and ¼ teaspoon salt; cook 2 to 3 minutes. Serve over steaks. **Yield:** 4 servings.

♥ Per serving: Calories 214
Fat 8.4g Cholesterol 71mg
Sodium 366mg

Red Wine Garlic Sauce

1 (750-milliliter) bottle dry red wine
1 head garlic, crushed (about 12 cloves)

• **Combine** wine and garlic in a large saucepan; simmer 45 minutes or until mixture is reduced to about 1 cup.
• **Pour** mixture through a wire-mesh strainer into a small container, discarding garlic. Store sauce in refrigerator up to 1 week or freeze up to 3 months. **Yield:** 1 cup.

Note: You can serve this slow-simmered, fat-free sauce over cooked mushrooms, beef, chicken, pork, or firm-fleshed fish like tuna or swordfish.

FILLET OF BEEF WITH RED PEPPER BUTTER

QUICK!

⅓ cup butter, softened
¼ cup finely chopped red bell pepper
¾ teaspoon seasoned salt
¼ to ½ teaspoon ground red pepper
2 (2½-inch-thick) beef tenderloin steaks

• **Combine** first 4 ingredients, stirring well. Shape into 4 (2-inch) rounds on a wax paper-lined baking sheet; cover and chill 1 hour or until firm.
• **Place** beef tenderloin steaks on a rack in broiler pan.

● **Broil** 5½ inches from heat (with electric oven door partially opened) 6 minutes. Turn steaks over, and top each with a butter round.

● **Broil** 6 to 7 additional minutes (with electric oven door partially opened) or until meat thermometer inserted in thickest portion registers 145° (medium-rare), 160° (medium), or to desired degree of doneness. Turn steaks over, and transfer to a serving platter; top with remaining butter rounds. **Yield:** 2 servings.

Kira F. Giffin
Houston, Texas

BEEF AND SHRIMP STIR-FRY

1 cup beef broth
1 cup chicken broth
1 tablespoon chopped green
    onions
1 tablespoon soy sauce
1 bay leaf
3 black peppercorns
½ teaspoon dried thyme
⅛ teaspoon dried oregano
1 tablespoon cornstarch
1½ tablespoons cold water
½ pound unpeeled medium-size
    fresh shrimp
1 tablespoon olive oil
½ pound beef tenderloin, cut into
    1-inch strips
¾ cup fresh broccoli flowerets
½ cup sliced zucchini
½ red bell pepper, cut into thin
    strips
½ cup snow pea pods
½ cup sliced fresh mushrooms
Hot cooked rice

● **Combine** first 8 ingredients in a medium saucepan, and bring to a boil; reduce heat, and simmer, uncovered, 30 minutes. Remove from heat, and pour liquid through a wire-mesh strainer into a 2-cup liquid measuring cup, discarding solids. Return broth mixture to saucepan.

● **Combine** cornstarch and water, stirring until smooth; stir into broth mixture, and bring to a boil. Cook 1 minute; remove from heat. Set aside.

● **Peel** and devein shrimp; set aside.

● Pour oil around top of preheated wok, coating sides; heat at medium-high (375°) for 2 minutes. Add shrimp, beef, and broccoli; cook 1 to 2 minutes, stirring constantly. Add zucchini and next 3 ingredients; cook 2 minutes, stirring constantly. Add broth mixture, and cook until thoroughly heated. Serve over rice. **Yield:** 4 servings.

Sue-Sue Hartstern
Louisville, Kentucky

FLAVORFUL FLANK STEAK

1 tablespoon butter or margarine
¼ cup chopped onion
1 clove garlic, minced
½ teaspoon chili powder
½ cup tomato sauce
2 tablespoons white vinegar
1 tablespoon honey
¼ teaspoon salt
¼ teaspoon pepper
1 (1½-pound) flank steak (¾ inch
    thick)

● **Melt** butter in a medium saucepan over medium-high heat; add onion, garlic, and chili powder, and cook, stirring constantly, until onion is tender.

● **Stir** in tomato sauce and next 4 ingredients; bring to a boil. Reduce heat, and simmer 5 minutes or until slightly thickened; cool.

● **Make** ¼-inch-deep cuts on both sides of steak; place steak in a shallow dish or heavy duty, zip-top plastic bag. Pour tomato sauce mixture over steak, turning to coat. Cover or seal, and chill at least 2 hours and up to 8 hours.

● **Cook** steak, without grill lid, over medium-hot coals (350° to 400°) about 7 minutes on each side or to desired degree of doneness. To serve, slice diagonally across grain. **Yield:** 4 servings.

Karen Peacock
Black Mountain, North Carolina

MARINATED FLANK STEAK

QUICK!

Cutting grilled flank steak diagonally across the grain into thin strips helps keep the slices of meat tender.

1 cup vegetable oil
½ cup soy sauce
⅓ cup red wine vinegar
¼ cup lemon juice
3 tablespoons Worcestershire
    sauce
2 tablespoons Dijon mustard
1 teaspoon freshly ground
    pepper
1 large onion, sliced
1 clove garlic, minced
2 (1-pound) flank steaks

● **Combine** first 9 ingredients in a shallow dish or a large heavy-duty, zip-top plastic bag; add steaks. Cover or seal, and chill 8 to 12 hours, turning steaks occasionally.

● **Remove** steaks and onion slices from marinade, discarding marinade. Wrap onion in heavy-duty aluminum foil.

● **Cook** steaks and onion, covered with grill lid, over medium-hot coals (350° to 400°) about 15 minutes or to desired degree of doneness, turning steaks and onion occasionally.

● **Cut** steaks diagonally across grain into thin strips; serve with onion slices. **Yield:** 4 to 6 servings.

Karen Dibble
Dallas, Texas

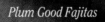
Plum Good Fajitas

PLUM GOOD FAJITAS
(pictured at left)

1 (16-ounce) can purple plums in heavy syrup, undrained
½ cup butter or margarine
1 large onion, chopped
1 (6-ounce) can frozen lemonade concentrate, thawed and undiluted
½ cup chili sauce
¼ cup soy sauce
1 tablespoon dry mustard
1 teaspoon ground ginger
1 teaspoon Worcestershire sauce
2 drops of hot sauce
8 (8-inch) flour tortillas
1 red bell pepper, cut into strips
1 green bell pepper, cut into strips
1 large onion, sliced
2 (1-pound) flank steaks
Sliced green onions
Sour cream or guacamole
Garnish: fresh cilantro sprigs

• **Drain** plums, reserving syrup; remove pits from plums. Place plums and syrup in container of an electric blender; process until smooth, stopping once to scrape down sides. Set plum puree aside.
• **Melt** butter in a saucepan over medium-high heat; add chopped onion, and cook, stirring constantly, until tender. Stir in puree, lemonade concentrate, and next 6 ingredients. Bring sauce to a boil; reduce heat, and simmer 15 minutes.
• **Heat** tortillas according to package directions; keep warm.
• **Place** peppers and sliced onion in a greased grill basket. Place basket and steaks on grill rack; baste with sauce. Cook, without grill lid, over hot coals (400° to 500°), 10 minutes on each side or to desired degree of doneness, basting often.
• **Cut** steaks diagonally across grain into thin strips.
• **Serve** steak and grilled vegetables in tortillas; top with green onions and sour cream or guacamole. Garnish, if desired. **Yield:** 8 servings.

Mary Tom Harper
Corpus Christi, Texas

JAVA FAJITAS

Brewed coffee gives these fajitas their unique flavor.

⅓ cup tomato paste
1¼ cups strongly brewed coffee
½ cup Worcestershire sauce
1 tablespoon sugar
2 teaspoons ground red pepper
1 teaspoon ground black pepper
3 tablespoons fresh lime juice
1 tablespoon vegetable oil
2 (1½-pound) flank steaks
24 (10-inch) flour tortillas
Pico de Gallo
Garnishes: fresh cilantro sprigs, lime wedges, serrano chile peppers, avocado slices

• **Combine** first 8 ingredients in a shallow dish or large heavy-duty, zip-top plastic bag; add steaks. Cover or seal; chill 8 hours, turning occasionally.
• **Remove** steaks from marinade, reserving marinade.
• **Cook** steaks, covered with grill lid, over hot coals (400° to 500°) about 6 minutes on each side or to desired degree of doneness.
• **Cut** steaks diagonally across grain into thin slices; keep warm.
• **Bring** marinade to a boil; boil 10 to 15 minutes or until reduced to 1 cup.
• **Place** steak down center of tortillas; drizzle with marinade. Top with Pico de Gallo. Roll up; serve immediately. Garnish, if desired. **Yield:** 12 servings.

♥ Per serving: Calories 590
Fat 20.7g Cholesterol 62mg
Sodium 1038mg

Pico de Gallo

2 medium tomatoes, chopped
½ onion, chopped
3 serrano chile peppers, chopped
½ cup fresh cilantro, chopped
¼ teaspoon salt
¼ teaspoon ground white pepper
2 tablespoons lemon juice

• **Combine** all ingredients. Cover and chill at least 3 hours. **Yield:** 3 cups.

Janie Baur
Spring, Texas

BLACKENED 'N' PEPPERED STEAK
QUICK!

This recipe generates plenty of pepper-scented smoke, so you may want to cook outdoors. We seared the steaks in an iron skillet over a propane cooker (like one used for a fish fry; you can purchase one at a hardware store). You can also prepare the steaks with the fan on in a well-ventilated kitchen.

4 (1½-inch-thick) New York strip steaks
¾ cup whole black peppercorns, crushed
¼ cup olive oil
¼ cup butter or margarine
1 cup chopped green onions
3 cups dry red wine
1 (3½-ounce) jar capers, drained

• **Trim** all visible fat from steaks; cut steaks in half crosswise. Dredge in peppercorns, coating all sides of steaks. Set aside.
• **Pour** olive oil in a large cast-iron skillet; place on burner of a propane cooker. Heat until hot, following manufacturer's instructions. Brown steaks on each edge in skillet. Cook 4 minutes on each side or to desired degree of doneness. Remove steaks to serving plate; keep warm. Discard drippings.
• **Melt** butter in skillet; add green onions, and cook 1 minute, stirring constantly. Add wine and capers; cook until liquid is reduced to 1½ cups. Serve with steak. **Yield:** 8 servings.

Note: Do not leave skillet unattended. Hot oil and wine can ignite. If mixture ignites, immediately cover skillet with a large lid to extinguish flames, and reduce heat.

Dave Christy
Pine Mountain, Georgia

GRECIAN SKILLET RIB EYES

QUICK!

This olive-feta topping works great on chicken and lamb, too.

1½ teaspoons garlic powder
1½ teaspoons dried basil, crushed
1½ teaspoons dried oregano, crushed
½ teaspoon salt
⅛ teaspoon pepper
2 (1-inch-thick) rib-eye steaks (1¾ to 2 pounds)
1 tablespoon olive oil
1 tablespoon fresh lemon juice
2 tablespoons crumbled feta cheese
1 tablespoon chopped kalamata or ripe olives

• **Combine** first 5 ingredients; rub onto all sides of steaks.
• **Pour** oil into a large nonstick skillet; place over medium heat until hot. Add steaks, and cook 10 to 14 minutes or to desired degree of doneness, turning once. Sprinkle with lemon juice; top with cheese and olives. **Yield:** 2 to 4 servings.

Fran Yuhas
Scotrun, Pennsylvania

GRILLADES AND BAKED CHEESE GRITS

4½ pounds round steak
2 teaspoons salt
2 teaspoons pepper
Vegetable oil
⅔ cup all-purpose flour
2 cups chopped onion
1½ cups chopped green bell pepper
½ cup chopped green onions
½ cup chopped celery
½ cup chopped fresh parsley
4 cloves garlic, minced
2 (14½-ounce) cans stewed tomatoes, undrained
1 teaspoon dried thyme
3 bay leaves
2 cups water
Garnish: fresh parsley sprigs
Baked Cheese Grits

• **Cut** meat into serving-size pieces; sprinkle with salt and pepper.
• **Pour** ½ cup oil into a Dutch oven. Fry steak in hot oil over medium-high heat until browned (about 2 minutes on each side). Remove to platter, and repeat until all meat is browned.
• **Measure** pan drippings; add enough oil to drippings to measure ⅔ cup; return to Dutch oven. Add flour; cook over medium heat, stirring constantly, 10 minutes or until roux is caramel-colored.
• **Stir** in onion and next 5 ingredients; cook over medium heat until tender; stirring often. Add tomatoes and next 3 ingredients, stirring well.
• **Return** meat to Dutch oven. Bring to a boil; cover, reduce heat, and simmer 1½ hours, stirring occasionally. Remove and discard bay leaves.
• **Transfer** mixture to a serving dish; garnish, if desired. Serve with Baked Cheese Grits. **Yield:** 12 servings.

Baked Cheese Grits

5 cups boiling water
1 teaspoon salt
⅔ cup quick-cooking yellow grits, uncooked
⅔ cup quick-cooking white grits, uncooked
1 (15½-ounce) can yellow hominy, undrained
½ cup butter or margarine
2 cups (8 ounces) shredded sharp Cheddar cheese
½ cup grated Parmesan cheese

• **Bring** water and salt to a boil in a heavy Dutch oven; stir in grits. Return to a boil; reduce heat, and cook 4 to 5 minutes, stirring occasionally.
• **Stir** in hominy, butter, and Cheddar cheese; spoon into a lightly greased 13- x 9- x 2-inch baking dish. Sprinkle with Parmesan cheese.
• **Bake** at 350° for 45 minutes or until set. **Yield:** 12 servings.

Wilder Selman
New Orleans, Louisiana

PEANUTTY BEEF STIR-FRY

QUICK!

1¼ pounds lean boneless top sirloin steak
3 tablespoons reduced-sodium soy sauce
2 to 3 tablespoons brown sugar
2 tablespoons creamy peanut butter
2 teaspoons lemon juice
½ teaspoon garlic powder
¼ teaspoon dried crushed red pepper
¼ teaspoon ground black pepper
2 teaspoons sesame or vegetable oil
1 medium-size red bell pepper, cut into 1-inch pieces
4 green onions, cut into 1-inch pieces
Hot cooked rice
Garnish: chopped peanuts

• **Trim** fat from steak, and slice steak diagonally across grain into ⅛-inch strips; set aside.
• **Combine** soy sauce and next 6 ingredients, stirring with a whisk until blended; set aside.
• **Pour** oil around top of a preheated nonstick wok or large skillet, coating sides; heat at medium-high (375°) 1 minute. Add steak strips; cook 2 minutes, stirring constantly. Add red bell pepper and green onions; cook 2 minutes, stirring constantly. Stir in soy sauce mixture; cover and cook 3 minutes or until thoroughly heated. Serve over rice. Garnish, if desired. **Yield:** 4 servings.

INDIVIDUAL MEAT LOAVES

1½ pounds lean ground beef
½ pound hot ground pork
    sausage
1 small onion, finely chopped
1 teaspoon salt
¼ teaspoon pepper
½ teaspoon poultry seasoning
2 tablespoons Worcestershire
    sauce
5 slices white bread
2 large eggs
½ cup milk
1½ cups soft breadcrumbs
1½ cups chili sauce
½ cup boiling water
Garnish: fresh parsley sprigs

• **Combine** first 7 ingredients; set meat mixture aside.
• **Remove** crust from bread, and reserve for another use; cut bread into cubes. Combine bread cubes, eggs, and milk in a large mixing bowl; beat at medium speed with an electric mixer until smooth. Stir in meat mixture, and shape into 6 individual loaves; roll each loaf in breadcrumbs.
• **Place** in a lightly greased 13- x 9- x 2-inch pan. Spread chili sauce over loaves. Pour boiling water into dish. Bake, uncovered, at 350° for 1 hour. Transfer loaves to a serving platter; garnish, if desired. **Yield:** 6 servings.

Leanne Baker
Johnson City, Tennessee

MEAT LOAF WITH CHUNKY TOMATO SAUCE

1 pound ground chuck
1 medium onion, chopped
1 medium-size green bell pepper,
    chopped
2 cloves garlic, minced
¾ cup quick-cooking oats,
    uncooked
½ cup ketchup
2 large eggs, lightly beaten
1 tablespoon steak sauce
¼ teaspoon salt
¼ teaspoon seasoned salt
¼ teaspoon pepper
Chunky Tomato Sauce

• **Combine** all ingredients except Chunky Tomato Sauce; press meat mixture into a 9- x 5- x 3-inch loafpan or shape into a loaf, and place on a rack in broiler pan.
• **Bake** at 350° for 50 to 60 minutes or until done. Serve with Chunky Tomato Sauce. **Yield:** 4 servings.

Chunky Tomato Sauce

QUICK!

1 (14½-ounce) can diced
    tomatoes, undrained
1 (5½-ounce) can spicy vegetable
    juice
½ cup chopped celery
½ cup chopped green bell
    pepper
½ cup chopped onion
½ teaspoon garlic powder
1 teaspoon dried basil
1 teaspoon dried marjoram
1 teaspoon dried oregano
1 teaspoon dried parsley flakes

• **Combine** all ingredients in a large saucepan, stirring well; bring mixture to a boil. Reduce heat, and simmer 15 minutes, stirring sauce occasionally. **Yield:** 2 cups.

Kathy Rogers
Cary, North Carolina

INDIVIDUAL BARBECUED BEEF LOAVES

½ cup ketchup
⅓ cup cider vinegar
3 tablespoons brown sugar
1 teaspoon beef-flavored bouillon
    granules
1½ pounds lean ground beef
1 cup fine, dry breadcrumbs
2 tablespoons finely chopped
    onion
½ teaspoon salt
¼ teaspoon pepper
1 cup evaporated milk

• **Combine** first 4 ingredients in a saucepan, stirring well; cook mixture over medium heat, stirring constantly, until bouillon granules dissolve. Set barbecue sauce aside.
• **Combine** beef and remaining 5 ingredients, stirring until mixture is thoroughly blended.
• **Shape** mixture into 6 loaves; place loaves in a lightly greased 11- x 7- x 1½-inch baking dish. Spoon barbecue sauce over loaves.
• **Bake** at 350° for 45 minutes. Serve immediately. **Yield:** 6 servings.

Peggy C. Brown
Winston-Salem, North Carolina

SPINACH MEAT LOAF

*We added the steak sauce to
Ann's recipe; it helps to keep
the meat loaf moist.*

2 large eggs, lightly beaten
1½ pounds ground round
½ cup regular oats, uncooked
½ cup wheat germ
½ cup shredded carrot
¼ cup chopped onion
1 (10-ounce) package frozen
    chopped spinach, thawed and
    well drained
½ cup milk
1 teaspoon salt
½ teaspoon pepper
½ cup steak sauce

• **Combine** all ingredients except steak sauce, stirring well; shape into a 9- x 5- x 3-inch loaf, and place on a lightly greased rack in broiler pan.
• **Bake** at 350° for 40 minutes. Spread steak sauce over meat loaf; bake 20 additional minutes or until a meat thermometer inserted in center registers 160°. **Yield:** 6 to 8 servings.

Ann Birkmire
Sharon, Massachusetts

MEATBALL KABOBS

1½ pounds ground chuck
1 cup regular oats, uncooked
1 large egg, lightly beaten
1 teaspoon curry powder
1 teaspoon Worcestershire
      sauce
1 (4¾-ounce) jar pimiento-stuffed
      olives, drained
16 cherry tomatoes
2 medium-size green bell peppers,
      quartered
8 new potatoes, cooked
8 mushrooms
¼ cup barbecue sauce
Vegetable cooking spray
Barbecue sauce

● **Combine** first 5 ingredients; divide meat mixture into 24 equal portions. Shape each portion into a ball around an olive.
● **Alternate** meatballs, tomatoes, green pepper, potatoes, and mushrooms on six 14-inch skewers. Brush with ¼ cup barbecue sauce.
● **Coat** food rack with cooking spray; place rack on grill over medium-hot coals (350° to 400°), and place kabobs on rack.
● **Cook**, covered with grill lid, 10 minutes or until done, turning once. Serve with additional barbecue sauce. **Yield:** 4 to 6 servings.

Peggy Huffstetler
Lebanon, Tennessee

QUICKER ENCHILADAS

◄QUICK!►

1 pound ground chuck
1 small onion, chopped
1 (10¾-ounce) can cream of
      mushroom soup, undiluted
2 (4.5-ounce) cans chopped
      green chiles, undrained and
      divided
8 (8-inch) flour tortillas
1 (8-ounce) package shredded
      colby-Monterey Jack cheese
      blend, divided
1 (10¾-ounce) can Cheddar
      cheese soup, undiluted
Salsa

● **Brown** ground chuck and onion in a large skillet, stirring until meat crumbles; drain. Stir in mushroom soup and 1 can green chiles.
● **Spoon** ½ cup beef mixture down center of each tortilla; sprinkle each with 2½ tablespoons cheese blend. Roll up tortillas, and place each, seam side down, in a lightly greased 13- x 9- x 2-inch baking dish. Pour Cheddar cheese soup over tortillas.
● **Drain** remaining can green chiles; sprinkle chiles and remaining ¾ cup cheese over soup.
● **Cover** and bake at 350° for 20 minutes; uncover and bake 5 additional minutes. Serve enchiladas with salsa. **Yield:** 4 servings.

Mrs. Joe Ford
Hamlin, Texas

SAUSAGE AND BEAN DINNER

◄QUICK!►

If you're serving a crowd, spoon this entrée over hot cooked rice or pasta.

1 pound reduced-fat smoked
      sausage, cut into ¼-inch slices
1 large green bell pepper, chopped
1 medium onion, chopped
1 tablespoon vegetable oil
2 (14½-ounce) cans stewed
      tomatoes, undrained
1 (16-ounce) can pink beans,
      drained
1 (16-ounce) can pinto beans,
      drained
1 (15-ounce) can Great Northern
      beans, drained
½ teaspoon garlic powder

● **Brown** sausage in a Dutch oven over medium-high heat; remove sausage, and set aside. Discard drippings.
● **Cook** pepper and onion in oil in Dutch oven over medium heat, stirring constantly, until tender.
● **Add** cooked sausage, tomatoes, and remaining ingredients. Bring mixture to a boil; reduce heat, and simmer 30 minutes. **Yield:** 6 servings.

Michele C. Harrington
Chesapeake, Virginia

SAUSAGE-VEGETABLE SKILLET

◄QUICK!►

Kielbasa sausage is usually sold precooked, but brown the sausage in the skillet anyway – it brings out its smoky flavor.

1 tablespoon butter or margarine
1 pound kielbasa sausage, cut into
      ½-inch slices
1 head cauliflower, broken into
      flowerets
3 zucchini, thinly sliced
3 carrots, scraped and thinly
      sliced
1 medium onion, thinly sliced
½ teaspoon salt
¼ teaspoon pepper
1 cup (4 ounces) shredded
      Monterey Jack cheese

● **Melt** butter in a 12-inch skillet over medium-high heat; add sausage, and cook until browned, stirring often. Remove with a slotted spoon, reserving drippings in skillet; set sausage aside.
● **Add** cauliflower and next 3 ingredients to skillet; cook, stirring constantly, 5 minutes or until crisp-tender. Stir in salt and pepper; cover, reduce heat, and simmer 5 minutes. Stir in sausage; cook just until thoroughly heated.
● **Spoon** mixture into individual baking dishes, and sprinkle with cheese. Cover and let stand until cheese melts. **Yield:** 6 servings.

Betty Levine
Loudon, Tennessee

CREOLE LIVER

QUICK!

2 tablespoons all-purpose flour
½ teaspoon dried thyme
¼ teaspoon pepper
1 pound thinly sliced beef liver
2 tablespoons vegetable oil
1 medium onion, chopped
1 large green bell pepper,
    chopped
1 clove garlic, pressed
1 (14.5-ounce) can diced
    tomatoes, undrained
1 bay leaf
½ teaspoon salt
Hot cooked grits

● **Combine** first 3 ingredients in a shallow dish; dredge liver in flour mixture.
● **Cook** liver in hot oil in a large skillet over medium-high heat until browned, turning once. Remove liver, reserving drippings in skillet.
● **Add** onion, bell pepper, and garlic to drippings, and cook until tender, stirring often. Add liver, tomatoes, bay leaf, and salt; cover, reduce heat, and simmer 10 minutes. Remove and discard bay leaf. Serve over grits. **Yield:** 4 servings.

Debbie E. Ipock
Charlotte, North Carolina

AMARETTO-LIME VEAL

QUICK!

4 slices bacon, chopped
⅓ cup sliced almonds
Vegetable oil
1 pound (¼-inch-thick) veal
    cutlets
¼ teaspoon salt
½ teaspoon coarsely ground
    pepper
½ cup all-purpose flour
½ cup amaretto
1½ tablespoons fresh lime juice
½ cup sliced green onions
¼ cup butter or margarine

● **Cook** bacon in a large skillet until crisp; remove bacon, reserving drippings in skillet. Set bacon aside.
● **Add** almonds to drippings, and cook over medium heat, stirring constantly, until lightly browned; remove almonds, reserving drippings in skillet. Drain almonds on paper towels; set aside.
● **Add** oil to drippings to make ¼ cup; set aside.
● **Sprinkle** cutlets evenly with salt and pepper; dredge in flour. Heat 2 tablespoons drippings mixture in skillet; add half of cutlets, and cook 1 minute on each side or until lightly browned. Remove to a serving dish; keep warm. Repeat procedure with remaining 2 tablespoons drippings mixture and cutlets. Drain excess drippings from skillet.
● **Add** amaretto, lime juice, and green onions to skillet; bring to a boil, deglazing skillet by scraping particles that cling to bottom. Boil 2 minutes, stirring often. Remove from heat; add butter, 1 tablespoon at a time, stirring until butter melts. Stir in almonds, and spoon over cutlets. Sprinkle with bacon. **Yield:** 4 servings.

VEAL CUTLETS WITH LEEKS AND ZINFANDEL CREAM

QUICK!

Wrap leftover leek tops in cheesecloth and use them to flavor soups.

3 leeks
3 tablespoons all-purpose flour
¾ teaspoon salt
½ teaspoon freshly ground
    pepper
1 pound veal cutlets
3 tablespoons olive oil, divided
½ cup white Zinfandel
½ cup whipping cream

● **Remove** and discard green tops from leeks. Cut white portions diagonally into thin slices; set aside.
● **Combine** flour, salt, and pepper in a shallow bowl; dredge cutlets in flour mixture.
● **Cook** cutlets in 2 tablespoons hot oil in a large skillet 2 minutes on each side or until golden. Transfer cutlets to a serving platter, and keep warm.
● **Cook** leeks in remaining 1 tablespoon olive oil in skillet 1 minute; add wine, and cook 1 minute or until most of liquid evaporates, stirring often.

● **Add** whipping cream to leek mixture, and cook, stirring constantly, about 2 minutes or until mixture is reduced by half. Serve with veal. **Yield:** 4 servings.

Louise W. Mayer
Richmond, Virginia

STUFFED VEAL CUTLETS

6 (4-ounce) veal cutlets
6 slices prosciutto (about
    5 ounces)
4 ounces fontina cheese, cut into
    5 strips
¼ teaspoon salt
¼ teaspoon pepper
½ cup all-purpose flour
1 tablespoon butter or margarine,
    melted
1 tablespoon vegetable oil
1 cup dry white wine
Hot cooked spaghetti

● **Place** cutlets between two sheets of heavy-duty plastic wrap, and flatten to ⅛-inch thickness, using a meat mallet or rolling pin.
● **Wrap** a prosciutto slice around each cheese strip, and place in center of each cutlet. Fold ends of veal cutlets over prosciutto and cheese; fold sides over, and secure with a wooden pick.
● **Sprinkle** veal with salt and pepper, and dredge in flour. Brown on all sides in butter and oil in a heavy skillet. Remove veal from skillet; set aside, and keep warm.
● **Add** wine to skillet; boil until wine is reduced by half. Return veal to skillet; cover and simmer 5 minutes. Serve over spaghetti. **Yield:** 6 servings.

Sue-Sue Hartstern
Louisville, Kentucky

LEMON VEAL

The long cooking time tenderizes this lean cut of veal, and infuses it with the flavors of rosemary, lemon, and wine.

1 tablespoon all-purpose flour
1 teaspoon beef-flavored bouillon
　　granules
½ teaspoon paprika
½ teaspoon chopped fresh
　　parsley
¼ teaspoon dried rosemary
⅛ teaspoon pepper
½ pound boneless round rump
　　veal, trimmed and cut into
　　1-inch cubes
Vegetable cooking spray
2 medium carrots, scraped and
　　cut into thin strips
¼ cup dry white wine
¼ cup water
1 tablespoon lemon juice
2 cups hot cooked rice (cooked
　　without salt or fat)

• **Combine** first 6 ingredients in a heavy-duty, zip-top plastic bag; add veal; seal bag, and shake to coat.
• **Coat** a nonstick skillet with cooking spray; place over medium heat until hot. Add veal, and cook, stirring constantly, until lightly browned.
• **Add** carrot and next 3 ingredients to veal in skillet; bring to a boil, stirring constantly. Cover, reduce heat, and simmer 40 minutes. Serve over rice. **Yield:** 2 servings.

Terri Cohen
North Potomac, Maryland

❤ Per serving: Calories 472
Fat 7.3g　Cholesterol 100mg
Sodium 577mg

VEAL MEAT LOAF

2 pounds ground veal *
½ cup soft breadcrumbs
⅓ to ½ cup finely chopped green
　　or red bell pepper
3 large eggs
1½ teaspoons salt
¼ teaspoon finely chopped fresh
　　thyme or ⅛ teaspoon dried
　　thyme
¼ teaspoon finely chopped fresh
　　or dried rosemary
¼ teaspoon pepper
1¼ cups thinly sliced fresh
　　mushrooms
Vegetable cooking spray

• **Combine** first 8 ingredients; stir in mushrooms.
• **Divide** meat mixture into 6 equal portions; place each portion in a 4- x 2½- x 1½-inch loafpan coated with cooking spray. Place loafpans in a shallow baking pan.
• **Bake** at 350° for 25 to 30 minutes or until done. Let stand 5 minutes. **Yield:** 6 servings.

* Substitute 2 pounds ground pork for ground veal.

Note: For 1 large loaf, place meat mixture in a 7½- x 3- x 2-inch loafpan coated with cooking spray. Bake at 350° for 1 hour and 5 minutes or until done. Let stand 5 minutes.

Prime Time Cafe
Disney MGM Studios
Lake Buena Vista, Florida

MARINATED RACK OF LAMB

4 (6- to 8-rib) lamb rib roasts,
　　trimmed (about 8 pounds)
1 cup dry white vermouth
1 cup steak seasoning sauce *
3 tablespoons garlic powder
2 tablespoons dried Italian
　　seasoning
Garnish: fresh parsley sprigs

• **Place** lamb in a large shallow dish or large heavy-duty, zip-top plastic bags.

• **Combine** vermouth and next 3 ingredients; pour 1 cup marinade over lamb. Cover and chill remaining marinade. Cover dish or seal bags, and chill 8 hours, turning lamb often.
• **Remove** meat from marinade, discarding marinade. Place lamb, fat side up, on a rack in a shallow roasting pan.
• **Bake** at 325° for 1 hour and 15 minutes or until a meat thermometer inserted in thickest portion registers 150° (medium-rare), basting often with reserved marinade. Garnish, if desired. **Yield:** 12 servings.

* For steak seasoning sauce, we used Dale's. Substitute 1 cup any brand of soy sauce-based marinade.

Note: Remove lamb from oven at 160° if you desire medium doneness or at 170° (well doneness).

Helen Shores Lee
Birmingham, Alabama

GRILLED LEG OF LAMB

1 head garlic
1 (6- to 7-pound) leg of lamb,
　　trimmed
1 (750-milliliter) bottle dry red
　　wine
¼ cup olive oil
1 tablespoon dried oregano
1 tablespoon dried rosemary
2 teaspoons paprika

• **Peel** garlic; cut 5 cloves into thin slices, and crush remaining cloves.
• **Make** 1-inch-deep cuts into lamb, using a small paring knife; insert a garlic slice into each cut. Place lamb in a large shallow dish.
• **Combine** crushed garlic, wine, and remaining 4 ingredients; reserve 1 cup wine mixture in the refrigerator. Pour remaining wine mixture over lamb; cover and marinate in refrigerator 8 hours, turning occasionally.
• **Remove** lamb from marinade, discarding marinade. Insert meat thermometer in thickest portion, making sure it does not touch fat or bone.
• **Cook** lamb over low coals under 300° for 1½ hours, or until thermometer

registers 145°, turning and basting with reserved wine mixture every 15 minutes. Remove lamb from heat; cover and let stand 30 minutes or until thermometer registers 150° (medium-rare). **Yield:** 8 servings.

Michael Spanos
Birmingham, Alabama

GRILLED LAMB WITH MANGO SALSA

Occasionally you can find boneless leg of lamb; if you can't, ask your butcher to remove the bone from a leg of lamb.

1 teaspoon cumin seeds
1 teaspoon coriander seeds
1 cup olive oil
½ cup dry white wine
¼ cup tequila
2 tablespoons fresh lime juice
2 tablespoons minced fresh garlic
2 tablespoons chopped fresh cilantro
2 jalapeño peppers, seeded and finely chopped
½ teaspoon salt
½ teaspoon freshly ground pepper
1 (4- to 4½-pound) boneless leg of lamb
Mango Salsa
Garnish: fresh cilantro sprigs

• **Cook** cumin seeds in a heavy skillet, stirring constantly, until browned; remove from heat, and crush. Repeat procedure with coriander seeds.
• **Combine** crushed cumin and coriander seeds, olive oil, and next 8 ingredients in a large heavy-duty, zip-top plastic bag or a large shallow dish. Add lamb, turning to coat. Seal bag or cover dish, and chill 8 hours, turning occasionally.
• **Cook** lamb, without grill lid, over medium-hot coals (350° to 400°) about 40 minutes or until meat thermometer inserted in thickest portion of meat registers 150° (medium-rare) or to desired degree of doneness, turning meat once.
• **Cut** lamb into thin slices; serve with Mango Salsa. Garnish, if desired. **Yield:** 8 servings.

Mango Salsa

4 medium mangoes, peeled and chopped
⅓ cup chopped fresh cilantro
¼ cup chopped celery
¼ cup finely chopped green onions
¼ cup chopped yellow or red bell pepper
1 jalapeño pepper, seeded and minced
¼ cup honey
¼ cup olive oil
2 tablespoons fresh lime juice
¼ teaspoon salt

• **Combine** first 6 ingredients in a small bowl. Combine honey and remaining 3 ingredients; pour over mango mixture. Toss gently to coat; cover and chill 30 minutes. **Yield:** about 4 cups.

Sue Sims
San Angelo, Texas

ROLLED LAMB ROAST

1 clove garlic, sliced
1 tablespoon chopped fresh parsley
1 teaspoon salt
½ teaspoon pepper
½ teaspoon chopped fresh thyme
1 (5-pound) lamb shoulder, boned
2 tomatoes, chopped
2 onions, chopped
1 green bell pepper, chopped
3 tablespoons olive oil
8 small turnips, peeled
½ cup Madeira
2 bay leaves

• **Combine** first 5 ingredients; sprinkle over lamb. Top with half of chopped vegetables. Roll roast, starting at shortest end; tie securely.
• **Pour** oil in a large Dutch oven; place over medium-high heat until hot. Brown lamb in hot oil about 20 minutes. Add remaining half of chopped vegetables, turnips, wine, and bay leaves.
• **Cover** and bake at 325° for 2 hours and 15 minutes or until meat thermometer inserted in thickest portion registers

150° (medium-rare). Remove and discard bay leaves. **Yield:** 10 servings.
Irma Seidensticker
Comfort, Texas

LEG OF LAMB WITH HUNTER SAUCE

1 (5-pound) leg of lamb
3 cloves garlic, thinly sliced
3 tablespoons Dijon mustard
1 tablespoon chopped fresh rosemary
2 teaspoons cracked pepper
Hunter Sauce

• **Cut** small slits in lamb with a sharp knife; insert garlic slices into slits. Place lamb in a large shallow dish.
• **Combine** mustard, rosemary, and pepper; spread over lamb. Cover and chill at least 1 and up to 2 days. Remove lamb from refrigerator, and place in a roasting pan; let stand at room temperature 30 minutes.
• **Bake** at 450° for 15 minutes; reduce oven temperature to 350°, and bake 1 additional hour or until meat thermometer inserted in thickest portion registers 145°. Remove from oven; cover lamb loosely with aluminum foil, and let stand 20 minutes or until thermometer registers 150° (medium-rare). Serve with Hunter Sauce. **Yield:** 8 to 10 servings.

Hunter Sauce

▸QUICK!◂

½ cup firmly packed brown sugar
½ cup ketchup
¼ cup butter or margarine
¼ cup apple jelly
3 tablespoons lemon juice
1 teaspoon ground cinnamon
½ teaspoon ground allspice
½ teaspoon pepper
¼ teaspoon ground cloves

• **Combine** all ingredients in a medium saucepan; cook over low heat, stirring until smooth. **Yield:** 1⅓ cups.

Sissy Nash and Kathy Nash Cary
Louisville, Kentucky

GRILLED LAMB WITH SWEET PEPPER RELISH

Lightly grill an extra red or yellow bell pepper or two with the lamb. Cut off the top, remove and discard the seeds, and use as a container to serve Sweet Pepper Relish.

4 (8-ounce) lamb rib sections
    (2 ribs per section)
¼ teaspoon salt
¼ teaspoon garlic powder
¼ teaspoon pepper
½ teaspoon chopped fresh
    basil
½ teaspoon chopped fresh
    rosemary
Sweet Pepper Relish
Garnish: fresh herbs

• **Trim** fat from rib sections, and set lamb aside.
• **Combine** salt, garlic powder, and pepper; sprinkle evenly over lamb. Press basil and rosemary evenly onto lamb rib sections.
• **Cook**, covered with grill lid, over medium-hot coals (350° to 400°) 12 minutes on each side or until meat thermometer inserted in thickest portion registers 150° (medium-rare) to 160° (medium).
• **Serve** lamb with Sweet Pepper Relish. Garnish, if desired. **Yield:** 4 servings.

Sweet Pepper Relish

2 red bell peppers, cut into thin
    strips
2 yellow bell peppers, cut into thin
    strips
¾ cup firmly packed brown sugar
8 serrano chile peppers, seeded
    and cut into thin strips

• **Combine** all ingredients in a small bowl, stirring gently. Cover relish mixture, and chill 8 hours.
• **Place** relish mixture in a small saucepan; bring to a boil over medium-low heat, stirring constantly. Reduce heat, and simmer 40 minutes, stirring often. Remove from heat, and let cool completely. **Yield:** 1 cup.

Gert Rausch
Austin, Texas

ROSEMARY-MARINATED LAMB KABOBS

Cubes of lamb soak up the vibrant flavors of orange juice, lime juice, and soy and teriyaki sauces. Green onions, rosemary, garlic, and black peppercorns further pique the palette of the marinade.

½ cup orange juice
¼ cup lime juice
¼ cup soy sauce
2 tablespoons teriyaki sauce
¼ cup finely chopped green
    onions
2 teaspoons dried rosemary
1 teaspoon minced garlic
5 to 7 black peppercorns
1 pound lean lamb, cut into 1-inch
    cubes
2 to 4 green bell peppers,
    quartered
1 large purple onion, cut into 8
    slices
1 navel orange, cut into 8
    slices
Hot cooked rice

• **Combine** first 8 ingredients in a shallow container or heavy-duty, zip-top plastic bag. Add lamb; cover or seal, and chill 8 hours, turning once.
• **Drain** lamb, discarding marinade. Arrange lamb on skewers. Place green bell pepper and onion in a grilling basket. Cook lamb and vegetables, covered with grill lid, over hot coals (400° to 500°) 10 minutes, turning often.
• **Place** orange slices on grill rack, and cook just until thoroughly heated, turning slices once.
• **Serve** lamb, vegetables, and orange slices over rice. **Yield:** 4 servings.

Alex Saied
Hoover, Alabama

DIJON-ROSEMARY LAMB CHOPS

QUICK!

¼ cup Dijon mustard
8 lamb chops (4 pounds)
1 tablespoon dried rosemary,
    crushed
All-purpose flour
2 tablespoons olive oil
1 cup dry white wine, divided
½ cup whipping cream
Salt and pepper

• **Spread** mustard over lamb chops; sprinkle evenly with rosemary. Dredge chops in flour, shaking off excess flour.
• **Pour** oil into a large skillet; place over medium-high heat until hot. Add chops, and cook until browned, turning once. Reduce heat to medium; cover and cook 10 minutes.
• **Turn** chops over, and add ¼ cup dry white wine. Cook 10 additional minutes or to desired degree of doneness. Remove from skillet, and keep warm.
• **Add** remaining ¾ cup wine to pan drippings, stirring to loosen browned particles that cling to bottom.
• **Cook** 10 minutes or until liquid is reduced to about 1 cup, stirring occasionally. Add whipping cream; simmer 2 minutes. Season with salt and pepper to taste. Serve sauce with lamb chops. **Yield:** 4 servings.

Chef J. R. Contway
Bentwood Country Club
San Angelo, Texas

SAGE LAMB CHOPS

QUICK!

Lamb chops from the microwave? We were pleasantly surprised.

1 tablespoon red wine vinegar
1 teaspoon dark brown sugar
½ teaspoon rubbed sage
⅛ teaspoon garlic powder
⅛ teaspoon salt
⅛ teaspoon pepper
4 (1-inch-thick) lamb chops

• **Combine** first 6 ingredients in a 9-inch pieplate or microwave-safe dish. Add chops, turning to coat; arrange chops with bones toward center of dish. Cover and chill 2 to 3 hours.

• **Microwave** at MEDIUM-HIGH (70% power) 3 to 5 minutes or until chops are pink in the center (do not overcook). Cover with aluminum foil; let stand 3 minutes. **Yield:** 2 servings.

LaJuan Coward
Jasper, Texas

GREEK MEAT LOAF

Leftovers taste luxurious drizzled with yogurt sauce and stuffed inside pita bread.

2½ pounds lean ground lamb
1 large onion, diced
1 green bell pepper, diced
½ cup quick-cooking oats, uncooked
¼ cup chopped fresh parsley
2½ teaspoons dried oregano
2 teaspoons chopped fresh mint or ½ teaspoon dried mint flakes
2 teaspoons pepper
½ teaspoon salt
1 (8-ounce) can tomato sauce
2 large eggs, lightly beaten

• **Combine** all ingredients in a large bowl; shape mixture into a loaf, and place in a lightly greased 9- x 5- x 3-inch loafpan.
• **Bake** at 350° for 1½ hours or until meat thermometer inserted in center registers 160°, and serve immediately. **Yield:** 8 servings.

Toni Reed Rashid
Birmingham, Alabama

CROWN PORK ROAST WITH CRANBERRY-PECAN STUFFING

1 tablespoon salt
1 tablespoon pepper
2 teaspoons dried thyme
1 (16-rib) crown pork roast, trimmed
2 cups Cranberry-Pecan Stuffing
¼ cup butter or margarine
⅓ cup all-purpose flour
2 (14½-ounce) cans chicken broth
2 tablespoons Grand Marnier or other orange-flavored liqueur *
2 tablespoons grated orange rind
¼ teaspoon salt
¼ teaspoon pepper
Garnishes: kumquat leaves, sugared kumquats, grape clusters, crabapples

• **Combine** first 3 ingredients; rub over all sides of roast.
• **Fold** a piece of aluminum foil into an 8-inch square; place on a rack in a roasting pan. Place roast, bone ends up, on foil-lined rack.
• **Bake** at 350° for 1 hour.
• **Spoon** 2 cups Cranberry-Pecan Stuffing into center of roast; cover with a 12-inch square of heavy-duty foil, and fold over tips of ribs.
• **Bake** at 350° for 1½ hours or until a meat thermometer inserted in thickest portion registers 160°. Remove foil; let roast stand 15 minutes before slicing.
• **Pour** pan drippings into a skillet; add butter, and cook over medium heat until butter melts. Add flour, whisking until smooth; cook, whisking constantly, until caramel-colored.
• **Stir** in chicken broth and next 4 ingredients; cook, whisking constantly, until smooth and thickened. Serve with roast. Garnish, if desired. **Yield:** 12 servings.

* You can substitute an equal amount of orange juice for liqueur.

Note: To make sugared fruit, sprinkle 4 envelopes unflavored gelatin over 4 cups warm water; stir with a wire whisk until gelatin dissolves. Dip fruit into gelatin mixture, shaking to remove excess; sprinkle all sides of fruit with superfine sugar, covering completely. Place on baking sheets; let stand 30 minutes or until dry and firm.

Cranberry-Pecan Stuffing

You can make the stuffing ahead. Place it in a large bowl; cover and chill until ready to bake. If not preparing a roast, spoon all stuffing into two lightly greased 11- x 7- x 1½-inch baking dishes; bake as directed.

2 cups dried cranberries
1 cup Grand Marnier or other orange-flavored liqueur *
2 pounds mild ground pork sausage
4 cups coarsely chopped celery
1½ cups chopped onion
½ cup butter or margarine
2 (14½-ounce) cans chicken broth
1 teaspoon salt
½ teaspoon pepper
1 teaspoon dried thyme
2 (6-ounce) packages pork stuffing mix
2 tablespoons grated orange rind
2 cups chopped pecans

• **Combine** cranberries and liqueur in a small saucepan; bring to a boil over medium-high heat. Remove from heat, and set aside.
• **Brown** sausage in a large skillet, stirring until it crumbles; drain, reserving 2 tablespoons drippings in skillet. Set sausage aside.
• **Cook** celery and onion in drippings over medium-high heat 10 minutes, stirring constantly. Add butter and next 4 ingredients; cook, stirring constantly, 3 minutes or until butter melts.
• **Combine** cranberry mixture, sausage, stuffing mix and seasoning packet, orange rind, and pecans in a large bowl, stirring well.
• **Spoon** 2 cups stuffing mixture into roast; spoon remainder of stuffing mixture into a lightly greased 13- x 9- x 2-inch baking dish.
• **Cover** and bake at 350° for 20 minutes; uncover and bake 10 additional minutes or until lightly browned. **Yield:** 12 servings.

SAUSAGE-STUFFED PORK RIB ROAST

1 (3- to 5-pound) center-cut pork
   rib roast (8 bone)
½ to 1 pound smoked sausage
¼ cup butter, softened
2 tablespoons red port wine
2 tablespoons cane syrup
2 tablespoons muscadine jelly
¼ cup minced garlic
1 tablespoon chopped fresh
   tarragon
1 tablespoon chopped fresh
   thyme
1 tablespoon chopped fresh
   basil
1 tablespoon chopped fresh
   rosemary
1 teaspoon salt
1 teaspoon pepper
10 pearl onions
1 cup chicken broth
Brown Sauce
Muscadine jelly
Garnish: fresh rosemary sprigs

• **Push** a boning knife through center of pork roast, making a slit from end to end. Cut sausage the length of roast; prick sausage at ½-inch intervals, and insert into slit in roast. Place the stuffed roast in a lightly greased roasting pan.
• **Combine** butter and next 3 ingredients; spread over roast.
• **Combine** garlic and next 6 ingredients; sprinkle over roast. Add onions and chicken broth to roasting pan.
• **Cover** and bake at 350° for 45 minutes. Uncover and bake 15 to 20 additional minutes or until meat thermometer registers 160°. Remove roast, reserving 1 cup pan drippings for Brown Sauce. Serve roast with Brown Sauce and additional muscadine jelly. Garnish, if desired. **Yield:** 8 servings.

Brown Sauce

> QUICK!

2 tablespoons butter
2 tablespoons all-purpose flour
2½ cups beef broth
1 cup reserved pan drippings
2 tablespoons muscadine jelly
1 tablespoon tomato sauce
¼ cup red port wine

• **Melt** butter in a heavy saucepan over medium heat, and add flour, stirring until smooth. Cook 1 minute, stirring constantly. Gradually stir in broth and 1 cup reserved pan drippings.
• **Bring** to a boil, stirring constantly, and cook until slightly thickened. Stir in jelly, tomato sauce, and port.
• **Pour** through a fine wire-mesh strainer into a container for a smoother consistency, if desired. **Yield:** 3½ cups.

Chef John Folse
Lafitte's Landing
Donaldsonville, Louisiana

APRICOT-PECAN STUFFED PORK LOIN

The bourbon sauce for this roast requires "flaming" on the cooktop before pouring over the pork and baking. This is to burn off the alcohol and to prevent the sauce from flaming in the oven. (Beware: Skipping this step could mean a call to the fire department.)

1½ cups dried apricots halves
½ cup pecans
1 clove garlic
½ teaspoon salt
¼ teaspoon pepper
2 tablespoons dried thyme, divided
¼ cup molasses, divided
¼ cup peanut or vegetable oil,
   divided
1 (5-pound) rolled boneless pork
   loin roast, well trimmed
1 cup bourbon
1 cup chicken broth
¼ cup whipping cream
¼ teaspoon salt

• **Position** knife blade in food processor bowl; add first 5 ingredients, and process until coarsely chopped. Add 1 tablespoon thyme, 1 tablespoon molasses, and 2 tablespoons oil; process until mixture is finely chopped.
• **Remove** pork loin halves from elastic net. (There should be 2 pieces.) Trim excess fat. Make a cut lengthwise down center of each piece, cutting to, but not through, bottom. Starting from center cut, slice horizontally toward 1 side, stopping ½ inch from edge. Repeat on opposite side. Unfold meat so that it's flat. Repeat with other loin half.
• **Flatten** to ½-inch thickness, using a meat mallet or rolling pin. Repeat with remaining loin half.
• **Spread** apricot mixture evenly on top of pork. Roll each loin half, separately, jellyroll fashion, starting with long side. Secure with string, and place seam side down in a shallow roasting pan. Brush with remaining 2 tablespoons oil; sprinkle with remaining 1 tablespoon thyme.
• **Bring** remaining 3 tablespoons molasses, bourbon, and chicken broth to a boil in a large saucepan. Remove from heat. Carefully ignite bourbon mixture with a long match. When flames die, pour over pork roasts.
• **Bake** at 350° for 1 to 1½ hours or until meat thermometer inserted in thickest portion registers 160°. Remove pork from pan, reserving drippings in pan, and keep pork warm.
• **Add** whipping cream and salt to drippings in pan, and cook over medium-high heat, stirring constantly, until slightly thickened.
• **Slice** pork, and serve with sauce. **Yield:** 10 servings.

FRUITCAKE-STUFFED PORK LOIN

Fruitcake breaks tradition as a delicious stuffing for this elegant entrée.

⅓ cup chopped onion
1 clove garlic, minced
1 tablespoon olive oil
3 cups crumbled fruitcake
1 (5-pound) rolled boneless pork
   loin roast
¼ teaspoon salt
¼ teaspoon pepper
2 tablespoons dried thyme, divided
1 cup apple juice
1 cup chicken broth
¼ cup bourbon
¼ cup honey
2 tablespoons butter or margarine
2 tablespoons all-purpose flour
2 tablespoons bourbon
¼ cup whipping cream
Garnishes: fresh grapes, kumquats,
   fresh thyme sprigs, canned
   crabapples

- **Cook** onion and garlic in olive oil in a skillet over medium-high heat, stirring constantly, until tender. Remove skillet from heat; add fruitcake, and stir well.
- **Remove** pork loin from elastic net. (There should be 2 pieces.) Trim excess fat. Make a cut lengthwise down the center of each piece, cutting to, but not through, bottom. Starting from center cut of each piece, slice horizontally toward 1 side, stopping ½ inch from edge. Repeat on opposite side. Unfold each piece of meat so that it lies flat.
- **Flatten** to ½-inch thickness, using a meat mallet or rolling pin.
- **Sprinkle** salt, pepper, and 1 tablespoon thyme evenly over pork. Sprinkle fruitcake mixture evenly over pork.
- **Roll** each loin half, jellyroll fashion, starting with long side. Secure with string, and place seam side down in a shallow roasting pan.
- **Pour** apple juice and chicken broth around rolled pork loins in pan.
- **Combine** ¼ cup bourbon and honey. Brush lightly over rolled pork loins. Sprinkle with remaining 1 tablespoon thyme.
- **Bake** at 350° for 50 minutes or until meat thermometer inserted in thickest portion registers 160°, basting with bourbon mixture every 20-minutes. Remove pork loins from pan, reserving pan drippings. Place pork on a serving platter, and keep warm.
- **Pour** pan drippings into a saucepan; bring to a boil, and cook 10 to 15 minutes until mixture is reduced to 1 cup. Set aside.
- **Melt** butter in a small heavy saucepan over low heat; add flour, stirring until smooth. Cook 1 minute, stirring constantly. Gradually add reduced drippings and 2 tablespoons bourbon; cook over medium heat, stirring constantly, until mixture thickens and boils. Remove from heat; stir in whipping cream. Serve with sliced pork. Garnish, if desired. **Yield:** 10 servings.

ROLLED PORK WITH RHUBARB SAUCE

A honeyed glaze of rhubarb and raspberries balanced with tangy apple cider vinegar and mustard tops this pork roast. Snippets of fresh rosemary and thyme provide fragrant flavor contrast.

1 (3-pound) rolled boneless pork loin roast
2 tablespoons chopped fresh rosemary, divided
2 tablespoons chopped fresh thyme, divided
3 cloves garlic, cut into fourths
Olive oil-flavored cooking spray
2 cups fresh or frozen sliced rhubarb, thawed
1 (10-ounce) jar seedless raspberry preserves
⅔ cup honey
2 tablespoons apple cider vinegar
½ teaspoon dry mustard
¼ teaspoon ground cloves
Garnishes: fresh rosemary and thyme sprigs

- **Remove** string from pork roast; trim fat. Sprinkle half of chopped rosemary and thyme on top of half of pork roast; place other half of roast on top, and tie at 2-inch intervals with heavy string.
- **Place** roast in a shallow roasting pan. Cut 12 small slits in roast; insert garlic pieces. Sprinkle with remaining chopped rosemary and thyme, and coat with cooking spray.
- **Bake** at 325° for 1 hour.
- **Combine** rhubarb and next 5 ingredients in a saucepan; bring to a boil over medium heat. Reduce heat, and simmer 10 minutes; cool slightly.
- **Position** knife blade in food processor bowl; add rhubarb mixture, and pulse 4 times or until smooth, stopping once to scrape down sides. Reserve ⅔ cup mixture. Brush roast with remaining mixture.
- **Bake** roast 20 additional minutes or until meat thermometer inserted in thickest portion registers 160°. Let roast stand 10 minutes. Serve with reserved rhubarb mixture. Garnish, if desired. **Yield:** 10 servings.

ROASTED PORK LOIN

You'll love what the garlic-ginger marinade does for this tender pork.

½ cup soy sauce
¼ cup vegetable oil
2 tablespoons molasses
1 tablespoon ground ginger
2 teaspoons dry mustard
6 cloves garlic, minced
1 (4- to 5-pound) rolled boneless pork loin roast

- **Combine** first 6 ingredients in a bowl, stirring with a wire whisk until blended.
- **Remove** pork loin halves from elastic net. (There should be 2 pieces.) Trim excess fat from pork. Place pork in a shallow dish or heavy-duty, zip-top plastic bag; pour soy sauce mixture over pork, turning to coat. Cover and chill at least 8 hours.
- **Remove** pork loin from marinade, reserving marinade. Bring marinade to a boil; set aside. Place pork loin halves together, and secure with string. Place in a greased roasting pan.
- **Bake** at 325° for 2 hours or until meat thermometer inserted in thickest portion registers 160°, brushing with marinade during first hour of cooking. **Yield:** 10 to 12 servings.

Myrna M. Ruiz
Marietta, Georgia

HONEY-ROASTED PORK

1 (2- to 3-pound) boneless pork
   loin roast
¼ cup honey
2 tablespoons Dijon mustard
2 tablespoons mixed or black
   peppercorns, crushed
½ teaspoon dried thyme,
   crushed
½ teaspoon salt
Garnishes: fresh watercress, apple
   and orange slices

• **Place** roast on a lightly greased rack in shallow roasting pan.
• **Combine** honey and next 4 ingredients; brush about half of mixture over roast.
• **Bake** at 325° for 1 hour; brush with remaining honey mixture. Bake 30 additional minutes or until a meat thermometer inserted in thickest portion registers 160°. Garnish, if desired. **Yield:** 8 servings.

Janie Wallace
Seguin, Texas

ROAST PORK LOIN WITH APPLES AND MUSHROOMS

1 (3-pound) rolled boneless pork
   loin roast, well trimmed
1 teaspoon dried thyme
¼ teaspoon salt
¼ teaspoon pepper
⅓ cup apple cider
2 tablespoons dry white vermouth
1 cup chicken broth
1 cup whipping cream
3 tablespoons butter or margarine,
   divided
3 small cooking apples, peeled,
   cored, and cut into eighths
¾ pound fresh mushrooms, sliced
Garnish: fresh thyme sprigs

• **Sprinkle** pork roast with seasonings, and place in a lightly greased 13- x 9- x 2-inch baking pan. Bake at 450° for 20 minutes; reduce oven temperature to 325°, and bake 1 hour and 15 minutes or until a meat thermometer registers 160°. Transfer roast to platter; let stand 10 minutes before slicing.

• **Place** baking pan over medium heat; add apple cider, stirring to loosen any particles that cling to bottom. Add vermouth, chicken broth, and whipping cream. Bring mixture to a boil; cook 15 minutes or until thickened, stirring often. Remove from heat.
• **Melt** 1½ tablespoons butter in a large skillet; add apple, and cook until golden, turning once. Remove from skillet; set aside, and keep warm. Melt remaining 1½ tablespoons butter in skillet over medium heat; add mushrooms, and cook until tender. Stir in cream mixture, and cook over low heat until thoroughly heated.
• **Place** 3 slices of pork roast on individual plates; spoon about ¼ cup sauce over meat, and serve with apple slices. Garnish, if desired. **Yield:** 8 servings.

Ouida Hamilton
Birmingham, Alabama

TROPICAL PORK LOIN

2 (15-ounce) cans sliced mangoes,
   drained
1 small onion, chopped
2 cloves garlic, minced
½ cup honey
⅓ cup soy sauce
¼ cup chopped crystallized ginger
¾ cup lemon-lime carbonated
   beverage
1 (2½- to 3-pound) boneless pork
   loin roast, well trimmed
¼ cup flaked coconut, toasted

• **Position** knife blade in food processor bowl; add mangoes. Process until smooth, stopping once to scrape down sides. Pour 2 cups mango puree into a large shallow dish or heavy-duty, zip-top plastic bag; chill remaining puree.
• **Add** onion and next 5 ingredients to dish or bag, stirring well; add roast, turning to coat. Cover or seal, and chill 6 to 8 hours, turning roast occasionally.
• **Remove** roast, reserving ½ cup marinade. Place roast on a rack in lightly greased broiler pan; pour reserved ½ cup marinade over roast.
• **Bake** at 325° for 1½ hours or until a meat thermometer inserted in thickest portion registers 160°.

• **Broil** 5½ inches from heat (with electric oven door partially opened) 5 minutes or until lightly browned. Remove roast to a serving platter, and keep warm; reserve ¼ cup drippings in broiler pan.
• **Add** remaining mango puree to reserved pan drippings; cook over medium heat until sauce is thoroughly heated, stirring occasionally.
• **Sprinkle** coconut over roast; serve with sauce. **Yield:** 8 servings.

Nita and Harold Norman
Coral Gables, Florida

GRANDMA RUTH'S GRILLED PORK LOIN

Bottled Italian dressing makes the marinade for this pork loin so easy.

1 (3- to 4-pound) boneless pork
   loin roast
1 (8-ounce) bottle Italian dressing
1 cup dry white wine
3 cloves garlic, minced
10 black peppercorns
Vegetable cooking spray

• **Pierce** roast at 1-inch intervals with a fork; set aside. (Piercing allows marinade to penetrate the meat better.)
• **Combine** dressing and next 3 ingredients in a large heavy-duty, zip-top plastic bag. Reserve ½ cup wine mixture in refrigerator for basting during grilling.
• **Add** roast to remaining wine mixture in bag; seal bag, and chill 8 hours, turning occasionally.
• **Remove** roast from marinade, discarding marinade.
• **Coat** a grill rack with cooking spray, and place over medium-hot coals (350° to 400°); place roast on rack.
• **Cook**, covered with grill lid, 35 minutes or until meat thermometer inserted in thickest portion registers 160°, turning and basting with reserved ½ cup wine mixture after 20 minutes. **Yield:** 8 to 10 servings.

Diane Buescher
Jackson, Missouri

HONEY-GRILLED PORK LOIN

An Asian blend of honey, sesame oil, soy sauce, garlic, and ginger imparts character to the pork. If you prefer, have your butcher butterfly the roast for you to simplify preparation.

1 (3-pound) boneless pork loin
      roast
⅔ cup soy sauce
1 teaspoon ground ginger
3 cloves garlic, crushed
¼ cup firmly packed brown
      sugar
⅓ cup honey
1½ tablespoons sesame oil
Vegetable cooking spray

• **Trim** fat from roast. Butterfly roast by making a lengthwise cut, cutting to within ½ inch of other side, and open roast. Place in a shallow dish or large heavy-duty, zip-top plastic bag.
• **Combine** soy sauce, ginger, and garlic, stirring well; pour over roast. Cover or seal, and chill at least 3 hours, turning roast occasionally.
• **Remove** roast from marinade, discarding marinade; set aside.
• **Combine** brown sugar, honey, and sesame oil in a small saucepan; cook over low heat, stirring constantly, until sugar dissolves.
• **Coat** grill rack with cooking spray. Brush roast with honey mixture. Cook, without grill lid, over medium-hot coals (350° to 400°) 20 to 25 minutes or until meat thermometer registers 160°, turning twice and basting often. **Yield:** 10 to 12 servings.

SPINACH AND BACON STUFFED PORK TENDERLOIN

½ cup finely chopped onion
1 clove garlic, minced
Vegetable cooking spray
1 cup sliced fresh mushrooms
1 (10-ounce) package frozen
      chopped spinach, thawed and
      drained
4 slices bacon, cooked and
      crumbled
1 tablespoon Dijon mustard
¼ teaspoon salt
¼ teaspoon pepper
2 (¾-pound) pork tenderloins,
      trimmed
2 tablespoons Dijon mustard
2 teaspoons dried rosemary,
      crushed
1 teaspoon dried oregano
1 teaspoon dried thyme
1 teaspoon pepper
¼ teaspoon salt
½ cup dry white wine

• **Cook** onion and garlic in a large nonstick skillet coated with cooking spray over medium heat, stirring constantly, until vegetables are tender. Add mushrooms; cook 3 minutes, stirring constantly. Stir in spinach and next 4 ingredients; set aside.
• **Slice** each pork tenderloin lengthwise down center, cutting to, but not through, bottom. Place between sheets of heavy-duty plastic wrap; pound into a 12- x 8-inch rectangle.
• **Spoon** half of spinach mixture over 1 tenderloin; spread to within ½ inch of sides. Roll tenderloin, jellyroll fashion, starting with short side. Tie with heavy string at 1½-inch intervals. Repeat procedure with remaining tenderloin and spinach mixture.
• **Combine** 2 tablespoons mustard and next 5 ingredients; spread evenly over tenderloins. Place seam side down in a shallow baking pan coated with cooking spray. Add wine to pan.
• **Bake** at 325° for 45 minutes. Let stand 10 minutes; remove strings. Cut into ½-inch slices. **Yield:** 6 servings.

❤ Per serving: Calories 227
Fat 7.6g Cholesterol 88mg
Sodium 504mg

GRILLED PORK TENDERLOIN WITH APPLES, CELERY, AND POTATOES

6 small new potatoes (10 ounces)
⅓ cup chopped purple onion
Vegetable cooking spray
2 Granny Smith apples, chopped
⅓ cup dry white wine
2 (10-ounce) pork tenderloins,
      trimmed
¼ teaspoon salt
¼ teaspoon freshly ground pepper
1 shallot, finely chopped
1 tablespoon olive oil
2 stalks celery, thinly sliced
1 tablespoon chopped fresh
      rosemary
⅔ cup white wine vinegar
2 tablespoons sugar
1 tablespoon chopped fresh
      parsley

• **Bake** potatoes at 350° for 20 minutes or until tender; cool. Cut potatoes into quarters; set aside.
• **Cook** onion in a saucepan coated with cooking spray over medium heat until tender. Add apple and wine; bring to a boil. Reduce heat, and simmer 10 minutes. Remove from heat, and set aside.
• **Sprinkle** pork with salt and pepper.
• **Cook** pork, covered with grill lid, over medium-hot coals (350° to 400°) about 15 to 20 minutes or until meat thermometer inserted in thickest portion registers 160°, turning once.
• **Cook** shallot in olive oil in a large nonstick skillet over medium-high heat, stirring constantly, until lightly browned. Stir in potato, apple mixture, celery, and rosemary. Cook 1 minute or until thoroughly heated. Place on serving plates, top with sliced pork, and keep warm.
• **Add** vinegar and sugar to skillet, stirring to dissolve sugar and scraping any particles that cling to bottom. Cook 3 to 5 minutes or until reduced by half.
• **Drizzle** over sliced pork and apple; sprinkle with chopped parsley. **Yield:** 4 servings.

*Chefs' Café
Atlanta, Georgia*

❤ Per serving: Calories 446
Fat 20.1g Cholesterol 101mg
Sodium 255mg

GRILLED PORK TENDERLOIN

QUICK!

½ cup soy sauce
½ cup dry sherry or orange juice
2 tablespoons brown sugar
1 teaspoon ground ginger
2 cloves garlic, pressed
2 (¾-pound) pork tenderloins

• **Combine** first 5 ingredients in a shallow dish or heavy-duty, zip-top plastic bag. Add tenderloins; cover dish or seal bag, and chill 8 hours, turning often.
• **Remove** tenderloins from marinade, discarding marinade.
• **Cook** tenderloins, covered with grill lid, over hot coals (400° to 500°) 12 to 15 minutes or until a meat thermometer inserted in thickest portion registers 160°, turning once.
• **Cut** into slices. **Yield:** 4 to 6 servings.

Cathy Robinson
Columbia, South Carolina

HONEY-MUSTARD PORK TENDERLOIN

QUICK!

2 (¾-pound) pork tenderloins, trimmed
Vegetable cooking spray
¼ cup honey
2 tablespoons apple cider vinegar
1 tablespoon Dijon mustard
½ teaspoon paprika

• **Place** tenderloins on a rack coated with cooking spray; place rack in broiler pan, and set aside.
• **Combine** honey and remaining 3 ingredients; spoon one-third of honey mixture over tenderloins, and set remaining honey mixture aside.
• **Bake** at 350° for 30 minutes or until a meat thermometer inserted in thickest portion registers 160°, basting occasionally with honey mixture. Cut tenderloins into thin slices. **Yield:** 6 servings.

Marie Davis
Charlotte, North Carolina

♥ Per serving: Calories 183
Fat 4.3g Cholesterol 64mg
Sodium 121mg

APPLE-MUSHROOM PORK TENDERLOIN

2 (¾-pound) pork tenderloins, trimmed *
¾ cup all-purpose flour
½ teaspoon salt
¼ teaspoon pepper
Vegetable cooking spray
1 clove garlic, minced
1 cup sliced fresh mushrooms
¾ cup frozen apple juice concentrate, thawed and undiluted

• **Cut** each tenderloin crosswise into 6 medaillons. Place medaillons, cut side down, between two sheets of heavy-duty plastic wrap; flatten each medaillon to ¼-inch thickness, using a meat mallet or rolling pin.
• **Combine** flour, salt, and pepper; coat pork slices with flour mixture.
• **Coat** a large nonstick skillet with cooking spray; place skillet over medium heat until hot.
• **Arrange** pork in skillet, and cook until browned on both sides.
• **Remove** pork from pan; set aside. Add garlic and mushrooms; cook 30 seconds, stirring constantly. Add apple juice concentrate and pork; simmer 3 minutes until thoroughly heated. **Yield:** 6 servings.

* You can substitute 6 skinned and boned chicken breast halves for pork tenderloins.

♥ Per serving: Calories 275
Fat 4.2g Cholesterol 74mg
Sodium 253mg

PORK MEDAILLONS WITH PORT WINE AND DRIED CRANBERRY SAUCE

Port wine is a sweet, fortified wine that balances with the tartness of the dried cranberries, orange rind, and balsamic vinegar in this dish.

1 large red bell pepper
1 teaspoon olive oil
1 medium-size purple onion, finely chopped
2 shallots, finely chopped
2 tablespoons minced fresh ginger
½ cup port wine
⅓ cup balsamic vinegar
2 tablespoons sugar
1 ripe pear, peeled and chopped
2 teaspoons grated orange rind
½ cup dried cranberries
1 cup fat-free chicken broth
2 tablespoons fresh thyme leaves
¼ teaspoon ground red pepper
2 (1-pound) pork tenderloins, trimmed
½ teaspoon salt
½ teaspoon freshly ground pepper
Garnish: fresh thyme sprigs

• **Place** red bell pepper on an aluminum foil-lined baking sheet. Bake at 500° for 20 minutes or until skin looks blistered, turning once.
• **Place** pepper immediately into a heavy-duty, zip-top plastic bag; seal and let stand 10 minutes to loosen skin. Peel pepper; remove and discard seeds. Cut pepper into strips; set aside.
• **Pour** oil into a large skillet; place over medium heat until hot. Add onion and shallot, and cook 10 minutes, stirring often.
• **Add** ginger and next 3 ingredients; bring to a boil. Reduce heat, and simmer 10 minutes or until liquid is reduced by three-fourths, stirring often.
• **Add** pepper strips, pear, and next 5 ingredients; simmer 10 minutes or until pear is tender, stirring occasionally. Remove from heat; keep warm.
• **Cut** each tenderloin into 8 slices. Place each slice between two sheets of heavy-duty plastic wrap, and flatten slightly with a meat mallet or rolling pin.

Sprinkle each side of slices with salt and pepper; arrange in a single layer on a rack in broiler pan.

• **Broil** 5½ inches from heat (with electric oven door partially opened) 3 minutes on each side or until meat thermometer inserted in thickest portion registers 160°. Garnish, if desired, and serve with sauce. **Yield:** 8 servings.

Ray Overton
Roswell, Georgia

♥ Per serving: Calories 254
Fat 9g Cholesterol 66.1mg
Sodium 204mg

PORK SCALOPPINE MARSALA

QUICK!

Imported from Italy, Marsala is a fortified wine with a rich, smoky flavor that can range from sweet to dry. The dry Marsala in this pork recipe enhances the simple, straightforward flavors of butter and freshly ground pepper.

2 (¾-pound) pork tenderloins
½ cup all-purpose flour
¼ cup butter or margarine, divided
1⅓ cups dry Marsala *
2 teaspoons beef-flavored bouillon granules
⅛ teaspoon freshly ground pepper
Hot cooked rice

• **Cut** each tenderloin into 6 (2-ounce) medaillons. Place pork, cut side down, between two sheets of heavy-duty plastic wrap; flatten to ¼-inch thickness, using a meat mallet or rolling pin.
• **Dredge** pork in flour. Cook half of pork medaillons in 2 tablespoons butter in a large skillet over medium heat about 2 minutes on each side or until lightly browned. Remove from skillet; keep warm. Repeat procedure with remaining 2 tablespoons butter and pork medaillons. Pour off excess butter, if necessary, leaving pan drippings.
• **Add** Marsala, bouillon granules, and pepper to skillet, and simmer mixture 3 to 4 minutes.

• **Return** pork medaillons to skillet; cover and simmer 2 minutes. Serve with rice. **Yield:** 6 servings.

✳ Substitute 1¼ cups dry white wine plus 2 tablespoons brandy for dry Marsala.

Mike Singleton
Memphis, Tennessee

EASY PORK PARMIGIANA

QUICK!

Using your favorite brand of spaghetti sauce makes quick work of this classic Italian dish. Buy grated and shredded cheeses to cut preparation time even further.

1 large egg
1 tablespoon water
2 tablespoons grated Parmesan cheese
⅓ cup Italian-seasoned breadcrumbs
4 (1¼-inch-thick) slices pork tenderloin (about 8 ounces)
2 tablespoons vegetable oil
1 cup spaghetti sauce
½ cup (2 ounces) shredded mozzarella cheese

• **Combine** egg and water; set aside.
• **Combine** Parmesan cheese and breadcrumbs; set aside.
• **Place** each piece of pork between two sheets of heavy-duty plastic wrap; flatten to ¼-inch thickness, using a meat mallet or rolling pin.
• **Dip** pork in egg mixture, and dredge in crumb mixture.
• **Cook** pork slices in hot oil in a large skillet over medium heat just until browned, turning once. Arrange pork in a lightly greased 8-inch square baking dish; top with spaghetti sauce.
• **Bake** at 350° for 25 minutes; top with mozzarella cheese. Bake 5 additional minutes. **Yield:** 4 servings.

Linda Sutton
Winston-Salem, North Carolina

PORK PICCATA

QUICK!

This pork-inspired version of the timeless Italian veal dish boasts the traditional ingredients of lemon juice and chopped parsley, but adds a twist by including capers and serving the mixture on a bed of fettuccine.

2 (¾-pound) pork tenderloins
½ cup all-purpose flour
½ teaspoon salt
¼ teaspoon pepper
3 tablespoons olive oil, divided
½ cup dry white wine
½ cup lemon juice
3 tablespoons butter or margarine
¼ cup chopped fresh parsley
1½ tablespoons capers
Hot cooked fettuccine
Garnishes: lemon slices, fresh parsley sprigs

• **Cut** each tenderloin into 6 (2-ounce) medaillons. Place, cut side down, between two sheets of heavy-duty plastic wrap; flatten to ¼-inch thickness, using a meat mallet or rolling pin.
• **Combine** flour, salt, and pepper; dredge pork in flour mixture.
• **Cook** half of pork in 1½ tablespoons oil in a large skillet over medium heat about 2 minutes on each side or until lightly browned. Remove from skillet; keep warm. Repeat procedure with remaining 1½ tablespoons oil and pork.
• **Add** wine and lemon juice to skillet; cook until thoroughly heated. Add butter, chopped parsley, and capers, stirring until butter melts.
• **Arrange** pork over pasta; drizzle with wine mixture. Garnish, if desired. Serve immediately. **Yield:** 6 servings.

KUNG PAO PORK

QUICK!

Dried crushed red pepper turns up the heat in this stir-fry favorite.

1 small red bell pepper
½ small onion
¾ pound lean pork
¼ cup soy sauce, divided
¼ cup water
2 tablespoons lemon juice
2 tablespoons sugar
2 teaspoons cornstarch
¼ teaspoon dried crushed red
     pepper
2 tablespoons olive oil
2 cloves garlic, minced
¼ cup unsalted roasted peanuts
Hot cooked rice

● **Cut** bell pepper and onion into 1-inch pieces; set aside. Cut pork into ½-inch cubes; drizzle with 2 tablespoons soy sauce.
● **Combine** remaining 2 tablespoons soy sauce, water, and next 4 ingredients, stirring until blended; set aside.
● **Pour** olive oil around top of a preheated wok or large skillet, coating sides; heat at medium-high (375°) 2 minutes. Add pork and garlic, and stir-fry 3 minutes or until lightly browned. Add bell pepper and onion; stir-fry 3 minutes or until vegetables are tender.
● **Add** soy sauce mixture; stir-fry 2 minutes or until thickened. Stir in peanuts, and serve over rice. **Yield:** 3 servings.

Sandra Enwright
Winter Park, Florida

APRICOT-MUSHROOM STUFFED PORK CHOPS

Ask your butcher to cut pockets in the pork chops – it's one less thing you'll have to worry about.

4 tablespoons butter or margarine,
     divided
1 (8-ounce) package sliced fresh
     mushrooms
⅓ cup chopped onion
⅓ cup chopped celery
1 cup soft breadcrumbs
½ cup dried apricot halves,
     chopped
½ cup chopped fresh parsley
½ teaspoon rubbed sage
8 (1-inch-thick) center-cut pork
     loin chops, cut with pockets
2 teaspoons salt
1 teaspoon freshly ground pepper
1 cup dry white wine
1½ tablespoons cornstarch
2 tablespoons cold water

● **Melt** 2 tablespoons butter in a large skillet over medium-high heat; add mushrooms, onion, and celery, and cook, stirring constantly, 5 minutes or until tender. Stir in breadcrumbs and next 3 ingredients; remove from heat.
● **Sprinkle** both sides and pocket of each pork chop with salt and pepper. Spoon vegetable mixture evenly into pockets, and secure with wooden picks.
● **Melt** remaining 2 tablespoons butter in skillet; add chops, and cook until browned, turning once. Place chops in a lightly greased roasting pan or large shallow baking dish; add white wine.
● **Cover** and bake at 350° for 45 minutes or until done. Remove from pan; discard wooden picks. Keep chops warm.
● **Remove** and discard fat from pan drippings; place 1½ cups drippings in a small saucepan.
● **Combine** cornstarch and water, stirring until smooth; stir into reserved drippings.
● **Cook** over medium heat, stirring constantly, until mixture thickens and boils. Boil 1 minute, stirring constantly. Remove from heat; serve with chops. **Yield:** 8 servings.

Margert Stewart
Murfreesboro, Tennessee

BONELESS PORK CHOPS WITH ANCHO CREAM SAUCE
(pictured at right)

4 (½-inch-thick) boneless pork
     loin chops
¼ teaspoon salt
¼ teaspoon pepper
4 slices bacon
Vegetable cooking spray
¼ cup Ancho Base
¾ cup whipping cream

● **Sprinkle** chops with salt and pepper. Wrap 1 slice bacon around each chop; secure with wooden picks, if desired.
● **Coat** food rack with cooking spray; place on grill over medium coals (300° to 350°). Place pork chops on rack, and cook, covered with grill lid, 8 minutes on each side or until done.
● **Combine** ¼ cup Ancho Base and whipping cream in a saucepan, whisking until smooth. Bring to a boil over medium heat, whisking constantly. Reduce heat, and simmer, whisking constantly, 5 minutes or until thickened.
● **Spoon** Ancho Cream Sauce onto plates; top each with a pork chop. Serve immediately. **Yield:** 4 servings.

Ancho Base

3 dried ancho chile peppers
4 ounces dried tomatoes
3 tablespoons minced garlic
½ cup chopped onion
4 beef-flavored bouillon cubes
1 tablespoon dried oregano
1 tablespoon brown sugar
2 tablespoons Worcestershire
     sauce
¼ cup tomato paste
1½ cups water

● **Combine** all ingredients in a saucepan. Bring to a boil over medium heat; reduce heat, and simmer 10 minutes, stirring occasionally. Cool 15 minutes.
● **Position** knife blade in food processor bowl; add pepper mixture. Process until smooth, stopping often to scrape down sides. Chill up to 1 week or freeze up to 3 months. **Yield:** 2¼ cups.

Chef Ron Brannon
Austin Central Markets Cooking School
Austin, Texas

Boneless Pork Chops With
Ancho Cream Sauce

Cassoulet

Boneless Pork Chops With Ancho Cream Sauce

PECAN-BREADED PORK CHOPS WITH BEER SAUCE

Chef Pfeifer uses a local product – Abita beer – to give pork chops a Louisiana twist. If you can't find it in your area, use another dark beer.

2 slices white bread
1 teaspoon dry mustard
1 teaspoon celery salt
¼ teaspoon pepper
1 cup pecan pieces
6 (¾-inch-thick) bone-in pork loin chops
¾ cup all-purpose flour
2 large eggs, lightly beaten
¼ cup milk
3 tablespoons butter or margarine
Beer Sauce

• **Position** knife blade in food processor bowl; add first 4 ingredients. Process 30 seconds or until bread is in fine crumbs. Add pecan pieces, and process until finely chopped; place pecan mixture in a shallow dish.
• **Dredge** chops in flour. Combine eggs and milk. Dip chops in egg mixture, and dredge in pecan mixture, coating all sides and shaking off excess.
• **Melt** butter in a large nonstick skillet over medium-high heat; add chops, and cook 2 minutes on each side or until browned. Transfer to a baking sheet.
• **Bake** at 350° for 10 to 15 minutes. Serve with sauce. **Yield:** 6 servings.

Beer Sauce

QUICK!

1 cup chopped onion
1 tablespoon caraway seeds
1 clove garlic, minced
1 tablespoon vegetable oil
1 (12-ounce) bottle Abita or other dark beer
1 (10½-ounce) can condensed beef consommé, undiluted
¼ teaspoon pepper
1½ tablespoons cornstarch
1½ tablespoons cold water

• **Cook** first 3 ingredients in oil in a large skillet over medium heat, stirring constantly, until tender.

• **Add** beer, beef consommé, and pepper. Bring mixture to a boil; reduce heat, and simmer 15 minutes.
• **Combine** cornstarch and water, stirring until smooth; add to beer mixture.
• **Cook** over medium heat, stirring constantly, until mixture thickens and boils. Boil sauce 1 minute, stirring constantly. **Yield:** 2 cups.

Chef Horst Pfeifer
Bella Luna
New Orleans, Louisiana

TAMARIND-GLAZED PORK CHOPS WITH GREEN MOLE SAUCE

The ingredients for this recipe are many, but most are processed into a seasoning paste and a sauce. (Chef Lagasse uses tamarind, but it's hard to find. So we used apricots, dates, and lemon juice.)

2½ tablespoons Southwest Seasoning, divided
⅛ teaspoon pepper
⅓ cup cane syrup or molasses
2 tablespoons ketchup
2 tablespoons water
2 teaspoons lemon juice
6 dried apricot halves
2 pitted dates
1 clove garlic
6 (1-inch-thick) boneless pork loin chops
1 tablespoon olive oil
Green Mole Sauce
Garnish: fresh cilantro sprigs

• **Position** knife blade in food processor bowl; add 1 tablespoon Southwest Seasoning, pepper, and next 7 ingredients. Process until smooth, stopping once to scrape down sides; set aside.
• **Coat** chops with remaining Southwest Seasoning. Cook in oil in a skillet over medium-high heat 2 minutes on each side or until browned. Remove to an aluminum foil-lined baking sheet; brush with syrup mixture.
• **Broil** 5½ inches from heat (with electric oven door partially opened) 15 minutes, turning and basting chops with syrup mixture every 5 minutes. Serve

with Green Mole Sauce. Garnish, if desired. **Yield:** 6 servings.

Southwest Seasoning

QUICK!

2 tablespoons chili powder
2 tablespoons paprika
1 tablespoon salt
1 tablespoon garlic powder
1 tablespoon ground coriander
2 teaspoons ground cumin
2 teaspoons ground red pepper
1 teaspoon dried oregano
1 teaspoon ground black pepper

• **Combine** all ingredients; store in an airtight container. **Yield:** ½ cup.

Green Mole Sauce

QUICK!

1 poblano chile pepper
3 dried apricot halves
1 pitted date
1 cup pistachio nuts or pine nuts
1 tablespoon cane syrup or molasses
1 teaspoon chili powder
1 teaspoon ground cumin
¼ teaspoon salt
1 teaspoon white vinegar
1 teaspoon lemon juice
1 tablespoon olive oil
¾ cup chicken broth
½ cup whipping cream

• **Place** chile pepper on an ungreased baking sheet. Broil 5½ inches from heat (with electric oven door partially opened) about 5 minutes on each side or until pepper looks blistered. Cool.
• **Peel** chile pepper; remove and discard seeds and membranes.
• **Position** knife blade in food processor bowl; add chile pepper, apricot halves, and next 9 ingredients. Process until smooth, stopping once to scrape down sides.
• **Combine** pepper mixture, broth, and whipping cream in a medium saucepan. Bring mixture to a boil; reduce heat, and simmer 2 minutes, stirring constantly. **Yield:** 1 cup.

Chef Emeril Lagasse
Emeril's
New Orleans, Louisiana

PORK CHOPS WITH WHITE BEAN PUREE

QUICK!

2 (6-ounce) boneless pork loin
    chops (½ inch thick)
2 teaspoons Cajun spice for pork
    and veal *
1 teaspoon olive oil
½ cup chopped onion
2 cloves garlic, minced
½ cup chicken broth
¼ cup currant jelly
2 tablespoons balsamic vinegar
2 cloves garlic
1 (15-ounce) can Great Northern
    beans, rinsed and drained
2 tablespoons chicken broth
1 tablespoon chopped fresh
    cilantro
½ teaspoon pepper

• **Rub** pork chops evenly with Cajun spice, and cook in oil in a large skillet over medium-high heat until browned on both sides. Remove from skillet, reserving drippings in skillet.
• **Add** onion and 2 minced cloves garlic to drippings in skillet, and cook until tender. Return pork chops to skillet.
• **Add** ½ cup broth, jelly, and vinegar to skillet; cover and simmer 10 to 15 minutes or until pork chops are tender. Transfer to a serving plate; set aside, and keep warm.
• **Combine** 2 cloves garlic and remaining 4 ingredients in container of an electric blender or food processor; process until smooth, stopping once to scrape down sides. Pour into a heavy saucepan; cook over low heat, stirring constantly, until thoroughly heated. Serve with pork chops. **Yield:** 2 servings.

* For Cajun spice for pork and veal we used Paul Prudhomme brand.

Mrs. William Alvine
Casselberry, Florida

♥ Per serving: Calories 576
Fat 14.5g Cholesterol 93mg
Sodium 167mg

PORK CHOPS WITH SWEET POTATOES

QUICK!

Butterflied pork chops partner with thick slices of sweet potato and Rome apple plus a savory blend of sage and green onions.

4 (½-inch-thick) butterflied
    boneless pork chops
1 cup apple cider, divided
4 sweet potatoes, peeled and cut
    into ½-inch-thick slices
2 green onions, chopped
2 tablespoons chopped fresh sage
    leaves
¾ teaspoon salt
¼ teaspoon pepper
2 large Rome or other cooking
    apples, sliced
1 teaspoon cornstarch

• **Brown** pork chops on both sides in a large nonstick skillet; remove chops from skillet, and set aside.
• **Add** ¾ cup apple cider, sweet potato, and next 4 ingredients to skillet. Bring mixture to a boil; cover, reduce heat, and simmer 10 minutes.
• **Add** pork chops and apple; cover and simmer 10 to 15 minutes or until sweet potato is tender and pork chops are done. Remove apple, sweet potato, and pork chops to serving platter, reserving drippings in skillet.
• **Combine** remaining ¼ cup cider with cornstarch, stirring until smooth. Stir into drippings. Cook over medium heat, stirring constantly, until mixture thickens and boils. Boil 1 minute, stirring constantly. Pour over pork chops. **Yield:** 4 servings.

Janie Wallace
Seguin, Texas

PORK CHOPS AND GRAVY

QUICK!

Cooking with electric slow cookers is making a comeback. You'll see why when you try this easy pork chop recipe. The common ingredients yield uncommonly delicious results.

½ cup all-purpose flour
1½ teaspoons dry mustard
½ teaspoon salt
½ teaspoon garlic powder
6 (1-inch-thick) lean pork chops
1 (10¾-ounce) can condensed
    chicken broth, undiluted
2 tablespoons vegetable oil

• **Combine** first 4 ingredients in a shallow dish; dredge pork chops in flour mixture, and set aside.
• **Combine** remaining flour mixture and chicken broth in a 3½-quart electric slow cooker.
• **Pour** oil into a large skillet; place over medium-high heat until hot. Cook chops in hot oil just until browned on both sides; place in slow cooker.
• **Cook**, covered, on HIGH 2 to 2½ hours or until chops are tender. Serve with hot cooked rice or mashed potatoes. **Yield:** 6 servings.

Carol S. Noble
Burgaw, North Carolina

Cassoulet

CASSOULET
(pictured at left)

1 pound dried Great Northern
   beans
2½ quarts water
½ pound salt pork with skin
3 cloves garlic, crushed
1 onion
2 carrots, scraped and cut in half
2 stalks celery, cut in half
1 teaspoon dried thyme
1 bay leaf
1 (6- to 7-pound) chicken
1 teaspoon salt
2 teaspoons freshly ground
   pepper
1 pound andouille sausage, cut
   into 2-inch pieces *
2 pounds boneless center-cut pork
   chops
1 medium onion, chopped
4 cloves garlic, minced
1 cup dry white wine
1 (14.5-ounce) can diced
   tomatoes, undrained
½ teaspoon dried thyme
2 teaspoons freshly ground
   pepper
1 cup fresh French breadcrumbs
¼ cup chopped fresh parsley

● **Sort** and wash beans; place in an 8-quart ovenproof Dutch oven. Cover with water 2 inches above beans; let soak 8 hours. Drain.
● **Add** 2½ quarts water to beans; stir in salt pork and next 6 ingredients. Bring to a boil; cover and cook 2 hours or until beans are tender, adding water if necessary. Remove and discard salt pork, onion, carrot, celery, and bay leaf; set beans aside.
● **Place** chicken in a roasting pan; sprinkle with salt and 2 teaspoons pepper.
● **Bake** at 350° for 2 hours or until meat thermometer inserted in meaty portion of thigh registers 180°; cool completely, reserving 3 tablespoons drippings. Cut chicken into serving-size pieces; set aside.
● **Cook** sausage in a skillet over medium-high heat until browned; remove sausage, reserving drippings in skillet. Set sausage aside.
● **Add** pork chops to skillet, and cook until browned on both sides; remove

pork chops, reserving drippings in skillet. Set pork chops aside.
● **Add** reserved chicken drippings to skillet. Add chopped onion and minced garlic, and cook over medium-high heat, stirring constantly, until tender. Add wine, and cook 6 minutes or until reduced by half.
● **Add** tomatoes, ½ teaspoon thyme, and 2 teaspoons pepper; stir into beans.
● **Spoon** half each of beans, sausage, chicken, and pork chops into a Dutch oven; repeat layers with remaining ingredients. Sprinkle with breadcrumbs.
● **Bake** at 325° for 1½ hours. Sprinkle with parsley. **Yield:** 8 to 10 servings.

✳ Substitute any spicy smoked sausage for andouille.

BARBECUED COUNTRY-STYLE RIBS

Thanks to Mildred Bickley of Bristol, Virginia, we have Rollin Johnson's recipe for ribs. He served these at family gatherings for decades.

1 small onion, finely chopped
1 cup finely chopped celery
1½ tablespoons bacon
   drippings
1 (15-ounce) can tomato sauce
¾ cup honey
½ cup water
¼ cup dry red wine
2 tablespoons lemon juice
2 tablespoons Worcestershire
   sauce
1 teaspoon salt
½ teaspoon pepper
¼ teaspoon garlic powder
1 cup water
2 tablespoons white vinegar
4 pounds boneless country-style
   pork ribs *

● **Cook** onion and celery in bacon drippings in a large saucepan over medium-high heat, stirring constantly, until tender. Add tomato sauce and next 8 ingredients. Bring mixture to a boil; reduce heat, and simmer 1 hour, stirring occasionally. Reserve 1½ cups tomato sauce mixture.

● **Combine** water and vinegar in a spray bottle.
● **Cut** ribs apart; cook, covered with grill lid, over medium coals (300° to 350°) 1 to 1½ hours or until done, spraying with vinegar solution and turning ribs occasionally. Baste with remaining 1 cup tomato sauce mixture after 30 minutes. Serve with reserved 1½ cups tomato sauce mixture. **Yield:** 8 servings.

✳ You can substitute 4 pounds bone-in country-style pork ribs. Cook as directed. Yield: 6 servings.

Rollin Johnson
Bristol, Virginia

GINGER PORK RIBS

1 tablespoon butter or margarine
1 medium onion, chopped
1 cup ginger marmalade or
   preserves
¼ cup soy sauce
2½ tablespoons honey
2½ tablespoons dry sherry
1 tablespoon grated fresh
   ginger
1 tablespoon grated orange rind
4 to 5 pounds baby-back pork
   ribs

● **Melt** butter in a large skillet over medium-high heat; add onion, and cook, stirring constantly, until tender. Add marmalade and next 5 ingredients; cook over medium heat, stirring constantly, until thoroughly heated.
● **Arrange** ribs in a shallow dish; pour ginger mixture over ribs. Cover and chill at least 8 hours.
● **Remove** ribs from marinade, discarding marinade. Place ribs on a rack in a roasting pan.
● **Bake** at 350° for 45 minutes or until tender. **Yield:** 4 servings.

Note: You can find ginger marmalade at specialty supermarkets.

Mike Singleton
Memphis, Tennessee

ADAMS' RIBS

Adams' Ribs is the hot and spicy product of a marriage. Anne-Marie's Cajun background is the source of the spicy heat. Her husband's commitment to the best equipment and a perfectly built fire contributes the smoky tenderness. A spice rub and two adapted sauces yield a taste and texture that give the ribs their signature.

2 tablespoons pepper
1 tablespoon garlic powder
1 tablespoon Creole seasoning
1 tablespoon Worcestershire
   sauce
8 pounds pork spareribs
Hickory wood chunks
Grill Basting Sauce
The Sauce

• **Combine** first 4 ingredients; rub on all sides of ribs.
• **Soak** wood chunks in water to cover 30 minutes.
• **Prepare** charcoal fire in grill; drain wood chunks, and place on coals.
• **Cook** ribs, covered with grill lid, over medium coals (300° to 350°) about 3 hours or until done, turning ribs after 1 hour and basting with Grill Basting Sauce after 2 hours. Turn once more after basting. Serve with The Sauce. **Yield:** 10 to 12 servings.

Grill Basting Sauce

QUICK!

¼ cup firmly packed brown
   sugar
¼ cup Worcestershire sauce
¼ cup prepared mustard
¾ cup ketchup
2 tablespoons ground black
   pepper
2 tablespoons dried crushed red
   pepper
2¾ cups red wine vinegar
1¾ cups water
¾ cup dry white wine
2 to 4 tablespoons salt

• **Combine** all ingredients in a saucepan; stir well. Cook sauce over medium heat 1 hour, stirring occasionally. **Yield:** 6 cups.

The Sauce

QUICK!

1 tablespoon butter or margarine
1 medium onion, finely chopped
½ tablespoon minced garlic
1 cup ketchup
½ cup white vinegar
¼ cup fresh lemon juice
¼ cup steak seasoning sauce *
2 tablespoons brown sugar
1 tablespoon Cajun seasoning **
2 tablespoons liquid smoke

• **Melt** butter in a large skillet over medium-high heat; add onion, and cook, stirring constantly, until tender. Add garlic and remaining ingredients; reduce heat, and simmer about 15 minutes. **Yield:** 2½ cups.

* For steak seasoning sauce, we used Dale's.
** For Cajun seasoning, we used Luzianne.

Anne-Marie Adams
Birmingham, Alabama

SOUTHERN SPARERIBS

1 (12-ounce) can beer
¼ cup soy sauce
2 tablespoons brown sugar
2 tablespoons chili sauce
2 tablespoons ketchup
2 tablespoons lemon juice
1 teaspoon onion powder
½ teaspoon salt
¼ teaspoon pepper
1 (4-pound) rack pork spareribs
Hickory wood chunks

• **Combine** first 9 ingredients. Place ribs in a shallow dish; pour beer mixture over ribs, turning to coat. Cover and chill 8 hours.
• **Soak** wood chunks in water 1 hour.
• **Prepare** charcoal fire in smoker; let burn 15 to 20 minutes.
• **Drain** wood chunks, and place on coals. Place water pan in smoker.
• **Remove** ribs from marinade; pour marinade into water pan. Add water to pan to depth of fill line. Place ribs on lower food rack; cover with smoker lid.

• **Cook** 5 hours or until done. **Yield:** 6 servings.

Jane Cooper
Washington Court House, Ohio

BISCUITS AND SAUSAGE GRAVY

3 cups self-rising soft wheat flour
¼ teaspoon baking soda
1 teaspoon sugar
½ cup butter-flavored shortening
1¼ cups buttermilk
Butter or margarine, melted
Sausage Gravy

• **Combine** first 3 ingredients in a large bowl; cut in shortening with pastry blender until mixture is crumbly.
• **Add** buttermilk, stirring just until dry ingredients are moistened.
• **Turn** dough out onto a lightly floured surface, and knead lightly 4 or 5 times.
• **Roll** to ¾-inch thickness; cut with a 2½-inch round cutter. Place on a greased baking sheet. Bake at 425° for 12 minutes or until golden. Brush tops with butter. Split biscuits open; serve with gravy. **Yield:** 12 to 14 servings.

Sausage Gravy

QUICK!

½ pound ground pork sausage
¼ cup butter or margarine
⅓ cup all-purpose flour
3¼ cups 1% low-fat milk or whole
   milk
½ teaspoon salt
½ teaspoon pepper
⅛ teaspoon Italian seasoning

• **Brown** sausage in a skillet, stirring until sausage crumbles. Drain, reserving 1 tablespoon drippings in skillet. Set sausage aside.
• **Add** butter to drippings; cook over low heat until butter melts. Add flour; stir until smooth. Cook 1 minute, stirring constantly. Gradually add milk; cook over medium heat, stirring constantly, until thickened and bubbly. Stir in sausage and seasonings. Cook, stirring constantly, until heated. **Yield:** 3¾ cups.

Diane Hogan
Chelsea, Alabama

CREAMY HAM AND CHICKEN MEDLEY

1 tablespoon butter or margarine
½ cup sliced fresh mushrooms
⅓ cup butter or margarine
⅓ cup all-purpose flour
2½ to 3 cups milk, divided
1 cup whipping cream
1 cup freshly grated Parmesan
    cheese
½ teaspoon salt
¼ teaspoon freshly ground black
    pepper
¼ teaspoon ground nutmeg
Dash of ground red pepper
2 cups chopped cooked chicken
2 cups chopped cooked ham
2 (10-ounce) packages frozen puff
    pastry shells, baked
Paprika

● **Melt** 1 tablespoon butter in a large saucepan over medium heat; add mushrooms, and cook, stirring constantly, until tender. Remove from saucepan; set aside.
● **Melt** ⅓ cup butter in saucepan over low heat; add flour, stirring until smooth. Cook 1 minute, stirring constantly. Gradually add 2½ cups milk; cook over medium heat, stirring constantly, until thickened and bubbly. Stir in whipping cream and next 5 ingredients. Cook, stirring constantly, until cheese melts and mixture is smooth; stir in reserved mushrooms, chicken, and ham. Add enough of remaining ½ cup milk for a thinner consistency, if desired. To serve, spoon mixture into shells, and sprinkle with paprika. **Yield:** 12 servings.

Note: You can serve Creamy Ham and Chicken Medley over hot cooked angel hair pasta instead of pastry shells. Sprinkle with freshly grated Parmesan cheese, if desired.

Jane Cairns
Birmingham, Alabama

HAM STROGANOFF ON CHEESY ONION BISCUITS

Use leftover or deli ham to make this creamy topping for a savory shortcake. Add a tossed green salad, and supper is ready.

2 tablespoons butter or margarine
2 cups chopped cooked ham
¼ cup finely chopped onion
1 (10¾-ounce) can cream of
    chicken soup, undiluted
½ cup milk
1 (8-ounce) carton sour cream
⅛ teaspoon pepper
Cheesy Onion Biscuits

● **Melt** butter in a heavy skillet over medium-high heat; add ham and onion, and cook, stirring constantly, until onion is tender.
● **Stir** in soup and milk; cover and cook over medium heat 3 to 4 minutes. Stir in sour cream and pepper; cook over low heat until mixture is thoroughly heated. Serve between split Cheesy Onion Biscuits. **Yield:** 4 servings.

Lea Davis
Dallas, Texas

Cheesy Onion Biscuits

QUICK!

2 cups all-purpose flour
3 tablespoons instant nonfat dry
    milk powder
4 teaspoons baking powder
¾ teaspoon salt
⅓ cup butter or margarine
½ cup grated Parmesan cheese
2 tablespoons finely chopped
    green onions
¾ cup water

● **Combine** first 4 ingredients in a large bowl; cut in butter with pastry blender until mixture is crumbly.
● **Stir** in Parmesan cheese and green onions. Add water, stirring with a fork until dry ingredients are moistened.
● **Turn** biscuit dough out onto a lightly floured surface, and knead lightly 5 or 6 times.
● **Roll** to ½-inch thickness; cut with a 3-inch round cutter. Place on a lightly greased baking sheet.

● **Bake** at 400° for 15 minutes or until biscuits are lightly browned. **Yield:** 8 biscuits.

Charlotte Pierce Bryant
Greensburg, Kentucky

BUTTERMILK BISCUITS WITH VIRGINIA HAM

4 cups all-purpose flour
2 tablespoons Single-Acting
    Baking Powder
1½ teaspoons salt
½ cup lard, chilled and cut up
1½ cups buttermilk
Unsalted butter, softened
½ pound cooked Virginia country
    ham, thinly sliced

● **Combine** first 3 ingredients in a large bowl; cut in lard with pastry blender until mixture is crumbly. Add buttermilk, stirring just until dry ingredients are moistened.
● **Turn** dough out onto a lightly floured surface; knead 3 or 4 times.
● **Roll** dough to ½-inch thickness; cut into 18 rounds with a 2½-inch round cutter, and place on an ungreased baking sheet.
● **Bake** at 500° for 8 to 10 minutes or until lightly browned. Split and spread with butter; serve with ham. **Yield:** 1½ dozen.

Single-Acting Baking Powder

QUICK!

This baking powder releases its gases when moistened, making it different from the more popular and readily available double-acting variety, which releases some gases when wet and the rest when it's heated.

¼ cup cream of tartar
3 tablespoons cornstarch
2 tablespoons baking soda

● **Combine** all ingredients in a jar; cover tightly, and shake vigorously. Store mixture at room temperature up to 1 month. **Yield:** ½ cup.

Chefs Edna Lewis and Scott Peacock
Atlanta, Georgia

COUNTRY HAM WITH GRITS STUFFING

1 (6-pound) country ham half, bone removed
4 cups unbaked Grits Stuffing
2 cups apple cider

• **Soak** ham in water to cover 24 hours; drain and pat dry. Remove center portion of ham with a sharp knife, leaving a 1½-inch border. Reserve center portion for another use or chop and substitute for oysters in stuffing, if desired.
• **Spoon** 4 cups unbaked Grits Stuffing into ham cavity; tie ham at 1-inch intervals with heavy string. Wrap ham in cheesecloth, and place, small end down, in large roasting pan. Add cider to pan. Spoon remaining stuffing into a greased shallow 2-quart baking dish; set aside.
• **Bake** ham at 325° for 1 hour, basting every 20 minutes with pan drippings; place dish of stuffing into oven, and bake ham and stuffing 30 minutes or until stuffing is lightly browned and a meat thermometer inserted in thickest portion of ham registers 140°. Remove dish of stuffing, and keep warm.
• **Remove** cheesecloth from ham, and return ham to roasting pan; baste ham with pan drippings.
• **Broil** 8 inches from heat (with electric oven door partially opened) until browned. Serve with baked stuffing. **Yield:** 12 servings.

Grits Stuffing

QUICK!

If you don't care for oysters, try this stuffing without them. Also, you can use fresh oysters if the smoked flavor is too strong for your taste.

3 cups water
1½ teaspoons salt
¼ teaspoon ground red pepper
½ cup butter or margarine
1 cup regular grits, uncooked
1 pound smoked or fresh oysters, drained (optional)
½ cup grated Parmesan cheese
1 red bell pepper, diced
1 bunch green onions, chopped
3 large eggs, lightly beaten
1 cup fine, dry breadcrumbs

• **Bring** first 4 ingredients to a boil in a large saucepan. Stir in grits; return to a boil. Cover, reduce heat, and simmer 10 minutes or until grits are cooked and liquid is absorbed, stirring occasionally. Remove from heat; cool. Stir in oysters, if desired.
• **Combine** Parmesan cheese and remaining 4 ingredients; stir into grits. **Yield:** about 12 cups.

Note: You can bake Grits Stuffing in a greased 3-quart baking dish at 325° for 45 minutes.

John Fleer
The Inn at Blackberry Farm
Walland, Tennessee

BAKED BURGUNDY HAM

1 (6- to 8-pound) smoked fully cooked ham half, well trimmed
6 cups water
2 cups cranberry juice cocktail, divided
2 cups dry red wine, divided
2 cups firmly packed dark brown sugar, divided
2 (3-inch) sticks cinnamon
1 tablespoon whole cloves

• **Place** ham in a large Dutch oven. Add water, 1 cup cranberry juice cocktail, 1 cup wine, 1 cup brown sugar, cinnamon sticks, and cloves.
• **Bring** to a boil; cover, reduce heat, and simmer 20 minutes. Cool.
• **Remove** ham and marinade from Dutch oven, and place in a large nonmetallic bowl. Cover and chill 8 hours, turning once.
• **Remove** ham from marinade; reserve 2 cups marinade. Discard remaining marinade.
• **Place** ham in a lightly greased shallow roasting pan; cover.
• **Bake** at 325° for 1½ hours, basting ham occasionally with reserved marinade. Uncover and bake 15 additional minutes or until meat thermometer registers 140°, basting ham occasionally with pan juices. Remove ham, reserving pan juices.
• **Combine** pan juices, remaining 1 cup cranberry juice, 1 cup wine, and 1 cup brown sugar in a saucepan. Bring to a boil; reduce heat, and cook 20 minutes. Serve with ham. **Yield:** 12 to 14 servings.

PEACHY GLAZED HAM

QUICK!

1 (16-ounce) can sliced peaches in light syrup, undrained
2 tablespoons dark brown sugar
2 to 3 teaspoons Dijon mustard
1 (1-pound) center-cut ham slice
⅓ cup sliced green onions

• **Drain** peaches, and reserve ½ cup syrup in a large skillet; set peaches aside.
• **Add** sugar and mustard to skillet; bring to a boil over medium-high heat. Cook 2 minutes or until mixture is slightly reduced.
• **Add** ham, and cook 2 minutes on each side. Add peaches and green onions; cover and cook over low heat 3 minutes or until peaches are thoroughly heated. **Yield:** 3 to 4 servings.

Robin Creed
Glade Valley, North Carolina

PRALINE HAM

QUICK!

⅓ cup chopped pecans
2 (½-inch-thick) ham slices (about 2½ pounds)
½ cup maple syrup
3 tablespoons sugar
2 teaspoons butter or margarine

• **Place** pecans in a shallow pan, and bake at 325° for 5 to 10 minutes or until toasted, stirring occasionally; set aside.
• **Bake** ham slices in a shallow pan at 325° for 10 minutes.
• **Bring** syrup, sugar, and butter to a boil in a small saucepan, stirring often. Stir in pecans, and spoon over ham.
• **Bake** 30 additional minutes. **Yield:** 4 servings.

Nancy Woodall
Bellaire, Texas

EASY GRILLED HAM

QUICK!

1 (2-inch-thick) boneless fully
　　cooked ham steak
½ cup ginger ale
½ cup orange juice
¼ cup firmly packed brown
　　sugar
1 tablespoon vegetable oil
1½ teaspoons white vinegar
1 teaspoon dry mustard
¼ teaspoon ground ginger
⅛ teaspoon ground cloves

● **Place** ham steak in a large shallow
dish or heavy-duty, zip-top plastic bag.
● **Combine** ginger ale and remaining 7
ingredients, stirring until sugar dissolves; pour over ham steak. Cover or
seal, and chill 8 hours, turning ham
steak occasionally.
● **Drain** ham steak, discarding marinade. Cook, covered with grill lid, over
medium-hot coals (350° to 400°) 15 minutes on each side or until a meat thermometer registers 140°. **Yield:** 10 to 12
servings.

Judy Grimes
Brandon, Mississippi

MUSHROOM-CRUSTED VENISON LOIN

1 (3½-ounce) package fresh
　　shiitake mushrooms
1 (8-ounce) package fresh crimini
　　mushrooms
¼ cup olive oil
1 teaspoon sea or table salt
½ teaspoon pepper
1 pound skinned and boned
　　chicken breast halves
¼ cup loosely packed fresh
　　parsley leaves
¼ cup loosely packed fresh chervil
　　leaves
1 (20-ounce) boneless venison
　　loin *
Garnishes: grilled purple onion
　　strips, asparagus spears, red
　　bell pepper strips

● **Wash** mushrooms thoroughly; remove
and discard shiitake stems.

● **Place** oil in a large skillet; add mushrooms, salt, and pepper. Cover and cook
over medium heat until mushrooms are
tender. Drain and set aside.
● **Position** knife blade in food processor bowl; add chicken, and process until
finely chopped, stopping occasionally to
scrape down sides. Add mushrooms,
parsley, and chervil; process until mixture is thoroughly blended, stopping occasionally to scrape down sides.
● **Cut** two sheets of heavy-duty plastic
wrap long enough to fit around venison
loin. Place chicken mixture on one
sheet, and top with remaining sheet.
Roll mixture to about ¼-inch thickness,
covering entire sheet. Remove top layer
of plastic wrap.
● **Place** venison in center of chicken
mixture. Using plastic wrap to lift
chicken mixture, cover entire venison
with chicken mixture; remove plastic
wrap, and place venison, seam side
down, on a greased baking sheet.
● **Bake** at 350° until a meat thermometer inserted in thickest portion registers
150° (medium-rare) or 160° (medium).
Let stand 10 minutes before slicing. Garnish, if desired. **Yield:** 8 servings.

✱ Substitute 1 (20-ounce) beef tenderloin, trimmed, for venison loin. Bake as
directed.

Chef David Everett
Dining Room at Ford's Colony
Williamsburg, Virginia

GRILLED VENISON ROAST

8½ pounds bone-in venison
　　saddle, trimmed
2 cloves garlic, halved
½ cup Worcestershire sauce
2 tablespoons soy sauce
2 teaspoons garlic powder
2 teaspoons lemon-pepper
　　seasoning
Hickory chips
Juniper Sauce
Garnishes: fresh bay leaves,
　　kumquats

● **Place** venison in a roasting pan. Cut 4
slits in venison, and insert garlic halves.

● **Combine** Worcestershire sauce and
soy sauce, and pour over venison in
pan; sprinkle all sides with garlic powder and lemon-pepper seasoning. Cover
and chill 2 hours.
● **Soak** hickory chips in water 30 minutes. Prepare charcoal fire on sides of
grill around a drip pan; let burn 30 minutes. Place venison on grill rack over
pan. Cook, covered with grill lid, over
low coals (under 300°) 3 hours or until
meat thermometer inserted in thickest
portion of meat registers 160° or to
desired degree of doneness. Carefully
remove drip pan, and reserve 2 tablespoons drippings to use in Juniper
Sauce. Serve venison with Juniper
Sauce, and garnish, if desired. **Yield:** 12
servings.

Juniper Sauce

4 (14½-ounce) cans chicken broth
1 (10-ounce) jar red currant jelly
½ cup bourbon
2 tablespoons dried juniper
　　berries, coarsely crushed ✱
2 tablespoons black peppercorns
¼ teaspoon dried thyme
2 tablespoons reserved pan
　　drippings

● **Combine** first 6 ingredients in a
saucepan; bring to a boil. Reduce heat,
and simmer, uncovered, 1 hour or until
liquid is reduced to 4 cups.
● **Pour** mixture through a large wiremesh strainer into a 4-cup liquid measuring cup, discarding seeds. Stir in 2
tablespoons reserved pan drippings.
Yield: 4 cups.

✱ Substitute 1 tablespoon gin for juniper berries.

Molly Griffin
Natchez, Mississippi

GAME POT PIE WITH PARMESAN CRUST

This hearty three-meat stew works just as well out of the crust and spooned over hot biscuits or cornbread.

4 cloves garlic, minced
1 small shallot, minced
¼ cup olive oil
1 pound boneless venison, cut into 1-inch pieces
1 pound boneless rabbit, cut into 1-inch pieces
1 pound boneless duck breasts, cut into 1-inch pieces
1 cup dry red wine
1 cup crème de cassis or other black currant-flavored liqueur
½ cup dried apricot halves, chopped
¼ teaspoon salt
¼ teaspoon pepper
1 bay leaf
4 cups Venison Stock (see recipe on page 378)
1 small turnip, peeled and chopped
1 medium carrot, scraped and chopped
1 cup chopped rutabaga
1 cup pearl onions, peeled
1 medium-size red potato, cut into ½-inch cubes
½ cup fresh shiitake mushrooms, sliced (3 whole)
1 (15½-ounce) can white beans, rinsed and drained
1½ teaspoons fresh thyme leaves
1½ teaspoons chopped fresh chives
1½ teaspoons chopped fresh parsley
Whipped Celery Potatoes (see recipe on page 398)
Parmesan Crust

• **Cook** garlic and shallot in olive oil in a large Dutch oven over medium-high heat, stirring constantly, until tender.
• **Add** venison, rabbit, and duck; cook, stirring constantly, until meat is browned. Stir in wine and next 5 ingredients. Bring mixture to a boil; reduce heat, and simmer 30 minutes.

• **Stir** in Venison Stock and next 6 ingredients. Bring to a boil; reduce heat, and simmer 30 minutes or until vegetables are tender. Add beans and next 3 ingredients; cook until mixture is thoroughly heated. Remove and discard bay leaf.
• **Ladle** into bowls. Pipe or dollop Whipped Celery Potatoes into 4 rosettes evenly spaced around rim of each bowl. Top each with Parmesan Crust. **Yield:** 8 servings.

Parmesan Crust

12 sheets frozen phyllo pastry, thawed
½ cup butter or margarine, melted
¾ cup grated Parmesan cheese

• **Place** 1 sheet of pastry on a large cutting board, keeping remaining pastry covered with a slightly damp towel until ready to use. Brush pastry sheet with butter, and sprinkle with 1 tablespoon Parmesan cheese. Repeat procedure 2 times, layering pastry, butter, and cheese.
• **Cut** 2 (6- to 8-inch) circles from stacked pastry, and place on a lightly greased baking sheet. Lightly grease bottom of a second baking sheet, and place on top of pastry circles to keep phyllo flat during baking.
• **Bake** at 350° for 10 minutes or until golden. Cool crusts on baking sheet on a wire rack.
• **Repeat** procedure 3 times, using remaining pastry, butter, and cheese. **Yield:** 8 crusts.

Chef David Everett
Dining Room at Ford's Colony
Williamsburg, Virginia

SANTA FE SPANISH RABBIT

A rich tomato sauce tenderizes and flavors extra-lean rabbit. Bill serves this game dish with black beans and rice.

¼ cup all-purpose flour
¼ teaspoon freshly ground pepper
1 (3-pound) rabbit, cleaned and cut into pieces
2 to 4 tablespoons olive oil
1 small onion, chopped
1 stalk celery, chopped
2 cloves garlic, minced
1 cup dry white wine
1 (10¾-ounce) can condensed beef broth, undiluted
4 medium tomatoes, coarsely chopped
⅓ cup ripe olives, cut in half
⅓ cup green olives, cut in half
1 to 2 tablespoons chopped fresh oregano
Garnish: roasted red bell pepper slices

• **Combine** flour and ground pepper in a large, heavy-duty, zip-top plastic bag; add rabbit, shaking to coat.
• **Brown** rabbit in olive oil in a large Dutch oven over medium-high heat; remove rabbit, reserving drippings in Dutch oven.
• **Cook** onion, celery, and garlic in drippings over medium heat, stirring constantly, 3 minutes or until tender. Add wine, and simmer until liquid is reduced by half (about 15 minutes).
• **Stir** in beef broth; bring to a boil. Reduce heat; add rabbit, tomato, olives, and oregano.
• **Simmer**, stirring occasionally, 30 minutes or until rabbit is tender. (For a thicker sauce, remove rabbit, and keep warm. Continue simmering sauce until thickened.) Garnish, if desired. **Yield:** 4 servings.

Bill Hall
Nashville, Tennessee

At right: *Late-Night Pasta Chez Frank* (page 223)

PASTA, GRAINS, AND RICE

TOMATO-GARLIC PASTA

QUICK!

12 ounces angel hair pasta,
      uncooked
20 cloves garlic, coarsely
      chopped
2 tablespoons olive oil
3 large tomatoes, peeled, seeded,
      and diced
¼ cup fresh basil, cut into ¼-inch
      strips
½ cup dry white wine
3 to 4 tablespoons balsamic
      vinegar
1 teaspoon pepper
1 cup grated Parmesan or Romano
      cheese

• **Cook** pasta according to package directions; drain. Keep warm.
• **Cook** garlic in olive oil in a large skillet over medium-high heat until lightly browned; add tomato and next 4 ingredients. Cook until thoroughly heated.
• **Spoon** tomato mixture over pasta; sprinkle with cheese. Serve immediately. **Yield:** 4 main-dish servings or 6 side-dish servings.

Caroline Wallace Kennedy
Newborn, Georgia

CREAMY FETTUCCINE
(pictured on page 181)

QUICK!

6 ounces fettuccine, uncooked
¼ cup butter or margarine
2 tablespoons all-purpose flour
½ cup half-and-half
½ cup water
½ cup freshly grated Parmesan
      cheese
2 teaspoons dried parsley flakes
½ teaspoon coarsely ground
      pepper
½ teaspoon garlic powder
½ teaspoon poppy seeds
¼ teaspoon salt

• **Cook** fettuccine according to package directions, omitting salt; drain and set aside.
• **Melt** butter in a heavy saucepan over low heat; add flour, stirring until

smooth. Cook 1 minute, stirring constantly. Gradually add half-and-half and water; cook over medium heat, stirring constantly, until mixture is thickened and bubbly. Stir in Parmesan cheese and remaining 5 ingredients. Toss with fettuccine. Serve immediately. **Yield:** 2 servings.

Lynne Teal Weeks
Columbus, Georgia

SPINACH FETTUCCINE
WITH MUSTARD GREENS

1½ pounds fresh mustard greens
10 ounces spinach fettuccine,
      uncooked *
1 cup whipping cream
4 ounces goat cheese
¼ teaspoon salt
½ teaspoon freshly ground pepper
2 tablespoons butter or margarine
2 cloves garlic, minced
¼ cup water
½ cup coarsely chopped walnuts,
      toasted

• **Remove** and discard stems and any discolored spots from greens. Wash greens thoroughly, and drain. Cut into 1-inch strips; set aside.
• **Cook** fettuccine according to package directions; drain and set aside.
• **Bring** whipping cream to a boil in a heavy saucepan; boil until cream is reduced to ¾ cup. Remove from heat; add goat cheese, salt, and pepper, stirring with a wire whisk until smooth. Set aside.
• **Melt** butter in a large heavy skillet over medium heat; add garlic, and cook 1 minute. Gradually add greens, stirring after each addition until leaves wilt. Add water; cover and cook 10 minutes or until tender, stirring occasionally. Drain.
• **Return** greens to skillet; add cream mixture. Cook over medium heat, stirring constantly, 1 minute or until thoroughly heated.
• **Combine** greens mixture, fettuccine, and walnuts; toss gently. Serve immediately. **Yield:** 3 to 4 main-dish servings or 6 to 8 side-dish servings.

*Substitute spaghetti for fettuccine.

PASTA WITH GREENS

QUICK!

Toasted pine nuts add satisfying crunch to this meatless entrée.

1 (8-ounce) package fettuccine
1 (16-ounce) package frozen
      collards or other greens
2 to 3 cloves garlic, minced
3 tablespoons olive oil
½ teaspoon salt
¼ teaspoon freshly ground pepper
½ cup freshly grated Parmesan
      cheese
⅓ cup pine nuts, toasted
Garnishes: freshly grated Parmesan
      cheese, toasted pine nuts

• **Cook** pasta according to package directions; drain and set aside.
• **Cook** greens according to package directions; drain and set aside.
• **Cook** garlic in olive oil in a large skillet over medium-high heat until tender, but not brown. Add greens, salt, and pepper; cook until heated.
• **Combine** pasta, greens, ½ cup Parmesan cheese, and ⅓ cup pine nuts in a large serving bowl. Garnish, if desired. **Yield:** 2 main-dish servings or 4 side-dish servings.

Melinda Clement
Kingsville, Texas

PARTY PASTA WITH PROSCIUTTO

QUICK!

½ cup butter or margarine,
      divided
2 cups thin prosciutto strips
      (about ⅓ pound) *
1 (12-ounce) package spinach
      fettuccine
1½ cups whipping cream
½ cup freshly grated Parmesan
      cheese
1 (14-ounce) can artichoke hearts,
      drained and halved
½ cup chopped fresh or frozen
      chives, divided

• **Melt** ¼ cup butter in a skillet. Add prosciutto, and cook over medium heat until browned, stirring often; drain.

- **Cook** pasta according to package directions; drain.
- **Melt** remaining ¼ cup butter in a Dutch oven over medium heat. Add pasta, whipping cream, cheese, artichoke hearts, and ¼ cup chives; toss gently. Arrange on a serving platter.
- **Sprinkle** with prosciutto and remaining ¼ cup chives. Serve immediately. **Yield:** 6 servings.

✳ If prosciutto isn't available, substitute cooked, crumbled bacon, and reduce butter to ¼ cup.

Thru the Grapevine
Junior League of Greater Elmira-Corning,
New York

CAJUN CHICKEN FETTUCCINE

1 (10-ounce) package tomato-basil
    fettuccine
1 teaspoon Cajun seasoning
½ teaspoon cracked pepper
4 skinned and boned chicken
    breast halves
1 cup water
½ teaspoon salt
1 pound broccoli, cut into
    flowerets
¼ cup butter or margarine
1 clove garlic, minced
1 tablespoon cornstarch
1½ tablespoons cold water
2 cups half-and-half
¼ teaspoon salt
¼ teaspoon ground red pepper
¼ teaspoon ground black
    pepper
⅓ cup freshly grated Parmesan
    cheese
Grated Parmesan cheese
    (optional)

- **Cook** pasta according to package directions; drain and keep warm.
- **Sprinkle** Cajun seasoning and cracked pepper over chicken; place chicken in a lightly greased 13- x 9- x 2-inch pan.
- **Bake** at 350° for 15 to 20 minutes or until done; cool slightly. Cut chicken crosswise into thin strips.
- **Combine** 1 cup water and ½ teaspoon salt in a large skillet; bring to a boil. Add broccoli; cover and cook 3 to 4 minutes or until crisp-tender. Drain.
- **Melt** butter in skillet; add minced garlic, and cook 2 minutes, stirring often. Set aside 1 cup broccoli flowerets; add remaining broccoli flowerets to garlic in skillet, and cook 2 minutes.
- **Combine** cornstarch and 1½ tablespoons water, stirring until smooth; stir in half-and-half. Gradually add cornstarch mixture to broccoli mixture.
- **Bring** to a boil over medium heat, stirring constantly. Boil 1 minute, stirring constantly. Add ¼ teaspoon salt, red pepper, black pepper, and ⅓ cup Parmesan cheese, stirring until cheese melts. Spoon over pasta; top with remaining 1 cup broccoli. Sprinkle with additional Parmesan cheese, if desired. Serve immediately. **Yield:** 4 servings.

Jill Ann Kelley
Essex, Missouri

CRAWFISH FETTUCCINE

If you prefer, you can use shrimp instead of crawfish in this recipe.

2 pounds crawfish meat
2 teaspoons Cajun seasoning
1 (12-ounce) package fettuccine
2 (½-ounce) envelopes butter-
    flavored granules
1 teaspoon chicken-flavored
    bouillon granules
¾ cup water
2 medium onions, chopped
1 green bell pepper, chopped
3 cloves garlic, pressed
½ teaspoon dried basil
½ teaspoon dried thyme
1 tablespoon cornstarch
1 (12-ounce) can evaporated
    skimmed milk
½ (16-ounce) loaf reduced-fat
    process cheese spread, cubed
¼ cup chopped fresh parsley
3 tablespoons freshly grated
    Parmesan cheese
Garnish: chopped fresh parsley

- **Combine** crawfish and Cajun seasoning; cover and chill 30 minutes.
- **Cook** pasta according to package directions; drain and keep warm.
- **Combine** butter granules, bouillon granules, and water in a large deep skillet or Dutch oven; cook over medium heat until granules dissolve.
- **Add** onion, bell pepper, and garlic; cook over medium-high heat, stirring constantly, 10 minutes or until tender. Stir in crawfish mixture, basil, and thyme; cook 5 minutes.
- **Combine** cornstarch and evaporated milk, stirring well; stir into crawfish mixture. Add cheese spread, stirring well. Bring to a boil over medium heat; boil 1 minute, stirring constantly.
- **Stir** in pasta and ¼ cup chopped parsley. Serve immediately; sprinkle servings evenly with Parmesan cheese. Garnish, if desired. **Yield:** 8 servings.

Holli Cramm
Tomball, Texas

❤ Per serving: Calories 400
Fat 5.9g   Cholesterol 171mg
Sodium 844mg

FETTUCCINE WITH
SHRIMP AND TOMATOES

QUICK!

1½ pounds unpeeled medium-size
    fresh shrimp
8 ounces fettuccine, uncooked
2 (14.5-ounce) cans diced
    tomatoes, undrained
1 teaspoon dried basil
3 cloves garlic, minced
2 tablespoons minced shallot
½ teaspoon freshly ground pepper
¼ teaspoon salt
¼ cup olive oil
Freshly grated Romano cheese

- **Peel** shrimp, and devein, if desired.
- **Cook** pasta according to package directions; drain and keep warm.
- **Drain** diced tomato, reserving ¼ cup liquid.
- **Cook** shrimp, tomato, reserved liquid, basil, and next 4 ingredients in oil in a large skillet 5 to 7 minutes or until shrimp turn pink, stirring often. Spoon over pasta; sprinkle with cheese. Serve immediately. **Yield:** 4 servings.

Gail B. Weller
St. Louis, Missouri

BOURBON-PECAN ALFREDO

QUICK!

6 ounces linguine, uncooked
2 tablespoons butter or margarine
3 cloves garlic, minced
¾ cup bourbon, divided
1 cup whipping cream
1 cup freshly grated Parmesan
   cheese
½ cup pecan pieces, toasted
2 tablespoons chopped parsley

• **Cook** linguine according to package directions; drain and keep warm.
• **Melt** butter in a skillet over medium-high heat; add garlic, and cook, stirring constantly, until tender.
• **Add** ½ cup bourbon, and cook 3 to 5 minutes, stirring constantly. Stir in whipping cream and cheese. Cook over low heat, stirring constantly, until cheese melts. Gradually stir in remaining ¼ cup bourbon; stir in pecans and parsley. Pour over pasta; toss. Serve immediately. **Yield:** 2 main-dish servings or 4 side-dish servings.

Megen McCully
Knoxville, Tennessee

LINGUINE WITH
RED PEPPER SAUCE

8 ounces linguine, uncooked
Vegetable cooking spray
2 tablespoons olive oil
6 cups chopped red bell pepper
3 cloves garlic, crushed
½ cup balsamic vinegar or red
   wine vinegar
⅔ cup chopped fresh basil
½ teaspoon salt
¼ teaspoon pepper

• **Cook** linguine according to package directions, omitting salt or fat; drain and keep warm.
• **Coat** a nonstick skillet with cooking spray; add olive oil, red bell pepper, and garlic. Cook over low heat 30 minutes, stirring occasionally.
• **Place** mixture in container of an electric blender or food processor. Add vinegar and remaining 3 ingredients to container; process until smooth,

stopping once to scrape down sides. Spoon over linguine. Serve immediately. **Yield:** 4 servings.

♥ Per serving: Calories 337
Fat 8.9g   Cholesterol 0mg
Sodium 304mg

PESTO PRIMAVERA

Ruth captures the season's freshness with this vegetable-packed dish.

3 quarts water
1 cup sliced carrot
1 cup dried tomatoes, cut into
   fourths
1 (16-ounce) package linguine
2 yellow squash, cut into thin
   strips
1 red bell pepper, cut into thin
   strips
⅓ cup Ruth's Pesto
Toasted pine nuts

• **Bring** water to a boil in a large Dutch oven; add carrot, tomato, and linguine; cook 8 minutes.
• **Add** squash and bell pepper; cook 2 minutes. Drain well, and stir in ⅓ cup Ruth's Pesto. Sprinkle with pine nuts; serve immediately. **Yield:** 8 servings.

Ruth's Pesto

QUICK!

4 cups loosely packed fresh basil
   leaves
1½ cups olive oil
1 cup freshly grated Parmesan
   cheese
½ cup pine nuts, toasted
3 cloves garlic
¼ teaspoon pepper

• **Combine** all ingredients in container of an electric blender or food processor; process until smooth, stopping once to scrape down sides. **Yield:** 2 cups.

Note: Freeze pesto in 2-tablespoon portions in sections of ice cube trays. Allow 1 cube per 2 ounces pasta.

Ruth Davidon
Arlington, Virginia

TRAVELING LINGUINE WITH
ROASTED VEGETABLES
(pictured at right)

Although this pasta recipe was designed to cook over a campfire while "roughing it," you're sure to enjoy it equally as much when prepared in the comfort of your own kitchen.

2 yellow squash, cut into
   chunks
2 zucchini, cut into chunks
1 purple onion, quartered
1 small eggplant, unpeeled and
   cut into chunks
1 red bell pepper, quartered
⅓ cup butter or margarine
2 to 3 teaspoons dried Italian
   seasoning
½ teaspoon pepper
2 teaspoons chicken-flavored
   bouillon granules
2 quarts water
8 ounces linguine, uncooked
¼ cup grated Parmesan cheese

• **Place** first 5 ingredients on a lightly greased 24- x 18-inch piece of heavy-duty aluminum foil; dot with butter, and sprinkle with Italian seasoning and pepper. Seal securely.
• **Cook** over hot coals (400° to 500°) 20 to 30 minutes or until vegetables are tender. Remove from heat, and keep sealed.
• **Combine** bouillon granules and 2 quarts water in a stockpot; cover and place in hot coals. Bring to a boil; add linguine, and cook until tender. Drain. Top with vegetables; sprinkle with cheese. **Yield:** 2 to 3 servings.

C. M. Rodes
Louisville, Kentucky

*Traveling Linguine With
Roasted Vegetables*

ARTICHOKE AND SHRIMP LINGUINE

QUICK!

8 ounces linguine, uncooked
1 pound unpeeled medium-size
    fresh shrimp
¼ cup olive oil
3 cloves garlic, minced
½ teaspoon dried crushed red
    pepper
1 (14-ounce) can artichoke hearts,
    drained and quartered
½ cup ripe olives, sliced
¼ cup fresh lemon juice
⅛ teaspoon salt
⅛ teaspoon pepper
½ cup grated Parmesan cheese

• **Cook** linguine according to package directions; drain and keep warm.
• **Peel** shrimp, and devein, if desired.
• **Heat** oil in a skillet over medium-high heat; add shrimp, garlic, and red pepper, and cook, stirring constantly, 5 minutes or until shrimp turn pink.
• **Stir** in artichoke hearts and next 4 ingredients. Add to pasta, and sprinkle with cheese. **Yield:** 3 to 4 servings.

Ann Winniford
Dallas, Texas

SAUTÉED SHRIMP AND PASTA

8 ounces linguine, uncooked
2 pounds unpeeled medium-size
    fresh shrimp
1 small onion, chopped
2 cloves garlic, minced
1 tablespoon hot sesame oil
6 plum tomatoes, peeled and
    chopped
1 teaspoon dried oregano
½ teaspoon salt
½ teaspoon dried basil
½ teaspoon freshly ground
    pepper
¼ cup chopped fresh parsley
¼ cup kalamata olives, sliced
¼ cup lemon juice
2 ounces crumbled feta cheese

• **Cook** linguine according to package directions; drain and keep warm.

• **Peel** shrimp, and devein, if desired.
• **Cook** onion and garlic in oil in a large skillet until tender, stirring often. Stir in tomato and next 4 ingredients; cook 3 minutes, stirring constantly. Add shrimp, and cook 3 minutes or until shrimp turn pink, stirring occasionally.
• **Stir** in parsley, olives, and lemon juice; cook just until thoroughly heated. Serve over linguine; sprinkle with cheese. **Yield:** 4 servings.

Carol Barclay
Portland, Texas

❤ Per serving: Calories 449
Fat 10.6g   Cholesterol 185mg
Sodium 708mg

PASTA WITH PEANUT SAUCE

QUICK!

Be sure to use dark sesame oil in this recipe. It has a more intense sesame taste than light sesame oil, and it stands up well to the peanut and pepper flavor accents of this pasta dish.

8 ounces spaghetti, uncooked
12 green onions
3 yellow squash
1 red bell pepper
1 tablespoon dark sesame oil
1 tablespoon minced garlic
¼ cup creamy peanut butter
¼ cup reduced-sodium soy
    sauce
3 tablespoons lime juice
1 tablespoon sugar
1 teaspoon dried crushed red
    pepper

• **Cook** spaghetti according to package directions, omitting salt and fat; drain and keep warm.
• **Cut** white portion of green onions into 2-inch pieces; reserve green tops for another use. Cut squash in half lengthwise; cut halves into slices. Remove and discard seeds from red pepper, and cut red pepper into thin strips.
• **Cook** vegetables in a saucepan in boiling water to cover 3 minutes; drain vegetables, and set aside.

• **Pour** oil into a large skillet; place over medium heat until hot. Add garlic; cook 1 minute, stirring constantly. Add peanut butter, stirring until smooth. Stir in soy sauce and next 3 ingredients.
• **Add** vegetables to skillet, and toss gently to coat; remove vegetables from skillet with a slotted spoon.
• **Add** spaghetti to sauce in skillet, tossing to coat; transfer to a serving platter, and top with vegetables. Serve immediately. **Yield:** 4 servings.

Bruce Messer
Middlesboro, Kentucky

❤ Per serving: Calories 400
Fat 13g   Cholesterol 0mg
Sodium 577mg

LEMON-GARLIC PASTA

QUICK!

2 tablespoons butter or
    margarine
2 tablespoons olive oil
4 to 5 cloves garlic, minced
¼ cup lemon juice
¼ teaspoon salt
½ to 1 teaspoon pepper
8 ounces thin spaghetti, cooked
⅓ cup chopped fresh parsley

• **Melt** butter in a large skillet over medium-high heat; add olive oil and minced garlic. Cook 1 minute, stirring constantly. Add lemon juice, salt, and pepper.
• **Bring** to a boil; pour mixture over pasta. Add parsley; toss gently. Serve immediately. **Yield:** 4 servings.

Nina Page Winkler
Orlando, Florida

LATE-NIGHT PASTA CHEZ FRANK
(pictured on page 217)

6 cloves garlic, pressed
2 tablespoons olive oil
4 jalapeño peppers or other chile
   peppers, seeded and minced
8 plum tomatoes, chopped
½ teaspoon salt
⅓ to ½ cup chopped fresh basil
1 (8-ounce) package spaghettini
   or vermicelli, cooked
Freshly grated Parmesan
   cheese
Garnish: fresh basil sprigs

• **Cook** garlic in oil in a large nonstick skillet over medium heat, stirring constantly, 1 to 2 minutes or until golden. Add pepper, and cook 1 minute, stirring constantly.
• **Add** tomato and salt; cook 3 minutes or until thoroughly heated. Stir in chopped basil. Serve immediately over pasta, and sprinkle with Parmesan cheese. Garnish, if desired. **Yield:** 2 to 3 servings.

Chef Frank Stitt
Highlands Bar & Grill
Birmingham, Alabama

CHICKEN-VEGETABLE SPAGHETTI

4 skinned and boned chicken
   breast halves, cut into 2-inch
   strips
2 tablespoons olive oil
3 medium zucchini, cut in half
   lengthwise and sliced (about
   1 pound)
1 large green bell pepper, coarsely
   chopped
½ pound fresh mushrooms,
   sliced
¼ cup chopped onion
1 clove garlic, minced
1 (30-ounce) jar spaghetti
   sauce
2 cups (8 ounces) shredded
   mozzarella cheese, divided
12 ounces spaghetti, uncooked
2 tablespoons chopped fresh
   parsley

• **Cook** chicken in oil in a large skillet over medium-high heat, stirring constantly, until no longer pink. Drain and set aside, reserving 1 tablespoon drippings in skillet.
• **Add** zucchini and next 4 ingredients to skillet; cook over medium heat, stirring constantly, until crisp-tender.
• **Stir** in chicken and spaghetti sauce; cook until thoroughly heated, stirring occasionally. Stir in 1 cup cheese; cook until cheese melts, stirring often.
• **Cook** spaghetti according to package directions; drain. Arrange on a large platter; top with sauce mixture, and sprinkle with remaining 1 cup cheese and parsley. **Yield:** 4 to 6 servings.

Yvonne M. Greer
Mauldin, South Carolina

CASSEROLE SPAGHETTI

*As one parent stated during
taste testing of this recipe,
"Kids will vacuum up this recipe."*

1½ pounds ground chuck
1 green bell pepper, chopped
1 large onion, chopped
½ cup chopped celery
2 cloves garlic, crushed
1 (10¾-ounce) can cream of
   mushroom soup, undiluted
¾ cup water
1 (16-ounce) can tomatoes,
   undrained and chopped
2 tablespoons chili powder
½ teaspoon salt
¼ teaspoon pepper
1 (8-ounce) package spaghetti
2 ounces sharp Cheddar cheese,
   cut into ½-inch cubes
1 (5-ounce) jar pimiento-stuffed
   olives, drained
¾ cup (3 ounces) shredded sharp
   Cheddar cheese

• **Cook** first 5 ingredients in a Dutch oven, stirring until meat crumbles; drain well, and return meat mixture to Dutch oven.
• **Stir** in soup and next 5 ingredients.
• **Bring** to a boil over medium heat. Cover, reduce heat, and simmer 1 hour, stirring occasionally.
• **Cook** spaghetti according to package directions; drain.
• **Stir** spaghetti, cheese cubes, and olives into meat sauce. Spoon mixture into a lightly greased 11- x 7- x 1½-inch baking dish.
• **Cover** and bake at 325° for 20 minutes or until thoroughly heated. Sprinkle with ¾ cup shredded cheese, and bake, uncovered, 10 additional minutes. **Yield:** 6 to 8 servings.

Note: You can prepare Casserole Spaghetti ahead, omitting shredded cheese. Cover and chill 8 hours. Remove from refrigerator; let stand at room temperature 30 minutes. Cover and bake at 325° for 45 minutes or until thoroughly heated. Uncover and sprinkle with shredded cheese; bake 10 additional minutes.

QUICK CHICKEN AND PASTA
QUICK!

2 quarts water
½ teaspoon salt
4 ounces vermicelli, uncooked
¾ cup frozen English peas
⅓ cup Italian salad dressing
1 cup chopped cooked chicken
¼ teaspoon sweet red pepper
   flakes
2 tablespoons grated Parmesan
   cheese

• **Combine** water and salt in a large saucepan; bring to a boil. Add vermicelli and peas. Return to a boil; reduce heat, and cook 10 minutes. Drain and set aside.
• **Heat** salad dressing in saucepan. Add chopped chicken and red pepper flakes, and cook 2 minutes, stirring constantly. Add reserved pasta mixture, and cook until thoroughly heated. Sprinkle with Parmesan cheese, tossing mixture well. **Yield:** 2 servings.

Jennifer Shupe
Raleigh, North Carolina

Bow Ties, Black Beans,
and Key Limes

BOW TIES, BLACK BEANS, AND KEY LIMES
(pictured at left)

6 ounces bow tie pasta, uncooked
    (2½ cups)
4 cloves garlic, minced
2 tablespoons olive oil
⅓ cup fresh Key lime juice
¼ cup dry sherry
1 cup sliced green onions
½ pound plum tomatoes, peeled
    and chopped
1 (15-ounce) can black beans,
    rinsed and drained
½ teaspoon salt
¼ teaspoon freshly ground pepper
2 teaspoons grated Key lime rind
¼ cup chopped fresh flat-leaf
    parsley
Garnish: fresh flat-leaf parsley
    sprigs

• **Cook** pasta according to package directions; drain and keep warm.
• **Cook** garlic in oil in a skillet over medium-high heat, stirring constantly, 2 minutes or until tender. Add lime juice and sherry; cook over high heat 5 minutes or until reduced to ¼ cup.
• **Add** green onions and chopped tomato; cook over medium heat 5 to 8 minutes, stirring occasionally.
• **Stir** in beans and next 3 ingredients; pour over pasta, tossing to coat. Sprinkle with chopped parsley, and garnish, if desired. Serve immediately. **Yield:** 3 servings.

Mike Adams
Naples, Florida

PEPPERY PASTA

3 pounds ripe plum tomatoes,
    peeled and quartered
8 green onions, thinly sliced
8 cloves garlic, minced
1 tablespoon olive oil
2 small sweet banana peppers,
    thinly sliced
⅓ cup chopped fresh oregano or
    2 tablespoons dried oregano
¼ cup chopped fresh basil or 1½
    teaspoons dried basil
½ teaspoon sea or table salt
8 green onions, thinly sliced
3 yellow bell peppers, cut into thin
    strips
3 red or orange bell peppers, cut
    into thin strips
3 tablespoons chopped fresh or
    1 tablespoon dried oregano
1 tablespoon olive oil
10 to 12 crimini or button
    mushrooms, coarsely chopped
1 teaspoon sea or table salt
1 teaspoon dried crushed red
    pepper
1 (16-ounce) package mostaccioli
    pasta
8 ounces fontina or mozzarella
    cheese, shredded

• **Position** knife blade in food processor bowl; add one-third of tomato. Pulse 5 or 6 times or until finely chopped. Remove tomato from processor bowl, and set aside. Repeat procedure twice.
• **Cook** 8 green onions and garlic in 1 tablespoon olive oil in a large heavy saucepan, stirring constantly, 10 minutes or until tender.
• **Stir** in tomato, banana pepper, and next 3 ingredients.
• **Bring** mixture to a boil over medium heat, stirring constantly; reduce heat, and simmer, uncovered, 1 hour, stirring occasionally. Remove from heat; keep tomato mixture warm.
• **Cook** 8 green onions, bell pepper strips, and 3 tablespoons fresh oregano in 1 tablespoon olive oil in a large skillet over medium heat, stirring constantly, 12 to 15 minutes or until vegetables are crisp-tender. Add mushrooms, 1 teaspoon salt, and crushed red pepper; cook about 7 minutes or until mushrooms are tender, stirring often.

• **Cook** pasta according to package directions; drain and place on a large serving platter.
• **Pour** tomato mixture over pasta; spoon mushroom mixture over sauce, and sprinkle with shredded cheese. **Yield:** 8 servings.

Joelle Diorio
Orlando, Florida

ORZO PRIMAVERA
QUICK!

3 quarts water
1 teaspoon salt
2 cups orzo, uncooked
1 pound fresh asparagus, cut into
    1-inch pieces
3 cloves garlic, minced
½ cup chopped red bell pepper
1 tablespoon olive oil
1 teaspoon butter or margarine,
    melted
1 cup frozen English peas, thawed
½ cup chicken broth
1 teaspoon grated lemon rind
¼ teaspoon ground white pepper
½ cup freshly grated Parmesan
    cheese

• **Combine** water and salt in a large Dutch oven; bring to a boil. Add orzo, and cook 5 minutes. Add asparagus, and cook 4 minutes. Drain and set mixture aside in a large serving bowl.
• **Cook** garlic and red bell pepper in oil and butter in Dutch oven over medium heat, stirring constantly, 1 minute or until crisp-tender. Add peas; cook 1 minute, stirring constantly. Add chicken broth, lemon rind, and white pepper; bring to a boil, and cook 1 minute.
• **Add** vegetable mixture to orzo mixture, tossing well. Sprinkle with Parmesan cheese. Serve immediately. **Yield:** 6 to 8 servings.

Note: Orzo is a rice-shaped pasta.
Preserving Our Italian Heritage
Sons of Italy Florida Foundation of Tampa

PASTA POTPOURRI

QUICK!

4 ounces penne or rigatoni,
    uncooked
1 teaspoon sesame oil
1½ tablespoons olive oil
1½ tablespoons sesame oil
1 small purple onion, chopped
2 medium carrots, scraped and
    diagonally sliced
2 medium zucchini, halved
    lengthwise and sliced
2 cloves garlic, pressed
1½ teaspoons grated ginger
½ teaspoon dried crushed red
    pepper
2 tablespoons soy sauce
2 teaspoons rice wine vinegar
1 tablespoon freshly grated
    Parmesan cheese
2 teaspoons chopped fresh
    cilantro

• **Cook** pasta according to package directions; drain and toss with 1 teaspoon sesame oil. Set aside.
• **Pour** olive oil and 1½ tablespoons sesame oil around top of a preheated wok, coating sides; heat at medium-high (375°) 1 minute. Add onion and carrot; cook, stirring constantly, 2 minutes or until onion is tender.
• **Add** zucchini and next 3 ingredients; cook 1 minute, stirring constantly.
• **Stir** in cooked pasta, soy sauce, and vinegar; cook 1 minute or until thoroughly heated.
• **Transfer** to a serving dish; sprinkle with cheese and cilantro. **Yield:** 4 to 6 servings.

Note: To create a quick main dish, add leftover chopped cooked chicken, beef, or pork.

Nan Rasor
San Antonio, Texas

HOT BROWN PASTA CASSEROLES

QUICK!

8 ounces penne pasta, uncooked
    (2½ cups)
6 ounces sliced cooked ham, cut
    into ½-inch strips
6 ounces sliced smoked turkey,
    cut into ¼-inch strips
1 (10¾-ounce) can Cheddar
    cheese soup, undiluted
½ cup milk
¼ teaspoon pepper
8 slices tomato
8 slices bacon, cooked
¼ cup freshly grated Parmesan
    cheese

• **Cook** pasta according to package directions; drain. Combine pasta, ham, and turkey in a bowl.
• **Combine** soup, milk, and pepper; stir into pasta mixture. Spoon into four lightly greased individual baking dishes; top with tomato slices.
• **Bake** at 350° for 15 minutes. Top with bacon slices, sprinkle with cheese; bake 5 additional minutes or until thoroughly heated. Serve immediately. **Yield:** 4 servings.

Lillian Harris
Mayfield, Kentucky

BASIL-CHEESE PASTA

QUICK!

1 (12-ounce) package rotini
2 cloves garlic, minced
2 tablespoons olive oil
1 (3-ounce) package cream cheese,
    softened
½ cup cottage cheese
⅓ cup grated Parmesan cheese
½ cup dry white wine
½ cup chopped fresh basil

• **Cook** rotini according to package directions, and drain well. Set aside, and keep warm.
• **Cook** garlic in oil in a skillet over medium-high heat 1 minute, stirring constantly. Add cheeses; reduce heat and cook, stirring constantly, until blended.

• **Stir** in wine and basil; cook 3 minutes or until mixture is slightly thickened, stirring often. Spoon over rotini. **Yield:** 4 servings.

Betty Rabe
Plano, Texas

ZITI WITH SAUSAGE AND BROCCOLI

QUICK!

1 pound Italian link sausage
2 cloves garlic, crushed
½ teaspoon dried crushed red
    pepper
1 teaspoon olive oil
2 (14.5-ounce) cans diced
    tomatoes, undrained
8 ounces ziti pasta, uncooked
2 cups broccoli flowerets
½ cup freshly grated Romano or
    Parmesan cheese

• **Cut** sausage diagonally into ½-inch-thick slices. Cook sausage in a large nonstick skillet over medium-high heat until browned; remove sausage, and set aside. Wipe skillet with paper towels.
• **Cook** garlic and red pepper in oil in skillet, stirring constantly, until lightly browned; add tomatoes, and cook until thoroughly heated. Remove from heat; keep warm.
• **Cook** pasta according to package directions, adding broccoli during last 5 minutes of cooking time. Drain and toss gently with sausage mixture and cheese. Serve immediately. **Yield:** 3 servings.

Candace Reed
Dallas, Texas

SAUSAGE-STUFFED SHELLS

½ (12-ounce) package jumbo
    pasta shells (about 20)
1 pound mild Italian link
    sausage
1 large egg, lightly beaten
¾ cup Italian-seasoned
    breadcrumbs
1 (30-ounce) jar spaghetti
    sauce
¼ cup grated Parmesan cheese

- **Cook** pasta shells according to package directions; drain and set aside.
- **Remove** and discard casings from sausage. Brown sausage in a large skillet, stirring until it crumbles; drain.
- **Combine** sausage, egg, and breadcrumbs in skillet; set aside.
- **Spread** 1 cup spaghetti sauce in bottom of a lightly greased 13- x 9- x 2-inch baking dish. Spoon sausage mixture into shells, and place in baking dish. Pour remaining sauce over stuffed shells.
- **Cover** and bake at 350° for 15 minutes; sprinkle with Parmesan cheese, and bake, uncovered, 5 additional minutes or until thoroughly heated. **Yield:** 4 to 6 servings.

Note: To make ahead, store stuffed shells in the refrigerator, without sauce or cheese, at least 8 hours. Assemble shells and sauce in baking dish as directed, and let stand at room temperature 30 minutes. Cover and bake at 350° for 20 minutes; sprinkle evenly with Parmesan cheese, and bake, uncovered, 5 additional minutes or until thoroughly heated.

Christine Johnston
Bossier City, Louisiana

RAVIOLI WITH CREAMY PESTO SAUCE

QUICK!

1 cup whipping cream
1 (2.82-ounce) jar pesto
1 (3-ounce) jar capers, drained (optional)
2 (9-ounce) packages refrigerated cheese-filled ravioli, uncooked
2 tablespoons pine nuts, toasted

- **Combine** whipping cream and pesto in a saucepan; add capers, if desired. Cook over low heat until thoroughly heated, stirring often.
- **Cook** pasta according to package directions, and drain. Toss pasta with sauce, and sprinkle with toasted pine nuts. Serve immediately. **Yield:** 4 to 6 servings.

CREAMY MACARONI AND CHEESE

2 quarts water
1 teaspoon salt
1 (8-ounce) package elbow macaroni
4 cups (16 ounces) shredded Cheddar or Jarlsberg cheese
1 (8-ounce) carton sour cream
1 cup mayonnaise
2 tablespoons chopped onion
1 cup cheese crackers, crushed
Garnish: green onion fan

- **Bring** water and salt to a boil in a large Dutch oven; stir in macaroni. Return to a rapid boil, and cook 8 to 10 minutes or until tender; drain. Rinse with cold water; drain.
- **Combine** macaroni, cheese, and next 3 ingredients. Spoon into a lightly greased 11- x 7- x 1½-inch baking dish; sprinkle with crushed crackers.
- **Bake** at 325° for 30 to 35 minutes, and garnish, if desired. **Yield:** 6 to 8 servings.

♥ To reduce fat and calories, substitute nonfat sour cream, fat-free mayonnaise, and reduced-fat Cheddar cheese.

Nat Holland
Columbia, South Carolina

MUSHROOM-MACARONI CASSEROLE

2 quarts water
1 teaspoon salt
1 (8-ounce) package elbow macaroni
1 (10¾-ounce) can cream of mushroom soup, undiluted
1 cup mayonnaise
2 cups (8 ounces) shredded sharp Cheddar cheese
1 (4-ounce) can sliced mushrooms, drained
1 (2-ounce) jar diced pimiento, drained (optional)
¾ cup crushed round buttery crackers (about 15 crackers)
1 tablespoon butter, melted

- **Bring** water and salt to a boil in a large Dutch oven; stir in macaroni. Return to

a rapid boil, and cook 8 to 10 minutes or until tender; drain. Rinse with cold water; drain.
- **Combine** macaroni, soup, and next 3 ingredients; add pimiento, if desired. Spoon into a lightly greased 2-quart casserole. Combine cracker crumbs and butter; sprinkle evenly over macaroni mixture.
- **Bake** at 300° for 30 minutes or until mixture is thoroughly heated. **Yield:** 6 to 8 servings.

Melba Edwards-Johnson
Sunset Beach, North Carolina

SAUSAGE AND NOODLE CASSEROLE

1 (8-ounce) package medium egg noodles
1 (16-ounce) package mild ground pork sausage
1 (10¾-ounce) can cream of chicken soup, undiluted
1 (8-ounce) carton sour cream
½ cup crumbled blue cheese
1 (4½-ounce) jar sliced mushrooms, drained
1 (2-ounce) jar diced pimiento, drained
2 tablespoons finely chopped green bell pepper
½ cup soft breadcrumbs
1 tablespoon butter or margarine, melted

- **Cook** noodles according to package directions; drain and set aside.
- **Brown** sausage in a large nonstick skillet, stirring until it crumbles; drain and set aside.
- **Combine** soup, sour cream, and blue cheese in a large saucepan; cook over medium heat, stirring constantly, until cheese melts.
- **Add** noodles, sausage, mushrooms, pimiento, and green pepper, tossing to coat. Spoon mixture into a lightly greased 11- x 7- x 1½-inch baking dish.
- **Combine** breadcrumbs and butter; sprinkle over casserole.
- **Bake** at 350° for 30 minutes. **Yield:** 6 servings.

Claudia Barnes
Birmingham, Alabama

Pasta   227

VEGETABLE-NOODLE KUGEL

*Traditionally, kugel is served as a
side dish on the Jewish Sabbath. Our
version adds carrot and zucchini
to the baked pudding.*

1 (8-ounce) package medium egg
    noodles
1 onion, chopped
2 carrots, scraped and coarsely
    shredded
1 zucchini, coarsely shredded
1 tablespoon vegetable oil
1 (16-ounce) carton sour cream
1 (12-ounce) carton cottage
    cheese
1 teaspoon dried rosemary,
    crushed
½ teaspoon salt
¾ teaspoon pepper
¼ cup grated Parmesan cheese

• **Cook** noodles according to package
directions; drain.
• **Cook** onion, carrot, and zucchini in
hot oil in a large skillet until tender; stir
in noodles, sour cream, and next 4 ingredients. Spoon into a lightly greased 2-
quart baking dish.
• **Cover** and bake at 350° for 25 minutes; sprinkle with Parmesan cheese,
and bake, uncovered, 5 additional minutes. **Yield:** 6 to 8 servings.

LASAGNA SUPREME

12 lasagna noodles, uncooked
1 pound ground beef
1 small onion, chopped
1 clove garlic, minced
2 (6-ounce) cans tomato
    paste
1 (16-ounce) can whole tomatoes,
    undrained and chopped
1½ cups water
1 tablespoon dried basil
1 teaspoon salt
½ teaspoon dried rosemary
2 bay leaves
2 large eggs, lightly beaten
2 cups ricotta cheese
1 (8-ounce) carton sour cream
2 tablespoons dried parsley flakes
    or ¼ cup chopped fresh
    parsley
½ teaspoon salt
¼ teaspoon pepper
1 cup (4 ounces) shredded
    Cheddar cheese
½ cup grated Parmesan cheese
½ cup grated Romano cheese
2 (8-ounce) packages mozzarella
    cheese slices

• **Cook** lasagna noodles according to
package directions. Drain well, and set
aside.
• **Cook** ground beef, onion, and garlic in
a large skillet over medium heat until
meat is browned and onion is tender,
stirring until meat crumbles. Drain well.
Wipe pan drippings from skillet with a
paper towel.
• **Combine** tomato paste and next 6 ingredients in skillet; return meat mixture
to skillet. Bring mixture to a boil, stirring occasionally; reduce heat, and simmer, uncovered, 1 hour and 15 minutes,
stirring often. Remove and discard bay
leaves.
• **Combine** eggs and next 5 ingredients;
set aside.
• **Arrange** 4 lasagna noodles in bottom
of a lightly greased 13- x 9- x 2-inch baking dish. Layer with one-third each of
meat mixture, egg mixture, and Cheddar, Parmesan, and Romano cheeses.
Repeat layers twice.
• **Bake**, uncovered, at 375° for 30 to 35
minutes or until bubbly. Arrange mozzarella cheese slices over top of lasagna;

bake 5 additional minutes. Let stand 10
minutes. **Yield:** 8 to 10 servings.

Note: To freeze half of lasagna, prepare
half of lasagna in an 8-inch square baking dish, and bake as directed above.
Prepare remaining half of lasagna in an
8-inch square aluminum pan; freeze, unbaked, up to 2 months. To bake, thaw in
refrigerator 24 hours; let stand at room
temperature 30 minutes. Bake at 375°
for 35 to 40 minutes; add mozzarella
cheese slices, and bake 5 additional
minutes.

*Betty Beske
Arlington, Virginia*

GOURMET WHITE LASAGNA

8 lasagna noodles, uncooked
1 pound ground beef
½ pound ground pork sausage
1 cup chopped onion
½ cup chopped celery
1 clove garlic, minced
2 teaspoons dried basil
1 teaspoon dried oregano
½ teaspoon dried Italian
    seasoning
½ teaspoon salt
1 cup half-and-half
1 (3-ounce) package cream cheese,
    softened
½ cup dry white wine
2 cups (8 ounces) shredded
    Cheddar cheese
1½ cups (6 ounces) shredded
    Gouda cheese
1 (12-ounce) carton small-curd
    cottage cheese
1 large egg, lightly beaten
2 cups (8 ounces) shredded
    mozzarella cheese

• **Cook** noodles according to package
directions; drain and set aside.
• **Cook** ground beef and next 4 ingredients in a large skillet, stirring until
meats crumble; drain. Stir in basil and
next 5 ingredients. Stir in wine and
Cheddar and Gouda cheeses; cook, stirring constantly, until cheeses melt. Set
aside.
• **Combine** cottage cheese and egg; set
aside.

• **Arrange** half of noodles in a lightly greased 13- x 9- x 2-inch baking dish; top with half each of meat mixture, cottage cheese mixture, and mozzarella cheese. Repeat layers with remaining meat mixture, cottage cheese mixture, and mozzarella cheese.

• **Bake**, uncovered, at 350° for 40 minutes; let stand 10 minutes before serving. **Yield:** 6 servings.

Mrs. Larry Coppernoll
Linden, North Carolina

MICROWAVE LASAGNA

QUICK!

1 pound ground beef
1 (28-ounce) jar spaghetti sauce
½ cup water
1½ cups cottage cheese
1 large egg, lightly beaten
1½ teaspoons pepper
8 lasagna noodles, uncooked
1 (10-ounce) package frozen chopped spinach, thawed
2 cups (8 ounces) shredded mozzarella cheese
½ cup grated Parmesan cheese

• **Crumble** beef in a 2-quart bowl. Microwave at HIGH 4 minutes or until browned, stirring once; drain. Stir in spaghetti sauce and water.

• **Combine** cottage cheese, egg, and pepper.

• **Spread** ½ cup meat sauce in a 13- x 9- x 2-inch baking dish. Top with half each of uncooked noodles, cottage cheese mixture, spinach, meat sauce, and mozzarella cheese. Repeat layers with remaining half of noodles, cottage cheese mixture, spinach, meat sauce, and mozzarella cheese; cover with heavy-duty plastic wrap.

• **Microwave** at HIGH 8 minutes; microwave at MEDIUM (50% power) 30 to 32 minutes or until noodles are tender, turning dish occasionally.

• **Sprinkle** with Parmesan cheese; cover and let stand 15 minutes before serving. **Yield:** 6 servings.

Queever Bronssard
New Iberia, Louisiana

CHICKEN LASAGNA FLORENTINE

6 lasagna noodles, uncooked
1 (10-ounce) package frozen chopped spinach, thawed
2 cups chopped cooked chicken
2 cups (8 ounces) shredded Cheddar cheese
⅓ cup finely chopped onion
¼ to ½ teaspoon freshly ground nutmeg
1 tablespoon cornstarch
½ teaspoon salt
¼ teaspoon pepper
1 tablespoon soy sauce
1 (10¾-ounce) can cream of mushroom soup, undiluted
1 (8-ounce) carton sour cream
1 (4.5-ounce) jar sliced mushrooms, drained
⅓ cup mayonnaise or salad dressing
1 cup freshly grated Parmesan cheese
Butter-Pecan Topping

• **Cook** noodles according to package directions; drain and set aside.

• **Drain** spinach well, pressing between layers of paper towels.

• **Combine** spinach, chicken, and next 11 ingredients in a large bowl; stir well.

• **Arrange** 2 noodles in a lightly greased 11- x 7- x 1½-inch baking dish. Spread half of chicken mixture over noodles. Repeat procedure with remaining noodles and chicken mixture. Sprinkle with Parmesan cheese and Butter-Pecan Topping.

• **Cover** and bake at 350° for 55 to 60 minutes or until hot and bubbly. Let stand 15 minutes before cutting. **Yield:** 8 servings.

Butter-Pecan Topping

QUICK!

2 tablespoons butter or margarine
1 cup chopped pecans

• **Melt** butter in a skillet over medium heat; add pecans, and cook 3 minutes. Cool completely. **Yield:** 1 cup.

CHICKEN LASAGNA

1 (8-ounce) package medium egg noodles
½ cup butter or margarine
½ cup all-purpose flour
1 teaspoon dried basil
1 teaspoon salt
½ teaspoon pepper
4 cups chicken broth
4 cups chopped cooked chicken
1 (24-ounce) carton cottage cheese
1 large egg, lightly beaten
2 cups (8 ounces) shredded mozzarella cheese
¾ cup freshly grated Parmesan cheese

• **Cook** noodles according to package directions; drain and set aside.

• **Melt** butter in a large saucepan over medium heat; stir in flour and next 3 ingredients. Cook 1 to 2 minutes, stirring constantly.

• **Add** chicken broth, stirring until smooth; bring to a boil. Reduce heat, and simmer 5 to 8 minutes or until mixture is thickened and bubbly. Stir in chicken, and remove from heat.

• **Combine** cottage cheese and egg in a bowl, stirring well.

• **Spoon** one-third chicken mixture into a lightly greased 13- x 9- x 2-inch baking dish. Top with half each of noodles, cottage cheese mixture, and mozzarella cheese. Repeat layers, ending with chicken mixture. Sprinkle with Parmesan cheese.

• **Bake** at 350° for 1 hour. **Yield:** 8 servings.

Yvonne M. Greer
Mauldin, South Carolina

CRABMEAT LASAGNA

6 lasagna noodles, uncooked
¼ cup butter or margarine
1 cup shredded carrot
½ cup finely chopped celery
½ cup finely chopped onion
⅓ cup chopped yellow bell pepper
⅓ cup chopped red bell pepper
3 cloves garlic, minced
1 teaspoon coriander seeds,
    crushed
1 (8-ounce) carton plain yogurt
¼ cup chopped fresh cilantro
¼ teaspoon salt
⅛ teaspoon ground white pepper
⅛ teaspoon ground nutmeg
1 pound fresh lump crabmeat
2 cups (8 ounces) shredded
    mozzarella cheese
2 cups (8 ounces) shredded
    process American cheese

• **Cook** noodles according to package directions; drain.
• **Melt** butter in a large skillet over medium-high heat; add carrot and next 6 ingredients. Cook 4 to 5 minutes or until vegetables are tender, stirring often.
• **Combine** yogurt and next 4 ingredients in a bowl; stir in vegetable mixture.
• **Drain** crabmeat, removing any bits of shell. Add to yogurt mixture, and toss.
• **Combine** shredded cheeses.
• **Arrange** 3 lasagna noodles in bottom of a lightly greased 13- x 9- x 2-inch baking dish; top with half of crabmeat mixture, and sprinkle with half of cheese mixture. Repeat layers with remaining noodles and crabmeat mixture.
• **Cover** and bake at 350° for 30 minutes or until thoroughly heated. Sprinkle with remaining cheese mixture, and bake, uncovered, 5 additional minutes. **Yield:** 6 servings.

Carolene and Richard Martinez
Natchez, Mississippi

VEGETABLE LASAGNA

Sunny serves any leftover slices of this garden-fresh favorite chilled. "It's even better the second day," she says.

10 lasagna noodles, uncooked
2 cups sliced fresh mushrooms
1 cup grated carrot (about 1 large)
½ cup chopped onion
1 tablespoon olive oil
1 (15-ounce) can tomato sauce
1 (12-ounce) can tomato paste
1 (4¼-ounce) can chopped ripe
    olives, drained
1 (4.5-ounce) can chopped green
    chiles, undrained
1½ teaspoons dried oregano
2 cups cottage cheese
1 (10-ounce) package frozen
    chopped spinach, thawed and
    well drained
4 cups (16 ounces) shredded
    Monterey Jack cheese
1 (3-ounce) package refrigerated
    grated Parmesan cheese

• **Cook** noodles according to package directions. Drain and set aside.
• **Cook** mushrooms, carrot, and onion in olive oil over medium-high heat, stirring constantly, until tender. Stir in tomato sauce and next 4 ingredients.
• **Place** half of cooked lasagna noodles in a greased 13- x 9- x 2-inch baking dish or pan. Layer with half each of cottage cheese, spinach, tomato sauce mixture, Monterey Jack cheese, and Parmesan cheese. Repeat layers.
• **Bake** at 375° for 45 minutes or until bubbly. Let stand 10 minutes before serving. **Yield:** 8 servings.

Sunny Tiedemann
Bartlesville, Oklahoma

LEMON COUSCOUS

QUICK!

1 tablespoon grated lemon rind
2 tablespoons fresh lemon
    juice
1 tablespoon butter or margarine
⅛ teaspoon salt
1 cup chicken broth
⅔ cup couscous, uncooked
2 tablespoons pecan pieces,
    toasted
2 tablespoons chopped fresh
    parsley
2 tablespoons finely chopped red
    bell pepper
Garnishes: fresh mint sprigs, lemon
    slices

• **Combine** first 5 ingredients in a saucepan; bring to a boil over medium-high heat. Add couscous, stirring well; cover, remove from heat, and let stand 10 minutes. Stir in pecans, parsley, and bell pepper. Garnish, if desired. **Yield:** 2 servings.

GARLIC AND HERB
CHEESE GRITS

QUICK!

Serve this flavorful 10-minute side dish with grilled or broiled beef or chicken.

4 cups fat-free chicken broth
1 cup quick-cooking grits,
    uncooked
1 (5-ounce) package light garlic-
    and-herb soft, spreadable
    cheese
¼ teaspoon freshly ground
    pepper

• **Bring** broth to a boil in a medium saucepan over high heat; gradually stir in grits. Cook, stirring constantly, 5 to 7 minutes or until thickened.
• **Remove** from heat, and stir in cheese and pepper. Serve immediately. **Yield:** 5 cups.

♥ Per ¾-cup serving: Calories 161
Fat 4.1g   Cholesterol 12mg
Sodium 112mg

GRITS AND GREENS

If you don't have stone-ground grits on hand or can't find them at your grocery store, substitute regular grits.

1 cup whipping cream
4 cups chicken broth, divided
1 cup stone-ground grits,
      uncooked
¼ to ½ cup milk
1 pound fresh collard greens
¼ cup butter or margarine
1 to 1½ cups freshly grated
      Parmesan cheese
¼ to ½ teaspoon freshly ground
      pepper
Garnish: chopped cooked bacon or
      cubed cooked ham

• **Combine** whipping cream and 3 cups chicken broth in a large saucepan. Bring to a boil, and gradually stir in grits.
• **Cook** over medium heat until mixture returns to a boil; cover, reduce heat, and simmer 25 to 30 minutes, stirring often. Gradually add milk, if necessary, for desired consistency.
• **Remove** and discard stems and any discolored spots from greens. Wash greens thoroughly; drain and cut into ½-inch strips.
• **Combine** greens and remaining 1 cup chicken broth in a large skillet; bring to a boil. Cover, reduce heat, and simmer 5 minutes or until greens are tender. Drain and plunge into ice water to stop the cooking process. Drain well on paper towels.
• **Add** butter, cheese, and pepper to grits, stirring until butter and cheese melt. Stir in greens.
• **Cook**, stirring constantly, until thoroughly heated. Garnish, if desired. **Yield:** 6 to 8 servings.

Marion Sullivan
Charleston, South Carolina

CHEESE GRITS WITH GREEN CHILES

6 cups water
1½ cups quick-cooking grits,
      uncooked
2 teaspoons salt
1 teaspoon paprika
1 teaspoon ground red pepper
3 large eggs
4 cups (16 ounces) shredded sharp
      Cheddar cheese
1 (4.5-ounce) can chopped green
      chiles, undrained

• **Bring** water to a boil in a saucepan; stir in grits and salt. Return to a boil; cover, reduce heat, and simmer 10 minutes or until thickened, stirring often. Stir in paprika and ground red pepper.
• **Beat** eggs in a large bowl. Gradually stir about one-fourth of hot grits mixture into eggs; add to remaining hot grits mixture, stirring constantly.
• **Stir** in cheese and chiles; pour into a greased 11- x 7- x 1½-inch baking dish.
• **Bake** at 325° for 45 minutes or until set. Serve immediately, or spoon into 10 lightly greased (6-ounce) custard cups; cool. Invert onto a greased baking sheet; remove cups.
• **Bake** at 300° for 5 minutes or until heated. **Yield:** 8 to 10 servings.

Note: For grits with more fire, substitute 5 pickled jalapeño peppers, unseeded and chopped, for the green chiles. For milder grits, use ½ (4.5-ounce) can chopped green chiles, undrained.

Jean Andrews
Red Hot Peppers (Macmillan)

HOT TOMATO GRITS

2 slices bacon, chopped
2 (14½-ounce) cans chicken broth
½ teaspoon salt
1 cup quick-cooking grits, uncooked
2 large ripe tomatoes, peeled and
      chopped
2 tablespoons canned chopped
      green chiles
1 cup (4 ounces) shredded
      Cheddar cheese

• **Cook** bacon in a large heavy saucepan until crisp, reserving drippings in pan. Gradually add broth and salt, and bring to a boil.
• **Stir** in grits, tomato, and chiles; return to a boil, stirring often. Reduce heat; simmer 15 to 20 minutes, stirring often.
• **Stir** in cheese; cover and let stand 5 minutes. **Yield:** 6 servings.

Lucy S. Wheaton
Birmingham, Alabama

SKILLET POLENTA SQUARES

Serve this enhanced version of polenta as a first course or side dish.

2 cups water
2 cups chicken broth
1 cup white cornmeal
½ cup whipping cream
1 cup (4 ounces) shredded
      Monterey Jack cheese with
      peppers
White cornmeal
Vegetable oil
Salsa
Garnish: fresh cilantro sprigs

• **Bring** water and broth to a boil in a saucepan; gradually whisk in 1 cup cornmeal. Return to a boil; reduce heat, and cook 5 minutes, stirring constantly.
• **Add** whipping cream, and cook 20 minutes, stirring often. Stir in cheese.
• **Spoon** mixture into a lightly greased 9-inch square pan. Cover and chill at least 2 hours or until firm.
• **Cut** into 3-inch squares, and dredge in cornmeal.
• **Pour** oil to depth of ½ inch into a large heavy skillet. Fry polenta in hot oil over medium heat 2 minutes on each side or until golden. Drain on paper towels. Serve immediately with salsa. Garnish, if desired. **Yield:** 9 servings.

Spoonbread Grits With Savory
Mushroom Sauce

SPOONBREAD GRITS WITH SAVORY MUSHROOM SAUCE
(pictured at left)

1 (14½-ounce) can chicken
   broth
½ cup quick-cooking grits,
   uncooked
¼ cup butter or margarine
1 cup milk
1 cup buttermilk
3 large eggs, lightly beaten
1 cup yellow cornmeal
1 teaspoon baking powder
1 teaspoon salt
¼ teaspoon baking soda
⅛ teaspoon ground red pepper
   (optional)
Savory Mushroom Sauce
Garnish: fresh thyme sprigs

• **Bring** broth to a boil in a large sauce-pan; stir in grits. Reduce heat, and sim-mer 5 to 7 minutes or until thickened, stirring occasionally. Stir in butter and next 3 ingredients.
• **Combine** cornmeal and next 4 ingre-dients; stir into grits mixture. Pour mix-ture into a lightly greased 11- x 7- x 1½-inch baking dish.
• **Bake** at 425° for 45 minutes or until lightly browned. Cut into triangles, if de-sired, and serve with Savory Mushroom Sauce; garnish, if desired. **Yield:** 4 to 6 servings.

Savory Mushroom Sauce

QUICK!

2 tablespoons butter or margarine
3 (3½-ounce) packages fresh
   shiitake mushrooms, sliced
1 clove garlic, minced
2 tablespoons all-purpose flour
¼ cup dry white wine
1 cup chicken broth
½ teaspoon salt
¼ teaspoon pepper

• **Melt** butter in a skillet; add mush-rooms and garlic, and cook until tender, stirring often. Remove mushrooms with a slotted spoon, reserving drippings in skillet.
• **Whisk** flour into reserved drippings until smooth. Cook, whisking con-stantly, until lightly browned. Gradually add wine and broth; cook over medium heat, whisking constantly, until thick-ened and bubbly. Stir in salt and pepper. Add mushrooms, and cook, stirring constantly, until thoroughly heated. **Yield:** 2 cups.

Mrs. Charles DeHaven
Owensboro, Kentucky

SOUTHWESTERN GRITS CAKES

4 cups water
1 teaspoon salt
1 cup quick-cooking grits,
   uncooked
½ cup chopped green onions
1 (4.5-ounce) can chopped green
   chiles, drained
2 tablespoons diced pimiento,
   drained
⅛ teaspoon hot sauce
2 tablespoons butter or margarine,
   divided
1 (15-ounce) can black beans,
   rinsed and drained
1 (8-ounce) jar picante sauce
1 medium tomato, seeded and
   chopped
2 tablespoons chopped fresh
   cilantro

• **Bring** water and salt to a boil in a medium saucepan. Stir in grits; return to a boil over medium heat, stirring con-stantly. Cover, reduce heat, and simmer 5 minutes. Remove from heat; stir in green onions and next 3 ingredients.
• **Pour** mixture into a buttered 9-inch square pan; cover and chill 3 hours or until firm. Invert pan to remove grits; cut grits into 4 squares. Cut each square into 2 triangles.
• **Heat** 1 tablespoon butter over medium heat; add 4 triangles, and cook 5 to 7 minutes on each side or until lightly browned. Gently transfer to a serving platter; keep warm. Repeat with remaining butter and triangles.
• **Combine** black beans and picante sauce in a small saucepan; cook over medium heat until thoroughly heated, stirring often. Spoon over grits cakes; sprinkle with chopped tomato and cilantro. Serve immediately. **Yield:** 4 servings.

Note: You can bake grits cakes (or tri-angles) at 350° for 7 minutes or broil 5½ inches from heat (with electric oven door partially opened) 7 minutes on 1 side. (Do not turn.)

Janice Elder
Charlotte, North Carolina

RICE WITH SPRING VEGETABLES

Substitute Swiss or Parmesan cheese for the fontina and Gruyère cheeses.

2 tablespoons unsalted butter
1 small onion, finely chopped
1 clove garlic, chopped
1½ cups Arborio rice,
   uncooked
½ cup 1-inch fresh asparagus
   pieces
½ cup small Sugar Snap peas
½ cup finely chopped leek
½ cup thinly sliced carrot
3 (14½-ounce) cans chicken or
   vegetable broth
1 teaspoon chopped fresh mint
2 ounces prosciutto or cooked
   ham, cut into thin strips
⅓ cup grated Parmesan cheese
½ cup (2 ounces) shredded
   fontina cheese
2 ounces grated Gruyère cheese
¼ teaspoon freshly ground
   pepper
Pinch of ground nutmeg
Garnishes: fresh flat-leaf parsley
   and thyme sprigs

• **Melt** butter in a large skillet over medium-low heat; add onion and garlic, and cook, stirring constantly, 10 min-utes or until tender.
• **Stir** in rice and next 5 ingredients; cook over medium-high heat 25 min-utes, stirring often.
• **Add** mint; cook 5 minutes or until liq-uid is absorbed and rice is tender, stir-ring often.
• **Stir** in prosciutto and next 5 ingredi-ents; garnish, if desired. **Yield:** 3 main-dish servings or 6 appetizer servings.

Jerry Mauri
Baltimore International Culinary College
Baltimore, Maryland

RISOTTO WITH GREENS

If you can't find peppery arugula, use more watercress in its place.

1   tablespoon butter or margarine
1   tablespoon olive oil
1   small onion, chopped
1   clove garlic, minced
1½ cups Arborio rice, uncooked
½   cup dry white wine
1   cup fresh watercress, chopped
1   cup fresh arugula, chopped
3   (14½-ounce) cans chicken broth
    or vegetable broth, heated
5   plum tomatoes, seeded and
    chopped
1   teaspoon chopped fresh thyme
1   teaspoon chopped fresh
    oregano
1   teaspoon chopped fresh mint
½   cup freshly grated Parmesan
    cheese
2   tablespoons butter or margarine
½   teaspoon freshly ground
    pepper

• **Melt** 1 tablespoon butter in a large saucepan over medium-low heat; add oil, onion, and garlic, and cook 10 minutes or until garlic is tender (do not brown), stirring often.
• **Add** rice; cook over medium-high heat 3 minutes, stirring constantly. Stir in wine, and cook 2 to 3 minutes or until liquid evaporates. Stir in watercress and arugula.
• **Add** ½ cup hot broth; cook, stirring constantly, until liquid is absorbed. Repeat procedure with remaining broth, adding ½ cup at a time.
• **Stir** in tomato and remaining ingredients. **Yield:** 3 main-dish servings or 6 appetizer servings.

Jerry Mauri
Baltimore International Culinary College
Baltimore, Maryland

RISOTTO WITH SHELLFISH AND PEAS

Leave a few of the mussels and clams in their shells to use as a garnish.

3   pounds fresh mussels
2   dozen fresh littleneck clams
1   cup dry white wine, divided
2   (14½-ounce) cans vegetable
    broth
1   medium onion, finely chopped
1   clove garlic, finely chopped
2   tablespoons olive oil
1½ cups Arborio rice, uncooked
1   cup frozen English peas,
    thawed
⅛   teaspoon threads of saffron
Pinch of ground red pepper
¼   cup chopped fresh flat-leaf
    parsley
½   teaspoon salt
½   teaspoon freshly ground black
    pepper

• **Scrub** mussels and clams with a brush, removing beards from mussels. Discard any opened shells.
• **Bring** ½ cup wine to a boil in a large saucepan; add mussels and clams, and cook just until shells open. Reserve cooking liquid. Discard any unopened shells. Remove mussels and clams from shells, and set aside.
• **Pour** cooking liquid through a fine wire-mesh strainer into a liquid measuring cup, and add enough water to measure 1 cup; return to saucepan. Add vegetable broth; bring to a boil over medium-high heat. Reduce heat, and simmer.
• **Cook** onion and garlic in oil in a large saucepan over medium-low heat, stirring constantly, 10 minutes or until tender (do not brown).
• **Add** rice, and cook over medium-high heat 3 minutes, stirring constantly. Add remaining ½ cup wine, and cook until liquid evaporates.
• **Add** ½ cup hot broth mixture to rice; cook, stirring constantly, until liquid is absorbed. Repeat procedure with remaining hot broth mixture, adding ½ cup at a time. Add peas, saffron, and ground red pepper after 15 minutes of cooking.

• **Stir** in mussels, clams, parsley, salt, and black pepper. **Yield:** 3 main-dish servings or 6 appetizer servings.

Jerry Mauri
Baltimore International Culinary College
Baltimore, Maryland

SOUTHWESTERN RISOTTO

½   cup chopped onion
2   cloves garlic, crushed
2   tablespoons butter or margarine,
    melted
1   cup medium-grain rice,
    uncooked
½   cup dry white wine
6   cups chicken broth, divided
½   cup whipping cream
2   medium tomatoes, seeded and
    chopped
1   jalapeño pepper, seeded and
    minced
½   cup sliced green onions
½   cup grated Parmesan cheese
2 to 3 tablespoons minced fresh
    cilantro
Garnish: fresh cilantro sprigs,
    cubed tomatoes

• **Cook** onion and garlic in butter in a large skillet or saucepan over medium heat, stirring constantly, until tender.
• **Add** rice; cook 2 to 3 minutes, stirring often with a wooden spoon. Add wine, and cook, uncovered, until liquid is absorbed. Add 1 cup broth; cook over medium-high heat, stirring constantly, 5 minutes or until broth is absorbed. Add remaining broth, 1 cup at a time, stirring constantly until each cup is absorbed, about 25 to 30 minutes. (Rice will be tender and have a creamy consistency.) Stir in whipping cream and next 5 ingredients; cook 2 minutes. Garnish, if desired, and serve immediately. **Yield:** 6 servings.

Note: For a party of 10 to 12, make two batches.

Jade and Charlie McCulloch
Houston, Texas

BAKED MUSHROOM RICE

¼ cup butter or margarine, melted
1 cup long-grain rice, uncooked
1 (10½-ounce) can condensed
    chicken broth, undiluted
1 (10½-ounce) can condensed
    French onion soup, undiluted
1 (2½-ounce) jar sliced
    mushrooms, drained

• **Combine** all ingredients in an un-
greased 2-quart baking dish.
• **Cover** and bake at 350° for 1 hour.
Yield: 4 servings.

BAKED SPICY RICE

1 cup long-grain rice, uncooked
2 (10-ounce) cans diced tomatoes
    and green chiles, undrained
1 cup water
1 teaspoon salt
⅔ cup pimiento-stuffed olives,
    sliced
¼ cup vegetable oil
½ cup chopped onion
1 cup (4 ounces) shredded
    Monterey Jack cheese

• **Combine** all ingredients in a shallow
greased 2-quart baking dish.
• **Cover** and bake at 350° for 45 minutes. Stir well, and bake, uncovered, 15
additional minutes or until liquid is absorbed and rice is tender. **Yield:** 6 to 8
servings.

Note: To double recipe, prepare it in 2
batches, and bake in separate baking
dishes.

Stop and Smell the Rosemary:
Recipes and Traditions to Remember
Junior League of Houston, Texas

GREEN RICE CASSEROLE
QUICK!

1¼ cups (5 ounces) shredded
    Monterey Jack or Swiss
    cheese, divided
1 cup ricotta cheese
1 cup mayonnaise or salad
    dressing
½ teaspoon garlic salt
¼ teaspoon pepper
3 cups cooked rice
1 (10-ounce) package frozen
    chopped broccoli, thawed and
    drained
1 cup frozen English peas, thawed
¼ cup sliced green onions
    (optional)

• **Combine** 1 cup shredded Monterey
Jack cheese, ricotta, and next 3 ingredients in a large bowl; stir in rice, broccoli, peas, and green onions, if desired.
• **Spoon** rice mixture into a lightly
greased 2-quart casserole.
• **Bake**, uncovered, at 375° for 20 minutes. Sprinkle with remaining ¼ cup
Monterey Jack cheese, and bake 5 additional minutes. **Yield:** 8 servings.

ARABIC RICE
QUICK!

1½ pounds lean ground beef
3 tablespoons garlic powder
2 tablespoons ground cinnamon
1 tablespoon ground allspice
2 cups long-grain rice, uncooked
1 tablespoon beef-flavored
    bouillon granules
4 cups water
¼ cup pine nuts, toasted
Rice wine vinegar or lemon juice

• **Combine** first 4 ingredients in a skillet; cook over medium heat until meat is
browned, stirring until it crumbles. Stir
in rice, bouillon granules, and water.
• **Bring** to a boil. Cover, reduce heat,
and cook 20 minutes or until liquid is absorbed and rice is tender.
• **Sprinkle** with pine nuts, and serve
with vinegar. **Yield:** 6 servings.

Van Chaplin
Birmingham, Alabama

INDIAN RICE
QUICK!

If you don't have saffron on hand
or can't find it at your grocery store,
use ⅛ teaspoon ground turmeric.

1½ cups basmati rice or other
    long-grain rice *
3 cups chicken broth
3 tablespoons butter or margarine
3 cups chopped onion
1 clove garlic, minced
¼ cup finely chopped mango
    chutney
⅓ cup slivered almonds, toasted
½ cup currants or raisins
¼ teaspoon threads of saffron or
    ⅛ teaspoon ground saffron
¼ teaspoon salt
¼ teaspoon pepper

• **Combine** all ingredients in a large
saucepan; bring mixture to a boil over
high heat, stirring occasionally. Cover,
reduce heat, and simmer 20 to 25 minutes or until liquid is absorbed and rice
is tender. **Yield:** 6 servings.

* Substitute 1½ cups yellow rice for
basmati rice; omit saffron.

Myrna M. Ruiz
Marietta, Georgia

SWEET JAMAICAN RICE
QUICK!

2 cups hot cooked rice
1 (11-ounce) can mandarin
    oranges, drained and chopped
1 (8-ounce) can crushed
    pineapple, drained
½ cup chopped red bell pepper
½ cup slivered almonds, toasted
⅓ cup sliced green onions
¼ cup flaked coconut, toasted
2 tablespoons hot mango chutney
¼ teaspoon ground ginger

• **Combine** all ingredients in a large skillet; cook over medium-high heat, stirring constantly, 5 minutes or until
thoroughly heated. **Yield:** 4 servings.

Andy Jones
New Port Richey, Florida

SPANISH RICE

3 tablespoons vegetable oil
2 cups long-grain rice, uncooked
2 large green bell peppers, chopped
2 large celery stalks, chopped
2 medium onions, finely chopped
2 teaspoons cumin seeds, crushed
1 to 1½ teaspoons salt
½ teaspoon pepper
¼ teaspoon garlic powder
6 cups water
1 (8-ounce) can tomato sauce

• **Heat** oil over medium-high heat in a heavy Dutch oven; add rice and next 7 ingredients, and cook until rice is browned, stirring often.
• **Stir** in water and tomato sauce; bring to a boil. Reduce heat to medium; cover and cook 25 minutes or until rice is tender. **Yield:** 8 to 10 servings.

King Ranch
Kingsville, Texas

BAKED RICE

1 cup wild rice, uncooked
1½ cups brown rice, uncooked
1 tablespoon butter or margarine
1 (10½-ounce) can condensed beef broth
2½ to 3 cups water
3 tablespoons butter or margarine
1 (8-ounce) package mushrooms, sliced
2 carrots, scraped and finely chopped
1 bunch green onions, sliced
1 (8-ounce) can sliced water chestnuts, drained
¼ teaspoon salt
¼ cup dry white vermouth (optional)
2 tablespoons cold butter or margarine, cut into small pieces

• **Place** wild rice in a large bowl; add water to depth of 1 inch above rice. Cover and let stand at least 8 hours. Drain rice. Rinse and drain again.

• **Combine** wild rice, brown rice, 1 tablespoon butter, beef broth, and 2½ cups water in a large heavy saucepan.
• **Bring** to a boil; cover, reduce heat, and simmer about 45 minutes or until water is absorbed and rice is tender. (Add additional water to prevent sticking or burning, if necessary.)
• **Melt** 3 tablespoons butter in a large heavy skillet. Add mushrooms and next 3 ingredients; cook over medium heat until all liquid is absorbed (about 3 minutes), stirring often.
• **Stir** vegetables and salt into rice mixture, and spoon into a lightly greased 13- x 9- x 2-inch baking dish.
• **Drizzle** with vermouth, if desired, and dot with butter; cover.
• **Bake** at 350° for 40 minutes or until thoroughly heated. **Yield:** 12 servings.

Note: To make ahead, prepare casserole, omitting vermouth and butter. Cover and chill overnight. Remove from refrigerator, and let stand at room temperature 30 minutes. To serve, add vermouth, if desired, and butter, and bake at 350° for 50 minutes or until thoroughly heated. To prepare casserole without soaking wild rice, cook wild rice as directed on package.

PECAN-LEMON WILD RICE

3 cups chicken broth
1½ tablespoons lemon rind, divided
1 tablespoon fresh lemon juice
1 tablespoon butter or margarine
1 cup wild rice, uncooked
½ cup chopped pecans, toasted
¼ cup chopped fresh parsley
3 tablespoons chopped green onions

• **Combine** broth, 2¼ teaspoons lemon rind, lemon juice, and butter in a medium saucepan. Bring to a boil; stir in rice. Cover, reduce heat, and simmer 50 to 60 minutes or until liquid is absorbed and rice is tender. Stir in pecans, remaining 2¼ teaspoons lemon rind, parsley, and green onions. **Yield:** 4 to 6 servings.

Sandi Pichon
Slidell, Louisiana

WILD RICE CASSEROLE

2 (6-ounce) packages long-grain-and-wild rice mix
1 (8-ounce) jar process cheese spread
1 (8-ounce) can sliced water chestnuts, drained
1 (6-ounce) jar sliced mushrooms, drained
1 (2-ounce) jar diced pimiento, drained
1 (2.8-ounce) can French fried onions, crushed

• **Cook** rice mix according to package directions.
• **Stir** in cheese spread and next 3 ingredients. Spoon into a lightly greased 11- x 7- x 1½-inch baking dish.
• **Cover** and bake at 325° for 20 minutes; uncover and sprinkle with crushed onions.
• **Bake**, uncovered, 10 additional minutes. **Yield:** 8 servings.

June Smith
Covington, Georgia

MIAMI RICE

QUICK!

1⅓ cups orange juice
1½ cups water
1 (10-ounce) package yellow rice
1 cup chopped dates

• **Bring** orange juice and water to a boil in a saucepan; stir in rice.
• **Cover**, reduce heat, and simmer 25 minutes or until liquid is absorbed and rice is tender. Stir in chopped dates. **Yield:** 8 servings.

Nita and Harold Norman
Coral Gables, Florida

At right: *Spicy Blueberry Pie (page 238)*

PIES AND PASTRIES

APPLE-BOURBON PIE

"I started making desserts when I was 10 years old. My first was a yellow cake from a baking powder recipe booklet. My uncle wants that cake each year for our reunion. Now, my recipe inspiration comes from travels to bed-and-breakfast and country inns." – Eugenia

½ cup raisins
½ cup bourbon
3 pounds cooking apples
¾ cup sugar
2 tablespoons all-purpose flour
1 teaspoon ground cinnamon
¼ teaspoon salt
⅛ teaspoon ground nutmeg
½ cup chopped pecans or walnuts, toasted
1 (15-ounce) package refrigerated piecrusts
2 teaspoons apricot preserves, melted
1 tablespoon buttermilk
1 tablespoon sugar

• **Combine** raisins and bourbon, and let soak at least 2 hours.
• **Peel** apples, and cut into ½-inch slices; arrange apple slices in a steamer basket over boiling water. Cover and steam 10 minutes or until apple slices are tender.
• **Combine** ¾ cup sugar and next 4 ingredients in a large bowl; add apple slices, raisin mixture, and pecans, stirring to combine.
• **Fit** 1 piecrust into a 9-inch pieplate according to package directions; brush preserves over piecrust. Spoon apple mixture into piecrust.
• **Roll** remaining piecrust to press out fold lines; cut with a 3-inch leaf-shaped cutter. Mark veins on leaves with a pastry wheel or sharp knife. Arrange pastry leaves over apple mixture; brush leaves with buttermilk, and sprinkle pie with 1 tablespoon sugar.
• **Bake** at 450° on lower rack of oven 15 minutes. Shield edges of pie with strips of aluminum foil to prevent excessive browning. Reduce oven temperature to 350°, and bake 30 to 35 additional minutes. **Yield:** 1 (9-inch) pie.

Eugenia W. Bell
Lexington, Kentucky

MEXICAN APPLE PIE

1½ cups sugar
2 cups water
½ cup butter or margarine, melted
4 cups peeled, chopped Golden Delicious apples (about 1½ pounds)
2 teaspoons ground cinnamon
10 (6-inch) flour tortillas
Whipped cream
Ground cinnamon (optional)

• **Combine** sugar and water in a saucepan; cook over medium heat, stirring constantly, until sugar melts. Set aside.
• **Place** butter in a 13- x 9- x 2-inch baking dish; set aside.
• **Combine** apples and 2 teaspoons cinnamon, stirring to coat.
• **Place** about ½ cup apple mixture down center of each tortilla. Roll up, and place seam side down in baking dish. Pour sugar mixture over top of tortillas, and cover with aluminum foil.
• **Bake** at 350° for 30 minutes.
• **Uncover** and bake 25 to 30 minutes. Let stand 10 minutes. Serve warm with whipped cream; sprinkle with additional cinnamon, if desired. **Yield:** 10 servings.

Diane Dawson Martin
Summerville, Georgia

SPICY BLUEBERRY PIE
(pictured on page 237)

Discover the thrill of picking your own blueberries. Enjoy them by the handful or, even better, served under a hot, flaky crust in this easy-to-make pie.

¾ cup sugar
¼ cup firmly packed brown sugar
½ cup all-purpose flour
½ teaspoon ground cinnamon
¼ teaspoon ground allspice
5 cups fresh blueberries
1 tablespoon lemon juice
1 tablespoon butter or margarine, melted
1 (15-ounce) package refrigerated piecrusts
1 tablespoon milk
1 teaspoon sugar

• **Combine** first 8 ingredients, tossing gently.
• **Fit** 1 piecrust into a 9-inch pieplate according to package directions. Spoon blueberry mixture into pastry shell.
• **Roll** remaining piecrust to ⅛-inch thickness; cut into 6 (2½-inch-wide) strips. Arrange strips in a lattice design over filling; fold edges under, and crimp. Brush pastry with milk; sprinkle with 1 teaspoon sugar.
• **Bake** at 400° for 40 to 45 minutes or until golden, shielding edges with strips of aluminum foil during last 20 minutes of baking to prevent excessive browning. **Yield:** 1 (9-inch) pie.

Nan Ferguson
Atlanta, Georgia

LEMONY CHERRY PIE
(pictured at right)

2 (16-ounce) cans pitted tart red cherries, undrained
1 cup sugar
3 tablespoons cornstarch
2 tablespoons butter or margarine
1 tablespoon lemon juice
⅛ teaspoon red liquid food coloring (optional)
Pastry for double-crust 9-inch pie

• **Drain** cherries, reserving ½ cup juice. Set both aside.
• **Combine** sugar and cornstarch in a large saucepan; stir in reserved cherry juice. Cook over medium heat, stirring constantly, until mixture comes to a boil; boil 1 minute, stirring constantly. Remove from heat, and stir in cherries, butter, lemon juice, and, if desired, food coloring; cool.
• **Roll** half of pastry to ⅛-inch thickness on a lightly floured surface. Place in a 9-inch pieplate; trim off excess pastry along edges. Pour cherry mixture into pastry shell.
• **Roll** remaining pastry to ⅛-inch thickness; cut into ½-inch strips. Arrange in lattice design over cherries; trim strips even with edges. Make shaped cutouts with remaining pastry. Moisten edge of piecrust with water, and gently press cutouts around edges. Bake at 375° for 30 to 35 minutes. **Yield:** 1 (9-inch) pie.

Lemony Cherry Pie

CRANBERRY-PECAN PIE

1 (15-ounce) package refrigerated
  piecrusts
1 teaspoon all-purpose flour
3½ cups fresh or frozen
  cranberries, divided
½ cup raisins, divided
¾ cup chopped pecans
1½ cups sugar
3 tablespoons all-purpose flour
¼ cup light corn syrup
1 teaspoon grated orange rind
Garnish: fresh or frozen cranberries

• **Unfold** 1 piecrust, and press out fold
lines; sprinkle with 1 teaspoon flour,
spreading over surface. Place piecrust,
floured side down, in a 9-inch pieplate;
fold edges under, and flute. Set aside.
• **Roll** remaining piecrust to press out
fold lines; cut with a 3¾-inch leaf-
shaped cutter, and mark veins, using a
pastry wheel or sharp knife. Drape
leaves over small balls of aluminum foil
on an ungreased baking sheet. Bake at
350° for 7 minutes; remove foil balls,
and bake 3 additional minutes. Let cool.
• **Position** knife blade in food processor bowl, and add 1¾ cups cranberries
and ¼ cup raisins. Pulse 5 or 6 times or
until coarsely chopped, stopping once
to scrape down sides. Transfer to a large
bowl. Repeat procedure with remaining
1¾ cup cranberries and ¼ cup raisins.
• **Combine** cranberry mixture, pecans,
and next 4 ingredients; spoon into pastry shell. Bake at 350° for 20 minutes;
cover edges of pastry with strips of aluminum foil to prevent excessive browning, and bake 20 additional minutes. Let
cool on a wire rack. Arrange pastry
leaves around edges, and garnish, if desired. **Yield:** 1 (9-inch) pie.

KENTUCKY MINCEMEAT PIE

1 (23-ounce) can mincemeat pie
  filling
1 (8-ounce) can crushed
  pineapple, drained
2 cups sliced cooking apples
1 (15-ounce) package refrigerated
  piecrusts
1 tablespoon sugar

• **Combine** first 3 ingredients in a large
bowl; set aside.
• **Fit** 1 piecrust into a 9-inch pieplate according to package directions. Spoon
mincemeat mixture into piecrust.
• **Roll** remaining piecrust to press out
fold lines; cut with a 3-inch leaf-shaped
cutter. Mark veins on leaves with a pastry wheel or sharp knife. Arrange pastry
leaves over mincemeat mixture; sprinkle pie with sugar.
• **Bake** at 425° for 30 to 32 minutes or
until golden. Shield edges of pie with
strips of aluminum foil after 12 minutes
to prevent excessive browning. **Yield:** 1
(9-inch) pie.

Betty Lee Long
Chapel Hill, North Carolina

SPIRITED MINCE PIE

¾ cup raisins
3 tablespoons brandy *
1 (15-ounce) package refrigerated
  piecrusts
1 teaspoon all-purpose flour
1 (29-ounce) jar mincemeat
1 large cooking apple, cored and
  finely chopped
1 cup chopped walnuts
¼ cup firmly packed brown
  sugar
1 teaspoon grated lemon or orange
  rind
1 tablespoon fresh lemon juice

• **Combine** raisins and brandy in a large
bowl; let stand 2 hours.
• **Unfold** 1 piecrust, and press out fold
lines; sprinkle with flour, spreading over
surface. Place piecrust, floured side
down, in a 9-inch pieplate; fold edges
under, and flute. Set aside.
• **Combine** raisin mixture, mincemeat,
and remaining 5 ingredients; spoon into
pastry shell.
• **Roll** remaining piecrust on a lightly
floured surface to press out fold lines;
cut with a 3¼-inch leaf-shaped cutter,
and mark veins, using a pastry wheel or
sharp knife. Roll pastry scraps into
balls. Arrange leaves and balls on top of
filling as desired.
• **Bake** at 375° for 10 minutes; cover
edges with strips of aluminum foil to

prevent excessive browning, and bake
25 additional minutes. Cool on a wire
rack. **Yield:** 1 (9-inch) pie.

❋ Substitute orange juice for brandy.
Robert W. Nolen
Falls Church, Virginia

ELIZABETH AND PHOEBE'S FRESH PEACH PIE
(pictured at right)

QUICK!

*"Betty Edge was my college
roommate. I named this pie after
her daughters. Assemble it at the
last minute so the crust will remain
crisp," Marion advises.*

¼ cup unsalted butter, softened
1 cup sifted powdered sugar
1 tablespoon brandy
1 baked 9-inch pastry shell
6 large fresh peaches, peeled and
  sliced
3 tablespoons fresh lemon
  juice
¼ cup sugar
1½ cups whipping cream
3 tablespoons sifted powdered
  sugar
1 teaspoon vanilla extract

• **Beat** butter at medium speed with an
electric mixer until creamy; gradually
add 1 cup powdered sugar and brandy,
beating well. Spread in bottom of pastry
shell; chill.
• **Combine** peaches, lemon juice, and ¼
cup sugar; cover and chill.
• **Beat** whipping cream at high speed
with an electric mixer until foamy; gradually add 3 tablespoons powdered sugar
and vanilla, beating until soft peaks
form. Cover and chill.
• **Drain** peaches; arrange over butter
mixture. Dollop whipped cream mixture over peaches; serve immediately.
Yield: 1 (9-inch) pie.

Marion Sullivan
Charleston, South Carolina

*Elizabeth and Phoebe's
Fresh Peach Pie*

BACKYARD PEAR PIE

4 large pears, peeled, cored, and
    thinly sliced
¼ to ⅓ cup lemon juice
3 tablespoons butter or margarine
½ cup firmly packed brown sugar
½ cup sugar
1 teaspoon ground cinnamon
½ teaspoon salt
½ teaspoon ground nutmeg
2 tablespoons all-purpose flour
1 (15-ounce) package refrigerated
    piecrusts
1 teaspoon all-purpose flour

• **Combine** first 8 ingredients in a large
saucepan; cook over medium heat
about 12 minutes or until pears are tender, stirring occasionally.
• **Gradually** sprinkle in 2 tablespoons
flour, stirring constantly; cook, stirring
constantly, about 2 minutes or until
slightly thickened.
• **Unfold** 1 piecrust, and press out fold
lines; sprinkle with 1 teaspoon flour,
spreading over surface. Place piecrust,
floured side down, in a 9-inch pieplate;
spoon pear mixture into pastry shell.
• **Roll** remaining piecrust on a lightly
floured surface to press out fold lines;
place over pear mixture. Fold edges
under, and crimp. Cut slits in top crust
to allow steam to escape. Bake at 350°
for 45 minutes. **Yield:** 1 (9-inch) pie.

Chip Smith
Houston, Texas
and
Paul Frederick
Huntsville, Alabama

GINGER-PEAR PIE

1 unbaked 9-inch pastry shell
1 cup gingersnap crumbs
¼ cup firmly packed brown sugar
1 tablespoon all-purpose flour
½ teaspoon ground cinnamon
⅛ teaspoon salt
¼ cup butter or margarine,
    softened
5 medium pears, peeled, cored,
    and thinly sliced (about 2½
    pounds)
1 medium pear (optional)
1 tablespoon finely chopped
    pecans (optional)

• **Bake** pastry shell at 450° for 9 to 11
minutes; set aside.
• **Combine** gingersnap crumbs and next
5 ingredients. Layer half of pear slices in
pastry shell; sprinkle half of gingersnap
mixture over pears. Repeat procedure
with remaining pears and gingersnap
mixture. Cover loosely with aluminum
foil, and bake at 375° for 40 minutes. Uncover and bake 10 additional minutes, if
you do not plan to garnish.
• **To** garnish, peel optional pear; cut
in half, leaving stem intact in 1 half.
Remove core; thinly slice half of pear
with stem, cutting to, but not through,
stem end. Reserve half without stem for
other use. After baking pie 40 minutes,
fan and arrange pear half with stem
on pie; sprinkle with pecans. Bake, uncovered, 10 additional minutes. **Yield:** 1
(9-inch) pie.

LaJuan Coward
Jasper, Texas

PEAR-MACADAMIA PIE

*Grated lemon rind adds a
subtle hint of citrus to the tender
pastry crust of this rich pie.*

Hint-of-Citrus Pastry *
½ cup pear preserves
2 tablespoons Frangelico or other
    hazelnut-flavored liqueur
⅔ cup macadamia nuts
½ cup sugar
1½ tablespoons all-purpose flour
¼ cup butter or margarine,
    softened
1 large egg
2½ pounds ripe pears, peeled,
    cored, and thinly sliced

• **Prepare** pastry; set aside, and keep
pastry warm.
• **Combine** preserves and Frangelico in
a small heavy saucepan; cook over
medium heat, stirring constantly, until
warm. Pour mixture through a wire-
mesh strainer into a small bowl, discarding solids. Gently brush a thin layer
of glaze over warm pastry, reserving remaining glaze.
• **Position** knife blade in food processor bowl; add nuts, sugar, and flour.
Process until ground. Add butter and
egg; process until smooth. Spread mixture evenly over pastry, and freeze 15
minutes.
• **Arrange** pear slices over nut mixture;
bake at 350° for 30 minutes. Cover
loosely with aluminum foil, and bake 40
additional minutes or until pears are
tender and golden. Remove from oven;
immediately brush pears with reserved
glaze. Cool. **Yield:** 1 (10-inch) pie.

Hint-of-Citrus Pastry

1½ cups all-purpose flour
¼ cup sugar
1 teaspoon grated lemon rind
⅛ teaspoon salt
3 tablespoons butter
3 tablespoons shortening
6 to 7 tablespoons cold water

• **Combine** first 4 ingredients in a bowl;
cut in butter and shortening with pastry
blender until mixture is crumbly. Sprinkle cold water, 1 tablespoon at a time,

evenly over surface; stir with a fork until dry ingredients are moistened. Shape into a ball; cover and chill.

- **Roll** pastry to ⅛-inch thickness on a lightly floured surface. Gently place in a 10-inch pieplate; trim off excess pastry along edges. Fold edges under, and crimp; bake at 350° for 5 minutes. **Yield:** 1 (10-inch) pastry shell.

✻ Substitute ½ of a 15-ounce package refrigerated piecrusts, if desired. Unfold 1 piecrust, and lightly roll to fit a 10-inch pieplate. Sprinkle with 1 teaspoon flour, spreading over surface. Place piecrust, floured side down, in a 10-inch pieplate; fold edges under, and crimp. Bake piecrust as directed.

Men's Gourmet
Raleigh, North Carolina

MAMA'S PUMPKIN PIE

Mary, who shared this recipe, usually makes pastry from scratch, but we give you the easy way out here with refrigerated piecrusts. We use them a lot in our own homes.

½ (15-ounce) package
  refrigerated piecrusts
1¾ cups canned pumpkin
1¾ cups sweetened condensed
  milk
2 large eggs, lightly beaten
⅔ cup firmly packed light brown
  sugar
2 tablespoons sugar
1¼ teaspoons ground cinnamon
½ teaspoon salt
½ teaspoon ground ginger
½ teaspoon ground nutmeg
¼ teaspoon ground cloves

- **Fit** piecrust into a 9-inch pieplate according to package directions; fold edges under, and crimp.
- **Combine** pumpkin and remaining 9 ingredients in a large bowl; beat at medium speed with an electric mixer 2 minutes. Pour pumpkin mixture into prepared piecrust.
- **Bake** at 425° for 15 minutes. Reduce oven temperature to 350°; bake 50 additional minutes or until a knife inserted in center comes out clean. Cool on a wire rack. **Yield:** 1 (9-inch) pie.

Note: You should always store pumpkin pie in the refrigerator.

Mary White
Birmingham, Alabama

SWEET POTATO PIE

Serve this pie chilled with low-fat vanilla ice cream for a cooling dessert.

1 (14½-ounce) can mashed sweet
  potatoes
¾ cup milk
¾ cup firmly packed brown
  sugar
2 large eggs
1 tablespoon butter or margarine,
  melted
½ teaspoon salt
½ teaspoon ground cinnamon
1 unbaked 9-inch pastry shell

- **Combine** all ingredients except pastry shell in container of an electric blender; process until smooth, stopping once to scrape down sides. Pour into pastry shell.
- **Bake** at 400° for 10 minutes. Reduce oven temperature to 350°, and bake 35 additional minutes or until a knife inserted in center comes out clean, shielding edges with aluminum foil after 20 minutes to prevent excessive browning. **Yield:** 1 (9-inch) pie.

Jerry Mauri
Baltimore International Culinary College
Baltimore, Maryland

PINEAPPLE-GRITS PIE

If you think grits are only for breakfast or as a receptacle for redeye gravy, this recipe will make you think again.

2 cups water
½ cup quick-cooking grits,
  uncooked
¼ teaspoon salt
1 (8-ounce) can crushed
  pineapple, drained
½ (8-ounce) package cream
  cheese, softened
3 large eggs
1 cup sugar
½ cup milk
¼ teaspoon vanilla extract
2 (9-inch) graham cracker
  crusts

- **Bring** water to a boil in a saucepan; add grits and salt, and return to a boil. Cover, reduce heat to low, and cook 5 minutes, stirring occasionally. Remove from heat.
- **Combine** grits, crushed pineapple, and cream cheese in container of an electric blender, and process until smooth, stopping once to scrape down sides. With blender running, add eggs, one at a time.
- **Add** sugar, milk, and vanilla, and process until smooth, stopping once to scrape down sides. Pour pineapple mixture evenly into crusts.
- **Bake** at 300° for 1 hour or until mixture is set; cool on a wire rack. **Yield:** 2 (9-inch) pies.

Pineapple-Coconut Chess Pie

PINEAPPLE-COCONUT CHESS PIE
(pictured at left)

1½ cups sugar
3 tablespoons cornmeal
2 tablespoons all-purpose flour
¼ teaspoon salt
4 large eggs, lightly beaten
1 teaspoon vanilla extract
¼ cup butter or margarine,
   melted
1 (15¼-ounce) can crushed
   pineapple, well drained
1 (3½-ounce) can flaked coconut
1 unbaked 9-inch pastry shell

● **Combine** first 4 ingredients in a large bowl; add eggs and vanilla, stirring until blended. Stir in butter, pineapple, and coconut; pour into unbaked pastry shell.
● **Bake** at 350° for 1 hour or until set, covering with aluminum foil after 40 minutes to prevent excessive browning. Cool pie on a wire rack. **Yield:** 1 (9-inch) pie.

Joy Knight Allard
San Antonio, Texas

CHOCOLATE-PECAN CHESS PIE

1¼ cups sugar
¼ cup cocoa
1 tablespoon all-purpose flour
1 tablespoon cornmeal
Pinch of salt
¾ cup chopped pecans
4 large eggs, lightly beaten
½ cup milk
1 tablespoon vanilla extract
1 unbaked 9-inch deep-dish pastry
   shell

● **Combine** first 5 ingredients in a medium bowl; stir in pecans.
● **Combine** eggs, milk, and vanilla, and stir into sugar mixture; pour into pastry shell.
● **Bake** at 350° for 45 minutes or until set. Cool on a wire rack. **Yield:** 1 (9-inch) pie.

Nuttin' 'Cept Pecan Pies
Charles Wallace
Austin, Texas

LEMON-PECAN PIE

1 unbaked 9-inch deep-dish pastry
   shell
4 large eggs, lightly beaten
6 tablespoons butter or margarine,
   softened
1 cup light corn syrup
½ cup firmly packed brown sugar
2 teaspoons grated lemon rind
¼ cup lemon juice
3 tablespoons all-purpose flour
1¼ cups coarsely chopped pecans
Whipped cream

● **Bake** pastry shell at 450° for 5 to 7 minutes. Remove from oven, and let cool completely.
● **Combine** eggs and next 6 ingredients; stir in pecans, and pour into prepared crust.
● **Bake** at 350° for 40 minutes, shielding edges with strips of aluminum foil after 25 minutes to prevent excessive browning. Cool on a wire rack. Serve with whipped cream. **Yield:** 1 (9-inch) pie.

Nuttin' 'Cept Pecan Pies
Charles Wallace
Austin, Texas

OLD PECAN STREET SPECIAL

4 large eggs, lightly beaten
1 cup light corn syrup
⅔ cup sugar
3 tablespoons butter or margarine,
   melted
1 tablespoon vanilla extract
1½ cups coarsely chopped pecans
1 unbaked 9-inch deep-dish pastry
   shell

● **Combine** first 5 ingredients; stir in chopped pecans, and pour into pastry shell.
● **Bake** at 350° for 50 to 55 minutes. Let pie cool on a wire rack. **Yield:** 1 (9-inch) pie.

Nuttin' 'Cept Pecan Pies
Charles Wallace
Austin, Texas

BUTTERMILK-COCONUT PIE

3 large eggs, lightly beaten
1½ cups sugar
½ cup flaked coconut
½ cup buttermilk
½ cup butter or margarine,
   melted
2 tablespoons all-purpose flour
1 teaspoon vanilla extract
1 unbaked 9-inch deep-dish pastry
   shell

● **Combine** first 7 ingredients; pour into pastry shell.
● **Bake** at 350° for 45 minutes; shield with aluminum foil after 25 minutes to prevent excessive browning, if necessary. **Yield:** 1 (9-inch) pie.

Barbara and Tommy Glenn
Huntsville, Alabama

MAGNOLIA PIE

This go-with-everything buttermilk pie is sure to please. If desired, top with your favorite fresh berries.

1½ cups sugar
¼ cup all-purpose flour
⅓ cup butter or margarine,
   softened
3 large eggs
1 cup buttermilk
1 teaspoon vanilla extract
½ teaspoon lemon extract
1 unbaked 9-inch pastry shell
Garnishes: whipped cream, lemon
   slices

● **Combine** first 3 ingredients; beat at medium speed with an electric mixer until blended. Add eggs, buttermilk, and flavorings. Beat at low speed until blended. Pour into pastry shell.
● **Bake** at 325° for 1 hour or until a knife inserted in center comes out clean. Cool on a wire rack. Garnish, if desired. **Yield:** 1 (9-inch) pie.

Mrs. H. W. Walker
Richmond, Virginia

QUICK 'N' EASY CUSTARD PIE

QUICK!

2 cups milk
3 large eggs
½ cup sugar
¾ teaspoon vanilla extract
¼ teaspoon freshly grated
    nutmeg
Dash of salt
1 unbaked 9-inch pastry shell
Freshly grated nutmeg

• **Heat** milk in a medium saucepan until hot. (Do not boil.)
• **Combine** eggs and sugar; beat at high speed with an electric mixer until thickened. Add vanilla, ¼ teaspoon nutmeg, and salt; beat until blended. Gradually stir in hot milk, stirring constantly. Pour into pastry shell; sprinkle with additional nutmeg.
• **Bake** on lower rack of oven at 400° for 25 minutes or until a knife inserted in center of pie comes out clean. Cool completely on a wire rack; cover and chill at least 2 hours before serving. **Yield:** 1 (9-inch) pie.

Claudine M. Moore
Lenoir, North Carolina

WEIDMANN'S BLACK BOTTOM PIE

1½ cups gingersnap crumbs
    (about 26 cookies)
⅓ cup butter or margarine,
    melted
½ cup sugar
¼ cup cornstarch
2 cups milk
4 large egg yolks, beaten
1 teaspoon vanilla extract
1 (1-ounce) square unsweetened
    chocolate
1 envelope unflavored gelatin
2 tablespoons cold water
1 tablespoon meringue powder
¼ cup cold water
½ cup sugar, divided
2 tablespoons bourbon
¾ cup whipping cream,
    whipped
Grated unsweetened chocolate

• **Combine** gingersnap crumbs and butter, and press mixture in bottom and up sides of a 9-inch pieplate.
• **Bake** at 375° for 6 to 8 minutes; cool completely.
• **Combine** ½ cup sugar, cornstarch, and milk in a heavy saucepan. Cook over medium heat, stirring constantly, 8 to 10 minutes or until mixture thickens and boils. Boil 1 minute, stirring constantly. Remove from heat.
• **Stir** about one-fourth of hot mixture gradually into yolks; add to remaining hot mixture, stirring constantly. Stir in vanilla.
• **Melt** chocolate in a small heavy saucepan over low heat, stirring often; set aside.
• **Sprinkle** gelatin over 2 tablespoons cold water; let stand 1 minute. Add gelatin to milk mixture in saucepan. Cook over low heat, stirring until gelatin dissolves (about 2 minutes).
• **Add** 1 cup milk mixture to melted chocolate, stirring with a wire whisk until smooth. Spread over crust. Cool remaining milk mixture.
• **Beat** meringue powder, ¼ cup cold water, and 2 tablespoons sugar at high speed with an electric mixer 5 minutes. Gradually add remaining 6 tablespoons sugar, beating until stiff peaks form (about 3 minutes).
• **Fold** remaining milk mixture and bourbon into meringue mixture; spread over chocolate mixture in crust. Cover and chill pie at least 4 hours.
• **Spread** whipped cream over pie; sprinkle with grated chocolate. **Yield:** 1 (9-inch) pie.

Weidmann's Restaurant
Meridian, Mississippi

CHOCOLATE CREAM PIE

1¼ cups sugar
½ cup all-purpose flour
¼ cup cocoa
Dash of salt
4 egg yolks
2 cups milk
¼ cup butter or margarine
1 teaspoon vanilla extract
1 baked 9-inch pastry shell
Meringue

• **Combine** first 4 ingredients in a large heavy saucepan; set aside.
• **Combine** egg yolks and milk; stir into sugar mixture. Add butter.
• **Cook** over medium heat, stirring constantly, until mixture thickens and boils. Remove from heat. Stir in vanilla. Spoon into pastry shell.
• **Spread** Meringue over hot filling, sealing to edge of pastry.
• **Bake** at 325° for 25 to 28 minutes. **Yield:** 1 (9-inch) pie.

Maryanne I. Kachelhofer
Birmingham, Alabama

Meringue

QUICK!

4 to 6 egg whites
½ to ¾ teaspoon cream of tartar
½ cup sugar
½ teaspoon vanilla extract

• **Beat** egg whites and cream of tartar at high speed with an electric mixer just until foamy.
• **Gradually** add sugar, 1 tablespoon at a time, beating until stiff peaks form and sugar dissolves (2 to 4 minutes). Add vanilla, beating well. **Yield:** enough for 1 (9-inch) pie.

CHOCOLATE-BANANA-PECAN CREAM PIE

¼ cup butter or margarine,
    softened
1 (3-ounce) package cream cheese,
    softened
1½ cups sifted powdered sugar
¼ cup whipping cream
½ teaspoon vanilla extract
3 bananas, sliced
1 (6-ounce) can pineapple juice
1 baked 9-inch pastry shell
½ cup chopped pecans, toasted
2 (1-ounce) squares semisweet
    chocolate
1 cup whipping cream
3 tablespoons powdered sugar

• **Beat** butter and cream cheese at medium speed with an electric mixer until creamy; gradually add 1½ cups powdered sugar alternately with ¼ cup whipping cream, beginning and ending with powdered sugar. Stir in vanilla. Set filling aside.

• **Toss** banana slices in pineapple juice; drain. Pat slices dry with paper towels.

• **Spoon** half of filling into pastry shell. Arrange banana slices over top of filling. Top with remaining filling, and sprinkle with pecans. Set pie aside.

• **Melt** chocolate in a heavy saucepan over low heat. Spoon into a small heavy-duty, zip-top plastic bag. Snip a tiny hole in one corner of bag; drizzle melted chocolate over pecans and filling. Set aside.

• **Beat** 1 cup whipping cream at low speed with an electric mixer until foamy; gradually add 3 tablespoons powdered sugar, beating until soft peaks form.

• **Spoon** whipped cream into a large heavy-duty, zip-top plastic bag. Snip ½ inch from corner of bag. Pipe dollops around outside edge of pie. **Yield:** 1 (9-inch) pie.

Joel Allard
San Antonio, Texas

WHITE CHOCOLATE-BANANA CREAM PIE

1 (4-ounce) bar white chocolate, finely chopped and divided *
1 cup milk
½ vanilla bean
3 tablespoons sugar
2 tablespoons cornstarch
3 egg yolks
1 tablespoon butter or margarine
2 tablespoons white crème de cacao
2 tablespoons crème de bananes
1 cup whipping cream
2 to 3 bananas, sliced
3 tablespoons lemon juice
1 baked 9-inch pastry shell
Cocoa
Garnish: strawberry fan

• **Place** half of white chocolate in top of a double boiler; place over boiling water. Cook until chocolate melts, stirring often. Pour onto an aluminum foil-lined baking sheet. Let stand at room temperature until chocolate cools and

feels slightly tacky but is not firm. (If chocolate is too hard, curls will break; if too soft, chocolate will not curl.) Pull a cheese plane across chocolate until curl forms. Repeat until chocolate is curled. Chill curls.

• **Combine** milk and vanilla bean in a small saucepan; bring to a boil. Remove and discard vanilla bean. Set hot milk aside.

• **Combine** sugar, cornstarch, and egg yolks in a heavy saucepan; gradually stir in hot milk.

• **Cook** over medium heat, stirring constantly, until mixture comes to a boil. Boil 1 minute. Remove from heat. Add butter and remaining half of white chocolate, stirring until chocolate melts. Place plastic wrap directly over surface of white chocolate mixture, and let cool completely.

• **Add** liqueurs to white chocolate mixture, stirring until smooth.

• **Beat** whipping cream until soft peaks form, and fold gently into white chocolate mixture.

• **Coat** banana slices with lemon juice; drain. Pat banana slices dry with paper towels. Gently stir into white chocolate mixture. Spoon into pastry shell. Top with white chocolate curls, and dust lightly with cocoa. Garnish, if desired. **Yield:** 1 (9-inch) pie.

* For white chocolate, we use Ghiradelli Classic White Confection.

COFFEE CREAM PIE
(pictured on page 249)

¼ cup butter or margarine
⅔ cup semisweet chocolate morsels
1⅓ cups graham cracker crumbs
½ cup sugar
3 tablespoons cornstarch
1 teaspoon instant coffee granules
¼ cup boiling water
1¼ cups milk
5 egg yolks, lightly beaten
1¾ cups whipping cream
¼ cup sifted powdered sugar
Garnish: chocolate-covered coffee beans

• **Melt** butter and chocolate morsels in a heavy saucepan over low heat. Stir in graham cracker crumbs. Firmly press into a lightly greased 9-inch pieplate. Bake at 375° for 8 minutes. Cool completely on a wire rack.

• **Combine** ½ cup sugar and cornstarch in a large heavy saucepan; set sugar mixture aside.

• **Combine** coffee granules and boiling water, stirring until coffee granules dissolve. Gradually stir coffee, milk, and egg yolks into sugar mixture.

• **Cook** over medium heat, stirring constantly, until mixture thickens and boils. Boil 1 minute, stirring constantly. Remove from heat; whisk until smooth. Place plastic wrap directly on surface of mixture; chill 1 hour.

• **Beat** whipping cream at low speed with an electric mixer until foamy; gradually add powdered sugar, beating until soft peaks form.

• **Fold** 1½ cups whipped cream into coffee mixture, reserving remaining whipped cream for topping. Spoon filling into prepared crust.

• **Pipe** or dollop remaining cream on top of pie. Chill up to 8 hours. Garnish, if desired. **Yield:** 1 (9-inch) pie.

Agnes L. Stone
Ocala, Florida

RASPBERRY CREAM PIE
(pictured on opposite page)

1 cup sugar
⅓ cup all-purpose flour
2 large eggs, lightly beaten
1⅓ cups sour cream
1 teaspoon vanilla extract
3 cups fresh raspberries
1 unbaked 9-inch pastry shell
⅓ cup all-purpose flour
⅓ cup firmly packed brown
      sugar
⅓ cup chopped pecans
3 tablespoons butter, softened
Garnishes: whipped cream, fresh
      raspberries

• **Combine** first 5 ingredients in a large bowl, stirring until smooth. Gradually fold in raspberries. Spoon into pastry shell.
• **Bake** at 400° for 30 to 35 minutes or until a knife inserted in center comes out clean.
• **Combine** ⅓ cup flour and next 3 ingredients; sprinkle over hot pie.
• **Bake** at 400° for 10 minutes or until golden. Garnish, if desired. **Yield:** 1 (9-inch) pie.

Nell Hamm
Louisville, Mississippi

Note: Do not substitute frozen raspberries for fresh in this pie.

CARAMEL PIE

This recipe is so easy and wildly delicious. If you don't own a 1-quart electric slow cooker, borrow one and make this recipe. But don't try this in a 4- or 5-quart electric slow cooker – the caramel might burn.

2 (14-ounce) cans sweetened
      condensed milk
1 (9-inch) graham cracker crust
1 (8-ounce) container frozen
      whipped topping, thawed
1 (1.4-ounce) English toffee candy
      bar, coarsely chopped

• **Pour** condensed milk into a 1-quart electric slow cooker.

• **Cover** and cook 6 to 7 hours or until mixture is the color of peanut butter, stirring mixture with a wire whisk every 30 minutes.
• **Pour** into graham cracker crust; cool. Spread whipped topping over top, and sprinkle with chopped candy bar. Cover and chill. **Yield:** 1 (9-inch) pie.

♥ To reduce fat and calories, substitute 2 (14-ounce) cans nonfat sweetened condensed milk for regular.

Note: A 1-quart slow cooker has no LOW or HIGH setting, only OFF or ON setting.

Marla Highbaugh
Louisville, Kentucky

COFFEE PIE

Make-ahead tip: This pie holds up well in the refrigerator overnight. Top it with dollops of whipped cream an hour before serving, and keep chilled until guests arrive.

1 cup water
1 tablespoon instant coffee
      granules
1 tablespoon butter or margarine
30 large marshmallows, cut into
      fourths
1 cup whipping cream, whipped
1 baked 9-inch pastry shell
½ cup chopped walnuts or pecans,
      toasted
Garnishes: whipped cream,
      chocolate-covered coffee
      beans

• **Bring** water to a boil in a heavy saucepan; add coffee granules, stirring to dissolve. Add butter and marshmallows to pan.
• **Cook** over low heat until marshmallows melt, stirring occasionally. Cool completely.
• **Fold** whipped cream into coffee mixture; spoon into pastry shell. Sprinkle evenly with walnuts. Cover and chill at least 8 hours. Garnish, if desired. **Yield:** 1 (9-inch) pie.

Jodie McCoy
Tulsa, Oklahoma

BEST-EVER LEMON MERINGUE PIE
(pictured at right)

1½ cups sugar
½ cup cornstarch
⅛ teaspoon salt
4 egg yolks
1¾ cups water
½ cup fresh lemon juice
3 tablespoons butter or margarine
1 teaspoon grated lemon rind
1 baked 9-inch pastry shell
Meringue (see recipe on page 246)

• **Combine** first 3 ingredients in a large heavy saucepan; set sugar mixture aside.
• **Combine** egg yolks, water, and juice; stir into sugar mixture. Cook over medium heat, stirring constantly, until mixture thickens and boils. Boil 1 minute, stirring constantly. Remove from heat. Stir in butter and lemon rind. Spoon into pastry shell.
• **Spread** Meringue over hot filling, sealing to edge of pastry.
• **Bake** at 325° for 25 to 28 minutes. **Yield:** 1 (9-inch) pie.

Anne Galbraith
Knoxville, Tennessee

Note: This pie is very firm with a bright yellow color. If you prefer a less firm pie with a more translucent color, substitute ⅓ cup cornstarch for ½ cup cornstarch, and cook as directed.

Best-Ever Lemon Meringue Pie;
Coffee Cream Pie, page 247;
Raspberry Cream Pie

MANNY AND ISA'S KEY LIME PIE

½ (15-ounce) package
    refrigerated piecrusts
1 teaspoon all-purpose flour
5 large eggs, separated
1 (14-ounce) can sweetened
    condensed milk
½ cup fresh or bottled Key lime
    juice
¼ teaspoon cream of tartar
⅓ to ½ cup sugar

• **Unfold** piecrust, and press out fold lines; sprinkle with flour, spreading over surface. Place crust, floured side down, in a 9-inch pieplate; fold edges under, and flute. Prick bottom and sides of piecrust generously with fork.
• **Bake** at 450° for 9 to 11 minutes; cool on a wire rack.
• **Combine** yolks, condensed milk, and lime juice in a heavy nonaluminum saucepan. Cook over low heat, stirring constantly, 10 minutes or until mixture thickens and boils. Pour into piecrust.
• **Beat** egg whites and cream of tartar at high speed with an electric mixer until foamy. Gradually add sugar, 1 tablespoon at a time, beating until stiff peaks form and sugar dissolves (about 2 to 4 minutes).
• **Spread** meringue over warm filling, sealing to edge of pastry.
• **Bake** at 325° for 25 to 28 minutes. **Yield:** 1 (9-inch) pie.

Manny and Isa Oritz
Manny and Isa's
Islamorada, Florida

KEY LIME PIE

Morgan's idea of an excellent evening is joining friends for a meal that's finished with this refreshing Floridian dessert.

1¾ cups graham cracker crumbs
2 tablespoons sugar
6 tablespoons butter, melted
3 large eggs, separated
1 (14-ounce) can sweetened
    condensed milk
½ cup fresh Key lime juice *
1 tablespoon lemon juice
2 teaspoons grated Key lime rind *
2 tablespoons sugar
1 cup whipping cream
1 tablespoon powdered sugar
½ teaspoon vanilla extract
Garnish: quartered lime slices

• **Combine** first 3 ingredients; press in bottom and 1 inch up sides of a 9-inch springform pan. Cover and chill at least 1 hour.
• **Whisk** egg yolks; add condensed milk and next 3 ingredients, whisking until smooth.
• **Beat** egg whites at high speed until foamy; gradually add 2 tablespoons sugar, beating until soft peaks form. Fold into yolk mixture; spoon into prepared crust.
• **Bake** at 325° for 15 to 20 minutes or until set and lightly browned. Cool on a wire rack; cover and chill 8 hours.
• **Beat** whipping cream at high speed until slightly thickened; add powdered sugar and vanilla, beating until soft peaks form.
• **Remove** sides of springform pan; dollop whipped cream around top of pie. Garnish, if desired. **Yield:** 1 (9-inch) pie.

* You can substitute regular (Persian) lime juice and lime rind for the Key lime variety.

Morgan Reeser
Miami, Florida

PUMPKIN PIE WITH MERINGUE

1 (9-inch) refrigerated piecrust
1 (16-ounce) can pumpkin
3 large eggs, separated
1 (14-ounce) can sweetened
    condensed milk
½ cup flaked coconut
¼ cup water
1 teaspoon ground cinnamon
½ teaspoon ground ginger
½ teaspoon ground nutmeg
Dash of salt
¼ teaspoon cream of tartar
½ cup sugar

• **Place** piecrust in a 9-inch pieplate; trim off excess pastry along edges. Fold edges of pastry under, and crimp. Prick bottom and sides of pastry with a fork. Bake at 425° for 5 minutes on lowest oven rack.
• **Combine** pumpkin, egg yolks, condensed milk, and next 6 ingredients; pour into piecrust. Cover edges of pastry with strips of aluminum foil to prevent excessive browning, and bake pie at 400° for 30 minutes on middle oven rack.
• **Beat** egg whites and cream of tartar at high speed with an electric mixer until foamy. Gradually add sugar, 1 tablespoon at a time, beating until stiff peaks form and sugar dissolves (2 to 4 minutes). Spread over hot filling, sealing to edge of pastry. Cover edges of pastry with strips of aluminum foil to prevent excessive browning, and bake at 325° for 25 to 28 minutes or until golden; cool on a wire rack. **Yield:** 1 (9-inch) pie.

Sandra Russell
Gainesville, Florida

LEMON PARFAIT PIE

1 cup sugar
2 tablespoons cornstarch
¼ teaspoon salt
1 tablespoon grated lemon rind
⅓ cup fresh lemon juice
3 egg yolks, lightly beaten
¼ cup butter or margarine
2 pints vanilla ice cream,
    softened
Graham Cracker Crust
¾ cup sugar
½ cup boiling water
¼ cup meringue powder *

• **Combine** first 5 ingredients in a heavy saucepan, stirring until blended. Add egg yolks and butter. Bring mixture to a boil over medium heat, stirring constantly. Boil 1 minute; remove from heat, and let cool.
• **Spread** half of ice cream in Graham Cracker Crust, and top with half of lemon mixture. Cover and freeze until firm. Repeat procedure with remaining ice cream and lemon mixture, and freeze until firm.
• **Combine** ¾ cup sugar and boiling water, stirring until sugar dissolves. Remove from heat, and let cool.
• **Add** meringue powder; beat at high speed with an electric mixer until stiff peaks form. Spread meringue over filling, sealing to edge of crust.
• **Bake** at 425° for 5 to 7 minutes or until golden. Serve pie immediately or return to freezer. **Yield:** 1 (9-inch) pie.

* For meringue powder, we used Country Kitchen brand.

Graham Cracker Crust

QUICK!

1¼ cups graham cracker crumbs
¼ cup sugar
⅓ cup butter or margarine,
    melted

• **Combine** all ingredients, and press mixture in bottom and up sides of a 9-inch pieplate.
• **Bake** at 375° for 6 to 8 minutes. Cool. **Yield:** 1 (9-inch) crust.

A Taste of Georgia
Junior Service League of Newnan, Georgia

CARAMEL-NUT CRUNCH PIE

QUICK!

Use a squeeze bottle to drizzle the hot fudge and caramel toppings on this pie. The tip of a teaspoon or a zip-top plastic bag with a corner snipped off will also work.

2 cups cream-filled chocolate
    sandwich cookie crumbs
    (about 20 cookies, crushed)
½ cup unsalted dry roasted
    peanuts, coarsely chopped
¼ cup butter or margarine,
    melted
6 (2.07-ounce) chocolate-coated
    caramel-peanut nougat bars *
1½ quarts vanilla ice cream,
    slightly softened
1 (11.75-ounce) jar hot fudge
    sauce, divided
1 (12-ounce) jar hot caramel
    sauce, divided

• **Combine** first 3 ingredients; press in bottom and up sides of a 9-inch deep-dish pieplate.
• **Bake** at 350° for 10 minutes; cool completely on a wire rack.
• **Chop** candy bars into small pieces, and reserve 2 tablespoons. Fold remaining candy into ice cream, and spread evenly into prepared crust.
• **Drizzle** with 2 tablespoons fudge sauce and 2 tablespoons caramel sauce; sprinkle with reserved candy.
• **Cover** and freeze until firm.
• **Remove** pie from freezer 20 minutes before serving. Serve with remaining fudge and caramel sauces. **Yield:** 1 (9-inch) pie.

* For chocolate-coated caramel-peanut nougat bars, we used Snickers.

Lilann Taylor
Savannah, Georgia

FROZEN CHOCOLATE BROWNIE PIE

¼ cup margarine
⅔ cup firmly packed brown sugar
½ cup fat-free egg substitute
¼ cup buttermilk
¼ cup all-purpose flour
⅓ cup cocoa
¼ teaspoon salt
1 teaspoon vanilla extract
Vegetable cooking spray
½ gallon vanilla nonfat frozen
    yogurt, softened
1 quart chocolate nonfat frozen
    yogurt, softened
¾ cup chocolate syrup
Garnishes: fresh strawberries,
    chocolate curls

• **Melt** margarine in a large saucepan over medium-high heat; add brown sugar, stirring with a wire whisk to blend. Remove from heat, and let cool slightly.
• **Add** egg substitute and buttermilk to pan, stirring well.
• **Combine** flour, cocoa, and salt; add to buttermilk mixture, stirring until blended. Stir in vanilla. Pour into a 9-inch springform pan lightly coated with cooking spray.
• **Bake** at 350° for 15 minutes. Cool completely in pan on a wire rack.
• **Spread** half of vanilla yogurt over brownie layer; cover and freeze until firm. Spread chocolate yogurt over vanilla yogurt; cover and freeze until firm. Top with remaining vanilla yogurt. Cover and freeze at least 8 hours.
• **Remove** sides of pan. Cut into wedges. Serve each wedge with 1 tablespoon syrup; garnish, if desired. **Yield:** 1 (9-inch) pie (12 servings).

Karen Moneyhun
Centreville, Virginia

♥ Per serving: Calories 258
Fat 4.8g Cholesterol 0mg
Sodium 205mg

FROZEN CHOCOLATE-MACADAMIA NUT PIE

1 (8-ounce) package cream cheese, softened
½ cup sugar
1 teaspoon vanilla extract
1 cup (6 ounces) semisweet chocolate morsels, melted
1½ cups macadamia nuts, finely chopped
1½ cups whipping cream
½ cup sugar
Chocolate-Macadamia Crumb Crust
Garnish: sweetened whipped cream

● **Combine** first 3 ingredients; beat at high speed with an electric mixer until smooth and creamy. Add chocolate morsels; beat at lowest speed just until blended. Stir in chopped nuts.
● **Beat** whipping cream at high speed until foamy. Gradually add sugar, beating until firm peaks form; fold into chocolate mixture. Pour into Chocolate-Macadamia Crumb Crust; cover and freeze 8 hours. Garnish, if desired. **Yield:** 1 (9-inch) pie.

Chocolate-Macadamia Crumb Crust

QUICK!

1¼ cups chocolate wafer crumbs
½ cup macadamia nuts, finely chopped
⅓ cup butter or margarine, melted

● **Combine** all ingredients, and press in bottom and up sides of a 9-inch pieplate.
● **Bake** at 350° for 8 minutes; cool. **Yield:** 1 (9-inch) piecrust.

Kim McCully
Knoxville, Tennessee

TURTLE PECAN PIE

3 cups chocolate wafer crumbs
½ cup butter or margarine, melted
1¼ cups semisweet chocolate morsels
1 cup evaporated milk
1 cup miniature marshmallows
⅛ teaspoon salt
1 quart vanilla ice cream, divided
1 cup pecan halves, toasted

● **Combine** chocolate crumbs and butter; press firmly in a 9-inch deep-dish pieplate, and freeze 15 minutes.
● **Combine** chocolate morsels and next 3 ingredients in a heavy saucepan. Cook over low heat, stirring constantly, until thickened and smooth. Remove from heat, and set aside.

MOCHA PIE

1 (11.75-ounce) jar hot fudge sauce, divided
1 (6-ounce) chocolate-flavored crumb crust
1 pint coffee ice cream, softened
3 (2.07-ounce) chocolate-coated caramel-peanut nougat bars, chopped and divided *
1 pint chocolate ice cream, softened
¼ cup slivered almonds, toasted

● **Spread** half of fudge sauce into crumb crust; carefully spread coffee ice cream over sauce. Top with half of chopped candy bars.
● **Cover** and freeze 2 hours.
● **Spread** chocolate ice cream over candy bars; carefully spread remaining fudge sauce over ice cream. Top with remaining half of candy, and sprinkle with almonds.
● **Cover** and freeze until firm. **Yield:** 1 (9-inch) pie.

* For chocolate-coated caramel-peanut nougat bars, we used Snickers.

Sharon Dorris
Nashville, Tennessee

● **Spread** 2 cups ice cream into prepared crust; cover and freeze 30 minutes. Pour half of chocolate mixture over ice cream layer; cover and freeze 30 minutes. Spread remaining ice cream over chocolate mixture; cover and freeze 30 minutes. Spread remaining chocolate mixture over ice cream, and top with pecans. Cover and freeze until firm. **Yield:** 1 (9-inch) pie.

Nuttin' 'Cept Pecan Pies
Charles Wallace
Austin, Texas

APPLE-CREAM CHEESE TART

Cream Cheese Pastry
½ (8-ounce) package cream cheese, softened
¼ cup sour cream
1 egg yolk
2 tablespoons honey
⅛ teaspoon grated lemon rind
1 large Granny Smith apple, peeled and thinly sliced
1 tablespoon apple jelly
1½ teaspoons water
½ cup whipping cream
1½ teaspoons honey
⅛ teaspoon vanilla extract

● **Roll** Cream Cheese Pastry to ⅛-inch thickness on a lightly floured surface; fit into a 7½-inch round tart pan with removable bottom. Trim excess pastry along edges; freeze 10 minutes. Line pastry with aluminum foil, and fill with pie weights or dried beans.
● **Bake** at 400° for 10 minutes. Remove weights and foil, and prick bottom of crust with a fork. Bake 10 additional minutes. Cool on a wire rack (pastry will shrink).
● **Beat** cream cheese and next 4 ingredients in a mixing bowl at medium speed with an electric mixer until smooth. Spoon into tart shell, and arrange apple slices on top.
● **Combine** apple jelly and water in a small saucepan; cook over low heat, stirring constantly, until jelly melts. Brush half of jelly mixture over apples.
● **Bake** at 400° on lower rack of oven 35 minutes. Cool on wire rack 15 minutes. Brush with remaining jelly mixture; cool.

• **Beat** whipping cream at medium speed until soft peaks form; stir in 1½ teaspoons honey and vanilla. Serve with tart. **Yield:** 1 (7½-inch) tart.

Cream Cheese Pastry

QUICK!

The food processor makes quick work of this flaky pastry.

¼ cup butter, cut up
½ (8-ounce) package cream cheese, cut up
1 cup all-purpose flour
¼ teaspoon salt

• **Combine** all ingredients with pastry blender or in a food processor. Shape pastry into a ball; seal in plastic wrap, and chill at least 30 minutes (pastry will be dry). **Yield:** enough for 1 (7½-inch) tart shell.

Elizabeth Berek Ellis
Austin, Texas

APRICOT-APPLE CRUMB TART

2 (6-ounce) packages dried apricot halves
1 (8-ounce) package dried apples *
3 cups water
¼ cup sugar
1 tablespoon all-purpose flour
½ (15-ounce) package refrigerated piecrusts
1 teaspoon all-purpose flour
½ cup all-purpose flour
½ cup sugar
¼ cup butter or margarine
Ice cream or sweetened whipped cream

• **Combine** first 3 ingredients in a large saucepan; bring mixture to a boil. Reduce heat, and simmer 30 minutes. Drain well.
• **Combine** ¼ cup sugar and 1 tablespoon flour; stir into fruit mixture. Set aside.
• **Unroll** pie crust, and press out fold lines. Fit into bottom and up sides of a 9-inch tart pan; sprinkle with 1 teaspoon flour. Spoon fruit mixture into prepared pastry shell.

• **Combine** ½ cup flour and ½ cup sugar; cut in butter with pastry blender until mixture is crumbly. Sprinkle mixture over tart.
• **Bake** at 425° for 10 minutes; reduce oven temperature to 350°, and bake 35 additional minutes or until lightly browned. Serve within 12 hours with ice cream or sweetened whipped cream, if desired. **Yield:** 1 (9-inch) tart.

✳ To create a tarter dessert, substitute 1 (6-ounce) package dried apricot halves for the dried apples.

Mrs. Carl M. Schmieg
Annandale, Virginia

KING CAKE FRUIT TART

1 (20-ounce) package refrigerated sliceable sugar cookie dough
1 (8-ounce) package cream cheese, softened
1 (3-ounce) package cream cheese, softened
1 cup sifted powdered sugar
1 teaspoon vanilla extract
4 to 6 kiwifruit, peeled and sliced
4 to 6 carambola (star fruit), sliced
1 cup blueberries
1 cup seedless purple grapes, cut in half
1 (8-ounce) can pineapple chunks, drained
¾ cup apple jelly
2 tablespoons water
¼ cup chopped pecans, toasted

• **Line** 2 (9-inch) round cakepans with 12-inch squares of aluminum foil, allowing corners to extend outside pans.
• **Cut** cookie dough into ⅛-inch-thick slices; line each prepared pan with half of slices, pressing edges of dough together to seal.
• **Bake** at 325° for 15 to 20 minutes or until lightly browned; cool completely in pans on wire racks.
• **Remove** cookie crusts from pans, using foil corners. Remove foil from crusts; place crusts on serving plates.
• **Combine** cream cheese, powdered sugar, and vanilla; beat at medium speed with an electric mixer until

smooth and fluffy. Spread evenly over each crust. Arrange kiwifruit and next 4 ingredients on top.
• **Combine** apple jelly and 2 tablespoons water in a small saucepan; cook over medium heat, stirring constantly, until jelly melts. Remove from heat, and drizzle evenly over each tart. Sprinkle with pecans. Cover and chill at least 1 hour. **Yield:** 2 (9-inch) tarts.

Jami Gaudet
Macon, Georgia

CAKY FLAKY TART (TART LEMON TART)

A good rule of thumb: 1 medium lemon yields about 3 tablespoons of juice and 2 to 3 teaspoons zest or grated rind.

1½ cups sugar
1 tablespoon all-purpose flour
1 tablespoon cornmeal
3 large eggs
3 tablespoons butter or margarine, melted
3 tablespoons milk
1½ teaspoons grated lemon rind
½ cup fresh lemon juice
1 unbaked 9-inch pastry shell
Garnishes: whipped cream, fresh mint leaves

• **Combine** first 4 ingredients in a large bowl, stirring well. Stir in melted butter and next 3 ingredients. Pour into pastry shell.
• **Bake** at 375° for 35 minutes or until filling is set, shielding edges with strips of aluminum foil after 25 minutes to prevent excessive browning. Cool completely on a wire rack. Garnish, if desired. **Yield:** 1 (9-inch) tart.

Diane Pfeifer
Stand By Your Pan
Atlanta, Georgia

CARAMEL TURTLE-TRUFFLE TART

Sugar Cookie Crust
1½ cups semisweet chocolate morsels
¾ cup whipping cream, divided
1 (14-ounce) package caramels
3 cups chopped pecans

● **Prepare** Sugar Cookie Crust, and press in bottom and up sides of an 11-inch tart pan; prick bottom generously with a fork. Bake at 400° for 10 minutes or until golden; cool.
● **Combine** chocolate morsels and ¼ cup whipping cream in a small microwave-safe bowl; microwave on HIGH 1 to 1½ minutes until chocolate melts, stirring once. Spread 1 cup mixture evenly in bottom of baked pastry, reserving remaining chocolate mixture. Cover and chill pastry 30 minutes.
● **Combine** caramels and remaining ½ cup whipping cream in a heavy saucepan; cook over low heat, stirring constantly, until caramels melt and mixture is smooth. Stir in pecans, and spread evenly over chocolate layer.
● **Spoon** reserved chocolate mixture into a small zip-top plastic bag. (If chocolate is firm, microwave on HIGH 30 seconds or until soft.) Cut a small hole in one corner of bag; drizzle chocolate over tart. Cover and chill at least 1 hour. Let stand 30 minutes before serving. **Yield:** 1 (11-inch) tart.

Sugar Cookie Crust

QUICK!

1⅓ cups all-purpose flour
⅓ cup sugar
½ cup butter, cut into slices
1 large egg
1 teaspoon vanilla extract

● **Position** knife blade in food processor bowl; add first 3 ingredients. Process 1 minute or until mixture is crumbly. Remove food pusher. Add egg and vanilla through chute with processor running; process until mixture forms a smooth dough. **Yield:** enough pastry for 1 (11-inch) tart.

Margot Hahn
Washington, D.C.

CHOCOLATE-PECAN TART WITH CARAMEL SAUCE

2 cups pecan pieces
¼ cup firmly packed brown sugar
¼ teaspoon ground cinnamon
2 tablespoons butter or margarine, softened
2 cups (12 ounces) semisweet chocolate morsels
½ cup half-and-half
Caramel Sauce

● **Position** knife blade in food processor bowl; add pecans, and pulse 5 or 6 times or until finely chopped. Add brown sugar, cinnamon, and butter; process 30 seconds, stopping once to scrape down sides.
● **Press** pecan mixture evenly in bottom and about ½ inch up sides of a 9-inch tart pan.
● **Bake** at 325° for about 25 minutes; set aside.
● **Combine** chocolate morsels and half-and-half in a saucepan; cook over medium heat, stirring constantly, until chocolate melts and mixture is smooth. Pour into tart shell.
● **Cover** and chill at least 2 hours. Serve with warm Caramel Sauce. **Yield:** 1 (9-inch) tart.

Caramel Sauce

QUICK!

½ cup butter or margarine
1¼ cups sugar
2 cups half-and-half

● **Melt** butter in a heavy saucepan over medium heat; add sugar, and cook, stirring constantly with a wire whisk, about 10 minutes or until mixture is a deep golden brown.
● **Add** half-and-half (mixture will lump), and cook, stirring constantly, until mixture is smooth and reduced to 2¼ cups (about 10 minutes). **Yield:** 2¼ cups.

Louise Bodziony
Gladstone, Missouri

WHITE CHOCOLATE CHESS TART

½ (15-ounce) package refrigerated piecrusts
1 (4-ounce) bar white chocolate, chopped
½ cup buttermilk
3 large eggs, lightly beaten
1 tablespoon vanilla extract
1¼ cups sugar
Pinch of salt
3 tablespoons all-purpose flour
1 tablespoon cornmeal

● **Fit** 1 piecrust into a 9-inch tart pan with removable bottom according to package directions; trim edges. Line pastry with aluminum foil, and fill with pie weights or dried beans.
● **Bake** at 450° for 8 minutes. Remove weights and foil; bake 3 to 4 additional minutes. Let cool in pan on a wire rack.
● **Combine** chocolate and buttermilk in a small saucepan; cook over low heat, stirring constantly, until chocolate melts and mixture is smooth. Cool 15 minutes.
● **Combine** eggs and vanilla in a bowl; gradually stir in chocolate mixture.
● **Combine** sugar and remaining 3 ingredients; gradually add to chocolate mixture, stirring until blended. Pour mixture into piecrust.
● **Bake** at 325° for 50 minutes or until a knife inserted in center comes out clean. Cool on a wire rack. **Yield:** 1 (9-inch) tart.

BRANDIED APPLE TARTS

1 (17¼-ounce) package frozen puff pastry sheets, thawed
½ cup butter or margarine, softened
2 tablespoons sugar
1 cup sugar
6 Rome apples, thinly sliced
¼ teaspoon ground cinnamon
½ cup brandy
Vanilla ice cream

● **Cut** pastry into 6 (5-inch) circles, and place on a baking sheet. Spread evenly with butter, and sprinkle with 2 tablespoons sugar. Lightly grease bottom of

another baking sheet, and place directly on pastry circles.
- **Bake** at 400° for 10 minutes or until pastry is golden. Remove to wire racks to cool.
- **Sprinkle** 1 cup sugar in a large skillet; cook over medium heat, stirring constantly, until golden. Stir in apple slices and cinnamon; cook until tender, stirring occasionally. Remove apples with a slotted spoon.
- **Stir** brandy into sugar mixture; cook 10 to 15 minutes or until thickened, stirring occasionally.
- **Place** pastry circles on individual dessert plates. Arrange apple slices on top; drizzle with brandy mixture. Top with vanilla ice cream, and serve immediately. **Yield:** 6 (5-inch) tarts.

BLACKBERRY PUDDING TARTS

1 (15-ounce) package refrigerated piecrusts
2 quarts fresh or frozen blackberries, thawed
1 cup water
1½ cups sugar
½ cup self-rising flour
¼ cup butter or margarine
2 teaspoons vanilla extract
Whipped cream

- **Unfold** 1 piecrust, and roll into a 15-inch circle on a lightly floured surface; cut into 5 (5½-inch) circles. Fit each circle into a 5-inch round tart pan with removable bottom, and place pans on a baking sheet. Prick bottom and sides of pastry with a fork. Repeat procedure with remaining piecrust. Bake at 450° for 8 minutes or until lightly browned. Remove to wire racks; cool.
- **Combine** blackberries and water in a large saucepan; bring to a boil. Reduce heat, and simmer, uncovered, 5 minutes or until blackberries are soft. Mash berries with a fork; pour through a large wire-mesh strainer into a 4-cup liquid measuring cup, discarding pulp and seeds. (Measurement should be 2 cups blackberry juice. If necessary, boil berry juice to reduce to 2 cups.)
- **Combine** sugar and flour in a medium saucepan; gradually add juice, stirring

constantly until smooth. Bring to a boil over medium heat, stirring constantly. Reduce heat, and simmer, uncovered, 3 minutes or until slightly thickened. Remove from heat; stir in butter and vanilla. Spoon about ¼ cup mixture into each prepared tart shell. Cool; top with a dollop of whipped cream. **Yield:** 10 (5½-inch) tarts.

Jean King
Walnut Hill, Florida

PEAR TART

Butter-flavored cooking spray
3 sheets frozen phyllo pastry, thawed
¼ cup finely chopped blanched almonds
¼ cup fat-free egg substitute
2 tablespoons sugar
1½ cups water
2 tablespoons lemon juice
3 medium-size fresh pears
2 tablespoons sugar
¼ teaspoon ground cinnamon
1 tablespoon sliced almonds
¼ cup low-sugar apple jelly, melted

- **Coat** a 10-inch pieplate with cooking spray. Place 1 sheet of phyllo pastry over pieplate, leaving edges of phyllo overhanging; coat sheet with cooking spray. Place second sheet of phyllo on top in opposite direction, and coat with cooking spray. Top with third sheet; coat with cooking spray. Roll and fold edges loosely under themselves to form a ruffled edge, and set aside.
- **Combine** chopped almonds, egg substitute, and 2 tablespoons sugar; spread over bottom of shell.
- **Combine** water and lemon juice in a medium bowl. Peel and core pears; dip pears in lemon juice mixture, and drain well. Cut pears in half vertically; cut each half into ⅛- to ¼-inch slices, keeping slices in order as they are cut. Arrange slices over almond mixture in shape of 6 pear halves, letting slices fan out slightly.
- **Combine** 2 tablespoons sugar and cinnamon; sprinkle over pears. Coat lightly with cooking spray. Cover edges of

phyllo with aluminum foil to prevent excessive browning. Bake at 400° for 35 minutes. Remove foil from edges; sprinkle sliced almonds over tart. Bake 5 additional minutes or until edges of phyllo are golden. Remove from oven; brush pears with apple jelly. **Yield:** 1 (10-inch) tart (6 servings).

♥ Per serving: Calories 168
Fat 3.8g Cholesterol 0mg
Sodium 72mg

CRAN-RASPBERRY MERINGUE TARTS

3 egg whites
¼ teaspoon cream of tartar
1 cup sugar
1 teaspoon vanilla extract
½ cup no-sugar-added raspberry-cranberry fruit spread

- **Beat** egg whites and cream of tartar at high speed with an electric mixer 1 minute. Gradually add sugar, 1 tablespoon at a time, beating until stiff peaks form and sugar dissolves (about 2 to 4 minutes). Stir in vanilla.
- **Drop** by heaping teaspoonfuls onto cookie sheets lined with unglazed brown paper. (Do not use recycled paper.) Using back of a teaspoon, make a small indentation in center of each meringue. Bake at 250° for 45 minutes; turn off heat and leave meringues in oven, with door closed, at least 2 hours.
- **Carefully** peel meringues from brown paper. Just before serving, fill each with about ½ teaspoon fruit spread. **Yield:** 50 tarts.

♥ Per tart: Calories 19
Fat 0g Cholesterol 0mg
Sodium 4mg

BOWL-ME-OVER FRESH FRUIT TARTS

1 (15-ounce) package refrigerated
   piecrusts
1 cup fresh raspberries
1 cup fresh blackberries
1 cup fresh whole strawberries
1 cup fresh or canned apricots,
   halved
2 kiwifruit, peeled and sliced
1 tablespoon sugar (optional)
Lemon Cream Sauce

• **Unfold** 1 piecrust, and roll into a 13-inch circle on a lightly floured surface; carefully tear 3 (5½-inch) circles, leaving jagged edges. Repeat procedure with remaining piecrust.
• **Place** 6 (6-ounce) custard cups upside down on a 15- x 10- x 1-inch jellyroll pan; lightly grease bottom and sides of cups. Drape a pastry circle over each cup; pinch dough to make 6 pleats, conforming pastry to shape of cup. Prick bottom and sides with a fork. Bake at 425° for 10 minutes or until lightly browned. Remove to wire racks; cool 5 minutes. Carefully remove pastry from cups; turn right side up, and cool completely on wire racks.
• **Combine** fruit in a large bowl, and add sugar, if desired; cover and chill up to 2 hours.
• **To** serve, spoon about ¾ cup fruit mixture into each tart shell. Serve with Lemon Cream Sauce. **Yield:** 6 (5½-inch) tarts.

Lemon Cream Sauce

QUICK!

1 (12-ounce) jar lemon curd
1 cup whipping cream

• **Combine** lemon curd and whipping cream, beating with a wire whisk until smooth. Cover and chill up to 24 hours before serving. **Yield:** 2 cups.

Note: Look for lemon curd, a creamy mixture of lemon juice, sugar, butter, and egg yolks, at specialty food shops and large supermarkets. Serve any extra Lemon Cream Sauce over pound cake.

MIDNIGHT DELIGHTS

Make-ahead tip: Bake and freeze up to 3 months. Dollop with whipped cream mixture before serving.

⅔ cup boiling water
2 teaspoons instant coffee
   granules
1¾ cups all-purpose flour
⅓ cup cocoa
¼ cup sugar
Dash of salt
¾ cup butter, cut into small pieces
2 cups (12 ounces) semisweet
   chocolate morsels, melted
⅔ cup sugar
2 tablespoons butter, melted
2 tablespoons milk
2 teaspoons Kahlúa or other
   coffee-flavored liqueur or
   strongly brewed coffee
2 large eggs
½ cup chopped pecans or
   walnuts
½ cup whipping cream
1 tablespoon powdered sugar

• **Combine** water and coffee granules, stirring well; let cool. Reserve 2 teaspoons coffee mixture.
• **Combine** flour and next 3 ingredients; cut in butter with pastry blender until mixture is crumbly. Sprinkle remaining coffee mixture, 1 tablespoon at a time, over flour mixture, and stir with a fork until dry ingredients are moistened.
• **Turn** dough out onto a lightly floured surface, and knead 2 or 3 times. Wrap in wax paper, and chill at least 1 hour.
• **Shape** dough into ¾-inch balls; press into lightly greased miniature (1¾-inch) muffin pans, using a tart tamper or back of a spoon. Cover and chill slightly.
• **Combine** melted chocolate and next 4 ingredients, stirring until smooth; stir in eggs and chopped pecans. Spoon 1 rounded teaspoonful mixture into each tart shell.
• **Bake** at 350° for 20 minutes. Cool in pans on wire racks 15 minutes; remove from pans, and cool completely on wire racks.
• **Combine** reserved 2 teaspoons coffee mixture, whipping cream, and powdered sugar; beat at medium speed with an electric mixer until soft peaks form.

Pipe or dollop a small amount onto each tart just before serving. **Yield:** 4 dozen.

Yetta J. Burrell
Valdosta, Georgia

BOURBON-CHOCOLATE-PECAN TARTS

Try this wonderfully rich twist on a favorite Southern dessert.

Cream Cheese Pastry
¾ cup semisweet chocolate
   morsels
3 large eggs, lightly beaten
⅓ cup sugar
3 tablespoons firmly packed light
   brown sugar
1 tablespoon all-purpose flour
¾ cup light corn syrup
¼ cup butter or margarine,
   melted
3 tablespoons bourbon
2 teaspoons vanilla extract
2 cups pecan halves
Garnishes: whipped cream, pecan
   halves, chopped pecans

• **Divide** Cream Cheese Pastry into 6 equal portions; shape each portion into a ball, and press into a 4½-inch tart pan. Sprinkle chocolate morsels into tart shells; chill 30 minutes.
• **Beat** eggs and next 7 ingredients at medium speed with an electric mixer until blended. Pour batter into tart shells, filling each half full. Arrange pecan halves over filling; drizzle with remaining filling.
• **Bake** at 350° for 30 to 35 minutes or until set; cool. Garnish, if desired. **Yield:** 6 (4½-inch) tarts.

Cream Cheese Pastry

QUICK!

1 (3-ounce) package cream cheese,
   softened
½ cup butter or margarine,
   softened
1 cup all-purpose flour

• **Beat** cream cheese and butter at medium speed with an electric mixer until smooth. Add flour, and beat at low speed until a soft dough forms. **Yield:** pastry for 6 (4½-inch) tarts.

Note: You can bake tart filling in a 9-inch tart pan fitted with pastry crust. Prepare as directed, and bake at 350° for 55 minutes or until set.

Trenda Leigh
Richmond, Virginia

TOASTY SOUTHERN PECAN TARTS

1 tablespoon butter or
   margarine
1 cup chopped pecans
⅛ teaspoon salt
1 (15-ounce) package refrigerated
   piecrusts
½ cup butter or margarine
1 cup light corn syrup
1 cup sugar
¼ teaspoon ground cinnamon
3 large eggs, beaten
1 teaspoon vanilla extract
½ teaspoon lemon juice

• **Place** 1 tablespoon butter in a large shallow pan; bake at 350° until melted. Add pecans, stirring to coat; bake 8 to 10 minutes or until toasted, stirring once. Remove from oven, and sprinkle with salt; cool.
• **Roll** 1 piecrust on a lightly floured surface to press out fold lines. Cut into rounds with a 2½-inch round cutter. Fit pastry rounds into miniature (1¾-inch) muffin pans; do not trim edges. Repeat procedure with remaining piecrust. Sprinkle toasted pecans evenly into tart shells; set aside.
• **Place** ½ cup butter in a small heavy saucepan; cook over medium heat, stirring constantly, until lightly browned (do not burn). Remove from heat; cool 10 minutes.
• **Add** corn syrup and remaining 5 ingredients to butter, stirring well; spoon evenly over pecans into tart shells.
• **Bake** at 350° for 35 to 40 minutes or until set. Cool in pans 5 minutes. Remove from pans; cool completely on wire racks. **Yield:** 4½ dozen.

Palmer Ragsdale
Rockwall, Texas

APPLE DUMPLINGS WITH MAPLE-CIDER SAUCE

3 cups all-purpose flour
1 teaspoon salt
¾ cup butter, chilled and cut into
   pieces
5 tablespoons shortening
½ cup apple cider, chilled
8 large Granny Smith apples
½ cup firmly packed brown sugar
½ cup currants
½ cup chopped walnuts
⅓ cup butter, softened
1 large egg
1 tablespoon water
4 (3-inch) sticks cinnamon, broken
   in half
Maple-Cider Sauce

• **Combine** flour and salt; cut in ¾ cup butter and shortening with pastry blender until mixture is crumbly. Sprinkle cider, 1 tablespoon at a time, evenly over surface; stir with a fork until dry ingredients are moistened. Shape into 2 (½-inch-thick) squares; cover and chill.
• **Core** each apple, leaving ½ inch intact on bottom. Peel top two-thirds of each apple; set apples aside.
• **Combine** sugar, currants, and walnuts; stir in ⅓ cup softened butter, blending well. Spoon into each apple.
• **Roll** pastry squares to ⅛-inch thickness on a floured surface; cut each square into 4 (7-inch) squares.
• **Press** 1 pastry square around each apple; remove excess pastry from bottom so apple will sit level. Reroll scraps, if desired, and cut into leaf shapes.
• **Combine** egg and water, beating lightly with a fork. Brush over apples, and attach leaf shapes, if desired.
• **Place** a cinnamon stick half in top of each apple to resemble a stem. Place apples in a lightly greased 15- x 10- x 1-inch jellyroll pan.
• **Bake** at 375° for 40 minutes. Pour Maple-Cider Sauce over apples; bake 15 minutes or until apples are tender. Place apples on a serving plate; spoon sauce around apples. **Yield:** 8 servings.

Note: Serve maple whipped cream with the apples. To make it, combine 1 cup whipping cream and 3 tablespoons maple syrup in a medium bowl, and beat at high speed with an electric mixer until soft peaks form.

Maple-Cider Sauce
QUICK!

2 teaspoons cornstarch
1½ cups apple cider
⅔ cup maple syrup
¼ cup firmly packed brown sugar
¼ cup fresh lemon juice

• **Combine** cornstarch and cider in a saucepan, stirring until smooth; add maple syrup, sugar, and lemon juice. Bring to a boil over medium-high heat; boil 1 minute. **Yield:** 2 cups.

Mildred Bickley
Bristol, Virginia

APPLE SQUARES

4 cups all-purpose flour
1 teaspoon salt
2 cups shortening
1 (8-ounce) carton sour cream
6 large cooking apples, peeled,
   cored, and sliced
1 cup sugar
½ cup firmly packed brown sugar
1½ tablespoons lemon juice
¼ cup graham cracker crumbs
¼ cup fine, dry breadcrumbs

• **Combine** flour and salt; cut in shortening with pastry blender until mixture is crumbly. Add sour cream; stir with a fork until flour mixture is moistened. Cover and chill.
• **Combine** apple and next 3 ingredients; set aside.
• **Divide** flour mixture in half; roll 1 portion into a 15- x 10-inch rectangle on wax paper. Place in an ungreased 15- x 10- x 1-inch jellyroll pan. Sprinkle with graham cracker crumbs and breadcrumbs. Arrange apple mixture over crumbs. Roll remaining pastry into a 16- x 12-inch rectangle; place over apple mixture. Fold edges under, and crimp. Bake at 375° for 1 hour. Let cool in pan on a wire rack. Cut into 2-inch squares. **Yield:** about 3 dozen.

Mary Prischak
Ladson, South Carolina

APPLE STRUDEL

1 (17¼-ounce) package frozen
   puff pastry sheets, thawed
2 tablespoons butter or margarine,
   melted and divided
¼ cup firmly packed brown
   sugar
1 teaspoon grated lemon rind
½ cup chopped pecans, divided
½ cup raisins, divided
1 (21-ounce) can apple pie filling,
   chopped

• **Roll** each sheet of pastry into a 12- x 9-inch rectangle. Brush 1 rectangle with 1 tablespoon melted butter. Combine brown sugar and lemon rind; sprinkle half of brown sugar mixture on buttered pastry. Sprinkle half of pecans and raisins over brown sugar mixture. Brush remaining 1 tablespoon melted butter over second sheet of pastry, and place on top of first sheet. Sprinkle with remaining brown sugar mixture, chopped pecans, and raisins.

• **Spoon** pie filling down 1 (12-inch) edge of pastry; starting with long side, roll up, jellyroll fashion. Place strudel, seam side down, on a lightly greased baking sheet. With a knife, make diagonal 2-inch slits in top of pastry every 1 to 2 inches. Bake strudel at 400° for 40 minutes or until golden. **Yield:** 1 (12-inch) strudel.

FRIED APRICOT PIES

1 (6-ounce) package dried apricot
   halves, chopped
1¼ cups water
½ cup sugar
½ teaspoon ground cinnamon
½ teaspoon ground nutmeg
1 tablespoon lemon or orange
   juice
1 (15-ounce) package refrigerated
   piecrusts
Vegetable oil
Powdered sugar

• **Combine** apricot and water in a small saucepan; bring to a boil. Cover, reduce heat, and simmer 20 minutes or until apricot is tender. Drain, if necessary.

• **Mash** apricot. Stir in sugar, cinnamon, nutmeg, and lemon juice; set mixture aside.

• **Unfold** 1 piecrust, and press out fold lines. Roll piecrust to ⅛-inch thickness on a lightly floured surface. Cut into 5 (5-inch) circles; stack circles between wax paper. Repeat procedure with remaining piecrust.

• **Spoon** 2 tablespoons apricot mixture on half of each circle. Moisten edges with water; fold dough over apricot mixture, pressing edges to seal. Crimp edges with a fork.

• **Pour** oil to depth of 1 inch into a large heavy skillet. Fry pies in hot oil (375°) about 2 minutes or until golden, turning once. Drain well on paper towels. Sprinkle with powdered sugar. **Yield:** 10 pies.

One of a Kind
Junior League of Mobile, Alabama

SPECIAL APRICOT PIES

1 (6-ounce) package dried apricot
   halves
¾ cup water
½ teaspoon ground nutmeg
½ teaspoon vanilla extract
½ cup butter or margarine,
   softened
4 ounces cream cheese,
   softened
1½ cups all-purpose flour
½ teaspoon salt
Glaze

• **Position** knife blade in food processor bowl; add apricots. Process until finely chopped.

• **Combine** apricots, water, nutmeg, and vanilla in a small saucepan; cook over medium heat 5 minutes, stirring constantly. Set aside.

• **Beat** butter and cream cheese at medium speed with an electric mixer until creamy. Add flour and salt, beating at low speed until dough forms a ball.

• **Roll** dough to ⅛-inch thickness on a lightly floured surface. Cut with a 2½-inch round cutter.

• **Place** about 1 teaspoon apricot mixture on half of each circle. Moisten edges with water; fold dough over apricot mixture, pressing edges to seal.

Crimp edges with a fork, and prick top of each pie; place on ungreased baking sheets. Bake pies at 350° for 18 minutes or until lightly browned. Transfer to wire racks; brush with Glaze. **Yield:** 3 dozen.

Glaze

QUICK!

1 cup sifted powdered sugar
1½ tablespoons milk
½ teaspoon vanilla extract
¼ teaspoon butter-flavored
   extract

• **Combine** all ingredients in a small bowl. **Yield:** ⅓ cup.

Carol Barclay
Portland, Texas

CRANBERRY POCKETS

1 (15-ounce) package refrigerated
   piecrusts
1 (8-ounce) carton soft cream
   cheese
⅓ cup sugar
½ cup chopped fresh cranberries
½ cup chopped pecans
1 teaspoon grated orange rind
2 tablespoons powdered sugar

• **Unfold** piecrusts, and press out fold lines. Cut each piecrust into 4 squares, discarding scraps.

• **Combine** cream cheese and next 4 ingredients; spread ¼ cup mixture onto each pastry square, leaving a ½-inch border. Moisten edges with water; fold pastry diagonally over filling, pressing edges to seal.

• **Crimp** edges with a fork. Place on lightly greased baking sheets.

• **Bake** at 350° for 15 to 18 minutes or until golden. Sprinkle with powdered sugar; serve warm or at room temperature. **Yield:** 8 servings.

Note: You can freeze unbaked pockets in airtight containers up to 1 month. Bake frozen pastries at 350° for 25 minutes or until golden.

CRANBERRY DESSERT PIZZAS

Use any leftover holiday cranberries in this recipe. (For perfect streusel stripes lay strips of wax paper on the pizzas before sprinkling the topping.)

3½ cups all-purpose flour, divided
2½ cups sugar, divided
2 teaspoons cream of tartar
1 teaspoon baking soda
½ teaspoon salt
1 cup butter or margarine, softened
2 large eggs
½ teaspoon ground cinnamon
4 cups fresh cranberries
½ cup orange juice
1 tablespoon cornstarch
¼ cup regular oats, uncooked
¼ cup firmly packed light brown sugar
2 tablespoons butter or margarine, softened
¼ cup chopped pecans

• **Combine** 3 cups flour, 1 cup sugar, cream of tartar, soda, and salt; cut in 1 cup butter with pastry blender until mixture is crumbly. Stir in eggs with a fork until dry ingredients are moistened.
• **Shape** dough into a ball. Divide dough in half, and press into two greased 12-inch pizza pans.
• **Combine** ¼ cup sugar and cinnamon; sprinkle over dough.
• **Bake** at 350° for 15 minutes.
• **Combine** 1 cup sugar, cranberries, orange juice, and cornstarch in a saucepan, stirring well; bring to a boil over medium-high heat, stirring often. Cook 10 to 12 minutes or until thickened, stirring occasionally. Spread evenly over crusts.
• **Combine** remaining ½ cup flour, remaining ¼ cup sugar, oats, and brown sugar in a bowl; cut in 2 tablespoons butter with pastry blender until mixture is crumbly. Stir in pecans.
• **Cut** narrow strips of wax paper with scissors; lay at intervals over cranberry mixture. Sprinkle topping over pizzas; remove wax paper.
• **Bake** at 350° for 12 minutes; serve warm. **Yield:** 2 (12-inch) pizzas.

Agnes L. Stone
Ocala, Florida

BAKLAVA

This dessert, pronounced BAHK-lah-vah, has a delicate flavor and texture and makes a wonderful gift. It also freezes well when stored in an airtight container.

2 cups sugar
1 cup water
¾ cup honey
2 tablespoons brandy
1 tablespoon fresh lemon juice
1 (3-inch) stick cinnamon
12 cups finely chopped pecans (3 pounds, shelled)
1 cup sugar
1 tablespoon ground cinnamon
1 teaspoon ground cloves
1 (16-ounce) package frozen phyllo pastry, thawed
1 pound unsalted butter, melted
Whole cloves

• **Combine** first 6 ingredients in a saucepan; bring to a boil over medium-high heat, stirring constantly. Immediately remove from heat; cool.
• **Combine** pecans and next 3 ingredients, stirring well.
• **Cut** phyllo sheets in half crosswise; keep covered with a slightly damp towel.
• **Brush** 2 (13- x 9- x 2-inch) pans with butter. Place 8 phyllo sheets in 1 pan, brushing each sheet with butter; top with 2 cups pecan mixture.
• **Place** 3 phyllo sheets over pecan mixture, brushing each sheet with butter; top with 2 cups pecan mixture. Repeat with 3 phyllo sheets and 2 cups pecan mixture; top with 6 phyllo sheets, brushing all but top sheet with butter.
• **Repeat** procedure with remaining phyllo sheets, butter, and pecan mixture in second pan.
• **Cut** layers diagonally into ¾-inch diamonds; brush with butter. Insert a clove in center of each diamond.
• **Bake** at 300° for 1 hour. Remove from oven; pour syrup evenly over baklava. Cool in pans on wire racks.
• **Cut** again diagonally; remove from pans, and store in airtight containers at room temperature. **Yield:** about 10 dozen.

Jeannie Sfakianos
Birmingham, Alabama

CHOCOLATE ÉCLAIRS

1 (5.1-ounce) package vanilla instant pudding mix
2½ cups milk
1¾ cups frozen whipped topping, thawed
Cream Puff Pastry
½ cup butter
⅓ cup buttermilk
3 tablespoons cocoa
1 (16-ounce) package powdered sugar, sifted

• **Whisk** together pudding mix and milk in a large bowl, and chill 5 minutes. Fold in whipped topping. Spoon into a heavy-duty, zip-top plastic bag; seal and chill.
• **Place** Cream Puff Pastry in a heavy-duty, zip-top plastic bag; seal. Cut ½ inch off one corner, making a 1-inch-wide hole. Squeeze pastry into 4½-inch-long strips, 2 inches apart, on ungreased baking sheets.
• **Bake** at 400° for 30 to 40 minutes. Transfer to wire racks to cool.
• **Bring** butter, buttermilk, and cocoa to a boil over medium heat; remove from heat. Gradually add powdered sugar; stir until smooth.
• **Cut** a ½-inch hole in 1 end of each éclair with a sharp knife. Cut ¼ inch off one corner of bag with pudding mixture, making a ½-inch-wide hole. Squeeze pudding into éclairs. Spread frosting over tops. **Yield:** 12 to 15 éclairs.

Myrna Story
Waynesboro, Mississippi

Cream Puff Pastry

QUICK!

1 cup water
½ cup butter
1 cup all-purpose flour
4 large eggs

• **Bring** water and butter to a boil over medium heat; reduce heat to low. Add flour, and beat with a wooden spoon until mixture leaves sides of pan. Remove from heat. Add eggs, one at a time, beating until mixture is smooth. **Yield:** enough for 15 éclairs.

Terry Anderson
Brooksville, Florida

COFFEE NAPOLEONS

Make-ahead tip: Bake pastry, and store in an airtight container for a day or two. Make filling and chocolate sauce the day before, and chill. Assemble just before serving.

1 (3.4-ounce) package chocolate pudding mix (not instant)
1 cup milk
2 teaspoons instant coffee granules
1 (8-ounce) package cream cheese, cut into pieces and softened
½ cup whipping cream, whipped
1 (17¼-ounce) package frozen puff pastry sheets, thawed
¼ cup whipping cream
2 teaspoons instant coffee granules
6 (1-ounce) squares semisweet chocolate, chopped
1 tablespoon powdered sugar

• **Combine** pudding mix and milk in a saucepan, stirring well; stir in 2 teaspoons coffee granules. Bring to a boil over medium heat, stirring constantly; remove from heat. Add cream cheese, stirring until smooth; cool completely.
• **Fold** whipped cream into pudding mixture; cover and chill.
• **Unfold** 1 pastry sheet on a lightly floured baking sheet. Roll into a 12-inch square. Cut into 2 (12- x 6-inch) rectangles. Cut each rectangle into 6 (6- x 2-inch) strips. Prick each strip several times with a fork. Place another baking sheet directly on top of pastry strips (to prevent overpuffing).
• **Bake** at 425° for 10 minutes. Remove top baking sheet; bake 5 additional minutes or until golden. Cool on wire racks. Repeat procedure with remaining pastry sheet.
• **Combine** ¼ cup whipping cream, 2 teaspoons coffee granules, and chocolate in a heavy saucepan; cook over low heat, stirring constantly, until chocolate melts. Cool slightly; spoon into a heavy-duty, zip-top plastic bag, and snip a tiny hole in one corner of bag. Drizzle over 12 pastry strips.
• **Pipe** or spoon filling evenly on remaining 12 pastry strips, and top evenly with chocolate-drizzled strips. Sprinkle with powdered sugar, and serve immediately. **Yield:** 12 napoleons.

CREAM PUFF TREE

A holiday Cream Puff Tree is a dazzling dessert to crown your holiday meal – it's spectacular in presentation and sensational in taste. A foil-wrapped plastic cone provides the base for the elegant Cream Puff Tree. A simple sugar mixture provides the "glue" to attach the pastry puffs to the cone. Once the tree has cooled, remove the foil-wrapped cone. (Leave cone in place if using tree as decoration.)

3 cups water
1½ cups butter
3 cups all-purpose flour
1½ teaspoons salt
12 large eggs
2 cups sugar
½ cup water
1 cup light corn syrup
Dark Chocolate Sauce
White Chocolate Sauce
Caramel Sauce
Raspberry Sauce

• **Bring** 3 cups water and butter to a boil in a large saucepan over medium-high heat; reduce heat to low.
• **Add** flour and salt, and beat with a wooden spoon until mixture leaves sides of pan. Remove from heat, and cool slightly.
• **Add** eggs, one at a time, beating until smooth.
• **Spoon** batter into a decorating bag fitted with a large star tip; pipe 1½-inch mounds, 2 inches apart, onto lightly greased baking sheets.
• **Bake** at 450° for 10 minutes; reduce oven temperature to 375°, and bake 30 additional minutes or until puffed and golden. Pierce warm puffs on 1 side with a small sharp knife to let steam escape. Let cool.
• **Cover** a 12- or 15-inch plastic foam cone with aluminum foil, and place on an 18- x 12-inch piece of foil. Lightly grease foil.
• **Combine** sugar, ½ cup water, and corn syrup in a heavy saucepan; cook over low heat, stirring constantly, until sugar melts.
• **Bring** to a boil over high heat; cook, stirring constantly, 5 minutes or until mixture is light amber. Remove from heat; cool 2 minutes or until slightly thickened.
• **Dip** bottom of each cream puff into hot sugar mixture, using tongs; press puffs onto cone, starting at bottom and working toward top. Attach more cream puffs over first layer, hiding any gaps, and evenly shaping tree. If sugar mixture hardens, cook over low heat just until it melts. (Freeze any remaining cream puffs for another use.)
• **Drizzle** any remaining sugar mixture over top of tree, allowing it to flow down sides; cool.
• **Remove** and discard cone and foil. Serve with Dark Chocolate Sauce, White Chocolate Sauce, Caramel Sauce, or Raspberry Sauce. **Yield:** 12 servings.

Note: You can drop batter by rounded tablespoonfuls rather than piping it. Recipe makes about 3 dozen puffs.

Dark Chocolate Sauce
QUICK!

¾ cup whipping cream
8 (1-ounce) squares dark sweet or semisweet chocolate
2 tablespoons light corn syrup

• **Cook** whipping cream in a small heavy saucepan over medium-low heat just until thoroughly heated, stirring often. Add chocolate and corn syrup; cook until chocolate melts, stirring often. **Yield:** 1½ cups.

White Chocolate Sauce
QUICK!

¾ cup whipping cream
8 (1-ounce) squares white chocolate or baking bar
2 tablespoons light corn syrup

• **Cook** whipping cream in a small heavy saucepan over medium-low heat just until thoroughly heated, stirring often.

• **Add** white chocolate and corn syrup; cook until chocolate melts, stirring often. **Yield:** 1½ cups.

Caramel Sauce

QUICK!

½ cup butter
1 cup sugar
½ cup whipping cream
2 teaspoons vanilla extract

• **Combine** butter and sugar in a small heavy saucepan; cook over medium heat, stirring constantly, until sugar melts.
• **Stir** in whipping cream. Bring to a boil, and cook 1 minute, stirring constantly. Stir in vanilla. **Yield:** 1¼ cups.

Raspberry Sauce

QUICK!

This ruby sauce can also be drizzled over ice cream and is especially pretty coupled with fresh berries.

2 (10-ounce) packages frozen raspberries, thawed
4 teaspoons cornstarch

• **Place** raspberries in container of an electric blender; process until smooth, stopping once to scrape down sides. Pour through a wire-mesh strainer into a small saucepan, discarding seeds. Stir in cornstarch.
• **Bring** to a boil over medium heat, stirring constantly; boil 1 minute, stirring constantly. Cool. **Yield:** 1 cup.

CAJUN FIG COBBLER

¼ cup butter or margarine
1 cup all-purpose flour
1 cup sugar
2 teaspoons baking powder
1 cup milk
1 large egg
1 teaspoon vanilla extract
2 (11-ounce) jars fig preserves

• **Place** butter in a 2-quart baking dish. Bake at 375° until butter melts. Remove from oven, and set aside.

• **Combine** flour, sugar, and baking powder in a large bowl. Add milk, egg, and vanilla, stirring until smooth. Pour batter into baking dish; spoon preserves over batter.
• **Bake** at 375° for 40 minutes, covering dish with aluminum foil after 20 minutes. Serve warm with vanilla ice cream or whipped cream. **Yield:** 8 servings.

Joshua Pucheu
Ville Platte, Louisiana

BLUEBERRY UPSIDE-DOWN COBBLER

2½ cups fresh blueberries
1½ cups water
¼ cup shortening
1½ cups sugar, divided
1 cup all-purpose flour
2 teaspoons baking powder
⅛ teaspoon salt
½ cup milk
½ teaspoon ground nutmeg
Pinch of salt
3 tablespoons butter or margarine, cut into pieces
1 tablespoon lemon juice

• **Combine** blueberries and water in a nonaluminum saucepan; bring to a boil. Boil 5 minutes; let cool. Pour mixture through a wire-mesh strainer into a bowl; reserve blueberries and juice separately.
• **Beat** shortening and 1 cup sugar in a large mixing bowl at medium speed with an electric mixer until smooth.
• **Combine** flour, baking powder, and ⅛ teaspoon salt in a bowl; add to shortening mixture alternately with milk, beginning and ending with flour mixture.
• **Pour** batter into a greased 11- x 7- x 1½-inch baking dish; spoon reserved berries over batter.
• **Combine** remaining ½ cup sugar, nutmeg, and pinch of salt; sprinkle over berries. Dot with butter.
• **Combine** reserved blueberry juice and lemon juice, and pour over top of batter.
• **Bake** at 375° for 35 to 40 minutes. **Yield:** 6 servings.

Sandra Russell
Gainesville, Florida

PEACH COBBLER

1 (15-ounce) package refrigerated piecrusts
1 teaspoon all-purpose flour
4 cups frozen sliced peaches
½ cup sugar
½ teaspoon ground cinnamon
¼ cup cornstarch
½ cup water
2 tablespoons butter or margarine, melted
1 large egg
2 tablespoons milk
1 tablespoon sugar

• **Roll** 1 piecrust into a 12-inch circle. Sprinkle flour over surface. Place crust, floured side down, in a 9½-inch quiche dish. Place peaches in crust.
• **Combine** ½ cup sugar, cinnamon, and cornstarch; sprinkle over peaches, and drizzle with water and butter.
• **Unfold** remaining piecrust, and roll on a lightly floured surface into a 12-inch circle; place over peaches. Fold edges under, and flute.
• **Cut** 6 (1-inch) slits in top of piecrust with a sharp knife.
• **Combine** egg and milk, stirring well; brush over top piecrust, and sprinkle evenly with 1 tablespoon sugar. Place on a baking sheet.
• **Bake** at 350° for 1 hour or until golden. **Yield:** 8 servings.

RASPBERRY-CHERRY COBBLER

1 (16-ounce) package frozen
    unsweetened raspberries,
    thawed
1 (16-ounce) package frozen
    no-sugar-added pitted dark
    sweet cherries, thawed
1 cup sugar
¼ cup all-purpose flour
1 tablespoon lemon juice
⅛ teaspoon ground cinnamon
Vegetable cooking spray
2 cups all-purpose flour
1 tablespoon baking powder
1 teaspoon baking soda
1 teaspoon salt
2 tablespoons sugar
¼ cup reduced-calorie margarine
¾ cup plain nonfat yogurt
¼ cup evaporated skimmed milk

• **Combine** first 6 ingredients; spoon into an 11- x 7- x 1½-inch baking dish coated with cooking spray.
• **Combine** 2 cups flour and next 4 ingredients in a large bowl; cut in margarine with pastry blender until mixture is crumbly. Add yogurt and milk, stirring with a fork until dry ingredients are moistened.
• **Turn** dough out onto a lightly floured surface, and knead about 10 times.
• **Roll** dough to ½-inch thickness; cut into 12 circles, using a 2-inch round cutter. Cut 6 diamonds from remaining dough.
• **Arrange** rounds and diamond shapes on top of fruit mixture. Bake at 425° for 20 to 25 minutes or until bubbly and golden. Remove from oven; lightly coat each biscuit with cooking spray. **Yield:** 12 servings.

♥ Per serving: Calories 225
Fat 2.7g   Cholesterol 0mg
Sodium 403mg

APPLE-CHEESE CRISP

A hint of cinnamon and nutmeg brings out the fresh flavors of the apple, Cheddar cheese, and toasted almonds.

6 cups peeled, cored, and sliced
    cooking apples
1 tablespoon water
½ teaspoon lemon juice
1 cup (4 ounces) shredded
    Cheddar cheese
1 cup all-purpose flour
½ cup firmly packed brown
    sugar
2 tablespoons sugar
¼ teaspoon ground cinnamon
¼ teaspoon ground nutmeg
½ cup butter or margarine
Vanilla ice cream
Toasted sliced almonds
    (optional)

• **Arrange** apple slices in a lightly greased 8-inch square baking dish.
• **Combine** water and lemon juice; sprinkle evenly over apple slices. Top evenly with cheese.
• **Combine** flour and next 4 ingredients; cut in butter with pastry blender until mixture is crumbly. Sprinkle over cheese.
• **Bake** at 350° for 40 minutes or until tender. Serve warm topped with vanilla ice cream; sprinkle with almonds, if desired. **Yield:** 6 to 8 servings.

Valerie Stutsman
Norfolk, Virginia

STRAWBERRY-RHUBARB CRISP

3 cups fresh or frozen sliced
    rhubarb, thawed
1 quart fresh strawberries,
    mashed
2 tablespoons lemon juice
1 cup sugar
⅓ cup cornstarch
2 cups all-purpose flour
1 cup sugar
1 teaspoon baking powder
1 teaspoon baking soda
½ teaspoon salt
1 cup butter or margarine
1½ cups buttermilk
2 large eggs, lightly beaten
1 teaspoon vanilla extract
¼ cup butter or margarine,
    melted
¾ cup all-purpose flour
¾ cup sugar

• **Combine** first 3 ingredients in a saucepan; cover and cook over medium heat 5 minutes.
• **Combine** 1 cup sugar and cornstarch; gradually stir into rhubarb mixture. Bring mixture to a boil, stirring constantly; boil 1 minute. Remove from heat; set aside.
• **Combine** 2 cups flour and next 4 ingredients; cut in 1 cup butter with pastry blender until mixture is crumbly. Add buttermilk, eggs, and vanilla; stir with a fork until dry ingredients are moistened.
• **Spread** half of batter evenly in a greased 13- x 9- x 2-inch baking dish. Spoon rhubarb mixture evenly over batter, and drop remaining batter by tablespoonfuls over filling.
• **Combine** ¼ cup melted butter, ¾ cup flour, and ¾ cup sugar; sprinkle over batter.
• **Bake** at 350° for 40 to 45 minutes. Cool on a wire rack. Cut into squares. **Yield:** 15 servings.

Ellie Wells
Lakeland, Florida

At right: *Basil-Stuffed Chicken With Tomato-Basil Pasta (page 281)*

POULTRY

BAKED HEN WITH CRANBERRY PAN GRAVY

1 (5½- to 6-pound) hen
5 cups water
1 large onion, quartered
Leaves from 3 stalks celery
1 teaspoon salt
⅛ teaspoon dried thyme
1 cup frozen cranberry juice
    cocktail concentrate, thawed
    and undiluted
½ cup fresh cranberries, finely
    chopped
2½ tablespoons cornstarch
3 tablespoons cold water
Garnishes: fresh rosemary, fresh
    oregano, fresh thyme, fresh
    cranberries

• **Combine** giblets and neck from hen, 5 cups water, and next 4 ingredients in a 3-quart saucepan. Bring to a boil; cover, reduce heat, and simmer 1½ hours. Pour through a wire-mesh strainer into a container, reserving broth and discarding solids. Cover and chill broth.
• **Rinse** hen with cold water; drain and pat dry. Tie ends of legs together with string. Lift wingtips up and over back, and tuck under bird. Place hen, breast side up, in a 15- x 10- x 2-inch baking dish. Cover with foil.
• **Bake** at 325° for 3 hours; uncover and bake 30 minutes or until a meat thermometer inserted in meaty portion of thigh reaches 180°. Remove hen from dish, reserving drippings.
• **Remove** and discard fat from drippings in dish, and return 2 tablespoons drippings to dish.
• **Add** water to reserved broth to equal 1½ cups. Add broth to drippings in dish. Stir to loosen browned particles; add cranberry juice concentrate and chopped cranberries. Transfer mixture to a saucepan.
• **Bring** mixture to a boil; reduce heat, and cook, stirring occasionally, 3 to 5 minutes.
• **Combine** cornstarch and water, stirring until smooth. Stir into gravy mixture; return to a boil. Cook 1 minute, stirring constantly. Serve with hen. Garnish, if desired. **Yield:** 8 to 10 servings.

Estelle Gilbert
Stanardsville, Virginia

FORTY-CLOVES-OF-GARLIC CHICKEN

So much garlic sounds like a mistake, but it's fantastic. And true garlic lovers will welcome the rich gravy that tops this piquant chicken.

1 (2½- to 3-pound) broiler-fryer
40 cloves garlic, unpeeled
½ cup dry white wine
½ to ⅔ cup chicken broth,
    divided
½ cup whipping cream
¼ teaspoon salt
⅛ teaspoon pepper

• **Place** chicken, breast side up, on a rack in a shallow roasting pan. Place 5 garlic cloves in cavity, and arrange remaining garlic cloves around chicken.
• **Bake** at 375° for 20 minutes.
• **Pour** wine over chicken, and bake 40 minutes or until done, basting occasionally with pan juices.
• **Remove** chicken from pan, reserving garlic and pan drippings; keep chicken warm. Remove garlic cloves, and set aside.
• **Remove** and discard fat from pan drippings; add enough broth to drippings to measure ½ cup.
• **Combine** drippings mixture and whipping cream in a small saucepan. Cook over medium-high heat 2 to 3 minutes, stirring occasionally.
• **Squeeze** pulp from garlic cloves into container of an electric blender or food processor. Add 2 tablespoons broth; process until smooth, stopping once to scrape down sides. Stir garlic mixture, salt, and pepper into hot drippings mixture. Serve chicken immediately with garlic mixture. **Yield:** 4 servings.

Mrs. Harland J. Stone
Ocala, Florida

LEMON-ROASTED CHICKEN

Always roast chicken with the skin on. The skin keeps the chicken moist, and the fat won't absorb into the meat. Be sure to remove the skin before serving.

1½ teaspoons salt
2 teaspoons freshly ground pepper
2 to 3 teaspoons dried rosemary,
    crushed
1 (3-pound) broiler-fryer
1 medium lemon, cut in half

• **Combine** first 3 ingredients; set aside.
• **Loosen** skin from chicken breast by running fingers between the two; rub 1 teaspoon seasoning mixture under skin. Rub remaining seasoning mixture over outside of chicken. Place chicken in a heavy-duty, zip-top plastic bag; seal and store in refrigerator 8 hours.
• **Remove** chicken from bag. Insert lemon halves into cavity; tie ends of legs together with string. Lift wing tips up and over back, and tuck under bird. Place chicken, breast side down, in a lightly greased shallow pan.
• **Bake** at 450°, turning over every 15 minutes, for 50 minutes or until meat thermometer inserted in thickest part registers 180°. Let chicken stand 10 minutes. Remove skin before serving. **Yield:** 4 servings.

Clay Nordan
Birmingham, Alabama

♥ Per 3-ounce serving without skin:
    Breast meat: Calories 116
    Fat 2g   Cholesterol 72mg
    Sodium 719mg

    Drumstick meat: Calories 132
    Fat 3g   Cholesterol 79mg
    Sodium 734mg

    Thigh meat: Calories 150
    Fat 7g   Cholesterol 81mg
    Sodium 728mg

CREOLE CHICKEN

This dish is great for a fall leaf-raking day. It cooks for a total of 3 hours and requires you to occasionally take a break from raking to add ingredients to the pot and stir.

1 (3½-pound) broiler-fryer
2 quarts water
1 teaspoon salt
1 tablespoon butter or margarine
1 medium onion, chopped
2 cloves garlic, minced
2 (16-ounce) cans whole tomatoes, undrained and chopped
2 teaspoons curry powder
2 teaspoons dried thyme
¼ teaspoon salt
Dash of ground red pepper
1 cup currants
8 ounces blanched almonds, toasted
Hot cooked rice

● **Combine** first 3 ingredients in a large Dutch oven; bring to a boil. Cover, reduce heat, and simmer 1 hour or until tender.
● **Remove** chicken, reserving 1 cup liquid; let chicken cool. Skin, bone, and cut chicken into large chunks. Cover and chill reserved liquid and chicken.
● **Melt** butter in a large skillet over medium-high heat; add onion and garlic, and cook, stirring constantly, until crisp-tender. Add tomatoes and next 4 ingredients; cover and cook over low heat 1 hour, stirring occasionally.
● **Add** currants, almonds, and chicken; cover and cook over low heat 1 hour, adding reserved liquid as needed to prevent sticking. Serve over rice. **Yield:** 6 servings.

John Feagin
Birmingham, Alabama

SIMPLY GOOD CHICKEN CASSEROLE

1 (3-pound) broiler-fryer
1 quart water
1 teaspoon salt
1 teaspoon pepper
1 (10¾-ounce) can cream of chicken soup, undiluted
1 (10¾-ounce) can cream of celery soup, undiluted
1 (8-ounce) carton sour cream
½ teaspoon pepper
½ (16-ounce) package oval-shaped buttery crackers, crushed (2 stacks)
¼ cup butter or margarine, melted

● **Combine** first 4 ingredients in a large Dutch oven; bring to a boil. Cover, reduce heat, and simmer 1 hour or until tender. Remove chicken, and cool slightly.
● **Skin** and bone chicken; cut chicken into bite-size pieces. Combine chicken, chicken soup, and next 3 ingredients, stirring well.
● **Place** half of crushed crackers in a lightly greased 11- x 7- x 1½-inch baking dish; spoon chicken mixture over crackers. Top with remaining crackers, and drizzle with butter.
● **Bake** at 325° for 35 minutes or until lightly browned. **Yield:** 6 to 8 servings.

♥ To reduce fat and calories, substitute 6 skinned chicken breast halves, reduced-fat cream of chicken and cream of celery soups, reduced-fat sour cream, and reduced-fat buttery crackers. Reduce butter to 2 tablespoons, and coat dish and top of casserole with butter-flavored cooking spray.

Note: You can add ½ teaspoon salt for additional flavor, if desired.

Jane Harber
Decatur, Georgia

CHICKEN-SQUASH CASSEROLE

1 (2½- to 3-pound) broiler-fryer
2 pounds yellow squash, cut into ¼-inch-thick slices
½ cup water
2 large carrots, scraped and shredded
1 medium onion, finely chopped
1 (8-ounce) carton sour cream
1 (10¾-ounce) can cream of mushroom soup, undiluted
½ teaspoon salt
¼ teaspoon pepper
1½ cups chicken-flavored one-step stuffing mix ✻
¼ cup butter or margarine, melted

● **Cook** chicken in a Dutch oven in boiling water to cover 45 minutes or until tender; drain. Cool chicken; skin and bone. Cut meat into bite-size pieces.
● **Combine** squash and ½ cup water in a medium saucepan; bring to a boil. Cover, reduce heat, and simmer 8 minutes or until tender; drain between paper towels.
● **Combine** squash, carrot, and onion; toss gently, and set aside.
● **Combine** sour cream and next 3 ingredients in a large bowl. Add chicken and squash mixture to sour cream mixture, stirring to blend.
● **Spoon** mixture into a lightly greased 13- x 9- x 2-inch baking dish.
● **Combine** stuffing mix and butter; sprinkle over casserole.
● **Bake** at 350° for 25 minutes or until bubbly. **Yield:** 8 servings.

✻ For chicken-flavored one-step stuffing mix, we used Stove Top One-Step Stuffing Mix.

Dorothy Burgess
Huntsville, Texas

CHICKEN POT PIE

1 (3½-pound) broiler-fryer
2 quarts water
½ teaspoon salt
½ teaspoon pepper
1 stalk celery, cut into 2-inch
    pieces
1 medium onion, quartered
1 bay leaf
3½ cups peeled, cubed red potato
    (1½ pounds)
1 (16-ounce) package frozen
    mixed vegetables
1 cup skim milk
½ cup all-purpose flour
¾ teaspoon salt
1 teaspoon pepper
½ teaspoon poultry seasoning
Butter-flavored cooking spray
5 sheets frozen phyllo pastry,
    thawed

• **Combine** first 7 ingredients in a large Dutch oven; bring to a boil. Cover, reduce heat, and simmer 1 hour or until chicken is tender.
• **Remove** chicken, reserving broth in Dutch oven; remove and discard vegetables and bay leaf. Let chicken cool to touch; skin, bone, and cut into bite-size pieces.
• **Remove** and discard fat (oily liquid) from chicken broth, reserving 3½ cups broth.
• **Bring** reserved broth to a boil in Dutch oven. Add potato and mixed vegetables; return to a boil. Cover, reduce heat, and cook about 8 minutes or until vegetables are tender.
• **Combine** milk and flour in a jar; cover tightly, and shake vigorously. Gradually add milk mixture in a slow, steady stream to broth mixture, stirring constantly. Cook, stirring constantly, 1 minute or until thickened. Stir in ¾ teaspoon salt, 1 teaspoon pepper, poultry seasoning, and chicken.
• **Spoon** mixture into a 13- x 9- x 2-inch baking dish coated with cooking spray; set aside.
• **Place** 1 phyllo sheet horizontally on a flat surface, keeping remaining sheets covered with a slightly damp towel until ready for use. Coat sheet with cooking spray. Layer remaining 4 sheets on first sheet, coating each with cooking spray.

Place on top of baking dish, loosely crushing edges around the dish.
• **Bake** at 400° for 20 minutes. **Yield:** 8 servings.

Note: Remove fat by chilling the broth and removing congealed layer of fat or by pouring the broth through a large fat separator.

♥ Per serving: Calories 249
Fat 5.5g   Cholesterol 50mg
Sodium 465mg

EASY CHICKEN DIVAN

*We liked this casserole
just as well without dotting the
top with 2 tablespoons of
butter, as recommended in
the original recipe.*

1 (3½- to 4-pound) broiler-fryer,
    cut in half
2 (10-ounce) packages frozen
    broccoli spears, thawed and
    coarsely chopped
2 (10¾-ounce) cans cream of
    chicken soup, undiluted
1 cup mayonnaise
1½ teaspoons lemon juice
¾ teaspoon curry powder
½ cup (2 ounces) shredded sharp
    Cheddar cheese
¾ cup herb-seasoned stuffing mix

• **Combine** chicken and enough water to cover in a Dutch oven; bring to a boil. Cover, reduce heat, and simmer 40 minutes or until tender. Remove chicken, reserving broth for another use. Let chicken cool. Skin, bone, and cut chicken into bite-size pieces. Set aside.
• **Place** broccoli in a lightly greased 11- x 7- x 1½-inch baking dish. Top with chicken.
• **Combine** soup and next 3 ingredients; spoon over chicken. Sprinkle with cheese and stuffing mix.
• **Bake** at 400° for 25 to 30 minutes or until thoroughly heated. **Yield:** 6 to 8 servings.

♥ To reduce fat and calories, substitute reduced-sodium, reduced-fat cream of

chicken soup and reduced-fat mayonnaise for the regular products.

A Taste of Georgia
Junior Service League of Newnan, Georgia

CHICKEN IN FOIL

1 (2½-pound) broiler-fryer,
    quartered and skinned
¼ teaspoon garlic salt
⅛ teaspoon paprika
1 large onion, cut into 4 slices
1 large baking potato, cut into 8
    slices
2 carrots, scraped and cut into
    ¾-inch pieces
2 stalks celery, cut into ¾-inch
    pieces
1 (4-ounce) can sliced mushrooms,
    drained
1 (10¾-ounce) can cream of
    chicken soup, undiluted

• **Cut** 4 (24- x 18-inch) pieces of heavy-duty aluminum foil.
• **Place** a chicken quarter in center of each piece of foil; sprinkle with garlic salt and paprika.
• **Top** chicken evenly with onion and next 4 ingredients.
• **Spoon** soup evenly over each portion. Seal bundles, and place on a 15- x 10- x 1-inch jellyroll pan.
• **Bake** at 400° for 1 hour and 15 minutes or until chicken is done. **Yield:** 4 servings.

*Margaret Jahns
Tarpon Springs, Florida*

GRILLED HERBED
CHICKEN QUARTERS

*Although sherry adds a sweet
kiss to this recipe, you can
substitute less-expensive soy
sauce with good results.*

2 (0.7-ounce) envelopes Italian-
   style dressing mix ✳
½ cup vegetable oil
½ cup dry sherry
2 (2½- to 3-pound) broiler-fryers,
   quartered and skinned

● **Combine** first 3 ingredients in a shallow dish or heavy-duty, zip-top plastic bag; add chicken. Cover or seal, and chill 8 hours or overnight, turning chicken occasionally.
● **Remove** chicken from marinade, discarding marinade.
● **Cook**, covered with grill lid, over medium-hot coals (350° to 400°) 50 to 60 minutes or until a meat thermometer inserted in thickest part of chicken registers 180°, turning occasionally. **Yield:** 8 servings.

✳ For Italian-style dressing mix, we used Good Seasons.

Rita W. Cook
Corpus Christi, Texas

LEMON-HERB
GRILLED CHICKEN

1 cup vegetable oil
¾ cup lemon juice
¼ cup honey
2 tablespoons dried oregano
1 tablespoon dried rosemary
1 teaspoon salt
½ teaspoon pepper
4 cloves garlic
2 (2½- to 3-pound) broiler-fryers,
   quartered and skinned

● **Combine** all ingredients except chicken in container of an electric blender, and process mixture until smooth, stopping occasionally to scrape down sides.
● **Place** chicken in a large heavy-duty, zip-top plastic bag; pour oil mixture over chicken. Seal bag, and marinate chicken in refrigerator at least 8 hours.
● **Drain** chicken, discarding marinade.
● **Cook** chicken, covered with grill lid, over medium-hot coals (350° to 400°) about 35 minutes or until meat thermometer inserted in thickest part registers 180°, turning occasionally. **Yield:** 8 servings.

SMOKY HERB CHICKEN

Hickory or fruitwood chips
1½ teaspoons dried oregano
1 tablespoon dried rosemary
1 tablespoon dried tarragon
1 tablespoon salt
1½ teaspoons pepper
1½ teaspoons onion powder
1½ teaspoons garlic powder
1½ teaspoons paprika
6 chicken quarters
½ cup olive oil
6 sprigs fresh sage

● **Soak** wood chips in water at least 30 minutes.
● **Combine** oregano and next 7 ingredients; set dried herb mixture aside.
● **Brush** chicken with olive oil, and rub with dried herb mixture, coating all sides. Place chicken in a 15- x 10- x 1-inch jellyroll pan.
● **Broil** 5½ inches from heat (with electric oven door partially open) 10 minutes on each side.
● **Prepare** charcoal fire in smoker; let burn 15 to 20 minutes.
● **Drain** chips, and place on coals. Place water pan in smoker; add sage and water to pan to depth of fill line.
● **Place** chicken on food racks; cover with smoker lid.
● **Cook** 2½ hours or until meat thermometer inserted in thickest part registers 180°. **Yield:** 6 servings.

OUR BEST SOUTHERN
FRIED CHICKEN

3 quarts water
1 tablespoon salt
1 (2- to 2½-pound) broiler-fryer,
   cut up
1 teaspoon salt
1 teaspoon pepper
1 cup all-purpose flour
2 cups vegetable oil
¼ cup bacon drippings

● **Combine** water and 1 tablespoon salt in a large bowl; add chicken. Cover and chill 8 hours.
● **Drain** chicken; rinse with cold water, and pat dry.
● **Combine** 1 teaspoon salt and pepper; sprinkle half of mixture over all sides of chicken.
● **Combine** remaining mixture and flour in a large heavy-duty, zip-top plastic bag.
● **Place** 2 pieces of chicken in bag; seal. Shake to coat completely. Remove chicken, and repeat procedure with remaining pieces.
● **Combine** vegetable oil and bacon drippings in a 12-inch cast-iron skillet or chicken fryer; heat to 360°.
● **Add** chicken, a few pieces at a time, skin side down. Cover and cook 6 minutes; uncover and cook 9 additional minutes.
● **Turn** chicken pieces; cover and cook 6 additional minutes. Uncover and cook 5 to 9 additional minutes, turning pieces during the last 3 minutes for even browning, if necessary.
● **Drain** chicken on a paper towel-lined plate placed over a large bowl of hot water. **Yield:** 4 servings.

Note: For best results, keep the oil temperature between 300° to 325°. Also, you can substitute 2 cups buttermilk for the saltwater solution to soak the chicken pieces. Proceed as directed.

John Egerton
Nashville, Tennessee

VIRGINIA PAN-FRIED CHICKEN

2 quarts cold water
½ cup kosher salt or coarse-grain
    sea salt
1 (3½-pound) broiler-fryer, cut up
1 quart buttermilk
¾ cup all-purpose flour
2 tablespoons cornstarch
2 tablespoons potato starch *
¾ teaspoon fine-grain sea salt
    or salt
¼ teaspoon freshly ground pepper
1 pound lard
½ cup unsalted butter
4 slices bacon

• **Combine** water and kosher salt in a large bowl; add chicken. Cover and chill 4 to 8 hours. Drain chicken, and pat dry; rinse bowl.
• **Return** chicken pieces to bowl; add buttermilk. Cover chicken, and chill 4 to 8 hours.
• **Drain** chicken on a wire rack; discard buttermilk.
• **Combine** flour and next 4 ingredients in a heavy-duty, zip-top plastic bag; add 2 pieces of chicken. Seal and shake to coat. Remove chicken; repeat procedure with remaining chicken pieces.
• **Place** lard, unsalted butter, and bacon evenly in two large cast-iron or heavy skillets; heat to 350°. Remove and discard bacon.
• **Add** chicken, skin side down (fat will come halfway up sides of chicken). Cook over medium-high heat 10 to 12 minutes on each side or until chicken is done. Drain on paper towels. **Yield:** 4 to 6 servings.

* We used Manischewitz potato starch, but you can substitute all-purpose flour.

Note: You can crush coarse-grain sea salt in a heavy-duty, zip-top plastic bag with a rolling pin to create the fine-grain sea salt.

Chefs Edna Lewis and Scott Peacock
Atlanta, Georgia

OVEN-BARBECUED CRANBERRY CHICKEN

1 (2½- to 3-pound) broiler-fryer,
    cut up and skinned
¼ cup vegetable oil
¼ teaspoon salt
¼ teaspoon pepper
½ cup chopped onion
¼ cup chopped celery
1 cup whole-berry cranberry
    sauce
½ cup ketchup
1 tablespoon brown sugar
2 tablespoons lemon juice
1 tablespoon Worcestershire sauce
1 tablespoon prepared mustard
1 tablespoon red wine vinegar

• **Cook** chicken in hot oil in a large skillet over medium-high heat until lightly browned on all sides. Drain on paper towels, discarding oil.
• **Arrange** chicken in a lightly greased 11- x 7- x 1½-inch baking dish; sprinkle with salt and pepper.
• **Cook** onion and celery in skillet over medium heat until tender, stirring often. Stir in cranberry sauce and remaining 6 ingredients. Bring to a boil; remove from heat, and spoon over chicken. Bake, uncovered, at 325° for 1 hour, basting with pan juices every 15 minutes. **Yield:** 4 servings.

Mildred T. Hurst
Mathews, Virginia

CHICKEN PIQUANT

1 pound fresh mushrooms, sliced
1 (3-pound) broiler-fryer, cut up
    and skinned
2 tablespoons cornstarch
¼ cup water
2 tablespoons olive oil (optional)
¾ cup rosé wine
¼ cup soy sauce
1 clove garlic, pressed
2 tablespoons brown sugar
¼ teaspoon dried oregano
Hot cooked rice

• **Place** sliced mushrooms in a lightly greased 13- x 9- x 2-inch baking dish. Arrange chicken over mushrooms.

• **Combine** cornstarch and water in a small bowl, stirring until smooth. Stir in olive oil, if desired, and next 5 ingredients; pour over chicken.
• **Bake**, uncovered, at 350° for 1 hour or until chicken is done. Serve with rice. **Yield:** 4 servings.

Out of Our League
Junior League of Greensboro,
North Carolina

KING RANCH CHICKEN

1 (3½- to 4-pound) broiler-fryer,
    cut up
1 (10-ounce) package corn
    tortillas, cut into quarters
1 large onion, thinly sliced or
    chopped
1 large green bell pepper,
    chopped
2 cups (8 ounces) shredded
    Cheddar cheese
1½ teaspoons chili powder
½ teaspoon garlic salt
1 (10¾-ounce) can cream of
    chicken soup, undiluted
1 (10¾-ounce) can cream of
    mushroom soup, undiluted
1 (10-ounce) can diced tomatoes
    and green chiles, undrained

• **Cook** chicken in a Dutch oven in boiling water to cover 45 minutes or until tender. Remove chicken, reserving 3 cups broth in pan. Let chicken cool; skin, bone, and cut into bite-size pieces. Set aside.
• **Bring** broth to a boil; dip tortillas in broth 5 seconds to soften. Set aside.
• **Place** half of tortillas in a lightly greased 13- x 9- x 2-inch baking dish. Layer with half each of chicken, onion, and green bell pepper. Repeat layers.
• **Sprinkle** with cheese, chili powder, and garlic salt.
• **Combine** soups, and spread over cheese; top with tomatoes. (Mixture will be wet on top.)
• **Bake** at 350° for 45 minutes or until mixture is thoroughly heated. **Yield:** 6 to 8 servings.

Variation 1: Substitute 2 cups (8 ounces) Monterey Jack cheese for

Cheddar cheese. Decrease chili powder to 1 teaspoon, and add 1 teaspoon ground cumin.

Variation 2: Substitute 6 skinned chicken breast halves for broiler-fryer. Add 1 large red bell pepper, chopped, in addition to the green bell pepper.

Variation 3: Substitute 2 cups (8 ounces) Monterey Jack cheese for Cheddar cheese. Add 1 large red bell pepper, chopped, and cook with onion and green bell pepper in 2 tablespoons butter or margarine.

King Ranch
Kingsville, Texas

BOURBON CHICKEN WITH GRAVY

¼ cup butter or margarine
4 pounds chicken pieces, skinned
¾ cup bourbon, divided
1 medium onion, finely chopped
2 tablespoons dried parsley flakes
1 teaspoon dried thyme
½ teaspoon salt
⅛ teaspoon pepper
¼ cup whipping cream

• **Melt** butter in a large heavy skillet over medium heat; add chicken, and brown on all sides. Add ¼ cup bourbon. Carefully ignite bourbon with a long match, and let burn until flames die.
• **Add** onion and next 4 ingredients. Stir in remaining ½ cup bourbon, stirring until blended. Bring to a boil; cover, reduce heat, and simmer 30 minutes or until chicken is done. Remove to serving plate, reserving liquid in skillet.
• **Add** whipping cream to skillet; bring to a boil, stirring constantly. Cook over medium heat until thickened. Serve with chicken. **Yield:** 4 servings.

Hazel Sellers
Albany, Georgia

PRETZEL-CRUSTED CHICKEN

1 (6.5-ounce) container pretzel twists
5 slices bacon, cooked
½ cup grated Parmesan cheese
2 teaspoons dried parsley flakes
⅓ cup all-purpose flour
1 teaspoon paprika
1 teaspoon salt
¼ teaspoon pepper
¼ teaspoon ground ginger
½ cup beer
1 large egg, lightly beaten
3 pounds chicken pieces

• **Position** knife blade in food processor bowl; add first 4 ingredients. Process until pretzels resemble fine crumbs. Place in a large heavy-duty, zip-top plastic bag; set aside.
• **Combine** flour and next 4 ingredients in a medium bowl; stir well. Stir in beer and egg.
• **Dip** chicken pieces, one at a time, in batter; place in bag of pretzel mixture, shaking to coat. Place on a lightly greased baking sheet.
• **Bake** at 350° for 1 hour or until done. **Yield:** 4 servings.

Janice M. France
Louisville, Kentucky

BARBECUED CHICKEN LEGS AND THIGHS

4 chicken legs, skinned
4 chicken thighs, skinned
¾ cup ketchup
⅓ cup firmly packed brown sugar
3 tablespoons Worcestershire sauce
2 tablespoons orange juice
1 tablespoon dried onion flakes
1 tablespoon prepared mustard
½ teaspoon garlic powder

• **Place** chicken in a greased 13- x 9- x 2-inch baking dish; set aside.
• **Combine** ketchup and remaining 6 ingredients; pour over chicken.
• **Bake** at 350° for 1 hour, turning chicken once. **Yield:** 8 servings.

LEMON BARBECUED CHICKEN

So satisfying and simple to prepare, this grilled drumstick dish picks up its fabulous flavor from a few simple ingredients and dried spices you likely have on hand.

20 chicken drumsticks (about 3 pounds)
1½ cups vegetable oil
1 cup lemon juice
1½ tablespoons onion powder
1½ tablespoons dried basil
1 tablespoon salt
2 teaspoons paprika
1 teaspoon dried thyme
2 cloves garlic, pressed

• **Place** chicken drumsticks in a heavy-duty, zip-top plastic bag; set aside.
• **Combine** oil and remaining 7 ingredients in a jar. Cover tightly, and shake vigorously. Pour 2 cups marinade mixture over drumsticks; cover and chill remaining ½ cup marinade mixture. Seal bag, and chill 4 hours, turning occasionally.
• **Remove** drumsticks from marinade, discarding marinade. Cook, covered with grill lid, over medium coals (300° to 350°) 15 minutes on each side, basting occasionally with reserved marinade. **Yield:** 8 to 10 servings.

Ed and Cathy Robinson
Columbia, South Carolina

HOT AND SPICY CHICKEN DINNER

QUICK!

2 cups quick-cooking rice,
 uncooked
2 (10-ounce) cans diced tomatoes
 and chiles, undrained
1 (10¾-ounce) can Cheddar
 cheese soup, undiluted
1 small onion, chopped
1 teaspoon dried basil
½ teaspoon salt
⅛ teaspoon pepper
2 pounds chicken legs and thighs,
 skinned

• **Combine** all ingredients except chicken; pour mixture into a greased 11- x 7- x 1½-inch baking dish. Arrange chicken in dish, and cover loosely with wax paper.
• **Microwave**, uncovered, at HIGH 15 minutes. Turn chicken pieces over. Microwave at HIGH 11 to 15 minutes or until done. **Yield:** 4 to 6 servings.

Note: Bake the casserole at 350° for 45 minutes.

Hettie Morgan
Shreveport, Louisiana

SWISS CHICKEN THIGHS

8 chicken thighs, skinned (about
 3 pounds)
4 slices Swiss cheese, cut
 in half
1 (10¾-ounce) can cream of
 mushroom soup, undiluted
¼ cup skim milk
8 thin slices green bell pepper
¾ cup herb-seasoned stuffing
 mix, crushed
3 tablespoons butter, melted

• **Arrange** chicken thighs in an 8-inch square baking dish. Top each thigh with Swiss cheese.
• **Combine** soup and milk, stirring well; pour over cheese. Top evenly with pepper slices.
• **Combine** stuffing mix and butter; sprinkle over casserole.

• **Bake** at 400° for 1 hour or until done. **Yield:** 4 servings.

Linda A. Bowman
Cordele, Georgia

♥ Per serving: Calories 529
Fat 22.4g Cholesterol 236mg
Sodium 769mg

♥ To save 100 calories and 12 fat grams per serving, substitute reduced-fat Swiss cheese, reduced-sodium, reduced-fat cream of mushroom soup, and reduced-calorie margarine.

CHICKEN AND DUMPLINGS WITH HERBED BROTH

1 cup self-rising flour
1 teaspoon pepper
3 pounds chicken legs and thighs
¼ cup vegetable oil
1 medium onion, chopped
2 cloves garlic, minced
1 tablespoon self-rising flour
3 (14½-ounce) cans chicken
 broth
2 tablespoons chopped fresh basil
 or 2 teaspoons dried basil
2 tablespoons chopped fresh
 thyme or 2 teaspoons dried
 thyme
1 tablespoon chopped fresh or
 dried rosemary
½ teaspoon grated lemon rind
2 tablespoons lemon juice
2 cups self-rising flour
1 cup whipping cream
¼ cup reduced-fat sour cream
 (optional)
Garnish: fresh herb sprigs

• **Combine** 1 cup flour and pepper. Dredge chicken in flour mixture.
• **Heat** oil in a large Dutch oven over medium heat; add chicken, and cook until golden, turning once. Add additional oil, if needed. Remove chicken from Dutch oven, reserving drippings in Dutch oven.
• **Cook** onion and garlic in drippings, stirring constantly, until tender.
• **Add** 1 tablespoon flour, and cook 1 minute, stirring constantly; gradually add broth, stirring constantly.

• **Add** chopped basil and next 4 ingredients; bring to a boil. Return chicken to Dutch oven; cover, reduce heat, and simmer 30 minutes.
• **Remove** chicken from Dutch oven, and keep warm.
• **Combine** 2 cups flour and whipping cream in a large bowl, stirring with a fork (mixture will be dry and crumbly). Gently pat mixture into 2-inch balls, handling dough as little as possible.
• **Bring** broth mixture to a rolling boil; add dumplings. Cover, reduce heat, and simmer, without stirring, 7 to 10 minutes or until dumplings are firm in center.
• **Remove** broth mixture from heat. Stir in sour cream, if desired. Serve dumplings and broth over chicken, and garnish, if desired. **Yield:** 4 servings.

Note: Adding the sour cream makes this broth creamy – like a Hungarian-style dish. The texture is more traditional without the sour cream.

BAKED BREAST OF CHICKEN WITH MARINATED BERMUDA ONIONS

1 large head garlic
Olive oil
½ pound goat cheese, softened
1 tablespoon chopped fresh basil
1 tablespoon chopped fresh
 parsley
¼ teaspoon salt
⅛ teaspoon pepper
8 boned whole chicken breasts,
 with skin
Marinated Bermuda Onions

• **Chop** off bottom of garlic head, and separate whole cloves, leaving tight outer covering intact. Place in an 8-inch square pan, and drizzle with olive oil. Bake at 350° for 20 minutes. Cool and drain; squeeze out pulp from cloves. Set aside.
• **Position** knife blade in food processor bowl; add garlic, goat cheese, and next 4 ingredients. Process 30 seconds or until almost smooth, stopping occasionally to scrape down sides.
• **Loosen** skin from chicken breasts, forming a pocket without detaching

skin. Spread 2 tablespoons cheese mixture under skin of each piece of chicken. Place in a 15- x 10- x 1-inch jellyroll pan. Bake, uncovered, at 400° for 30 minutes or until done. Serve on a bed of Marinated Bermuda Onions. **Yield:** 8 servings.

Marinated Bermuda Onions

1 cup balsamic vinegar
¼ cup olive oil
3 cloves garlic, minced
3 tablespoons chopped fresh basil
¼ teaspoon salt
⅛ teaspoon pepper
3 large Bermuda onions, thinly sliced and separated into rings
2 tablespoons olive oil

• **Combine** first 6 ingredients; pour over onions. Cover and chill 1 hour; drain.
• **Cook** onions in 2 tablespoons olive oil in a large nonstick skillet over medium-high heat, stirring constantly, 3 to 5 minutes or until crisp-tender. **Yield:** 4 cups.

Morrison House
Alexandria, Virginia

OVEN-FRIED CHICKEN

If you want to eat crispy chicken on a frequent basis, we recommend this oven-fried version. The secret is baking the chicken at a high temperature, ensuring that almost-fried crispness.

1 quart water
1 teaspoon salt
6 chicken drumsticks
4 chicken breast halves, skinned
½ cup nonfat buttermilk
3 cups corn flake crumbs
2 to 3 teaspoons Creole seasoning
2 teaspoons dried Italian seasoning
½ teaspoon garlic powder
⅛ teaspoon freshly ground black pepper
⅛ teaspoon ground red pepper (optional)
Vegetable cooking spray

• **Combine** water and salt in a bowl; add chicken. Cover and chill 8 hours.

• **Drain** chicken; rinse with cold water, and pat dry. Place chicken in a shallow dish; pour buttermilk over chicken, turning pieces to coat.
• **Combine** corn flake crumbs and next 4 ingredients in a large heavy-duty, zip-top plastic bag. Add red pepper, if desired. Place 2 pieces chicken in bag; seal. Shake to coat completely. Remove chicken, and repeat procedure with remaining pieces.
• **Place** coated chicken, bone side down, in a 15- x 10- x 1-inch jellyroll pan coated with cooking spray, and spray chicken with cooking spray. Place pan on lowest rack in oven.
• **Bake** at 400° for 45 minutes (do not turn). **Yield:** 6 to 8 servings.

♥ Per breast half: Calories 281
Fat 3.6g Cholesterol 68mg
Sodium 635mg

Per drumstick: Calories 176
Fat 3.6g Cholesterol 48mg
Sodium 427mg

SEASONED CHICKEN BAKE

8 skinned and boned chicken breast halves
1 (8-ounce) bottle Italian dressing
¾ cup herb-seasoned stuffing mix, crushed
¼ cup grated Parmesan cheese
1 teaspoon dried parsley flakes
¼ teaspoon salt
⅛ teaspoon pepper

• **Combine** chicken and dressing in a shallow dish; cover and chill 8 hours.
• **Remove** chicken, discarding marinade. Set chicken aside.
• **Combine** stuffing mix and remaining 4 ingredients; coat chicken with stuffing mixture. Arrange chicken in a lightly greased 15- x 10- x 2-inch baking dish.
• **Bake** at 350° for 30 minutes or until chicken is done.
• **Broil** 4 to 6 inches from heat (with electric oven door partially opened) 2 minutes. **Yield:** 8 servings.

Kaye Mabry Adams
Birmingham, Alabama

HERB-SEASONED CHICKEN BREASTS

8 skinned and boned chicken breast halves
1½ cups herb-seasoned stuffing mix
1 tablespoon butter or margarine, melted
¼ cup orange juice
Hot cooked wild rice
Sweet Orange Sauce

• **Arrange** chicken in a lightly greased 13- x 9- x 2-inch baking dish. Sprinkle with stuffing mix; drizzle with butter. Pour orange juice over chicken; cover and bake at 350° for 1 hour. Serve over wild rice with Sweet Orange Sauce. **Yield:** 8 servings.

Sweet Orange Sauce

QUICK!

1 (6-ounce) can frozen orange juice concentrate, thawed and undiluted
½ cup orange marmalade
2 tablespoons steak sauce

• **Combine** all ingredients in a microwave-safe container. Microwave on HIGH 6 minutes or until hot and bubbly, stirring once. **Yield:** 1⅓ cups.

Snookie and Bill Dixon
Arkadelphia, Arkansas

Pepper-Sage Chicken

PEPPER-SAGE CHICKEN
(pictured at left)

QUICK!

While the chicken marinates, wash a bunch of your favorite greens and put them on to boil. Peel, chop, and roast a few sweet potatoes, and you've got a meal your whole family will enjoy.

¼ cup water
¼ cup lemon juice
2 tablespoons white wine
   vinegar
2 tablespoons olive oil
2 teaspoons Dijon mustard
¼ cup chopped fresh sage
1 teaspoon cracked pepper
4 skinned and boned chicken
   breast halves
Vegetable cooking spray
Garnish: fresh sage sprigs

• **Combine** first 7 ingredients in a large heavy-duty, zip-top plastic bag, and add chicken. Seal and chill 1 hour, turning occasionally.
• **Remove** chicken from marinade, reserving marinade.
• **Cook** chicken in a skillet coated with cooking spray over medium-high heat until browned, turning once. Add reserved marinade, and bring to a boil. Reduce heat, and simmer 15 minutes. Slice chicken into strips. Garnish, if desired. **Yield:** 4 servings.

Patsy Bell Hobson
Liberty, Missouri

BAKED CHICKEN WITH TARRAGON SAUCE

8 skinned and boned chicken
   breast halves
½ teaspoon salt
¼ teaspoon pepper
3 tablespoons lemon juice
½ cup mayonnaise or salad
   dressing
1 cup finely chopped celery
1 teaspoon dried tarragon
1 pound fresh spinach
3 medium tomatoes, cut into
   wedges
Garnish: celery leaves

• **Sprinkle** chicken breasts with salt and pepper. Arrange in a lightly greased 13- x 9- x 2-inch pan; sprinkle chicken breasts with lemon juice.
• **Bake** at 375° for 20 minutes or until done. Chill 1 hour.
• **Combine** mayonnaise, celery, and tarragon; set aside.
• **Remove** stems from spinach. Wash leaves thoroughly, and pat dry. Arrange spinach on individual plates. Arrange chicken and tomato wedges on top of spinach. Spoon mayonnaise mixture over chicken. Garnish, if desired. **Yield:** 8 servings.

Note: For chicken salad, coarsely chop cooked chicken, and combine with mayonnaise mixture.

Gina Holmes
Andrews, Texas

MUSTARD CHICKEN

QUICK!

Mustard lovers will thrill to this three-ingredient recipe. Preparing a flavor-packed entrée doesn't get much easier than this.

4 skinned and boned chicken
   breast halves
1 (8-ounce) jar sweet brown
   mustard *
1 teaspoon mustard seeds

• **Place** chicken on a lightly greased rack; place rack in broiler pan.
• **Combine** mustard and mustard seeds; brush on chicken breasts. Broil 5½ inches from heat (with electric oven door partially opened) 15 to 20 minutes or until done. **Yield:** 4 servings.

* For sweet brown mustard, we used Honeycup prepared mustard.

Alice Pahl
Raleigh, North Carolina

PAPRIKA CHICKEN

QUICK!

1 tablespoon margarine
4 skinned and boned chicken
   breast halves
1 (10¾-ounce) can reduced-
   sodium cream of mushroom
   soup, undiluted
1 tablespoon paprika
½ teaspoon dried tarragon
½ teaspoon salt
½ teaspoon ground red pepper
⅓ cup reduced-fat sour cream
Hot cooked egg noodles
Chopped fresh parsley

• **Melt** margarine in a large nonstick skillet over medium-high heat; add chicken, and cook until browned on both sides.
• **Combine** soup and next 4 ingredients; add to skillet, turning chicken to coat. Cover and cook over medium heat 8 minutes or until chicken is done.
• **Remove** chicken; keep warm. Stir sour cream into pan drippings, and cook 1 minute.
• **Place** chicken on noodles; top with sour cream mixture. Sprinkle with parsley. **Yield:** 4 servings.

Denise Gee
Birmingham, Alabama

SALSA-TOPPED CHICKEN BREASTS

Don't let the long list of ingredients fool you. The first 10 are simply tossed together to make the salsa topping.

1 (15-ounce) can black beans, rinsed and drained
1¼ cups frozen whole kernel corn, thawed
¾ cup finely chopped purple onion
¾ cup finely chopped red bell pepper
2 jalapeño peppers, seeded and finely chopped
½ cup balsamic vinegar
¼ cup olive oil
1½ tablespoons Dijon mustard
¼ teaspoon salt
⅛ teaspoon pepper
1 tablespoon chili powder
1 teaspoon ground cumin
¼ teaspoon salt
⅛ teaspoon pepper
4 skinned and boned chicken breast halves *
1 tablespoon butter or margarine
¼ cup chopped fresh cilantro

● **Combine** first 10 ingredients; cover and chill at least 2 hours.
● **Combine** chili powder and next 3 ingredients; sprinkle over chicken.
● **Melt** butter in a nonstick skillet. Add chicken, and cook 5 to 7 minutes on each side or until done.
● **Stir** cilantro into black bean mixture. Serve over chicken. **Yield:** 4 servings.

* Substitute 4 (4-ounce) orange roughy fillets for chicken. Cook 5 minutes on each side or until fish flakes easily when tested with a fork.

Margot Hahn
Washington, D.C.

CHAMPAGNE-POACHED CHICKEN WITH CREAMY MUSTARD SAUCE

QUICK!

1 cup champagne or sparkling wine
½ cup chicken broth
4 skinned and boned chicken breast halves
1 cup whipping cream
1 to 2 teaspoons stone-ground mustard
¼ teaspoon ground red pepper

● **Combine** champagne and broth in a large heavy skillet; bring to a boil. Add chicken; cover, reduce heat, and simmer 10 to 12 minutes or until tender. Remove chicken from skillet; set aside.
● **Stir** whipping cream, mustard, and pepper into skillet. Cook over medium heat 8 to 10 minutes or until thickened, stirring occasionally.
● **Add** chicken to skillet, and cook until thoroughly heated. **Yield:** 4 servings.

POACHED CHICKEN BREAST WITH TURNED VEGETABLES AND CHIVE SAUCE

"Turned" vegetables, pieces of carrot and zucchini trimmed into small football shapes, give this dish a chef's signature.

2 (6-inch-long) zucchini, cut into 2-inch pieces
4 (8-inch-long) carrots, scraped and cut into 2-inch pieces
3 (10½-ounce) cans low-sodium chicken broth
2¼ cups water
½ teaspoon salt
½ teaspoon freshly ground pepper
4 (4- to 5-ounce) skinned and boned chicken breast halves
1 teaspoon chicken-flavored bouillon granules
1½ tablespoons cornstarch
3 tablespoons unsalted butter, cut into ½-inch pieces and chilled
1 teaspoon lemon juice
1 tablespoon finely chopped fresh chives
⅛ teaspoon freshly ground pepper
Garnishes: lemon twist, fresh chives

● **Cut** zucchini pieces in half lengthwise.
● **Trim** zucchini and carrot pieces to resemble football shapes, using a paring knife, and set aside.
● **Place** carrots in boiling water to cover; remove from heat, cover and let stand 10 minutes. Add zucchini; cover and let stand 5 minutes. Drain and set aside.
● **Reserve** 2 tablespoons chicken broth.
● **Combine** remaining chicken broth, water, salt, and ½ teaspoon pepper in a large Dutch oven; bring to a boil. Add chicken; reduce heat to low, and cook 5 minutes. Turn chicken, and cook 5 additional minutes.
● **Remove** 2 cups chicken broth mixture from Dutch oven; set aside.
● **Add** carrots and zucchini to Dutch oven; cover and let stand while making sauce.
● **Place** 2 cups chicken broth mixture in a 2-quart saucepan; bring to a boil over medium heat, and cook 6 to 8 minutes or until liquid is reduced to 1 cup. Reduce heat, and add bouillon granules, stirring until granules dissolve.
● **Combine** cornstarch and reserved 2 tablespoons chicken broth; gradually stir into reduced liquid. Return to a boil, and cook 1 minute, stirring constantly, or until thickened. Remove from heat; add butter pieces, one at a time, and stir with a wire whisk until butter melts. (Do not boil mixture after butter is added.)
● **Stir** in lemon juice, chopped chives, and ⅛ teaspoon pepper. Set aside.
● **Drain** chicken and vegetables; cut chicken diagonally into ½-inch-wide slices. Arrange with vegetables on serving plates; spoon sauce over chicken. Garnish, if desired. **Yield:** 4 servings.

CHICKEN À LA RUSSELL

*The easy béarnaise sauce drizzled
over the top of this dish ties the
ingredients together nicely.*

1 pound ground pork sausage with
    sage
¾ cup all-purpose flour
1 teaspoon dried thyme
1 teaspoon salt
1 teaspoon cracked pepper
8 skinned and boned chicken
    breast halves
⅓ cup vegetable oil
2 (0.9-ounce) envelopes béarnaise
    sauce mix
1 (14-ounce) can artichoke hearts,
    drained and halved
⅓ cup chopped pecans
Garnishes: pecan halves, fresh sage
    sprigs
Wild Rice Casserole (see recipe on
    page 236)

● **Brown** sausage in a large skillet, stirring until it crumbles. Drain sausage,
and set aside. Discard drippings from
skillet.
● **Combine** flour, thyme, salt, and pepper; dredge chicken in flour mixture.
● **Heat** oil in skillet over medium heat.
● **Add** chicken to skillet, and brown on
both sides. Drain chicken, and set aside.
● **Prepare** béarnaise sauce according to
package reduced-calorie directions;
keep warm.
● **Spread** sausage in a lightly greased 11-
x 7- x 1½ -inch baking dish. Top with
chicken, artichokes, béarnaise sauce,
and chopped pecans.
● **Bake** at 325° for 20 minutes or until
thoroughly heated. Garnish, if desired.
Serve with Wild Rice Casserole. **Yield:** 8
servings.

*Irene Smith
Covington, Georgia*

GREEK CHICKEN BREASTS

QUICK!

¼ cup all-purpose flour
1 tablespoon dried oregano
4 skinned and boned chicken
    breast halves
3 tablespoons olive oil
⅓ cup dry white wine
⅓ cup chicken broth
2 medium-size ripe tomatoes,
    peeled and chopped
3 tablespoons sliced ripe olives
2 tablespoons capers
2 tablespoons crumbled feta
    cheese

● **Combine** flour and oregano in a shallow dish; dredge chicken breasts in
flour mixture.
● **Heat** olive oil in a large skillet over
medium heat; add chicken breasts, and
cook 10 minutes, turning once.
● **Add** wine and broth; simmer 10 to 15
minutes. Add chopped tomato, olives,
and capers; cook until thoroughly
heated.
● **Spoon** into serving dish; sprinkle with
feta cheese. **Yield:** 4 servings

JAMAICAN JERK CHICKEN

*The distinguishing flavors
in Jamaican jerk seasoning are
thyme, allspice, and pepper. Rub
the seasoning on chicken or
pork, and pan-fry or grill. (As a
bonus, the seasoning is fat free.)*

½ cup coarsely chopped onion
6 green onions, chopped
2 cloves garlic, coarsely chopped
1 to 2 jalapeño peppers, unseeded
    and coarsely chopped
2 tablespoons fresh thyme leaves
1 tablespoon light brown sugar
1 teaspoon salt
1 teaspoon freshly ground pepper
1 teaspoon ground allspice
½ teaspoon ground cinnamon
¼ teaspoon ground nutmeg
6 skinned and boned chicken
    breast halves or boneless
    pork loin chops
Vegetable cooking spray

● **Position** knife blade in food processor bowl; add first 11 ingredients,
and process until blended.
● **Rub** 1 tablespoon mixture onto each
chicken breast. Cover and chill 1 hour.
● **Cook** chicken in a nonstick skillet
coated with cooking spray 5 to 7 minutes on each side or cook, without grill
lid, over medium coals (300° to 350°) 10
minutes on each side or until chicken is
done. **Yield:** 6 servings.

SMOKY CAJUN JAMBALAYA

QUICK!

1 pound andouille or Cajun-style
    sausage
4 skinned and boned chicken
    breast halves
2 tablespoons peanut oil
1 cup chopped cooked ham
2 teaspoons Cajun seasoning
1 large onion, finely chopped
1 medium-size green bell pepper,
    chopped
½ cup chopped celery
3 cloves garlic, minced
1 (14½-ounce) can Cajun-style
    stewed tomatoes, undrained
½ cup chicken broth
1 tablespoon Worcestershire sauce
½ teaspoon hot sauce
3 cups hot cooked rice
1 cup finely chopped green onions

● **Cut** sausage into ½-inch slices; cut
chicken into ½-inch pieces.
● **Cook** sausage in oil in a large Dutch
oven over medium-high heat 3 minutes
or until browned. Add chicken, and
cook, stirring constantly, 3 minutes or
until browned.
● **Stir** in ham, and cook until thoroughly
heated. Remove meat mixture, reserving 1 tablespoon drippings in Dutch
oven. Return meat mixture to pan; stir
in Cajun seasoning and next 5 ingredients. Cook 5 minutes, stirring mixture
constantly.
● **Stir** in chicken broth and remaining
ingredients; cook, stirring constantly, 2
minutes or until thoroughly heated.
Yield: 6 servings.

*Margaret Jones
Birmingham, Alabama*

MEDITERRANEAN CHICKEN

QUICK!

4 skinned and boned chicken
   breast halves
3 tablespoons all-purpose flour
2 tablespoons olive oil
1 (14½-ounce) can chicken
   broth
¼ cup sliced ripe olives
2 tablespoons capers
⅛ teaspoon pepper
1 (14-ounce) can artichoke hearts,
   halved

• **Dredge** chicken in flour; set aside.
• **Heat** olive oil in a large skillet over medium-high heat. Add chicken, and cook 3 minutes on each side or until lightly browned.
• **Add** chicken broth and next 3 ingredients. Bring to a boil; reduce heat, and simmer 20 minutes or until thickened and bubbly.
• **Stir** in artichoke hearts, and cook until mixture is thoroughly heated. **Yield:** 4 servings.

BANANA CHICKEN WITH BLACK BEAN SAUCE

QUICK!

This unusual combination of ingredients is a delicious surprise – part southwestern, part tropical.

2 large medium-ripe bananas
1 tablespoon ground cumin,
   divided
4 skinned and boned chicken
   breast halves
2 teaspoons vegetable oil
½ cup chopped red bell
   pepper
½ cup chopped green onions
1 medium tomato, chopped
2 cloves garlic, minced
1 (11-ounce) can black bean soup,
   undiluted *
¼ teaspoon pepper
¼ teaspoon dried oregano
½ teaspoon chicken-flavored
   bouillon granules
½ cup water

• **Cut** bananas in half crosswise, and then in half lengthwise; sprinkle with ½ teaspoon cumin.
• **Sprinkle** chicken with remaining cumin; set aside.
• **Heat** oil in a large nonstick skillet over medium-high heat; add bananas, and cook until lightly browned, turning often. Transfer to a serving platter, and keep warm.
• **Add** chicken to skillet; cook 4 to 5 minutes on each side or until done. Add to bananas; keep warm.
• **Add** bell pepper and next 3 ingredients to skillet; cook, stirring constantly, 2 to 3 minutes or until almost crisp-tender.
• **Add** soup and remaining 4 ingredients; cook, stirring constantly, until thoroughly heated. Spoon over chicken and bananas. **Yield:** 4 servings.

✳ Substitute 1 (15-ounce) can black beans, drained, for black bean soup.

Peggy Fowler Revels
Woodruff, South Carolina

COCONUT CHICKEN WITH FRESH FRUIT

2 tablespoons butter or
   margarine
8 skinned and boned chicken
   breast halves
1 tablespoon finely chopped fresh
   ginger *
½ teaspoon salt
⅓ cup flaked coconut, toasted
   and divided
1 cup whipping cream
2 to 3 bananas, quartered
1 large papaya, peeled, seeded,
   and sliced
Garnishes: lime wedges, fresh
   flat-leaf parsley sprigs

• **Melt** butter in a large skillet over medium-high heat; add chicken, and cook 4 minutes on each side or until lightly browned. Sprinkle with ginger, salt, and half of coconut; add whipping cream. Cover and cook over low heat 10 minutes.
• **Arrange** chicken, bananas, and papaya on a large serving platter. Pour warm sauce over chicken, and sprinkle

with remaining coconut. Garnish, if desired. **Yield:** 8 servings.

✳ Substitute ¾ teaspoon ground ginger for fresh, if desired.

A Taste of Aloha
Junior League of Honolulu, Hawaii

BRAISED CHICKEN BREAST IN LEMON CREAM SAUCE

QUICK!

⅓ cup butter or margarine,
   divided
1 (12-ounce) package fresh
   mushrooms, sliced
6 skinned and boned chicken
   breast halves
½ teaspoon salt
½ teaspoon ground white pepper
½ cup all-purpose flour
1 cup chicken broth
1 cup whipping cream
3 tablespoons lemon juice

• **Melt** 3 tablespoons butter in a large skillet over medium heat. Add sliced mushrooms, and cook until browned, stirring often. Drain mushrooms, and set aside.
• **Sprinkle** chicken breasts with salt and white pepper; dredge in flour, shaking off excess.
• **Melt** remaining butter in skillet over medium heat; add chicken, and cook about 8 minutes on each side. Remove chicken from skillet, reserving 1 tablespoon drippings in skillet. Add broth.
• **Bring** broth mixture to a boil. Cook over high heat about 15 minutes or until mixture is reduced to ⅓ cup.
• **Combine** whipping cream and lemon juice; add to broth mixture. Cook over medium heat about 5 minutes. Add mushrooms and chicken breasts.
• **Bring** sauce to a boil; reduce heat, and simmer 4 to 5 minutes or until chicken is heated, spooning sauce over chicken as it cooks. **Yield:** 6 servings.

Freida Merrell
Magnolia, Arkansas

LEMON CHICKEN

QUICK!

4 skinned and boned chicken
     breast halves
½ cup all-purpose flour
¼ cup butter or margarine
2 tablespoons minced garlic
1 cup apple juice
2 tablespoons lemon juice
½ teaspoon pepper

● **Coat** chicken with flour; set aside.
● **Melt** butter in a large skillet over
medium heat; add chicken and garlic.
Cook 8 minutes or until chicken is
browned, turning once. Remove
chicken from skillet, and keep warm.
● **Add** apple juice, lemon juice, and pepper to skillet, stirring to loosen particles
that cling to bottom. Bring to a boil;
cook 10 minutes or until reduced to ½
cup. Pour over chicken; serve immediately. **Yield:** 4 servings.

Marge Killmon
Annandale, Virginia

SKILLET-SEARED
ORANGE CHICKEN

¾ cup fine, dry breadcrumbs
1½ teaspoons chopped fresh
      mint
1½ teaspoons chopped fresh
      cilantro
1½ teaspoons chopped fresh
      basil
4 (5-ounce) skinned and boned
     chicken breast halves
Vegetable cooking spray
1 cup broccoli flowerets
1 cup cauliflower flowerets
1 cup sliced carrot
½ cup fresh shiitake mushrooms
¼ pound fresh spinach, torn
½ cup coarsely chopped purple
     onion
Blended Rice
Mandarin-Teriyaki Sauce

● **Combine** first 4 ingredients in a shallow dish. Dredge chicken in mixture.
● **Place** a large cast-iron skillet over
medium-high heat until very hot. Remove from heat; carefully coat with

cooking spray, and return to heat. Add
chicken, and cook 4 to 5 minutes on
each side. Remove from heat; set aside,
and keep warm.
● **Arrange** broccoli and next 3 ingredients in a steamer basket over boiling
water; cover and steam 8 minutes or
until crisp-tender.
● **Cook** spinach in a small amount of
boiling water 5 to 8 minutes or until tender; drain well.
● **Place** chicken on individual serving
plates; arrange steamed vegetables,
spinach, and purple onion on plates.
Serve with Blended Rice and Mandarin-
Teriyaki Sauce. **Yield:** 4 servings.

♥ Per serving: Calories 566
Fat 4.8g Cholesterol 60mg
Sodium 1760mg

Blended Rice

½ cup basmati rice, uncooked
½ cup wild rice, uncooked
Vegetable cooking spray
½ cup peeled, finely chopped
     plum tomato
½ cup sliced green onions
¼ cup reduced-sodium soy
     sauce

● **Cook** basmati and wild rice separately
according to package directions.
● **Coat** a skillet with cooking spray; add
cooked rice, tomato, green onions, and
soy sauce. Cook over medium heat, stirring constantly, until thoroughly heated.
Yield: 2½ cups.

Mandarin-Teriyaki Sauce

QUICK!

1 tablespoon cornstarch
½ cup reduced-sodium soy sauce
1 cup unsweetened pineapple juice
2 tablespoons brown sugar
1 tablespoon minced garlic
1 tablespoon minced fresh
     ginger
1 tablespoon chopped fresh
     cilantro
2 (11-ounce) cans mandarin
     oranges, drained

● **Combine** cornstarch and soy sauce,
stirring until smooth. Set aside.

● **Combine** pineapple juice and next 4
ingredients in a skillet; bring to a boil
over medium-high heat, stirring constantly. Stir in cornstarch mixture; boil 1
minute, stirring constantly. Remove
from heat; stir in oranges, and let cool.
Yield: 3 cups.

PGA National Resort & Spa
Palm Beach Gardens, Florida

SESAME-CRUSTED CHICKEN
WITH PINEAPPLE SALSA

½ cup sesame seeds
2 tablespoons minced fresh ginger
2 teaspoons vegetable oil
4 (4-ounce) skinned and boned
     chicken breast halves
½ teaspoon salt
Pineapple Salsa

● **Bake** sesame seeds in a shallow pan at
350° for 5 minutes or until toasted, stirring often; cool.
● **Combine** sesame seeds, ginger, and
oil, stirring well.
● **Sprinkle** chicken with salt; coat with
sesame seed mixture, and place on a
lightly greased rack in broiler pan.
● **Bake** at 400° for 20 to 25 minutes or
until tender. Top evenly with Pineapple
Salsa, and serve immediately. **Yield:** 4
servings.

♥ Per serving: Calories 572
Fat 15.5g Cholesterol 196mg
Sodium 519mg

Pineapple Salsa

QUICK!

1 (15¼-ounce) can pineapple
     tidbits, drained
½ cup chopped red bell pepper
1 teaspoon grated fresh ginger
1 tablespoon fresh lime juice
Pinch of ground cloves
¼ cup chopped fresh cilantro
¼ teaspoon hot sauce

● **Combine** all ingredients in a medium
bowl; cover and chill 15 minutes. **Yield:**
1½ cups.

Judy Carter
Winchester, Tennessee

Chicken With Orange, Lime, and Ginger Sauce

CHICKEN WITH ORANGE, LIME, AND GINGER SAUCE

(pictured at left)

QUICK!

2½ tablespoons reduced-calorie orange marmalade
⅛ teaspoon grated lime rind
1½ tablespoons fresh lime juice
½ tablespoon grated fresh ginger
4 (4-ounce) skinned and boned chicken breast halves

● **Combine** first 4 ingredients. Place chicken on grill, and brush with half of marmalade mixture. Cook, covered with grill lid, over medium-hot coals (350° to 400°) 6 minutes. Turn chicken, and brush with remaining marmalade mixture; cook, covered with grill lid, 6 minutes or until done. Serve with grilled vegetables, if desired. **Yield:** 4 servings.

Beth Evins
Atlanta, Georgia

♥ Per serving: Calories 191
Fat 4.0g Cholesterol 96mg
Sodium 85mg

HONEY-LIME GRILLED CHICKEN

QUICK!

½ cup honey
⅓ cup soy sauce
¼ cup lime juice
4 skinned and boned chicken breast halves

● **Combine** first 3 ingredients in a heavy-duty, zip-top plastic bag; add chicken, turning to coat. Seal bag, and chill 30 minutes.
● **Remove** chicken from marinade, discarding marinade.
● **Cook** chicken, without grill lid, over medium-hot coals (350° to 400°) 5 to 6 minutes on each side or until done. **Yield:** 4 servings.

Karen Lapidus
Hampton, Alabama

CHICKEN PROVOLONE

QUICK!

6 skinned and boned chicken breast halves
6 slices prosciutto
6 ounces shredded provolone cheese
Garnish: fresh purple basil leaf or fresh rosemary sprig

● **Cook** chicken, without grill lid, over medium coals (300° to 350°) 15 to 20 minutes, turning once.
● **Place** chicken on a baking sheet; top each breast with a prosciutto slice, and sprinkle evenly with cheese. Bake at 300° for 6 minutes. Garnish, if desired. **Yield:** 6 servings.

Randall Yearwood
Nashville, Tennessee

EASY CHICKEN JALAPEÑO

QUICK!

4 skinned and boned chicken breast halves
2 tablespoons butter or margarine, melted
½ cup jalapeño jelly

● **Place** chicken breasts between two sheets of heavy-duty plastic wrap, and flatten to ¼-inch thickness, using a meat mallet or rolling pin.
● **Cook** chicken in butter in a large skillet over medium-high heat 5 minutes on each side. Transfer to a serving platter; set aside, and keep warm. Add jelly to pan drippings; bring to a boil, stirring until smooth. Spoon over chicken. **Yield:** 4 servings.

Juanita Alexander
Bradenton, Florida

CHICKEN IN MUSTARD CREAM SAUCE

QUICK!

A splash of whipping cream blended with white wine, Dijon mustard, and green peppercorns works magic spooned over quickly browned chicken breast halves.

4 skinned and boned chicken breast halves
⅛ teaspoon pepper
1 tablespoon Dijon mustard
2 tablespoons olive oil
¼ cup whipping cream
¼ cup dry white wine
2 teaspoons Dijon mustard
1 teaspoon green peppercorns in vinegar

● **Place** chicken between two sheets of heavy-duty plastic wrap, and flatten to ¼-inch thickness, using a meat mallet or rolling pin. Sprinkle with pepper, and spread 1 side of chicken breasts with 1 tablespoon mustard. Cook chicken in hot oil in a large skillet over medium heat 10 minutes, turning often. Remove from skillet; set aside, and keep warm.
● **Combine** whipping cream and remaining 3 ingredients in skillet. Bring to a boil, and cook until mixture thickens. Spoon sauce over chicken. **Yield:** 4 servings.

Carol Durr
Pasadena, Maryland

CHICKEN PARMESAN

QUICK!

6 skinned and boned chicken
   breast halves
1 large egg, lightly beaten
¼ cup water
½ cup Italian-seasoned
   breadcrumbs
½ cup grated Parmesan cheese
3 tablespoons butter or margarine
1 (30-ounce) jar spaghetti sauce
Hot cooked egg noodles
1 cup (4 ounces) shredded
   mozzarella cheese
2 teaspoons grated Parmesan
   cheese

• **Place** each chicken breast half between two sheets of heavy-duty plastic wrap, and flatten each to ¼-inch thickness, using a meat mallet or rolling pin.
• **Combine** egg and water in a bowl. Combine breadcrumbs and Parmesan cheese in a separate bowl. Dip chicken in egg mixture; dredge in breadcrumb mixture.
• **Melt** butter in a large skillet over medium heat; add half of chicken, and cook, turning once, until browned. Repeat procedure with remaining chicken.
• **Return** chicken to skillet; add spaghetti sauce. Cover and simmer 10 minutes. Place noodles on platter. Spoon chicken and sauce over noodles; sprinkle with mozzarella and Parmesan cheeses. Cover and let stand until cheese melts. **Yield:** 6 servings.

Kimberly D. Newcomb
Augusta, Georgia

CELEBRITY CHICKEN BREASTS

1 (6-ounce) package long-grain-
   and-wild rice mix
6 ounces fresh goat cheese
   (chèvre)
¼ teaspoon garlic powder
¼ teaspoon dried basil
¼ teaspoon pepper
6 skinned and boned chicken
   breast halves
2 ounces fresh goat cheese
   (chèvre)
2 tablespoons water
¾ cup crushed corn flakes cereal
Garnishes: tomato wedges, fresh
   basil sprigs

• **Cook** rice according to package directions; set aside.
• **Combine** 6 ounces cheese and next 3 ingredients, stirring until blended. Add 1 cup cooked rice mix, stirring well; set aside.
• **Place** each breast half between two sheets of heavy-duty plastic wrap; flatten each to ¼-inch thickness, using a meat mallet or rolling pin.
• **Spoon** about ¼ cup cheese-rice mixture onto center of each chicken breast half. Fold edges of chicken to center to enclose mixture, and secure with a wooden pick.
• **Combine** 2 ounces of cheese and water, stirring until smooth and the consistency of sour cream. Spread mixture on all surfaces of chicken bundles; coat with crushed cereal. Place chicken bundles, seam side down, on a lightly greased baking sheet.
• **Bake** chicken at 375° for 25 minutes. Remove and discard wooden picks; serve warm chicken bundles over remaining rice mix. Garnish, if desired. **Yield:** 6 servings.

Fleming and Brit Pfann
Celebrity Dairy
Greensboro, North Carolina

GOLD NUGGET CHICKEN

A delicious surprise awaits you when you cut into this attractive bundle.

8 skinned and boned chicken
   breast halves
8 to 10 ounces sharp Cheddar
   cheese, cut into 8 equal pieces
2 large eggs, lightly beaten
¾ cup dry breadcrumbs
1 chicken-flavored bouillon cube
1 cup boiling water
½ cup margarine, divided
½ cup chopped onion
½ cup chopped green bell pepper
2 tablespoons all-purpose flour
1 teaspoon salt
½ teaspoon pepper
3 cups cooked rice
1 (4-ounce) can sliced mushrooms,
   drained
1 (2-ounce) jar diced pimiento,
   drained
Garnish: fresh oregano sprigs

• **Place** chicken between two sheets of heavy-duty plastic wrap, and flatten to ¼-inch thickness, using a meat mallet or rolling pin. Place a piece of cheese in center of each breast; fold over all sides of breast, enclosing cheese, and secure with wooden picks.
• **Dip** chicken bundles in egg; dredge in breadcrumbs, coating all sides.
• **Combine** bouillon cube and boiling water; set aside.
• **Melt** ¼ cup margarine in a large skillet over medium-high heat. Cook chicken bundles on both sides until browned; remove from skillet.
• **Melt** remaining ¼ cup margarine in skillet; add onion and green pepper, and cook, stirring constantly, until tender.
• **Add** flour to skillet; cook 1 minute, stirring constantly. Add salt, pepper, and bouillon to skillet; cook, stirring constantly, until mixture is thickened.
• **Add** cooked rice, mushrooms, and pimiento; pour into a greased 13- x 9- x 2-inch baking dish. Place chicken on top.
• **Bake** at 400° for 20 minutes. Garnish, if desired. **Yield:** 8 servings.

The Nashville Cookbook
Nashville Area Home Economics
Association
Nashville, Tennessee

CHICKEN AND HAM ROLLS À LA SWISS

1 large egg, beaten
2 tablespoons water
2 tablespoons Dijon mustard, divided
½ cup fine, dry breadcrumbs
¼ cup grated Parmesan cheese
1 teaspoon salt, divided
½ teaspoon ground white pepper, divided
6 skinned and boned chicken breast halves
6 (4-inch-square) slices cooked ham
¼ cup butter or margarine, melted
2 tablespoons butter or margarine
2 tablespoons all-purpose flour
1½ cups milk
½ cup dry white wine
1 cup (4 ounces) shredded Swiss cheese

• **Combine** egg, water, and 1 tablespoon mustard, mixing well; set aside.
• **Combine** breadcrumbs, Parmesan cheese, ½ teaspoon salt, and ¼ teaspoon ground white pepper; set aside.
• **Place** each piece of chicken between two sheets of heavy-duty plastic wrap, and flatten to ¼-inch thickness, using a meat mallet or rolling pin. Place a ham slice on each chicken breast. Roll up from short side, and secure rolls with wooden picks. Dip chicken rolls in egg mixture, and dredge in breadcrumb mixture. Place chicken rolls in a lightly greased 11- x 7- x 1½-inch baking dish. Drizzle chicken rolls with ¼ cup melted butter. Bake, uncovered, at 350° for 45 minutes or until tender.
• **Melt** 2 tablespoons butter in a heavy saucepan over low heat; add flour, remaining 1 tablespoon mustard, remaining ½ teaspoon salt, and remaining ¼ teaspoon ground white pepper, stirring until smooth. Gradually add milk; cook over medium heat, stirring constantly, until mixture is thickened and bubbly. Stir in wine and Swiss cheese; cook 1 minute, stirring constantly, or until cheese melts. Serve over chicken. **Yield:** 6 servings.

Jeanne S. Hotaling
Augusta, Georgia

MEXICAN CHICKEN ROLLS

½ cup fine, dry breadcrumbs
¼ cup grated Parmesan cheese
1 teaspoon chili powder
¼ teaspoon ground cumin
¼ teaspoon pepper
8 skinned and boned chicken breast halves
1 (8-ounce) package Monterey Jack cheese with peppers, cut crosswise into 8 equal slices
⅓ cup butter or margarine, melted

• **Combine** first 5 ingredients in a shallow dish; set aside.
• **Place** each chicken breast between two sheets of heavy-duty plastic wrap; flatten to ¼-inch thickness, using a meat mallet or rolling pin.
• **Place** a slice of cheese on each chicken breast. Roll up from short side, and secure with wooden picks.
• **Dip** chicken rolls in butter, and dredge in breadcrumb mixture. Place rolls, seam side down, on a baking sheet. Cover and freeze until firm; transfer to a large heavy-duty plastic freezer bag, and return to freezer. Freeze up to 6 months.
• **To** serve, place frozen chicken rolls in a lightly greased 11- x 7- x 1½-inch baking dish; bake at 400° for 30 minutes. **Yield:** 8 servings.

Valynda Kingsley
Woodbridge, Virginia

BASIL-STUFFED CHICKEN WITH TOMATO-BASIL PASTA
(pictured on page 263)

4 (4-ounce) skinned and boned chicken breast halves
¼ teaspoon salt
¼ teaspoon garlic powder
2 bunches fresh basil (about 20 large basil leaves)
Tomato-Basil Pasta
Garnish: fresh basil sprigs

• **Place** each piece of chicken between two sheets of heavy-duty plastic wrap; flatten to ¼-inch thickness, using a meat mallet or rolling pin.
• **Sprinkle** chicken breasts evenly with salt and garlic powder.
• **Arrange** basil leaves in a single layer over chicken breasts. Starting at short end, roll up 2 chicken breasts. Place each roll on top of a remaining chicken breast, and roll up, forming 2 larger rolls. Secure chicken with wooden picks.
• **Cook**, covered with grill lid, over medium-hot coals (350° to 400°) 18 to 20 minutes, turning once.
• **Wrap** in aluminum foil, and chill at least 8 hours.
• **Remove** chicken rolls from refrigerator, and unwrap. Place chicken rolls on a microwave-safe plate, and cover with wax paper.
• **Microwave** at MEDIUM-HIGH (70% power) 1½ minutes, turning once. Remove wooden picks.
• **Cut** each chicken roll into thin slices. Serve on individual plates with Tomato-Basil Pasta. Garnish, if desired. **Yield:** 4 servings.

♥ Per serving: Calories 636
Fat 7.9g Cholesterol 70mg
Sodium 296mg

Tomato-Basil Pasta
QUICK!

1 tablespoon reduced-calorie margarine
2 cloves garlic, minced
¼ cup lemon juice
¼ cup dry white wine
¼ cup chopped fresh basil
1 cup peeled, seeded, and finely chopped tomato
8 ounces thin spaghetti, cooked without salt or fat

• **Melt** margarine in a large saucepan over medium heat; add minced garlic, and cook 1 minute, stirring constantly. Add lemon juice and remaining ingredients; toss gently. **Yield:** 4 servings.

PESTO-STUFFED CHICKEN ROLLS

6 large skinned and boned chicken
   breast halves
¼ teaspoon salt
¼ teaspoon pepper
1 (3-ounce) package cream cheese,
   softened
¼ cup pesto
½ cup finely chopped red bell
   pepper
¾ cup corn flake crumbs
½ teaspoon paprika
Vegetable cooking spray
Garnish: fresh basil sprigs

• **Place** each piece of chicken between two sheets of heavy-duty plastic wrap; flatten to ¼-inch thickness, using a meat mallet or rolling pin. Sprinkle with salt and pepper; set aside.
• **Combine** cream cheese, pesto, and red bell pepper in a small bowl, stirring with a fork until blended. Spread 2 tablespoons cheese mixture over each chicken breast; roll up lengthwise, securing with wooden picks.
• **Combine** corn flake crumbs and paprika; dredge chicken rolls in crumb mixture. Place in an 11- x 7- x 1½-inch baking dish coated with cooking spray. Cover and chill 8 hours.
• **Remove** chicken from refrigerator, and let stand at room temperature 30 minutes. Bake, uncovered, at 350° for 35 minutes; let stand 10 minutes. Remove wooden picks, and slice into 1-inch rounds. (An electric knife works best.) Garnish, if desired. **Yield:** 6 servings.

Note: To make and bake on the same day, prepare according to above directions, omitting the 8-hour chilling time.

CHICKEN BREASTS WITH PECAN-SAUSAGE STUFFING

⅓ pound ground pork sausage
⅓ cup butter or margarine
⅓ cup finely chopped celery
⅓ cup finely chopped green bell
   pepper
1 small onion, finely chopped
½ cup chopped pecans, divided
¼ teaspoon pepper
⅛ teaspoon salt
3 cups dry bread cubes (¼-inch
   pieces)
1 large egg, lightly beaten
1½ tablespoons milk
4 skinned and boned whole
   chicken breasts
1½ tablespoons butter or
   margarine, melted
3 tablespoons fine, dry
   breadcrumbs
Garnish: chopped fresh parsley

• **Brown** sausage in a Dutch oven, stirring until it crumbles. Remove from pan, and set aside; discard drippings.
• **Melt** ⅓ cup butter in Dutch oven over medium-high heat; add celery, green bell pepper, and onion. Cook, stirring constantly, until vegetables are tender.
• **Add** ⅓ cup pecans, pepper, and salt; cook 3 minutes, stirring constantly. Remove from heat; stir in sausage, bread cubes, egg, and milk. Set aside.
• **Place** each chicken breast between two sheets of heavy-duty plastic wrap, and flatten to ¼-inch thickness, using a meat mallet or rolling pin.
• **Place** chicken breasts on a flat surface. Spoon sausage mixture evenly into center of each chicken breast. Fold long sides over filling, and secure with wooden picks. Place chicken, seam side down, in a baking pan lined with aluminum foil.
• **Combine** 1½ tablespoons melted butter, remaining 2 tablespoons plus 2 teaspoons pecans, and breadcrumbs; press evenly onto chicken breasts.
• **Bake** at 350° for 30 minutes or until golden. Garnish, if desired. **Yield:** 4 servings.

Jeanne S. Hotaling
Augusta, Georgia

SPINACH-STUFFED CHICKEN IN PUFF PASTRY

4 skinned and boned chicken
   breast halves *
½ teaspoon salt
½ teaspoon pepper
1 (10-ounce) package frozen
   spinach, thawed and
   drained
¾ cup (3 ounces) shredded
   Gruyère or Swiss cheese
½ cup finely chopped prosciutto
   or cooked ham (3 ounces)
¼ teaspoon salt
⅛ teaspoon pepper
Dash of ground nutmeg
1 (17¼-ounce) package frozen
   puff pastry sheets, thawed
1 large egg, lightly beaten
1 teaspoon water
1 (0.9-ounce) package béarnaise
   sauce mix

• **Place** chicken between two sheets of heavy-duty plastic wrap, and flatten to ⅛-inch thickness, using a meat mallet or rolling pin. Sprinkle chicken with ½ teaspoon each of salt and pepper, and set aside.
• **Combine** spinach and next 5 ingredients; shape into 4 balls, placing 1 ball in center of each chicken breast. Fold chicken over spinach.
• **Roll** each sheet of puff pastry into a 12-inch square. Cut a 1-inch strip from side of each sheet, setting aside for garnish. Cut each sheet in half, making 4 (5½- x 6-inch) rectangles.
• **Place** stuffed chicken breasts in center of pastry rectangles; fold sides over chicken. Combine egg and water, and brush on pastry seams, pinching to seal. Place seam side down on a lightly greased 15- x 10- x 1-inch jellyroll pan.
• **Cut** decorative stems and leaves or desired shapes from reserved pastry strips. Brush back of cutouts with egg mixture, and arrange on chicken bundles. Chill chicken bundles and remaining egg mixture 1 hour. Brush bundles with egg mixture, and bake, uncovered, at 400° for 20 to 25 minutes or until golden.
• **Prepare** béarnaise sauce according to package directions. Spoon 2 tablespoons sauce in each of four plates; top

each with chicken bundle. Serve immediately. **Yield:** 4 servings.

✳ Substitute 12 (1-ounce) slices of veal scaloppine for 4 chicken breasts. Overlap 3 slices of veal, and place on each puff pastry rectangle.

Missy Wilson
Birmingham, Alabama

CHICKEN FAJITA SPUDS

2 teaspoons ground cumin
1 teaspoon dried oregano,
      crushed
¼ teaspoon ground red pepper
½ teaspoon salt
6 skinned and boned chicken
      breast halves
6 large baked potatoes
1½ cups (6 ounces) shredded
      Mexican-style cheese blend,
      divided
1 (8-ounce) carton sour cream,
      divided
2 tablespoons butter or
      margarine
3 tablespoons milk
½ teaspoon salt
¼ teaspoon ground black pepper
1 (16-ounce) jar chunky salsa
Garnishes: chopped fresh cilantro,
      fresh cilantro sprigs

● **Combine** first 4 ingredients; rub onto all sides of chicken. Place chicken in a lightly greased 13- x 9- x 2-inch baking dish, and let stand 15 minutes.
● **Bake** at 400° for 6 minutes on each side. Cut into strips.
● **Cut** a 1-inch-wide strip from top of each baked potato. Carefully scoop out pulp, leaving shells intact; set shells aside. Mash pulp; stir in 1 cup cheese blend, ½ cup sour cream, butter, and next 3 ingredients. Spoon into shells, and place on a baking sheet.
● **Bake** potatoes at 350° for 20 minutes. Sprinkle with remaining cheese blend, and top with chicken. Bake 5 additional minutes or until cheese melts. Serve with remaining sour cream and salsa. Garnish, if desired. **Yield:** 6 servings.

Molly Connally
Annandale, Virginia

CHICKEN ENCHILADAS VERDE

14 skinned chicken breast halves
      (about 7 pounds)
3 quarts water
2 tablespoons ground red pepper
1 tablespoon salt
14 fresh tomatillos
1½ cups chopped onion
3 cloves garlic, minced
2 tablespoons vegetable oil
1 teaspoon salt
¼ cup chopped fresh cilantro
4 cups (16 ounces) shredded
      Monterey Jack cheese,
      divided
1 cup vegetable oil
20 corn tortillas
Verde Sauce
8 ounces feta cheese, crumbled
Red Pepper Puree
Garnish: fresh cilantro leaves

● **Combine** first 4 ingredients in a large Dutch oven; bring to a boil. Cover, reduce heat, and simmer 35 minutes or until chicken is done. Remove chicken, discarding broth; cool. Bone and shred chicken; set aside.
● **Remove** husks from tomatillos, and cook tomatillos in a saucepan in boiling water to cover 5 minutes; drain and set aside.
● **Cook** onion and garlic in 2 tablespoons oil in Dutch oven over medium-high heat until tender, stirring often. Add tomatillos and 1 teaspoon salt. Bring to a boil; reduce heat, and simmer 5 minutes. Add chicken and cilantro; cook 10 minutes. Stir in 1 cup Monterey Jack cheese.
● **Heat** 1 cup vegetable oil in a medium skillet. Fry tortillas, one at a time, 3 or 4 seconds on each side; drain on paper towels. Dip each tortilla in Verde Sauce, coating well. Place about ½ cup chicken mixture down center of each tortilla, and roll up. Repeat procedure with each tortilla. Place tortillas, seam side down, into two 13- x 9- x 2-inch baking dishes; top with remaining sauce, spreading to cover ends of tortillas. Sprinkle with remaining 3 cups Monterey Jack cheese and feta cheese. Cover and bake at 425° for 20 to 30 minutes or until thoroughly heated. Serve with Red Pepper Puree. Garnish, if desired. **Yield:** 10 servings.

Verde Sauce

8 poblano chile peppers
32 fresh tomatillos
3 cups chicken broth, divided
1 medium onion, chopped
4 cloves garlic, minced
6 romaine lettuce leaves, torn
½ cup chopped fresh cilantro
2½ teaspoons salt

● **Wash** and dry peppers; place on an aluminum foil-lined baking sheet. Broil 5 inches from heat (with electric oven door partially opened) about 5 minutes on each side or until peppers look blistered, turning once. Immediately place in a heavy-duty, zip-top plastic bag; seal and let stand 10 minutes to loosen skins. Peel peppers, and remove seeds; set aside.
● **Remove** husks from tomatillos, and cook tomatillos in a Dutch oven in boiling water to cover 5 minutes; drain. Position knife blade in food processor bowl. Add peppers, tomatillos, 1 cup chicken broth, onion, and remaining 4 ingredients; process 20 to 30 seconds or until smooth, stopping once to scrape down sides. Transfer to a Dutch oven, and cook, over medium heat 5 minutes, stirring constantly. Slowly stir in remaining 2 cups chicken broth, and simmer until thickened (about 10 to 12 minutes). **Yield:** 6 cups.

Red Pepper Puree

5 red bell peppers
1 teaspoon salt

● **Wash** and dry peppers; place on an aluminum foil-lined baking sheet. Broil 5½ inches from heat (with electric oven door partially opened) 5 minutes on each side or until peppers look blistered, turning once. Immediately place in a heavy-duty, zip-top plastic bag; seal and let stand 10 minutes to loosen skins. Peel peppers, and remove seeds.
● **Position** knife blade in food processor bowl. Add peppers and salt; process until smooth, stopping once to scrape down sides. Cover and chill, if desired. **Yield:** 2 cups.

Libby and Jim Collet
Dallas, Texas

CHICKEN ENCHILADAS WITH TOMATILLO SAUCE

1 (6½-ounce) package 6-inch corn
   tortillas
3½ cups chopped cooked chicken
3 cups (12 ounces) shredded
   Monterey Jack cheese,
   divided
Tomatillo Sauce

• **Wrap** tortillas in aluminum foil; bake at 325° for 15 minutes or until thoroughly heated.
• **Place** about ⅓ cup chicken and ¼ cup cheese down center of each tortilla; roll up, and place seam side down in a 13- x 9- x 2-inch baking dish. Repeat procedure with each tortilla. Top with 2 cups Tomatillo Sauce. Sprinkle with remaining 1 cup Monterey Jack cheese.
• **Bake** at 350° for 15 to 20 minutes. **Yield:** 4 to 5 servings.

Tomatillo Sauce

1 pound fresh tomatillos
2 cups water
1 chicken-flavored bouillon cube
¼ cup finely chopped onion
12 to 15 cloves garlic, minced
¼ cup finely chopped fresh
   cilantro
1 tablespoon finely chopped
   jalapeño pepper
1 tablespoon finely chopped
   roasted red bell pepper
1½ tablespoons brown sugar
2 tablespoons lime juice
¼ teaspoon salt

• **Remove** and discard tomatillo husks, and wash tomatillos.
• **Combine** tomatillos, water, bouillon cube, and onion in a saucepan. Bring to a boil over medium heat; reduce heat, and simmer 50 minutes or until mixture is thickened.
• **Add** garlic and remaining ingredients; cool. **Yield:** 3 cups.

Note: Serve remaining Tomatillo Sauce over grilled chicken or fish or hot cooked pasta.

Chef Ron Brannon
Austin Central Market's Cooking School
Austin, Texas

ORIENTAL CHICKEN KABOBS

QUICK!

1½ pounds skinned and boned
   chicken breast halves, cut into
   1-inch cubes
¼ teaspoon salt
¼ teaspoon pepper
1 medium-size yellow bell pepper,
   seeded and cut into 1-inch
   pieces
1 medium-size red bell pepper,
   seeded and cut into 1-inch
   pieces
1 (15-ounce) jar baby corn,
   drained and cut in half
⅓ cup hoisin or teriyaki sauce
⅓ cup honey
1 clove garlic, pressed
½ teaspoon minced fresh ginger

• **Sprinkle** chicken evenly with salt and pepper.
• **Alternate** chicken, pepper pieces, and corn on 8 (14-inch) skewers.
• **Combine** hoisin sauce and remaining 3 ingredients; brush on kabobs.
• **Cook**, covered with grill lid, over medium-hot coals (350° to 400°) 12 minutes, turning and basting with sauce mixture. **Yield:** 4 servings.

CHICKEN AND VEGETABLE STIR-FRY

QUICK!

2 tablespoons vegetable oil
1 pound chicken breast strips
2 tablespoons water
1 (16-ounce) package broccoli
   stir-fry mix
1 purple onion, cut into strips
2 red bell peppers, cut into strips
1 (11.75-ounce) bottle stir-fry
   sauce
Hot cooked rice

• **Pour** oil around top of a preheated wok, coating sides; heat at medium-high (375°) for 2 minutes. Add chicken, and stir-fry 2 minutes or until lightly browned.
• **Add** water and vegetables, stirring gently. Cover and cook 8 minutes or until vegetables are crisp-tender, stirring once. Add sauce, and stir-fry 2 additional minutes. Serve over rice. **Yield:** 4 servings.

CHOW MEIN CHICKEN CASSEROLE

QUICK!

This clever casserole comes together quickly thanks to convenience products. A can of chow mein noodles makes a quick and crunchy topping.

1 tablespoon butter or margarine
1 small red bell pepper,
   chopped
2 cloves garlic, minced
2 (8-ounce) packages sliced fresh
   mushrooms
⅓ cup slivered almonds
3 green onions, chopped
1 (10¾-ounce) can cream of
   mushroom soup, undiluted
¾ cup mayonnaise
2 teaspoons soy sauce
3 cups chopped cooked chicken
¼ teaspoon pepper
1 (3-ounce) can chow mein
   noodles

• **Melt** butter in a large skillet over medium heat. Add bell pepper, garlic, and mushrooms; cook until tender, stirring often. Stir in almonds and next 6 ingredients; pour into a lightly greased 11- x 7- x 1½-inch baking dish. Sprinkle with chow mein noodles.
• **Bake** at 350° for 30 minutes or until bubbly. **Yield:** 6 servings.

Louise W. Mayer
Richmond, Virginia

SPAGHETTI SQUASH AND CHICKEN SKILLET CASSEROLE

3 tablespoons butter or margarine
1 cup sliced fresh mushrooms
⅓ cup chopped leeks
¼ cup chopped celery
3 tablespoons chopped red bell
     pepper
3 tablespoons finely chopped fresh
     parsley
2 cups cooked spaghetti squash
4 skinned and boned chicken
     breast halves, cooked and
     cut into thin strips
¼ cup crushed seasoned croutons
¼ teaspoon salt
¼ teaspoon seasoned pepper
⅛ teaspoon garlic powder
Pinch of dried summer savory
½ cup sour cream
½ cup (2 ounces) shredded Swiss
     cheese

• **Melt** butter in a large skillet over medium heat. Add mushrooms and next 4 ingredients; cook, stirring constantly, 5 minutes or until tender.
• **Add** squash and next 6 ingredients; cook 4 minutes, stirring constantly.
• **Stir** in sour cream; cook, stirring constantly, just until thoroughly heated. Remove from heat.
• **Sprinkle** with cheese. Cover and let stand 1 minute. **Yield:** 3 to 4 servings.

Spaghetti Squash Tortillas: Prepare recipe according to directions; omit chicken and cheese. Spoon onto 8 (6-inch) flour tortillas, and fold. Place seam side down in a lightly greased 11- x 7- x 1½-inch baking dish. Cover and bake at 350° for 20 minutes. Uncover; sprinkle with cheese. Bake 5 additional minutes.

Fresh Ideas For Vegetable Cooking
Georgia Massie
Seagoville, Texas

TURBAN CHICKEN CURRY

1 (7¾-pound) turban squash
3½ cups chicken broth, divided
1 cup long-grain rice, uncooked
1 (6-ounce) package chopped
     dried tropical fruit mix
3 green onions, cut into ½-inch
     pieces
2 tablespoons vegetable oil
1½ tablespoons all-purpose
     flour
1 tablespoon curry powder
½ teaspoon salt
¼ teaspoon ground red pepper
½ cup unsweetened coconut
     milk
3 cups chopped cooked chicken
¼ cup flaked coconut, toasted
½ cup cashews, toasted
Garnish: fresh cilantro sprigs

• **Remove** squash crown by cutting around it with a sharp knife angled toward the center; set crown aside. Remove and discard fiber and seeds.
• **Place** base and crown, cut sides down, in a large baking pan. Add water to pan to depth of 1 inch.
• **Bake** at 350° for 1 hour or until tender. Remove from water, reserving pan of water.
• **Bring** 2½ cups chicken broth to a boil in a medium saucepan; add rice. Cover, reduce heat, and cook 20 minutes or until liquid is absorbed and rice is tender. Stir in fruit mix; cover and set aside.
• **Cook** green onions in oil in a large skillet 3 minutes; stir in flour and next 3 ingredients. Cook 1 minute, stirring constantly. Gradually add remaining 1 cup chicken broth; cook 1 minute or until mixture is slightly thickened. Stir in coconut milk.
• **Add** rice mixture and chicken to skillet, stirring just until blended. Spoon into squash base; top with crown. Place in pan with water.
• **Bake** at 350° for 20 minutes or until thoroughly heated.
• **Set** crown to the side, and sprinkle rice mixture with coconut and cashews before serving. Garnish, if desired. **Yield:** 6 servings.

Kinsey Mills
Birmingham, Alabama

CHICKEN DUMPLING PIE

An easy blend of biscuit mix, sour cream, and milk blankets this easy-to-prepare casserole with down-home goodness. Canned ingredients and a few simple additions make this recipe a dependable one-dish meal your family is sure to enjoy.

3 cups chopped cooked chicken or
     turkey
2 (10¾-ounce) cans cream of
     chicken soup, undiluted
1 (10½-ounce) can condensed
     chicken broth, undiluted
1 (15-ounce) can mixed
     vegetables, drained
½ teaspoon poultry seasoning
2 cups biscuit mix
1 (8-ounce) carton sour cream
1 cup milk

• **Combine** first 5 ingredients in a bowl, and pour chicken mixture into a lightly greased 13- x 9- x 2-inch baking dish.
• **Combine** biscuit mix, sour cream, and milk in a medium bowl; pour over chicken mixture.
• **Bake** at 350° for 50 to 60 minutes or until topping is golden. **Yield:** 6 to 8 servings.

Lilann Taylor
Savannah, Georgia

CHICKEN POT PIE

¼ cup butter or margarine
¼ cup all-purpose flour
1½ cups chicken broth
1½ cups half-and-half
¾ teaspoon salt
½ teaspoon freshly ground
   pepper
2 tablespoons butter or margarine
1 (8-ounce) package sliced fresh
   mushrooms
1 small onion, chopped
3 stalks celery, sliced
3½ cups chopped cooked
   chicken
2 hard-cooked eggs, chopped
1 (15-ounce) package refrigerated
   piecrusts

● **Melt** ¼ cup butter in a heavy sauce-pan over low heat; add flour, stirring until smooth. Cook 1 minute, stirring constantly. Gradually add chicken broth and half-and-half; cook over medium heat, stirring constantly, until thickened and bubbly. Stir in salt and pepper; set sauce aside.
● **Melt** 2 tablespoons butter in a skillet over medium-high heat; add mushrooms, onion, and celery, and cook, stirring constantly, until vegetables are tender. Drain and stir vegetable mixture, chicken, and chopped egg into sauce.
● **Fit** 1 piecrust into a 9-inch deep-dish pieplate according to package directions. Spoon filling into crust; top with remaining piecrust. Trim off excess pastry. Fold edges under, and flute. Cut slits in top.
● **Bake** at 375° for 30 to 40 minutes or until top is golden, covering edges with strips of aluminum foil after 20 minutes to prevent excessive browning. **Yield:** 6 servings.

Angie Williams
Montgomery, Alabama

CHICKEN ON EGG BREAD

Nashville cooks often rely on this dish for easy entertaining. You can substitute your favorite cornbread for the Egg Bread.

3 tablespoons butter or margarine
2 tablespoons finely chopped
   celery
2 tablespoons finely chopped
   onion
3 tablespoons all-purpose flour
2 cups chicken broth
¾ cup whipping cream
¼ teaspoon salt
Egg Bread
3 cups coarsely chopped cooked
   chicken
Freshly ground pepper

● **Melt** butter in a large skillet over medium-high heat; add celery and onion, and cook, stirring constantly, until tender.
● **Add** flour; cook, stirring constantly, 1 minute. Gradually add chicken broth, whipping cream, and salt; bring to a boil, stirring constantly. Reduce heat, and simmer until slightly thickened (about 3 minutes). Remove from heat, and keep warm.
● **Cut** Egg Bread into wedges or squares; slice in half horizontally. Top with chicken and sauce. Sprinkle with pepper. **Yield:** 6 servings.

Egg Bread

1 cup milk
1 cup water
2¼ cups yellow cornmeal, divided
3 large eggs
1 teaspoon salt
2 cups buttermilk
1 teaspoon baking soda
2 tablespoons shortening

● **Combine** milk and water in a large saucepan; bring to a boil over high heat. Reduce heat, and stir in 2 cups cornmeal. Remove from heat.
● **Beat** eggs at high speed with an electric mixer until foamy; add salt, and beat until light and fluffy.
● **Combine** buttermilk and soda; add to cornmeal mixture with egg mixture, and beat until smooth.

● **Place** shortening in a 10-inch cast-iron skillet; place skillet in a 400° oven for 5 minutes. Pour melted shortening into cornmeal mixture, stirring well. Add remaining ¼ cup cornmeal, stirring until smooth. Pour cornmeal mixture into hot skillet.
● **Bake** at 400° for 25 to 30 minutes or until firm. Remove from skillet immediately. **Yield:** 6 to 8 servings.

The Nashville Cookbook
Nashville Area Home Economics
Association
Nashville, Tennessee

CHICKEN RAGOÛT WITH CHEDDAR DUMPLINGS

2 cups diagonally sliced carrot
1 cup sweet red pepper strips
3 tablespoons butter or margarine
¼ cup all-purpose flour
2 cups chicken broth
1 cup milk
1 tablespoon lemon juice
½ teaspoon salt
½ teaspoon pepper
3 cups chopped cooked chicken
1 cup frozen English peas, thawed
   and drained
2 cups biscuit mix
⅔ cup milk
¾ cup (3 ounces) shredded
   Cheddar cheese
1 (2-ounce) jar diced pimiento,
   drained

● **Arrange** sliced carrot and sweet red pepper strips in a steamer basket; place over boiling water. Cover; steam 8 minutes or until vegetables are crisp-tender; set aside.
● **Melt** butter in a large heavy saucepan over low heat; add flour, stirring until mixture is smooth. Cook 1 minute, stirring constantly. Gradually add chicken broth and 1 cup milk; cook over medium heat, stirring constantly, until mixture is thickened and bubbly. Remove from heat.
● **Stir** in lemon juice, salt, and pepper. Add chicken, steamed vegetables, and peas, stirring gently. Spoon into a lightly greased 11- x 7- x 1½-inch baking dish; set aside.

• **Combine** biscuit mix and ⅔ cup milk, stirring until dry ingredients are moistened. Stir vigorously 30 seconds. Turn out onto a lightly floured surface, and knead 4 or 5 times.

• **Roll** dough into a 12- x 9-inch rectangle. Sprinkle with cheese and pimiento, leaving a ½-inch border; roll up jellyroll fashion, starting with a long side, and turn seam side down. Cut into 1-inch-thick slices, and place over chicken mixture.

• **Bake** at 400° for 30 minutes or until golden brown. **Yield:** 6 servings.

Sue Deck
Ellenwood, Georgia

CHICKEN PACKETS

These chicken bundles are a snap to make with convenience products.

2 tablespoons olive oil
4 skinned and boned chicken
    breast halves, cut into 1-inch
    pieces
1 cup chopped onion
½ cup chopped green bell pepper
½ cup sour cream
½ (10¾-ounce) can cream of
    mushroom soup, undiluted
½ teaspoon garlic salt
¼ teaspoon pepper
3 (8-ounce) cans refrigerated
    crescent dinner rolls
1 cup (4 ounces) shredded
    mozzarella cheese
Garnish: fresh parsley sprigs

• **Pour** oil into a medium skillet, and place over medium-high heat until hot. Add chicken, onion, and bell pepper; cook, stirring constantly, 5 minutes or until chicken is tender. Drain.

• **Combine** chicken mixture, sour cream, and next 3 ingredients in a small bowl, stirring well.

• **Unroll** crescent rolls, and separate into 12 rectangles; press perforations to seal. Spoon 2 tablespoons chicken mixture in center of each rectangle, and sprinkle evenly with cheese. Bring corners of rectangles together and twist, pinching seams to seal; place on lightly greased baking sheets.

• **Bake** at 350° for 20 minutes or until lightly browned. Garnish, if desired. **Yield:** 1 dozen.

Note: You can freeze unbaked packets in airtight containers up to 3 days. Remove from freezer, and bake, unthawed, at 350° for 30 minutes or until lightly browned.

Cathy Ruark
Brandon, Mississippi

CHICKEN AND BLACK BEAN QUESADILLAS

The ubiquitous Tex-Mex appetizer becomes a hearty meal with main-dish ingredients.

1 tablespoon fajita seasoning
2 (4-ounce) skinned and boned
    chicken breast halves, cut
    into thin strips
Vegetable cooking spray
½ onion, cut into strips
½ green bell pepper, cut into
    strips
2 cloves garlic, minced
1 to 2 jalapeño peppers,
    minced
1 (15-ounce) can black beans,
    rinsed and drained
½ cup chopped fresh cilantro
4 (10-inch) flour tortillas
1½ cups (6 ounces) shredded
    reduced-fat Monterey Jack
    cheese

• **Rub** fajita seasoning on all sides of chicken; cover and chill 30 minutes.

• **Cook** chicken in a large nonstick skillet over medium-high heat, stirring constantly, 4 minutes or until done. Remove from skillet, and keep warm.

• **Coat** skillet with cooking spray; add onion and next 3 ingredients, and cook until tender, stirring often. Stir in black beans and cilantro; cook, stirring constantly, until thoroughly heated.

• **Coat** 1 side of each tortilla with cooking spray; layer chicken, vegetable mixture, and cheese evenly on uncoated side of 2 tortillas. Top with remaining tortillas, coated side up. Cook in skillet over medium heat until lightly browned,

turning once. Serve immediately. **Yield:** 2 servings.

Patty Messer
Middlesboro, Kentucky

♥ Per serving: Calories 697
Fat 22.2g Cholesterol 93mg
Sodium 911mg

SPICY CHICKEN QUESADILLAS

4 skinned and boned chicken
    breast halves, cut into ¼-inch-
    thick strips
1 (1¼-ounce) package taco
    seasoning mix
2½ cups (10 ounces) shredded
    Monterey Jack cheese
⅔ cup picante sauce
1 medium-size red bell pepper,
    chopped
10 (10-inch) flour tortillas
Melted butter

• **Combine** chicken and taco seasoning mix in a heavy-duty, zip-top plastic bag; toss to coat. Cover and chill 1 hour.

• **Place** chicken in a 15- x 10- x 1-inch jellyroll pan.

• **Broil** chicken 5½ inches from heat (with electric oven door partially opened) 5 minutes.

• **Cool** chicken, and cut breasts into bite-size pieces.

• **Combine** chicken, cheese, picante sauce, and red pepper; set aside.

• **Brush** 1 side of each tortilla with melted butter; place 2 tortillas, buttered side down, on a lightly greased baking sheet. Top each tortilla with about 1 cup chicken mixture, spreading to edges of tortilla. Top each with another tortilla, buttered side up.

• **Bake** at 375° for 10 minutes or until golden. Cut into wedges. Repeat with remaining tortillas and chicken mixture. Serve immediately. **Yield:** 5 main-dish servings or 30 appetizers.

Note: Cook quesadillas on the cooktop in a cast-iron skillet or on a griddle. Cook quesadillas, one at a time, 3 minutes on each side.

Amy Cromwell
Atlanta, Georgia

CHICKEN-CHILE CHEESECAKE

1⅓ cups finely crushed tortilla
  chips
¼ cup butter or margarine, melted
3 (8-ounce) packages cream
  cheese, softened
4 large eggs
1 teaspoon chili powder
1 teaspoon Worcestershire sauce
¼ teaspoon salt
3 tablespoons minced green
  onions
1½ cups finely shredded cooked
  chicken
2 (4.5-ounce) cans chopped green
  chiles, drained
1½ cups (6 ounces) shredded
  Monterey Jack cheese
1 (16-ounce) carton sour cream
1 teaspoon seasoned salt
Garnish: minced green onions
Picante sauce

● **Combine** tortilla chips and butter;
press in bottom and 1 inch up sides of a
9-inch springform pan. Set aside.
● **Beat** cream cheese at high speed with
an electric mixer until light and fluffy;
add eggs, one at a time, beating well
after each addition. Stir in chili powder
and next 3 ingredients.
● **Pour** half of cream cheese mixture
into prepared pan. Sprinkle with
chicken, chiles, and cheese; carefully
pour remaining cream cheese mixture
on top. Bake at 350° for 10 minutes; reduce oven temperature to 300°, and
bake 1 additional hour or until set. Cool
completely in pan on a wire rack.
● **Combine** sour cream and seasoned
salt, stirring well; spread evenly on top
of cheesecake. Cover and chill at least 8
hours. Garnish, if desired. Serve with picante sauce. **Yield:** 8 to 10 servings.

GRANDMA ROSE'S
CHOPPED CHICKEN LIVERS

QUICK!

*Art Meripol shares his grandmother's
recipe. Although the original uses
schmaltz – rendered chicken fat – olive
oil makes a fine substitute.*

2 tablespoons olive oil
1 pound chicken livers
2 cloves garlic, minced
1 medium onion, chopped and
  divided
1 hard-cooked egg, chopped
¼ teaspoon salt
¼ teaspoon pepper

● **Pour** oil into a large skillet; place over
medium-high heat until hot. Add livers,
garlic, and half of onion; cook, stirring
constantly, 10 minutes or until livers are
done. Remove from heat.
● **Position** knife blade in food processor bowl; add remaining onion, liver
mixture, egg, salt, and pepper. Pulse 5
times or until livers are chopped. Cover
and chill. Serve with rye or pumpernickel bread. **Yield:** ¾ cup.

Art Meripol
Birmingham, Alabama

FRIED CHICKEN LIVERS

1 pound chicken livers
2 cups all-purpose flour
1½ teaspoons seasoned salt
1 teaspoon pepper
1 cup buttermilk
Vegetable oil

● **Pierce** chicken livers several times
with a fork.
● **Combine** flour, salt, and pepper in a
shallow dish; dredge livers in flour mixture. Dip livers in buttermilk, and
dredge in flour mixture again.
● **Pour** oil to depth of 2 inches into a
Dutch oven or electric fryer; heat to
365°. Fry livers, a few at a time, 4 to 5
minutes or until golden. Serve immediately. **Yield:** 4 to 5 servings.

CRANBERRY-CORNBREAD
STUFFED CORNISH HENS
(pictured at right)

1 (6-ounce) package cornbread
  stuffing mix
½ cup water
½ cup thinly sliced celery
1 (8-ounce) container soft cream
  cheese with chives and onions,
  divided
½ cup fresh or frozen cranberries,
  halved
¼ cup coarsely chopped pecans
4 (1- to 1½-pound) Cornish hens
1 tablespoon vegetable oil

● **Combine** seasoning packet from stuffing mix, water, and celery in a large
saucepan; bring to a boil. Cover, reduce
heat, and simmer 5 minutes.
● **Add** ¼ cup cream cheese, stirring until
blended. Stir in stuffing mix, cranberries, and pecans. Remove from heat;
cover and let stand 5 minutes.
● **Loosen** skin from hens without totally
detaching skin; place remaining cream
cheese under skin of hens. Lightly
spoon stuffing mixture into hens; close
opening with skewers. Place hens,
breast side up, in a roasting pan; brush
with oil.
● **Bake** at 350° for 1 hour or until thermometer inserted in stuffing registers
165°. Remove skewers, and serve immediately. **Yield:** 4 servings.

Betty E. Taylor
Piqua, Ohio

Cranberry-Cornbread Stuffed
Cornish Hens

CAJUN-FRIED CORNISH HENS

You like fried chicken, right? Why not try Cajun-Fried Cornish Hens? We loved 'em. (It's nice to have a whole bird to yourself.)

3 tablespoons Cajun seasoning
1 teaspoon ground red pepper
4 (1¼-pound) Cornish hens
½ cup Italian dressing
1 cup all-purpose flour
1½ gallons vegetable oil

• **Combine** seasoning and pepper; rub over inside and outside of hens.
• **Fill** the injector needle of a bulb baster with dressing, and squirt under skin of hens. Tie legs together with one end of a 30-inch string.
• **Place** flour in a large plastic bag; add hens, one at a time, and shake to coat thoroughly.
• **Pour** oil to depth of 4 inches into a deep pot of a propane cooker; heat to 350°. Carefully lower hens into hot oil, using string.
• **Fry** 18 to 20 minutes or until meat thermometer inserted in thickest part registers 180°. Remove hens from oil, and drain on paper towels; remove string. **Yield:** 4 servings.

Denise Boudreaux Schexnayder
Houma, Louisiana

JELLY-GLAZED CORNISH HENS

3 (1½-pound) Cornish hens, split
½ teaspoon salt
¼ teaspoon pepper
1 (10½-ounce) jar jalapeño jelly
2 teaspoons grated lime rind
⅓ cup lime juice
¼ cup vegetable oil
1 tablespoon chopped fresh
    cilantro

• **Sprinkle** hens with salt and pepper, and place, cut side down, in a large shallow dish; set aside.
• **Melt** jelly in a small saucepan over low heat; add lime rind and remaining 3 ingredients. Pour marinade mixture over hens; cover and chill 3 hours, turning occasionally.

• **For** a charcoal grill, prepare fire, and let burn until coals are white. Rake coals to opposite sides of grill, and place a drip pan between coals. For a gas grill, light one burner, placing drip pan on opposite side.
• **Drain** hens, reserving marinade. Bring marinade to a boil; set aside. Arrange hens on food rack over drip pan. Cook, covered with grill lid, over medium-hot coals (350° to 400°) 35 minutes. Brush with marinade; cook 40 additional minutes. **Yield:** 6 servings.

CORNISH HENS À L'ORANGE

1 navel orange, sliced
6 leaves fresh basil *
2 (1½-pound) Cornish hens, split
1 teaspoon salt
1 teaspoon ground white pepper
2 teaspoons grated orange rind
2 teaspoons dried thyme
¼ cup orange juice concentrate,
    thawed and undiluted
¾ cup water
1 tablespoon all-purpose flour
2 tablespoons water

• **Arrange** orange slices in a single layer in a lightly greased 11- x 7- x 1½-inch baking dish; top with basil.
• **Sprinkle** hens with salt and pepper; place hens, breast side down, in dish. Sprinkle evenly with orange rind and thyme.
• **Bake** at 375° for 40 minutes.
• **Combine** orange juice concentrate and ¾ cup water. Remove hens from oven, and turn hens breast side up; pour juice mixture over hens. Increase oven temperature to 400°, and bake 20 additional minutes. Transfer hens to a serving platter, reserving drippings; keep hens warm. Pour pan drippings into a saucepan, and place over medium heat.
• **Combine** flour and 2 tablespoons water, stirring well; add to pan drippings, stirring constantly. Bring to a boil; boil 1 minute. Serve with hens. **Yield:** 2 servings.

* Substitute 4 teaspoons dried basil.
Georgie O'Neill-Massa
Welaka, Florida

CORNISH HENS TARRAGON

Marinating the split Cornish hens in a tarragon-garlic based blend of olive oil, lemon juice, soy sauce, and vermouth infuses them with lots of flavor. Tarragon sprinkled on the hens before baking refreshes the herbal element.

4 (1½-pound) Cornish hens, split
¼ cup olive oil
¼ cup fresh lemon juice
¼ cup soy sauce
¼ cup dry vermouth
2 cloves garlic, crushed
1½ teaspoons salt
½ teaspoon coarsely ground black
    pepper
3 teaspoons dried tarragon,
    divided
Vegetable cooking spray

• **Place** hens, breast side down, in a large baking dish or heavy-duty zip-top plastic bag.
• **Combine** oil and next 6 ingredients; pour over hens. Sprinkle with 1½ teaspoons tarragon; cover or seal, and store in refrigerator at least 8 hours.
• **Arrange** hens, breast side up, on a rack coated with cooking spray; place rack in broiler pan. Sprinkle remaining 1½ teaspoons tarragon over hens.
• **Bake** at 350° for 1 hour or until tender. **Yield:** 4 servings.

Lisa Conlon
Crystal River, Florida

ROASTED TURKEY WITH SAUSAGE AND WILD MUSHROOM STUFFING

1 cup butter, softened
1 tablespoon dried thyme, crushed
1 (14- to 16-pound) turkey
1 tablespoon salt
1 tablespoon pepper
Sausage and Wild Mushroom
  Stuffing
2 tablespoons soy sauce
2 tablespoons sesame oil
½ cup dry white wine
¼ cup all-purpose flour
1 (16-ounce) carton half-and-half
½ teaspoon soy sauce
½ teaspoon salt
½ teaspoon pepper
Garnish: fresh sage sprigs

• **Combine** butter and thyme; stir well.
• **Remove** giblets and neck from turkey; set aside. Rinse turkey with cold water, and pat dry. Loosen skin from breast without detaching it; carefully spread butter mixture under skin. Rub outside of turkey with 1 tablespoon salt and 1 tablespoon pepper.
• **Spoon** 4 cups Sausage and Wild Mushroom Stuffing into cavity; truss turkey, and tie ends of legs together with string. Lift wingtips up and over back, and tuck under bird. Place turkey, breast side up, in a large roasting pan; rub with 2 tablespoons soy sauce and oil.
• **Bake** at 375° for 2½ hours or until meat thermometer inserted in turkey thigh registers 180° and stuffing registers 165°, shielding turkey with aluminum foil after 1 hour and basting with pan juices every 30 minutes.
• **Cook** giblets and neck in boiling water to cover 45 minutes or until tender. Drain, reserving 1 cup broth. Chop neck meat and giblets; chill.
• **Transfer** turkey to a serving platter, reserving drippings in pan. Remove and discard fat from drippings; pour ¼ cup drippings into a heavy saucepan. Stir wine and reserved broth into roasting pan, stirring to loosen particles that cling to bottom.
• **Place** ¼ cup drippings over medium heat. Add flour, and cook, whisking constantly, until browned. Gradually add wine mixture and half-and-half; cook,

whisking constantly, until bubbly. Stir in neck meat and giblets, ½ teaspoon soy sauce, ½ teaspoon salt, and ½ teaspoon pepper; simmer to desired thickness, stirring often. Serve with turkey. Garnish, if desired. **Yield:** 8 servings.

Sausage and Wild Mushroom Stuffing

½ pound ground pork sausage
½ cup butter or margarine
3 pounds mixed wild mushrooms
   (shiitake, portobello, enoki),
   sliced
1 large onion, sliced
1 bunch green onions, sliced
1 (14½-ounce) can chicken broth
1 (8-ounce) package herb-
   seasoned stuffing mix
1 poultry herb bouquet, chopped
   (see note)
½ teaspoon salt
½ teaspoon pepper

• **Brown** sausage in a large skillet, stirring until it crumbles. Drain; set aside.
• **Melt** butter in skillet; add mushrooms, onion, and green onions, and cook until tender. Stir in sausage, broth, and remaining 4 ingredients. Spoon 4 cups stuffing into cavity of turkey, if desired; place remaining stuffing in a lightly greased 13- x 9- x 2-inch baking dish.
• **Bake** at 375° for 45 minutes or until lightly browned. **Yield:** 8 to 10 servings.

Note: A poultry herb bouquet contains 2 sprigs each of fresh sage, rosemary, and thyme. Or you can substitute 1 teaspoon of each dried herb for fresh.

Sudi Swirles and Jan Hryharrow
Durham, North Carolina

DEEP-FRIED TURKEY

1 (8-ounce) bottle Caesar dressing
1 (8- to 10-pound) turkey
1 to 2 gallons vegetable oil or
   peanut oil

• **Fill** the injector needle of a bulb baster with dressing, and squirt under skin. Tie legs together with one end of a 30-inch string.

• **Pour** oil to depth of 5 to 6 inches into a deep pot of a propane cooker; heat to 325°. Carefully lower turkey into oil, using string; fry 30 minutes or until thermometer inserted into meaty portion of thigh registers 180°. (Temperature of oil drops immediately after turkey is placed in it; oil may not reach 325° again.) Remove from oil; cool slightly before slicing. **Yield:** 12 to 14 servings.

Kreis Beall
The Inn at Blackberry Farm
Walland, Tennessee

CITRUS-MARINATED TURKEY BREAST

1 (6- to 7-pound) turkey breast
1 cup orange juice
¼ cup lime juice
¼ cup olive oil
3 tablespoons apple cider vinegar
2 teaspoons salt
2 teaspoons dried oregano
1 teaspoon pepper
Garnishes: fresh sage, oregano, and
   rosemary sprigs

• **Remove** and discard skin and breast bone. Place turkey in a jumbo heavy-duty, zip-top plastic bag; set aside.
• **Combine** orange juice and next 6 ingredients in a jar; cover tightly, and shake vigorously. Reserve ½ cup marinade in refrigerator. Pour remaining marinade over turkey; seal bag. Chill 8 hours, turning turkey occasionally.
• **Remove** turkey from marinade; discard marinade.
• **Cook** turkey, covered with grill lid, over hot coals (400° to 500°) for 18 minutes on each side or until a meat thermometer inserted in thickest part registers 170°, brushing occasionally with reserved marinade. Let stand 10 minutes before slicing. Garnish, if desired. **Yield:** 8 servings.

Note: To cook turkey in oven, place on a rack in a roasting pan; bake at 325° for 1 hour and 10 minutes or until a meat thermometer registers 170°, brushing occasionally with the marinade.

Carolyn Gaskins
Cherryville, North Carolina

GRILLED MARINATED TURKEY STEAKS

1 (5-pound) bone-in turkey
   breast *
½ cup soy sauce
¼ cup vegetable oil
1 tablespoon ground ginger
1 teaspoon dry mustard
3 cloves garlic, pressed

• **Purchase** turkey breast. Ask butcher to cut in half lengthwise, and then cut each half crosswise into 1-inch-thick "steaks" resembling large pork chops.
• **Combine** soy sauce and remaining 4 ingredients; pour over turkey. Cover and chill 8 hours. Remove turkey from marinade, discarding marinade.
• **Cook** turkey, covered with grill lid, over medium-hot coals (350° to 400°) 8 to 10 minutes on each side. **Yield:** 12 servings.

* Substitute 1 (5-pound) boneless turkey breast. Cut turkey in same manner yourself.

Jesse and Violet Rhinehart
Raleigh, North Carolina

GRILLED TURKEY BREAST WITH CRANBERRY SALSA

1 (6-pound) turkey breast
1 cup cranberry juice cocktail
¼ cup orange juice
¼ cup olive oil
1 teaspoon salt
1 teaspoon pepper
¼ cup chopped fresh cilantro
3 cups frozen cranberries
½ cup honey
2 tablespoons fresh lime juice
½ cup coarsely chopped purple
   onion
2 jalapeño peppers, seeded and
   coarsely chopped
½ cup coarsely chopped dried
   apricot halves
½ cup fresh cilantro leaves
2 large oranges, peeled, seeded,
   and coarsely chopped

• **Remove** and discard skin and breast bone from turkey breast, separating breast halves; place turkey in a large heavy-duty, zip-top plastic bag.
• **Combine** cranberry juice cocktail and next 5 ingredients in a jar; cover tightly, and shake vigorously. Reserve ½ cup marinade, and chill. Pour remaining marinade over turkey. Seal bag, and chill 8 hours, turning occasionally.
• **Position** knife blade in food processor bowl; add cranberries and remaining 7 ingredients. Pulse until chopped, stopping once to scrape down sides (do not overprocess). Transfer cranberry mixture to a serving bowl; chill.
• **Remove** turkey from marinade, discarding marinade.
• **Cook** turkey, covered with grill lid, over medium-hot coals (350° to 400°), about 15 minutes on each side or until a meat thermometer inserted in thickest part registers 170°, basting occasionally with reserved marinade. Let stand 10 minutes before slicing. Serve with cranberry mixture. **Yield:** 8 servings.

Julie Downey
Houston, Texas

♥ Per serving: Calories 322
Fat 5.6g Cholesterol 79mg
Sodium 240mg

TURKEY CUTLETS WITH SAGE GRAVY

Turkey cutlets for company? You bet. A rich, creamy sauce, well worth the calories and time invested, makes this dish fit for any special occasion.

4 (5-ounce) boneless turkey
   breast cutlets
1 tablespoon finely chopped fresh
   sage leaves or 1 teaspoon
   dried leaf sage, crumbled
¼ teaspoon salt
⅛ teaspoon pepper
⅛ teaspoon paprika
½ cup all-purpose flour
2 tablespoons butter
2 tablespoons olive oil
Sage Gravy
Garnish: fresh sage leaves

• **Place** turkey cutlets between two sheets of heavy-duty plastic wrap; flatten to ¼-inch thickness, using a meat mallet or rolling pin.
• **Combine** sage, salt, pepper, and paprika; rub evenly on each side of cutlets. Cover and chill 1 to 2 hours.
• **Dredge** cutlets in flour, and shake off excess.
• **Melt** butter in a large nonstick skillet over medium heat; add olive oil. Add cutlets; cook 3 minutes on each side or until lightly browned. Transfer cutlets to a serving plate; keep warm.
• **Reserve** drippings in skillet for Sage Gravy.
• **Serve** cutlets with Sage Gravy. Garnish, if desired. **Yield:** 4 servings.

Sage Gravy

½ cup finely chopped onion
½ cup finely chopped carrot
¼ cup finely chopped celery
1 tablespoon finely chopped
   fresh sage leaves or
   1 teaspoon dried leaf sage,
   crumbled
Reserved drippings
⅓ cup dry white wine
½ cup chicken broth
1 cup half-and-half
½ teaspoon lemon juice
½ teaspoon salt
½ teaspoon pepper
2 tablespoons cold butter, cut
   into pieces

• **Add** first 4 ingredients to reserved drippings in skillet.
• **Cook** over medium heat, stirring constantly, until onion is tender. Add wine; bring mixture to a boil, and cook until liquid in skillet is reduced to about 2 tablespoons.
• **Add** broth, and cook until liquid is reduced by half. Stir in half-and-half. Return to a boil; cook until slightly thickened.
• **Pour** mixture through a wire-mesh strainer into a bowl; discard vegetables. Return mixture to skillet. Stir in lemon juice, salt, and pepper.
• **Add** butter pieces, one at a time, stirring with a wire whisk until blended. (If butter is difficult to work into gravy, place skillet over low heat for a few seconds, being careful not to get mixture too hot.) **Yield:** 1 cup.

TURKEY CUTLETS WITH TARRAGON-MUSTARD SAUCE

QUICK!

4 turkey cutlets
1 teaspoon garlic salt
¼ teaspoon pepper
2 tablespoons olive oil
½ cup plain yogurt
2 tablespoons Dijon mustard
¼ teaspoon dried tarragon
¼ teaspoon sugar
⅛ teaspoon hot sauce

• **Sprinkle** turkey cutlets with garlic salt and pepper. Cook in hot oil in a large skillet over medium-high heat 2 minutes on each side. Remove turkey, and keep warm.
• **Combine** yogurt and remaining 4 ingredients in skillet; cook over low heat until thoroughly heated. Serve over turkey. **Yield:** 4 servings.

Cathy Darling
Grafton, West Virginia

TURKEY-BASIL PICCATA

QUICK!

2 tablespoons all-purpose flour
¼ teaspoon salt
¼ teaspoon pepper
1¾ pound turkey cutlets
2 tablespoons olive oil
4 cloves garlic, minced
1½ teaspoons dried basil or 1½ tablespoons chopped fresh basil
½ cup dry white wine
1½ tablespoons fresh lemon juice
1 lemon, sliced

• **Combine** first 3 ingredients in a shallow dish; dredge cutlets in flour mixture, shaking off excess.
• **Pour** olive oil into a large skillet; place over medium-high heat until hot. Add cutlets, and cook 1½ minutes or until done, turning once. Remove cutlets from skillet.
• **Add** garlic and basil to skillet, and cook 45 seconds, stirring to loosen particles that cling to bottom. Add wine, lemon juice, and lemon slices; cook 45

seconds, stirring constantly. Return cutlets to pan; cook just until heated. Serve immediately. **Yield:** 3 to 4 servings.

Deborah Holley
Patterson, Louisiana

EASY TURKEY SCALOPPINE

QUICK!

1 tablespoon butter or margarine
2 teaspoons lemon juice
1 large egg, lightly beaten
¼ cup Italian-seasoned breadcrumbs
2 tablespoons grated Parmesan cheese
½ teaspoon dried basil
⅛ teaspoon garlic salt
⅛ teaspoon ground black pepper
⅛ teaspoon ground red pepper
4 slices fresh turkey cutlets (about ½ pound)
⅓ cup pasta sauce

• **Place** butter in a microwave-safe bowl, and microwave at MEDIUM (50% power) 1 minute or until butter melts. Add lemon juice and egg, stirring well.
• **Combine** breadcrumbs and next 5 ingredients in a shallow dish.
• **Dip** turkey in egg mixture; dredge in breadcrumb mixture. Place in a lightly greased 8-inch square baking dish.
• **Microwave** at HIGH 4 minutes, giving dish a half-turn after 2 minutes. Spoon pasta sauce evenly over turkey. **Yield:** 2 servings.

TURKEY AND PEPPERS IN CORNBREAD CRUST

2 cups chopped cooked turkey
1 (7-ounce) jar roasted red bell peppers, drained and sliced
1 (4.5-ounce) can chopped green chiles, undrained
1 (10¾-ounce) can cream of chicken soup, undiluted
½ cup sour cream
¼ cup milk
1 teaspoon chili powder
1 (11.5-ounce) can refrigerated cornbread twists

• **Combine** all ingredients except cornbread twists. Spoon into a lightly greased 8-inch square baking dish; set aside.
• **Prepare** cornbread twists according to package directions, but do not bake. Place over turkey mixture. Cover loosely with aluminum foil.
• **Bake** at 375° for 30 minutes. Uncover and bake 10 additional minutes or until cornbread is lightly browned. **Yield:** 4 to 6 servings.

Beppy Hassey
Montgomery, Alabama

EASY TURKEY EMPANADAS

QUICK!

1 (15-ounce) package refrigerated piecrusts
2 cups cooked yellow rice
1 cup chopped smoked turkey
1 cup (4 ounces) shredded Monterey Jack cheese with peppers
½ cup sliced green onions
1 (2.25-ounce) can sliced ripe olives, drained
1 to 2 teaspoons fajita seasoning
Cornmeal
Sour cream
Picante sauce

• **Unfold** piecrusts, and press out fold lines.
• **Combine** rice and next 5 ingredients; spoon evenly onto half of each piecrust. Fold piecrusts over filling, pressing edges to seal. Crimp edges with a fork. Place on a baking sheet sprinkled with cornmeal.
• **Bake** at 400° for 25 minutes or until lightly browned. Cut in half. Serve with sour cream and picante sauce. **Yield:** 4 servings.

Sandra Stewart
Northport, Alabama

HOME-STYLE TURKEY TURNOVERS

½ cup quartered fresh mushrooms
½ cup chopped fresh green
    beans
1 small onion, finely chopped
1 clove garlic, crushed
½ teaspoon dried thyme
½ teaspoon dried rosemary
2 tablespoons vegetable oil
1 tablespoon all-purpose flour
⅓ cup whipping cream
1 cup chopped cooked turkey
¼ teaspoon salt
¼ teaspoon pepper
1 (17¼-ounce) package frozen
    puff pastry sheets, thawed

• **Cook** first 6 ingredients in oil in a skillet over medium-high heat until crisptender, stirring often. Add flour, and cook 1 minute, stirring constantly. Add whipping cream, and cook, stirring constantly, until thickened; remove from heat. Stir in turkey, salt, and pepper; cool 5 minutes.
• **Unfold** pastry sheets, and cut each sheet into 4 squares.
• **Spoon** turkey mixture evenly in center of each square. Brush pastry edges lightly with water; fold in half to form triangles. Press edges to seal; crimp with a fork. Place on an ungreased baking sheet.
• **Bake** at 400° for 15 minutes or until golden. **Yield:** 8 servings.

Lilann Taylor
Savannah, Georgia

DOVE AU VIN

1 cup all-purpose flour
1 teaspoon salt
1 teaspoon pepper
12 doves, dressed
⅓ cup butter or margarine
1 cup chopped celery
1 cup chopped onion
1 small green bell pepper,
    chopped
1 (10½-ounce) can beef
    consommé
½ cup dry red wine
Hot cooked egg noodles or rice

• **Combine** first 3 ingredients in a large heavy-duty, zip-top plastic bag. Add doves, a few at a time; seal bag, and shake to coat.
• **Melt** butter in a large nonstick skillet over medium-high heat; add doves, and cook until browned, turning once.
• **Place** doves in a lightly greased 13- x 9- x 2-inch baking dish. Sprinkle celery, onion, and green pepper evenly over doves; add consommé. Cover with aluminum foil.
• **Bake** at 350° for 1½ hours. Pour wine over doves; cover and bake 30 additional minutes. Serve with noodles or rice. **Yield:** 6 servings.

Party Potpourri
Junior League of Memphis, Tennessee

GAME BIRDS IN WINE MARINADE

12 skinned dove breasts
¾ cup dry red wine
¼ cup vegetable oil
¼ cup soy sauce
1 tablespoon brown sugar
2 tablespoons water
1 teaspoon dried oregano
1 teaspoon ground ginger
1 clove garlic, pressed
1 (8-ounce) can sliced mushrooms,
    undrained
1 tablespoon vegetable oil
Hot cooked rice
Garnishes: chopped fresh parsley,
    fresh whole mushrooms

• **Place** dove breasts in a large shallow dish or heavy-duty, zip-top plastic bag.
• **Combine** wine and next 8 ingredients; pour over dove, turning to coat. Cover dish, or seal bag. Chill 8 hours, turning dove occasionally. Drain, reserving marinade.
• **Brown** dove in 1 tablespoon hot oil in a small Dutch oven. Add reserved marinade. Bring to a boil; cover, reduce heat, and simmer 1 hour.
• **Remove** dove from Dutch oven, reserving liquid in pan; cool slightly. Remove and discard bones from dove; return meat to pan.
• **Bring** mixture to a boil; reduce heat, and simmer 3 minutes or until mixture

is thoroughly heated. Serve over rice. Garnish, if desired. **Yield:** 4 servings.

Jill Fortney
Fort Worth, Texas

BLACKENED DUCK BREASTS

The blackening in this recipe is best done outdoors on a propane cooker due to the heavy smoke produced. If you haven't been duck hunting lately or can't find duck breasts, use 12 skinned and boned chicken breast halves, instead. They're great, too.

3 (6-ounce) packages long-grain-
    and-wild rice mix *
2 (0.9-ounce) envelopes béarnaise
    sauce mix
12 duck breast halves, skinned
    and boned
⅓ cup butter or margarine,
    melted
3 tablespoons Cajun blackened
    seasoning
2 (14-ounce) cans artichoke
    hearts, drained
½ pound fresh mushrooms,
    sliced
1 cup dry white wine
2 cloves garlic, crushed
Garnishes: lemon slices, fresh
    parsley sprigs

• **Prepare** rice mix according to package directions; keep warm.
• **Prepare** béarnaise sauce mix according to package directions; keep warm.
• **Place** a large, greased cast-iron skillet over an outdoor propane cooker until very hot (about 10 minutes), following manufacturer's instructions.
• **Brush** duck with butter; sprinkle with seasoning, and cook in hot skillet about 4 minutes on each side or until done. Remove from skillet, and keep warm.
• **Combine** artichokes and next 3 ingredients in a heavy saucepan; cook over medium heat until mushrooms are tender, stirring occasionally.
• **To** serve, slice duck into thin strips, and place on a bed of cooked rice mix. Using a slotted spoon, spoon artichoke

mixture evenly over duck strips. Top with béarnaise sauce, and serve immediately. Garnish, if desired. **Yield:** 12 servings.

Men's Gourmet
Raleigh, North Carolina

* Substitute 12 ounces angel hair pasta, cooked according to package directions, for the long-grain-and-wild rice mix.

BAKED QUAIL WITH CORNBREAD STUFFING

12 quail
Cornbread Stuffing
12 slices bacon
¼ cup Worcestershire sauce
1 (14½-ounce) can beef broth, divided

● **Cut** a pocket on each side of quail backbone, measuring about 2 inches long and 1½ inches deep.
● **Stuff** quail pockets with unbaked Cornbread Stuffing, spooning about 1 tablespoon stuffing into each pocket. Reserve remaining Cornbread Stuffing for baking.
● **Wrap** a bacon slice around each quail; place in a roasting pan, breast side down, and drizzle evenly with Worcestershire sauce.
● **Reserve** 1¼ cups beef broth.
● **Cover** and bake at 350° for 1 hour, uncovering and basting quail with remaining beef broth every 10 minutes during the first 30 minutes of cooking time.
● **Uncover** and turn quail, breast side up. Brush with pan drippings.
● **Broil** quail, uncovered, 5 inches from heat (with electric oven door partially opened) 3 to 5 minutes or until browned. Remove quail from roasting pan, reserving drippings in a pan. Keep quail warm.
● **Add** reserved 1¼ cups beef broth to drippings, stirring to loosen browned particles that cling to bottom. Cook over high heat about 15 minutes or until liquid is reduced by one-third; skim fat from liquid. Serve quail with sauce and baked Cornbread Stuffing. **Yield:** 6 servings.

Cornbread Stuffing

2 (8½-ounce) packages cornbread muffin mix
1 pound ground pork sausage
¼ cup butter or margarine
3 cups finely chopped celery
½ cup chopped onion
½ cup chopped green onions
1 (8-ounce) package herb-seasoned stuffing mix
2 (14½-ounce) cans chicken broth
3 large eggs, lightly beaten

● **Prepare** cornbread mix according to package directions; cool and crumble in a large bowl. Set aside.
● **Brown** sausage in a large skillet, stirring until it crumbles. Drain well, and stir into cornbread.
● **Melt** butter in a large skillet, and add celery and onions. Cook over medium-high heat, stirring constantly, until tender. Stir vegetables into cornbread mixture.
● **Stir** stuffing mix, broth, and eggs into cornbread mixture. Remove 1½ cups for stuffing quail. Spoon remaining mixture into a greased 13- x 9- x 2-inch baking dish.
● **Bake** at 350° for 1 hour or until golden. **Yield:** 6 to 8 servings.

Jill Fortney
Fort Worth, Texas

MAPLE-GLAZED QUAIL WITH WHITE BEAN RAGOÛT

4 (4-ounce) dressed quail
2 medium onions, diced
1 tablespoon sugar
4 fresh mushrooms, sliced
1 teaspoon white vinegar
⅓ cup fine, dry breadcrumbs
¼ teaspoon salt
¼ teaspoon pepper
¼ teaspoon dried thyme
3 tablespoons butter or margarine, melted
White Bean Ragoût
Maple Brown Sauce

● **Remove** breast and back bones from quail; set quail aside.

● **Cook** onion in a nonstick skillet over low heat 10 minutes or until browned, stirring often; add sugar and mushrooms, and cook until tender, stirring mixture often. Stir in vinegar and next 4 ingredients.
● **Spoon** into quail cavities, and secure with wooden picks. Tuck wings under, and place, breast side up, in a buttered 2-quart casserole. Brush with melted butter.
● **Bake** at 350° for 20 minutes or until done. Serve over a bed of White Bean Ragoût; drizzle with Maple Brown Sauce. **Yield:** 2 servings.

White Bean Ragoût

1 cup dried Great Northern or navy beans
½ cup diced onion
1 bay leaf
3 tablespoons diced carrot
2 cups beef broth

● **Sort** and wash beans; drain.
● **Combine** beans and water to cover in a large saucepan; let stand 1 hour. Drain beans, and return to pan. Add onion and remaining ingredients; bring to a boil. Reduce heat, and simmer 2 hours or until beans are tender, stirring occasionally. Remove and discard bay leaf. **Yield:** 2 cups.

Maple Brown Sauce

QUICK!

1 teaspoon butter or margarine
1 teaspoon all-purpose flour
½ cup beef broth
1 tablespoon maple syrup

● **Melt** butter in a small heavy saucepan over low heat; whisk in flour until smooth. Cook 1 minute, whisking constantly. Whisk in broth; cook over medium heat, whisking constantly, 5 minutes or until thickened and bubbly. Stir in maple syrup. **Yield:** ½ cup.

Devil's Pool Restaurant
Big Cedar Lodge
Ridgedale, Missouri

ROASTED QUAIL ÉTOUFFÉE

1 medium potato, peeled and cut
   into ½-inch pieces
1 large fresh leek, chopped
4 cups loosely packed fresh
   spinach
1 tablespoon vegetable oil
½ teaspoon salt
¼ teaspoon ground black pepper
8 quail, dressed
8 large plum tomatoes
½ cup vegetable oil
½ cup all-purpose flour
1½ cups chopped onion
½ cup finely chopped green bell
   pepper
½ cup finely chopped celery
2 cloves garlic, minced
4 bay leaves
3 cups chicken broth
2 teaspoons salt
2 teaspoons fresh thyme or
   ¾ teaspoon dried thyme
1 teaspoon Worcestershire
   sauce
½ teaspoon sugar
⅓ cup chopped green onions
2 tablespoons chopped fresh
   parsley
2 teaspoons ground black pepper
½ teaspoon ground red pepper
2 teaspoons hot sauce
Soufflé Cornbread (see recipe on
   page 40)

• **Cook** potato in boiling water to cover 8 minutes or until potato is tender; drain and let cool.
• **Cook** leek and spinach in 1 tablespoon oil in a large skillet over medium heat, stirring constantly, 3 minutes or until wilted; cool.
• **Combine** potato, leek mixture, ½ teaspoon salt, and ¼ teaspoon black pepper; spoon into cavities of quail. Place 1 leg over the other, and secure with a wooden pick. Place quail and tomatoes in a large roasting pan.
• **Bake** at 400° for 45 minutes; cool tomatoes slightly. Chop tomatoes, reserving liquid; set aside.
• **Pour** ½ cup oil into a large skillet or Dutch oven; place over medium-high heat until very hot. Add flour, and cook, stirring constantly, 2 to 3 minutes or until golden (do not burn).

• **Add** 1½ cups onion and next 4 ingredients; cook 4 to 5 minutes or until onion is tender. Gradually add chicken broth, stirring constantly.
• **Add** tomato, reserved liquid, 2 teaspoons salt, and next 3 ingredients; bring to a boil. Reduce heat, and simmer, uncovered, 1 hour.
• **Stir** in green onions and next 4 ingredients. Add quail, breast side up; simmer 15 minutes. Remove and discard bay leaves. Serve quail mixture over Soufflé Cornbread. **Yield:** 8 servings.

Chef Johnny Earles
Criolla's
Destin, Florida

GRILLED QUAIL

16 quail, dressed
16 jalapeño peppers
16 slices bacon
1 (8-ounce) bottle Italian
   dressing
½ cup dry white wine
⅓ cup soy sauce
¼ cup lemon juice
¼ teaspoon pepper
Garnish: banana peppers

• **Rinse** quail thoroughly with cold water; pat dry. Place a jalapeño pepper into body cavity of each quail. Wrap 1 bacon slice around each quail, and secure with a wooden pick. Place quail in a large shallow dish.
• **Combine** Italian dressing and next 4 ingredients; pour over quail. Cover and chill 8 hours. Remove quail from dish, reserving marinade. Bring leftover marinade to a boil, and set aside.
• **Prepare** charcoal fire in one end of grill; let burn 15 to 20 minutes or until flames disappear and coals are white. Cook, covered with grill lid, on opposite end 1 hour, turning once, and basting often with marinade. Garnish, if desired. **Yield:** 8 servings.

Note: You can bake quail on a rack in a roasting pan in the oven at 350° for 1 hour, turning once, and basting often with marinade.

Bee and Michael Fitzpatrick
New Orleans, Louisiana

COUNTRY-FRIED WILD TURKEY

An overnight soak in milk tenderizes these strips of wild turkey.

3 pounds boneless wild turkey
   breast
2 to 2½ cups milk
1½ cups all-purpose flour
1 to 1¼ teaspoons salt
½ teaspoon pepper
Vegetable oil
Turkey Gravy

• **Cut** turkey into 1-inch slices; cut each slice into 3- x ½-inch strips, and place in an 11- x 7- x 1½-inch baking dish. Pour milk over strips; cover and chill 8 hours. Drain turkey, discarding milk, and set aside.
• **Combine** flour, salt, and pepper in a large heavy-duty, zip-top plastic bag. Add 6 to 8 turkey strips; seal bag, and shake to coat. Place turkey strips in a single layer on wax paper; repeat procedure with remaining turkey strips.
• **Pour** oil to depth of 2 to 3 inches in a large Dutch oven; heat to 350°. Cook turkey strips, 8 to 10 at a time, until golden. Drain on paper towels; keep warm. Repeat procedure with remaining strips. Reserve ⅓ cup drippings for Turkey Gravy. Serve turkey strips with gravy. **Yield:** 8 to 10 main-dish servings or 16 to 18 appetizer servings.

Turkey Gravy

QUICK!

⅓ cup reserved turkey drippings
⅓ cup all-purpose flour
2 cups milk
½ teaspoon salt
½ teaspoon pepper

• **Pour** reserved drippings into a heavy skillet. Stir in flour; cook over medium heat, stirring constantly, until dark golden. Gradually stir in milk; cook, stirring constantly, until thickened. Stir in salt and pepper. **Yield:** 2 cups.

Jill Fortney
Fort Worth, Texas

At right: *Summer Tomato Salad (page 307)*

SALADS

BLUE CHEESE ASPIC

1 (3-ounce) package lemon-
   flavored gelatin
1¼ cups boiling water
¼ cup dry white wine
½ cup sour cream
1 cup finely chopped Rome
   apple
¼ cup crumbled blue cheese

● **Dissolve** gelatin in boiling water; stir in wine. Add sour cream, stirring well with a wire whisk.
● **Chill** until gelatin mixture is the consistency of unbeaten egg white. Fold in apple and cheese. Spoon mixture into a lightly oiled 3-cup mold; cover and chill until firm.
● **Unmold** onto a serving platter. **Yield:** 6 servings.

Charlotte Pierce Bryant
Greensburg, Kentucky

GAZPACHO ASPIC

A twist on traditional tomato aspic,
this recipe is brimming with vegetables.

1 envelope unflavored gelatin
1 tablespoon sugar
¼ teaspoon salt
1 beef-flavored bouillon cube
1¼ cups water, divided
3 tablespoons lemon juice
⅛ teaspoon hot sauce
1 (14.5-ounce) can diced Italian-
   style tomatoes, well drained
½ cup finely chopped celery
¼ cup finely chopped green bell
   pepper
2 tablespoons sliced green
   onions
Lettuce leaves
Mayonnaise (optional)

● **Combine** first 4 ingredients and ¼ cup water in a small saucepan; let stand 1 minute. Cook over low heat, stirring until gelatin and bouillon cube dissolve. Remove from heat.
● **Combine** remaining 1 cup water, lemon juice, hot sauce, and gelatin mixture in a bowl; chill until the consistency of unbeaten egg white.

● **Stir** in tomatoes and next 3 ingredients; spoon into six lightly oiled ½-cup molds. Chill until firm.
● **Unmold** onto lettuce leaves; dollop each serving with mayonnaise, if desired. **Yield:** 6 servings.

Becky Schuford
Wilmington, North Carolina

FRESH FRUIT WITH MINT-BALSAMIC TEA

Serve this versatile compote on
lettuce leaves as a salad, in a large bowl
for a brunch or breakfast buffet, or
in individual dishes as a dessert.

1½ cups water
¼ cup sugar
1 regular-size tea bag
½ cup loosely packed fresh mint
   sprigs
1 tablespoon balsamic vinegar
2 cups cubed fresh pineapple
1 cup cubed honeydew
1 cup cubed cantaloupe
1 cup orange sections
1 cup fresh blueberries

● **Combine** water and sugar in a heavy saucepan; bring to a boil. Add tea bag and mint; remove from heat, and let steep 5 minutes. Remove tea bag. Stir in balsamic vinegar; let stand 5 minutes.
● **Pour** mixture through a wire-mesh strainer into a large bowl, discarding mint. Add fruit, stirring gently to coat. Cover mixture, and chill at least 1 hour. **Yield:** 5 cups.

Susan Mack and Andy Armstrong
Atlanta, Georgia

♥ Per 1-cup serving: Calories 158
Fat 0.7g   Cholesterol 0mg
Sodium 11mg

BERRY-CITRUS TWIST

QUICK!

2 quarts fresh strawberries,
   halved
2 fresh pineapples, peeled, cored,
   and cut into chunks ✳
½ cup orange marmalade
¼ cup orange juice
2 tablespoons lemon juice
½ cup fresh or frozen blueberries

● **Combine** strawberries and pineapple in a bowl; set aside.
● **Combine** orange marmalade, orange juice, and lemon juice; pour over fruit, and toss gently. Stir in blueberries just before serving. **Yield:** 10 cups.

✳ Substitute 2 (20-ounce) cans of pineapple chunks in juice, drained, for fresh.

Ruth Sherrer
Fort Worth, Texas

FRUIT SALAD WITH CITRUS-CILANTRO DRESSING

3 cups fresh pineapple chunks or
   1 (20-ounce) can pineapple
   chunks in juice, drained
2 cups pink grapefruit sections
   (about 3 grapefruit)
2 cups fresh strawberry slices
1 mango, peeled and sliced
Citrus-Cilantro Dressing
1 tablespoon chopped fresh
   cilantro

● **Combine** first 4 ingredients in a bowl; toss with Citrus-Cilantro Dressing, and sprinkle with cilantro.
● **Cover** and chill 1 hour. Serve with a slotted spoon. **Yield:** 6 to 8 servings.

Citrus-Cilantro Dressing

QUICK!

⅓ cup orange juice
⅓ cup fresh lime juice
3 tablespoons chopped fresh
   cilantro
2 tablespoons honey

● **Combine** orange juice, lime juice, and cilantro in a small saucepan.

- **Bring** to a boil; reduce heat, and simmer 5 minutes.
- **Pour** mixture through a wire-mesh strainer into a bowl; discard cilantro. Stir in honey. **Yield:** about ½ cup.

GRILLED MELON SALAD WITH ORANGE-RASPBERRY VINAIGRETTE

½ cup orange marmalade
2 tablespoons lemon juice
2 tablespoons soy sauce
2 teaspoons grated fresh ginger
½ cantaloupe, cut into 1-inch cubes
½ honeydew melon, cut into 1-inch cubes
2 cups fresh strawberries, halved
1 cup fresh raspberries
Orange-Raspberry Vinaigrette
Lettuce leaves

- **Combine** first 4 ingredients in a large bowl; add cantaloupe and honeydew, tossing gently. Arrange melon in a grill basket or thread onto skewers.
- **Cook**, covered with grill lid, over hot coals (400° to 500°) 2 to 3 minutes on each side. Remove melon to a large bowl; cover and chill.
- **Combine** chilled melon, strawberries, and raspberries. Drizzle with Orange-Raspberry Vinaigrette, and toss gently. Serve in a lettuce-lined bowl. **Yield:** 4 servings.

Orange-Raspberry Vinaigrette
QUICK!

½ cup orange marmalade
¼ cup raspberry vinegar
2 tablespoons seeded, finely chopped jalapeño pepper
2 tablespoons finely chopped fresh cilantro

- **Combine** all ingredients in a small bowl. **Yield:** 1 cup.

JEWELED CONGEALED FRESH FRUIT

1 pint strawberries, hulled and halved
3 envelopes unflavored gelatin
4½ cups unsweetened pineapple juice, divided
2 (15¼-ounce) cans pineapple tidbits, drained
2 (11-ounce) cans mandarin oranges, drained
1 grapefruit, peeled, sectioned, and well drained
1 cup fresh blueberries
1 cup seedless green grapes
Lettuce leaves
Poppyseed dressing

- **Arrange** strawberry halves, cut side up, in the bottom of a lightly greased 12-cup Bundt pan. Set aside.
- **Sprinkle** gelatin over ½ cup pineapple juice in a small saucepan; stir and let stand 1 minute. Cook over low heat, stirring until gelatin dissolves (about 2 minutes). Combine gelatin mixture and remaining 4 cups pineapple juice in a large bowl.
- **Pour** about ½ cup pineapple juice mixture over strawberries in Bundt pan; chill until firm.
- **Chill** remaining pineapple juice mixture until the consistency of unbeaten egg white. Stir in pineapple tidbits and remaining fruit; spoon into Bundt pan. Chill until firm.
- **Line** a large serving plate with lettuce leaves.
- **Unmold** fruit mold onto lettuce leaves. Cut with an electric knife, and serve with poppyseed dressing. **Yield:** 10 to 12 servings.

Note: To unmold, insert a flat knife between the salad and edge of the Bundt pan to break the suction. Invert salad (still in pan) onto a lettuce-lined plate. If it won't come out, place hot towels around the pan for a minute or two, and try again.

AMBROSIA SALAD

Rosé wine and sliced strawberries add the festive ruby color to this congealed version of a holiday favorite.

2 (6-ounce) packages apricot-flavored gelatin
2 cups boiling water
1 cup rosé wine or dry white wine, chilled
¾ cup cold water
1 (10-ounce) package frozen sliced strawberries, thawed and undrained
1 (8-ounce) can crushed pineapple, undrained
2 bananas, cut in half lengthwise and sliced
1 (8-ounce) carton sour cream
2 tablespoons brown sugar
1 to 2 tablespoons coconut, toasted
Lettuce leaves

- **Combine** gelatin and boiling water in a large bowl; stir 2 minutes or until gelatin dissolves. Add wine and cold water; chill until the consistency of unbeaten egg white.
- **Stir** in strawberries, pineapple, and banana; pour mixture into a lightly oiled 6-cup mold.
- **Cover** and chill at least 8 hours.
- **Combine** sour cream and brown sugar; spoon into a serving dish. Sprinkle with toasted coconut.
- **Unmold** salad onto lettuce leaves; serve with sour cream mixture. **Yield:** 12 servings.

Martha Myers
Manchester, Maryland

Holiday Cranberry Salad

HOLIDAY CRANBERRY SALAD
(pictured at left)

2 cups fresh or frozen cranberries, thawed
1 cup sugar
1 (3-ounce) package lemon-flavored gelatin
1 cup boiling water
1 cup chopped celery
1 cup chopped walnuts, toasted
Lettuce leaves
Garnishes: lemon slices, celery leaves, cranberries

• **Position** knife blade in food processor bowl; add cranberries. Process 30 seconds or until chopped.
• **Combine** cranberries and sugar in a large bowl; let stand 1 hour or until sugar dissolves.
• **Combine** gelatin and boiling water in a large bowl; stir 2 minutes or until gelatin dissolves. Chill until the consistency of unbeaten egg white.
• **Stir** cranberry mixture, celery, and walnuts into gelatin mixture. Pour into a lightly oiled 4-cup mold. Cover and chill until firm.
• **Unmold** salad onto a lettuce-lined plate. Garnish, if desired. **Yield:** 6 to 8 servings.

Sunny Tiedemann
Bartlesville, Oklahoma

ORANGE-BUTTERMILK SALAD

"This very light dish can be made the day before and is always a hit. People cannot believe it's made with buttermilk." – Juanita

1 (20-ounce) can unsweetened crushed pineapple, undrained
1 (6-ounce) package orange-flavored gelatin
2 cups buttermilk
1 (8-ounce) container frozen whipped topping, thawed
1 cup chopped pecans, toasted
Lettuce leaves

• **Bring** pineapple and liquid to a boil in a medium saucepan. Remove from heat; stir in gelatin. Stir until gelatin dissolves; let cool.
• **Add** buttermilk to pineapple mixture; cover and chill until mixture is the consistency of unbeaten egg white. Fold in whipped topping and chopped pecans.
• **Spoon** mixture into a lightly oiled 9-cup mold; cover and chill until mixture is firm.
• **Unmold** onto a lettuce-lined plate. **Yield:** 14 to 16 servings.

Juanita B. Hutto
Richmond, Virginia

FROZEN STRAWBERRY SALAD

QUICK!

1 (8-ounce) package fat-free cream cheese product, softened
½ cup sugar
1 (8-ounce) container reduced-fat frozen whipped topping, thawed
2 cups frozen no-sugar-added whole strawberries, thawed and halved
1 (15¼-ounce) can unsweetened crushed pineapple, undrained
1½ cups sliced banana (2 medium)

• **Beat** cream cheese at medium speed with an electric mixer until creamy; gradually add sugar, beating until smooth.
• **Fold** in whipped topping and remaining ingredients; spoon into a 13- x 9- x 2-inch dish. Cover with aluminum foil.
• **Freeze** until firm. **Yield:** 12 servings.

Linda S. Zachry
Dallas, Texas

♥ Per serving: Calories 138
Fat 2.6g   Cholesterol 4mg
Sodium 128mg

ALMOND-CITRUS SALAD

⅔ cup vegetable oil
2 teaspoons grated grapefruit rind
½ cup fresh grapefruit juice
1 (0.7-ounce) envelope Italian salad dressing mix
1 grapefruit
2 oranges
1 avocado, sliced
3 cups torn spinach
3 cups torn leaf lettuce
3 cups torn iceberg lettuce
½ cup sliced celery
½ cup chopped green bell pepper
¼ cup Sweet and Spicy Almonds

• **Combine** oil, grapefruit rind, grapefruit juice, and salad dressing mix in a jar; cover tightly, and shake vigorously.
• **Peel** and section grapefruit and oranges, and place in a large bowl. Add avocado and next 5 ingredients.
• **Add** dressing, tossing to coat. Sprinkle with Sweet and Spicy Almonds. **Yield:** 8 servings.

Sweet and Spicy Almonds

QUICK!

Make a double batch of these almonds to serve as an appetizer or hostess gift.

1 cup sliced almonds
1 tablespoon butter or margarine, melted
1½ teaspoons sugar
¼ teaspoon ground cumin
¼ teaspoon chili powder
⅛ teaspoon dried crushed red pepper
Pinch of salt

• **Combine** almonds and butter, stirring well. Combine sugar and remaining 4 ingredients; sprinkle over almonds, tossing to coat. Spread on a lightly greased baking sheet.
• **Bake** at 325° for 15 minutes, stirring occasionally; cool. **Yield:** 1 cup.

Nora Henshaw
Okemah, Oklahoma

CITRUS AND GREENS WITH ORANGE-GINGER DRESSING

3 oranges
2 pink grapefruit
1 pineapple
½ cup orange marmalade
¼ cup raspberry vinegar
1 tablespoon grated fresh
    ginger
1 (16-ounce) package mixed
    salad greens (8 cups torn)

• **Section** oranges and grapefruit; peel and cut pineapple into chunks.
• **Melt** marmalade in a small saucepan over low heat, stirring constantly; remove from heat, and stir in vinegar and ginger.
• **Arrange** salad greens evenly on individual serving plates; top with fruit, and drizzle with marmalade mixture. **Yield:** 4 servings.

RASPBERRY-WALNUT SALAD

4 cups torn Boston lettuce
4 cups torn red leaf lettuce
¾ cup walnuts, chopped and
    toasted
1 cup fresh raspberries
1 avocado, cubed
1 kiwifruit, sliced
Raspberry Salad Dressing

• **Combine** all ingredients except dressing in a large bowl; toss gently. Serve with Raspberry Salad Dressing. **Yield:** 12 servings.

Raspberry Salad Dressing

QUICK!

⅓ cup seedless raspberry jam
⅓ cup raspberry vinegar
1 cup vegetable oil
1 tablespoon poppy seeds

• **Combine** jam and vinegar in container of an electric blender; process 20 seconds. With blender on high, gradually add oil in a slow, steady stream.
• **Stir** in poppy seeds. **Yield:** 1½ cups.

Kelli and Jim Silliman
Dallas, Texas

GARDEN SALAD WITH BUTTERMILK DRESSING

¾ cup mayonnaise or salad
    dressing
½ cup buttermilk
1 tablespoon chopped fresh
    parsley
1 tablespoon finely chopped
    onion
1 clove garlic, minced
¼ teaspoon salt
Dash of pepper
4 cups mixed salad greens

• **Combine** first 7 ingredients; stir with a wire whisk until blended. Cover and chill 2 hours. Serve with salad greens. **Yield:** 4 servings.

Janice M. France
Louisville, Kentucky

MIXED GREENS WITH PARMESAN WALNUTS

"Experiment with flavors when you make salad by using lots of different greens. Wild watercress has become one of my favorite salad ingredients." – Rublelene

2 tablespoons butter or
    margarine
¼ teaspoon hickory salt
1½ cups chopped walnuts
3 tablespoons freshly grated
    Parmesan cheese
1 medium head iceberg lettuce,
    torn
1 medium head leaf lettuce,
    torn
½ bunch curly endive, torn
½ bunch fresh watercress, torn
½ pound fresh spinach, torn
½ cup vinegar and oil salad
    dressing

• **Combine** butter and salt in a 8-inch square pan.
• **Bake** at 350° for 2 to 3 minutes or until butter melts. Stir in walnuts, and bake 5 minutes. Sprinkle with cheese, tossing to coat; bake 4 to 5 additional minutes or until cheese is lightly browned. Cool completely.

• **Combine** iceberg lettuce and remaining 5 ingredients; toss gently to coat. Top mixture with walnuts, and serve immediately. **Yield:** 12 servings.

Rublelene Singleton
Scotts Hill, Tennessee

BAKED GOAT CHEESE SALAD

"Goat cheese releases more flavor when it's warm and creamy," says Paula, founder of Mozzarella Company in Dallas.

3 sprigs fresh rosemary
3 sprigs fresh thyme
3 sprigs fresh oregano
½ cup olive oil
1 (11-ounce) log fresh goat cheese
½ teaspoon Dijon mustard
3 tablespoons balsamic vinegar
¼ teaspoon salt
¼ teaspoon freshly ground pepper
½ cup dry breadcrumbs
½ bunch fresh watercress,
    trimmed
½ head Bibb lettuce, torn
1 small head radicchio, torn
Garnish: fresh thyme sprigs

• **Combine** first 4 ingredients in a small saucepan over medium-high heat. Bring to a boil; remove from heat, and let cool.
• **Cut** cheese log into 8 rounds, and place rounds on a plate; drizzle with oil mixture. Let stand 30 minutes.
• **Pour** oil from cheese into a bowl; discard herbs. Chill cheese rounds 15 minutes or until firm.
• **Add** mustard and next 3 ingredients to oil, stirring with a wire whisk.
• **Coat** cheese with breadcrumbs; place on a baking sheet. Bake at 350° for 10 minutes; set aside.
• **Combine** greens in a bowl; drizzle with oil mixture, tossing to coat. Place evenly on four individual salad plates; top each serving with 2 cheese rounds. Garnish, if desired. **Yield:** 4 servings.

Paula Lambert
Mozzarella Company
Dallas, Texas

BALSAMIC-PESTO SALAD

QUICK!

½ cup pine nuts
1 (0.5-ounce) package pesto sauce mix
½ cup water
¼ cup balsamic vinegar
3 tablespoons olive oil
8 cups mixed salad greens

• **Place** pine nuts in a shallow pan, and bake at 350° for 5 to 10 minutes or until toasted, stirring occasionally; set aside.
• **Combine** sauce mix and next 3 ingredients in a jar; cover tightly, and shake vigorously. Pour over greens, tossing to coat. Sprinkle with pine nuts; serve immediately. **Yield:** 6 servings.

Donna M. DiRicco
Woodbridge, Virginia

CARAMELIZED SHALLOT SALAD

If you prefer, you can caramelize the shallots, make the dressing, and wash the greens a day ahead.

2 pounds shallots, peeled
1 cup chicken broth
2 tablespoons brown sugar
½ cup balsamic vinegar
2 cloves garlic, minced
½ teaspoon salt
½ teaspoon freshly ground pepper
¾ cup olive oil
2 heads romaine lettuce
2 heads Bibb lettuce
2 heads Belgian endive
12 radicchio leaves
2 (4-ounce) packages crumbled blue cheese

• **Place** shallots in a large skillet; add broth and brown sugar. Cover and cook over medium heat 25 minutes or until shallots are tender, stirring occasionally with a rubber spatula.
• **Uncover,** reduce heat, and simmer 20 minutes or until shallots are golden, stirring often. Carefully transfer shallots to a large shallow dish.
• **Whisk** together vinegar and next 3 ingredients; add oil in a slow, steady stream, whisking constantly. Reserve ½ cup mixture; pour remaining vinegar mixture over shallots. Cover and chill 8 hours.
• **Tear** romaine and Bibb lettuces, and shred 6 small endive leaves; toss with reserved ½ cup vinegar mixture.
• **Arrange** whole endive leaves, lettuces, and radicchio leaves on individual serving plates; drain shallots, and place in radicchio leaves. Sprinkle with blue cheese. **Yield:** 12 servings.

ROASTED ONION SALAD

5 medium onions, unpeeled and cut into ½-inch-thick slices
¼ cup olive oil
8 cups mixed baby lettuces
½ cup chopped walnuts, toasted
1 (4-ounce) package crumbled blue cheese
Garlic Vinaigrette

• **Arrange** onion slices in a lightly greased roasting pan. Drizzle evenly with olive oil.
• **Bake** at 500° for 10 minutes or until onion slices are lightly charred; cool. Remove and discard outer skin of onion slices. Set onion slices aside.
• **Combine** lettuces, walnuts, and blue cheese; toss gently. Top with roasted onion slices; drizzle with Garlic Vinaigrette. **Yield:** 8 servings.

Garlic Vinaigrette

QUICK!

4 cloves garlic
2 shallots
¼ cup chopped fresh parsley
½ teaspoon dried crushed red pepper
½ teaspoon salt
½ teaspoon freshly ground black pepper
2 tablespoons white wine vinegar
⅔ cup olive oil

• **Position** knife blade in food processor bowl; add garlic and shallots, and pulse 3 or 4 times. Add parsley and next 4 ingredients; process 20 seconds, stopping once to scrape down sides.
• **Pour** oil through food chute in a slow, steady stream with processor running, and process until blended. **Yield:** 1 cup.

W. N. Cottrell II
New Orleans, Louisiana

MOCK CAESAR SALAD

(pictured on page 181)

1 clove garlic
¼ cup water
⅛ teaspoon salt
1 tablespoon white wine vinegar
½ teaspoon Dijon mustard
¼ cup olive oil
2 cups firmly packed torn romaine lettuce
2 tablespoons freshly grated Parmesan cheese
2 tablespoons pine nuts, toasted
⅛ teaspoon freshly ground pepper

• **Combine** garlic and water in a small saucepan; bring to a boil. Cover, reduce heat, and simmer 10 minutes or until garlic is soft; drain.
• **Place** garlic in a salad bowl; add salt. Mash into a paste, using back of a spoon. Stir in vinegar and mustard with a wire whisk. Add olive oil in a slow, steady stream, whisking until blended. Add lettuce, and toss gently. Sprinkle with cheese, pine nuts, and pepper. **Yield:** 2 servings.

Nicka Thornton
Greensboro, North Carolina

CAESAR MARGARITA SALAD

A frosty salted rim frames this Caesar salad inspired by the margarita.

Lime wedges (optional)
Kosher salt (optional)
1 large head romaine lettuce, torn
1 cup (4 ounces) shredded Monterey Jack cheese
¼ cup finely chopped fresh cilantro
1 red bell pepper, cut into thin strips
Margarita Dressing
Tortilla Triangles
Garnish: lime wedges

• **Rub** rims of six chilled salad plates with lime wedges, if desired; place salt in saucer, and roll rim of each plate in salt, if desired. Set aside.
• **Combine** lettuce and next 3 ingredients in a large bowl; add Margarita Dressing, tossing gently.
• **Arrange** salad on plates, and sprinkle with Tortilla Triangles. Garnish, if desired. **Yield:** 6 servings.

Margarita Dressing

QUICK!

⅓ cup canola or safflower oil
¼ cup lime juice
2 tablespoons fat-free egg substitute
1½ tablespoons tequila
1½ teaspoons Triple Sec or other orange-flavored liqueur
1 clove garlic, minced
1 serrano chile pepper, seeded and finely chopped
¼ teaspoon salt
¼ teaspoon ground cumin

• **Combine** all ingredients in a small bowl; stir well with a wire whisk. Cover and chill. **Yield:** 1 cup.

Tortilla Triangles

QUICK!

6 (6-inch) corn tortillas, cut into small triangles
½ cup canola or vegetable oil
Kosher salt

• **Fry** tortilla triangles in hot oil in a small skillet until golden; drain on paper towels, and sprinkle immediately with kosher salt. **Yield:** 1½ cups.

GREEK CAESAR SALAD

¾ cup olive oil
¼ cup lemon juice
¼ cup fat-free egg substitute
2 cloves garlic, pressed
1 teaspoon dried oregano
¼ teaspoon salt
⅛ teaspoon pepper
1 head romaine lettuce, torn
¾ cup kalamata olives, pitted
1 small purple onion, thinly sliced
½ cup crumbled feta cheese
Pita Croutons

• **Combine** first 7 ingredients in a small bowl, stirring with a wire whisk. Cover and chill.
• **Combine** lettuce and next 3 ingredients in a large bowl; gradually add enough dressing to coat leaves, tossing gently. Sprinkle with Pita Croutons, and serve with remaining dressing. **Yield:** 6 servings.

Pita Croutons

QUICK!

2 tablespoons olive oil
1 teaspoon dried oregano
¼ teaspoon crushed garlic
Dash of salt
1 (8-inch) pita bread round, split into 2 circles

• **Combine** first 4 ingredients, and brush olive oil mixture over the inside of each pita bread circle.
• **Cut** each pita bread circle into bite-size pieces, and place on a baking sheet.
• **Bake** at 400° for 5 to 7 minutes or until golden. **Yield:** 1⅓ cups.

SOUTHERN CAESAR SALAD

Caesar comes to Dixie in this stately salad, dressed in the flavors of the South.

⅓ cup peanut oil
3 tablespoons cider vinegar
2 tablespoons fat-free egg substitute
2 tablespoons honey mustard
¼ teaspoon pepper
4 ounces thinly sliced country ham, cut into ¼-inch strips
1 tablespoon peanut oil
1 large head romaine lettuce, torn
¾ cup pecans, toasted and coarsely chopped
Honeyed Cornbread Croutons

• **Combine** first 5 ingredients, and stir well with a wire whisk. Cover and chill at least 1 hour.
• **Cook** ham in peanut oil in a skillet over medium-high heat, stirring constantly, until browned. Drain on paper towels.
• **Combine** lettuce, pecans, and ham in a large bowl; add dressing, tossing gently. Sprinkle with Honeyed Cornbread Croutons. **Yield:** 6 servings.

Honeyed Cornbread Croutons

1 (11.5-ounce) package refrigerated cornbread twists
¼ cup butter or margarine, melted
1 tablespoon honey

• **Unroll** dough; separate at perforations to form 16 strips. Place on an ungreased baking sheet.
• **Combine** butter and honey; brush on strips.
• **Bake** at 375° for 11 minutes. Transfer to wire racks to cool.
• **Cut** each strip diagonally into ½-inch slices, and place on an ungreased baking sheet.
• **Bake** at 225° for 20 minutes, stirring every 5 minutes. Cool.
• **Store** in airtight container up to 1 month. **Yield:** 4 cups.

SPINACH-APRICOT SALAD

1 cup boiling water
1 (6-ounce) package dried apricot
    halves
1 pound fresh spinach or
    1 (10-ounce) package fresh
    spinach
3 tablespoons cider vinegar
3 tablespoons apricot preserves
½ cup vegetable oil
¾ cup coarsely chopped
    macadamia nuts, toasted

• **Pour** boiling water over apricots; let
stand 30 minutes. Drain well; set aside.
• **Remove** stems from spinach; wash
leaves thoroughly, and pat dry. Tear into
bite-size pieces. Set aside.
• **Combine** vinegar and preserves in
container of an electric blender; process
until smooth, stopping once to scrape
down sides. With blender on high, gradually add oil in a slow, steady stream.
• **Combine** spinach, half of apricot
halves, half of nuts, and dressing, and
toss gently. Sprinkle with remaining
apricot halves and nuts. Serve immediately. **Yield:** 8 servings.

SPINACH SALAD WITH
SAUTÉED PEARS

1 (10-ounce) package fresh
    spinach
1 cup water
¼ cup lemon juice
2 Bosc pears
4 slices bacon, chopped
¼ cup olive oil
1 medium onion, sliced
1 medium-size red or yellow bell
    pepper, sliced
1 cup white wine or red wine
    vinegar
2 tablespoons sugar
1 teaspoon grated orange rind
1 teaspoon dried thyme
½ teaspoon dried basil
1 teaspoon salt
½ teaspoon cracked pepper
½ to 1 teaspoon hot sauce

• **Wash** spinach, and remove and discard stems; set spinach aside.

• **Combine** water and lemon juice in a
bowl; peel, core, and chop pears. Place
chopped pear in lemon-water mixture,
and set aside.
• **Cook** bacon in olive oil over medium-
high heat in a large skillet until crisp.
Add onion and pepper slices; cook 3
minutes or until tender.
• **Drain** pears; add to skillet, and cook
just until tender.
• **Add** vinegar, sugar, and orange rind;
bring to a boil. Remove mixture from
heat, and stir in thyme and remaining 4
ingredients.
• **Place** spinach in a large bowl; add
vinegar mixture, and toss gently. Serve
immediately with a slotted spoon.
Yield: 6 to 8 servings.

Chef John Folse
Lafitte's Landing
Donaldsonville, Louisiana

SPINACH SALAD
WITH THE BLUES

Spoon the salad dressing on
the plate, and arrange the salad
on top. To shred fresh spinach,
roll several leaves together. Use
kitchen scissors or a sharp knife to
cut the roll at ¼-inch intervals.

½ cup chopped walnuts
⅓ cup olive oil
¼ cup white wine vinegar
1 tablespoon prepared
    mustard
1 teaspoon sugar (optional)
1 (10-ounce) bag fresh spinach,
    washed, trimmed, and
    shredded
1 head Belgian endive, washed
    and trimmed
2 Red Delicious apples, cored
    and thinly sliced
1 (4-ounce) package crumbled
    blue cheese

• **Spread** walnuts in a shallow pan.
Bake at 350° for 5 minutes, stirring occasionally. Set aside.
• **Combine** olive oil, vinegar, mustard,
and sugar, if desired, in a jar. Cover
tightly, and shake vigorously. Pour
evenly onto six salad plates.

• **Arrange** spinach on top of dressing.
• **Arrange** endive leaves and thin apple
slices evenly beside shredded spinach.
• **Sprinkle** with walnuts and blue
cheese. **Yield:** 6 servings.

Agnes L. Stone
Ocala, Florida

GREEN BEAN, WALNUT,
AND FETA SALAD

1 cup coarsely chopped walnuts
¾ cup olive oil
¼ cup white wine vinegar
1 tablespoon chopped fresh dill
½ teaspoon minced garlic
¼ teaspoon salt
¼ teaspoon pepper
1½ pounds fresh green beans
1 small purple onion, thinly sliced
1 (4-ounce) package crumbled feta
    cheese

• **Place** walnuts in a shallow pan, and
bake at 350° for 5 to 10 minutes or until
toasted, stirring occasionally; set aside.
• **Combine** oil and next 5 ingredients;
cover and chill.
• **Wash** beans, trim ends, and remove
strings. Cut green beans into thirds, and
arrange in a steamer basket over boiling
water. Cover and steam 15 minutes or
until crisp-tender. Immediately plunge
into cold water to stop the cooking
process; drain and pat dry.
• **Combine** walnuts, beans, onion, and
cheese in a large bowl; toss well. Cover
and chill.
• **Pour** oil mixture over bean mixture 1
hour before serving; toss just before
serving. **Yield:** 6 servings.

Judi Grant
El Paso, Texas

MARINATED BEAN SALAD

QUICK!

This salad is best made the day before you want to serve it.

1 (15.8-ounce) can great Northern beans, drained and rinsed
1 (15-ounce) can black beans, drained and rinsed
1 (15-ounce) can kidney beans, drained and rinsed
1 (8-ounce) can whole kernel corn, drained and rinsed
1 (2-ounce) jar diced pimiento, drained
1 carrot, scraped and chopped
½ cup olive oil
½ cup cider vinegar
1 clove garlic, pressed
½ teaspoon salt
½ teaspoon pepper
½ teaspoon chili powder

• **Combine** first 6 ingredients in a large bowl. Set aside.
• **Combine** olive oil and remaining 5 ingredients; pour over bean mixture. Spoon into an airtight container, and chill up to 4 days. **Yield:** 6 servings.

Toasted Appetizers: Place 1 cup Marinated Bean Salad into container of an electric blender; process until smooth, adding 1 to 2 tablespoons marinating liquid, if necessary. Spread evenly on 10 thin slices of toasted French bread; top with thin slices of mozzarella or goat cheese. Bake at 350° for 3 to 5 minutes. **Yield:** 4 appetizer servings.

BROCCOLI SALAD

½ cup raisins
2 pounds broccoli, cut into flowerets
1 cup purple seedless grapes, halved
3 green onions, thinly sliced
⅔ cup mayonnaise
2 tablespoons tarragon vinegar
¼ cup slivered almonds, toasted
8 slices bacon, cooked and crumbled

• **Soak** raisins in hot water to cover 5 minutes; drain.
• **Combine** raisins, broccoli, grapes, and green onions in a large bowl. Combine mayonnaise and vinegar; stir into broccoli mixture. Cover and chill.
• **Stir** in almonds and bacon just before serving. **Yield:** 6 to 8 servings.

Ruth J. Carnes
Victoria, Texas

CONFETTI CORN SALAD

QUICK!

2 cups fresh corn, cut from cob
¾ cup water
1 (14½-ounce) can black beans, rinsed and drained
½ cup sliced green onions
½ cup chopped red bell pepper
1 small cucumber, seeded and chopped
2 cloves garlic, minced
¼ cup chopped fresh cilantro
1 teaspoon sweet red pepper flakes
¼ teaspoon salt
¼ teaspoon ground ginger
2 tablespoons corn oil
2 tablespoons rice vinegar
1 tablespoon sesame oil
1 tablespoon lime juice

• **Combine** corn and ¾ cup water in a saucepan; bring to a boil. Cover, reduce heat, and simmer 7 to 8 minutes or just until corn is tender. Drain. Combine corn, black beans, and next 5 ingredients in a large bowl.
• **Whisk** together red pepper flakes and remaining 6 ingredients until blended; pour over corn mixture. Cover and chill at least 2 hours. **Yield:** 4 to 6 servings.

Kitty Jones
Greeneville, Tennessee

MEDITERRANEAN LENTIL SALAD

QUICK!

1 cup dried lentils
1 small onion, chopped
1 quart water
1 small red bell pepper
1 small green bell pepper
1 tomato
3 green onions
1 (2¼-ounce) can sliced ripe olives, drained
½ cup Italian dressing
2 tablespoons lemon juice
½ teaspoon pepper
1 (4-ounce) package crumbled tomato-basil feta cheese

• **Bring** first 3 ingredients to a boil in a Dutch oven; reduce heat, and simmer, partially covered, 15 to 20 minutes or just until lentils are tender. Drain.
• **Chop** bell peppers, tomato, and green onions; add to lentil mixture. Stir in olives and next 3 ingredients; cover and chill. Sprinkle with cheese; serve immediately. **Yield:** 5 cups.

Donna F. Bearden
Gibsonville, North Carolina

HOPPIN' JOHN SALAD

The mint in this Southern black-eyed pea and rice salad makes it exceptionally original.

2 cups cooked black-eyed peas
3 cups cooked long-grain rice
½ cup chopped purple onion
¼ cup chopped celery
1 jalapeño pepper, seeded and minced
¼ cup loosely packed fresh chervil or parsley
¼ cup loosely packed fresh mint
1 clove garlic
½ teaspoon salt
3 tablespoons fresh lemon juice
¼ cup olive oil
¼ teaspoon freshly ground pepper

• **Combine** first 5 ingredients in a bowl.
• **Place** herbs and garlic on a cutting board, and sprinkle evenly with salt;

finely chop herbs and garlic. Sprinkle over rice mixture, and stir gently.

● **Combine** lemon juice, olive oil, and pepper in a bowl; stir into rice mixture. **Yield:** 6 servings.

John Martin Taylor
Charleston, South Carolina
The New Southern Cook
(Bantam)

GREEN PEA SALAD

QUICK!

This recipe halves easily.

2 (16-ounce) packages frozen
    English peas, thawed
2 green onions, sliced
2 (8-ounce) cans sliced water
    chestnuts, drained
⅔ cup reduced-fat sour cream
⅔ cup reduced-fat mayonnaise
1 teaspoon freshly ground black
    pepper
Garnishes: sliced green onions,
    cashew halves

● **Combine** all ingredients except garnishes, stirring gently. Garnish, if desired. **Yield:** 8 servings.

Toni Spanos Nordan and Clay Nordan
Birmingham, Alabama

CRUNCHY SPROUT SALAD

1 (3-ounce) package chicken
    ramen noodle soup mix
¼ cup vegetable oil
1½ tablespoons rice wine
    vinegar
1 tablespoon sesame oil
1 teaspoon chili-flavored oil
1 (3.2-ounce) package enoki
    mushrooms
2 carrots, scraped and shredded
1 cucumber, peeled, seeded, and
    chopped
½ cup bean sprouts
¼ pound fresh snow pea pods, cut
    into thin strips
1 avocado, chopped
4 leaves radicchio or red cabbage
¼ cup sesame seeds, toasted

● **Place** noodles in a 9-inch square pan; discard seasoning packet.
● **Bake** at 375° for 7 minutes or until browned, stirring twice. Cool.
● **Combine** vegetable oil and next 3 ingredients, stirring with a wire whisk until blended.
● **Combine** half of noodles, mushrooms, and next 5 ingredients. Add oil mixture; toss gently to coat.
● **Place** radicchio on individual serving plates; spoon vegetable mixture evenly on radicchio. Sprinkle with remaining half of noodles and sesame seeds. **Yield:** 4 servings.

Daisy Trippeer
Germantown, Tennessee

TOMATO AND CUCUMBER SUMMER SALAD

¼ cup mayonnaise or salad
    dressing
3 tablespoons white vinegar
1 green onion, chopped
1 clove garlic, pressed
1 teaspoon sugar
½ to ¾ teaspoon salt
1 teaspoon Worcestershire
    sauce
½ teaspoon hot sauce
½ cup vegetable oil
1 cup chopped fresh parsley
Leaf lettuce
3 medium tomatoes, thinly
    sliced
2 cucumbers, thinly sliced

● **Combine** first 8 ingredients in container of an electric blender; process until smooth, stopping once to scrape down sides. With blender on high, gradually add oil in a slow, steady stream. Stir in parsley. Cover and chill.
● **Arrange** lettuce on chilled salad plates. Top with tomato slices and cucumber slices. Drizzle evenly with dressing. **Yield:** 6 to 8 servings.

SUMMER TOMATO SALAD

(pictured on page 297)

2 medium-size ripe tomatoes,
    sliced
8 ounces fresh mozzarella cheese
    or goat cheese, thinly sliced
6 large fresh basil leaves, finely
    chopped and divided
½ teaspoon freshly ground pepper,
    divided
Tarragon Vinaigrette
1 medium cucumber, thinly
    sliced
1 sweet onion, thinly sliced
Fresh basil leaves (optional)

● **Layer** tomato and cheese slices in a shallow dish; sprinkle with half of chopped basil and ¼ teaspoon pepper. Drizzle with ¼ cup Tarragon Vinaigrette. Top with cucumber and onion slices; sprinkle with remaining half of chopped basil and ¼ teaspoon pepper, and drizzle with remaining ¼ cup Tarragon Vinaigrette.
● **Cover** and chill 4 hours. Serve on a basil leaf-lined plate, if desired. **Yield:** 4 to 6 servings.

Note: Fresh mozzarella cheese is available at gourmet grocery stores and large supermarkets.

Tarragon Vinaigrette

QUICK!

¼ cup Tarragon Vinegar (see
    recipe on page 354)
¼ cup olive oil
1 tablespoon chopped fresh
    basil
½ teaspoon lemon juice
½ teaspoon finely chopped green
    onions
½ teaspoon honey
¼ teaspoon Dijon mustard

● **Combine** all ingredients in container of an electric blender; process until smooth. **Yield:** ½ cup.

Cindie Hackney
Longview, Texas

Grilled Vegetable Salad

GRILLED VEGETABLE SALAD
(pictured at left)

⅓ cup white balsamic vinegar
2 tablespoons olive oil
2 shallots, finely chopped
1 teaspoon dried Italian
     seasoning
¼ teaspoon salt
¼ teaspoon pepper
1½ teaspoons molasses
½ pound carrots, scraped
1 red bell pepper
1 yellow bell pepper
2 zucchini
2 yellow squash
1 large onion

● **Combine** first 7 ingredients in a large bowl. Set aside.
● **Cut** carrots and remaining vegetables into large pieces.
● **Add** vegetables to vinegar mixture, tossing to coat. Let stand 30 minutes, stirring occasionally.
● **Drain** vegetables, reserving vinegar mixture. Arrange vegetables in a grill basket.
● **Cook**, covered with grill lid, over medium-hot coals (350° to 400°) 15 to 20 minutes, turning occasionally.
● **Return** vegetables to reserved vinegar mixture, tossing gently.
● **Cover** and chill at least 8 hours. **Yield:** 6 servings.

Margaret Jordan
Birmingham, Alabama

♥ Per serving: Calories 103
Fat 4.9g Cholesterol 0mg
Sodium 116mg

AVOCADO-POTATO SALAD WITH HORSERADISH DRESSING

1 pound baking potatoes
3 avocados, cubed
2 medium-size red apples,
     cubed
¾ cup chopped green onions
½ cup chopped walnuts or pecans,
     toasted
1 tablespoon chopped fresh
     parsley
Horseradish Dressing

● **Cook** potatoes in boiling salted water to cover 20 to 30 minutes or until tender; drain. Cool; peel and cube.
● **Combine** potato, avocado, apple, and green onions in a large bowl; toss gently. Sprinkle with walnuts and parsley; cover and chill. Serve immediately with Horseradish Dressing. **Yield:** 6 servings.

Horseradish Dressing
QUICK!

1 (8-ounce) carton sour cream
1 tablespoon prepared horseradish
1 tablespoon lemon juice
½ teaspoon salt
½ teaspoon freshly ground pepper

● **Combine** all ingredients; cover and chill. **Yield:** 1 cup.

GREEN BEAN-RED POTATO SALAD

Leave the skins on the red potatoes for pretty color and to help them keep their shape after they're cooked.

1½ pounds round red potatoes
1 (9-ounce) package frozen whole
     green beans
2 tablespoons white vinegar
1 tablespoon sugar
¾ cup mayonnaise
2 tablespoons chopped onion
½ teaspoon dried dillweed or
     1½ teaspoons finely chopped
     fresh dill

● **Cook** potatoes in boiling salted water to cover 10 minutes or until tender.

Drain potatoes, and cool to touch. Cut into slices.
● **Cook** green beans according to package directions; drain and rinse with cold water.
● **Combine** potato slices and green beans in a bowl. Combine vinegar and remaining 4 ingredients; pour over potato mixture, and toss gently. Cover and chill 4 hours. **Yield:** 4 servings.
Linda Kirkpatrick
Westminster, Maryland

NEW POTATO SALAD

3 pounds new potatoes,
     unpeeled
⅓ cup finely chopped purple
     onion
⅓ cup olive oil
⅓ cup red wine vinegar
¼ cup stone-ground mustard
2 teaspoons sugar
½ teaspoon salt
½ teaspoon freshly ground
     pepper
½ pound thick-sliced bacon,
     cooked and crumbled
1 cup chopped fresh parsley

● **Cook** potatoes in boiling water to cover 15 minutes or until tender. Drain and cool slightly. Cut into ¼-inch slices. Combine potato and onion in a large bowl; set aside.
● **Combine** olive oil and next 5 ingredients; stir well with a wire whisk. Pour dressing over potato mixture; toss gently. Cover and chill.
● **Add** bacon and chopped parsley just before serving, and toss gently. **Yield:** 12 servings.

Rebecca and Don Farris
Dallas, Texas

WARM GOAT CHEESE AND POTATO SALAD

4 large Yukon gold or red
    potatoes
Vegetable or corn oil
1 teaspoon salt, divided
1 teaspoon cracked pepper,
    divided
1 cup balsamic vinegar
8 bacon slices
1½ tablespoons balsamic
    vinegar
½ pound torn frisée or gourmet
    salad greens
1 tablespoon chopped fresh
    parsley
1 tablespoon chopped chives
1 tablespoon chopped fresh
    thyme
1 Granny Smith apple, cut into
    thin wedges
Warm Goat Cheese Fondue
Parsley Oil
Chili Oil

• **Cut** potatoes into rectangular blocks; dice trimmings.
• **Pour** oil to depth of 3 inches into a Dutch oven; heat to 375°. Fry diced potato in oil 2 minutes or until golden. Drain and set aside. Fry potato blocks 6 minutes or until golden. Drain and place in a shallow pan.
• **Bake** at 375° for 10 minutes or until tender.
• **Sprinkle** diced potato and potato blocks with ½ teaspoon salt and ½ teaspoon pepper; cool.
• **Boil** 1 cup balsamic vinegar in a heavy nonstick skillet until reduced to ½ cup; set aside.
• **Cook** bacon in skillet until crisp; remove bacon, reserving 1½ tablespoons drippings in skillet. Crumble bacon, and set aside.
• **Add** remaining ½ teaspoon salt, ½ teaspoon pepper, and 1½ tablespoons balsamic vinegar to reserved drippings, stirring balsamic dressing well.
• **Combine** diced potato, bacon, frisée, and next 3 ingredients in a large salad bowl; drizzle with balsamic dressing, and toss gently.
• **Arrange** salad evenly on individual salad plates; stand potato blocks upright in center. Cut a slit in top of potato blocks; insert 3 or 4 apple wedges into each slit.
• **Spoon** Warm Goat Cheese Fondue onto plates; spoon over potato, if desired. Drizzle plate with reduced vinegar, Parsley Oil, and Chili Oil. Serve immediately. **Yield:** 4 servings.

Warm Goat Cheese Fondue

QUICK!

2 tablespoons minced shallots
1 tablespoon corn oil
2 tablespoons chopped fresh
    thyme
¾ cup whipping cream
1 (5.3-ounce) package goat cheese,
    crumbled
½ teaspoon salt
½ teaspoon cracked pepper

• **Cook** shallot in oil in a large skillet until tender, stirring often; stir in thyme and cream. Bring to a boil, stirring constantly; remove from heat. Add goat cheese, salt, and pepper, whisking until smooth. **Yield:** about 1½ cups.

Parsley Oil

QUICK!

1 bunch flat-leaf parsley, chopped
½ cup corn oil

• **Combine** parsley and oil in container of an electric blender, and process until combined, stopping once to scrape down sides; pour through a wire-mesh strainer into a small bowl, discarding parsley. Store any leftover oil in refrigerator. **Yield:** ¼ cup.

Chili Oil

QUICK!

1 tablespoon chili powder
½ cup corn oil

• **Cook** chili powder in a nonstick skillet over high heat 1 minute, stirring constantly; remove from heat. Stir in oil; let stand 30 minutes. Pour through a fine-mesh strainer into a small bowl, discarding chili powder. Store any leftover oil in refrigerator. **Yield:** ½ cup.

*James At The Mill
Johnson, Arkansas*

HOT GERMAN POTATO SALAD

9 medium-size round red potatoes,
    (about 4¼ pounds)
6 slices bacon
1 medium onion, chopped
2 tablespoons all-purpose flour
2 tablespoons sugar
2 to 3 teaspoons salt
⅛ teaspoon pepper
½ teaspoon celery seeds
¾ cup water
⅓ cup apple cider vinegar

• **Cook** potatoes in boiling water to cover 25 to 30 minutes or until tender. Drain and cool 10 minutes. Cut potatoes into ½-inch-thick slices; set aside.
• **Cook** bacon in a large skillet until crisp; remove bacon, reserving drippings in skillet. Crumble bacon, and set aside.
• **Cook** onion in drippings over medium heat, stirring constantly, until tender. Add flour and next 4 ingredients, stirring until blended. Cook 1 minute, stirring constantly. Gradually stir in ¾ cup water and vinegar; cook until sauce is thickened and bubbly.
• **Layer** one-third each of potato and bacon in a 2½-quart serving bowl; drizzle with one-third of sauce mixture. Repeat procedure twice; serve immediately. **Yield:** 8 servings.

*Theresa Sheldon
Ponca City, Oklahoma*

WARM POTATO AND SAUSAGE SALAD

3 pounds red potatoes
4 green onions, sliced
½ cup chopped dill pickle
¼ cup chopped fresh parsley
1 pound kielbasa sausage,
    sliced
½ cup olive oil, divided
¼ cup white wine vinegar
3 cloves garlic, pressed
1 tablespoon chopped fresh
    tarragon or 1 teaspoon dried
    tarragon
1 tablespoon Dijon mustard
1 teaspoon freshly ground pepper
½ teaspoon salt

- **Cook** potatoes in boiling water to cover in a Dutch oven 10 to 15 minutes or until tender; drain and cool slightly. Cut into 1-inch pieces.
- **Combine** potato, green onions, dill pickle, and parsley in a large bowl.
- **Cook** sausage in 1 tablespoon oil in Dutch oven over medium-high heat 4 minutes or until browned; drain. Stir sausage into potato mixture.
- **Combine** remaining oil, vinegar, and remaining 5 ingredients in Dutch oven; bring to a boil over medium heat. Pour over potato mixture; toss gently to coat. **Yield:** 6 servings.

Edith Askins
Greenville, Texas

HAM AND POTATO SALAD

1 pound small round red potatoes, cut into ½-inch wedges (about 3 cups)
1 (16-ounce) package frozen mixed vegetables
⅓ cup mayonnaise or salad dressing
⅓ cup sour cream
½ cup sliced green onions
1 teaspoon pepper
½ teaspoon salt
3 cups chopped cooked ham (about 1 pound)

- **Cook** potato, covered, in boiling water to cover 10 minutes or until tender (do not overcook); drain and set aside.
- **Cook** mixed vegetables according to package directions; drain vegetables, and set aside.
- **Combine** mayonnaise and next 4 ingredients in a large bowl; stir well. Gently stir in potato, vegetables, and ham. Cover and chill at least 8 hours. **Yield:** 6 to 8 servings.

Charlotte Pierce Bryant
Greensburg, Kentucky

SHRIMP AND POTATO SALAD

2 medium potatoes, unpeeled
6 cups water
2 pounds unpeeled medium-size fresh shrimp
½ cup finely chopped green onions
4 stalks celery, finely chopped
4 large hard-cooked eggs
½ cup mayonnaise
2 tablespoons prepared mustard
¼ teaspoon salt
½ teaspoon pepper
½ teaspoon hot sauce
Lettuce leaves

- **Cube** potatoes, and place in a saucepan; add enough water to cover, and bring to a boil over medium-high heat. Cook 6 to 7 minutes or until tender. Drain and place in a large bowl; cool.
- **Bring** 6 cups water to a boil in saucepan; add shrimp, and cook 3 to 5 minutes or just until shrimp turn pink. Drain shrimp, and rinse with cold water.
- **Peel** shrimp, and devein, if desired. Coarsely chop shrimp, if desired. Add shrimp, green onions, and celery to potato.
- **Chop** egg whites, and add to shrimp mixture. Mash egg yolks; stir in mayonnaise and mustard. Add mayonnaise mixture, salt, pepper, and hot sauce to shrimp mixture, tossing gently to coat; cover and chill. Serve on lettuce leaves with fresh fruit and tomato wedges. **Yield:** 6 to 8 servings.

"THINK PINK" SLAW

Tuck leaf lettuce under individual servings of this slaw for colorful contrast.

3 medium-size firm pears, unpeeled and cored
1 (16-ounce) can whole beets, drained *
⅓ cup mayonnaise or salad dressing
⅓ cup sour cream
1 tablespoon raspberry vinegar
1 tablespoon honey
Garnish: leaf lettuce

- **Position** medium-size shredding disk in food processor bowl; process pears and beets until shredded. Place in a large bowl.
- **Combine** mayonnaise and next 3 ingredients; add to pear mixture, tossing to coat. Cover and chill at least 1 hour. Toss before serving. Garnish, if desired. **Yield:** 8 servings.

* Substitute 2 medium-size fresh beets, peeled, for canned.

Note: Use a handheld grater instead of a food processor to shred pears and beets.

BLUE CHEESE COLESLAW

For crisp slaw, first soak the shredded cabbage in ice water for an hour. Then drain the cabbage, pat dry, and store in the refrigerator in a plastic bag until ready to use.

3 tablespoons apple cider vinegar
2 tablespoons finely chopped onion
1 tablespoon sugar
¾ teaspoon celery seeds
¼ teaspoon salt
⅛ teaspoon dry mustard
¼ teaspoon pepper
1 clove garlic, minced
¼ cup vegetable oil
1 pound cabbage, finely shredded
1 (4-ounce) package crumbled blue cheese

- **Combine** first 8 ingredients in a small bowl; add oil in a slow, steady stream, stirring constantly with a wire whisk until mixture is blended. Cover and chill at least 1 hour.
- **Combine** cabbage and blue cheese; cover and chill 1 hour.
- **Drizzle** vinegar mixture over cabbage mixture; toss gently, and serve immediately. **Yield:** 6 servings.

Janie Baur
Spring, Texas

SWEET BROCCOLI SLAW

QUICK!

1 cup sugar
½ cup apple cider vinegar
¼ cup water
½ teaspoon mustard seeds
½ teaspoon celery seeds
1 (16-ounce) package broccoli
   slaw mix

● **Combine** first 5 ingredients in a small saucepan; bring to a boil, stirring constantly, until sugar dissolves. Remove from heat. Pour over broccoli slaw mix, stirring gently.
● **Cover** and chill at least 4 hours, stirring occasionally. Serve with a slotted spoon. **Yield:** 4 to 6 servings.

Trenda Leigh
Richmond, Virginia

CHINESE PEANUT SLAW

1 (3-ounce) package chicken
   ramen noodle soup mix
⅓ cup peanut oil
3 tablespoons rice wine vinegar
2 tablespoons sugar
1 small cabbage, shredded (about
   1½ pounds)
½ cup sliced green onions
1 cup dry roasted peanuts
¼ cup sesame seeds, toasted

● **Remove** seasoning packet from noodles; set aside. Break noodles into pieces; place in a shallow baking pan. Bake at 400° for 5 minutes or until golden, stirring once; set aside.
● **Combine** seasoning packet, peanut oil, vinegar, and sugar in a small bowl; beat with a wire whisk until well blended. Cover and chill.
● **Just** before serving, combine dressing, cabbage, and remaining 3 ingredients, tossing well. Sprinkle with toasted noodles. **Yield:** 8 to 10 servings.

Mary Catherine Crowe
Birmingham, Alabama

BROCCOLI-CHEESE-PASTA SALAD

8 ounces rigatoni, uncooked
4 cups fresh broccoli flowerets
4 ounces mozzarella cheese, cubed
⅓ cup chopped fresh parsley
2 tablespoons chopped fresh basil
Mustard Vinaigrette
Lettuce leaves
Garnish: cherry tomato halves

● **Cook** pasta according to package directions; drain. Rinse with cold water; drain.
● **Cook** broccoli in a small amount of boiling water 2 to 3 minutes or until slightly tender; drain. Rinse with cold water; drain.
● **Combine** pasta, broccoli, mozzarella cheese, and herbs in a large bowl; toss gently with Mustard Vinaigrette, and serve on a lettuce-lined platter. Garnish, if desired. **Yield:** 8 servings.

Mustard Vinaigrette

QUICK!

½ cup vegetable oil
⅓ cup lemon juice
2 teaspoons Dijon mustard
3 cloves garlic, minced
½ teaspoon salt
½ teaspoon pepper

● **Combine** all ingredients in a jar; cover tightly, and shake vigorously. Chill. **Yield:** about 1 cup.

Heather Check
Oxford, Alabama

CAESAR RAVIOLI SALAD

1 (9-ounce) package refrigerated
   light cheese ravioli
2 cups cherry tomato halves
1 medium cucumber, thinly
   sliced
½ cup chopped purple onion
¼ cup sliced ripe olives
¼ cup freshly grated Parmesan
   cheese
½ teaspoon freshly ground pepper
¾ cup reduced-calorie Caesar
   dressing
4 cups shredded romaine lettuce

● **Cook** ravioli according to package directions; drain. Rinse with cold water; drain.
● **Combine** ravioli, tomato halves, and next 6 ingredients. Cover and chill. Serve over lettuce. **Yield:** 4 servings.

MEDITERRANEAN SALAD

For a new twist, use fusilli (spiral-shaped noodles) in place of spaghetti. We liked both versions a lot.

1 (8-ounce) package spaghetti
1 (6-ounce) jar marinated
   artichoke hearts, drained and
   coarsely chopped
1 (4-ounce) can sliced ripe olives,
   drained
1 cup frozen English peas, thawed
1 medium-size red bell pepper,
   chopped
1 small zucchini, chopped
½ small purple onion, thinly
   sliced
½ cup freshly grated Parmesan
   cheese
½ cup mayonnaise or salad
   dressing
½ cup Italian dressing
1 teaspoon dried parsley flakes
½ teaspoon dried dillweed
½ teaspoon coarsely ground
   pepper

● **Cook** spaghetti according to package directions; drain. Rinse with cold water, and drain.
● **Combine** artichokes and next 6 ingredients in a large bowl. Add spaghetti, tossing well.
● **Combine** mayonnaise and remaining 4 ingredients, stirring with wire whisk; add to spaghetti mixture, and stir well. Cover and chill. **Yield:** 8 servings.

Janice Rinks
Bluff City, Tennessee

PASTA-VEGGIE SALAD

1 (9-ounce) package refrigerated cheese-filled tortellini
3 ounces fettuccine, uncooked
2 cups fresh snow pea pods, trimmed
2 cups broccoli flowerets
1 pint cherry tomatoes, cut in half
2 cups sliced fresh mushrooms
1 (7.5-ounce) can pitted whole ripe olives, drained
2 tablespoons freshly grated Parmesan cheese
Herbed Pasta Salad Dressing
Garnish: freshly grated Parmesan cheese

• **Cook** tortellini and fettuccine separately according to package directions; drain and set aside.
• **Cook** snow peas in boiling water to cover 1 minute; remove and plunge peas immediately into cold water to stop the cooking process. Repeat procedure with broccoli.
• **Combine** snow peas, broccoli, cherry tomatoes, mushrooms, and olives in a large salad bowl; add pasta and 2 tablespoons Parmesan cheese, tossing gently to combine. Add Herbed Pasta Salad Dressing, and toss well. Cover and chill. Garnish, if desired. **Yield:** 8 to 10 servings.

Herbed Pasta Salad Dressing

½ cup chopped fresh chives
2 tablespoons chopped fresh parsley
2 tablespoons chopped fresh basil
1 tablespoon chopped fresh dill
2 cloves garlic, minced
1 teaspoon salt
½ teaspoon pepper
½ teaspoon sugar
½ teaspoon chopped fresh oregano
½ teaspoon Dijon mustard
⅓ cup red wine vinegar
⅔ cup olive oil

• **Combine** all ingredients in a jar; cover jar tightly, and shake vigorously. **Yield:** 1¼ cups.

Rachel Kilpatrick
Houston, Texas

PASTA-VEGETABLE SALAD

This easy make-ahead pasta salad can be assembled quickly; chill the mixture at least six hours to give the flavors a chance to blend.

6 ounces tricolor rotini pasta, uncooked (about 3 cups)
1 pound fresh broccoli, cut into flowerets
3 stalks celery, sliced
1 bunch radishes, sliced
1 (8-ounce) can sliced water chestnuts, drained
1 (2¼-ounce) can sliced ripe olives, drained
1 (0.6-ounce) envelope zesty Italian salad dressing mix
2 tablespoons chopped fresh oregano
½ cup crumbled feta cheese

• **Prepare** pasta according to package directions; drain. Rinse with cold water; drain.
• **Combine** pasta, broccoli, and next 4 ingredients in a bowl; set aside.
• **Prepare** dressing mix according to package directions; stir in oregano. Pour over pasta mixture, stirring to coat. Sprinkle with cheese. Cover and chill at least 6 hours. **Yield:** 8 to 10 servings.

Gayle Gardner
Owensboro, Kentucky

ARTICHOKE-PASTA SALAD

Orzo, rice-shaped pasta, is tossed with artichoke hearts, vinaigrette, and basil, and then topped with prosciutto, an Italian salt-cured ham. (If your deli doesn't carry prosciutto, ask for a good smoked ham, sliced paper thin.)

2 tablespoons white wine vinegar
2 tablespoons lemon juice
1 teaspoon Dijon mustard
⅓ cup olive oil
¼ cup chopped fresh parsley
2 tablespoons chopped fresh basil
1½ cups orzo, uncooked
1 (14-ounce) can artichoke hearts, drained and quartered
⅔ cup grated Parmesan cheese
Lettuce leaves
4 ounces prosciutto, cut into ½-inch strips
4 green onions, thinly sliced

• **Combine** first 3 ingredients in container of an electric blender or food processor; process until blended. With blender or processor running, add oil in a slow, steady stream; process until blended. Stir in parsley and basil. Set dressing aside.
• **Cook** orzo according to package directions; drain and rinse with cold water.
• **Combine** orzo, artichoke hearts, Parmesan cheese, and dressing; toss gently. Cover and chill.
• **Arrange** orzo mixture on a lettuce-lined platter; sprinkle with prosciutto and green onions. **Yield:** 6 servings.

Fran Baker
Rockledge, Florida

ORZO SALAD WITH SESAME DRESSING

1 pound orzo, uncooked
1 tablespoon sesame oil
4 carrots, cut into thin strips
2 cups raisins
1 cup sunflower kernels, toasted
Sesame Dressing
2 tablespoons chopped fresh
   parsley
2 tablespoons sliced green onions

• **Cook** orzo in boiling salted water to cover 8 minutes or until tender; drain. Rinse with cold water; drain. Combine orzo and oil, tossing gently.
• **Spoon** half of orzo into a large glass bowl; top with half each of carrot strips, raisins, and sunflower kernels. Repeat layers; drizzle 1 cup Sesame Dressing over top.
• **Combine** parsley and green onions; sprinkle evenly over salad. Serve with remaining Sesame Dressing. **Yield:** 10 servings.

Sesame Dressing

QUICK!

¾ cup corn oil
½ cup rice vinegar
¼ cup sesame oil
1 tablespoon salt
1 tablespoon sugar
2 tablespoons grated orange rind
1 teaspoon pepper
1 teaspoon minced fresh ginger
1 teaspoon soy sauce
½ teaspoon minced garlic
¼ teaspoon dried crushed red
   pepper

• **Place** all ingredients in container of an electric blender or food processor. Process until smooth, stopping once to scrape down sides. **Yield:** 1⅔ cups.

Sally Harris Whatley
Margate, Florida

PINE NUT, RICE, AND FETA SALAD

1 (7-ounce) package long-grain-
   and-wild rice mix
1 (4-ounce) package crumbled
   feta cheese
½ cup chopped green bell
   pepper
½ cup chopped yellow bell
   pepper
½ cup chopped onion
⅔ cup pine nuts, toasted
1 (2-ounce) jar diced pimiento,
   drained
⅓ cup olive oil
2 tablespoons tarragon wine
   vinegar
⅛ teaspoon pepper
Lettuce leaves (optional)

• **Cook** rice according to package directions; let cool.
• **Combine** cheese and next 5 ingredients in a large bowl; stir in rice.
• **Combine** oil, vinegar, and pepper, stirring well; pour over rice mixture. Toss gently. Cover and chill up to 24 hours. Serve on lettuce leaves, if desired. **Yield:** 6 to 8 servings.

Betty Joyce Mills
Birmingham, Alabama

SPINACH-RICE SALAD

1 cup long-grain rice, uncooked
½ cup Italian dressing
1 tablespoon soy sauce
½ teaspoon sugar
2 cups shredded fresh spinach
½ cup sliced celery
½ cup sliced green onions
6 slices bacon, cooked and
   crumbled

• **Cook** rice according to package directions; rinse and drain. Set aside.
• **Combine** dressing, soy sauce, and sugar in a large bowl. Stir in rice. Cover and chill 2 hours.
• **Stir** spinach and remaining 3 ingredients into rice mixture. Serve immediately. **Yield:** 6 to 8 servings.

Nancy Bremer
Fallston, Maryland

BOOT SCOOT TABBOULI (TABBOULEH SALAD)

Mint and parsley are essential ingredients in this Lebanese favorite. Serve it with a crisp bread such as lavosh to scoop up every delicious morsel.

2 cups boiling water
1 teaspoon salt
1 cup bulgur wheat
1 cup finely chopped fresh
   parsley
½ cup finely chopped green onion
   tops
2 tablespoons finely chopped
   fresh mint or 2 teaspoons
   dried mint
¼ cup olive oil
¼ cup fresh lemon juice
½ teaspoon salt
¼ teaspoon pepper
1 cup peeled, finely chopped
   tomato

• **Combine** boiling water and 1 teaspoon salt; pour over bulgur. Let stand 30 minutes.
• **Drain** bulgur; add chopped parsley and next 6 ingredients, stirring well. Gently fold in chopped tomato; cover and chill salad at least 4 hours. **Yield:** 4¾ cups.

Diane Pfeifer
Stand By Your Pan
Atlanta, Georgia

BASIL AND TOMATO COUSCOUS SALAD

QUICK!

1¼ cups water
1¼ cups couscous, uncooked
2 cups chopped tomato
1 cup finely chopped fresh
   basil
⅓ cup finely chopped purple
   onion
3 slices bacon, cooked and
   crumbled
¼ cup apple cider vinegar
2 tablespoons olive oil
¼ teaspoon salt
¼ teaspoon pepper

- **Bring** water to a boil in a saucepan; stir in couscous. Cover, remove from heat, and let stand 5 minutes. Uncover and fluff with a fork; cool.
- **Combine** couscous, tomato, and next 3 ingredients; set aside.
- **Combine** vinegar and remaining 3 ingredients in a jar; cover tightly, and shake vigorously. Drizzle over salad, and toss gently.
- **Cover** and chill. Toss before serving. **Yield:** 6 servings.

Constance Ober
Port Haywood, Virginia

♥ Per serving: Calories 216
Fat 6g   Cholesterol 2mg
Sodium 149mg

TABBOULEH COUSCOUS

QUICK!

1   (14½-ounce) can chicken
     broth
¼   cup fresh lemon juice
1½ cups couscous, uncooked
10 plum tomatoes, seeded and
     chopped
1   cup diced green onions
1   cup minced fresh flat-leaf
     parsley
1   cup minced fresh mint
½   cup frozen whole kernel corn,
     thawed
2   cloves garlic, pressed
1   tablespoon grated lemon rind
⅓   cup olive oil
¼   cup fresh lemon juice
1   teaspoon salt
Garnish: fresh flat-leaf parsley
     sprigs

- **Bring** chicken broth and ¼ cup lemon juice to a boil in a large saucepan; stir in couscous. Cover, remove from heat, and let stand 5 minutes. Uncover and fluff with a fork; cool.
- **Stir** in chopped tomato and next 9 ingredients; garnish, if desired. **Yield:** 4 servings.

Jolie Peacock
Birmingham, Alabama

COUSCOUS SALAD WITH DRIED TOMATO VINAIGRETTE

Toasted spices and dried tomatoes give this salad added flavor. You can substitute rice or orzo for the couscous or add chopped cooked chicken or shrimp to make it a main dish.

1   red bell pepper
½   medium-size purple onion
1   medium cucumber
¼   cup olive oil
3   tablespoons red wine vinegar
¼   teaspoon salt
⅛   teaspoon ground red pepper
1   tablespoon mustard seeds
1   tablespoon cumin seeds
⅓   cup minced dried tomato
¼   cup minced fresh cilantro
1½ cups water
½   teaspoon salt
½   teaspoon pepper
1   clove garlic, pressed
1   cup couscous, uncooked

- **Place** bell pepper on an aluminum foil-lined baking sheet.
- **Broil** 5½ inches from heat (with electric oven door partially opened) about 5 minutes on each side or until pepper looks blistered.
- **Place** pepper in a heavy-duty, zip-top plastic bag; seal and let stand 10 minutes to loosen skin. Peel pepper; remove and discard seeds. Dice pepper and onion; peel, seed, and dice cucumber. Set vegetables aside.
- **Whisk** oil and next 3 ingredients in a small bowl.
- **Cook** mustard and cumin seeds in a small skillet over medium heat, stirring constantly, 5 minutes or until toasted; immediately stir into oil mixture. Add tomato and cilantro, stirring well.
- **Bring** water and next 3 ingredients to a boil in a saucepan; stir in couscous. Cover, remove from heat, and let stand 5 minutes or until liquid is absorbed. Transfer to a serving bowl; stir in diced vegetables. Drizzle with dressing; toss gently. **Yield:** 6 servings.

♥ Per serving: Calories 231
Fat 10.2g   Cholesterol 0mg
Sodium 364mg

PITA BREAD SALAD

4   (6-inch) pita bread rounds
1   bunch fresh parsley, finely
     chopped
4   medium tomatoes, finely
     chopped
1   large green bell pepper, finely
     chopped
1   bunch green onions, finely
     chopped
1   medium cucumber, peeled,
     seeded, and finely chopped
3   cloves garlic, minced
⅓   cup fresh lemon juice (about
     2 large lemons)
⅓   cup olive oil
2   tablespoons finely chopped fresh
     mint
¼   teaspoon salt
¼   teaspoon pepper
2   cups shredded romaine lettuce
4   ounces feta cheese, crumbled

- **Cut** each pita round into 6 wedges, and separate each wedge into 2 triangles. Place triangles in a single layer on a baking sheet.
- **Bake** at 400° for 10 minutes or until crisp and brown. Cool completely; place pita triangles in a zip-top plastic bag, and set aside.
- **Combine** chopped parsley and next 10 ingredients; toss gently. Cover and chill 1 hour.
- **Toss** parsley mixture with shredded lettuce; sprinkle with feta cheese. Serve with toasted pita triangles. **Yield:** 6 to 8 servings.

Shirley Awood Glaab
Hattiesburg, Mississippi

MEXICAN CORNBREAD SALAD

1 (6-ounce) package Mexican cornbread mix
1 (4.5-ounce) can chopped green chiles, undrained
Dash of ground sage
1 (1-ounce) package Ranch-style salad dressing mix
1 (8-ounce) carton reduced-fat sour cream
1 cup reduced-fat mayonnaise
2 (16-ounce) cans pinto beans, drained
1 cup chopped green bell pepper
2 (15¼-ounce) cans whole kernel corn, drained
3 large tomatoes, chopped
10 slices bacon, cooked and crumbled
1 (8-ounce) package shredded reduced-fat Cheddar cheese
1 cup sliced green onions
Lettuce leaves
Tomato wedges (optional)

• **Prepare** cornbread mix according to package directions, adding green chiles and sage; cool.
• **Combine** salad dressing mix, sour cream, and mayonnaise; set aside.
• **Crumble** half of cornbread into a bowl. Top with half each of beans, sour cream mixture, green pepper, and next 5 ingredients. Repeat layers.
• **Cover** and chill 2 hours. Serve in individual lettuce-lined salad bowls, and top with tomato wedges, if desired. **Yield:** 8 servings.

Anne Ringer
Warner Robins, Georgia

SALAD ANTIPASTO

½ (8-ounce) package mozzarella cheese
18 slices salami
12 cherry tomatoes, halved
3 dozen whole ripe olives
12 pickled banana peppers
1 small purple onion, thinly sliced and separated into rings
½ cup olive oil
¼ cup lemon juice
¼ cup white wine vinegar
4 cloves garlic, minced
2 tablespoons dried oregano
½ teaspoon salt
¼ teaspoon pepper
½ cup crumbled feta cheese
Fresh spinach leaves

• **Cut** mozzarella cheese into 18 thin sticks. Wrap each with a salami slice; secure with a wooden pick. Place in a shallow container. Add tomatoes and next 3 ingredients.
• **Whisk** together oil and next 6 ingredients. Drizzle over salad ingredients. Cover and chill at least 8 hours, turning ingredients occasionally. Drain.
• **Arrange** salad ingredients and feta on a spinach-lined serving plate. Serve with breadsticks. **Yield:** 6 servings.

GRILLED SIRLOIN SALAD

½ to 1 jalapeño pepper, unseeded
⅓ cup chopped onion
1 green onion, chopped
2 cloves garlic
1 tablespoon brown sugar
1 teaspoon ground ginger
1 teaspoon lime rind
¼ cup lime juice
¼ cup reduced-sodium soy sauce
1 (1¼-pound) boneless top sirloin steak, trimmed
½ cup peanut oil
1 teaspoon sea or table salt
3 to 4 cups mixed salad greens
½ cup fresh mint leaves, chopped
2 tablespoons coarsely chopped fresh cilantro
6 yellow pear tomatoes, halved
Garnishes: green onion fans, lime slices

• **Place** first 9 ingredients in container of an electric blender. Process until smooth, stopping once to scrape down sides. Set jalapeño pepper mixture in blender aside.
• **Place** steak in a shallow container; pour ¼ cup jalapeño pepper mixture over steak, reserving remaining pepper mixture in blender. Cover steak, and chill 3 hours.
• **Turn** blender on high; gradually add oil to remaining pepper mixture in a slow, steady stream. Cover pepper dressing, and chill.
• **Remove** steak from marinade, discarding marinade. Sprinkle steak evenly with salt. Cook steak, covered with grill lid, over medium-hot coals (350° to 400°) 8 to 10 minutes on each side. Remove steak from grill, and let stand 5 minutes.
• **Slice** steak diagonally across grain into ¼-inch-thick slices.
• **Combine** salad greens and next 3 ingredients; arrange evenly on individual plates. Place 5 steak slices on each plate. (Reserve remaining steak slices for another use.)
• **Serve** salad with jalapeño pepper dressing, and garnish, if desired. **Yield:** 2 servings.

STIR-FRY BEEF SALAD

1 pound boneless round steak
2 cloves garlic, minced
3 tablespoons minced fresh ginger, divided
2 tablespoons reduced-sodium soy sauce, divided
3 cloves garlic, minced
3 tablespoons white vinegar
2 tablespoons creamy peanut butter
1 tablespoon molasses
½ teaspoon dark sesame oil
1 teaspoon canola oil
½ cup fresh cilantro leaves
8 cups mixed salad greens
1 red bell pepper, cut into strips
½ cup fresh bean sprouts
4 cherry tomatoes, quartered

- **Trim** excess fat from steak; cut steak into thin strips.
- **Combine** 2 cloves garlic, 1 tablespoon ginger, and 1 tablespoon soy sauce in a heavy-duty, zip-top plastic bag; add steak. Seal and chill at least 1 hour, turning steak occasionally.
- **Combine** remaining 2 tablespoons ginger, 1 tablespoon soy sauce, 3 cloves garlic, and next 4 ingredients in container of an electric blender; process until smooth, stopping once to scrape down sides. Set aside.
- **Remove** steak from marinade, discarding marinade.
- **Pour** canola oil into a large nonstick skillet; place over medium-high heat until hot. Add steak, and stir-fry 1 to 2 minutes or until browned.
- **Combine** cilantro and salad greens; place evenly on individual serving plates. Top evenly with steak, bell pepper strips, bean sprouts, and tomatoes, and drizzle with ginger mixture. **Yield:** 4 servings.

♥ Per serving: Calories 267
Fat 10.8g Cholesterol 65mg
Sodium 361mg

"PIG IN THE GARDEN" SALAD

9   cups mixed salad greens
¾   cup sliced celery
¾   cup chopped green bell pepper
1   cup (4 ounces) shredded Monterey Jack cheese
1   cup (4 ounces) shredded Cheddar cheese
3   cups warm shredded or chopped, grilled or smoked pork
6   small tomatoes, cut into wedges
Cheesy Barbecue Salad Dressing

- **Combine** first 3 ingredients in a large bowl; toss and arrange evenly on plates.
- **Combine** cheeses; sprinkle over mixed greens. Top with pork; arrange tomato wedges on plates. Serve with Cheesy Barbecue Salad Dressing. **Yield:** 6 servings.

Cheesy Barbecue Salad Dressing

◀QUICK!▶

1   cup John Wills's Barbecue Sauce
1   (9-ounce) can Cheddar cheese dip
⅓   cup sour cream
½   cup buttermilk
½   cup mayonnaise or salad dressing
1   tablespoon sugar

- **Combine** all ingredients, stirring well with a wire whisk; cover and chill. **Yield:** 3 cups.

John Wills's Barbecue Sauce

1   (8-ounce) can tomato sauce
½   cup spicy honey mustard
1   cup ketchup
1   cup red wine vinegar
½   cup Worcestershire sauce
¼   cup butter or margarine
2   tablespoons hot sauce
1   tablespoon lemon juice
2   tablespoons brown sugar
1   tablespoon paprika
1   tablespoon seasoned salt
1½ teaspoons garlic powder
⅛   teaspoon chili powder
⅛   teaspoon ground red pepper
⅛   teaspoon black pepper

- **Combine** all ingredients in a Dutch oven. Bring to a boil; reduce heat, and simmer, uncovered, 30 minutes, stirring occasionally. **Yield:** 1 quart.

John Wills
John Wills Bar-B-Que Bar and Grill
Memphis, Tennessee

MEXICAN CHICKEN TORTILLA SALADS

Fresh cilantro and a wonderful creamy sauce brushed on the chicken give the typical taco salad a lift.

¼   cup mayonnaise, divided
¾   cup (3 ounces) shredded Monterey Jack cheese
3   tablespoons sour cream
2   tablespoons chopped fresh cilantro or parsley
1   tablespoon finely chopped pickled jalapeño peppers
1   clove garlic, minced
6   skinned and boned chicken breast halves
1   (10-ounce) bag tortilla chips
1   head leaf lettuce, shredded
3   plum tomatoes, sliced
Garnishes: sour cream, fresh cilantro sprigs

- **Combine** 3 tablespoons mayonnaise, cheese, and next 4 ingredients. Set aside.
- **Place** chicken between two sheets of heavy-duty plastic wrap, and flatten to ¼-inch thickness, using a meat mallet or rolling pin.
- **Brush** both sides of chicken with remaining 1 tablespoon mayonnaise; place on a rack in broiler pan.
- **Broil** 5½ inches from heat (with electric oven door partially opened) 5 minutes on each side.
- **Spread** cheese mixture evenly on top of chicken.
- **Broil** 5 additional minutes or until mixture is browned; keep warm.
- **Layer** chips, lettuce, and tomato on individual plates; top with chicken. Garnish, if desired. **Yield:** 6 servings.

LaJuan Coward
Jasper, Texas

♥ Reduce fat and calories by using reduced-fat mayonnaise and reduced-fat sour cream.

Summery Chicken Salad;
Honey Angel Biscuit, page 63

SUMMERY CHICKEN SALAD
(pictured at left)

A splash of dry white wine plus a dash of curry powder infuse this fruit-studded chicken salad with unexpected flavor.

6 cups chopped cooked chicken
1¼ cups sliced celery
1 (8-ounce) can pineapple tidbits, drained
1¼ cups reduced-fat mayonnaise or salad dressing
2½ tablespoons dry white wine
¾ teaspoon salt
¾ teaspoon curry powder
2 Red Delicious apples, thinly sliced
1 cantaloupe, thinly sliced
½ pound green grapes
1 pint strawberries
1 cup blackberries
Lettuce leaves
¼ cup chopped walnuts, toasted
Garnish: celery leaves

• **Combine** first 3 ingredients in a large bowl; set aside.
• **Combine** mayonnaise and next 3 ingredients. Add to chicken mixture, tossing to coat. Cover and chill 1 to 2 hours.
• **Arrange** apples and next 4 ingredients on a lettuce-lined platter; top with chicken mixture. Sprinkle with toasted walnuts. Garnish, if desired. **Yield:** 6 servings.

Mrs. Wallace Cupit
Seminole, Florida

ROYAL CURRIED CHICKEN SALAD

½ cup sliced almonds, toasted
2 cups chopped cooked chicken
¼ cup chopped water chestnuts
½ pound seedless green grapes, halved
1 (8-ounce) can pineapple chunks, drained
½ cup chopped celery
¾ cup mayonnaise
1 teaspoon curry powder
2 teaspoons lemon juice
2 teaspoons soy sauce
2 avocados

• **Combine** first 6 ingredients; set aside.
• **Combine** mayonnaise, curry powder, lemon juice, and soy sauce in a bowl; spoon mixture over chicken mixture, and toss gently to coat. Cover and chill at least 4 hours.
• **Peel** and chop avocados; sprinkle over salad, and serve immediately. **Yield:** 6 servings.

Cindy Sullivan
Tallahassee, Florida

GRILLED CHICKEN AND FRUIT SALAD

Flavor contrasts abound in this grilled chicken salad. The sweetness of orange marmalade plays off nicely against the bold characteristics of soy sauce, raspberry vinegar, and jalapeño pepper.

¾ cup orange marmalade
3 tablespoons soy sauce
3 tablespoons lemon juice
3 teaspoons chopped fresh ginger
4 skinned and boned chicken breast halves
1 pineapple
2 medium jícamas
Vegetable cooking spray
2 cups fresh strawberry halves
1 cup fresh raspberries
Orange-Raspberry Vinaigrette
Lettuce leaves

• **Combine** first 4 ingredients; reserve ¼ cup marmalade mixture, and chill. Pour remaining mixture into a heavy-duty, zip-top plastic bag; add chicken. Seal bag, and marinate in refrigerator 8 hours, turning bag occasionally.
• **Peel**, core, and cut pineapple into spears; peel jícamas, and cut into ½-inch-thick slices. Combine reserved ¼ cup marmalade mixture, pineapple, and jícama, tossing to coat. Set aside.
• **Coat** a grill basket with cooking spray; place on grill over hot coals (400° to 500°). Remove chicken from marinade, discarding marinade.
• **Add** chicken and pineapple mixture to basket; cook, covered with grill lid, 3 minutes on each side or until chicken is done. Remove from grill, and cool.
• **Cut** chicken and jícama into thin strips; cut pineapple into bite-size pieces.
• **Combine** chicken, jícama, pineapple, strawberries, and raspberries; drizzle with Orange-Raspberry Vinaigrette, and toss gently. Serve in a lettuce-lined bowl. **Yield:** 4 servings.

Orange-Raspberry Vinaigrette

QUICK!

Always wear rubber gloves when seeding and chopping a member of the pepper family. Pepper oils contain a fiery heat that can irritate even a small cut; the oils are difficult to wash away with soap and water.

½ cup orange marmalade
¼ cup raspberry vinegar
1 medium jalapeño pepper, seeded and minced
2 tablespoons finely chopped fresh cilantro
2 tablespoons olive oil

• **Whisk** together all ingredients in a bowl. **Yield:** 1 cup.

ORIENTAL CHICKEN SALAD

3 tablespoons soy sauce
2 teaspoons grated fresh
  ginger
2 skinned and boned chicken
  breast halves
5 cups coarsely chopped mixed
  salad greens
1 cup fresh bean sprouts
1 cup fresh snow pea pods,
  trimmed
½ green bell pepper, thinly
  sliced
½ red bell pepper, thinly sliced
1 cucumber, thinly sliced
1 cup sliced green onions
1 (3-ounce) package ramen
  noodles
Oriental Salad Dressing
2 teaspoons sesame seeds,
  toasted
Spicy Peanut Sauce

• **Combine** soy sauce and ginger in a shallow dish or heavy-duty, zip-top plastic bag; add chicken. Cover or seal, and marinate in refrigerator up to 4 hours.
• **Remove** chicken from marinade, discarding marinade. Place chicken on a rack in broiler pan.
• **Broil** 4 inches from heat (with electric oven door partially opened) 7 minutes on each side or until tender. Cool slightly, and slice.
• **Combine** salad greens and next 6 ingredients. Break uncooked noodles into small pieces, and sprinkle on top; reserve seasoning packet for another use. Add ½ cup Oriental Salad Dressing, tossing to coat.
• **Arrange** chicken on top; pour remaining Oriental Salad Dressing over chicken, and sprinkle with sesame seeds. Serve with Spicy Peanut Sauce. **Yield:** 4 servings.

Oriental Salad Dressing

QUICK!

⅓ cup pineapple juice
¼ cup rice vinegar
1 tablespoon reduced-sodium soy
  sauce
2 teaspoons brown sugar
1½ teaspoons sesame oil
¼ teaspoon pepper

• **Combine** all ingredients in a small jar; cover jar tightly, and shake vigorously. **Yield:** ⅔ cup.

Spicy Peanut Sauce

QUICK!

½ cup chunky peanut butter
⅓ cup coconut milk
2 tablespoons reduced-sodium soy
  sauce
1 tablespoon grated fresh ginger
1 tablespoon sesame oil
¼ teaspoon dried crushed red
  pepper
¼ cup chicken broth

• **Combine** all ingredients in a bowl, stirring well with a wire whisk. **Yield:** 1⅓ cups.

Fran Pointer
Kansas City, Missouri

THAI CHICKEN SALAD

4 skinned and boned chicken
  breast halves
Peanut-Ginger Dressing
3 ounces vermicelli, uncooked
4 cups torn romaine lettuce
2 cups thinly sliced Chinese
  cabbage
2 medium carrots, coarsely
  shredded
1 medium cucumber, thinly
  sliced
1 large red bell pepper, cut into
  strips
¼ cup chopped fresh cilantro
Chopped peanuts (optional)
Sliced cucumber (optional)

• **Cook** chicken, without grill lid, over medium coals (300° to 350°) 15 to 20 minutes, turning once. Cut into thin strips. Combine chicken and 3 tablespoons Peanut-Ginger Dressing, tossing to coat; cover and chill 8 hours.
• **Cook** vermicelli according to package directions; drain.
• **Combine** vermicelli and 3 tablespoons Peanut-Ginger Dressing, tossing to coat. Cover and chill 8 hours.
• **Combine** romaine and next 5 ingredients, tossing well; arrange on a serving

platter. Top with vermicelli and chicken; sprinkle salad with peanuts, if desired. Arrange cucumber slices around vermicelli, if desired. Serve with remaining dressing. **Yield:** 6 servings.

Peanut-Ginger Dressing

QUICK!

½ cup rice wine vinegar
2 cloves garlic
⅓ cup creamy peanut butter
¼ cup lime juice
¼ cup chopped fresh cilantro
2 tablespoons apple cider
  vinegar
1 tablespoon honey
1 tablespoon molasses
1 tablespoon hot sauce
2 teaspoons grated fresh
  ginger
2 teaspoons soy sauce

• **Combine** all ingredients in container of an electric blender; process until smooth, stopping once to scrape down sides. **Yield:** 1½ cups.

Cindie Hackney
Longview, Texas

FRUIT AND SPICE
TURKEY SALAD

1 cup long-grain basmati brown
  rice, uncooked
1½ cups chopped cooked turkey
  breast
2 green onions, sliced
1 small Red Delicious apple,
  chopped
1 small Granny Smith apple,
  chopped
½ cup seedless green grape halves
¼ cup pecan halves, toasted
¼ cup raisins
¼ cup white wine vinegar
1½ teaspoons sugar
¼ teaspoon salt
¼ teaspoon ground cinnamon
¼ cup olive oil
Red leaf lettuce

• **Cook** brown rice according to package directions. Rinse with cold water, and drain well.

- **Combine** brown rice, turkey, and next 6 ingredients in a large bowl; set aside.
- **Combine** vinegar and next 3 ingredients. Add oil, stirring with a wire whisk. Pour over rice mixture; toss gently. Cover and chill at least 2 hours. Serve on lettuce. **Yield:** 4 to 6 servings.

SMOKED TURKEY SALAD

1 (10-ounce) package fresh
    spinach
1 pound smoked turkey, chopped
1 red bell pepper, cut into strips
4 green onions, diagonally sliced
½ cup walnut halves
½ cup vegetable oil
¼ cup raspberry or red wine
    vinegar
1 teaspoon seasoned salt
1 teaspoon dried Italian seasoning
¼ teaspoon freshly ground pepper

- **Remove** stems from spinach; wash leaves thoroughly, and pat dry. Set spinach aside.
- **Combine** turkey and next 3 ingredients in a bowl. Combine oil and remaining 4 ingredients in a jar; cover tightly, and shake vigorously. Pour over turkey mixture; toss to coat. Cover and chill.
- **Place** spinach on individual salad plates; top with turkey mixture. **Yield:** 4 servings.

Peggy Fowler Revels
Woodruff, South Carolina

ORIENTAL SALMON AND WILD RICE SALAD

1 (8-ounce) fillet salmon
⅓ cup rice wine vinegar
¼ cup orange marmalade
2 tablespoons teriyaki sauce
1 tablespoon grated fresh ginger
2 teaspoons sesame oil
1 (6-ounce) package wild rice,
    cooked without salt
¾ cup fresh snow pea pods
½ cup sliced green onions
½ cup finely chopped red bell
    pepper
Bibb lettuce leaves

- **Place** salmon in an 8-inch square dish; set aside.
- **Combine** vinegar and next 4 ingredients in a jar; cover tightly, and shake vigorously. Pour half of marinade over salmon, turning to coat well. Set remaining marinade aside.
- **Cover** salmon, and chill 1 hour.
- **Drain** salmon, discarding marinade; place salmon on a rack in broiler pan.
- **Broil** 5½ inches from heat (with electric oven door partially opened) 3 to 5 minutes on each side or until fish flakes easily when tested with a fork.
- **Separate** salmon into chunks. Cool.
- **Combine** salmon, rice, and next 3 ingredients in a large bowl; drizzle with reserved marinade, tossing gently.
- **Cover** and chill at least 3 hours. Serve on lettuce leaves. **Yield:** 5 servings.

♥ Per serving: Calories 323
Fat 6.5g   Cholesterol 31mg
Sodium 389mg

BROILED SALMON SALAD

2 (6-ounce) salmon steaks
1 cup Lemon and Herb Dressing,
    divided
1 medium zucchini
1 medium-size yellow squash
1 carrot, scraped
½ red bell pepper
1 tablespoon chopped fresh
    cilantro or parsley
2 cups torn fresh spinach
2 cups torn Bibb lettuce
1 tomato, cut into wedges
1 small avocado, sliced
Garnishes: lemon twists, fresh
    parsley sprigs

- **Place** salmon steaks in a shallow dish; pour ¼ cup dressing over steaks. Cover and chill 1 hour, turning once.
- **Cut** zucchini and next 3 ingredients into thin strips; combine with cilantro and ¼ cup dressing, tossing gently.
- **Remove** steaks from marinade, reserving marinade. Bring marinade to a boil, and set aside.
- **Place** steaks on a lightly greased rack of broiler pan. Broil 4 inches from heat

(with electric oven door partially opened) 5 to 6 minutes; turn and brush with marinade. Broil 5 to 6 additional minutes or until fish flakes easily when tested with a fork. Cool slightly.
- **Arrange** salad greens and marinated vegetables on serving plates. Top with salmon steaks, tomato wedges, and avocado slices. Garnish, if desired, and serve with remaining dressing. **Yield:** 2 servings.

Lemon and Herb Dressing

¾ cup lemon juice
½ cup vegetable oil
1 teaspoon chopped fresh
    parsley
¼ teaspoon minced garlic
1½ tablespoons sugar
¾ teaspoon paprika
¾ teaspoon dried basil
½ teaspoon dried tarragon
½ teaspoon seasoned salt
⅛ teaspoon pepper

- **Combine** all ingredients in a jar; cover tightly, and shake mixture vigorously. **Yield:** 1⅓ cups.

Joyce M. Maurer
Christmas, Florida

Spinach Salad With Oysters and Red Wine Vinaigrette

SPINACH SALAD WITH OYSTERS AND RED WINE VINAIGRETTE
(pictured at left)

Wolf Hanau, of North Miami, Florida, won the 1991 Buck Briscoe Memorial Award at the National Oyster Cook-Off in Leonardtown, Maryland, with a similar version of this recipe.

1 (10-ounce) package fresh spinach
2 (12-ounce) containers fresh oysters, drained
2 egg whites, lightly beaten
1½ cups Italian-seasoned breadcrumbs
1½ cups vegetable oil
4 large fresh mushrooms, sliced
Red Wine Vinaigrette
1 small purple onion, thinly sliced
4 slices bacon, cooked and crumbled

• **Remove** stems from spinach; wash leaves thoroughly, and pat dry. Set aside.
• **Dip** oysters in egg white; coat with breadcrumbs. Set aside.
• **Pour** oil into a large heavy skillet; heat to 350°. Fry oysters about 1 minute on each side or until golden; drain on paper towels.
• **Place** spinach on individual plates. Arrange mushrooms evenly over spinach, and drizzle with half of Red Wine Vinaigrette. Top evenly with oysters, onion slices, and bacon. Serve immediately with remaining Red Wine Vinaigrette. **Yield:** 6 servings.

Red Wine Vinaigrette
QUICK!

¾ cup olive oil
3 tablespoons dry red wine
3 tablespoons red wine vinegar
1 tablespoon Dijon mustard
½ teaspoon sugar
½ teaspoon Worcestershire sauce
⅛ teaspoon pepper

• **Combine** all ingredients in container of an electric blender or food processor; process until blended. **Yield:** 1 cup.

GREEK SALAD

Jane adapted this salad from one of her favorite Florida books, The Gasparilla Cookbook. *If you dig to the bottom of the mound of vegetables, you'll discover creamy potato salad.*

2 cups water
½ pound unpeeled medium-size fresh shrimp
1 large head leaf lettuce
Potato Salad
1 bunch watercress, chopped
3 tomatoes, cut into wedges
1 to 2 cucumbers, peeled and cut into spears
½ cup crumbled feta cheese
2 avocados, cut into wedges
1 green bell pepper, cut into rings
1 red bell pepper, cut into rings
1 (16-ounce) jar sliced beets, drained
12 pitted ripe olives
8 radishes
8 green onions
6 to 8 Greek pickled peppers
¾ cup olive oil
¼ cup red wine vinegar
2 teaspoons dry mustard
1 teaspoon dried oregano

• **Bring** water to a boil; add shrimp, and cook 3 to 5 minutes or until shrimp turn pink. Drain well, and rinse with cold water. Chill. Peel shrimp, and devein, if desired. Set aside.
• **Remove** large outer leaves from lettuce, and line a large platter. Shred remaining lettuce, and arrange on lettuce-lined platter.
• **Spoon** Potato Salad in center of shredded lettuce; sprinkle with watercress. Arrange tomato and cucumber alternately around edge. Sprinkle with cheese. Top with shrimp, avocado, and next 7 ingredients.
• **Combine** olive oil and remaining 3 ingredients in a jar; cover tightly, and shake vigorously. Drizzle dressing over salad, and serve immediately. **Yield:** 20 servings.

Note: Increase shrimp to 2 pounds for 8 main-dish servings.

Potato Salad

2 pounds medium-size round red potatoes
1 cup finely chopped purple onion
3 tablespoons red wine vinegar
¾ to 1 cup mayonnaise
2 teaspoons salt

• **Cook** potatoes in boiling water to cover 25 to 30 minutes or until tender; drain. Let cool to touch; peel and cut into ¾-inch cubes.
• **Combine** onion and vinegar; let stand 10 minutes. Stir in mayonnaise and salt; pour over potatoes, tossing gently. Cover and chill. **Yield:** about 6 cups.

Jim and Jane Bowyer
Maitland, Florida

ALOHA SHRIMP SALAD

6 cups water
2 pounds unpeeled medium-size fresh shrimp
1 cup finely chopped celery
1 (20-ounce) can unsweetened pineapple chunks, drained
⅓ cup raisins
½ cup reduced-calorie mayonnaise
2 teaspoons curry powder
Leaf lettuce or pita bread rounds

• **Bring** water to a boil; add shrimp, and cook 3 to 5 minutes or until shrimp turn pink. Drain; rinse with cold water. Peel shrimp, and devein, if desired.
• **Combine** shrimp, celery, and next 4 ingredients. Cover and chill at least 1 hour before serving. Serve on lettuce or in pita bread. **Yield:** 3 to 4 servings.

SHRIMP AND COUSCOUS SALAD

4¼ cups water
1 lemon, sliced
1¼ pounds unpeeled large fresh
 shrimp
½ cup couscous, uncooked
½ red bell pepper, chopped
1 (14-ounce) can artichoke hearts,
 drained and coarsely
 chopped
¼ cup reduced-fat mayonnaise
⅓ cup fresh lemon juice
3 tablespoons chopped fresh dill
¼ teaspoon salt
½ teaspoon pepper

• **Combine** water and lemon slices in a Dutch oven; bring to a boil. Add shrimp; cook 3 to 5 minutes or until shrimp turn pink. Drain well, discarding lemon; rinse shrimp with cold water. Peel shrimp, and devein, if desired. Cut shrimp in half lengthwise. Cover and chill.
• **Cook** couscous according to package directions; place in a large bowl to cool. Stir with a fork; add shrimp, bell pepper, and artichoke hearts.
• **Combine** mayonnaise and remaining 4 ingredients, stirring well. Pour dressing over shrimp mixture, tossing to coat. Cover and chill at least 2 hours. **Yield:** 4 servings.

Janil K. Miller
Beaufort, North Carolina

❤ Per serving: Calories 234
Fat 6.2g Cholesterol 113mg
Sodium 367mg

ASIAN SALAD DRESSING

QUICK!

1 cup vegetable oil
⅓ cup rice wine vinegar
2 tablespoons soy sauce
2 tablespoons dark sesame oil
2 teaspoons dry mustard
4 teaspoons sugar
2 teaspoons grated fresh ginger

• **Combine** all ingredients in a jar; cover tightly, and shake vigorously. Chill. **Yield:** about 1½ cups.

CURRY SALAD DRESSING

QUICK!

1 cup olive oil
¼ cup lemon juice
1 tablespoon white wine vinegar
1 tablespoon mango chutney
1 teaspoon Dijon mustard
½ teaspoon curry powder
¼ teaspoon salt
¼ teaspoon pepper

• **Combine** all ingredients in container of an electric blender; process until smooth, stopping once to scrape down sides. Chill. **Yield:** 1¾ cups.

Carol Scheder
Roswell, Georgia

GREEN ONION DRESSING
(pictured on page 375)

QUICK!

4 green onions, cut into 1-inch
 pieces
1 cup vegetable oil
½ cup red wine vinegar
2 tablespoons sugar
¾ teaspoon Worcestershire
 sauce
½ teaspoon dry mustard

• **Combine** all ingredients in container of an electric blender or food processor; pulse 3 times or until green onions are chopped. Chill. **Yield:** 1¾ cups.

Kim Uding
Sainte Genevieve, Missouri

LEMON-HONEY VINAIGRETTE

QUICK!

1 cup white wine vinegar
¾ cup vegetable oil
¼ cup honey
1 tablespoon grated lemon rind
3 tablespoons fresh lemon juice
1 teaspoon salt
2 cloves garlic, minced

• **Combine** all ingredients in a jar; cover tightly, and shake vigorously. Chill. **Yield:** 2 cups.

PAPAYA SEED DRESSING

When preparing fresh papayas, don't throw away seeds. Their peppery flavor adds mysterious pungency to this dressing.

1 tablespoon cornstarch
1 (7.1-ounce) can papaya nectar
½ cup sugar
½ teaspoon salt
½ teaspoon dry mustard
½ cup white wine vinegar
2 tablespoons chopped onion
3 tablespoons fresh papaya seeds

• **Combine** cornstarch and nectar in a saucepan; bring to a boil over medium heat, stirring constantly. Boil 1 minute, stirring constantly; cool.
• **Combine** sugar and remaining 5 ingredients in container of an electric blender; process until seeds resemble coarsely ground pepper. Stir into nectar mixture; cover and chill at least 2 hours. Serve over mixed fruit. **Yield:** 2 cups.

❤ Per tablespoon: Calories 18
Fat 0g Cholesterol 0mg
Sodium 37mg

VANILLA VINAIGRETTE

QUICK!

¼ cup sugar
2 tablespoons white wine vinegar
2 teaspoons grated onion
½ teaspoon dry mustard
¼ teaspoon salt
¼ vanilla bean or 2 teaspoons
 vanilla extract
½ cup vegetable oil

• **Combine** first 6 ingredients in container of an electric blender; process mixture until smooth. With blender on high, add oil in a slow, steady stream. Serve with fresh fruit or salad greens. **Yield:** ⅔ cup.

Carol Lundy
New Tazewell, Tennessee

At right: *Grilled Chili Con Queso Sandwiches (page 326)*

SANDWICHES AND SNACKS

SANDWICHES AND SNACKS

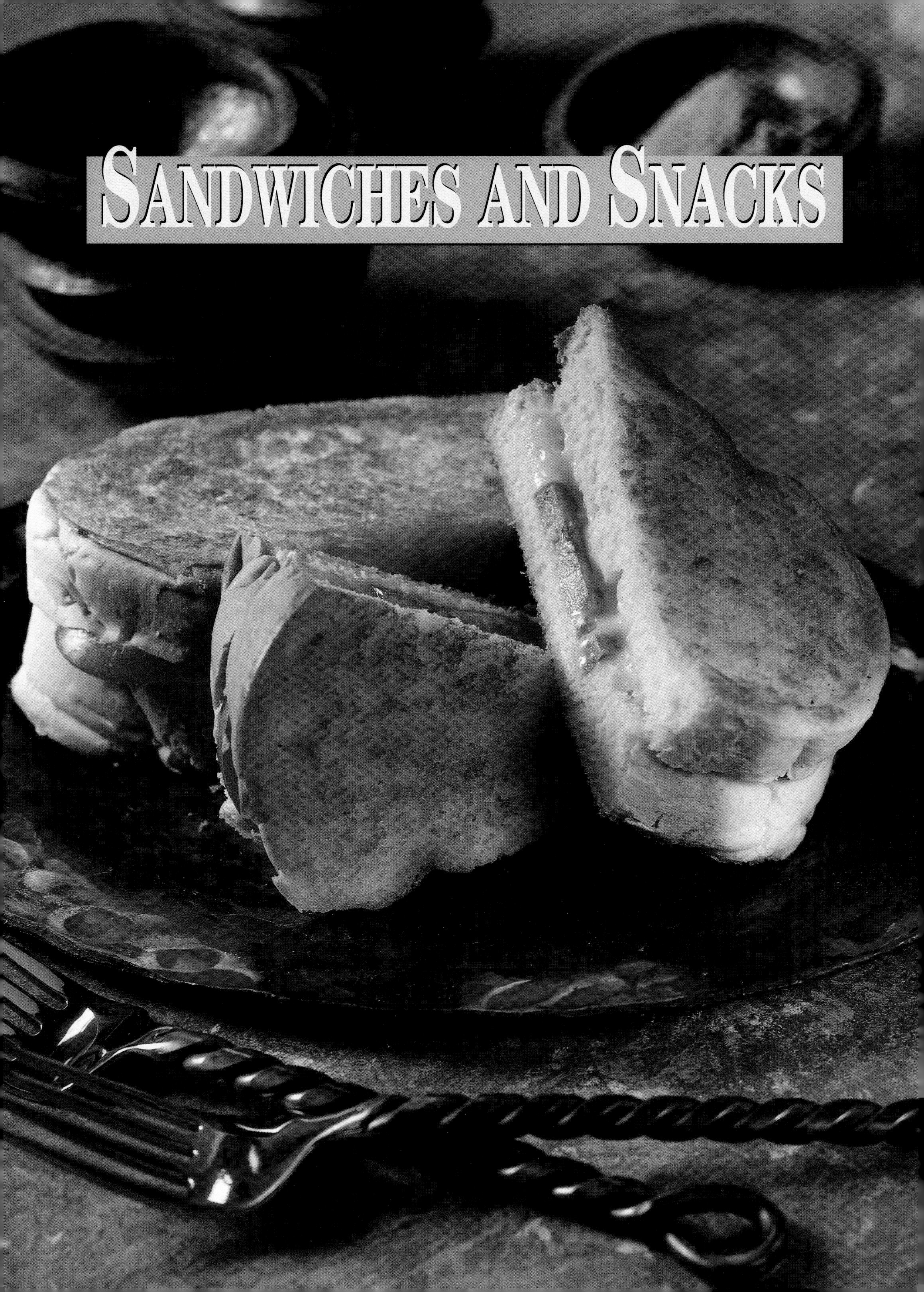

GRILLED POUND CAKE DESSERT SANDWICH

QUICK!

¼ cup strawberry-flavored cream cheese
1 tablespoon chopped sliced almonds, toasted
4 (½-inch-thick) slices frozen pound cake, thawed
2 teaspoons butter or margarine, softened
1 tablespoon powdered sugar

• **Combine** cream cheese and almonds in a small bowl.
• **Spread** on 1 side of half of pound cake slices. Top with remaining cake slices.
• **Spread** half of butter evenly on outside of 1 side of each sandwich. Place sandwiches, buttered side down, onto a hot nonstick skillet or griddle. Cook over medium heat until golden.
• **Spread** remaining butter evenly on ungrilled side of sandwiches; turn and cook until golden.
• **Sprinkle** with powdered sugar. **Yield:** 2 servings.

GRILLED CHILI CON QUESO SANDWICHES

(pictured on previous page)

QUICK!

4 ounces process cheese spread with peppers
1 tablespoon butter or margarine, softened
4 (1-inch-thick) slices French bread
¼ teaspoon ground cumin
6 plum tomato slices

• **Cut** cheese into 4 slices. Spread butter evenly on 1 side of bread slices; sprinkle with cumin.
• **Place** a nonstick skillet or griddle over medium heat until hot; place 2 bread slices, buttered side down, in skillet. Top each with a cheese slice, 3 tomato slices, second cheese slice, and remaining bread slice, buttered side up.
• **Cook** sandwiches until browned on both sides, turning once. **Yield:** 2 servings.

HERBED CHEESE SANDWICHES WITH ARTICHOKE-TOMATO SALSA

1 (15-ounce) carton part-skim ricotta cheese
1 (7-ounce) package crumbled feta cheese
½ cup chopped fresh parsley
2 tablespoons chopped green onions
1 teaspoon chopped fresh dill
16 slices rye bread
Artichoke-Tomato Salsa
8 lettuce leaves

• **Combine** first 5 ingredients, and spread on half of bread slices. Top with Artichoke-Tomato Salsa, lettuce, and remaining bread slices. Serve immediately. **Yield:** 8 servings.

♥ Per serving: Calories 294
Fat 11.4g Cholesterol 39mg
Sodium 653mg

Artichoke-Tomato Salsa

QUICK!

2 medium tomatoes, chopped
1 (14-ounce) can artichoke hearts, drained and chopped
2 teaspoons olive oil
2 cloves garlic, minced
3 tablespoons chopped fresh basil

• **Combine** all ingredients in a bowl; cover and chill. Serve with a slotted spoon. **Yield:** 3 cups.

Sarah Ryder
Lexington, Kentucky

FALAFEL SANDWICHES

Falafel (feh-LAH-fehl) sandwiches are to Israelis what hot dogs are to Americans.

2 (15-ounce) cans chickpeas, rinsed and drained
½ cup fine, dry breadcrumbs
4 cloves garlic, pressed
½ cup chopped fresh parsley
2 tablespoons ground cumin
1 teaspoon salt
½ teaspoon ground red pepper
2 large eggs
Vegetable oil
5 (8-inch) pita bread rounds
Tahini Sauce
Cucumber Relish

• **Position** knife blade in food processor bowl; add first 8 ingredients, and process until mixture is smooth, stopping once to scrape down sides. Shape mixture into 10 (½-inch-thick) patties.
• **Pour** oil to depth of ½ inch into a large heavy skillet; place over medium heat until hot.
• **Fry** patties in hot oil 3 to 5 minutes or until golden, turning once. Drain on paper towels.
• **Cut** pita bread rounds in half, and place 1 patty into each pita half. Top with Tahini Sauce and Cucumber Relish, and serve immediately. **Yield:** 5 servings.

Tahini Sauce

QUICK!

⅔ cup tahini *
½ cup lemon juice
¼ cup water
2 tablespoons olive oil
½ teaspoon salt
2 cloves garlic, minced

• **Combine** all ingredients in a small bowl, stirring until blended; cover and chill. **Yield:** 1¼ cups.

✽ You can find tahini (a thick paste made of ground sesame seeds commonly used in Middle Eastern cooking) near the peanut butter or specialty foods in most supermarkets.

Cucumber Relish

QUICK!

1 large cucumber, peeled, seeded, and chopped
4 plum tomatoes, chopped
2 cloves garlic, pressed
¼ cup chopped fresh parsley
2 tablespoons lemon juice
¼ teaspoon salt
¼ teaspoon pepper

● **Combine** all ingredients; cover and chill. **Yield:** 2 cups.

Sarah W. Meriwether
Montgomery, Alabama

MUSHROOM BAGEL SANDWICHES WITH CURRY-MUSTARD SAUCE

3 tablespoons olive oil
1 tablespoon red wine vinegar
1 tablespoon lemon juice
2 teaspoons Dijon mustard
½ teaspoon Worcestershire sauce
1 clove garlic, pressed
⅛ teaspoon salt
⅛ teaspoon dried oregano
⅛ teaspoon dried tarragon
⅛ teaspoon pepper
Dash of hot sauce
2 (8-ounce) packages sliced fresh mushrooms
1 small purple onion, thinly sliced
6 bagels, sliced
Curry-Mustard Sauce
2 cups (8 ounces) shredded Swiss cheese

● **Whisk** first 11 ingredients in a large bowl. Add mushrooms and onion, tossing to coat.
● **Arrange** bagels, cut side up, on a baking sheet; top bagels evenly with mushroom mixture, Curry-Mustard Sauce, and cheese.
● **Bake** at 350° for 10 to 15 minutes or until bubbly. **Yield:** 6 servings.

Curry-Mustard Sauce

QUICK!

2 tablespoons butter or margarine
2 tablespoons all-purpose flour
¾ cup milk
½ cup chicken broth
2 tablespoons dry sherry
2 teaspoons Dijon mustard
1 teaspoon curry powder

● **Melt** butter in a small saucepan over medium heat. Whisk in flour, and cook 1 minute, whisking constantly.
● **Whisk** in milk and remaining ingredients; cook, whisking constantly, 1 to 2 minutes or until mixture is thickened. **Yield:** 1⅓ cups.

Marie H. McNeil
Roswell, Georgia

BEEF, BACON, AND BLUE CHEESE SANDWICHES

½ (4-ounce) package crumbled blue cheese
¼ cup butter or margarine, softened
½ (8-ounce) package cream cheese
½ cup sour cream
1 tablespoon finely chopped onion
⅛ teaspoon ground white pepper
⅛ teaspoon garlic salt
1 (12-ounce) package bacon, cooked and crumbled
12 slices pumpernickel or sourdough bread, toasted
12 ounces thinly sliced cooked roast beef
1 tablespoon chopped fresh chives
2 tomatoes, thinly sliced
1 head endive, separated

● **Combine** blue cheese and butter; set aside.
● **Combine** cream cheese and next 4 ingredients in a small saucepan; cook over low heat, stirring constantly, until blended. Cool and stir in bacon.
● **Spread** blue cheese mixture over 6 bread slices; top evenly with roast beef.

● **Spread** cream cheese mixture on remaining 6 bread slices, and sprinkle with chives. Serve open-face with tomato slices and endive leaves. **Yield:** 6 servings.

Nancy Williams
Starkville, Mississippi

STEAK BAGEL SANDWICHES

⅔ cup beer
⅓ cup vegetable oil
1 teaspoon salt
¼ teaspoon garlic powder
¼ teaspoon pepper
1 (1½-pound) flank steak
2 tablespoons butter or margarine
2 large onions, sliced and separated into rings
¼ teaspoon salt
½ teaspoon paprika
6 bagels, sliced and toasted

● **Combine** first 5 ingredients in a heavy-duty, zip-top plastic bag; add steak, turning to coat. Seal and chill 8 hours, turning occasionally.
● **Remove** steak from marinade, discarding marinade. Place steak on a rack in a broiler in a pan.
● **Broil** 3 inches from heat (with electric oven door partially opened) 5 to 7 minutes on each side or to desired degree of doneness. Cut steak into thin slices, and keep warm.
● **Melt** butter in a medium saucepan. Add onion, salt, and paprika; cook until tender, stirring often.
● **Arrange** steak and onion on bagel bottoms. Cover with tops. Serve with horseradish. **Yield:** 6 servings.

Joann J. McKoane
Sarasota, Florida

SAVORY BEEF AND CHEESE ROLL-UPS

⟨QUICK!⟩

2 (5-ounce) containers vegetable-
    flavored soft spreadable
    cheese *
4 (10-inch) flour tortillas
1 cup shredded carrot
1 cup (4 ounces) shredded
    Monterey Jack cheese
8 lettuce leaves
1 pound thinly sliced roast beef

• **Spread** vegetable-flavored cheese
evenly over 1 side of each tortilla; top
each evenly with carrot, shredded
cheese, lettuce, and roast beef, leaving a
½-inch border around edges.
• **Roll** up tortillas tightly, and wrap in
plastic wrap. Store in refrigerator up to
8 hours.
• **Unwrap** roll-ups, and cut in half before serving. **Yield:** 4 servings.

* For the spreadable cheese, we used
Rondelé.

Jill Hilton
Cedar Rapids, Iowa

THE SEBASTIAN

⟨QUICK!⟩

*Serve this grilled ham and cheese
sandwich with gazpacho from the deli
or your favorite tomato soup.*

3 cups shredded cabbage
⅔ cup mayonnaise
⅓ cup chutney
1 tablespoon curry powder
⅛ teaspoon salt
12 (1-ounce) slices cooked ham
6 slices Cheddar cheese
12 slices rye bread
¼ cup butter, softened

• **Combine** first 5 ingredients; set aside.
• **Place** 2 ham slices, ½ cup slaw, and 1
cheese slice onto 6 bread slices; top
with remaining slices of bread.
• **Spread** half of butter on outside of 1
side of each sandwich. Place, buttered
side down, onto a hot griddle or skillet.
Cook 1 minute or until golden.

• **Spread** remaining butter on ungrilled
side, and cook until golden and cheese
begins to melt. Serve immediately.
Yield: 6 servings.

The Williamsburg Lodge
Williamsburg, Virginia

HAM AND PINEAPPLE SLAW SANDWICHES

⟨QUICK!⟩

2 cups chopped cooked ham
3 cups shredded cabbage
1 (8-ounce) can pineapple tidbits,
    undrained
⅔ cup mayonnaise
1 cup (4 ounces) shredded
    Cheddar cheese
½ teaspoon salt
½ teaspoon pepper
4 French sandwich rolls

• **Combine** all ingredients except rolls,
stirring gently. Spoon onto bottoms of
rolls; cover with tops, and serve immediately. **Yield:** 4 servings.

Dorsella Utter
Louisville, Kentucky

HOT CHICKEN SALAD SANDWICHES

⟨QUICK!⟩

2 (5-ounce) cans chunk white
    chicken, drained and flaked
1 (8-ounce) can pineapple tidbits,
    drained
1 cup (4 ounces) shredded
    Cheddar cheese
¼ cup finely chopped green bell
    pepper
2 tablespoons finely chopped
    celery
1 tablespoon finely chopped onion
⅓ cup mayonnaise or salad
    dressing
1 teaspoon salt
3 kaiser rolls, split

• **Combine** all ingredients except rolls,
stirring well; set aside.
• **Place** rolls, cut side up, on a baking
sheet. Broil 5½ inches from heat (with

electric oven door partially opened)
until lightly browned.
• **Spread** filling evenly over rolls. Bake
at 350° for 5 minutes or until thoroughly
heated. **Yield:** 6 servings.

Nancy Williams
Starkville, Mississippi

JAMAICAN CHICKEN SANDWICH

1 (20-ounce) can pineapple slices,
    undrained
¼ cup dark rum or pineapple juice
1 tablespoon chili powder
1 tablespoon molasses
¼ teaspoon hot sauce
4 skinned and boned chicken
    breast halves
Red Cabbage Slaw
4 sesame seed sandwich buns,
    toasted
Lettuce leaves
¼ cup flaked coconut, toasted
    (optional)
Red cabbage leaves
Garnish: green onions

• **Drain** pineapple, reserving 2 tablespoons juice for Red Cabbage Slaw,
and, if desired, ¼ cup juice for basting
mixture; set pineapple and juice aside.
• **Combine** rum or ¼ cup reserved
pineapple juice, chili powder, molasses,
and hot sauce; set mixture aside.
• **Cook** pineapple and chicken, covered
with grill lid, over medium-hot coals
(350° to 400°) 15 to 20 minutes or until
done, basting often with rum mixture.
• **Place** Red Cabbage Slaw on bottom
half of each bun; top each with chicken,
leaf lettuce, and 2 pineapple slices.
Sprinkle with coconut, if desired. Cover
with tops of buns. Serve each sandwich
on a red cabbage leaf, and garnish, if desired. **Yield:** 4 servings.

Red Cabbage Slaw

⟨QUICK!⟩

1 cup finely shredded red cabbage
2 green onions, finely chopped
2 tablespoons reserved pineapple
    juice
2 teaspoons vegetable oil
1 teaspoon sesame oil

- **Combine** all ingredients.
- **Cover** and chill. Serve with a slotted spoon. **Yield:** 1 cup.

Sandi Pichon
Slidell, Louisiana

CHICKEN-AVOCADO DAGWOODS

QUICK!

Mash avocados the clean and easy way: Place peeled halves in a heavy-duty, zip-top plastic bag; seal and squeeze.

8 slices sourdough bread, toasted
2 tablespoons mayonnaise
2 avocados, mashed
8 slices purple onion
4 slices Monterey Jack or provolone cheese
8 slices bacon, cooked
8 lettuce leaves
8 slices tomato
8 (¼-inch-thick) slices roasted chicken breast
⅛ teaspoon salt
⅛ teaspoon pepper

- **Spread** 1 side of each bread slice evenly with mayonnaise; spread half of slices with mashed avocado, and top with onion and next 5 ingredients. Sprinkle with salt and pepper. Top with remaining bread slices; serve sandwiches immediately. **Yield:** 4 servings.

Karen Lesemann
Charleston, South Carolina

TURKEY-CRANBERRY CROISSANT

QUICK!

1 (8-ounce) package cream cheese, softened
¼ cup orange marmalade
½ cup chopped pecans
6 large croissants, split
Lettuce leaves
1 pound thinly sliced cooked turkey
¾ cup whole-berry cranberry sauce

- **Combine** first 3 ingredients, stirring well. Spread evenly on cut sides of croissants.
- **Place** lettuce and turkey on croissant bottoms; spread with cranberry sauce, and cover with croissant tops. **Yield:** 6 servings.

Patricia Jones
Fairmont, North Carolina

SMOKED TURKEY-ROASTED PEPPER SANDWICHES

QUICK!

Smoked turkey breast is soaked in a salt solution before smoking. If you're watching your sodium, substitute roasted turkey breast for the smoked.

2 tablespoons fat-free cream cheese product, softened
1 tablespoon reduced-fat mayonnaise
1 tablespoon spicy brown mustard
⅛ teaspoon pepper
¼ cup chopped roasted red bell peppers, drained
2 tablespoons sliced green onions
8 slices pumpernickel bread
¾ pound sliced smoked turkey breast
¼ cup alfalfa sprouts

- **Combine** first 4 ingredients; stir in red pepper and green onions.
- **Spread** cream cheese mixture evenly on 1 side of bread slices. Layer turkey and alfalfa sprouts on 4 slices of bread; top with remaining bread slices. Cut sandwiches in half.
- **Serve** immediately or wrap each sandwich in heavy-duty plastic wrap, and chill. **Yield:** 4 servings.

♥ Per serving: Calories 280
Fat 2.9g Cholesterol 44mg
Sodium 1057mg

BATTER-FRIED GROUPER SANDWICHES

The Dill Mayonnaise is also great with crab cakes or cold steamed lobster.

1 cup all-purpose flour
¼ cup cornstarch
1 tablespoon garlic powder
½ teaspoon pepper
4 (4-ounce) grouper fillets
½ to ¾ cup buttermilk
Canola oil
Dill Mayonnaise
4 onion sandwich buns, toasted
Lettuce leaves
2 large tomatoes, sliced
Garnishes: fresh chives, lemon twists

- **Combine** first 4 ingredients in a shallow dish. Dredge grouper in flour mixture; dip into buttermilk, and dredge in flour mixture again.
- **Pour** oil to depth of 3 inches into a Dutch oven; heat to 350°. Fry fillets in hot oil 5 minutes or until golden; drain on paper towels.
- **Spread** Dill Mayonnaise on buns; place each fillet on a bun with lettuce and tomato, and add top half of bun. Garnish, if desired. Serve immediately. **Yield:** 4 sandwiches.

Dill Mayonnaise

QUICK!

½ cup mayonnaise
1 tablespoon chopped fresh parsley
1 tablespoon lemon juice
1 teaspoon chopped fresh dill
1 teaspoon capers
1 teaspoon chopped sweet pickle
⅛ teaspoon ground red pepper

- **Combine** all ingredients in a bowl, stirring well; cover and chill. **Yield:** about ⅔ cup.

Chef Chris McDonald,
Atlanta Fish Market
Atlanta, Georgia

HOT TUNA MELTS

QUICK!

If you're hooked on coffee shop tuna salad sandwiches, you'll love these heated versions.

1 (6-ounce) can solid white tuna in
     spring water, drained and
     flaked
⅓ cup mayonnaise
¼ cup sliced pimiento-stuffed
     olives, drained
3 hard-cooked eggs, chopped
3 tablespoons sweet pickle relish
2 tablespoons finely chopped
     onion
2 English muffins, split and lightly
     toasted
4 slices sharp Cheddar cheese

• **Combine** first 6 ingredients, stirring well. Spoon evenly onto muffin halves; place on a baking sheet.
• **Broil** 5½ inches from heat (with electric oven door partially opened) 2 minutes. Top each with a cheese slice; broil 1 additional minute or until cheese melts. **Yield:** 4 servings.

TUNA ROLL SANDWICHES

QUICK!

Brown bag tip: Pita bread pockets make this sandwich faster to prepare.

1 (3-ounce) package cream cheese,
     softened
2 tablespoons mayonnaise
1 tablespoon lemon juice
½ teaspoon pepper
¼ teaspoon salt
1 (10-ounce) can solid white tuna
     in spring water, drained and
     flaked *
½ cup chopped purple onion
6 large lettuce leaves
6 (8-inch) flour tortillas

• **Combine** first 5 ingredients, stirring until smooth; add tuna and onion, stirring well.
• **Place** lettuce on tortillas, and trim to fit. Spoon tuna mixture onto lettuce. Roll tortilla up, and tie with kitchen string. (Remove string before serving.) Serve with marinated vegetables. **Yield:** 6 servings.

* You can substitute 1 (10-ounce) can white chicken, drained and flaked, for the tuna.

Edith Askins
Greenville, Texas

SHRIMP AND EGG SALAD SANDWICHES

2 cups water
½ pound unpeeled medium-size
     fresh shrimp
6 large hard-cooked eggs, chopped
¼ cup finely chopped green onions
2 tablespoons finely chopped
     celery
1 tablespoon chopped fresh
     parsley
2 tablespoons capers (optional)
2 teaspoons chopped fresh dill
     (optional)
3 tablespoons mayonnaise or salad
     dressing
1 teaspoon lemon juice
1 teaspoon prepared mustard
¼ teaspoon salt
¼ teaspoon hot sauce
3 English muffins, split and
     toasted
Garnishes: fresh dill sprigs, whole
     cooked shrimp, lemon slices

• **Bring** water to a boil; add shrimp, and cook 3 to 5 minutes or until shrimp turn pink. Drain well, and rinse with cold water. Peel shrimp, and devein, if desired. Coarsely chop shrimp.
• **Combine** chopped shrimp, eggs, and next 3 ingredients; if desired, stir in capers and chopped dill. Set mixture aside.
• **Combine** mayonnaise and next 4 ingredients; gently fold into egg mixture.
• **Spoon** onto English muffins; garnish, if desired. **Yield:** 6 servings.

Virginia J. MacMillan
Summerland Key, Florida

GRILLED SEAFOOD PO'BOY
(pictured at right)

Grilling the seafood and using reduced-fat mayonnaise make this sandwich low fat.

1 pound unpeeled medium-size
     fresh shrimp
1 (10-ounce) farm-raised catfish
     fillet
2 teaspoons Creole seasoning
¼ cup lemon juice
1 teaspoon olive oil
½ cup roasted red bell pepper
     strips
1 jalapeño pepper
½ cup reduced-fat mayonnaise
2 tablespoons Creole mustard
2 tablespoons chopped fresh
     parsley
1 clove garlic, minced
2 tablespoons sliced green onions
Vegetable cooking spray
8 slices tomato
8 lettuce leaves
4 French sandwich rolls, split and
     toasted

• **Peel** shrimp, and devein, if desired.
• **Cut** fish crosswise into 1-inch slices. Combine shrimp and fish in a shallow dish, and sprinkle with Creole seasoning. Cover and chill 2 hours.
• **Combine** lemon juice and oil; pour mixture over seafood. Cover and chill 30 additional minutes.
• **Pat** red pepper strips dry. Seed and chop jalapeño pepper. Combine red pepper strips, jalapeño pepper, mayonnaise, and next 4 ingredients; set aside.
• **Drain** seafood, and place in a grill basket coated with cooking spray.
• **Cook**, covered with grill lid, over medium-hot coals (350° to 400°) 7 to 10 minutes, turning once.
• **Place** seafood, tomato, and lettuce evenly on bottom halves of rolls; spread top halves of rolls evenly with mayonnaise mixture, and place on sandwiches. **Yield:** 4 servings.

Clemie Barron
Panama City, Florida

♥ Per serving: Calories 405
Fat 15g   Cholesterol 112mg
Sodium 711mg

Grilled Seafood Po'Boy

FERTITTA'S "MUFFY" SANDWICH

3 tablespoons prepared mustard
1 (8-inch) round loaf Italian
    bread, cut in half horizontally
½ cup (2 ounces) shredded
    Cheddar cheese
½ cup (2 ounces) shredded
    mozzarella cheese
½ cup (2 ounces) shredded
    provolone cheese
2 to 3 ounces sliced cooked ham
2 to 3 ounces sliced Genoa
    salami
2 to 3 ounces sliced bologna
2 to 3 ounces sliced cooked turkey
1 to 1½ cups Muffy Salad Mix

• **Spread** mustard on cut slices of bread.
• **Combine** cheeses; place on bottom half of bread. Arrange meat on both halves; place on a baking sheet.
• **Bake** at 350° for 15 minutes or until thoroughly heated. Spread chilled Muffy Salad Mix on bottom half; cover with top half. Cut into quarters, and serve immediately. **Yield:** 2 to 4 servings.

Muffy Salad Mix

QUICK!

1½ cups pimiento-stuffed olives,
    drained
1 cup ripe olives, drained
1 cup coarsely chopped celery
1 cup mixed pickled garden
    vegetables, drained
6 cloves garlic
1 to 1½ teaspoons dried basil
1 to 1½ teaspoons dried
    oregano
⅓ cup olive oil
⅓ cup white dry wine or white
    wine vinegar

• **Position** knife blade in food processor bowl; add all ingredients.
• **Process** 20 seconds or until finely chopped.
• **Cover** and chill. Store remaining salad mix in refrigerator up to 1 week. **Yield:** 3 cups.

Agatha Wiley
Fertitta's Delicatessen
Shreveport, Louisiana

DOODLES MUFFULETTA

¼ pound thinly sliced cooked
    ham
¼ pound sliced Genoa salami
4 slices Swiss cheese
1 (6-ounce) package sliced
    provolone cheese
1 (10-inch) round loaf Italian
    bread, cut in half horizontally
1½ cups Doodles Olive Salad

• **Layer** first 4 ingredients on bottom half of bread; place bread halves on a baking sheet.
• **Bake** at 350° for 20 to 30 minutes or until thoroughly heated.
• **Top** with chilled Doodles Olive Salad and remaining bread half; cut into quarters. **Yield:** 2 to 4 servings.

Doodles Olive Salad

3 (10-ounce) jars pimiento-stuffed
    olives, drained and coarsely
    chopped
3 stalks celery, chopped
2 carrots, scraped and grated
2 cloves garlic, finely chopped
1 (4-ounce) jar diced pimiento,
    drained
3 tablespoons capers, drained
½ cup olive oil
¼ cup red wine vinegar

• **Combine** all ingredients; cover and chill. Store remaining salad in refrigerator up to 1 week. **Yield:** 7 cups.

Jerry Harris
Doodles
Birmingham, Alabama

NAPOLEON HOUSE MUFFULETTA

2 slices cooked ham (about
    2 ounces)
3 slices Genoa salami (about
    2½ ounces)
2 slices pastrami (about
    2 ounces)
¼ cup Italian Olive Salad
1 slice provolone cheese
1 slice Swiss cheese
1 (5-inch) sandwich bun with
    sesame seeds

• **Layer** first 6 ingredients on bottom half of bun; top with remaining bun half, and wrap in aluminum foil.
• **Bake** at 350° for 20 minutes or until thoroughly heated. **Yield:** 1 serving.

Italian Olive Salad

4 cups pimiento-stuffed olives,
    drained and coarsely chopped
1 cup canned mixed vegetables,
    drained
1 (14-ounce) can artichoke hearts,
    drained and coarsely chopped
1 (15-ounce) can chickpeas,
    drained and coarsely chopped
1 (8-ounce) jar cocktail onions,
    drained and coarsely chopped
¼ cup capers, drained
⅔ cup pickled vegetables, drained
    and coarsely chopped
1 large green bell pepper, chopped
3 stalks celery, chopped
2 cloves garlic, minced
1 cup olive oil
½ cup red wine vinegar
1½ tablespoons dried oregano
½ teaspoon pepper

• **Combine** all ingredients; cover and chill 8 hours.
• **Store** remaining salad in refrigerator up to 1 week. **Yield:** 12 cups.

Napoleon House
New Orleans, Louisiana

GIANT HAM AND PEPPER SANDWICH

2 Anaheim chile peppers
1 red bell pepper
1 green bell pepper
3 green onions
1 tablespoon butter or margarine
1 (10-ounce) can refrigerated
    pizza dough
1¼ pounds thinly sliced cooked
    ham
⅓ cup Thousand Island salad
    dressing
1½ cups (6 ounces) shredded
    sharp Cheddar cheese

• **Cut** peppers into thin strips; slice green onions.

- **Melt** butter in a 10-inch cast-iron skillet over medium-high heat; add peppers and green onions, and cook, stirring constantly, until tender. Remove from skillet; wipe drippings from skillet, and set skillet aside to cool.
- **Unroll** pizza dough, stretching to a 14½-inch square (do not tear dough). Gently place dough in cooled skillet, allowing edges to overhang.
- **Place** ham, pepper mixture, salad dressing, and cheese on dough; bring corners and sides of dough over cheese. Twist corners together in center, forming a knot, and pinch seams to seal.
- **Bake** at 425° for 15 to 20 minutes or until golden. Let sandwich stand 5 minutes before cutting into wedges. **Yield:** 6 servings.

Lee Barnett
Helena, Alabama

MEDITERRANEAN PICNIC LOAF

1 (16-ounce) round loaf peasant-style bread
3 large tomatoes
1 large purple onion, thinly sliced
1 green bell pepper, thinly sliced
4 ounces crumbled feta cheese
1 (6⅛-ounce) can solid white tuna in spring water, drained and flaked
½ cup kalamata olives, sliced
1 cup firmly packed fresh basil, chopped
2 tablespoons capers
2 tablespoons balsamic vinegar
1 tablespoon Dijon mustard
1 tablespoon olive oil
2 cloves garlic, minced

- **Cut** bread in half horizontally, and hollow out center of bottom half, leaving a 1-inch-thick shell. Set bread top and shell aside.
- **Slice** tomatoes; cut slices into fourths.
- **Layer** tomato, onion, bell pepper, and cheese in bread shell. Place tuna and next 3 ingredients in bread shell.
- **Combine** vinegar and remaining 3 ingredients; drizzle over mixture in bread shell, and cover with bread top.

- **Wrap** filled loaf in aluminum foil, and chill 2 hours. Cut into wedges to serve. **Yield:** 6 servings.

Janice Elder
Charlotte, North Carolina

♥ Per serving: Calories 311
Fat 9.2g   Cholesterol 30mg
Sodium 976mg

HAM AND CHEESE SANDWICH ROUND

1 (1-pound) round loaf sourdough bread *
½ cup mayonnaise or salad dressing
2½ teaspoons dried Italian seasoning
½ teaspoon pepper
1 large onion, thinly sliced
2 medium-size green or red bell peppers, cut into thin strips
1 stalk celery, sliced
1 tablespoon olive oil
1 pound cooked ham, thinly sliced (about 25 slices)
1½ cups (6 ounces) shredded Cheddar and mozzarella cheese blend

- **Slice** off top third of bread loaf; set top aside. Hollow out bottom section, leaving a ½-inch shell. (Reserve crumbs for another use.)
- **Combine** mayonnaise, Italian seasoning, and pepper. Brush inside of bread shell with half of mixture. Set shell and remaining mixture aside.
- **Cook** onion, pepper strips, and celery in oil in a large skillet over medium-high heat until tender, stirring often.
- **Arrange** half of ham in bread shell, and top with half of vegetable mixture; sprinkle with half of cheese. Spread remaining mayonnaise mixture over cheese. Repeat layers with remaining ham, vegetable mixture, and cheese. Replace bread top. Wrap sandwich in heavy-duty aluminum foil.
- **Bake** at 400° for 30 minutes or until thoroughly heated. Cut into wedges; serve immediately. **Yield:** 6 servings.

* Substitute 6 hoagie rolls for bread.

BRIE-MUSHROOM BURGERS

Brie brings sophistication to an ordinary burger. If the kids don't like it, slip Cheddar into theirs, and enjoy your gourmet version alone.

1½ pounds lean ground beef
3 tablespoons grated onion
2 teaspoons Worcestershire sauce
¾ teaspoon dry mustard
¼ teaspoon freshly ground pepper
6 ounces Brie cheese
2 tablespoons butter or margarine
1 cup sliced fresh mushrooms
1 medium onion, sliced
4 hamburger buns with sesame seeds
Olive oil
Garnish: fresh parsley sprigs

- **Combine** first 5 ingredients; shape into 8 (6-inch) patties, and set aside.
- **Set** one-third of Brie aside. Cut remaining Brie into 4 pieces, and place 1 piece on each of 4 patties. Top with remaining patties, and seal edges. Cover and chill.
- **Melt** butter in a large nonstick skillet over medium heat. Add mushrooms and onion; cook until tender, stirring often. Remove from heat; add remaining 2 ounces cheese to skillet, stirring until cheese melts. Remove from skillet, and keep warm.
- **Cook** patties in skillet over medium heat 8 minutes, turning once. Remove from skillet, and keep warm.
- **Brush** cut sides of buns with olive oil; place buns, cut side down, in skillet, and cook until lightly browned.
- **Place** bottom half of each bun on a plate; top with a patty, and spoon mushroom mixture over meat. Cover with bun tops; garnish, if desired. **Yield:** 4 servings.

Note: To grill burgers, cook, covered with grill lid, over medium-hot coals (350° to 400°) 7 to 8 minutes on each side. Toast buns on grill as well.

Lilann Taylor
Savannah, Georgia

OPEN-FACED CHICKEN-ONION BURGERS

1½ pounds ground chicken
½ cup finely chopped green bell
    pepper
⅓ cup finely chopped fresh
    mushrooms
10 large pimiento-stuffed green
    olives, finely chopped
1 (8-ounce) package shredded
    sharp Cheddar cheese
½ teaspoon salt
½ teaspoon pepper
1 tablespoon butter or margarine
2 medium onions, sliced and
    separated into rings
8 slices French bread
Garnishes: cherry tomatoes, fresh
    parsley sprigs

• **Combine** first 7 ingredients in a large bowl; shape chicken mixture into 8 patties. Cover and chill.
• **Melt** butter in a large skillet over medium-low heat. Add onion, and cook until tender and brown, stirring often. Keep warm.
• **Cook** patties, covered with grill lid, over medium-hot coals (350° to 400°) 5 minutes on each side or until done. Place bread slices on grill rack; cook until lightly browned, if desired. Place patties on bread; top with onion. Garnish, if desired. **Yield:** 8 servings.

TERIYAKI HAMBURGERS

1 pound lean ground beef
⅓ cup chopped water chestnuts
¼ cup chopped green bell
    pepper
2 green onions, finely chopped
1 tablespoon brown sugar
2 tablespoons water
1 tablespoon lemon juice
1 tablespoon soy sauce
½ teaspoon ground ginger
Vegetable cooking spray
4 sesame seed buns
Hoisin Ketchup
Garnish: green onion brushes

• **Combine** first 9 ingredients; shape into 4 patties.

• **Coat** grill rack with cooking spray; place rack on grill over medium-hot coals (350° to 400°).
• **Place** patties on rack, and cook, without grill lid, 5 minutes on each side or until done. Serve on buns with Hoisin Ketchup. Garnish, if desired. **Yield:** 4 servings.

Hoisin Ketchup

QUICK!

¼ cup ketchup
¼ cup hoisin sauce

• **Combine** ketchup and hoisin sauce. **Yield:** ½ cup.

Elaine McVinney
Alexandria, Virginia

FRIED GREEN TOMATO CHEESEBURGERS

½ cup mayonnaise
1 clove garlic, pressed
1½ pounds lean ground beef
½ pound ground pork sausage
½ cup Italian-seasoned
    breadcrumbs
2 large eggs
3 tablespoons white wine
    Worcestershire sauce
1 teaspoon fennel seeds,
    crushed
3 green tomatoes, cut into ¼-inch
    slices
½ teaspoon salt
¼ teaspoon pepper
1 cup yellow cornmeal
1 to 4 tablespoons vegetable oil
Vegetable cooking spray
8 kaiser rolls, split
Lettuce leaves
8 slices sharp Cheddar cheese
Purple onion slices
Garnish: pimiento-stuffed olives

• **Combine** mayonnaise and garlic; cover and chill.
• **Combine** ground beef and next 5 ingredients; shape into 8 patties. Cover and chill.
• **Sprinkle** tomato slices with salt and pepper; let stand 5 minutes. Dredge in cornmeal.

• **Cook** tomato slices in oil in a large skillet over medium heat until golden on each side. Drain on paper towels, and keep warm.
• **Place** patties in a grill basket coated with cooking spray.
• **Cook**, covered with grill lid, over medium-hot coals (350° to 400°) 4 to 5 minutes on each side or until done.
• **Spray** cut sides of rolls with cooking spray; place rolls, cut side down, on rack, and grill until lightly browned.
• **Place** a patty on lettuce on bottom half of each roll; top each patty with a cheese slice, green tomato slices, purple onion slices, mayonnaise mixture, and top half of bun. Garnish, if desired. **Yield:** 8 servings.

TUNA BURGERS

QUICK!

For a smokier flavor, try using hickory-flavored water-packed tuna.

3 tablespoons butter or margarine,
    melted
1 tablespoon lemon juice
2 drops of hot sauce
⅛ teaspoon pepper
3 (6-ounce) cans solid white tuna
    in spring water, drained and
    flaked
2 cups soft breadcrumbs
3 large eggs, lightly beaten
1 teaspoon Worcestershire sauce
1 medium onion, finely chopped
2 tablespoons dried parsley
    flakes
1 teaspoon lemon-pepper
    seasoning
½ teaspoon onion powder
½ teaspoon garlic powder
1 teaspoon cracked black
    pepper
½ teaspoon dried thyme
4 kaiser rolls, split
Lettuce leaves
Tomato slices

• **Combine** first 4 ingredients, and set mixture aside.
• **Combine** tuna and next 6 ingredients; shape into 4 patties. Brush patties lightly with half of butter mixture.

- **Combine** onion powder and next 3 ingredients; sprinkle evenly on patties.
- **Heat** remaining butter mixture in a skillet; add patties, and cook 4 minutes on each side or until done.
- **Place** each patty on a roll with lettuce and tomato slices; serve with mayonnaise, tartar sauce, or sweet pickle relish. **Yield:** 4 servings.

Note: To blacken patties, remove food rack from grill, and place a cast-iron skillet directly on hot coals; heat at least 5 minutes. (Do not add the remaining butter mixture.) Add patties, and cook 3 minutes on each side. Remove from heat, and drizzle with remaining butter mixture.

Kimberly R. Diamondidis
Germantown, Maryland

POTATO-CRUSTED CRAB BURGERS

2 tablespoons butter or margarine
1 red bell pepper, chopped
1 green bell pepper, chopped
1 purple onion, chopped
1 clove garlic, minced
1 pound fresh crabmeat, drained and flaked
2 cups soft breadcrumbs
3 large eggs, lightly beaten
¼ cup Dijon mustard
2 cups instant potato flakes
Vegetable oil
6 kaiser rolls, split
Lettuce leaves
Tomato slices
Rémoulade Sauce
Garnishes: fresh tarragon sprigs, lemon wedges

- **Melt** butter in a large skillet over medium heat. Add red bell pepper and next 3 ingredients; cook, stirring constantly, 3 minutes or until tender.
- **Combine** cooked vegetables, crabmeat, and next 3 ingredients. Shape into 6 patties, and coat with potato flakes. (Patties will be fragile and difficult to handle.)
- **Cook** patties, two at a time, in oil in a skillet over medium-high heat 2 minutes on each side or until golden. Drain on

paper towels, and place on a baking sheet.
- **Bake** at 350° for 15 minutes or until thoroughly heated. Serve each patty on a roll with lettuce, tomato slices, and Rémoulade Sauce; add top half of roll. Garnish, if desired. **Yield:** 6 servings.

Rémoulade Sauce

QUICK!

1½ cups mayonnaise or salad dressing
2 tablespoons Creole mustard
1 tablespoon capers, chopped
1 tablespoon chopped sweet pickle
1 tablespoon chopped fresh parsley
1 teaspoon dried tarragon

- **Combine** all ingredients; cover and chill. **Yield:** 1¾ cups.

Karen Lapidus
Huntsville, Alabama

ALL-STAR PIZZA CALZONES

1½ (32-ounce) packages frozen bread dough
1 pound ground pork sausage, cooked and drained
½ pound ground baked ham
½ pound ground salami
1 cup (4 ounces) shredded Swiss cheese
1 cup (4 ounces) shredded mozzarella cheese
1 cup (4 ounces) shredded provolone cheese
2 cups (8 ounces) shredded mild Cheddar cheese
¼ cup chopped ripe olives
1 cup chopped onion
3 jalapeño peppers, seeded and chopped
3 tablespoons butter or margarine, melted

- **Allow** dough to rise according to package directions.
- **Combine** sausage and next 9 ingredients, stirring well.
- **Roll** 1 loaf of dough into a 9- x 11-inch rectangle on a lightly floured surface.

Place 3½ cups sausage mixture on 1 short side of dough; fold dough over sausage mixture, and pinch edges to seal. Place on a lightly greased baking sheet, and brush with 1 tablespoon butter. Repeat with remaining dough, sausage mixture, and butter.
- **Bake** at 300° for 30 minutes or until golden. Let stand 5 minutes; slice each into 3 or 4 portions with an electric knife, and serve warm. **Yield:** 9 to 12 servings.

Note: These calzones may be frozen. Prepare as directed; bake at 300° for 15 minutes or until lightly browned. Let cool. Freeze in airtight containers. Bake on a greased baking sheet at 300° for 40 minutes or until golden.

Monica Pierce
Covington, Louisiana

EASY HERB PIZZA

QUICK!

1 (10-ounce) can refrigerated pizza crust
1 (8-ounce) can tomato sauce
⅓ cup chopped fresh basil
1½ cups (6 ounces) shredded provolone cheese

- **Shape** pizza crust in a lightly greased 12-inch pizza pan; bake at 425° for 7 minutes.
- **Spread** tomato sauce over pizza crust; sprinkle evenly with basil, and bake 8 minutes. Sprinkle with cheese, and bake 5 additional minutes. **Yield:** 1 (12-inch) pizza.

Shannon Gayle
Alexandria, Louisiana

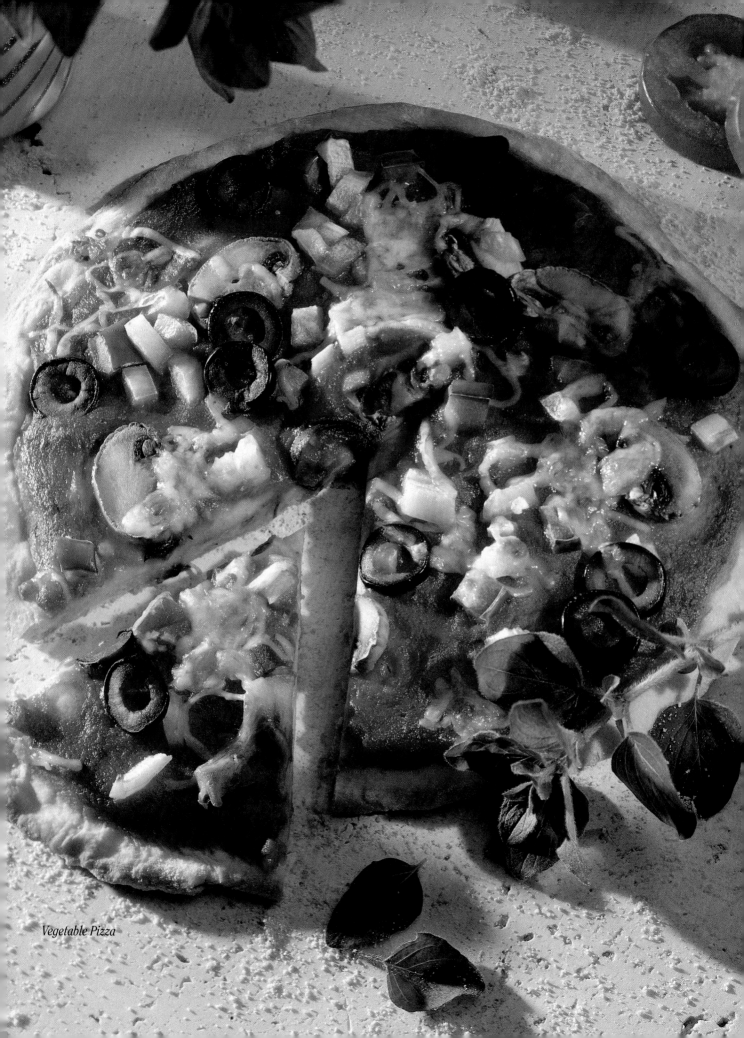

Vegetable Pizza

VEGETABLE PIZZA
(pictured at left)

QUICK!

6 (8-inch) Skillet Pizza Crusts
    (see recipe on page 62)
1½ cups reduced-fat pasta sauce
1 cup sliced fresh mushrooms
1 cup (4 ounces) shredded part-
    skim mozzarella cheese
¾ cup chopped green bell pepper
½ cup chopped onion
¼ cup sliced ripe olives, drained

• **Place** frozen pizza crusts on baking
sheets. Spread each crust with ¼ cup
pasta sauce, and sprinkle evenly with
toppings.
• **Bake** at 425° for 12 to 15 minutes or
until edges are lightly browned and
cheese melts. Cut into wedges. **Yield:** 6
servings.

Kathy Piques
Knoxville, Tennessee

♥ Per serving: Calories 391
Fat 10.3g Cholesterol 11mg
Sodium 607mg

BLAZING SUNSET PIZZA

QUICK!

⅔ cup Pesto Sauce (see recipe on
    page 345)
1 (12-inch) refrigerated pizza
    crust
2 plum tomatoes, sliced
½ red bell pepper, thinly sliced
½ yellow bell pepper, thinly sliced
½ orange bell pepper, thinly sliced
1 cup (4 ounces) shredded colby-
    Monterey Jack cheese blend
Garnish: fresh basil sprig

• **Spread** Pesto Sauce over crust; top
with tomato and next 4 ingredients.
• **Bake** at 425° for 10 minutes or until
bubbly. Garnish, if desired. **Yield:** 1 (12-
inch) pizza.

SOUTHWESTERN VEGGIE PIZZA

QUICK!

1 (10-ounce) Italian bread shell *
1 carrot, scraped and chopped
1 zucchini, sliced
1 clove garlic, minced
1 tablespoon olive oil
1 (11-ounce) jar black bean dip
½ cup salsa, drained
1 cup (4 ounces) shredded
    Monterey Jack cheese with
    peppers

• **Bake** bread shell on a baking sheet at
350° for 5 minutes; set aside.
• **Cook** carrot, zucchini, and garlic in
olive oil in a skillet over medium heat,
stirring constantly, 3 to 5 minutes or
until crisp-tender; drain.
• **Spread** bean dip over bread shell; top
with salsa and vegetables.
• **Bake** at 350° for 5 minutes; sprinkle
with cheese. Bake 5 additional minutes
or until cheese melts and pizza is thoroughly heated. **Yield:** 2 to 3 servings.

✳ For the bread shell, we used Boboli.
Susan Dosier
Birmingham, Alabama

FIVE-RING PIZZAS

QUICK!

1 (14-ounce) jar pizza sauce
1 teaspoon dried Italian seasoning
1 pound ground beef
3 (10-ounce) cans refrigerated
    biscuits
½ cup (2 ounces) shredded
    Cheddar cheese
½ cup (2 ounces) shredded
    mozzarella cheese
½ cup chopped onion (optional)
¼ cup chopped green bell pepper
    (optional)
1 (2.5-ounce) can sliced
    mushrooms, drained
    (optional)

• **Combine** pizza sauce and Italian seasoning; set aside.
• **Brown** ground beef in a large nonstick
skillet, stirring until it crumbles; drain.

• **Separate** biscuits; flatten to ¼-inch
thickness on baking sheets. Spread each
with 1 tablespoon pizza sauce mixture.
Top evenly with ground beef and
cheeses; if desired, add onion, bell pepper, and mushrooms.
• **Bake** at 400° for 10 to 12 minutes.
Yield: 30 mini pizzas.

Allison Mendoza
Arlington, Texas

THE KING HENRY PIZZA

QUICK!

*If he were alive today, Henry VIII
no doubt would have the well-known
drumstick in one hand and a slice of
this meaty pizza in the other.*

1¼ cups Traditional Pizza Sauce
    (see recipe on page 344)
1 (12-inch) refrigerated pizza
    crust
½ pound ground pork sausage,
    cooked and drained
½ (3.5-ounce) package sliced
    pepperoni
8 slices bacon, cooked and
    crumbled
1 (8-ounce) package shredded
    four-cheese blend

• **Spread** Traditional Pizza Sauce over
pizza crust, and top evenly with sausage
and remaining ingredients.
• **Bake** at 425° for 10 minutes or until
bubbly. **Yield:** 1 (12-inch) pizza.

SOUTHERN CLASSIC PIZZA
QUICK!

¼ pound thinly sliced country ham
⅔ cup Roasted Garlic Sauce (see recipe on page 345)
1 (12-inch) refrigerated pizza crust
1 (10-ounce) package frozen chopped turnip greens or spinach, cooked and well drained
1 cup (4 ounces) shredded mozzarella cheese
½ cup freshly grated Parmesan cheese

• **Cook** ham according to package directions, and cut into thin strips.
• **Spread** Roasted Garlic Sauce over pizza crust; top with ham, turnip greens, and cheeses.
• **Bake** at 425° for 10 minutes or until bubbly. **Yield:** 1 (12-inch) pizza.

HAM AND PINEAPPLE PIZZA

Bryan based this sweet-and-savory pizza on his favorite selection at Everybody's Pizza, near Emory University in Atlanta.

1 (12-inch) refrigerated baked pizza crust *
2 teaspoons olive oil
1 cup pizza sauce
2 cups chopped smoked ham
1 (20-ounce) can pineapple tidbits, well drained
½ cup (2 ounces) shredded mozzarella cheese
1 cup (4 ounces) shredded provolone cheese

• **Brush** pizza crust with olive oil, and spread pizza sauce evenly over crust. Top sauce evenly with ham and pineapple; sprinkle with cheeses.
• **Bake** at 425° for 10 minutes or until cheese melts and crust is lightly browned. **Yield:** 1 (12-inch) pizza.

* For pizza crust, we used Mama Mary's.

Bryan Jacob
Alpharetta, Georgia

MEXICAN PIZZA
QUICK!

1 cup sliced fresh mushrooms
½ cup chopped green bell pepper
1 tablespoon vegetable oil
1 cup chopped cooked ham
1 (2¼-ounce) can sliced ripe olives, drained
1 (12-inch) refrigerated pizza crust
1 (16-ounce) jar thick and chunky salsa, divided
1 (8-ounce) package shredded Monterey Jack and Cheddar cheese blend
Shredded lettuce
Sour cream

• **Cook** mushrooms and bell pepper in oil in a skillet over medium heat, stirring constantly, until crisp-tender; stir in ham and olives. Spoon over pizza crust. Reserve ½ cup salsa; spoon remaining salsa over vegetable mixture.
• **Bake** at 425° for 10 to 12 minutes. Sprinkle with cheese; bake 5 additional minutes. Serve with reserved ½ cup salsa, lettuce, and sour cream. **Yield:** 1 (12-inch) pizza.

Note: For a crispier crust, bake pizza on bottom rack of oven.

Kay C. Regnier
Newbern, North Carolina

CHICKEN AND THREE-CHEESE FRENCH BREAD PIZZAS
QUICK!

½ cup butter, softened
½ cup (2 ounces) shredded Cheddar cheese
⅓ cup freshly grated Parmesan cheese
1 clove garlic, pressed
¼ teaspoon dried Italian seasoning
1 (16-ounce) loaf sliced French bread
1 (10-ounce) can white chicken, drained and flaked *
1 cup (4 ounces) shredded mozzarella cheese
¼ cup chopped red bell pepper
¼ cup chopped green onions

• **Combine** first 5 ingredients in a small bowl, and spread evenly over bread slices. Top with chicken; sprinkle with mozzarella cheese, bell pepper, and green onions.
• **Bake** at 350° for 10 minutes or until cheese melts. **Yield:** 6 servings.

* Substitute 1½ cups chopped cooked chicken breast for canned.

M. B. Quesenbury
Dugspur, Virginia

SOUTHWEST DELUXE PIZZA

This one takes more time than the others, but it's worth it.

3 skinned and boned chicken breast halves
1 teaspoon cumin
½ teaspoon salt
2 tablespoons butter or margarine
Juice of 1 lime
4 poblano peppers
1 (12-inch) refrigerated pizza crust
⅔ cup Roasted Garlic Sauce (see recipe on page 345)
½ cup canned black beans, rinsed and drained
1 medium purple onion, thinly sliced and separated into rings
½ cup chopped fresh cilantro, divided
1½ cups (6 ounces) shredded Monterey Jack cheese with peppers

• **Sprinkle** chicken with cumin and salt. Melt butter in a skillet over medium heat; add chicken, and cook 10 minutes or until tender. Cut into 1-inch pieces, and pour lime juice over chicken. Set chicken aside.
• **Place** peppers on an aluminum foil-lined baking sheet. Broil 5½ inches from heat (with electric oven door partially opened) 5 minutes on each side or until peppers look blistered.
• **Place** peppers in a heavy-duty, zip-top plastic bag; seal and let stand 10 minutes. Peel peppers; remove and discard cores, membranes, and seeds. Chop peppers, and set aside.

- **Bake** pizza crust at 425° for 10 minutes. Spread Roasted Garlic Sauce over pizza crust; top with chicken, chopped pepper, black beans, onion, ¼ cup cilantro, and cheese.
- **Bake** at 425° for 15 minutes or until bubbly. Serve with remaining ¼ cup cilantro. **Yield:** 1 (12-inch) pizza.

THE BEST OF THE BAYOU PIZZA

1 pound unpeeled large fresh shrimp
½ cup chopped green bell pepper
½ cup chopped onion
½ cup chopped celery
2 teaspoons Creole seasoning *
1 tablespoon olive oil
⅔ cup Roasted Garlic Sauce (see recipe on page 345)
1 (12-inch) refrigerated pizza crust
1 cup (4 ounces) shredded mozzarella cheese
¼ cup freshly grated Parmesan cheese

- **Peel** shrimp, and devein, if desired.
- **Cook** shrimp, green pepper, and next 3 ingredients in oil in a large skillet over medium-high heat, stirring constantly, 3 to 5 minutes or until shrimp turn pink.
- **Spread** Roasted Garlic Sauce over pizza crust; top with shrimp mixture. Sprinkle with cheeses.
- **Bake** at 425° for 10 minutes or until bubbly. **Yield:** 1 (12-inch) pizza.

* For Creole seasoning, we used Tony Chachere's More Spice, Less Salt Creole Seasoning.

CRUNCHY MUNCHIES

6 cups corn-and-rice cereal *
1½ cups pecan pieces or peanuts
½ cup light corn syrup
⅓ cup butter or margarine, melted
½ cup sifted powdered sugar

- **Combine** cereal and pecans in a large bowl; set aside.

- **Combine** corn syrup, butter, and powdered sugar, stirring until smooth. Pour over cereal mixture, stirring to coat. Pour mixture into a lightly greased 15- x 10- x 1-inch jellyroll pan.
- **Bake** at 250° for 1 hour, stirring every 15 minutes.
- **Stir** carefully to loosen from pan; cool and break into pieces. Store in an airtight container. **Yield:** 7 cups.

* For corn-and-rice cereal, we used Crispix.

POP GRAHAM MUNCHIES

10 cups popped popcorn
3 cups honey graham cereal *
2 cups miniature marshmallows
1½ cups golden raisins
½ cup butter or margarine
¼ cup firmly packed brown sugar
1½ teaspoons ground cinnamon
¼ teaspoon ground ginger
¼ teaspoon freshly ground nutmeg

- **Combine** first 4 ingredients in a large roasting pan. Set aside.
- **Combine** butter and remaining 4 ingredients in a small saucepan; cook over low heat, stirring constantly, until butter melts. Pour over popcorn mixture, tossing to coat.
- **Bake** at 325° for 20 minutes, stirring every 5 minutes.
- **Pour** onto wax paper; cool. Store in airtight containers. **Yield:** about 3 quarts.

* For honey graham cereal, we used Golden Honey Graham Cereal.

POWER MUNCH
QUICK!

6 cups crispy corn cereal squares *
1 cup dry-roasted peanuts
3 tablespoons butter or margarine, melted
3 tablespoons honey
½ cup finely chopped dried apricot halves

- **Combine** cereal and peanuts in a 13- x 9- x 2-inch pan. Combine butter and honey; drizzle over cereal mixture, tossing gently to coat.
- **Bake** at 300° for 10 minutes, stirring once. Add apricots; bake 10 additional minutes, stirring twice. Cool on wax paper; store in airtight containers. **Yield:** 6 cups.

* For crispy corn cereal squares, we used Corn Chex.

Barbara Barnard
Birmingham, Alabama

CEREAL SNACK MIX

1 (13-ounce) package honey graham cereal *
1 (12.3-ounce) package corn-and-rice cereal *
1 (17-ounce) package O-shaped sweetened oat and wheat bran cereal *
1 (12-ounce) can mixed nuts
1 (7.5-ounce) package pretzel chips
1 cup butter or margarine, melted
2 tablespoons Worchestershire sauce
1 tablespoon seasoned salt

- **Combine** first 5 ingredients in a large heavy-duty, zip-top plastic bag.
- **Combine** butter, Worchestershire sauce, and seasoned salt; cool slightly, and pour into bag. Seal bag, and shake gently until well coated.
- **Divide** mixture into two large roasting pans; place pans on racks in oven, one above the other. Bake at 225° for 1 hour, stirring every 15 minutes. Remove from oven; spread on paper towels to cool. Store in airtight containers. **Yield:** 8 quarts.

* For honey graham cereal, we used Golden Honey Graham Cereal. For corn-and-rice cereal, we used Crispix. For O-shaped sweetened oat and wheat bran, we used Cracklin' Oat Bran.
Linda P. Jones
Mount Airy, North Carolina

GRANOLA MIX

2 (3-ounce) packages ramen
    noodles
4 cups regular oats, uncooked
1 (2⅛-ounce) jar sesame seeds
    (⅓ cup)
1 (3.75-ounce) package sunflower
    kernels (¾ cup)
½ cup dry-roasted peanuts
⅓ cup firmly packed brown sugar
¼ cup honey
¼ cup vegetable oil
1 teaspoon vanilla extract
½ cup raisins (optional)

• **Remove** seasoning packets from noodles, and reserve for another use; break noodles into small pieces.
• **Combine** noodles, oats, and next 3 ingredients in a large bowl; set aside.
• **Combine** brown sugar and next 3 ingredients; pour over noodle mixture, and stir well. Spread mixture evenly in a 15- x 10- x 1-inch jellyroll pan.
• **Bake** at 325° for 30 minutes or until golden, stirring every 10 minutes.
• **Stir** in raisins, if desired. Cool and store mixture in an airtight container. Serve with milk or over frozen yogurt. **Yield:** 8½ cups.

Fruit Crisp: Combine 4 cups sliced fresh peaches and 1 cup fresh or frozen blackberries or blueberries, thawed, in a 9-inch round cakepan; sprinkle with 2 tablespoons sugar and 1 cup Granola Mix. Bake at 375° for 35 minutes. Serve with frozen yogurt or ice cream. **Yield:** 6 servings.

CARAMEL CRUNCH

12 cups popped popcorn (about
    ½ cup unpopped)
1 (3-ounce) can chow mein
    noodles
1 cup dry-roasted peanuts
½ cup raisins
1½ cups firmly packed brown
    sugar
¾ cup butter or margarine
¾ cup light corn syrup
1 teaspoon ground cinnamon
½ teaspoon baking soda

• **Combine** first 4 ingredients in a lightly greased roasting pan, and set aside.
• **Combine** brown sugar and next 3 ingredients in a large saucepan; cook over medium heat, stirring constantly, 5 minutes or until mixture boils. Remove mixture from heat, and stir in soda (mixture will bubble).
• **Pour** brown sugar mixture over popcorn mixture; stir with a lightly greased long-handled spoon to coat.
• **Bake** at 250° for 1 hour, stirring every 15 minutes. Remove from oven, and immediately pour onto wax paper, breaking apart large clumps as they cool. Store in airtight containers. **Yield:** 4 quarts.

Ann Niedens
Kure Beach, North Carolina

TACO-CHEESE
ANIMAL CRACKERS

1 cup all-purpose flour
1½ cups (6 ounces) shredded
    taco-flavored Cheddar
    cheese
½ cup butter or margarine,
    softened
Paprika (optional)

• **Position** knife blade in food processor bowl; add flour, shredded cheese, and butter. Process until mixture forms a ball, stopping once to scrape down sides.
• **Wrap** dough in heavy-duty plastic wrap; chill 30 minutes.
• **Unwrap** dough, and roll to ¼-inch thickness on a lightly floured surface. Cut with 2½-inch animal-shaped cutters; place on ungreased baking sheets. Sprinkle with paprika, if desired.
• **Bake** at 375° for 10 to 12 minutes or until lightly browned; cool on wire racks. **Yield:** 3 dozen.

SOUP NUTS

Keep plenty of these little jewels on hand. They're great for snacking.

2 cups all-purpose flour
½ cup grated Parmesan cheese
1 teaspoon garlic salt
½ teaspoon dried Italian
    seasoning
3 large eggs
3 tablespoons olive oil

• **Combine** first 4 ingredients in a large mixing bowl; add eggs and oil, beating at medium speed with an electric mixer until blended.
• **Turn** dough out onto a lightly floured surface; knead lightly 3 or 4 times (dough may be crumbly). Divide dough into 6 portions. Shape each portion into a 12-inch log; cut each roll into ¼-inch-thick slices, and place on ungreased baking sheets.
• **Bake** at 375° for 12 minutes or until lightly browned. Transfer to wire racks to cool completely. **Yield:** 3 cups.

CRAN-ORANGE SURPRISE

QUICK!

1 quart orange sherbet, softened
2 cups cranberry juice cocktail
1 cup lemon-lime carbonated
    beverage

• **Combine** all ingredients. Spoon mixture into paper cups or pop molds.
• **Freeze** 1 hour.
• **Insert** a wooden craft stick into each paper cup; freeze until firm. For molds, insert base of mold into pop immediately. Freeze until firm. **Yield:** 6 cups.

Note: To make pops that are for adults only, substitute ¼ cup Grand Marnier for 1 cup lemon-lime beverage, and freeze as directed. Yield: about 5 cups.

At right: Traditional Pizza Sauce (page 344), Roasted Garlic Sauce (page 345), and Pesto Sauce (page 345)

Sauces and
Condiments

BUTTERMILK SAUCE

QUICK!

1 cup sugar
½ cup butter or margarine
½ cup buttermilk
1 tablespoon light corn syrup
2 teaspoons vanilla extract
½ teaspoon baking soda
Toasted sliced almonds (optional)

• **Combine** all ingredients except almonds in a heavy saucepan.
• **Bring** to a boil over medium heat, stirring constantly. Serve warm over fresh fruit, cake, or ice cream. Sprinkle with almonds, if desired. **Yield:** 1¾ cups.

Cindy Hinton
Franklin, Tennessee

MARASCHINO-ORANGE SAUCE

QUICK!

2 tablespoons sugar
1 tablespoon cornstarch
1 cup orange juice
1 teaspoon butter or margarine
⅓ cup drained maraschino
     cherries

• **Whisk** together first 3 ingredients in a small saucepan. Bring to a boil over medium heat, stirring constantly; boil 1 minute, stirring constantly. Remove from heat.
• **Add** butter and cherries; stir until butter melts; cool. Cover and chill 1 hour. Serve with ice cream. **Yield:** 1¼ cups.

PRALINE SAUCE

1 cup firmly packed brown sugar
½ cup chopped pecans
½ cup light corn syrup
¼ cup water
Dash of salt
1 tablespoon butter or margarine
1 teaspoon vanilla extract

• **Combine** first 5 ingredients in a small saucepan; bring to a boil, stirring constantly, until sugar dissolves. Remove from heat.

• **Stir** in butter and vanilla. Serve over waffles or ice cream. Store in refrigerator up to 2 weeks. **Yield:** 1½ cups.

LaJuan Coward
Jasper, Texas

TOFFEE SAUCE

5 (1.4-ounce) toffee-flavored
     candy bars
¾ cup sugar
½ cup whipping cream
¼ cup light corn syrup
2 tablespoons butter or margarine
Fresh strawberries
Sour cream
Garnish: fresh mint sprigs

• **Position** knife blade in food processor bowl; add candy bars. Process until finely crushed. Set aside.
• **Combine** sugar and next 3 ingredients in a heavy saucepan.
• **Cook** over medium heat, stirring constantly, until sugar dissolves. Bring mixture to a boil, and boil 2 minutes.
• **Remove** from heat; add crushed candy, stirring until smooth.
• **Serve** sauce with strawberries and sour cream. Garnish, if desired. **Yield:** 1⅔ cups.

Note: For a thinner sauce, stir in additional whipping cream.

Judy Laramy
Austin, Texas

DARK CHOCOLATE SAUCE

QUICK!

¾ cup cocoa
½ cup sugar
½ cup light corn syrup
¼ cup vegetable oil
¼ cup butter or margarine
¼ cup water
1 teaspoon vanilla extract

• **Combine** cocoa and sugar in a saucepan; stir in corn syrup and oil.
• **Cook** over low heat 8 to 10 minutes, stirring constantly, or until sugar dissolves. Add butter, water, and vanilla;

cook, stirring constantly, just until butter melts. Serve warm over ice cream. **Yield:** 1⅔ cups.

Anne Fowler Newell
Johnsonville, South Carolina

CHOCOLATE-PEPPERMINT SAUCE

QUICK!

1 cup (6 ounces) semisweet
     chocolate morsels
½ to ⅔ cup half-and-half, divided
¼ cup finely crushed hard
     peppermint candy

• **Combine** chocolate morsels, ½ cup half-and-half, and candy in a small saucepan; cook over low heat about 10 minutes or until chocolate and candy melt, stirring occasionally.
• **Stir** in enough remaining half-and-half for desired consistency. Serve over pound cake or ice cream. Store in refrigerator up to 2 weeks. **Yield:** 1¼ cups.

Marsha Littrell
Sheffield, Alabama

WHITE CHOCOLATE SAUCE

QUICK!

1 (6-ounce) white chocolate-
     flavored baking bar, chopped
¼ cup plus 2 tablespoons whipping
     cream
2 tablespoons light corn syrup
1½ teaspoons crème de cacao or
     other chocolate-flavored
     liqueur
½ teaspoon vanilla extract

• **Place** white chocolate in a small heavy saucepan; cook over low heat, stirring constantly, until chocolate melts. Remove from heat, and set aside.
• **Place** whipping cream in a saucepan, and bring to a boil; add corn syrup, stirring until blended. Remove from heat, and gradually add to melted white chocolate, stirring constantly, until smooth. Stir in crème de cacao and vanilla. Serve at room temperature with fresh berries. **Yield:** 1 cup.

SPICY SOUTHWEST BARBECUE SAUCE

6 cloves garlic, unpeeled
2 cups ketchup
2 stalks celery, chopped
1 cup water
½ cup chopped onion
½ cup firmly packed brown sugar
½ cup butter or margarine
½ cup Worcestershire sauce
½ cup apple cider vinegar
3 tablespoons chili powder
2 teaspoons instant coffee granules
1½ to 2 teaspoons dried crushed red pepper
½ teaspoon salt
½ teaspoon ground cloves

● **Bake** garlic in a baking pan at 350° for 20 minutes or until golden. Cool; peel.
● **Combine** garlic, ketchup, and remaining ingredients in a saucepan.
● **Bring** to a boil; reduce heat, and simmer 20 minutes. Cool.
● **Pour** mixture into container of an electric blender; process until smooth, stopping once to scrape down sides.
● **Divide** sauce into separate containers for basting and serving at the table. (Basting brushes used on raw food should not be dipped in table sauce.)
● **Use** as a basting sauce during last 30 minutes of cooking for chicken.
● **Store** any remaining table sauce in refrigerator, and discard any remaining basting sauce. **Yield:** 4½ cups.

THICK AND ROBUST BARBECUE SAUCE

¾ cup apple cider vinegar
½ cup ketchup
¼ cup chili sauce
¼ cup Worcestershire sauce
2 tablespoons chopped onion
1 clove garlic, minced
1 tablespoon brown sugar
1 tablespoon lemon juice
½ teaspoon dry mustard
Dash of ground red pepper

● **Combine** all ingredients in a saucepan; bring to a boil over medium heat,
stirring occasionally. Reduce heat, and simmer, uncovered, 40 minutes, stirring occasionally.
● **Divide** sauce into separate containers for basting and serving at the table. (Basting brushes used on raw food should not be dipped in table sauce.)
● **Use** as a basting sauce during last 10 minutes of cooking for steak, pork, or hamburgers.
● **Store** any leftover table sauce in refrigerator, and discard any remaining basting sauce. **Yield:** 1¾ cups.

THIN AND TASTY BARBECUE SAUCE

QUICK!

1 (8-ounce) bottle ketchup
1 cup apple cider vinegar
¼ cup water
1½ tablespoons pepper
1 tablespoon paprika
1½ teaspoons chili powder
½ teaspoon salt
½ teaspoon dry mustard
1½ teaspoons Worcestershire sauce
1½ teaspoons hot sauce

● **Combine** all ingredients in a bowl.
● **Divide** sauce into separate containers for basting and serving at the table. (Basting brushes used on raw food should not be dipped in table sauce.)
● **Use** as a basting sauce during last 10 minutes of cooking for hamburgers, chicken, or ribs.
● **Store** any remaining table sauce in refrigerator, and discard any remaining basting sauce. **Yield:** 2⅔ cups.

Mrs. P. D. Moore
Roanoke, Virginia

LEMONY BARBECUE SAUCE

QUICK!

½ cup ketchup
1 teaspoon grated lemon rind
2 teaspoons fresh lemon juice
2 teaspoons Worcestershire sauce
2 teaspoons prepared mustard
Dash of garlic powder

● **Combine** all ingredients in a bowl.
● **Divide** sauce into separate containers for basting and serving at the table. (Basting brushes used on raw food should not be dipped in table sauce.)
● **Use** as a basting sauce during last 10 minutes of cooking for chicken.
● **Store** any remaining table sauce in refrigerator, and discard any remaining basting sauce. **Yield:** about ⅔ cup.

MAPLE SYRUP BARBECUE SAUCE

1 cup maple syrup
1 cup ketchup
1 cup finely chopped onion
¼ cup firmly packed brown sugar
¼ cup apple cider vinegar
¼ cup lemon juice
¼ cup water
2 tablespoons olive oil
2 tablespoons Worcestershire sauce
2 teaspoons minced garlic
2 teaspoons grated lemon rind
1 teaspoon salt
¼ teaspoon hot sauce

● **Combine** all ingredients in a saucepan. Bring to a boil; reduce heat, and simmer 20 minutes. Cool.
● **Pour** mixture into container of an electric blender; process until smooth.
● **Divide** sauce into separate containers for basting and serving at the table. (Basting brushes used on raw food should not be dipped in table sauce.)
● **Use** as a basting sauce during last 30 minutes of cooking for chicken.
● **Store** any remaining table sauce in refrigerator, and discard any remaining basting sauce. **Yield:** 3½ cups.

Barbara Evans
Hendersonville, Tennessee

KLEBERG HOT SAUCE

QUICK!

6 to 8 ounces chile piquíns *
¼ cup coarsely chopped onion
2 cloves garlic
1 (28-ounce) can whole tomatoes,
    undrained
2 tablespoons white vinegar
¼ teaspoon salt
⅛ teaspoon pepper

• **Combine** all ingredients in container
of an electric blender; pulse 3 or 4 times
or until finely chopped. Store sauce in
refrigerator up to 1 week or freeze up to
1 month. **Yield:** 4½ cups.

* Substitute 10 ounces serrano chile
peppers for piquíns.

King Ranch
Kingsville, Texas

TACO SAUCE

½ teaspoon cumin seeds
1 (16-ounce) can whole tomatoes,
    undrained
2 jalapeño peppers, seeded
1 small onion, sliced
1 clove garlic, peeled
1 teaspoon salt
1 teaspoon pepper
Garnish: seeded jalapeño pepper
    slices

• **Place** a small skillet over medium-high
heat until hot; add cumin seeds, and
cook, stirring constantly, until seeds are
more fragrant and lightly browned. Let
seeds cool.
• **Combine** cumin seeds, tomatoes, and
next 5 ingredients in container of an
electric blender or food processor;
process until blended. Pour into a
medium saucepan.
• **Bring** to a boil; reduce heat, and simmer 5 minutes. Garnish, if desired.
Yield: 2 cups.

Becky Holzhaus
Castroville, Texas

TOMATO-BASIL SAUCE

QUICK!

1 pint cherry tomatoes, cut in half
1 cup fresh basil leaves, chopped
¼ cup olive oil
½ teaspoon salt
½ teaspoon pepper

• **Combine** all ingredients in a large
bowl, tossing gently to coat; let stand 30
minutes. Serve over angel hair pasta.
Yield: 2 cups.

Hilda Marshall
Bealeton, Virginia

SLOW-SIMMERED SPAGHETTI SAUCE

QUICK!

Reach for your slow cooker.
This sauce tastes every bit as good
as ones prepared on the cooktop.
You just don't have to stir it.

2 cloves garlic, minced
1 large onion, chopped
4 (14.5-ounce) cans Italian-style
    tomatoes, undrained and
    chopped
1 (15-ounce) can tomato sauce
1 (12-ounce) can tomato
    paste
2 to 3 teaspoons dried basil
2 to 3 teaspoons dried oregano
½ teaspoon dried crushed red
    pepper

• **Combine** all ingredients in a 4-quart
electric slow cooker.
• **Cover** and cook on HIGH 6 hours.
Serve over spaghetti, chicken, or pork.
Yield: 2½ quarts.

Note: You can freeze the spaghetti
sauce in airtight containers up to 2
weeks.

Cindy Sullivan
Tallahassee, Florida

TRADITIONAL PIZZA SAUCE

(pictured on page 341)

QUICK!

1 (14½-ounce) can pasta-style
    tomatoes, undrained
1 (8-ounce) can tomato sauce
1 clove garlic, pressed
½ teaspoon dried oregano
⅛ teaspoon garlic salt
⅛ teaspoon pepper

• **Combine** all ingredients in a saucepan. Bring to a boil, stirring constantly.
Reduce heat; simmer, uncovered, 5 minutes, stirring often. **Yield:** about 2 cups.

DRIED TOMATO PESTO

Use this sauce chilled as a dip for
raw vegetables or steamed shrimp or
serve it warm, tossed with pasta.

½ cup dried tomatoes
1 cup vegetable broth, divided
½ cup fresh basil leaves
1 clove garlic
¼ cup grated reduced-fat
    Parmesan cheese
2 tablespoons pine nuts
1 tablespoon olive oil
¼ teaspoon salt
¼ teaspoon ground white pepper
1 teaspoon cornstarch

• **Combine** tomatoes and ½ cup vegetable broth in a small saucepan, and
bring mixture to a boil. Remove from
heat; let stand 10 minutes.
• **Position** knife blade in food processor bowl; add tomato mixture, basil, and
next 6 ingredients. Process until
smooth, stopping twice to scrape down
sides. Set tomato mixture aside.
• **Combine** remaining ½ cup vegetable
broth and cornstarch in a saucepan;
bring to a boil over medium heat, stirring constantly. Cook 1 minute, stirring
constantly. Stir in tomato mixture.
Cover and chill up to 3 days or freeze up
to 3 months. **Yield:** 1 cup.

♥ Per ¼-cup serving: Calories 106
Fat 7.9g   Cholesterol 4mg
Sodium 390mg

PESTO SAUCE
(pictured on page 341)

QUICK!

Lemon juice keeps the basil from turning too dark and brightens the flavor of this pesto.

2 cloves garlic
½ cup walnuts, toasted
2 cups loosely packed fresh basil leaves
½ cup olive oil
¾ cup freshly grated Parmesan or Romano cheese
¼ teaspoon salt
2 teaspoons lemon juice
1 teaspoon hot water

• **Position** knife blade in food processor bowl; add first 3 ingredients. Process until smooth, stopping once to scrape down sides.
• **Pour** oil through food chute with processor running. Add cheese and remaining ingredients; process until smooth, stopping once to scrape down sides. Cover and chill up to 3 days or freeze up to 3 months. **Yield:** 1 cup.

BURNED BOURBON WITH MOLASSES SAUCE

⅓ cup bourbon
4 cups Beef Stock (see recipe on page 378)
¾ cup port wine
1 tablespoon molasses
2 tablespoons butter or margarine

• **Bring** bourbon to a boil over medium heat in a long-handled saucepan. Remove from heat; ignite and let stand until flames disappear. Combine bourbon, Beef Stock, wine, and molasses in a heavy saucepan.
• **Bring** to a boil; reduce heat, and simmer 50 minutes or until reduced to about ¾ cup. Remove from heat.
• **Add** butter, 1 teaspoon at a time, stirring until blended. Serve with beef or pork tenderloin. **Yield:** about ¾ cup.
Charles Walton IV
Birmingham, Alabama

ROASTED GARLIC SAUCE
(pictured on page 341)

That's 2 heads of garlic, not cloves. The flavor mellows with roasting.

2 heads garlic, unpeeled
1 teaspoon olive oil
1½ tablespoons butter or margarine
1½ tablespoons all-purpose flour
⅔ cup chicken broth

• **Place** garlic on a piece of aluminum foil, and drizzle with olive oil. Fold edges together to seal.
• **Bake** at 425° for 30 minutes; cool.
• **Melt** butter in a heavy saucepan over medium-high heat. Cut top off each garlic head, and squeeze cooked garlic into pan. (Garlic will be soft and sticky.)
• **Add** flour, and cook, stirring constantly with a wire whisk, 1 minute or until lightly browned.
• **Add** chicken broth. Cook, stirring constantly, until mixture is thick and bubbly. **Yield:** ⅔ cup.

SHALLOT-THYME SAUCE

Try this delicate yet rich sauce with grilled veal, lamb, or chicken, or steamed vegetables.

8 sprigs fresh thyme
2 shallots, finely chopped
1 clove garlic, minced
1 cup dry white wine
½ cup whipping cream
1 cup cold butter, cut into 8 pieces
Dash of salt
Dash of pepper

• **Combine** first 4 ingredients in a medium skillet, and cook over medium-high heat 15 minutes or until liquid is reduced to ⅓ cup.
• **Reduce** heat to simmer. Stir in whipping cream, and simmer 10 minutes or until mixture is reduced by half.
• **Remove** mixture from heat; immediately add butter, a few pieces at a time, stirring constantly with a wire whisk until smooth. If necessary, place skillet

over low heat for a few seconds to melt butter. (Do not melt butter before adding to sauce.)
• **Pour** sauce through a wire-mesh strainer into a bowl, discarding solids. Stir in salt and pepper. Serve immediately. (Do not reheat the sauce or it will separate.) **Yield:** 1⅓ cups.

VENISON REDUCTION SAUCE

1 tablespoon olive oil
2 cloves shallot, minced
1 clove garlic, minced
½ cup dry red wine
2 cups Venison Stock ✳ (see recipe on page 378)
½ teaspoon chopped fresh parsley or chervil

• **Heat** olive oil in a small saucepan; add shallot and garlic, and cook over medium-high heat, stirring constantly, until tender. Add wine and Venison Stock.
• **Bring** to a boil; reduce heat, and simmer 20 minutes. Stir in chopped parsley. **Yield:** 1½ cups.

✳ Substitute 2 cups no-salt-added beef broth for Venison Stock. If you substitute broth, add 1 tablespoon all-purpose flour while cooking shallot and garlic.
Chef David Everett
Dining Room at Ford's Colony
Williamsburg, Virginia

LEMONY TARTAR SAUCE

QUICK!

½ cup mayonnaise or salad dressing
2 tablespoons finely chopped green onions
2 tablespoons sweet pickle relish
1 teaspoon grated lemon rind
2 teaspoons fresh lemon juice

• **Combine** all ingredients. Serve sauce with seafood or as a sandwich spread. **Yield:** ⅔ cup.

TROPICAL SALSA

This exotic concoction turns fish or chicken into a marvelous meal.

1 ripe mango, chopped
½ cup chopped plum tomato
½ cup chopped red bell pepper
½ cup chopped purple onion
1 tablespoon minced garlic
1½ teaspoons minced jalapeño pepper
1 teaspoon ground cumin
1 tablespoon olive oil
1 tablespoon red wine vinegar
¼ cup fresh lime juice
½ teaspoon hot sauce
½ cup chopped fresh cilantro
¼ teaspoon salt
¼ teaspoon pepper

• **Combine** all ingredients. Store in refrigerator in an airtight container up to 3 days. **Yield:** 2½ cups.

Paul Stansel
Raleigh, North Carolina

PEACH SALSA

Chips, fish, or chicken will wake up to the fruity flavor of this salsa.

1 (16-ounce) can peaches in juice, drained and chopped
4 plum tomatoes, chopped
4 green onions, sliced
2 tablespoons chopped pickled jalapeño peppers
1 tablespoon finely chopped fresh cilantro
1 tablespoon olive oil
1 tablespoon lime juice
1 teaspoon honey
¼ teaspoon salt
¼ teaspoon pepper

• **Combine** all ingredients in a large bowl, stirring gently. Store in refrigerator in an airtight container up to 3 days. **Yield:** 3 cups.

Judy Carter
Winchester, Tennessee

AVOCADO-FETA SALSA

Serve this tangy version of guacamole with Tex-Mex combos, hamburgers, pasta, grilled fish, or chicken.

1 large avocado
2 plum tomatoes
¼ cup chopped purple onion
1 clove garlic, minced
1 tablespoon chopped fresh parsley
½ teaspoon chopped fresh oregano
1 tablespoon olive oil
½ tablespoon red wine vinegar
½ (4-ounce) package crumbled feta cheese

• **Peel** and seed avocado; chop avocado and tomatoes, and place in a large bowl. Add onion and next 5 ingredients, tossing to coat. Fold in cheese. Serve immediately. **Yield:** 2 cups.

Heather Riggins
Nashville, Tennessee

CORN-BLACK BEAN SALSA

QUICK!

This colorful salsa is good with just about anything.

1 (15-ounce) can black beans, rinsed and drained
1 cup frozen corn kernels, thawed
½ cup chopped red bell pepper
½ cup chopped fresh cilantro
8 green onions, sliced
3 tablespoons lime juice
2 tablespoons balsamic vinegar
½ teaspoon ground cumin
¼ teaspoon salt

• **Combine** all ingredients. Store in refrigerator in an airtight container up to 3 days. **Yield:** 4 cups.

Kenner Patton
Birmingham, Alabama

TOMATO SALSA

QUICK!

Pair this classic salsa with chips, pasta, or anything Tex-Mex.

1 (16-ounce) can crushed tomatoes, undrained
2 (14.5-ounce) cans diced tomatoes, undrained
1 (4.5-ounce) can chopped green chiles, undrained
1 medium onion, chopped
2 large jalapeño peppers, chopped
2 cloves garlic, minced
½ cup chopped fresh cilantro
2 tablespoons lime juice
1 tablespoon sugar

• **Combine** all ingredients. Store in refrigerator in an airtight container up to 3 days. **Yield:** 7 cups.

Sheila Fogle
Huntsville, Alabama

SALSA VERDE

QUICK!

½ cup coarsely chopped purple onion
¼ cup loosely packed fresh cilantro
1 jalapeño pepper, seeded
½ teaspoon salt
2 (11-ounce) cans tomatillos, drained

• **Position** knife blade in food processor; add all ingredients. Process until finely chopped. Store in refrigerator in an airtight container up to 3 days. **Yield:** 2 cups.

Ginny Munsterman
Garland, Texas

PEACH JAM

3 pounds fresh peaches
1 (1.75-ounce) package powdered
   pectin
2 tablespoons lemon juice
5 cups sugar
½ teaspoon whole allspice

• **Peel,** pit, and coarsely mash peaches to measure 4 cups. Combine peaches, pectin, and lemon juice in a Dutch oven; bring to a boil over high heat, stirring constantly. Stir in sugar and allspice; return to a boil, and cook 1 minute, stirring constantly. Remove from heat; skim off foam with a metal spoon.
• **Quickly** ladle hot mixture into hot, sterilized jars, filling to ¼ inch from top. Remove air bubbles; wipe jar rims. Cover at once with metal lids, and screw on bands.
• **Process** in boiling-water bath 5 minutes. **Yield:** 6 half-pints.

Azine G. Rush
Monroe, Louisiana

SPICED APPLE JELLY
(pictured on page 349)

4 pounds cooking apples
2 cups water
1½ cups apple cider vinegar
2 (3-inch) sticks cinnamon
2 teaspoons whole cloves
3 cups sugar

• **Remove** stem and blossom ends from apples. Cut apples into large slices. (Do not peel or core.)
• **Combine** apple slices, 2 cups water, and next 3 ingredients in a Dutch oven, and bring to a boil. Cover, reduce heat, and simmer 25 minutes or until apple slices are tender. Cool slightly.
• **Pour** apple mixture through a jelly bag or a colander lined with four layers of cheesecloth into a bowl, reserving apple liquid in bowl. (Do not press or squeeze mixture through bag or colander.) Add water to apple liquid to equal 4 cups.
• **Combine** apple liquid and sugar in a large saucepan; bring to a boil over medium heat, stirring until sugar dissolves. Boil 30 to 35 minutes or until

thermometer registers 220° and jelly sheets from a spoon. Remove from heat; skim off foam with a metal spoon.
• **Quickly** pour jelly into hot, sterilized jars, filling to ¼ inch from top; wipe jar rims. Cover at once with metal lids, and screw on bands.
• **Process** in boiling-water bath 5 minutes. **Yield:** 3 half-pints.

Anna Robinson
Oak Ridge, Tennessee

CHILE PIQUÍN JELLY

¼ cup red or green chile piquíns *
1 medium-size red or green bell
   pepper
6½ cups sugar
1½ cups white vinegar
   (5% acidity)
2 (3-ounce) envelopes liquid fruit
   pectin (6-ounce package)
Red or green liquid food coloring
   (optional)

• **Wash** chile piquíns and bell pepper; pat dry. Remove and discard seeds and membranes. Cut into quarters; set aside.
• **Position** knife blade in food processor bowl. Add chile and peppers; pulse 3 or 4 times or until finely chopped.
• **Combine** pepper, sugar, and vinegar in a Dutch oven; bring to a boil. Boil 2 minutes. Remove from heat, and cool 5 minutes.
• **Add** liquid pectin to pepper mixture; return to a boil, and boil 1 minute, stirring constantly. Remove from heat, and skim off foam with a metal spoon. Add food coloring, if desired.
• **Quickly** pour jelly into hot, sterilized jars, filling to ¼ inch from top; wipe jar rims. Cover at once with metal lids, and screw on bands.
• **Process** in boiling-water bath 5 minutes. **Yield:** 6 half-pints.

∗ Substitute serrano chile peppers, if desired.

Note: For a translucent jelly, pour through a wire-mesh strainer into a Dutch oven before adding pectin.

King Ranch
Kingsville, Texas

QUICK JALAPEÑO PEPPER JELLY

QUICK!

*Serve as an appetizer with cream
cheese and crackers.*

4 (16-ounce) jars lime marmalade
   or apple jelly
6 to 8 jalapeño peppers, minced
¼ cup apple cider vinegar

• **Combine** all ingredients in a large saucepan; bring to a boil. Reduce heat; simmer 5 minutes. Remove from heat; let cool. Cover and store in refrigerator up to 2 weeks. **Yield:** 4½ cups.

Judi Grigoraci
Charleston, West Virginia

BLUEBERRY MARMALADE

*This easy recipe uses only 4 cups
of berries and makes 6 half-pints.*

1 medium orange
1 lemon
¾ cup water
⅛ teaspoon baking soda
4 cups fresh blueberries, crushed
5 cups sugar
1 (6-ounce) package liquid fruit
   pectin

• **Peel** orange and lemon; finely chop rind, and place in a Dutch oven. Chop orange and lemon pulp, and set aside. Add water and baking soda to rind; bring to a boil. Reduce heat, and simmer 10 minutes, stirring occasionally.
• **Add** chopped orange and lemon pulp, blueberries, and sugar; return to a boil. Reduce heat, and simmer 5 minutes. Remove from heat; cool 5 minutes.
• **Add** pectin; return to a boil. Boil 1 minute, stirring constantly; remove from heat, and skim off foam with a metal spoon.
• **Quickly** pour into hot jars, filling to ¼ inch from top; wipe jar rims. Cover at once with metal lids; screw on bands.
• **Process** in boiling-water bath 10 minutes. **Yield:** 6 half-pints.

Adelyn Whiting
Albany, Georgia

QUICK STRAWBERRY FIG PRESERVES

3 cups mashed fresh figs (about 2 pounds)
1½ cups sugar
1 (3-ounce) package strawberry-flavored gelatin

• **Combine** figs and sugar in a heavy saucepan; cook over medium heat 2 minutes, stirring constantly. Gradually stir in gelatin, and cook over low heat 15 minutes, stirring constantly.
• **Spoon** preserves into hot, sterilized jars, filling to ¼ inch from top. Remove air bubbles; wipe jar rims. Cover at once with metal lids, and screw on bands.
• **Process** in boiling-water bath 5 minutes. **Yield:** 4 half-pints.

Nora Henshaw
Okemah, Oklahoma

CRANBERRY CHUTNEY

Serve with turkey or as an appetizer with gingersnaps and cream cheese.

8 (16-ounce) cans whole-berry cranberry sauce
2 cups firmly packed light brown sugar
2 cups chopped dates
2 cups currants or raisins
2 cups slivered almonds
2 cups apple cider vinegar
¼ cup minced crystallized ginger
2 teaspoons ground allspice

• **Combine** all ingredients in a large Dutch oven. Bring to a boil, stirring constantly; reduce heat, and simmer 30 minutes, stirring occasionally.
• **Cool**, place in jars, and store in refrigerator up to 2 weeks. For longer storage, pack chutney into hot, sterilized jars, filling to ½ inch from top; remove air bubbles, and wipe jar rims. Cover at once with metal lids, and screw on bands.
• **Process** in boiling-water bath 5 minutes. **Yield:** 10 pints.

Louise W. Mayer
Richmond, Virginia

BLUE-RIBBON MANGO CHUTNEY

3 large mangoes, chopped (about 2 pounds) *
1½ cups chopped onion
½ cup peeled, chopped cooking apple
½ cup raisins
1 cup apple cider vinegar
1¼ cups firmly packed brown sugar
½ cup sugar
¼ cup finely chopped fresh ginger
½ teaspoon grated lime rind
2 tablespoons fresh lime juice
1 tablespoon mustard seeds
1½ teaspoons celery seeds
¾ teaspoon salt
¼ teaspoon ground cinnamon
¼ teaspoon ground cloves

• **Combine** all ingredients in a glass bowl; cover and chill 8 hours.
• **Transfer** to a Dutch oven; bring to a boil over medium heat. Reduce heat; cook 1½ hours, stirring occasionally.
• **Divide** mango mixture into airtight containers; chill up to 1 week or freeze up to 6 months. **Yield:** 3 cups.

* Substitute 1 (26-ounce) jar mango, drained and chopped, for fresh.

Kathryn McKelvey Smith
Durham, North Carolina

PEAR CHUTNEY
(pictured on opposite page)

1 pound onions, quartered
9 cloves garlic
5 pounds firm pears, peeled, cored, and chopped
1 quart white vinegar (5% acidity)
6 cups sugar
1 (24-ounce) package raisins
½ teaspoon dry mustard
1½ cups chopped crystallized ginger
½ teaspoon ground ginger
3 tablespoons mustard seeds

• **Position** knife blade in food processor bowl; add half of onion quarters and garlic. Pulse 4 or 5 times or until onion quarters are chopped. Transfer to a

Dutch oven; repeat procedure with remaining onion quarters and garlic.
• **Add** pears and vinegar to onion mixture; bring to a boil. Reduce heat; simmer 20 to 25 minutes or until tender.
• **Add** sugar, stirring until dissolved; cook over medium heat 10 minutes, stirring occasionally. Add raisins and mustard; cook 20 minutes.
• **Add** crystallized ginger, ground ginger, and mustard seeds; cook over medium heat 10 minutes or until thickened.
• **Pour** hot mixture into hot jars, filling to ½ inch from top. Remove air bubbles, and wipe jar rims. Cover jars at once with metal lids, and screw on bands.
• **Process** in boiling-water bath 10 minutes. **Yield:** 7 pints.

Jean Graham
Wilmington, North Carolina

NANNIE'S CHOWCHOW
(pictured at right)

5½ pounds green tomatoes, chopped
2¼ pounds onions, chopped
2 pounds green bell peppers, chopped
1 pound red bell peppers, chopped
1 (5-pound) cabbage, shredded
½ cup salt
1 quart water
1½ quarts white vinegar (5% acidity)
1½ cups sugar
½ cup mustard seeds
2 tablespoons celery seeds
1 tablespoon whole allspice

• **Combine** first 5 ingredients in a large nonmetallic container. Combine salt and water; stir until salt dissolves. Pour over vegetables. Chill at least 8 hours. Drain vegetables; discard liquid.
• **Combine** vinegar and remaining 4 ingredients in a stockpot; add vegetables . Bring to a boil over medium heat; reduce heat, and simmer 10 minutes.
• **Pack** hot mixture into hot jars, filling to ½ inch from top. Remove air bubbles; wipe jar rims. Cover at once with metal lids, and screw on bands.
• **Process** in boiling-water bath 10 minutes. **Yield:** 12 pints.

Nannie's Chowchow; Spiced Apple Jelly, page 347; Apple Pie Filling in a Jar, page 350; Pear Chutney

SWEET ZUCCHINI RELISH

10 cups grated zucchini (about
    5 pounds)
4 cups chopped onion
¼ cup salt
5 cups sugar
2¼ cups white vinegar (5%
    acidity)
1 tablespoon celery seeds
1 tablespoon ground turmeric
1 tablespoon pepper

• **Combine** first 3 ingredients in a large bowl. Cover and chill at least 8 hours.
• **Transfer** zucchini mixture to a colander; rinse under cold running water. Drain well, and press between layers of paper towels.
• **Combine** zucchini mixture, sugar, and remaining ingredients in a Dutch oven. Bring to a boil over medium-high heat; reduce heat to medium, and simmer 30 minutes, stirring often.
• **Pack** hot mixture into hot jars, filling to ½ inch from top. Remove air bubbles; wipe jar rims. Cover at once with metal lids, and screw on bands.
• **Process** in boiling-water bath 15 minutes. **Yield:** 9 half-pints.

Marge Killmon
Annandale, Virginia

SPANISH CABBAGE RELISH

4 cups coarsely chopped cabbage
1 cup chopped onion
1 cup coarsely chopped celery
1 small green bell pepper, chopped
1 (14-ounce) bottle hot ketchup
½ cup apple cider vinegar
¼ cup vegetable oil
1 teaspoon salt
½ teaspoon pepper

• **Combine** all ingredients in a Dutch oven; bring to a boil over high heat, stirring often.
• **Cover,** reduce heat, and simmer 10 minutes, stirring occasionally. Serve warm or cold with hot dogs or black-eyed peas. Store leftovers in refrigerator. **Yield:** 4 cups.

Ann Winniford
Dallas, Texas

GREEN OLIVE RELISH WITH CORIANDER

QUICK!

1 (12-ounce) jar pimiento-stuffed
    olives, drained and chopped
¼ cup olive oil
¼ cup red wine vinegar
2 cloves garlic, pressed
1 tablespoon ground coriander

• **Combine** all ingredients in a bowl.
• **Cover** and chill at least 8 hours. Serve relish with cream cheese and crackers. Store leftovers in refrigerator. **Yield:** about 2 cups.

Caroline Wallace Kennedy
Newborn, Georgia

PINEAPPLE-COCONUT RELISH

This tropical topping stays fresh in the refrigerator up to 1 week.

1 fresh pineapple, chopped *
1 (7-ounce) can flaked coconut
1 large red bell pepper, chopped
¼ cup minced purple onion
2 jalapeño peppers, seeded and
    minced
3 tablespoons rice wine vinegar
1 teaspoon salt
1¼ teaspoons chili powder

• **Combine** all ingredients in a bowl.
• **Cover** and chill at least 4 hours. Serve relish with pork, chicken, or fish. Store leftovers in refrigerator. **Yield:** 5½ cups.

* You can substitute 1 (20-ounce) can of pineapple tidbits in juice, drained and chopped.

Linda Marco
Chapel Hill, North Carolina

APPLE PIE FILLING IN A JAR

(pictured on page 349)

2 quarts cold water
¼ cup ascorbic-citric powder *
10 pounds cooking apples
2 quarts water
5½ cups sugar
1½ cups ClearJel **
1 tablespoon ground cinnamon
1 teaspoon ground nutmeg
2½ cups water
5 cups apple juice
¾ cup lemon juice

• **Combine** 2 quarts cold water and ascorbic-citric powder in a large bowl.
• **Peel**, core, and cut apples into ½-inch slices; immediately add slices to ascorbic mixture.
• **Bring** 2 quarts water to a boil in a large Dutch oven. Remove 6 cups apple slices from ascorbic mixture, and add to Dutch oven; return to a boil. Boil 1 minute. Remove apple from boiling water; keep warm. Repeat procedure 3 times with remaining apple slices; keep warm. Discard ascorbic mixture.
• **Combine** sugar and next 3 ingredients in a Dutch oven; gradually stir in 2½ cups water and apple juice.
• **Cook** over medium-high heat, stirring constantly, until mixture thickens and boils. Add lemon juice, and boil 1 minute, stirring constantly. Add apple slices, stirring to coat.
• **Pack** hot fruit into hot jars, filling to 1 inch from top. Remove air bubbles; wipe jar rims. Cover at once with metal lids, and screw on bands.
• **Process** in boiling-water bath 25 minutes. **Yield:** 6 quarts (enough filling for 6 double-crust pies).

* For ascorbic-citric powder, we used Fruit-Fresh.

** ClearJel is available from Sweet Celebrations, Inc.; 1-800-328-6722.

Elizabeth Andress
Athens, Georgia

DILL GREEN BEANS

3 pounds fresh green beans
10 cloves garlic
10 fresh dill sprigs
5 teaspoons sweet red pepper
    flakes
5 teaspoons pickling spice
50 black peppercorns
5 (4- x ½-inch) carrot sticks
¼ cup pickling salt
3 cups white vinegar (5% acidity)
3 cups water

• **Wash** beans, and trim ends, and re-move strings; cut into lengths ½ inch shorter than jar. Cook beans in boiling water to cover 3 minutes; drain. Plunge into ice water; drain and set aside.
• **Place** 2 cloves garlic, 2 dill sprigs, 1 teaspoon red pepper flakes, 1 teaspoon pickling spice, 10 peppercorns, and 1 carrot stick into each hot jar. Pack beans tightly into jars, filling to ½ inch from top.
• **Combine** pickling salt, vinegar, and water; bring to a boil. Cover beans with boiling mixture, filling to ½ inch from top. Remove air bubbles; wipe jar rims. Cover at once with metal lids, and screw on bands.
• **Process** in boiling-water bath 15 min-utes. **Yield:** 5 pints.

Alice Byars
Mayfield, Kentucky

TOMATO SPREAD
QUICK!

20 oil-packed dried tomatoes,
    drained
1 (12-ounce) jar roasted red bell
    peppers, drained
5 fresh basil leaves
1 tablespoon balsamic vinegar
½ teaspoon salt
¼ teaspoon sugar

• **Combine** all ingredients in container of an electric blender; process until smooth, stopping once to scrape down sides. Store leftovers in refrigerator. **Yield:** 1¾ cups.

Helen Dowling
Birmingham, Alabama

GREEN TOMATO
SANDWICH SPREAD

3 large green tomatoes, quartered
    (1¼ pounds)
1 medium onion, coarsely chopped
1 large green bell pepper, coarsely
    chopped
1½ teaspoons salt
¾ cup sugar
½ cup white vinegar
2 tablespoons all-purpose flour
½ cup salad dressing or
    mayonnaise
2½ tablespoons prepared mustard
¼ cup chopped pimiento-stuffed
    olives

• **Position** knife blade in food proces-sor bowl; add first 3 ingredients. Process until finely chopped (do not puree), stopping once to scrape down sides.
• **Combine** tomato mixture and salt in a large nonaluminum saucepan; cover and let stand 2 to 3 hours.
• **Drain** tomato mixture, discarding liq-uid. Return mixture to saucepan, and stir in sugar and vinegar; bring to a boil. Reduce heat, and simmer 10 minutes, stirring occasionally.
• **Combine** ½ cup tomato mixture and flour, stirring well, and return to remain-ing tomato mixture in saucepan; cook, stirring constantly, 5 minutes or until thickened. Remove from heat.
• **Stir** in salad dressing and remaining ingredients; cool. Serve on hot dogs or hamburgers or as a relish with meats and vegetables. Store leftovers in refrig-erator. **Yield:** 3¼ cups.

Drexel Mills
Pontotoc, Mississippi

GARLIC BUTTER
QUICK!

1 cup butter, softened
2 to 3 cloves garlic, pressed
1 teaspoon dried Italian
    seasoning

• **Combine** all ingredients in a small mixing bowl, and beat at high speed with an electric mixer until creamy. Cover and chill until firm. Serve with Italian rolls or French bread. Store in refrigerator. **Yield:** 1 cup.

SAGE BUTTER
QUICK!

Try this savory butter on grilled chicken or fish, or tossed with steamed vegetables.

½ cup fresh sage leaves, loosely
    packed
1 large shallot
½ cup butter, softened
1 teaspoon grated lemon rind
½ teaspoon fresh lemon juice
¼ teaspoon freshly ground
    pepper

• **Position** knife blade in food proces-sor bowl; add sage and shallot, and process until chopped.
• **Add** butter and remaining ingredients; process until mixture is thoroughly blended, stopping occasionally to scrape down sides. Store in refrigerator. **Yield:** ½ cup.

Ian Tarica
Alabaster, Alabama

Thyme Mayonnaise,
Thyme-Lemon Butter

THYME-LEMON BUTTER
(pictured at left)

Put a pat on hot-off-the-grill pork chops, steak, or fish, or use it to top a baked potato or dinner roll. You can shape the butter, slice it, and freeze. Take out a little as you need it.

2 tablespoons fresh thyme leaves
1 cup butter, softened
1 teaspoon grated lemon rind
1 tablespoon fresh lemon juice

• **Position** knife blade in food processor bowl; add thyme, and pulse 10 times. Add butter, lemon rind, and lemon juice. Process until mixture is smooth, stopping once to scrape down sides.
• **Spoon** butter mixture onto plastic wrap. Shape butter mixture into a 1-inch-diameter log by folding wrap over mixture and rolling. (Work quickly to keep butter from melting.) Seal in wrap, and chill 4 hours or store in refrigerator up to 1 week. **Yield:** about 1 cup.

THYME MAYONNAISE
(pictured at left)

QUICK!

A little fresh thyme gives oomph to regular mayonnaise in potato salad, deviled eggs, and sandwiches. You can also brush it on fish, chicken, or pork chops before broiling or grilling.

1 cup mayonnaise
2 tablespoons fresh thyme leaves, chopped

• **Combine** mayonnaise and thyme; cover and chill 1 hour or store in refrigerator up to 1 week. **Yield:** about 1 cup.

PEACH KETCHUP

1 (16-ounce) can sliced peaches in heavy syrup, undrained
½ cup finely chopped onion
½ cup white vinegar
¼ teaspoon salt
½ teaspoon ground cinnamon
¼ teaspoon ground cloves
¼ teaspoon ground allspice
¼ teaspoon ground red pepper

• **Drain** peaches, reserving syrup in a small saucepan; set peaches aside.
• **Cook** syrup over medium heat 5 to 7 minutes or until reduced to ½ cup, stirring occasionally. Add peaches, onion, and remaining ingredients; bring to a boil. Reduce heat, and simmer 45 to 50 minutes or until thickened, stirring often; cool.
• **Position** knife blade in food processor bowl; add peach mixture. Process until mixture is smooth, stopping once to scrape down sides. Transfer mixture to a serving bowl; cover and chill at least 8 hours. Serve with poultry or pork. Store leftovers in refrigerator. **Yield:** about 1¼ cups.

Carole Miller Radford
Lincolnton, Georgia

PEPPERED HONEY MUSTARD

QUICK!

This mustard is excellent with chicken or mixed into a homemade vinaigrette salad dressing.

¾ cup Dijon mustard
¼ cup honey
1 tablespoon cracked pepper
⅛ teaspoon salt
Garnish: cracked pepper

• **Combine** first 4 ingredients in a small serving bowl, stirring well. Garnish, if desired. Store leftovers in refrigerator. **Yield:** 1 cup.

SWEET CIDER MUSTARD

QUICK!

Teri serves this mustard as a dip for pretzels.

½ cup sugar
¼ cup dry mustard
Dash of salt
1 large egg
⅓ cup apple cider vinegar

• **Combine** all ingredients in container of an electric blender; process 20 seconds or until smooth, stopping once to scrape down sides. Pour mixture into a heavy saucepan.
• **Cook** over medium heat, stirring constantly, 5 minutes or until mixture is thickened; cool completely. Store leftovers in refrigerator. **Yield:** about 1 cup.

Teri Schmid
Marietta, Georgia

RASPBERRY WINE VINEGAR

3 cups fresh or frozen raspberries
2 (17-ounce) bottles white wine vinegar
1 cup sugar

• **Combine** all ingredients in a large saucepan; bring to a boil. Cover, reduce heat, and simmer 10 minutes.
• **Pour** mixture through a wire-mesh strainer lined with two layers of cheesecloth, discarding pulp.
• **Pour** into decorative jars or bottles, and seal with an airtight lid or cork. Store in refrigerator up to 6 months. **Yield:** 5 cups.

Nancy Strother
Fredericksburg, Virginia

♥ Per tablespoon: Calories 13
Fat 0.0g Cholesterol 0mg
Sodium 1mg

TARRAGON VINEGAR

1 bunch fresh tarragon (about 14
   sprigs)
7 (17-ounce) bottles champagne
   wine vinegar
Fresh tarragon sprigs (optional)

• **Twist** tarragon gently, and place in a
large glass container. Set aside.
• **Bring** vinegar to a boil, and pour over
tarragon. Cover and store in a cool, dark
place at room temperature 2 weeks.
• **Pour** vinegar mixture through a wire-
mesh strainer into decorative bottles,
discarding solids. Add additional tarragon sprigs, if desired. Seal bottles, and
store in a cool, dark place up to 6
months. **Yield:** about 16 cups.

Cindie Hackney
Longview, Texas

TOMATO-HERB VINEGAR

10 large sprigs fresh rosemary
6 large sprigs fresh basil
4 large sprigs fresh oregano
12 cloves garlic, peeled and halved
10 dried tomato halves
1 teaspoon black peppercorns
3 (32-ounce) bottles red wine
   vinegar
Fresh rosemary sprigs (optional)

• **Twist** stems of herbs gently, and press
garlic with back of a spoon. Place herbs
and garlic in a large glass container. Add
tomatoes and peppercorns. Set aside.
• **Bring** vinegar to a boil, and pour over
herb mixture. Cover vinegar mixture,
and store in a cool, dark place at room
temperature 2 weeks.
• **Pour** vinegar mixture through a large
wire-mesh strainer into decorative bottles, discarding solids. Add additional
fresh rosemary sprigs, if desired. Seal
bottles, and store in a cool, dark place
up to 6 months. **Yield:** 11 cups.

Cindie Hackney
Longview, Texas

LEMON HONEY

QUICK!

4 large eggs
2 egg yolks
2 cups sugar
1 tablespoon grated lemon rind
½ cup fresh lemon juice
¼ cup butter

• **Combine** all ingredients in a heavy
saucepan; cook over low heat, stirring
constantly, 10 minutes or until mixture
is thickened. Let cool completely. Serve
with Hazelnut Scones (recipe on page
49). Store leftover honey in refrigerator.
Yield: 2½ cups.

Sharon McCullar
Victorian Room
Shreveport, Louisiana

LEMON-MINT SUGAR

QUICK!

2 cups sugar
3 tablespoons grated lemon rind
2 tablespoons dried mint flakes
¼ teaspoon salt

• **Combine** all ingredients; spread sugar
mixture in a thin layer in a 15- x 10- x 1-
inch jellyroll pan.
• **Bake** sugar mixture at 200° for 15 minutes. Cool in pan.
• **Place** sugar mixture in container of an
electric blender. Process to a fine powder. Store in an airtight container up to 6
months. Serve with hot or iced tea or
fresh fruit. **Yield:** 2 cups.

ORANGE SYRUP

2 cups sugar
1 tablespoon grated orange rind
½ cup fresh orange juice
⅓ cup light corn syrup
¼ cup Triple Sec or other orange-
   flavored liqueur
2 tablespoons butter or margarine
1 teaspoon clear vanilla extract

• **Combine** all ingredients in a heavy
saucepan, and bring to a boil over
medium heat. Reduce heat to low; simmer 5 minutes or until sugar dissolves,
stirring occasionally.
• **Pour** through a wire-mesh strainer
into a small pitcher, discarding orange
rind. Serve with orange sections over
ice cream or waffles. Store leftovers in
refrigerator. **Yield:** 2 cups.

Beverly Justice
Columbiana, Alabama

WEAVER D'S SEASONING MIX

QUICK!

*Dexter uses his mix for battered
fried chicken and pork chops. This recipe
is enough for about 3½ pounds of
fryer pieces. Tip: Just before serving,
sprinkle fried chicken or pork with
seasoned salt for added zest.*

3½ cups all-purpose flour
3 tablespoons garlic powder
3 tablespoons seasoned salt
3 tablespoons pepper
1 tablespoon salt

• **Combine** all ingredients; store in an
airtight container. **Yield:** 4 cups.

Dexter Weaver
Weaver D's Delicious Fine Foods
Athens, Georgia

At right: *Herbed Gazpacho (page 356)*

SOUPS AND STEWS

CHILLED MANGO-CANTALOUPE SOUP

¼ cup sugar
¼ cup boiling water
2 mangoes, peeled, seeded, and cut into chunks
½ medium cantaloupe, peeled, seeded, and cut into chunks
1½ cups milk, divided
¾ cup whipping cream, divided
2 tablespoons lemon juice
⅛ teaspoon ground cinnamon

• **Dissolve** sugar in boiling water; set aside to cool.
• **Position** knife blade in food processor bowl; add half of fruit and ¼ cup milk, and process until smooth, stopping once to scrape down sides.
• **Pour** fruit mixture through a wire-mesh strainer into a large bowl, discarding pulp. Set fruit mixture aside.
• **Repeat** procedure with remaining fruit and ¼ cup milk.
• **Stir** sugar mixture, remaining 1 cup milk, ½ cup whipping cream, lemon juice, and cinnamon into fruit mixture. Cover and chill until ready to serve.
• **Pour** remaining ¼ cup whipping cream into a small heavy-duty, zip-top plastic bag; snip a small hole in one corner of bag. Drizzle horizontal lines across each serving, and pull a wooden pick vertically through lines to make a wavy design. **Yield:** 5½ cups.

Carol Lundy
New Tazewell, Tennessee

TROPICAL GAZPACHO

Top each bowl of gazpacho with a small scoop of fruit-flavored sorbet for extra refreshment.

2 papayas, peeled, seeded, and chopped
2 mangoes, peeled, seeded, and chopped
2 kiwifruit, peeled and chopped
2 teaspoons grated lime rind
3 tablespoons fresh lime juice
¼ to ½ teaspoon ground cardamom
1 teaspoon vanilla extract
3 (8-ounce) bottles papaya nectar
Garnish: carambola or starfruit slices

• **Combine** all ingredients except carambola slices in a large bowl; cover mixture, and chill. Garnish, if desired. **Yield:** 5 cups.

♥ Per 1-cup serving: Calories 189
Fat 0.8g Cholesterol 0mg
Sodium 11mg

HERBED GAZPACHO
(pictured on previous page)

1 (46-ounce) can spicy-hot tomato vegetable juice
1 (16-ounce) can Italian-style tomatoes, undrained
1 (10½-ounce) can condensed beef broth, undiluted
2 tomatoes, seeded and chopped
1 cucumber, seeded and chopped
1 green bell pepper, chopped
3 green onions, chopped
2 tablespoons chopped fresh basil
2 tablespoons chopped fresh oregano
2 cloves garlic, minced
2 tablespoons white wine vinegar
1 tablespoon Worcestershire sauce
½ teaspoon salt
1 teaspoon pepper

• **Combine** all ingredients; cover and chill 2 hours. **Yield:** 12 cups.

Irene Smith
Covington, Georgia

SHRIMP-CREAM CHEESE GAZPACHO

Give the cream cheese a quick chill in the freezer before adding it to this soup; then it will be easy to cube.

5 cups water
1½ pounds unpeeled small fresh shrimp
2 quarts tomato juice
1 bunch green onions, chopped
2 cucumbers, peeled, seeded, and chopped
4 tomatoes, peeled, seeded, and chopped
1 avocado, chopped
1 (8-ounce) package cream cheese, cut into ½-inch cubes
¼ cup lemon juice or white wine vinegar
2 tablespoons sugar
½ teaspoon hot sauce
Garnishes: cucumber slices, sour cream, whole cooked shrimp

• **Bring** water to a boil; add shrimp, and cook 3 to 5 minutes or until shrimp turn pink. Drain; rinse with cold water. Chill.
• **Peel** shrimp, and devein, if desired. (Set aside about 10 shrimp for garnish, if desired.)
• **Combine** shrimp, tomato juice, and next 8 ingredients in a large bowl; cover and chill at least 3 hours. Garnish, if desired. **Yield:** 13 cups.

Carol Savage
Charleston, South Carolina

CHILLED CUCUMBER-BUTTERMILK SOUP

5 (7- to 8-inch-long) cucumbers (about 2¾ pounds)
½ teaspoon salt
6 green onions, chopped
½ cup chopped fresh parsley
1 tablespoon chopped fresh dill
1 quart buttermilk
1 (16-ounce) carton sour cream
¼ cup lemon juice
¼ teaspoon salt
¼ teaspoon ground white pepper
Garnishes: thinly sliced cucumber, fresh parsley sprigs

• **Peel** cucumbers; cut in half lengthwise, and scoop out seeds. Place cucumber shells on a paper towel; sprinkle ½ teaspoon salt evenly over both sides of cucumber. Let stand 30 minutes. Drain; coarsely chop.

• **Combine** cucumber, green onions, and next 7 ingredients. Place one-third of mixture in container of an electric blender; process 1 minute or until smooth, stopping once to scrape down sides. Pour into a 3-quart container. Repeat procedure twice with remaining mixture. Cover and chill at least 3 hours. Garnish, if desired. **Yield:** 9 cups.

Fran Jackson
Kansas City, Missouri

EGG-LEMON SOUP

2 quarts chicken broth
1 cup rice, uncooked
½ cup chopped green onions
½ cup chopped fresh parsley
1 tablespoon chopped fresh
　　dill
1 tablespoon chopped fresh
　　mint
6 large eggs
⅓ cup lemon juice
Garnish: fresh dill sprigs

• **Bring** broth to a boil in a Dutch oven over medium-high heat; add rice. Cover, reduce heat, and simmer 20 minutes or until rice is tender.

• **Stir** green onions and next 3 ingredients into broth mixture.

• **Beat** eggs with a wire whisk until frothy; gradually add lemon juice, stirring constantly.

• **Add** 2 cups hot broth mixture gradually to egg mixture, stirring constantly; gradually add to remaining broth mixture, stirring constantly. Cook over medium heat 5 minutes or until thermometer registers 160° (do not boil). Garnish, if desired. **Yield:** 8 cups.

Margie Spanos
Birmingham, Alabama

SPICY WHITE BEAN SOUP

QUICK!

1 large onion, chopped
2 tablespoons butter or margarine,
　　melted
2 (15½-ounce) cans Great
　　Northern beans, rinsed and
　　drained
2 (15½-ounce) cans yellow
　　hominy, rinsed and drained
2 (14½-ounce) cans chili-style
　　chopped tomatoes, undrained
2 (14½-ounce) cans vegetable
　　broth
1 teaspoon sugar
½ teaspoon ground cumin
¼ to ½ teaspoon ground red
　　pepper
¼ teaspoon ground cloves
2 tablespoons chopped fresh
　　cilantro

• **Cook** onion in butter in a Dutch oven over medium heat until tender. Add beans and remaining ingredients.

• **Bring** mixture to a boil; reduce heat, and simmer, uncovered, 20 minutes. **Yield:** 14 cups.

Wendy V. Kitchens
Charlotte, North Carolina

BLACK, WHITE, AND RED ALL OVER SOUP

QUICK!

1 (15½-ounce) can white hominy,
　　rinsed and drained
1 (15-ounce) can black beans,
　　rinsed and drained
1 (14½-ounce) can chili-style
　　diced tomatoes, undrained
1 (14½-ounce) can chicken
　　broth
1 teaspoon chopped fresh
　　cilantro
½ teaspoon chili powder
½ teaspoon ground cumin

• **Combine** all ingredients in a large saucepan; cook over medium heat until thoroughly heated, stirring occasionally. **Yield:** 5½ cups.

Julia Rutland
Cordova, Tennessee

MARGE CLYDE'S BLACK BEAN SOUP

1 pound dried black beans
4 hot peppers in vinegar, finely
　　chopped
½ cup chopped onion
¼ teaspoon minced garlic
½ cup fresh lemon juice
3 (14¼-ounce) cans fat-free
　　chicken broth
1½ cups chopped onion
1 tablespoon minced garlic
Vegetable cooking spray
1 (10-ounce) can diced tomatoes
　　and green chiles, undrained
½ teaspoon pepper
½ teaspoon hot sauce
⅔ cup cooked rice

• **Sort** and wash beans; place beans in a large Dutch oven. Cover with water to depth of 2 inches above beans; let soak overnight. Drain beans, and set aside.

• **Combine** hot pepper and next 3 ingredients; cover and chill.

• **Cook** chicken broth and beans in Dutch oven over medium-high heat 2½ hours, adding hot water as needed to keep beans covered with liquid.

• **Cook** chopped onion and garlic in a skillet coated with cooking spray over medium-high heat, stirring constantly, until tender. Reduce heat, and add tomatoes, pepper, and hot sauce; cook 5 additional minutes.

• **Position** knife blade in food processor bowl; add tomato mixture and 2 cups beans. Pulse 3 times or until blended; add to remaining beans.

• **Spoon** 2 tablespoons rice into each individual bowl; ladle 1½ cups soup over rice. Top each serving evenly with hot pepper mixture. **Yield:** 7½ cups.

Marge Clyde
San Antonio, Texas

♥ Per serving (1½ cups soup and
2 tablespoons rice): Calories 422
Fat 2.4g Cholesterol 0mg
Sodium 520mg

REFRIED BEAN SOUP

This dish is so filling, you need to add only tortilla chips and salsa to round out the meal.

1 small onion, chopped
2 cloves garlic, minced
1 tablespoon vegetable oil
1 (31-ounce) can refried beans
1 (16-ounce) can diced tomatoes, undrained
1 (10-ounce) can diced tomatoes and green chiles, undrained
1 (14½-ounce) can chicken broth
2 tablespoons chopped fresh cilantro (optional)
6 corn tortillas
2 cups (8 ounces) shredded Monterey Jack cheese
1 (8-ounce) carton sour cream

● **Cook** onion and garlic in oil in a Dutch oven over medium-high heat, stirring constantly, until tender. Add beans and next 3 ingredients, stirring until smooth; bring to a boil. Reduce heat, and simmer 15 minutes. Stir in cilantro, if desired.
● **Cut** tortillas into thin strips; spread in a single layer on a baking sheet. Bake at 350° for 15 minutes or until browned, stirring every 5 minutes. Cool.
● **Ladle** soup into individual soup bowls; top with tortilla strips, cheese, and sour cream. Serve immediately. **Yield:** 7 cups.

Shirley M. Draper
Winter Park, Florida

BUTTERNUT SQUASH SOUP

1 (2½-pound) butternut squash, peeled, seeded, and cut into 1-inch chunks
3 cups water
2 medium onions, chopped
1 large red bell pepper, finely chopped
2 cloves garlic, pressed
3 tablespoons vegetable oil
1 teaspoon ground cumin
1 teaspoon ground coriander
1 teaspoon ground ginger
1 teaspoon dry mustard
1 teaspoon curry powder
½ teaspoon salt
1 cup orange juice
1 teaspoon lemon juice
⅛ teaspoon ground red pepper
¼ cup fresh goat cheese (chèvre)
¼ cup water

● **Combine** squash and 3 cups water in a large saucepan. Bring to a boil over medium-high heat; cover, reduce heat, and simmer 10 minutes or until squash is tender. Drain, reserving cooking liquid; set both aside.
● **Cook** chopped onion, chopped red bell pepper, and garlic in oil in a Dutch oven over medium-high heat, stirring constantly, 10 minutes or until tender.
● **Add** cumin and next 5 ingredients, stirring mixture well.
● **Combine** half of squash and half of cooked onion mixture in container of an electric blender; process until smooth, stopping once to scrape down sides.
● **Pour** blended squash mixture into another container. Repeat procedure with remaining squash and onion mixture, and return blended squash mixture to Dutch oven.
● **Add** orange juice, lemon juice, ground red pepper, and cooking liquid to squash mixture. Cook over medium heat, stirring constantly, until thoroughly heated.
● **Combine** cheese and ¼ cup water, stirring until mixture is smooth and consistency of sour cream. Dollop onto the center of each serving. **Yield:** 7 cups.

Fleming and Brit Pfann
Celebrity Dairy
Greensboro, North Carolina

SHERRIED MUSHROOM SOUP

2 tablespoons butter or margarine
1 small onion, chopped
¼ teaspoon garlic powder
2 (10½-ounce) cans condensed chicken broth, undiluted
3 (10¾-ounce) cans cream of mushroom soup, undiluted
1 cup milk
2 tablespoons sour cream
1 tablespoon chopped fresh parsley
1 teaspoon chopped fresh thyme
1 cup quick brown rice, uncooked
½ cup dry sherry
¼ teaspoon pepper
1 (8-ounce) package sliced fresh mushrooms
Garnish: toast points

● **Melt** butter in a 3-quart saucepan over medium-high heat; add onion and garlic powder, and cook, stirring constantly, until tender. Add broth; reduce heat, and simmer 5 minutes.
● **Combine** soup and next 4 ingredients, whisking until blended; stir into broth mixture. Add rice and next 3 ingredients; cook 20 to 30 minutes or until rice is tender and soup is thickened. Garnish, if desired. **Yield:** 8 cups.

Marilyn W. Godsey
Fort Myers, Florida

FRENCH ONION SOUP

2 tablespoons butter
Vegetable cooking spray
6 large onions, thinly sliced (3 pounds)
2 (10½-ounce) cans beef consommé, undiluted
1 (13¾-ounce) can no-salt-added, fat-free beef broth
1⅓ cups water
¼ cup dry white wine
¼ teaspoon freshly ground pepper
7 (1-inch-thick) slices French bread
¼ cup grated Parmesan cheese

● **Melt** butter in a large Dutch oven coated with cooking spray. Add onion, and cook over medium heat 5 minutes, stirring often. Add 1 can beef consommé; cook over low heat 30 minutes. Gradually add remaining 1 can beef consommé and next 4 ingredients; bring to a boil, reduce heat, and simmer, uncovered, 10 minutes.

• **Place** bread slices on a baking sheet; sprinkle with cheese. Broil 6 inches from heat (with electric oven door partially opened) until cheese is golden.

• **Ladle** soup into serving bowls, and top each serving with a toasted bread slice. **Yield:** 7 cups.

♥ Per 1-cup serving: Calories 219
Fat 5.3g Cholesterol 28mg
Sodium 798mg

MARDI GRAS SOUP

English Pea Soup
Roasted Yellow Bell Pepper Soup
Shredded red cabbage

• **Pour** ¾ cup of each soup simultaneously down the sides of 5 shallow soup bowls, taking care not to mix soups. Place shredded red cabbage on top. **Yield:** 5 servings.

English Pea Soup

6 tablespoons unsalted butter
1½ cups chopped onion
3 cups vegetable or chicken broth
2 (1-pound) packages frozen
    English peas
¼ teaspoon salt
⅛ teaspoon ground white pepper

• **Melt** butter in a Dutch oven over medium heat; add onion, and cook, stirring constantly, until tender. Add broth, and bring to a boil.

• **Stir** in peas, salt, and pepper; reduce heat, and simmer 5 to 10 minutes or until peas are tender. Cool slightly.

• **Position** knife blade in food processor bowl; add soup, and process until smooth, stopping once to scrape down sides.

• **Pour** soup through a wire-mesh strainer into Dutch oven, discarding solids; cook over low heat just until thoroughly heated. **Yield:** 4 cups.

Roasted Yellow Bell Pepper Soup

3 yellow bell peppers
2 tablespoons unsalted butter
½ cup chopped onion
½ cup chopped leek
¼ teaspoon salt
¼ teaspoon freshly ground pepper
1 medium-size red potato, peeled
    and sliced
2½ cups vegetable or chicken
    broth

• **Cut** peppers in half; remove and discard seeds. Place peppers, cut side down, on an aluminum foil-lined baking sheet.

• **Broil** 5½ inches from heat (with electric oven door partially opened) 5 minutes or until bell peppers look blistered.

• **Place** bell peppers in a heavy-duty, zip-top plastic bag; seal and let stand 10 minutes to loosen skins. Peel peppers, and coarsely chop; set aside.

• **Melt** butter in a Dutch oven over medium heat; add onion and next 3 ingredients. Cook, stirring constantly, 10 minutes or until vegetables are tender.

• **Add** chopped bell pepper, potato, and broth; bring to a boil. Reduce heat, and simmer 10 minutes or until potato is tender, stirring occasionally. Cool slightly.

• **Position** knife blade in food processor bowl; add soup, and process until smooth, stopping once to scrape down sides. Return to Dutch oven, and cook over low heat just until soup is thoroughly heated. **Yield:** 4 cups.

Jami Gaudet
Macon, Georgia

EASY POTATO SOUP

½ (32-ounce) package frozen hash
    brown potatoes
1 cup chopped onion
1 (14½-ounce) can chicken broth
2 cups water
1 (10¾-ounce) can cream of celery
    soup, undiluted
1 (10¾-ounce) can cream of
    chicken soup, undiluted
2 cups milk
**Garnishes: shredded Cheddar
    cheese, diced cooked ham or
    bacon**

• **Combine** first 4 ingredients in a Dutch oven; bring to a boil. Cover, reduce heat, and simmer 30 minutes. Stir in soups and milk; cook until thoroughly heated. Garnish, if desired. **Yield:** 10 cups.

Harriett Blanford
Owensboro, Kentucky

BAKED POTATO SOUP

4 large baking potatoes
⅔ cup butter or margarine
⅔ cup all-purpose flour
6 cups milk
¾ teaspoon salt
½ teaspoon pepper
4 green onions, chopped and
    divided
12 slices bacon, cooked, crumbled,
    and divided
1¼ cups (5 ounces) shredded
    Cheddar cheese, divided
1 (8-ounce) carton sour cream

• **Wash** potatoes, and prick several times with a fork; bake at 400° for 1 hour or until done. Let cool. Cut potatoes in half lengthwise; scoop out pulp, and set aside. Discard skins.

• **Melt** butter in a heavy saucepan over low heat; add flour, stirring until smooth. Cook 1 minute, stirring constantly. Gradually add milk; cook over medium heat, stirring constantly, until mixture is thickened and bubbly.

• **Add** potato pulp, salt, pepper, 2 tablespoons green onions, ½ cup crumbled bacon, and 1 cup cheese to saucepan. Cook until thoroughly heated, and stir in sour cream. Add extra milk, if necessary, for desired consistency. Serve with remaining green onions, bacon, and ¼ cup cheese. **Yield:** 10 cups.

LaJuan Coward
Jasper, Texas

Creamy Onion and Potato Soup

Chili Verde;
Bodacious Chili

CREAMY ONION AND POTATO SOUP
(pictured at left)

QUICK!

2 tablespoons butter or margarine
2 tablespoons all-purpose flour
1 cup chopped onion
1 large clove garlic, minced
2 (14½-ounce) cans chicken broth
4 cups peeled, cubed baking potato (about 3 large)
½ cup sliced green onions
⅛ teaspoon salt
¼ teaspoon ground white pepper
1 cup liquid nondairy creamer or milk
Garnish: green onion strips

● **Melt** butter in a Dutch oven over low heat; add flour, stirring until smooth. Cook 1 minute, stirring constantly. Add onion and garlic; cook 1 minute or until onion is tender. Gradually add broth, stirring constantly.
● **Add** potato and next 3 ingredients. Bring to a boil; cover, reduce heat, and simmer 15 minutes or until potato is tender, stirring occasionally. Stir in nondairy creamer, and cook until thoroughly heated. Garnish, if desired. **Yield:** 7 cups.

Cathy Darling
Grafton, West Virginia

SWEET POTATO VELOUTÉ

A velouté is a stock-based sauce thickened with a roux (flour cooked in fat). Unlike Louisiana's medium to dark roux, this one is blond, which is easier and faster to prepare.

9 to 10 cups chicken broth
1¼ pounds sweet potatoes, peeled and finely chopped
1 bay leaf
1 teaspoon dried Italian seasoning
½ teaspoon ground white pepper
Dash of ground red pepper
Dash of ground nutmeg
½ cup butter or margarine
½ cup all-purpose flour
Garnishes: crème fraîche or sour cream, chopped fresh parsley
Fried Sweet Potato Strips

● **Combine** first 3 ingredients in a Dutch oven; bring to a boil over high heat. Reduce heat; simmer 20 minutes or until potato is tender. Remove from heat; stir in Italian seasoning and next 3 ingredients. Remove and discard bay leaf. Set aside.
● **Melt** butter in a heavy skillet over medium-high heat. Add flour, and cook, stirring constantly, 5 minutes or until light golden; stir into potato mixture.
● **Place** about one-fourth of potato mixture in container of an electric blender or food processor; process until smooth. Pour into a large bowl. Repeat procedure with remaining mixture. Return mixture to Dutch oven, and cook until thoroughly heated and slightly thickened.
● **Spoon** into soup bowls. Garnish, if desired. Top each serving with Fried Sweet Potato Strips just before serving. **Yield:** 11 cups.

Note: To make lines on soup with crème fraîche or sour cream, spoon it into a small heavy-duty, zip-top plastic bag. Snip a small hole in one corner of bag, and squeeze in straight lines onto soup. Pull a wooden pick through lines in opposite directions at intervals to create design.

Fried Sweet Potato Strips

1 large sweet potato, peeled and grated into long strips
1 cup vegetable oil

● **Fry** potato in hot oil in a skillet until lightly browned. (Watch carefully – the thin strips brown quickly.) Remove with a slotted spoon, and drain on paper towels. (Strips will be crisp when cooled.) **Yield:** about 1 cup.

Chefs Gary Schenk and William Wells
Juban's
Baton Rouge, Louisiana

PUMPKIN-CORN SOUP WITH GINGER-LIME CREAM

3 cups fresh or frozen corn kernels
1½ cups water
2 cloves garlic, minced
¾ teaspoon salt
½ to ¾ teaspoon ground white pepper
3 to 3½ cups chicken broth
3 cups cooked, mashed pumpkin *
Ginger-Lime Cream
Garnish: lime zest

● **Combine** corn and water; cover and cook over medium-high heat 10 minutes or until tender.
● **Position** knife blade in food processor bowl; add corn mixture, and process 2 minutes or until smooth, stopping once to scrape down sides. Pour mixture through a wire-mesh strainer into a bowl, discarding pulp.
● **Combine** corn mixture, garlic, salt, pepper, and 3 cups chicken broth in a Dutch oven; bring to a boil over medium-high heat. Reduce heat to low; stir in pumpkin. Simmer 10 minutes, adding additional chicken broth as necessary, stirring constantly.
● **Spoon** into individual bowls, and dollop with Ginger-Lime Cream. Garnish, if desired. **Yield:** 8 cups.

* Substitute 3 cups canned pumpkin.

Ginger-Lime Cream

¼ cup fresh lime juice
1 tablespoon grated fresh ginger
1½ teaspoons grated lime rind
½ cup whipping cream

● **Combine** lime juice and ginger in a small saucepan; cook over medium heat 2 minutes. Remove from heat; pour through a wire-mesh strainer into a small mixing bowl, discarding pulp.
● **Add** lime rind and whipping cream to juice mixture; beat at medium speed with an electric mixer until soft peaks form. **Yield:** 1 cup.

CREAMY ASPARAGUS SOUP

You can prepare the vegetable puree base ahead and store in the refrigerator up to 3 days or freeze up to 6 months. Dilute with milk, and heat to serve.

½ cup chopped onion
1 cup sliced celery
3 cloves garlic, pressed
3 tablespoons butter or margarine, melted
2 (14½-ounce) cans cut asparagus, undrained
1 (16-ounce) can sliced potatoes, drained *
1 (14½-ounce) can chicken broth
1 teaspoon white vinegar
1 teaspoon salt
½ teaspoon ground black pepper
¼ teaspoon ground red pepper
½ teaspoon dried basil
1 cup milk
½ cup sour cream (optional)
Garnish: celery leaves

• **Cook** first 3 ingredients in butter in a Dutch oven over medium-high heat, stirring constantly, until tender. Stir in asparagus and next 7 ingredients.
• **Bring** to a boil, stirring often. Reduce heat, and simmer, uncovered, 10 minutes, stirring often. Cool slightly.
• **Pour** half of mixture into container of an electric blender; process until smooth, stopping once to scrape down sides. Transfer mixture to another container. Repeat procedure.
• **Return** asparagus mixture to Dutch oven. Stir in milk; cook just until thoroughly heated (do not boil). Dollop each serving with sour cream, if desired. Garnish, if desired. **Yield:** 8 cups.

* Substitute 2 medium red potatoes, cooked, peeled, and sliced, for canned.
Sider Krison
Shreveport, Louisiana

CREAMY BUTTERNUT SOUP

4 cups cooked, mashed butternut squash
2 (14½-ounce) cans chicken broth
½ teaspoon sugar
½ teaspoon salt
¼ teaspoon pepper
1 cup whipping cream, divided
¼ teaspoon ground nutmeg

• **Combine** half of first 5 ingredients in container of an electric blender or food processor, and process until smooth, stopping once to scrape down sides; pour into a large saucepan. Repeat procedure with remaining half.
• **Bring** to a boil over medium heat; gradually stir in half of whipping cream, and cook until thoroughly heated. Remove from heat.
• **Beat** remaining whipping cream at high speed with an electric mixer until firm peaks form. Dollop on soup; sprinkle with nutmeg. **Yield:** 7 cups.

Creamy Acorn-Butternut Soup: Substitute 2 cups cooked, mashed acorn squash for 2 cups cooked, mashed butternut squash.

Acorn Squash Bowls: Cut off tops of squash; cut a thin slice from bottoms to stand squash upright. Remove seeds, and brown top of shells in a hot greased skillet.

Sandra Holmes-Kennedy
Atlanta, Texas

CREAM OF CAULIFLOWER SOUP

1 large onion
2 shallots
1 clove garlic
1 tablespoon olive oil
2 (14½-ounce) cans chicken broth
1 large cauliflower, cut into flowerets
1½ cups whipping cream
1 teaspoon salt
⅛ teaspoon ground white pepper
Garnishes: asparagus tips, cracked black pepper

• **Slice** first 3 ingredients; cook in oil in a Dutch oven until tender, stirring often. Stir in broth; bring to a boil. Add cauliflower; cook 15 minutes or until tender, stirring occasionally.
• **Process** soup in batches in container of an electric blender until smooth, stopping once to scrape down sides; return to pan. Stir in whipping cream, salt, and white pepper; cook over low heat until thoroughly heated, stirring often. Ladle into soup bowls; garnish, if desired. **Yield:** 8 cups.

Julia Rutland
Cordova, Tennessee

CREAMY KALE SOUP

Be sure to use green kale – variegated kale is better for garnishing than eating.

1¼ pounds fresh kale
2 (14½-ounce) cans chicken broth
1 cup water
1½ pounds red potatoes, chopped
1½ cups chopped cooked ham
¾ teaspoon salt
2 to 3 teaspoons pepper
1 large onion, cut in half and sliced
2 cups whipping cream
2 (15-ounce) cans white beans, rinsed and drained
2 tablespoons butter or margarine, softened
2 tablespoons all-purpose flour

• **Remove** and discard stems and discolored spots from kale; rinse with cold water, and drain. Tear into bite-size pieces; set aside.
• **Combine** broth, 1 cup water, and next 4 ingredients in a large Dutch oven; bring to a boil. Reduce heat, and simmer 20 minutes, stirring occasionally. Stir in kale and onion; simmer 20 minutes, stirring occasionally. Add whipping cream and beans; bring to a boil, stirring often.
• **Combine** butter and flour, stirring until blended. Stir into soup, and simmer 10 minutes, stirring occasionally. **Yield:** 16 cups.

Pat Pittman
Boone, North Carolina

CREAM OF MUSTARD GREEN SOUP

1 (1-pound) center-cut ham slice
   with bone
8 cups water
1 large bunch fresh mustard
   greens, washed and finely
   chopped (about 4½ cups)
¼ cup butter or margarine
2 cups chopped green onions
2 cups chopped celery
1 cup chopped onion
⅓ cup butter or margarine
⅓ cup all-purpose flour
5 cups half-and-half
½ teaspoon salt
⅛ teaspoon hot sauce

• **Combine** ham and water in a Dutch oven; bring to a boil. Cover, reduce heat, and simmer 3 hours. Remove ham, leaving liquid in Dutch oven. (Reserve ham for another use.)
• **Add** mustard greens to Dutch oven, and cook, uncovered, 1 hour, stirring occasionally. Set aside.
• **Melt** ¼ cup butter in a large skillet over medium heat; add green onions, celery, and onion, and cook, stirring constantly, until mixture is tender. Remove from heat.
• **Position** knife blade in food processor bowl; add onion mixture. Process onion mixture until smooth, stopping occasionally to scrape down sides. Set aside.
• **Melt** ⅓ cup butter in Dutch oven over low heat; gradually add flour, stirring until smooth. Cook 1 minute, stirring constantly. Gradually add half-and-half; cook over medium heat, stirring constantly, until thickened and bubbly. Stir in mustard green mixture, pureed vegetables, salt, and hot sauce. Cook just until thoroughly heated (do not boil). **Yield:** 10 cups.

CREAM OF SHIITAKE SOUP

QUICK!

½ pound fresh shiitake mushrooms
¼ cup butter or margarine
2 cups chopped onion
3 tablespoons all-purpose flour
2 (14½-ounce) cans chicken broth
2 cups whipping cream
¼ teaspoon pepper
¼ teaspoon ground nutmeg

• **Remove** stems from mushrooms; discard. Finely chop mushroom caps.
• **Melt** butter in a saucepan over medium-high heat; add chopped mushroom caps and onion, and cook, stirring constantly, until tender.
• **Add** flour; cook 1 minute, stirring constantly. Gradually add broth; cook, stirring constantly, until thickened. Remove from heat. Stir in whipping cream, pepper, and nutmeg. **Yield:** 7 cups.

Jean Hartgroves
Charlestown, West Virginia

CREAM OF ROASTED SWEET RED PEPPER SOUP

8 large red bell peppers
6 cloves garlic, minced
1 small onion, chopped
3 tablespoons butter, divided
2 (14½-ounce) cans chicken broth
2 cups dry white wine
1 bay leaf
½ teaspoon salt
¼ teaspoon pepper
2 tablespoons all-purpose flour
1½ cups whipping cream
Garnish: fresh basil, cut into strips

• **Place** peppers on an aluminum foil-lined baking sheet; broil 5½ inches from heat (with electric oven door partially opened) about 5 minutes on each side or until peppers look blistered.
• **Place** roasted peppers in a heavy-duty, zip-top plastic bag; seal and let stand 10 minutes. Peel; remove and discard stem and seeds. Set roasted peppers aside.
• **Cook** garlic and onion in 1 tablespoon butter in a Dutch oven over medium heat until crisp-tender. Add chicken broth and next 4 ingredients; bring to a boil. Reduce heat, and simmer 30 minutes. Pour broth mixture through a large wire-mesh strainer into a large container, reserving solids. Remove and discard bay leaf. Set broth mixture aside.
• **Position** knife blade in food processor bowl; add reserved solids and peppers. Process 30 seconds or until smooth, stopping once to scrape down sides; set pepper puree aside.
• **Melt** remaining 2 tablespoons butter in Dutch oven over low heat; add flour, stirring until smooth. Cook 1 minute, stirring constantly. Gradually add broth mixture; cook over medium heat, stirring constantly, until thickened and bubbly (about 3 minutes). Stir in pepper puree. Gradually stir in whipping cream. Cook over low heat until heated. Garnish, if desired. **Yield:** 8 cups.

Nicholas Rutyna
San Antonio, Texas

CREAM OF PIMIENTO SOUP

QUICK!

1 (4-ounce) jar diced pimiento,
   undrained
2 tablespoons butter or margarine
2½ tablespoons all-purpose flour
1 (14½-ounce) can chicken broth
1½ cups half-and-half
2 teaspoons grated onion
½ teaspoon salt
¼ teaspoon hot sauce

• **Place** pimiento in container of an electric blender; process until smooth, stopping once to scrape down sides. Set aside.
• **Melt** butter in a heavy saucepan over low heat; add flour, stirring until smooth. Cook 1 minute, stirring constantly.
• **Add** chicken broth and half-and-half gradually to flour mixture; cook over medium heat, stirring constantly, until mixture is thickened and bubbly.
• **Stir** in pureed pimiento, onion, salt, and hot sauce; cook over low heat, stirring constantly, until thoroughly heated. **Yield:** 3¾ cups.

Note: You can easily double the recipe.

Eugenia W. Bell
Lexington, Kentucky

CURRIED PUMPKIN SOUP

(pictured on page 2)

QUICK!

2　tablespoons butter or margarine
1　(8-ounce) package sliced fresh
　　mushrooms
½　cup chopped onion
2　tablespoons all-purpose flour
1　tablespoon curry powder
3　cups chicken broth
2　cups canned pumpkin
1　tablespoon honey
½　teaspoon salt
¼　teaspoon ground nutmeg
¼　teaspoon pepper
1　(12-ounce) can evaporated milk
Garnishes: sour cream, chopped
　　fresh chives

• **Melt** butter in a large saucepan; add mushrooms and onion, and cook until tender, stirring often.
• **Stir** in flour and curry powder; gradually add chicken broth, and cook over medium heat, stirring constantly, until mixture is thickened.
• **Stir** in pumpkin and next 4 ingredients; reduce heat, and simmer 10 minutes, stirring occasionally. Stir in milk, and cook, stirring constantly, until thoroughly heated. Garnish, if desired. **Yield:** 6½ cups.

Nancy Wilson
Houston, Texas

CREAM OF TOMATO SOUP WITH LEMON BASIL

3　pounds tomatoes, cut into
　　fourths
¼　cup chopped fresh lemon basil
2　tablespoons butter or margarine
2　tablespoons all-purpose flour
2　cups half-and-half
1　teaspoon sugar
1　teaspoon salt
¼　teaspoon freshly ground pepper
2　tablespoons chopped fresh
　　lemon basil

• **Combine** tomato and ¼ cup lemon basil in a large heavy saucepan; bring to a boil. Reduce heat, and simmer 10 to 15 minutes or until tomato is soft.

• **Pour** mixture through a wire-mesh strainer into a bowl, pressing mixture against sides of strainer with back of a spoon; discard pulp. Set tomato liquid aside.
• **Melt** butter in saucepan over low heat; add flour, stirring until smooth. Cook 1 minute, stirring constantly. Gradually add half-and-half; cook over medium heat, stirring constantly, until mixture is thickened and bubbly.
• **Stir** in sugar, salt, and pepper; gradually stir in tomato liquid and 2 tablespoons lemon basil. Cook just until thoroughly heated (do not boil). Serve immediately. **Yield:** 5½ cups.

CHEESE VELVET SOUP

6　ounces Brie cheese
½　cup finely chopped celery
½　cup finely chopped carrot
¼　cup finely chopped onion
½　cup butter or margarine, melted
½　cup all-purpose flour
2　cups chicken broth
1　teaspoon dried thyme
1　bay leaf
½　cup whipping cream
Garnish: shredded carrot

• **Carefully** cut rind from Brie, and discard; set cheese aside.
• **Cook** celery, carrot, and onion in butter in a saucepan over medium heat, stirring constantly, until tender. Add flour, and cook over low heat 1 minute, stirring constantly. Gradually stir in broth, thyme, and bay leaf. Cook, stirring constantly, until mixture is thickened and bubbly. Add cheese, stirring until smooth. Add whipping cream, and cook until thoroughly heated. Remove and discard bay leaf; serve immediately. Garnish, if desired. **Yield:** 3 cups.

Potluck on the Pedernales
Community Garden Club of
Johnson City, Texas

HERBED CHEESE SOUP

QUICK!

¼　cup butter or margarine
3　tablespoons all-purpose flour
1　tablespoon chopped fresh chives
1½　teaspoons paprika
½　teaspoon dry mustard
¼　teaspoon salt
Dash of freshly ground pepper
2　cups chicken broth
2　cups half-and-half
8　ounces fresh goat cheese
　　(chèvre), crumbled *
1　clove garlic, minced
¼　teaspoon caraway seeds, crushed
1　teaspoon dried basil
1　teaspoon dried dillweed
Garnish: fresh chives

• **Melt** butter in a large saucepan over medium-high heat. Whisk in flour and next 5 ingredients. Cook 3 minutes, whisking constantly. Gradually add broth and half-and-half, and cook, whisking constantly, until smooth.
• **Add** cheese and next 4 ingredients; reduce heat to low, and cook 10 minutes, whisking constantly. Garnish, if desired. **Yield:** 4 servings.

*Substitute 1 (8-ounce) package cream cheese, cubed, for fresh goat cheese.

Patricia Bell
Split Creek Farm
Anderson, South Carolina

MACARONI AND CHEESE SOUP

1　cup elbow macaroni, uncooked
¼　cup butter or margarine
½　cup finely chopped carrot
½　cup finely chopped celery
1　small onion, finely chopped
4　cups milk
1½　cups (6 ounces) shredded
　　process American cheese
2　tablespoons chicken-flavored
　　bouillon granules
½　teaspoon ground white pepper
2　tablespoons cornstarch
2　tablespoons cold water
1　(8-ounce) can whole kernel corn,
　　drained
½　cup frozen English peas

- **Cook** macaroni according to package directions, omitting salt; drain well. Rinse macaroni with cold water; drain and set aside.
- **Melt** butter in a large skillet over medium-high heat; add carrot, celery, and onion, and cook, stirring constantly, 5 to 7 minutes or until tender. Remove vegetable mixture from heat; set aside.
- **Combine** milk and cheese in a heavy Dutch oven, and cook over medium heat until cheese melts, stirring often. Stir in bouillon granules and pepper.
- **Combine** cornstarch and water in a small bowl, stirring well; stir into milk mixture. Cook over medium heat, stirring constantly, until mixture thickens and comes to a boil. Boil 1 minute, stirring constantly.
- **Stir** in macaroni, vegetable mixture, corn, and peas; cook over low heat, stirring constantly, until thoroughly heated. **Yield:** 8 cups.

W. N. Cottrell II
New Orleans, Louisiana

STONE CRAB BISQUE

½ cup butter or margarine, divided
½ cup finely chopped onion
½ cup finely chopped green bell pepper
2 green onions, finely chopped
¼ cup chopped fresh parsley
1 (8-ounce) package fresh mushrooms, chopped
¼ cup all-purpose flour
2 cups milk
2 teaspoons salt
¼ teaspoon pepper
1 teaspoon hot sauce
3 cups half-and-half
2½ cups stone crab claw meat (22 medium claws) *
¼ cup dry sherry

- **Melt** ¼ cup butter in a Dutch oven over medium-high heat; add onion and next 4 ingredients, and cook, stirring constantly, 5 minutes or until tender. Remove from Dutch oven, and set aside.
- **Melt** remaining ¼ cup butter in Dutch oven over low heat; add flour, stirring

until smooth. Cook 1 minute, stirring constantly. Gradually stir in milk. Cook over medium heat, stirring constantly, until thickened and bubbly.
- **Stir** in onion mixture, salt, and next 3 ingredients. Bring to a boil, stirring constantly; reduce heat, and gently stir in crab claw meat. Simmer 5 minutes, stirring often. Gently stir in sherry. **Yield:** 8 servings.

✳ Substitute 2½ cups flaked, back-fin crabmeat for claw meat.

Note: Stone crab is in season October 15 to May 15. You can mail-order it from Joe's Stone Crab in Miami Beach, 1-800-780-2722. The medium stone crab claws come in orders of six. Market prices vary, so call for specific prices. There's an additional charge for packing and shipping.

Nita and Harold Norman
Coral Gables, Florida

OYSTER BISQUE

QUICK!

¼ cup butter or margarine
3 cloves garlic, minced
2 shallots, finely chopped
3 tablespoons all-purpose flour
1 (8-ounce) bottle clam juice
½ cup dry sherry
¼ cup lemon juice
1 tablespoon Worcestershire sauce
⅛ teaspoon hot sauce
¼ teaspoon freshly ground pepper
1 quart whipping cream
2 (12-ounce) containers fresh oysters, drained

- **Melt** butter in a large Dutch oven over medium heat; add garlic and shallot, and cook until tender, stirring often.
- **Add** flour, and cook 1 minute. Add clam juice, sherry, and lemon juice; cook 2 to 3 minutes or until thickened and bubbly.
- **Stir** in Worcestershire sauce and next 3 ingredients; add oysters, and cook over medium heat 10 minutes or just until edges of oysters curl, stirring occasionally. **Yield:** 9 cups.

SHRIMP-CHILE BISQUE

QUICK!

2 (10¾-ounce) cans cream of shrimp soup, undiluted
3 cups milk
1 (14-ounce) can artichoke hearts, drained and chopped
½ (16-ounce) loaf mild Mexican-style process cheese spread, cubed
¼ teaspoon seasoned salt
¼ teaspoon ground white pepper
½ teaspoon Beau Monde seasoning (optional)
1 (5-ounce) package frozen cooked small shrimp
Garnishes: red bell pepper slices, fresh parsley sprigs

- **Combine** first 7 ingredients in a Dutch oven; cook over low heat until cheese melts and mixture is hot, stirring often.
- **Add** shrimp; cook 1 minute or until thoroughly heated, stirring often. Spoon into bowls, and garnish, if desired. **Yield:** 8 cups.

Note: You can prepare bisque a day ahead except adding shrimp. Reheat over low heat, stirring often. Stir in shrimp, and cook as directed.

Candy Stevens Smith
Texarkana, Texas

BELL PEPPER-CHEESE CHOWDER

⅓ cup butter or margarine
1 cup chopped red bell pepper
1 cup chopped yellow bell pepper
½ cup chopped carrot
½ cup sliced celery
½ cup chopped onion
2 cloves garlic, minced
½ cup all-purpose flour
1 quart half-and-half
2 (10½-ounce) cans condensed
   chicken broth, undiluted
1 (12-ounce) can beer
½ teaspoon dry mustard
¼ teaspoon dried rosemary,
   crushed
¼ teaspoon salt
¼ teaspoon ground red pepper
½ teaspoon freshly ground black
   pepper
2 cups (8 ounces) shredded sharp
   Cheddar cheese
Garnishes: fresh rosemary sprig,
   finely chopped red and yellow
   bell pepper

• **Melt** butter in a large Dutch oven over medium-high heat. Add chopped peppers and next 4 ingredients. Cook, stirring constantly, 5 minutes or until tender.
• **Add** flour, stirring constantly. Cook 1 minute, stirring constantly. Gradually add half-and-half, chicken broth, and beer; cook, stirring constantly, until thickened and bubbly.
• **Stir** in mustard and next 4 ingredients; gradually add cheese, stirring until cheese melts. Garnish, if desired, and serve immediately. **Yield:** 11 cups.

Elizabeth A. Crawley
New Orleans, Louisiana

OVEN-ROASTED VEGETABLE CHOWDER

1½ pounds red potatoes, cut into
   ½-inch cubes
2 large carrots, scraped and cut
   into ½-inch cubes
1 large onion, coarsely chopped
6 plum tomatoes, quartered
   lengthwise
3 (14½-ounce) cans chicken
   broth
Dash of salt (optional)
Dash of pepper (optional)

• **Combine** potato and carrot in a lightly greased aluminum foil-lined 13- x 9- x 2-inch pan. Bake at 375° for 15 minutes.
• **Stir** in onion. Place tomato at one end of pan, keeping separate from potato mixture. Bake 1 hour, stirring every 15 minutes.
• **Remove** from oven. Coarsely chop tomato; set aside.
• **Bring** broth to a boil in a large saucepan; add potato mixture. Reduce heat, and simmer 10 to 15 minutes.
• **Stir** in tomato; if desired, add salt and pepper. Serve immediately. **Yield:** about 7 cups.

Chef Marcel Desaulniers
Trellis Restaurant
Williamsburg, Virginia

SOUTHERN CORN AND BACON CHOWDER

1 pound bacon, chopped
1 large onion, thinly sliced
10 ears fresh corn
2 (14½-ounce) cans chicken broth
1 medium potato, peeled and cut
   into ½-inch cubes
2 carrots, scraped and shredded
¼ cup all-purpose flour
1½ cups milk
1½ cups half-and-half
1 tablespoon lemon juice
¼ teaspoon hot sauce
2 teaspoons salt
½ teaspoon pepper

• **Cook** bacon in a Dutch oven until crisp; remove bacon, reserving drippings. Set aside.

• **Cook** onion in 3 tablespoons reserved drippings in Dutch oven until tender; drain.
• **Cut** tips of corn kernels into a large bowl; scrape milk and remaining pulp from cobs. Add corn, broth, potato, and carrot to onion in Dutch oven.
• **Bring** to a boil; reduce heat, and simmer 10 minutes or until potato is tender. Set aside.
• **Whisk** together ⅓ cup reserved bacon drippings and flour in a 10-inch heavy skillet, and cook over medium-low heat, stirring constantly, 10 minutes or until browned. Remove from heat, and set aside.
• **Add** milk and half-and-half to vegetable mixture; cook over medium heat, whisking often, until thoroughly heated. Stir in lemon juice and next 3 ingredients. Whisk in flour mixture and three-fourths of cooked bacon.
• **Cook** until thickened, stirring often. Sprinkle with remaining bacon. **Yield:** about 14 cups.

Note: You can freeze chowder up to 1 month.

Gail Laughlin
Memphis, Tennessee

TURKEY-CORN CHOWDER

QUICK!

4 medium onions, sliced
¼ cup butter or margarine, melted
5 medium red potatoes, cubed
2 stalks celery, chopped
1 tablespoon salt
½ teaspoon pepper
1 chicken-flavored bouillon cube
2 cups water
5 cups milk
2 (15¼-ounce) cans whole kernel
   corn, drained
1 (14¾-ounce) can cream-style
   corn
1 cup half-and-half
1½ teaspoons paprika
¼ teaspoon dried thyme
3 cups chopped cooked turkey *
Chopped fresh parsley

• **Cook** onion in butter in a Dutch oven until tender, stirring often. Add cubed

potato and next 5 ingredients; bring to a boil. Cover, reduce heat, and simmer 15 minutes or until vegetables are tender.
• **Add** milk and next 6 ingredients; cook until heated. Sprinkle with parsley. **Yield:** 20 cups.

* You can substitute 3 cups chopped cooked chicken for turkey.
Marty Sprague
36 Best Christmas Party Ideas
Fort Worth, Texas

CLAM AND SAUSAGE CHOWDER

2 dozen fresh clams
2 pounds smoked Polish sausage, thinly sliced
1 medium onion, chopped
2 cloves garlic, minced
2 tablespoons olive oil
1½ pounds red potatoes, cubed
1 (10-ounce) package frozen whole kernel corn, thawed
4 (8-ounce) bottles clam juice
2 cups water
1 teaspoon fennel seeds, crushed
½ to 1 teaspoon ground red pepper
2 (16-ounce) cans crushed tomatoes, undrained
½ cup chopped fresh parsley

• **Wash** clams thoroughly, discarding any opened shells. Set aside.
• **Brown** sausage in a Dutch oven over medium heat; drain on paper towels, and set aside. Wipe pan drippings from Dutch oven.
• **Cook** onion and garlic in olive oil in Dutch oven over medium-high heat, stirring constantly, until tender. Add potato and next 5 ingredients.
• **Bring** to a boil; cover, reduce heat, and simmer 15 minutes or until potato is tender. Stir in tomatoes.
• **Remove** 2 cups potato mixture, and pour into container of an electric blender. Process until smooth, stopping once to scrape down sides. Return mixture to Dutch oven.
• **Bring** to a boil. Add clams; cover, reduce heat, and simmer 4 to 5 minutes or until clam shells open. (Discard any unopened shells.)

• **Stir** in sausage and parsley; cook until thoroughly heated. **Yield:** 12 cups.

CHILI BEAN SOUP

QUICK!

½ pound lean ground beef
1 small onion, finely chopped
1 (15-ounce) can pinto beans, undrained
1 (10-ounce) can diced tomatoes and green chiles, undrained
¼ cup dry red wine
2 teaspoons chili powder
¼ teaspoon garlic salt

• **Cook** beef and onion in a large skillet until browned, stirring until meat crumbles; drain well.
• **Combine** beef mixture, beans, and remaining ingredients in a 1-quart electric slow cooker.
• **Cover** and cook 3 hours. If desired, serve with a green salad and cornbread. **Yield:** 2 servings.

Note: A 1-quart slow cooker has no LOW or HIGH setting, only OFF and ON.

TACO SOUP

QUICK!

1 pound lean ground beef
1 large onion, chopped
3 (16-ounce) cans Mexican-style chili beans, undrained
1 (16-ounce) can whole kernel corn, undrained
1 (16-ounce) can chopped tomatoes, undrained
1 (15-ounce) can tomato sauce
1½ cups water
1 (4.5-ounce) can chopped green chiles, undrained
1 (1¼-ounce) package taco seasoning mix
1 (1-ounce) envelope Ranch-style salad dressing mix
Toppings: tortilla chips, shredded Cheddar cheese, shredded lettuce, chopped tomato, sour cream, chopped avocado

• **Brown** ground beef and onion in a large Dutch oven over medium-high heat, stirring until beef crumbles; drain. Stir in beans and next 7 ingredients. Bring to a boil; reduce heat, and simmer, uncovered, 15 minutes. Serve with desired toppings. **Yield:** 14 cups.

Note: You can freeze Taco Soup up to 3 months.

Bette Stevens
Texarkana, Texas

CAROLINA GUMBO

QUICK!

1 pound lean ground beef
1 large onion, chopped
1 (16-ounce) package frozen white corn, thawed
1 (15½-ounce) can Great Northern beans, drained
3 (14½-ounce) cans stewed tomatoes, undrained
1 (10-ounce) package frozen sliced okra, thawed
2 tablespoons chili powder
Hot cooked rice
Hot sauce (optional)

• **Brown** ground beef and onion in a Dutch oven over medium-high heat, stirring until beef crumbles. Drain, rinse with hot water, and return mixture to Dutch oven.
• **Stir** in corn and next 4 ingredients. Bring mixture to a boil over medium heat, stirring occasionally; cover, reduce heat, and simmer 20 minutes, stirring occasionally.
• **Serve** over rice. Sprinkle with hot sauce, if desired. **Yield:** 6 cups.

Dawn Poston
Elkin, North Carolina

BEANOLLA SOUP

1 pound boneless pork loin chops, cut into cubes
1 tablespoon butter or margarine, melted
1 tablespoon olive oil
2 medium onions, chopped
3 cloves garlic, minced
3 (14½-ounce) cans chicken broth
3 (16-ounce) cans pinto beans, rinsed and drained
1¼ teaspoons dried oregano
¾ teaspoon cumin seeds
½ teaspoon pepper
Vegetable oil
12 (6-inch) corn tortillas, cut into 2- x ¼-inch strips
2 (3-ounce) packages cream cheese, cut into ¼-inch cubes
Condiments: shredded lettuce, chopped tomato, sliced green onions, chopped fresh cilantro (optional)

• **Brown** pork in butter and olive oil in a Dutch oven over medium-high heat. Remove pork with a slotted spoon, reserving drippings in Dutch oven. Drain pork on paper towels; set aside.
• **Cook** onion and garlic in reserved drippings over medium heat, stirring constantly, 3 to 5 minutes or until onion is tender. Add pork, chicken broth, and next 4 ingredients.
• **Bring** to a boil; cover, reduce heat, and simmer 20 to 30 minutes.
• **Pour** vegetable oil to depth of 1 inch into a heavy skillet. Fry one-fourth of tortilla strips in hot oil over medium heat until browned. Remove strips; drain on paper towels. Repeat procedure with remaining tortilla strips.
• **Ladle** soup into bowls; top with tortilla strips and cream cheese cubes. Serve with condiments, if desired. **Yield:** 11 cups.

Joni Mosher
Arlington, Texas

NAVY BEAN SOUP

If you love the taste of ham hocks, but can't afford the fat, follow the directions here to make a fat-free ham broth. Freeze the broth in ice cube trays, and use a few cubes to season beans, soups, or greens.

2 ham hocks *
7 cups water
1 pound dried navy beans
1 cup chopped celery
1 cup chopped onion
1 carrot, scraped and sliced diagonally
1 teaspoon dried basil
1 teaspoon dried oregano
½ teaspoon salt
½ teaspoon ground nutmeg
¼ teaspoon pepper

• **Combine** ham hocks and water in a 6-quart pressure cooker.
• **Cover** cooker with lid, and seal securely; place pressure control over vent and tube. Cook over high heat until pressure control rocks back and forth quickly. Reduce heat until pressure control rocks occasionally; cook 45 additional minutes.
• **Remove** from heat; run cold water over cooker to reduce pressure. Carefully remove lid so that steam escapes away from you.
• **Pour** broth into a fat strainer; let stand until fat rises to top. Pour broth into a large bowl; discard fat. Remove meat from ham hocks; discard skin, bones, and fat.
• **Combine** broth, meat, beans, and remaining ingredients in cooker. Cook soup as directed above 30 minutes. **Yield:** 9 cups.

* Substitute 1 cup cubed ham for ham hocks. Decrease salt, if desired, and reduce broth cooking time to 30 minutes.

Deborah Moore Clark
Roanoke, Virginia

SPANISH-STYLE LENTIL SOUP

1 pound dried lentils
2 bay leaves
¼ pound ham, diced
1 large onion, chopped
2 carrots, scraped and sliced
4 cloves garlic, chopped
3 tablespoons olive oil
1 large potato, peeled and chopped
½ pound smoked sausage, sliced
1 (14½-ounce) can chicken broth
3 tablespoons red wine vinegar
½ teaspoon salt
½ teaspoon pepper
2 teaspoons paprika
2 tablespoons chopped fresh parsley

• **Combine** first 3 ingredients and enough water to cover in a Dutch oven; bring to a boil. Cover, reduce heat, and simmer 30 minutes.
• **Cook** onion, carrot, and garlic in oil in a large skillet until tender, stirring often; stir into lentil mixture. Add potato and next 6 ingredients. Cover and simmer 45 minutes or until done, stirring occasionally. Stir in parsley. Remove and discard bay leaves. **Yield:** 8 cups.

CREAMY ASPARAGUS AND CHICKEN SOUP

4 chicken breast halves (about 1¾ pounds)
4 cups water
1 medium onion, quartered
2 large stalks celery, cut into 1-inch pieces
1½ teaspoons salt
¼ teaspoon pepper
1½ pounds fresh asparagus
2 cups half-and-half
2 tablespoons butter or margarine
¼ teaspoon salt
¼ teaspoon pepper
Garnish: chopped fresh parsley

• **Combine** first 6 ingredients in a 3-quart saucepan. Bring to a boil over medium-high heat; cover, reduce heat, and simmer 35 minutes or until chicken is tender.

• **Remove** chicken, reserving broth and vegetables in pan. Let chicken cool slightly. Discard bones and skin; cut chicken into bite-size pieces.

• **Snap** off tough ends of asparagus; remove scales from stalks with a vegetable peeler, if desired. Cut asparagus into 2-inch pieces; add to reserved chicken broth and vegetables.

• **Bring** to a boil over medium-high heat; cover, reduce heat, and simmer 10 minutes or until asparagus is tender. Cool 10 minutes.

• **Pour** about one-third of asparagus mixture into container of an electric blender; process until smooth, stopping once to scrape down sides. Pour puree into a large container; repeat procedure twice with remaining asparagus mixture. Return all puree to saucepan.

• **Add** chicken, half-and-half, and next 3 ingredients to asparagus puree; cook over medium heat 5 minutes or until thoroughly heated, stirring occasionally. Garnish, if desired. **Yield:** 8½ cups.

Lilann Taylor
Savannah, Georgia

CHICKEN NOODLE SOUP

1 (3½- to 4-pound) broiler-fryer, halved
2 stalks celery, halved
1 large onion, quartered
1 carrot, scraped and halved
1 turnip, peeled and halved
2 cloves garlic, crushed
1¼ teaspoons salt
¾ teaspoon pepper
¼ teaspoon dried tarragon
4 cups water
3 cups chicken broth
4 ounces medium egg noodles, uncooked
1 large onion, chopped
2 stalks celery, sliced
2 carrots, scraped and sliced
½ teaspoon salt
½ teaspoon pepper
¼ teaspoon tarragon

• **Combine** first 11 ingredients in a large Dutch oven, and bring mixture to a boil over high heat. Reduce heat; cook 45 minutes or until chicken is tender.

• **Remove** chicken from broth; reserve broth. Let chicken cool slightly.

• **Pour** broth through a wire-mesh strainer into a bowl; discard vegetables. Remove and discard fat from broth; return broth to Dutch oven.

• **Cook** noodles according to package directions, omitting salt and fat; drain and set aside.

• **Skin** and bone chicken; chop chicken meat, and set aside.

• **Add** onion, celery, and carrot to chicken broth; bring to a boil. Reduce heat; simmer 15 minutes.

• **Stir** in chopped chicken and noodles; add ½ teaspoon salt, ½ teaspoon pepper, and ¼ teaspoon tarragon. Cook until thoroughly heated. **Yield:** 10 cups.

TORTILLA SOUP

This soup recipe is long on ingredients, but the effort you'll spend yields a richly seasoned, versatile stock. The flavor is best if the soup is made ahead and frozen.

16 medium tomatoes, unpeeled (about 8½ pounds)
2 large onions, peeled and quartered
½ cup vegetable oil, divided
2 poblano chile peppers
3 cloves garlic, minced
24 (6-inch) corn tortillas, cut into thin strips and divided
1 tablespoon ground cumin
1 teaspoon chili powder
1 bay leaf
5 (14½-ounce) cans chicken broth
4 (14½-ounce) cans beef broth
1 (8-ounce) can tomato sauce
½ teaspoon salt
¼ teaspoon ground red pepper
¼ teaspoon ground black pepper
Mesquite chips
8 (4-ounce) skinned and boned chicken breast halves
2 cups (8 ounces) shredded colby-Monterey Jack cheese blend
1 avocado, sliced
Garnish: fresh cilantro sprigs

• **Combine** tomatoes, onion, and 3 tablespoons vegetable oil, tossing to coat;

place in a shallow roasting pan. Broil 5½ inches from heat (with electric oven door partially opened) until tomatoes look blistered, stirring often.

• **Position** knife blade in food processor bowl; add about one-third of tomato mixture. Process until smooth. Transfer mixture to a large Dutch oven. Repeat process twice; set aside.

• **Place** peppers on an aluminum foil-lined baking sheet; broil 5 inches from heat (with electric oven door partially opened) about 5 minutes on each side or until peppers look blistered, turning once. Immediately place in a heavy-duty, zip-top plastic bag; seal and let stand 10 minutes to loosen skins. Peel peppers, and remove seeds; chop.

• **Cook** pepper and garlic in 2 tablespoons oil in a skillet over medium heat 3 minutes, stirring constantly.

• **Add** pepper mixture, half of tortilla strips, cumin, and next 5 ingredients to tomato mixture, and bring to a boil. Cover, reduce heat to low, and simmer 30 minutes. Stir in salt, red pepper, and black pepper. Pour mixture through a large wire-mesh strainer into a large container, discarding solids.

• **For** a charcoal grill, soak mesquite chips in water 1 to 24 hours; drain. (Do not soak chips if using a gas grill.) Wrap chips in heavy-duty aluminum foil; punch several holes in top of foil. Place on medium-hot coals or lava rocks (350° to 400°). Cook chicken, covered with grill lid, 15 minutes or until done, turning once. Cut into strips; keep warm.

• **Pour** remaining 3 tablespoons oil into a large skillet. Fry remaining half of tortilla strips in hot oil over high heat until crisp. Drain on paper towels.

• **To** serve, place small amounts of crisp tortilla strips, chicken strips, cheese, and avocado in individual bowls; ladle soup into bowls. Garnish, if desired. **Yield:** 22 cups.

Note: To make ahead, prepare soup with first 15 ingredients; cover and chill up to 3 days or freeze up to 3 months. Thaw soup in refrigerator. Prepare chicken and remaining tortilla strips; reheat soup. Serve soup according to directions.

Libby and Jim Collet
Dallas, Texas

CHICKEN AND SAUSAGE GUMBO

This low-fat gumbo uses an alternative fat-free roux method that browns all-purpose flour in the oven.

¾ cup all-purpose flour
½ pound 80% fat-free smoked sausage, cut into ¼-inch slices
Vegetable cooking spray
6 (6-ounce) skinned chicken breast halves
1 cup chopped onion
½ cup chopped green bell pepper
½ cup sliced celery
Vegetable cooking spray
2 quarts hot water
3 cloves garlic, minced
2 bay leaves
2 teaspoons reduced-sodium Cajun seasoning *
½ teaspoon dried thyme
1 tablespoon low-sodium Worcestershire sauce
1 teaspoon hot sauce
½ cup sliced green onions
4 cups cooked rice (cooked without salt or fat)

• **Place** flour in a 13- x 9- x 2-inch pan. Bake at 400° for 15 minutes or until the color of caramel, stirring flour every 5 minutes.
• **Brown** sausage in a Dutch oven coated with cooking spray over medium heat. Drain and pat dry with paper towels; wipe drippings from Dutch oven.
• **Brown** chicken in Dutch oven; drain and pat dry with paper towels. Wipe drippings from Dutch oven.
• **Cook** onion, green bell pepper, and celery in Dutch oven coated with cooking spray until tender; sprinkle with browned flour. Gradually stir in water; bring to a boil. Add chicken, garlic, and next 5 ingredients. Reduce heat; simmer, uncovered, 1 hour.
• **Remove** chicken; let cool. Add sausage, and cook, uncovered, 30 minutes. Stir in green onions; cook, uncovered, 30 additional minutes.
• **Bone** chicken, and cut into strips. Add to gumbo, and cook until heated.

Remove and discard bay leaves; serve gumbo over rice. **Yield:** 8 cups.

* For reduced-sodium Cajun seasoning, we used Tony Chachere's More Spice, Less Salt Cajun blend of spices.

♥ Per serving (1 cup gumbo with ½ cup rice):
Calories 336   Fat 8.8g
Cholesterol 69mg   Sodium 200mg

GULF COAST CIOPPINO

Plump clams and inky-shelled mussels are cradled in this colorful tomato-based soup.

20 fresh mussels
20 fresh clams
¼ cup butter or margarine
1 tablespoon olive oil
2 cups chopped celery
2 cups chopped green bell pepper
1 cup chopped green onions
2 cloves garlic, pressed
1 (16-ounce) can crushed tomatoes, undrained
1 (15-ounce) can tomato sauce
1 to 1½ tablespoons dried Italian seasoning
1 to 1½ teaspoons ground red pepper
1½ teaspoons paprika
1 teaspoon sugar
1 teaspoon salt
½ teaspoon ground black pepper
2 (14½-ounce) cans chicken broth
1 pound grouper, amberjack, or sea bass fillets, cut into bite-size pieces

• **Scrub** mussels with a brush, removing beards. Wash clams thoroughly. Discard any opened mussels and clams. Set aside.
• **Melt** butter in a large Dutch oven. Add olive oil and next 4 ingredients; cook, stirring constantly, 5 minutes or until tender.
• **Stir** in tomatoes and next 7 ingredients; cook 2 to 3 minutes, stirring occasionally. Stir in broth.
• **Bring** to a boil; reduce heat, and simmer 45 minutes, stirring occasionally.

• **Stir** in mussels, clams, and fish; cook 3 to 4 minutes, stirring mixture occasionally. (Mussels and clams should open during cooking. Discard any unopened shells.) Serve immediately. **Yield:** about 12 cups.

Malana Clark
Birmingham, Alabama

SPICY THAI LOBSTER SOUP

This soup hints of faraway places with a serendipitous blend of coconut milk, ground red pepper, and ginger.

2 fresh lobster tails *
1 tablespoon ground ginger
½ teaspoon ground red pepper
1 tablespoon peanut oil
5 cups chicken broth
1 tablespoon coarsely grated lime rind
⅓ cup long-grain rice, uncooked
1 cup unsweetened coconut milk
6 large fresh mushrooms, sliced
½ cup chopped onion
1 tablespoon chopped fresh cilantro
2 tablespoons lime juice
Garnishes: chopped green onions, fresh cilantro sprigs

• **Remove** lobster meat from shell; slice. Set aside.
• **Cook** ground ginger and ground red pepper in peanut oil in a large saucepan over medium heat 1 minute. Add chicken broth and lime rind.
• **Bring** mixture to a boil. Stir in rice; cover, reduce heat, and simmer 15 to 20 minutes.
• **Add** coconut milk, sliced mushrooms, chopped onion, and chopped cilantro; cook 5 minutes, stirring occasionally.
• **Add** lobster; cook 3 to 5 minutes. Remove from heat, and stir in lime juice. Spoon into bowls; garnish, if desired. **Yield:** 6½ cups.

* Substitute 1 pound unpeeled medium-size fresh shrimp for lobster. Peel shrimp, and devein, if desired.

Heather Riggins
Nashville, Tennessee

LOUISIANA OYSTER AND ARTICHOKE SOUP

QUICK!

2 (12-ounce) containers fresh
  Standard oysters
½ cup finely chopped shallot
1 bay leaf
⅛ to ¼ teaspoon ground red
  pepper
Pinch of dried thyme
3 tablespoons butter or margarine,
  melted
2 tablespoons all-purpose flour
1 (14½-ounce) can chicken
  broth
1 (14-ounce) can artichoke hearts,
  drained and cut into eighths
1 tablespoon chopped fresh
  parsley
½ teaspoon salt
⅛ to ¼ teaspoon hot sauce
½ cup whipping cream

• **Drain** oysters, reserving 1 cup oyster liquid. Cut oysters into fourths. Set aside.
• **Sauté** shallot and next 3 ingredients in butter in a Dutch oven until shallot is tender. Add flour, stirring well. Cook 1 minute, stirring constantly. Gradually add oyster liquid and broth; simmer 15 minutes, stirring occasionally. Remove and discard bay leaf. Add oysters, artichokes, parsley, salt, and hot sauce; simmer, uncovered, 10 minutes. Stir in whipping cream; cook until thoroughly heated. **Yield:** 6 cups.

Mary Adele Baus
New Orleans, Louisiana

SHRIMP ENCHILADA SOUP

*If you love the taste of Tex-Mex,
then this bowl's for you.*

5 cups chicken broth
4 ounces tortilla chips (3 cups)
1 pound unpeeled medium-size
  fresh shrimp
2 (4.5-ounce) cans chopped green
  chiles, undrained
1 (10-ounce) can diced tomatoes
  and green chiles, undrained
2 tablespoons butter or margarine
1 medium onion, chopped
2 cloves garlic, minced
1 cup sour cream
¼ cup chopped fresh cilantro
Shredded mozzarella cheese
Shredded Cheddar cheese

• **Bring** chicken broth to a boil in a large Dutch oven.
• **Add** tortilla chips. Remove from heat, and let stand 10 minutes.
• **Peel** shrimp, and devein, if desired. Set shrimp aside.
• **Position** knife blade in food processor bowl; add half of broth mixture. Process until smooth, stopping once to scrape down sides. Transfer mixture to another container. Repeat procedure with remaining broth mixture.
• **Return** blended broth mixture to Dutch oven; stir in green chiles and tomatoes. Set aside.
• **Melt** butter in a large skillet over medium-high heat. Add shrimp, onion, and garlic; cook, stirring constantly, 3 to 4 minutes or until shrimp turn pink.
• **Stir** shrimp mixture into broth mixture; cook over medium heat until thoroughly heated (do not boil).
• **Stir** in sour cream and cilantro. Serve soup immediately. Sprinkle each serving with mozzarella and Cheddar cheeses. **Yield:** 8 cups.

Laurie McIntyre
Houston, Texas

SEAFOOD GUMBO

2½ cups all-purpose flour
1 tablespoon olive oil
2 cups chopped celery
1 cup chopped green bell pepper
1 cup chopped onion
1 cup chopped green onions
5 cloves garlic, pressed
1 tablespoon gumbo filé
7 (14½-ounce) cans no-salt-added,
  fat-free chicken broth
1 tablespoon salt
½ teaspoon black pepper
½ teaspoon ground red pepper
1 tablespoon hot sauce
1 (10-ounce) package frozen cut
  okra
3 pounds unpeeled large fresh
  shrimp
2 pounds fresh crabmeat
1 pound crawfish meat
2 (12-ounce) containers fresh
  oysters, undrained
Gumbo filé (optional)
Hot cooked rice

• **Sprinkle** flour evenly in a 15- x 10- x 1-inch pan.
• **Bake** at 400° for 20 minutes or until caramel-colored (do not burn), stirring often; cool.
• **Pour** oil into a 12-quart stockpot; place over medium heat until hot. Add celery and next 5 ingredients; cook, stirring constantly, 5 to 7 minutes or until tender.
• **Add** toasted flour, broth, salt, pepper, red pepper, and hot sauce; bring to a boil. Reduce heat, and simmer, uncovered, 30 minutes. Add okra, and simmer, uncovered, 30 minutes.
• **Peel** shrimp, and devein, if desired. Drain and flake crabmeat, removing any bits of shell.
• **Add** shrimp, crabmeat, crawfish, and oysters to stockpot; cook 15 to 20 minutes or just until seafood is done. Stir in additional gumbo filé, if desired. Spoon over rice, and serve immediately. **Yield:** 9 quarts.

Beth Ann Spracklen
Arlington, Texas

♥ Per serving (1 cup gumbo and ½ cup rice):
Calories 223   Fat 2.1g
Cholesterol 82mg   Sodium 333mg

Chili Verde;
Bodacious Chili

BODACIOUS CHILI
(pictured at left)

With such a long list of ingredients, the name is obviously appropriate. But none of the items are terribly unusual or expensive, and it's easy to make. The flavor? Well, the name again applies.

2 pounds boneless beef chuck roast, cut into 1-inch cubes
2 large onions, chopped
3 stalks celery, cut into 1-inch pieces
1 large green bell pepper, coarsely chopped
1 large red bell pepper, coarsely chopped
1 cup sliced fresh mushrooms
2 jalapeño peppers, seeded and chopped
4 cloves garlic, minced
3 tablespoons olive oil
2 tablespoons cocoa
2 tablespoons chili powder
1 teaspoon ground cumin
1 teaspoon dried oregano
1 teaspoon paprika
1 teaspoon ground turmeric
½ teaspoon salt
½ teaspoon ground cardamom
¼ teaspoon pepper
1 tablespoon molasses
½ cup dry red wine
2 (16-ounce) cans whole tomatoes, undrained and chopped
1 (16-ounce) can kidney beans, drained
1 (15-ounce) can chickpeas, drained
Spicy Sour Cream Topping
Shredded Cheddar cheese

• **Cook** first 8 ingredients in olive oil in a large Dutch oven over medium-high heat, stirring constantly, until meat browns. Drain and return meat mixture to Dutch oven.
• **Stir** in cocoa and next 13 ingredients. Bring mixture to a boil; cover, reduce heat, and simmer 1½ hours, stirring occasionally. Serve chili with Spicy Sour Cream Topping and shredded cheese. **Yield:** 12 cups.

Spicy Sour Cream Topping

1 (8-ounce) carton sour cream
⅓ cup salsa
2 tablespoons mayonnaise
1 teaspoon chili powder
½ teaspoon onion powder
½ teaspoon curry powder
Dash of ground red pepper
1 tablespoon lemon juice
1 teaspoon Dijon mustard

• **Combine** all ingredients; cover and chill. **Yield:** 1⅔ cups.

Peggy Huffstetler
Lebanon, Tennessee

CINCINNATI CHILI

QUICK!

Because the meat in this chili is not browned and drained, use very lean ground beef.

2 pounds ground round
2 cups water
2 (6-ounce) cans no-salt-added tomato paste
1 large onion, finely chopped
1 clove garlic, minced
2 large bay leaves
3 tablespoons chili powder
1 tablespoon ground cumin
2 teaspoons ground allspice
1½ teaspoons ground cinnamon
1 teaspoon salt
1 teaspoon pepper
¼ teaspoon ground red pepper
1 teaspoon white wine vinegar
1 teaspoon Worcestershire sauce
Hot cooked spaghetti
Shredded Cheddar cheese
Chopped onion

• **Combine** beef and water in a 4-quart pressure cooker; stir with a fork until thoroughly blended. Stir in tomato paste and next 12 ingredients.
• **Cover** cooker with lid, and seal securely; place pressure control over vent and tube. Cook over high heat until pressure control rocks back and forth quickly. Reduce heat until pressure control rocks occasionally; cook 15 additional minutes.

• **Remove** from heat; run cold water over cooker to reduce pressure. Carefully remove lid so that steam escapes away from you.
• **Remove** and discard bay leaves. Stir chili well. Serve over hot spaghetti, and top with cheese and onion. Serve with oyster crackers. **Yield:** 6 to 8 servings.

Mary Blackmon
Lake Dallas, Texas

CHILI VERDE
(pictured on opposite page)

¾ pound beef chuck roast, cut into 1-inch cubes
¾ pound pork loin or shoulder roast, cut into 1-inch cubes
1 large onion, chopped
1 large green bell pepper, chopped
1 clove garlic, minced
2 tablespoons olive oil, divided
2 (16-ounce) cans whole tomatoes, undrained and chopped
2 (4.5-ounce) cans chopped green chiles, undrained
1 cup dry red wine
1 cup salsa
¼ cup chopped fresh cilantro
2 beef-flavored bouillon cubes
1 tablespoon brown sugar
3 tablespoons lemon juice
Hot cooked rice
Garnish: fresh cilantro sprigs

• **Combine** first 5 ingredients. Cook half of mixture in 1 tablespoon olive oil in a large Dutch oven over medium-high heat, stirring constantly, until browned. Remove from Dutch oven; set aside. Repeat procedure with remaining meat mixture and 1 tablespoon olive oil.
• **Combine** meat mixture, tomatoes, and next 7 ingredients. Bring to a boil; cover, reduce heat, and simmer 1 hour or until meat is tender, stirring occasionally. Serve over rice, and garnish, if desired. **Yield:** 11 cups.

Fran Pointer
Kansas City, Missouri

BLACK BEAN CHILI MARSALA

1 large onion, chopped
2 cloves garlic, minced
3 tablespoons vegetable oil
1 (2½-pound) boneless beef chuck
      roast, trimmed and chopped
1 (29-ounce) can tomato sauce
2 (6-ounce) cans tomato paste
1 cup Marsala *
1 cup water
2 or 3 (4-ounce) cans sliced
      mushrooms, drained
3 to 4 tablespoons chili powder
2 teaspoons seasoned salt
1 teaspoon freshly ground pepper
2 (15-ounce) cans black beans,
      undrained
Hot cooked rice
Garnish: strips of lime rind or fresh
      cilantro sprigs

• **Cook** onion and garlic in oil in a Dutch oven over medium-high heat, stirring constantly, until tender. Add chopped roast and next 8 ingredients.
• **Bring** mixture to a boil. Cover, reduce heat, and simmer 1 hour, stirring mixture occasionally.
• **Add** beans, and cook until thoroughly heated. Serve chili over rice. Garnish, if desired. **Yield:** 12 cups.

* Substitute 1 cup dry white wine plus 1½ tablespoons brandy for Marsala.

Walter C. Lund
Miami, Florida

RED CHILI STEW

1½ pounds lean beef chuck roast,
      cut into 1-inch cubes
2 cups water
3 tablespoons ground red chile
1 teaspoon salt
1 teaspoon ground oregano
1 clove garlic, pressed
3 large tomatoes, chopped

• **Combine** beef and water in a Dutch oven; bring to a boil over medium-high heat. Cover, reduce heat, and simmer 45 minutes or until meat is tender, stirring occasionally.

• **Stir** in ground chile and remaining ingredients; cook 30 additional minutes. **Yield:** 4 cups.

Rose Trujillo
Sante Fe, New Mexico

WHITE LIGHTNING TEXAS CHILI

1 pound dried navy beans
4 (14½-ounce) cans chicken broth,
      divided
1 large onion, chopped
2 cloves garlic, minced
1 tablespoon ground white
      pepper
1 tablespoon dried oregano
1 tablespoon ground cumin
1 teaspoon salt
½ teaspoon ground cloves
5 cups chopped cooked chicken
2 (4.5-ounce) cans chopped green
      chiles
1 cup water
1 jalapeño pepper, seeded and
      chopped
8 (8-inch) flour tortillas
Shredded Monterey Jack cheese
Salsa
Sour cream

• **Sort** and wash beans; place in a large Dutch oven. Cover with water 2 inches above beans. Soak 8 hours; drain beans, and return to Dutch oven. Discard liquid. Add 3 cans chicken broth, onion, and next 6 ingredients; bring to a boil. Cover, reduce heat, and simmer 2 hours or until beans are tender, stirring occasionally. Add remaining can of chicken broth, chicken, and next 3 ingredients. Cover and simmer 1 hour, stirring occasionally.
• **Make** 4 cuts in each tortilla toward, but not through, center, using kitchen shears. Line serving bowls with tortillas, overlapping cut edges of tortillas. Ladle chili into prepared bowls, and top with cheese, salsa, and sour cream. Serve immediately. **Yield:** 12 cups.

Beverly Germany
Fort Worth, Texas

BEEF STEW
(pictured at right)

1 (2¾-pound) boneless chuck
      roast *
¼ cup all-purpose flour
2 tablespoons vegetable oil
4 cups water
1 tablespoon Worcestershire
      sauce
2 teaspoons salt
1 teaspoon garlic salt
¾ teaspoon pepper
¼ teaspoon ground allspice
2 bay leaves
4 carrots, scraped
2 stalks celery
4 medium-size red potatoes
3 small onions
2 green bell peppers
3 tablespoons all-purpose flour
3 tablespoons water

• **Trim** fat from roast, and cut roast into 1-inch cubes. Place beef and ¼ cup flour in a plastic bag; seal bag, and shake vigorously to coat.
• **Pour** oil into a large Dutch oven; place over medium-high heat until hot. Add beef, and cook until browned, stirring occasionally.
• **Add** 4 cups water and next 6 ingredients; bring to a boil. Cover, reduce heat, and simmer 2 hours or until beef is tender. Remove and discard bay leaves.
• **Cut** carrots and celery into 2-inch lengths. Peel potatoes; cut potatoes and onions into eighths. Cut bell peppers into 1-inch pieces.
• **Add** carrot, celery, potato, onion, and bell pepper to beef mixture; cover and simmer 30 minutes or until vegetables are tender.
• **Combine** 3 tablespoons flour and 3 tablespoons water, stirring well; stir into stew. Bring to a boil; boil, stirring constantly, 1 minute or until thickened and bubbly. **Yield:** 6 to 8 servings.

* Substitute 2 pounds stew meat for roast.

Ann Winniford
Dallas, Texas

Beef Stew; Green Onion Dressing, page 324; Sour Cream Cornbread, page 39

VEAL AND ARTICHOKE RAGOÛT

3 tablespoons all-purpose flour
1 teaspoon paprika
½ teaspoon salt
½ teaspoon dried basil
½ teaspoon dried rosemary
¼ teaspoon pepper
2 pounds lean boneless veal stew
    meat, cut into 1-inch cubes *
¼ cup vegetable oil, divided
½ pound fresh mushrooms, sliced
1 (14½-ounce) can chicken broth
1 cup dry white wine
1 (14-ounce) can artichoke hearts,
    drained and quartered
Hot cooked wide egg noodles

• **Combine** first 6 ingredients in a bowl or zip-top plastic bag; add veal, tossing to coat. Set aside.
• **Heat** 2 tablespoons oil in a Dutch oven over medium heat; add half of veal. Cook until browned, stirring often. Remove veal. Repeat procedure with remaining oil and veal, reserving remaining flour mixture. Remove veal, and set aside.
• **Add** mushrooms to Dutch oven, and cook until tender, stirring often. Stir in reserved flour mixture; cook 1 minute, stirring constantly. Stir in veal, chicken broth, and wine.
• **Bring** to a boil. Cover, reduce heat, and simmer 1 hour.
• **Add** artichokes; cover and cook 10 to 15 minutes, stirring occasionally. Serve in individual bowls over noodles. **Yield:** 6 cups.

✻ Substitute 2 pounds boneless pork.
Jeanne S. Hotaling
Augusta, Georgia

EMERALD ISLE STEW

1 (4½-pound) leg of lamb ✻
1 (1-pound) trimmed lean
    boneless beef top sirloin
    steak, cut into 1-inch cubes
1 tablespoon vegetable oil
1 pound onions, chopped
1 clove garlic, minced
¾ cup stout beer ✻✻
4 bay leaves
1 (10½-ounce) can condensed
    beef broth, undiluted
1 tablespoon salt
1 teaspoon pepper
2 cups water
¾ pound carrots, cut into ¼-inch
    slices
1 pound new potatoes, cut into
    ¾-inch cubes
2 to 3 teaspoons dried tarragon
3 tablespoons all-purpose flour
¼ cup water
1 (17¼-ounce) package frozen
    puff pastry, thawed

• **Remove** meat from lamb bone; cut into 1-inch cubes. Set bone aside.
• **Brown** lamb and beef cubes in oil in a large Dutch oven over medium-high heat, stirring occasionally.
• **Add** lamb bone, onion, and next 7 ingredients; bring to a boil. Cover, reduce heat, and simmer 30 minutes.
• **Remove** lamb bone; add carrot, potato, and tarragon. Cover and simmer 30 minutes. Discard bay leaves.
• **Combine** flour and ¼ cup water; stir until mixture is smooth. Slowly add flour mixture to stew, stirring constantly. Cook over medium heat 3 minutes or until thickened and bubbly.
• **Cut** pastry into shapes with a 5-inch shamrock cookie cutter. Place shamrocks on an ungreased baking sheet.
• **Bake** at 400° for 5 minutes or until lightly browned.
• **Spoon** stew into bowls; top each with shamrock puff pastry. **Yield:** 14 cups.

✻ Substitute 3 pounds trimmed lean boneless beef top sirloin steak.

✻✻ For the stout beer, we used Guinness brand.
The Emerald Restaurant
Austin, Texas

LAMB STEW WITH POPOVERS

3 tablespoons olive oil
2 pounds boneless lamb, cut into
    1-inch cubes
1 medium onion, chopped
1 clove garlic, pressed
2 tablespoons all-purpose flour
1½ cups chicken broth
½ cup dry white wine
2 tablespoons lemon juice
1½ teaspoons salt
¼ teaspoon dried marjoram
¼ teaspoon dried rosemary
⅛ teaspoon pepper
1 bay leaf
12 pearl onions
6 to 8 small new potatoes, peeled
    and cut into ¼-inch slices
    (about 1 pound)
3 carrots, scraped and sliced
    diagonally into 1-inch pieces
Popovers
Garnish: fresh rosemary sprigs

• **Heat** oil in a Dutch oven over medium heat; add lamb, and cook until browned, stirring often. Remove lamb, reserving 2 tablespoons drippings in pan.
• **Cook** onion and garlic in drippings over medium heat, stirring constantly, 3 minutes or until onion is tender. Return lamb to Dutch oven, and sprinkle with flour; stir well. Stir in chicken broth and next 7 ingredients.
• **Bring** to a boil; cover, reduce heat, and simmer 30 minutes.
• **Add** pearl onions, potato, and carrot; cover and simmer 20 to 30 minutes or until tender. Remove and discard bay leaf. Serve stew in Popovers. Garnish, if desired. **Yield:** 7 cups.

Popovers

1 cup all-purpose flour
¼ teaspoon salt
1 cup milk
2 large eggs, lightly beaten

• **Combine** all ingredients in a mixing bowl; beat at low speed with an electric mixer just until smooth.
• **Place** well-greased 3½-inch muffin pans or popover pans in a 450° oven for 3 minutes or until a drop of water sizzles when dropped in them. Remove pans

from oven; spoon batter into cups, filling half full.

- **Bake** at 450° for 15 minutes. Reduce oven temperature to 350°, and bake 20 to 25 additional minutes. Serve immediately. **Yield:** 6 popovers.

Lynn Abbott
Southern Pines, North Carolina

PANCHO VILLA STEW

2 pounds pork loin, cut into 1-inch cubes
¼ cup all-purpose flour
2 tablespoons vegetable oil
2 (4-ounce) chorizo sausages, cut into ½-inch slices
3 (14½-ounce) cans chicken broth
1 (14½-ounce) can whole tomatoes, drained
3 (4.5-ounce) cans diced green chiles, undrained
1 large purple onion, sliced into rings
3 cloves garlic, pressed
2 teaspoons ground cumin
2 teaspoons cocoa
1 teaspoon dried oregano
¼ teaspoon salt
1 (2-inch) stick cinnamon
2 (15-ounce) cans black beans, rinsed and drained
1 (15½-ounce) can white hominy, rinsed and drained
1 (10-ounce) package frozen whole kernel corn
½ cup beer or tequila
Flour tortillas

- **Dredge** pork in flour; set aside.
- **Heat** oil in a large Dutch oven over medium heat; add pork, and cook until browned, stirring often. Add sausage, and cook 2 minutes, stirring often. Add broth and next 9 ingredients.
- **Bring** to a boil; reduce heat, and simmer 1 hour.
- **Stir** in black beans and next 3 ingredients; simmer 30 minutes. Remove and discard cinnamon stick. Serve with buttered flour tortillas. **Yield:** 12 cups.

Judith Hartley
Signal Mountain, Tennessee

SALMON AND VEGETABLE RAGOÛT

2 tablespoons olive oil, divided
2 tablespoons butter or margarine, divided
4 (6-ounce) salmon fillets (1½ inches thick)
⅛ teaspoon salt
⅛ teaspoon pepper
⅓ cup chopped purple onion
¼ cup chopped green bell pepper
2 green onions, cut diagonally into 1-inch pieces
2 tablespoons minced garlic
1 tablespoon chopped fresh cilantro
1 (11-ounce) can diced tomatoes and green chiles, undrained
1 (8-ounce) bottle clam juice
½ cup dry white wine
½ teaspoon salt
⅛ teaspoon pepper
Hot cooked rice
Garnishes: sliced green onions, chopped fresh cilantro, lemon wedges

- **Combine** 1 tablespoon oil and 1 tablespoon butter in an 11- x 7- x 1½-inch baking dish; place in a 375° oven for 5 minutes or until butter is lightly browned.
- **Sprinkle** fillets with ⅛ teaspoon salt and ⅛ teaspoon pepper; place salmon in baking dish, skin side up.
- **Bake** at 375° for 15 to 20 minutes or until fish flakes easily when tested with a fork, turning once. Remove and discard skin; break salmon into 1½-inch pieces.
- **Heat** remaining 1 tablespoon olive oil and 1 tablespoon butter in a heavy saucepan over medium-high heat until butter melts; add purple onion and next 3 ingredients, and cook, stirring constantly, 3 minutes or until tender.
- **Stir** cilantro and next 5 ingredients into onion mixture; bring to a boil. Cook mixture 10 to 15 minutes or until reduced to 1½ cups, stirring occasionally.
- **Add** salmon, and cook just until thoroughly heated, stirring gently. Serve over rice; garnish, if desired. **Yield:** 4 servings.

Carolynn St. Pierre
Winter Haven, Florida

VEGETARIAN CASSOULET

1 (16-ounce) package dried chickpeas
3 quarts water
3 tablespoons minced garlic, divided
1 bay leaf
¼ cup butter or margarine
½ pound whole fresh mushrooms
½ teaspoon dried thyme
¼ teaspoon dried rosemary, crushed
½ teaspoon dried oregano
1 cup dry white wine
3 tablespoons tomato paste
6 turnips, peeled and cut into fourths
4 large red potatoes, peeled and cut into fourths
1 rutabaga, peeled and cut into 1-inch pieces
2 onions, cut into eighths
6 carrots, scraped and cut into 2-inch pieces
½ teaspoon salt
½ teaspoon pepper
¼ cup olive oil
2 (14½-ounce) cans vegetable broth
½ cup fine, dry breadcrumbs

- **Sort** and wash chickpeas; place in an ovenproof 6-quart Dutch oven. Cover with water 2 inches above beans; let soak 8 hours. Drain.
- **Add** 3 quarts water, 1 tablespoon garlic, and bay leaf; cook over medium-high heat 2 hours or until beans are tender. Remove and discard bay leaf. Set beans aside.
- **Melt** butter in a large skillet over medium-high heat; add 1 tablespoon garlic, mushrooms, and next 3 ingredients. Cook 5 minutes, stirring constantly. Add wine and tomato paste; cook 2 minutes, stirring constantly. Add to beans.
- **Combine** remaining 1 tablespoon garlic, turnip, and next 7 ingredients; place in an aluminum foil-lined roasting pan.
- **Bake** at 500° for 20 minutes, stirring once. Spoon vegetables over beans in Dutch oven; pour broth over vegetables. Sprinkle with breadcrumbs.
- **Bake** at 325° for 1½ hours or until vegetables are tender. **Yield:** 8 servings.

REGGAE RUNDOWN

A rundown is a Jamaican dish reduced by slow cooking. This vegetable stew gets its kick from a Caribbean Scotch bonnet pepper.

1 (8-ounce) sweet potato
1 (8-ounce) baking potato
1 (14-ounce) can coconut milk
3 carrots, scraped and sliced
3 green onions, chopped
2 cloves garlic, minced
½ teaspoon salt
¼ teaspoon ground allspice
⅛ teaspoon dried thyme
1 cup peeled, chopped tomato
⅛ teaspoon minced Scotch bonnet
   or habanero pepper

• **Peel** potatoes; cut into ¾-inch cubes.
• **Bring** coconut milk to a boil in a large heavy saucepan over medium heat, stirring often; stir in potato, carrot, and next 5 ingredients. Return to a boil, stirring often; reduce heat, and simmer 7 minutes or until vegetables are almost tender, stirring often.
• **Stir** in tomato and pepper; cook 5 minutes or until thoroughly heated, stirring often. **Yield:** 4 servings.

CHICKEN STOCK

4 pounds chicken pieces
1 pound chicken wings
4 quarts water
2 onions, peeled and quartered
4 stalks celery with tops, cut into
   2-inch pieces
4 carrots, cut into 2-inch pieces
1 large bay leaf
6 sprigs fresh parsley
1 tablespoon fresh thyme or
   1 teaspoon dried thyme
6 sprigs fresh dill or ½ teaspoon
   dried dillweed
½ teaspoon black peppercorns

• **Combine** first 3 ingredients in a large stockpot; bring to a boil, skimming the surface to remove excess fat and foam.
• **Add** onion and remaining ingredients to stockpot. Return mixture to a boil; reduce heat, and simmer, uncovered,

2 hours, skimming surface to remove excess fat, if necessary. Let cool.
• **Line** a large wire-mesh strainer with a double layer of cheesecloth; place in a large bowl. Pour stock through strainer; reserve chicken for other uses, and discard remaining solids. Cool stock slightly.
• **Cover** and chill; remove and discard solidified fat from top of stock. Cover and chill stock up to 2 days or freeze up to 1 month. **Yield:** 8 cups.

BEEF STOCK

5 pounds beef or veal bones
2 large carrots, quartered
2 large onions, quartered
4 stalks celery, quartered
4 quarts water, divided
3 tablespoons tomato paste
6 to 8 sprigs fresh parsley
3 or 4 sprigs fresh thyme
4 whole cloves
½ teaspoon black peppercorns
1 bay leaf
2 cloves garlic, crushed

• **Place** first 4 ingredients in a large roasting pan; bake at 500° for 1 hour, turning occasionally.
• **Transfer** mixture to a large stockpot; discard drippings from roasting pan. Set aside.
• **Add** 1 quart water to roasting pan; bring to a boil over medium-high heat, stirring to loosen pieces that cling to bottom. Pour into stockpot; add remaining 3 quarts water, tomato paste, and remaining ingredients to stockpot.
• **Bring** to a boil; cover, reduce heat, and simmer 2 hours.
• **Line** a large wire-mesh strainer with a double layer of cheesecloth; place in a large bowl. Pour stock through strainer, discarding solids. Cool stock slightly.
• **Cover** and chill; remove and discard solidified fat from top of stock. Cover and chill stock up to 2 days or freeze up to 1 month. **Yield:** 8 cups.

VENISON STOCK

Ask your butcher or game processor to cut leg bones into smaller pieces.

5 pounds venison bones
2 (10¾-ounce) cans tomato puree
2 large carrots, scraped and
   coarsely chopped
4 stalks celery, coarsely chopped
2 large onions, coarsely chopped
2 cups dry red wine
3 quarts water
¼ teaspoon pepper
1 bay leaf
4 sprigs fresh thyme
8 sprigs fresh parsley

• **Combine** first 5 ingredients in a roasting pan; bake, uncovered, at 500° for 1 hour or until bones are well browned, turning bones over to prevent burning, if necessary. Transfer mixture to a large stockpot; set aside.
• **Add** wine to roasting pan, and bring to a boil, stirring to loosen browned particles that cling to bottom. Pour into stockpot. Add water and remaining ingredients.
• **Bring** to a boil; reduce heat, and simmer at least 3 hours.
• **Line** a large wire-mesh strainer or colander with a double layer of cheesecloth; place over a large bowl. Pour stock through strainer, discarding solids in strainer. Cool stock slightly.
• **Cover** and chill; remove and discard solidified fat from top of stock. Cover and chill stock up to 2 days or freeze up to 1 month. **Yield:** about 8 cups.

Chef David Everett
Dining Room at Ford's Colony
Williamsburg, Virginia

At right: *Skillet Zucchini Combo*
(page 409)

VEGETABLES AND SIDE DISHES

BRANDIED CRANBERRIES

Using brandy for the liquid in this cranberry relish recipe creates a bold new flavor for a traditional favorite.

3 (12-ounce) packages fresh or
   frozen cranberries, thawed
3 cups sugar
½ cup brandy
Garnish: fresh thyme sprigs

• **Place** cranberries in a single layer in two lightly greased 15- x 10- x 1-inch jellyroll pans; pour sugar over cranberries. Cover tightly with aluminum foil.
• **Bake** at 350° for 1 hour.
• **Spoon** cranberries into a large serving bowl; gently stir in brandy. Cool. Serve cranberries chilled or at room temperature. Garnish, if desired. Store in refrigerator up to 1 week. **Yield:** 5 cups.

Carole Miller Radford
Lincolnton, Georgia

BROILED GRAPEFRUIT

QUICK!

3 large pink grapefruit
½ cup apricot preserves
1 tablespoon brown sugar
½ cup flaked coconut

• **Peel**, section, and seed grapefruit; place in four lightly greased individual baking dishes. Place dishes on a large baking sheet.
• **Combine** apricot preserves and sugar in a small bowl, stirring well; spoon over grapefruit.
• **Broil** 5½ inches from heat (with electric oven door partially opened) 2 to 3 minutes or until bubbly.
• **Sprinkle** with coconut; broil 1 additional minute or until coconut is lightly toasted. **Yield:** 4 servings.

HOT CURRIED FRUIT

This side dish doubles as a dessert when served over ice cream or pound cake.

1 (29-ounce) can pear halves,
   drained
1 (29-ounce) can peach halves,
   drained
1 (20-ounce) can pineapple
   chunks, drained
2 (17-ounce) cans apricot halves,
   drained
½ cup butter or margarine,
   softened
1 cup firmly packed brown sugar
1 tablespoon cornstarch
1½ teaspoons curry powder

• **Place** first 4 ingredients in a 13- x 9- x 2-inch baking dish.
• **Combine** butter and remaining 3 ingredients; spoon over fruit.
• **Bake** at 325° for 1 hour, basting occasionally with cooking liquid.
• **Serve** with a slotted spoon. **Yield:** 8 to 10 servings.

Note: You can prepare casserole ahead and store it in the refrigerator up to 2 days; bake according to directions just before serving.

To Market, To Market
Junior League of Owensboro, Kentucky

PINEAPPLE BAKE

Serve this sweet side dish with sliced ham, pork, chicken, or turkey.

2 (20-ounce) cans sliced pineapple
   in juice, undrained
2 cups (8 ounces) shredded sharp
   Cheddar cheese
⅔ cup sugar
⅓ cup all-purpose flour
1 cup round buttery cracker
   crumbs
¼ cup butter or margarine, melted

• **Drain** sliced pineapple, reserving ⅓ cup juice.
• **Place** pineapple in a lightly greased 11- x 7- x 1½-inch baking dish; sprinkle with cheese.

• **Combine** reserved pineapple juice, sugar, and flour; pour over cheese. Combine cracker crumbs and butter; sprinkle over flour mixture.
• **Bake** at 350° for 25 minutes or until bubbly. **Yield:** 8 servings.

Sheryl Jennings
Uvalde, Texas

HERBED ARTICHOKE SAUTÉ
(pictured at right)

10 baby artichokes
1 tablespoon olive oil
1 red bell pepper, cut into thin
   strips
1 tablespoon fresh thyme leaves
½ cup dry white wine
½ teaspoon salt
2 tablespoons chopped shallots
2 cloves garlic, minced
2 tablespoons butter

• **Hold** each artichoke by stem, and wash by plunging up and down in cold water. Cut off stem ends. Remove dark-green outer leaves from baby artichokes until light-green leaves appear. Place artichokes in a large Dutch oven; cover with water, and bring to a boil. Cook 12 to 15 minutes or until tender; drain and cool slightly.
• **Cut** artichokes in half lengthwise.
• **Cook** artichokes in oil in a large non-stick skillet over medium-high heat 2 minutes, stirring constantly. Add bell pepper strips and thyme leaves. Cook 3 additional minutes, stirring constantly. Remove artichoke mixture from skillet; set aside.
• **Combine** wine and next 3 ingredients in skillet; bring to a boil over medium-high heat. Reduce heat to low, and simmer until reduced to 2 tablespoons (about 5 minutes).
• **Stir** in butter; add artichoke mixture, and cook until thoroughly heated. **Yield:** 2 servings.

Herbed Artichoke Sauté

HAM-MUSHROOM-STUFFED ARTICHOKES

2 medium-size fresh artichokes
Lemon wedge
1½ tablespoons fresh lemon juice
1 cup sliced fresh mushrooms
1 teaspoon olive or vegetable oil
3 ounces smoked ham, cut into strips (about ½ cup strips)
2 tablespoons dry vermouth or chicken broth
¼ cup whipping cream
2 tablespoons chopped fresh chives
½ cup (2 ounces) shredded Swiss cheese

• **Hold** artichokes by stems, and wash by plunging up and down in cold water. Cut off stem end; trim about ½ inch from top of each artichoke. Remove any loose bottom leaves. With kitchen scissors, trim one-fourth off top of each outer leaf, and rub top and edges of leaves with lemon wedge to prevent discoloring.
• **Place** artichokes in a large non-aluminum Dutch oven; cover with water, and add lemon juice.
• **Bring** to a boil; cover, reduce heat, and simmer 35 minutes or until lower leaves of artichoke pull out easily. Drain and place in a baking pan.
• **Cook** mushrooms in oil in a large skillet over medium-high heat 3 minutes, stirring often. Add ham, and cook 3 minutes, stirring often. Add vermouth and whipping cream; cook 3 minutes. Remove from heat; stir in chives and cheese.
• **Spoon** mixture into and over artichokes. Broil 5½ inches from heat (with electric oven door partially opened) 3 minutes or until golden. Serve immediately. **Yield:** 2 servings.

Chef José Guiterrez
Chez Phillipe
Memphis, Tennessee

MARINATED ASPARAGUS WITH PROSCIUTTO

Prosciutto is cured Italian ham sliced paper thin. If you can't find it, ask a butcher to slice regular ham as thinly as possible.

2 pounds fresh asparagus
¾ cup vegetable oil
¼ cup white wine vinegar
2 tablespoons Dijon mustard
2 tablespoons honey
2 teaspoons dried tarragon
¼ pound prosciutto or thinly sliced cooked ham, cut into thin strips

• **Snap** off tough ends of asparagus. Remove scales from stalks with a vegetable peeler, if desired.
• **Cover** and cook asparagus in a small amount of boiling water 4 minutes or until crisp-tender; drain. Plunge into ice water to stop the cooking process; drain. Place in a shallow baking dish; set aside.
• **Combine** oil and next 4 ingredients in a jar. Cover tightly, and shake vigorously. Pour over asparagus; cover and chill at least 2 hours.
• **Remove** asparagus, reserving marinade; arrange asparagus on a serving platter. Top asparagus with prosciutto, and drizzle with reserved marinade. **Yield:** 8 servings.

Gwyneth A. Jones-Rader
Ellicott City, Maryland

ASPARAGUS WITH WARM CITRUS DRESSING

QUICK!

2 pounds fresh asparagus
½ cup butter or margarine
2 teaspoons grated lime rind
2 tablespoons fresh lime juice

• **Snap** off tough ends of asparagus. Remove scales from stalks with a vegetable peeler, if desired.
• **Place** asparagus in an 11- x 7- x 1½-inch dish. Cover tightly with heavy-duty plastic wrap, and fold back a small corner to allow the steam to escape.

• **Microwave** at HIGH 6 to 7 minutes or until crisp-tender, giving dish a half-turn after 3 minutes. Set aside.
• **Place** butter in a 2-cup liquid measuring cup; microwave at HIGH 1 minute or just until melted. Stir in lime rind and juice; pour over asparagus. **Yield:** 8 servings.

Nita and Harold Norman
Coral Gables, Florida

SESAME ASPARAGUS

QUICK!

½ pound fresh asparagus
3 tablespoons red wine vinegar
1 tablespoon dark sesame oil
1 tablespoon sesame seeds, toasted

• **Snap** off tough ends of asparagus. Remove scales from stalks with a vegetable peeler, if desired.
• **Cover** and cook asparagus in a small amount of boiling water 2 minutes or until crisp-tender. Drain and rinse with cold water; drain well.
• **Combine** vinegar, oil, and sesame seeds in a large heavy-duty, zip-top plastic bag; add asparagus. Seal and chill 2 hours, turning occasionally.
• **Remove** asparagus from marinade, reserving marinade. Arrange asparagus on plates; drizzle with marinade. **Yield:** 2 servings.

ASPARAGUS STIR-FRY

QUICK!

Peanut oil is recommended for stir-frying because it can stand higher temperatures than other oils before it begins to smoke or taste "off."

1½ pounds fresh asparagus
1 tablespoon peanut oil
¾ cup chicken broth, divided
1 tablespoon cornstarch
1 teaspoon sugar
2 tablespoons soy sauce
1 (2-ounce) package cashews, coarsely chopped and toasted (about ½ cup)

• **Snap** off tough ends of asparagus. Remove scales from stalks with a vegetable peeler, if desired.

• **Diagonally** cut asparagus into 1-inch pieces, and set aside.

• **Cook** asparagus in peanut oil in a large skillet over medium-high heat 2 minutes, stirring constantly. Add ¼ cup chicken broth to skillet; cover and cook 4 minutes or until asparagus is crisp-tender.

• **Combine** remaining ½ cup chicken broth, cornstarch, sugar, and soy sauce, stirring until smooth. Add to asparagus mixture, stirring constantly.

• **Bring** to a boil, and boil 1 minute, stirring constantly. Sprinkle with cashews, and serve immediately. **Yield:** 4 to 6 servings.

Kathy Sellers
Nashville, Tennessee

DILLED GREEN BEANS

QUICK!

2 **pounds small fresh green beans, trimmed**
1 **cup white wine vinegar**
¼ **cup chopped fresh dill**
3 **tablespoons sugar**
2 **cloves garlic, crushed**
½ **teaspoon salt**
½ **teaspoon pepper**

• **Place** beans in boiling water to cover; reduce heat, and simmer 8 minutes or until crisp-tender. Drain; plunge beans into ice water to stop the cooking process, and drain again. Place beans in a large shallow dish.

• **Combine** vinegar and remaining 5 ingredients, stirring until sugar dissolves; pour over beans, stirring to coat. Cover and chill 8 hours, stirring occasionally. Serve with a slotted spoon. **Yield:** 8 servings.

Irene Smith
Covington, Georgia

GREEN BEANS WITH CARAMELIZED ONIONS

2 **pounds fresh green beans, trimmed ***
1 **pound pearl onions**
¼ **cup butter or margarine**
¼ **cup firmly packed brown sugar**

• **Arrange** beans in a steamer basket over boiling water. Cover and steam 15 minutes; set aside.

• **Place** onions in boiling water 3 minutes; drain and rinse with cold water. Cut off root ends of onions; peel onions.

• **Arrange** onions in steamer basket over boiling water. Cover and steam 5 minutes; set onions aside.

• **Melt** butter in a large heavy skillet over medium heat; add sugar, and cook, stirring constantly, until bubbly. Add onions; cook 3 minutes, stirring constantly. Add beans, and cook, stirring constantly, until thoroughly heated. **Yield:** 8 servings.

* Substitute 2 pounds fresh brussels sprouts for beans.

Sue P. Wilson
Etowah, North Carolina

GREEN BEAN ITALIANO

1 **(4½-ounce) package brown and wild rice mix ***
2 **tablespoons butter or margarine**
1 **medium onion, chopped**
1 **(16-ounce) carton sour cream**
1 **(8-ounce) package cream cheese, softened**
3 **(16-ounce) cans French-style green beans, drained**
1 **(4-ounce) jar diced pimiento, drained**
1 **(2¼-ounce) can sliced ripe olives, drained**
1 **teaspoon dried Italian seasoning**
1 **(8-ounce) package (2 cups) shredded mozzarella cheese**
¼ **cup grated Parmesan cheese**
½ **cup Italian-seasoned dried breadcrumbs**

• **Cook** rice mix according to package directions, and set aside.

• **Melt** butter in a Dutch oven over medium-high heat. Add onion, and cook until tender, stirring often. Stir in rice, sour cream, and next 5 ingredients. Spoon mixture into a greased 13- x 9- x 2-inch baking dish.

• **Sprinkle** with mozzarella and Parmesan cheeses; top with breadcrumbs.

• **Bake** at 350° for 20 to 25 minutes until cheese is bubbly and lightly browned. **Yield:** 12 servings.

* For the rice, we used Success Boil-in-Bag Rice Mix for the brown and wild rice mix.

Louise W. Mayer
Richmond, Virginia

BARBECUED BEANS

½ **pound ground beef**
½ **cup chopped onion**
⅓ **cup sugar**
⅓ **cup firmly packed brown sugar**
½ **cup barbecue sauce**
¼ **cup ketchup**
½ **teaspoon salt**
½ **teaspoon pepper**
½ **teaspoon chili powder**
2 **tablespoons molasses**
2 **teaspoons Dijon mustard**
1 **(15-ounce) can kidney beans, drained**
1 **(15-ounce) can butter beans, drained**
1 **(16-ounce) can pork and beans, undrained**
10 **slices bacon, cooked and crumbled**

• **Cook** ground beef and onion in a Dutch oven, stirring until meat crumbles; drain and place in a large bowl.

• **Stir** sugar and remaining ingredients into mixture. Spoon into a lightly greased 2½-quart baking dish.

• **Bake,** uncovered, at 350° for 1 hour, stirring once. **Yield:** 8 to 10 servings.

Patty Renwick
Mount Airy, Maryland

BOURBON BAKED BEANS

QUICK!

If you can't keep baked beans hot until they're served, chill and reheat just before mealtime.

4 (16-ounce) cans Boston baked beans
1 (16-ounce) can crushed pineapple, drained
1 (12-ounce) jar chili sauce
½ cup strongly brewed coffee
½ cup bourbon
¼ cup firmly packed brown sugar
1 tablespoon molasses
¾ teaspoon dry mustard

• **Combine** all ingredients in a 3½- or 4-quart electric slow cooker.
• **Cover** and cook on HIGH 2 hours; uncover and cook to desired consistency. Serve with a slotted spoon. **Yield:** 10 to 12 servings.

Note: To make strong coffee, dissolve 1 teaspoon instant coffee granules in ½ cup hot water.

LaJuan Coward
Jasper, Texas

BUTTERBEANS, BACON, AND TOMATOES

3 slices bacon, chopped
1 cup finely chopped onion
3 cloves garlic, minced
1 bay leaf
¾ cup chopped green bell pepper
7 plum tomatoes, seeded and chopped
4 cups chicken broth
4 cups fresh or frozen butterbeans, thawed
2 tablespoons finely chopped fresh parsley
1 teaspoon salt
1 teaspoon pepper
1 teaspoon Worcestershire sauce
½ teaspoon hot sauce
Vicksburg Cornbread (see recipe on page 39)

• **Cook** bacon in a skillet over medium heat, stirring constantly, 8 minutes or until crisp. Add onion, garlic, and bay leaf; cook 3 minutes or until onion is tender, stirring often.
• **Add** bell pepper; cook 3 minutes, stirring often. Add tomato, and cook 3 minutes, stirring constantly.
• **Add** broth and butterbeans; bring to a boil. Cover, reduce heat, and simmer 30 minutes, stirring occasionally.
• **Simmer**, uncovered, 20 minutes, stirring often. Stir in parsley and next 4 ingredients. Cook 5 minutes, stirring often. Remove and discard bay leaf. Serve over Vicksburg Cornbread. **Yield:** 6 servings.

Chef Johnny Earles
Criolla's
Destin, Florida

LIMA BEAN CASSEROLE

"This is my momma's recipe, and we usually had it with either turkey or ham for a special occasion." – Freda

2 cups water
4 cups fresh, shelled baby lima beans *
4 slices bacon
2 tablespoons all-purpose flour
3 tablespoons brown sugar
1½ teaspoons salt
¼ teaspoon pepper
1½ tablespoons dry mustard
1½ tablespoons lemon juice
½ cup dry breadcrumbs
2 tablespoons butter, melted
½ cup (2 ounces) shredded Cheddar cheese

• **Bring** water to a boil in a medium saucepan. Add lima beans; return to a boil. Reduce heat, and simmer 20 minutes or until tender; drain, reserving 1 cup liquid (add water to make 1 cup, if necessary). Place lima beans in a lightly greased 8-inch square baking dish; set aside.
• **Cook** bacon in a large skillet until crisp; remove bacon, reserving 2 tablespoons drippings in skillet. Crumble bacon, and set aside.

• **Heat** bacon drippings in skillet; add flour, stirring until smooth. Cook 1 minute, stirring constantly. Gradually add reserved bean liquid; cook over medium heat, stirring constantly, until mixture is thickened. Stir in brown sugar and next 4 ingredients. Pour sauce over beans. Combine breadcrumbs and butter; sprinkle over top.
• **Bake** at 350° for 25 minutes; sprinkle with cheese. Bake 5 additional minutes or until cheese melts. Sprinkle crumbled bacon over top. **Yield:** 6 servings.

✻ Substitute 2 (10-ounce) packages frozen baby lima beans for fresh. Simmer 14 to 16 minutes or until beans are tender.

Freda Wilkins
Wilmington, North Carolina

RED BEANS AND RICE

2 pounds dried red beans
6 cups water
2 large onions, chopped
4 cloves garlic, minced
1 large green bell pepper, chopped
1 large red bell pepper, chopped
½ pound salt pork
1 cup dry red wine
½ cup chopped fresh parsley
1 tablespoon chopped fresh oregano
1 tablespoon Old Bay seasoning
3 bay leaves
1 teaspoon celery seeds
1 teaspoon salt
1 teaspoon freshly ground black pepper
1 teaspoon paprika
½ to 1 teaspoon ground red pepper
½ to 1 teaspoon dried crushed red pepper
1 teaspoon hot sauce
1 pound smoked beef sausage, cut into ½-inch pieces
1 pound andouille sausage, cut into ½-inch pieces
2 (11-ounce) cans diced tomatoes and green chiles, undrained
1 tablespoon gumbo filé
Hot cooked rice

• **Sort** and wash beans. Combine beans, water, and next 17 ingredients in a large Dutch oven; bring to a boil. Cover, reduce heat, and simmer 3 hours or until mixture is thickened and beans are tender.

• **Add** sausages and tomatoes; cook 30 minutes.

• **Remove** and discard salt pork and bay leaves; stir in filé. Serve over rice. **Yield:** 10 to 12 servings.

Dail "Duke" Mullins, Jr.
Birmingham, Alabama

SPICY ORANGE BEETS

2 **pounds small fresh beets** *
¼ **cup firmly packed brown**
     sugar
1 **tablespoon grated orange rind**
2 **teaspoons cornstarch**
¼ **teaspoon salt**
¼ **teaspoon ground allspice**
⅛ **teaspoon pepper**
⅔ **cup orange juice**
2 **tablespoons butter or margarine**
1 **tablespoon chopped fresh**
     chives

• **Leave** root and 1 inch of stem on beets; scrub with a vegetable brush.

• **Cook** beets in boiling water to cover 30 minutes or until tender. Drain. Pour cold water over beets, and drain. Trim off roots and stems; rub off skins. Cut beets into ¼-inch slices; set aside.

• **Combine** sugar and next 5 ingredients in a saucepan; gradually add orange juice, stirring until smooth. Stir in butter; bring to a boil, stirring constantly. Boil 1 minute, stirring constantly. Add beets; cook until thoroughly heated. Sprinkle with chives just before serving. **Yield:** 4 to 6 servings.

* To save time, substitute 2 (16-ounce) cans sliced beets for fresh, and omit precooking them. Add beets to orange sauce mixture, and cook until thoroughly heated; sprinkle with chives.

Hilda Marshall
Bealeton, Virginia

BEETS 'N' GREENS

1½ **pounds smoked ham hocks**
8 **cups water**
¼ **pound chopped country ham**
1 **(3½-pound) bunch collard**
     greens, trimmed and chopped
     (about 16 cups)
1 **(3½-pound) bunch turnip**
     greens, trimmed and chopped
     (about 12 cups)
4 **medium-size fresh beets, peeled**
     and sliced
½ **teaspoon sugar**
½ **teaspoon liquid from hot**
     peppers in vinegar
¼ **teaspoon salt**
¼ **teaspoon pepper**

• **Place** ham hocks in a large Dutch oven; add water, and bring to a boil over high heat. Cover, reduce heat, and simmer 30 minutes. Remove and discard ham hocks.

• **Add** chopped ham to liquid; cook 5 minutes.

• **Add** collards, and cook 15 minutes.

• **Add** turnip greens and remaining ingredients; cook 15 minutes or until vegetables are tender, stirring occasionally. **Yield:** 6 to 8 servings.

GARLIC BROCCOLI

QUICK!

1½ **pounds fresh broccoli**
1½ **teaspoons dark sesame oil**
1½ **teaspoons vegetable oil**
½ **teaspoon dried crushed red**
     pepper
2 **cloves garlic, minced**
¼ **cup reduced-sodium soy**
     sauce
1 **tablespoon sugar**
1 **tablespoon lemon juice**
1 **tablespoon water**

• **Remove** and discard broccoli leaves and tough ends of stalks; cut broccoli into spears.

• **Arrange** broccoli spears in a steamer basket over boiling water. Cover and steam 5 minutes or until broccoli is crisp-tender. Remove from heat, and keep warm.

• **Heat** sesame and vegetable oils in a small saucepan until hot but not smoking; remove from heat.

• **Add** crushed red pepper, and let stand 10 minutes.

• **Add** garlic and remaining 4 ingredients, stirring until sugar dissolves.

• **Toss** broccoli spears gently with oil mixture just before serving. Serve hot or cold. **Yield:** 6 servings.

Patsy Bell Hobson
Liberty, Missouri

♥ Per serving: Calories 88
Fat 2.7g Cholesterol 0mg
Sodium 357mg

BROCCOLI WITH STUFFING

QUICK!

2 **(10-ounce) packages frozen**
     broccoli spears
1 **cup (4 ounces) shredded**
     Cheddar cheese
2 **large eggs, lightly beaten**
1 **(10¾-ounce) can cream of**
     mushroom soup, undiluted
½ **cup mayonnaise or salad**
     dressing
½ **cup finely chopped onion**
¾ **cup herb-seasoned stuffing**
     mix
2 **tablespoons butter or margarine,**
     melted

• **Cook** broccoli according to package directions; drain.

• **Arrange** broccoli in a lightly greased 11- x 7- x 1½-inch baking dish. Sprinkle with cheese.

• **Combine** eggs and next 3 ingredients; spread over cheese.

• **Combine** stuffing mix and butter; sprinkle over casserole.

• **Bake** at 350° for 30 minutes or until thoroughly heated. **Yield:** 8 servings.

♥ To reduce fat and calories, substitute reduced-fat Cheddar cheese, ½ cup fat-free egg substitute, reduced-fat cream of mushroom soup, reduced-fat mayonnaise, and butter-flavored cooking spray.

Sharon McClatchey
Muskogee, Oklahoma

BROCCOLI SOUFFLÉS

2 (10-ounce) packages frozen
    chopped broccoli, thawed
¼ cup butter or margarine
¼ cup all-purpose flour
1¼ cups milk
⅔ cup (2.6 ounces) shredded
    sharp Cheddar cheese
5 large eggs, separated
1½ teaspoons salt
¼ teaspoon minced garlic
2 tablespoons lemon juice

• **Cook** broccoli in a small amount of
boiling water 5 minutes, and drain.
• **Melt** butter in a heavy saucepan over
low heat; add flour, whisking until
smooth. Cook 1 minute, whisking constantly. Gradually add milk; cook over
medium heat, whisking constantly, until
thickened and bubbly. Add cheese, stirring until it melts. Remove from heat.
• **Beat** egg yolks at medium speed with
an electric mixer until thick and pale.
Add cooked broccoli, salt, garlic, and
lemon juice, beating until blended.
Gradually stir about one-fourth of hot
cheese mixture into yolk mixture; add
to remaining hot mixture, stirring mixture constantly.
• **Beat** egg whites at high speed until
stiff; fold one-third of egg whites into
broccoli mixture. Fold in remaining egg
whites. Pour into eight buttered individual soufflé dishes or 6-ounce custard
cups. Seal in aluminum foil, and freeze
up to 1 week.
• **Unwrap** soufflés, and place in a 13- x
9- x 2-inch pan; add hot water to pan to
depth of 1 inch.
• **Bake** at 400° for 10 minutes; reduce
heat to 350°, and bake 35 to 40 additional minutes or until puffed and
golden. Serve immediately. **Yield:** 8
servings.

Note: If not freezing soufflés, bake as
directed at 350° for 35 to 40 minutes.

BRUSSELS SPROUTS DIJON

QUICK!

⅔ cup mayonnaise or salad
    dressing
⅔ cup sour cream
¼ cup Dijon mustard
½ teaspoon garlic salt
1 tablespoon Worcestershire
    sauce
Dash of hot sauce
4 (10-ounce) packages frozen
    brussels sprouts
3 tablespoons butter or margarine,
    melted
¼ cup finely chopped pecans,
    toasted

• **Combine** first 6 ingredients in a small
saucepan; cook over low heat until
heated, stirring often. Keep warm.
• **Cook** brussels sprouts according to
package directions 5 minutes; drain.
• **Combine** brussels sprouts, butter, and
pecans, tossing to coat; serve with
sauce. **Yield:** 12 servings.

♥ To save 84 calories and 9.6 fat
grams, substitute reduced-fat mayonnaise and sour cream for the regular
versions, and reduced-calorie margarine for regular margarine. Analysis
below is for lightened version.

♥ Per serving: Calories 124
Fat 8.5g Cholesterol 10mg
Sodium 352mg

MARINATED BRUSSELS SPROUTS

QUICK!

3 (10-ounce) packages frozen
    brussels sprouts, thawed *
½ cup olive oil
¼ cup white vinegar
1 (2-ounce) jar sliced pimiento,
    drained
2 tablespoons diced onion
2 tablespoons minced fresh
    parsley
1 teaspoon dried thyme
1 teaspoon pepper
¾ teaspoon salt

• **Cook** brussels sprouts according to
package directions, omitting salt, and
drain well.
• **Whisk** oil and remaining 7 ingredients
until blended; pour over brussels
sprouts, stirring gently to coat. Cover
and chill 2 hours. **Yield:** 8 servings.

* You can substitute 2 pounds fresh
brussels sprouts for frozen brussels
sprouts. Cook fresh brussels sprouts in
1 cup boiling water 8 minutes or until
tender.

Leisla Sansom
Alexandria, Virginia

CABBAGE-ONION-SWEET PEPPER MEDLEY
(pictured at right)

QUICK!

½ small red bell pepper
½ small yellow bell pepper
½ small green bell pepper
1 onion
2 bacon slices
2 cups shredded cabbage
3 tablespoons white vinegar
1 tablespoon vegetable oil
1 tablespoon water
1½ teaspoons brown sugar
1½ teaspoons Dijon mustard
½ teaspoon salt
½ teaspoon pepper

• **Cut** bell peppers into 2-inch-long thin
strips; chop onion, and cut bacon into 1-
inch pieces.
• **Cook** bacon in a large skillet until
crisp. Add bell pepper, onion, and cabbage, tossing gently.
• **Combine** vinegar and remaining 6 ingredients in a jar; cover tightly, and
shake vigorously. Add to vegetable mixture, stirring gently.
• **Bring** to a boil; cover, reduce heat, and
simmer 8 minutes or until cabbage is
tender, stirring occasionally. Serve immediately. **Yield:** 2 to 4 servings.

Dorothy J. Callaway
Thomasville, Georgia

Cabbage-Onion-Sweet Pepper Medley

QUICK COOKED CABBAGE

QUICK!

2 slices bacon, cut into 1-inch
   pieces
¼ cup chopped onion
1¼ pounds cabbage, sliced
1 teaspoon dried parsley
   flakes
¾ teaspoon salt
¼ teaspoon dried basil
¼ teaspoon dried oregano
¼ teaspoon dried marjoram
¼ teaspoon ground black
   pepper
Dash of ground red pepper

• **Cook** bacon in a large skillet over medium heat until crisp; remove bacon, reserving drippings in skillet. Crumble bacon, and set aside.
• **Cook** chopped onion in reserved drippings over medium heat about 2 minutes, stirring often.
• **Add** cabbage and remaining 7 ingredients; cook 1 minute, stirring constantly. Cover and cook about 3 minutes. Sprinkle with bacon. **Yield:** 6 servings.

Sharon McClatchey
Muskogee, Oklahoma

GERMAN RED CABBAGE

QUICK!

¼ cup sugar
¼ cup firmly packed brown
   sugar
½ cup apple cider vinegar
1 medium-size red cabbage,
   shredded (about 2½ pounds)
2 slices bacon
1 medium Granny Smith apple,
   chopped
½ cup chopped onion
¼ cup water
2 tablespoons white wine
   vinegar
½ teaspoon salt
¼ teaspoon pepper
¼ teaspoon ground cloves

• **Combine** first 3 ingredients, stirring until sugar dissolves. Pour over cabbage; toss to coat. Let stand at room temperature 5 to 10 minutes.

• **Cook** bacon in a skillet until crisp; remove bacon, reserving drippings in skillet. Crumble bacon, and set aside.
• **Cook** apple and onion in reserved drippings in skillet, stirring constantly, until tender. Add cabbage mixture and water; bring to a boil. Cover, reduce heat, and simmer 10 minutes.
• **Add** wine vinegar and remaining 3 ingredients; simmer, uncovered, 5 minutes. Spoon into a serving dish, and sprinkle with reserved bacon. **Yield:** 6 to 8 servings.

Cindie Hackney
Longview, Texas

BRAISED CARROTS, APPLES, AND CELERY

QUICK!

3 carrots, scraped and cut into
   thin 2-inch strips
3 stalks celery, diagonally sliced
1 purple onion, chopped
1 teaspoon olive oil
2 Granny Smith apples, cored
   and thinly sliced
1 cup currants
½ cup apple juice
¼ cup cider vinegar
¼ cup honey
2 tablespoons Dijon mustard
2 tablespoons chopped fresh
   basil
¼ teaspoon salt
¼ teaspoon freshly ground
   pepper

• **Cook** first 3 ingredients in hot oil in a large skillet over medium-high heat 10 minutes or until vegetables begin to caramelize, stirring often.
• **Add** sliced apple and next 5 ingredients; cover, reduce heat to medium, and cook 10 minutes. Uncover and cook until liquid is absorbed and vegetables are glazed.
• **Add** basil, salt, and pepper. **Yield:** 6 servings.

GINGERED CARROTS

QUICK!

2 pounds carrots, scraped
2 tablespoons sugar
2 teaspoons cornstarch
½ teaspoon salt
½ teaspoon ground ginger
½ cup orange juice
2 tablespoons butter or margarine
Garnish: chopped fresh parsley

• **Cut** carrots diagonally into ¼-inch slices. Cook carrot in boiling water to cover 7 minutes or until tender; drain. Place in a serving dish; set aside, and keep warm.
• **Combine** sugar and next 3 ingredients in a saucepan; gradually add orange juice, stirring well. Bring to a boil over medium heat, stirring constantly. Boil 1 minute, stirring constantly; stir in butter. Pour over carrot; toss well. Garnish, if desired. **Yield:** 8 servings.

Romanza O. Johnson
Bowling Green, Kentucky

PARSNIP-CARROT MEDLEY

QUICK!

¾ cup water
1 pound carrots, scraped and
   shredded
1 pound parsnips, scraped and
   shredded
2 tablespoons butter or margarine
1 tablespoon maple syrup
1 teaspoon dried tarragon
½ teaspoon salt
¼ teaspoon pepper

• **Bring** water to a boil in a large saucepan; add carrot and parsnip. Cover and cook 5 to 7 minutes or until crisp-tender, stirring twice. Stir in butter and remaining ingredients; serve immediately. **Yield:** 8 servings.

Cathy Darling
Grafton, West Virginia

SCALLOPED CARROTS

4 cups sliced carrot
3 tablespoons butter or margarine
1 medium onion, chopped
1 (10¾-ounce) can cream of celery
   soup, undiluted
½ teaspoon salt
⅛ teaspoon pepper
½ cup (2 ounces) shredded
   Cheddar cheese
2 cups herb-seasoned stuffing mix
⅓ cup butter or margarine,
   melted

• **Cook** carrot in a small amount of boiling water 10 minutes or until tender; drain. Melt 3 tablespoons butter in a skillet over medium-high heat; add onion, and cook until tender, stirring constantly.
• **Stir** in soup and next 3 ingredients; spoon into a lightly greased 2-quart baking dish.
• **Combine** stuffing mix and ⅓ cup melted butter; spoon evenly over carrot mixture.
• **Bake** at 350° for 20 minutes or until thoroughly heated. **Yield:** 6 servings.

Carrie Triechel
Johnson City, Tennessee

CARROT SOUFFLÉS

3 pounds carrots, scraped and
   sliced
1½ cups butter or margarine
6 large eggs
½ cup all-purpose flour
1 tablespoon baking powder
3 cups sugar
¼ teaspoon ground cinnamon

• **Cook** carrot in boiling water to cover 15 minutes or until tender; drain.
• **Position** knife blade in food processor bowl; add carrot, butter, and remaining ingredients, and process until smooth, stopping once to scrape down sides.
• **Spoon** into two lightly greased 1½-quart soufflé or baking dishes.
• **Bake** at 350° for 1 hour or until set and lightly browned. Serve immediately. **Yield:** 12 servings.

CAULIFLOWER WITH CHINESE MUSTARD GRATIN

1 large cauliflower
½ cup mayonnaise
¼ cup hot Chinese mustard
½ cup (2 ounces) shredded Swiss
   cheese
2 tablespoons fine, dry
   breadcrumbs
Sautéed Cherry Tomatoes
Garnish: chopped fresh parsley

• **Remove** outer leaves and stalk, leaving cauliflower head whole. Place in boiling water to cover; cover and cook 10 to 15 minutes or until tender. Drain and place in a 9-inch square pan.
• **Combine** mayonnaise and mustard; spread over cauliflower.
• **Combine** cheese and breadcrumbs; sprinkle over mustard mixture.
• **Broil** 5½ inches from heat (with electric oven door partially opened) 3 minutes. Serve with Sautéed Cherry Tomatoes, and garnish, if desired. **Yield:** 6 servings.

Sautéed Cherry Tomatoes

QUICK!

1 pint cherry tomatoes, cut in half
2 tablespoons vegetable oil
¼ teaspoon salt
¼ teaspoon garlic powder

• **Cook** tomato halves in oil in a small saucepan over medium-high heat, stirring constantly, 3 minutes or until hot. Stir in salt and garlic powder. **Yield:** about 2 cups.

Nanette Wesley
Jackson, Georgia

MEXICAN CORN ON THE COB

QUICK!

8 slices bacon
8 ears fresh corn
¼ cup chili powder

• **Wrap** a bacon slice around each ear of corn; place each on a sheet of heavy-duty aluminum foil. Sprinkle with chili powder, and wrap in foil.

• **Cook**, covered with grill lid, over medium-hot coals (350° to 400°) 15 to 20 minutes, turning once. **Yield:** 8 servings.

Margie Kloeppel
Dallas, Texas

BUTTERMILK FRIED CORN

You can serve this as a side dish or sprinkle it on salads, soups, or casseroles.

2 cups fresh corn, cut from cob
1½ cups buttermilk
⅔ cup all-purpose flour
⅔ cup cornmeal
1 teaspoon salt
½ teaspoon pepper
Corn oil

• **Combine** corn and buttermilk in a large bowl; let stand 30 minutes. Drain.
• **Combine** flour and next 3 ingredients in a large heavy-duty, zip-top plastic bag. Add corn, a small amount at a time, to flour mixture, and shake bag to coat.
• **Pour** oil to depth of 1 inch in a Dutch oven; heat to 375°. Fry corn, a small amount at a time, in hot oil 2 minutes or until golden. Drain. **Yield:** 4 servings.

CURRIED CORN AND SWEET RED PEPPERS

QUICK!

3 tablespoons butter or margarine
¼ cup chopped red bell pepper
1 (15¼-ounce) can whole kernel
   corn, drained
1 teaspoon curry powder
⅛ teaspoon salt
⅛ teaspoon pepper
¼ cup whipping cream

• **Melt** butter in a skillet; add red pepper, and cook, stirring constantly, until tender. Stir in corn and next 3 ingredients; cook 3 minutes, stirring often. Stir in whipping cream; cook, stirring constantly, just until heated. Serve alone or over chicken breasts or sliced pork tenderloin. **Yield:** 3 to 4 servings.

Leanne McMullen
Natchez, Mississippi

FREEZER-FRESH CREAMED CORN

QUICK!

3 (16-ounce) packages frozen
   shoepeg corn, partially thawed
   and divided
½ cup butter or margarine
1¾ to 2 cups milk
1½ to 2 teaspoons salt
½ teaspoon pepper

• **Position** knife blade in food processor bowl; add 1 package corn. Process until smooth, stopping once to scrape down sides.
• **Melt** butter in a heavy skillet over medium heat; stir in pureed corn, remaining 2 packages corn, milk, salt, and pepper. Bring to a boil, stirring constantly; reduce heat, and simmer 20 minutes or until desired thickness, stirring often. **Yield:** 10 to 12 servings.

Sue George
Birmingham, Alabama

TEE'S CORN PUDDING

¼ cup sugar
3 tablespoons all-purpose flour
2 teaspoons baking powder
2 teaspoons salt
6 large eggs
2 cups whipping cream
½ cup butter or margarine,
   melted
6 cups fresh corn kernels *

• **Combine** first 4 ingredients.
• **Beat** eggs with a fork in a large bowl; stir in whipping cream and butter. Gradually add sugar mixture, stirring until smooth; stir in corn. Pour into a lightly greased 13- x 9- x 2-inch baking dish.
• **Bake** at 350° for 45 minutes or until deep golden and set. Let stand 5 minutes. **Yield:** 8 servings.

* Substitute 6 cups frozen whole kernel or canned shoepeg corn for fresh.

Kathy's Onion Pudding: Combine first 4 ingredients as in original recipe. Beat eggs with a fork in a large bowl; stir in whipping cream. Gradually add sugar

mixture, stirring until smooth. Substitute 6 cups thinly sliced onion for corn kernels. Combine onion and melted butter in a large skillet over medium heat. Cook 30 to 40 minutes or until onion is caramel-colored, stirring often; remove from heat. Add onion to cream mixture, stirring well. Pour into a lightly greased 11- x 7- x 1½-inch baking dish. Bake as directed, shielding with aluminum foil after 30 minutes to prevent excessive browning.

Sissy Nash and Kathy Nash Cary
Louisville, Kentucky

SAVORY SUCCOTASH

QUICK!

4 thick slices bacon
1 medium onion, chopped
½ teaspoon rubbed sage
1 (10-ounce) package frozen
   whole kernel corn, partially
   thawed
1 (10-ounce) package frozen lima
   beans, partially thawed
1½ cups half-and-half
1 teaspoon sugar
¼ to ½ teaspoon salt
¼ to ½ teaspoon pepper
3 cups hot cooked rice
1 cup chopped cooked ham

• **Cook** bacon in a large skillet until crisp; remove bacon, reserving 2 tablespoons drippings in skillet. Crumble bacon, and set aside.
• **Add** onion and sage to drippings; cook, stirring constantly, 3 to 5 minutes or until crisp-tender. Drain and return to skillet.
• **Add** corn and lima beans; cook, stirring constantly, 5 to 7 minutes or until tender. Add half-and-half and next 3 ingredients to skillet; reduce heat, and simmer until liquid is slightly reduced, stirring occasionally.
• **Stir** in rice and ham; cook 2 to 3 minutes or until thoroughly heated. Sprinkle with bacon, and serve immediately. **Yield:** 6 to 8 servings.

Stanlay Webber
Winston-Salem, North Carolina

CORN AND BLACK BEAN CAKES WITH SMOKED SALMON SALSA

Chef Susser cooks fresh corn and dried black beans when possible, but he offers shortcuts here.

1 cup all-purpose flour
1 teaspoon baking powder
2 large eggs
¼ cup butter or margarine, melted
¾ cup milk
¾ cup frozen whole kernel corn,
   thawed
¾ cup canned black beans, rinsed
   and drained
¾ teaspoon salt
¾ teaspoon coarsely ground
   pepper
Smoked Salmon Salsa

• **Combine** first 5 ingredients in a bowl; stir in corn, beans, salt, and pepper.
• **Pour** about ¼ cup batter for each pancake into a nonstick skillet over medium-high heat. Cook until tops are covered with bubbles and edges look cooked; turn and cook other side. Serve with Smoked Salmon Salsa. **Yield:** 6 servings.

Smoked Salmon Salsa

QUICK!

1 (8-ounce) package smoked
   salmon, diced
¼ cup diced purple onion
3 tablespoons chopped fresh
   cilantro
3 tablespoons chopped fresh
   parsley
1 tablespoon diced jalapeño
   pepper
2 tablespoons olive oil

• **Combine** all ingredients; let stand 30 minutes before serving. **Yield:** 2 cups.

Chef Allen Susser
Chef Allen's
North Miami Beach, Florida

BUTTERCRUST CORN PIE WITH FRESH TOMATO SALSA

Serve this as an entrée when you're planning a vegetable supper.

1¼ cups finely crushed saltine
    crackers
¼ cup grated Parmesan cheese
½ cup butter or margarine,
    melted
1¼ cups milk, divided
2 cups fresh or frozen corn
½ to 1 teaspoon onion salt
¼ teaspoon ground white
    pepper
1 teaspoon sugar (optional)
2 tablespoons all-purpose flour
¼ cup chopped ripe olives
½ cup sliced green onions
2 large eggs, lightly beaten
Paprika
Fresh Tomato Salsa

• **Combine** first 3 ingredients, stirring well; reserve 2 tablespoons.
• **Press** remaining cracker mixture in bottom and up sides of a 9-inch pieplate. Set aside.
• **Combine** 1 cup milk, corn, onion salt, pepper, and sugar, if desired, in a large saucepan; bring to a boil over medium heat. Reduce heat, and simmer mixture 3 minutes.
• **Combine** flour and remaining ¼ cup milk, stirring until smooth. Gradually add flour mixture to corn mixture, stirring constantly. Cook 1 minute, stirring constantly. (Mixture will be thick.) Remove from heat.
• **Stir** in olives and green onions. Gradually stir about one-fourth of hot mixture into eggs; add to remaining hot mixture, stirring constantly.
• **Spoon** mixture into prepared pieplate; sprinkle with reserved crumb mixture and paprika.
• **Bake** at 400° for 20 minutes or until set. Cut into wedges; serve with Fresh Tomato Salsa. **Yield:** 6 servings.

Fresh Tomato Salsa

QUICK!

2 cups peeled, chopped tomato
1 jalapeño pepper, seeded
    and finely chopped or
    1 (4.5-ounce) can chopped
    green chiles, drained
½ cup thinly sliced green onions
2 tablespoons lemon juice
½ teaspoon salt
½ teaspoon dried oregano
⅛ teaspoon pepper

• **Combine** all ingredients, stirring well. Cover and chill at least 3 hours. **Yield:** about 2 cups.

Linda Magers
Clemmons, North Carolina

ASIAN CUCUMBERS AND PASTA

Tired of green salad? Try cucumbers in this warm pasta side dish.

2 cloves garlic
1 tablespoon grated fresh ginger
⅓ cup creamy peanut butter
¼ cup soy sauce
2 tablespoons fresh lime juice
1 tablespoon molasses
8 ounces angel hair pasta,
    uncooked
3 medium cucumbers, peeled,
    seeded, and coarsely chopped
½ cup sliced green onions

• **Combine** first 6 ingredients in container of an electric blender; process until smooth, stopping once to scrape down sides.
• **Cook** pasta according to package directions; drain and return to pan. Add peanut butter mixture, and toss gently.
• **Spoon** onto a serving platter; top with cucumber and green onions. **Yield:** 4 servings.

Margaret Springer
Killen, Alabama

SPICY ORIENTAL EGGPLANT

QUICK!

Serve this as a side dish or toss it with pasta for a quick weeknight dinner.

½ cup ready-to-serve Oriental
    broth
1 large eggplant, peeled and cut
    into cubes (1 pound)
2 tablespoons reduced-sodium soy
    sauce
2 teaspoons chili puree with garlic
1 teaspoon sugar
1 teaspoon red wine vinegar
1 teaspoon dark sesame oil
2 cloves garlic, minced
2 tablespoons minced fresh ginger
1 bunch green onions, chopped

• **Combine** broth and eggplant in a large nonstick skillet; cover and cook over high heat 3 to 4 minutes or until tender. Drain and set aside. Wipe out skillet with paper towels.
• **Combine** soy sauce, chili puree, sugar, and vinegar in a small bowl, and set mixture aside.
• **Heat** oil in nonstick skillet; add garlic and ginger, and stir-fry 1 minute. Add eggplant and soy sauce mixture; stir-fry 2 additional minutes. Stir in green onions. **Yield:** 2 servings.

Betty Levine
Loudon, Tennessee

♥ Per serving: Calories 130
Fat 2.8g Cholesterol 0mg
Sodium 902mg

SAGE-GRILLED EGGPLANT

1 large eggplant, unpeeled
1½ teaspoons salt
⅓ cup Sage Butter (see recipe on
      page 351)
¼ teaspoon pepper

• **Cut** eggplant crosswise into ½-inch slices; sprinkle cut sides with salt. Place in a single layer on paper towels; let stand 1 hour.
• **Rinse** eggplant with water, and pat dry. Arrange in a single layer in a lightly greased grill basket.
• **Melt** Sage Butter over low heat; stir in pepper. Brush on eggplant.
• **Cook**, covered with grill lid, over medium-hot coals (350° to 400°) 12 to 15 minutes or until lightly browned, turning and brushing with butter mixture. **Yield:** 4 servings.

BALSAMIC-FLAVORED EGGPLANT

2 medium tomatoes, sliced
1 purple onion, sliced and
      separated into rings
1 (6-ounce) can medium pitted
      ripe olives, drained
¾ cup balsamic vinegar
1 medium eggplant
½ teaspoon salt
2 tablespoons olive oil
1 (8-ounce) package firm farmer
      cheese, cut into ½-inch cubes

• **Combine** first 3 ingredients in a shallow dish; drizzle with vinegar. Cover and chill 2 hours.
• **Cut** eggplant into 1-inch slices; sprinkle both sides of slices with salt, and drain on paper towels 30 minutes. Pat dry. Brush both sides of slices with oil.
• **Cook**, covered with grill lid, over medium-hot coals (350° to 400°) 3 minutes on each side or until tender. Cool.
• **Remove** vegetables from marinade, reserving marinade. Arrange vegetables and eggplant on a serving plate. Sprinkle with cheese; drizzle with ¼ cup marinade (discard any remaining marinade). **Yield:** 6 servings.

Sandy Davis
Emory, Virginia

EGGPLANT SAUTÉ

QUICK!

1 (12-ounce) package fettuccine
1 to 2 tablespoons olive oil
1 medium onion, chopped
3 cloves garlic, minced
1 medium eggplant, peeled and
      cubed
1 large red bell pepper, sliced
2 (14½-ounce) cans pasta-style
      tomatoes, undrained
½ cup freshly grated Parmesan
      cheese

• **Cook** fettuccine according to package directions; drain. Place in a large serving bowl, and keep warm.
• **Pour** oil into a large skillet; place over medium-high heat until hot. Add onion and next 3 ingredients; cook, stirring constantly, 10 minutes or until vegetables are tender.
• **Stir** in tomatoes; spoon mixture over fettuccine, and sprinkle with Parmesan cheese. **Yield:** 4 servings.

Michelle Henderson
Birmingham, Alabama

EGGPLANT CASSEROLE

1 eggplant, peeled and chopped
4 slices white bread, torn
1 (5-ounce) can evaporated
      milk
1 medium onion, chopped
2 cloves garlic, minced
¼ cup butter or margarine,
      melted
2 large eggs, separated
½ teaspoon salt
¼ teaspoon pepper
¼ cup grated Parmesan cheese

• **Cook** eggplant in boiling water to cover 10 minutes or until tender; drain well. Mash eggplant; set aside.
• **Combine** bread and milk; let stand 10 minutes.
• **Cook** onion and garlic in butter in a large skillet over medium-high heat, stirring constantly, until tender. Add eggplant, bread mixture, egg yolks, salt, and pepper. Set aside.
• **Beat** egg whites at high speed with an electric mixer until stiff peaks form; fold

into eggplant mixture. Pour into a well-greased 1½-quart baking dish; sprinkle with Parmesan cheese.
• **Bake** at 350° for 30 minutes or until set. Serve immediately. **Yield:** 4 to 6 servings.

Tad Cairns
Birmingham, Alabama

EGGPLANT PARMESAN

QUICK!

1 (1½-pound) eggplant, peeled
      and sliced into ¼-inch-thick
      slices
½ cup grated Parmesan cheese,
      divided
2 cups (8 ounces) shredded part-
      skim mozzarella cheese,
      divided
1½ cups spaghetti sauce, divided
Vegetable cooking spray

• **Layer** half of eggplant, ¼ cup Parmesan cheese, ¾ cup mozzarella cheese, and half of spaghetti sauce in a 2-quart shallow baking dish coated with cooking spray. Repeat with remaining eggplant, ¼ cup Parmesan cheese, ¾ cup mozzarella cheese, and spaghetti sauce.
• **Bake** at 350° for 35 minutes; sprinkle with ½ cup mozzarella cheese, and bake 5 minutes. **Yield:** 6 servings.

Gloria Stricklin
Winter Haven, Florida

COLLARD GREENS

5 to 6 pounds fresh collard greens
1 (10½-ounce) can condensed
      chicken broth, undiluted
⅔ cup water
½ cup chopped onion
1½ tablespoons bacon drippings
1 teaspoon seasoned salt
¼ teaspoon sugar
½ teaspoon freshly ground pepper

• **Remove** and discard stems and any discolored spots from greens. Wash greens thoroughly; drain and coarsely chop. Place in a large Dutch oven; add broth and remaining ingredients.

• **Bring** to a boil over medium-high heat. Cover, reduce heat, and simmer 1 hour or until tender. Serve with vinegar with green peppers. **Yield:** 6 to 8 servings.

Carol Barclay
Portland, Texas

EDNA'S GREENS

4½ pounds fresh greens (collard, mustard, or turnip)
1 pound salt pork (streak of lean) or smoked pork shoulder
3 quarts water
¼ teaspoon freshly ground pepper

• **Remove** and discard stems and discolored spots from greens. Wash greens thoroughly; drain and cut greens into strips. Set aside.
• **Slice** salt pork at ¼-inch intervals, cutting to, but not through, the skin.
• **Combine** salt pork, water, and pepper in a large Dutch oven; bring to a boil. Cover, reduce heat, and simmer 1 hour.
• **Add** greens, and cook, uncovered, 17 minutes or until tender. Serve with a slotted spoon. **Yield:** 2 to 4 servings.

Chef Edna Lewis
Atlanta, Georgia

GRILLED SHIITAKES

QUICK!

The simple ingredients of this recipe belie its fabulous flavor.

1 pound large fresh shiitake mushrooms
½ cup butter or margarine, melted
4 cloves garlic, minced
¼ cup chopped fresh parsley
½ teaspoon freshly ground pepper
¼ teaspoon salt

• **Remove** stems from mushrooms; discard. Combine butter and remaining 4 ingredients; spread on mushroom caps.
• **Cook**, without grill lid, over medium-hot coals (350° to 400°) 8 minutes, turning once. **Yield:** 4 servings.

Dale Glennon
Florence, Alabama

MUSHROOM DELUXE CASSEROLE

QUICK!

½ cup butter or margarine, divided
3 (8-ounce) packages sliced fresh mushrooms
1½ cups herb-seasoned stuffing mix
2 cups (8 ounces) shredded sharp Cheddar cheese, divided
½ cup half-and-half

• **Melt** ¼ cup butter in a large skillet over medium-high heat; add mushrooms, and cook, stirring constantly, until tender. Stir in stuffing mix.
• **Spoon** half of mushroom mixture into an 8-inch square baking dish; sprinkle with half of cheese. Repeat layers; dot with remaining ¼ cup butter. Pour half-and-half over casserole.
• **Bake** at 325° for 30 minutes. **Yield:** 6 servings.

Arlene Cox
Elizabethton, Tennessee

RAGOÛT OF WILD MUSHROOMS WITH CREAMY GRITS

QUICK!

2 cups fresh wild mushrooms, sliced
¼ cup olive oil
¼ cup finely chopped shallots
3 cups chicken broth
2 tablespoons chopped fresh parsley
2 tablespoons chopped fresh chervil
3 tablespoons unsalted butter, softened
¼ teaspoon salt
¼ teaspoon pepper
Creamy Grits
Shaved fresh Parmesan cheese

• **Cook** mushrooms in oil in a large skillet over medium heat 2 minutes, stirring constantly. Add shallot; cook 1 minute. Gradually add broth; increase heat to high, and cook 25 minutes (broth will be reduced and slightly thickened). Stir in parsley and next 4 ingredients. Serve

over Creamy Grits, and top with Parmesan cheese. **Yield:** 4 main-dish servings or 6 appetizer servings.

Creamy Grits

QUICK!

4 cups milk
1 teaspoon salt
¼ teaspoon pepper
1 cup regular white grits, uncooked
1 cup whipping cream
3 tablespoons unsalted butter

• **Combine** first 3 ingredients in a large saucepan; bring to a boil over medium heat. Stir in grits; cook 10 minutes or until soft. Add whipping cream and butter, stirring mixture until smooth. (Grits may be thinned with a few drops of water if they are too thick.) Serve immediately. **Yield:** 4 cups.

Chef Louis Osteen
Louis's Charleston Grill
Charleston, South Carolina

STIR-FRIED OKRA

QUICK!

3 tablespoons vegetable oil
1 pound fresh okra, sliced
1 large onion, finely chopped
1 large green bell pepper, finely chopped
1 cup finely chopped celery
¼ teaspoon salt
¼ teaspoon pepper
½ teaspoon dried thyme, crushed
3 tablespoons soy sauce

• **Place** oil in a large skillet over medium-high heat until hot. Add okra and next 6 ingredients, and stir-fry mixture 8 to 10 minutes or until okra is crisp-tender.
• **Add** soy sauce to vegetable mixture, and cook, stirring constantly, 2 minutes or until okra is tender. **Yield:** 6 to 8 servings.

Sherida Eddlemon
Memphis, Tennessee

BALSAMIC CARAMELIZED FLORIDA SWEET ONIONS

"Caramelize" means to heat sugar until it becomes liquid or syrupy. In this recipe, the onions' natural sugar becomes caramelized while they're baking.

1 cup balsamic vinegar
2 large sweet onions, cut in half crosswise (about 1½ pounds)
2 tablespoons butter or margarine
1 cup walnut halves
¼ cup firmly packed brown sugar
¼ cup chopped red bell pepper
¼ cup chopped yellow bell pepper
1 to 1½ teaspoons ground red pepper
Garnish: fresh pineapple sage sprigs

• **Bring** vinegar to a boil in a cast-iron skillet over medium-high heat.
• **Remove** from heat; place onions, cut side down, in skillet.
• **Bake** at 400° for 55 to 60 minutes or until onions are tender and vinegar turns the color of dark chocolate.
• **Melt** butter in a skillet over medium heat. Add walnuts; cook 2 minutes, stirring often. Add sugar and next 3 ingredients; cook until bubbly, stirring often.
• **Place** an onion half, cut side up, on each plate. Sprinkle walnut mixture evenly around onions; drizzle onions with vinegar. Garnish, if desired. Serve immediately. **Yield:** 4 servings.

Note: Look for balsamic (dark, aged) vinegar next to the more common vinegars at your grocery store.

Chef Mark Rodriguez
Jordan's Grove
Maitland, Florida

GRILLED STUFFED ONIONS

1½ cups herb-seasoned stuffing mix
1 cup (4 ounces) shredded sharp Cheddar cheese
1 teaspoon poultry seasoning
⅓ cup butter or margarine, melted
⅓ cup hot water
6 medium-size sweet onions
Vegetable cooking spray
Garnish: fresh oregano sprigs

• **Combine** first 5 ingredients, stirring until well blended; set aside.
• **Cut** each onion into 3 horizontal slices. Spread 2 tablespoons stuffing mixture between slices, and reassemble onions. Place each onion on a 12-inch-square piece of heavy-duty aluminum foil coated with cooking spray. Bring opposite corners together, and twist foil to seal.
• **Cook**, covered with grill lid, over medium-hot coals (350° to 400°) 25 minutes or until onions are tender. Garnish, if desired. **Yield:** 6 servings.

Note: For an alternative, cover and bake onions, unwrapped, in a lightly greased 11- x 7- x 1½-inch baking dish at 350° for 1 hour or until tender.

Margaret Johns
Tarpon Springs, Florida

RATATOUILLE-STUFFED ONIONS

6 large onions, cut in half crosswise
1½ cups finely chopped green bell pepper
¾ cup peeled, finely chopped eggplant
¾ cup finely chopped zucchini
¾ cup thinly sliced fresh mushrooms
¼ cup olive oil
1½ cups peeled, seeded, chopped tomato
½ cup dry white wine
¼ cup tomato paste
1½ teaspoons dried thyme
1 teaspoon dried rosemary
½ teaspoon salt
½ teaspoon freshly ground pepper
½ teaspoon garlic powder
⅓ cup pine nuts, toasted and divided
2 tablespoons grated Parmesan cheese

• **Cut** a thin slice from bottom of onion halves, if necessary, for onions to sit upright. Scoop out onions, leaving a ½-inch-thick shell. Chop onion centers to measure 1½ cups; reserve remaining onion for another use.

• **Place** shells, upright, in a 13- x 9- x 2-inch baking dish; add hot water to dish to depth of 1 inch.
• **Cover** and bake at 400° for 35 minutes or until tender. Remove shells; drain and keep warm.
• **Cook** reserved 1½ cups chopped onion, bell pepper, and next 3 ingredients in olive oil in a large skillet over medium-high heat, stirring constantly, 3 minutes or until tender.
• **Add** tomato and next 7 ingredients; bring to a boil, stirring constantly. Reduce heat, and simmer 12 minutes or until most of liquid evaporates, stirring often. Remove from heat; stir in 3 tablespoons pine nuts.
• **Spoon** evenly into onion shells; sprinkle with cheese and remaining pine nuts. Serve immediately. **Yield:** 12 servings.

SOUTH-OF-THE-BORDER ONION RINGS
(pictured at right)

The batter's spicy sweetness stems from the unexpected – sweetened condensed milk.

2 medium onions
1 cup self-rising flour
⅓ cup self-rising cornmeal
1 large egg, lightly beaten
½ cup sweetened condensed milk
¼ cup club soda
⅓ cup minced jalapeño pepper
Vegetable oil
Salt

• **Cut** onions into ¼-inch-thick slices, and separate into rings.
• **Combine** flour and cornmeal in a bowl. Combine egg, condensed milk, and club soda; add to dry ingredients, stirring until smooth. Stir in pepper.
• **Pour** oil to depth of 3 inches into a Dutch oven; heat to 375°.
• **Dip** onion rings in batter, coating well; fry, a few rings at a time, until golden. Drain on paper towels, and sprinkle with salt. Serve immediately. **Yield:** 4 to 6 servings.

Charlotte Pierce Bryant
Greensburg, Kentucky

South-of-the-Border Onion Rings

FRENCH ONION CASSEROLE

Your family will think the creamy sauce in this casserole was hard to make – only you will know that you relied on canned products.

3 medium-size sweet onions
2 tablespoons butter or margarine
1 (8-ounce) package sliced fresh mushrooms
2 cups (8 ounces) shredded Swiss cheese, divided
1 (10¾-ounce) can cream of mushroom soup, undiluted
1 (5-ounce) can evaporated milk
2 teaspoons soy sauce
6 (½-inch-thick) slices French bread
¼ cup finely chopped fresh parsley

● **Cut** onions crosswise into ¼-inch slices; cut each of the slices in half.
● **Melt** butter in a large skillet over medium-high heat; add onion and mushrooms, and cook, stirring constantly, until tender.
● **Spoon** mixture into a lightly greased 2-quart baking dish. Sprinkle with 1 cup cheese.
● **Combine** soup, milk, and soy sauce; pour over cheese. Top with bread slices, and sprinkle with remaining 1 cup cheese and parsley.
● **Cover** and chill 4 to 8 hours. Remove baking dish from refrigerator, and let stand at room temperature 30 minutes.
● **Cover** and bake at 375° for 30 minutes. Uncover and bake 15 to 20 additional minutes or until thoroughly heated. Let stand 5 minutes before serving. **Yield:** 6 servings.

Ellie Wells
Lakeland, Florida

SWEET ONION TARTS

½ (15-ounce) package refrigerated piecrusts
4 cups thinly sliced sweet onion (about 1¼ pounds)
2 tablespoons butter or margarine
1½ teaspoons fresh thyme or ½ teaspoon dried thyme
2½ tablespoons whipping cream
1 egg yolk
Dash of salt (optional)
Dash of pepper (optional)
2 tablespoons crumbled goat cheese (optional)
Garnish: fresh thyme sprigs

● **Unfold** piecrust; press out fold lines with a rolling pin on a lightly floured surface. Cut 2 (5½-inch) circles out of piecrust; fit circles into 2 (5-inch) round tart pans with removable bottoms. Place pans on a baking sheet. Prick bottom and sides of crusts with a fork.
● **Bake** at 450° for 8 minutes; transfer to wire racks to cool.
● **Cook** sliced onion in butter in a large heavy skillet over medium heat 30 minutes or until onion is tender, stirring often. Stir in thyme; remove from heat.
● **Combine** whipping cream, egg yolk, and, if desired, salt and pepper; stir into onion. Pour mixture into prepared crusts.
● **Bake** at 350° for 20 to 30 minutes or until golden, sprinkling with goat cheese after 15 minutes, if desired. Garnish, if desired. **Yield:** 2 (5-inch) tarts.

Note: You can double the recipe, but onion mixture will take longer to brown and become tender.

Chef Louis Osteen
Louis's Charleston Grill
Charleston, South Carolina

SPECIAL PEAS

QUICK!

2 pounds fresh unshelled English peas *
½ cup chopped purple onion
¼ cup chopped red bell pepper
2 tablespoons butter, melted
2 cups coarsely shredded iceberg lettuce
½ teaspoon salt
¼ teaspoon pepper
¼ teaspoon dried tarragon

● **Shell** peas; rinse well, and drain.
● **Cook** peas, onion, and red pepper in butter in a large saucepan over medium-high heat, stirring constantly, 6 minutes or until peas are crisp-tender. Reduce heat; gently stir in lettuce and remaining ingredients. Cover and simmer 5 minutes. Serve immediately. **Yield:** 4 servings.

* Substitute 1 (10-ounce) package frozen English peas for fresh.

Jane Maloy
Wilmington, North Carolina

SUGAR SNAP PEAS WITH BASIL AND LEMON

QUICK!

1 teaspoon olive oil
¾ pound Sugar Snap peas
¼ cup coarsely chopped fresh basil
½ teaspoon grated lemon rind
¼ teaspoon salt
¼ teaspoon ground white pepper
Lemon wedges

● **Heat** oil in a nonstick skillet over medium heat. Add peas; stir-fry 3 minutes or until crisp-tender. Sprinkle with basil and next 3 ingredients; stir-fry 1 minute. Serve immediately with lemon wedges. **Yield:** 2 servings.
Exchanges per serving: 2 Vegetable and 2 Fat.

Family Cookbook, Volume IV:
The American Tradition
Chicago, Illinois

♥ Per serving: Calories 95
Fat 2.6g   Cholesterol 0mg
Sodium 300mg

CAJUN BLACK-EYED PEAS

1 pound dried black-eyed peas
8 cups water
6 slices bacon
1 bunch green onions, chopped
1 large onion, chopped
1 green bell pepper, chopped
1 cup chopped fresh parsley
1 small jalapeño pepper, seeded
     and minced
3 cloves garlic, pressed
2 tablespoons Worcestershire
     sauce
¼ teaspoon hot sauce
1½ teaspoons salt
1 teaspoon pepper
¼ teaspoon dried oregano
¼ teaspoon dried thyme
1 pound smoked sausage, sliced
1½ cups chopped smoked ham
     (about ½ pound)
1 (14½-ounce) can Cajun-style
     stewed tomatoes, undrained

• **Sort** and wash peas; place in a large Dutch oven, and add water to depth of 2 inches above peas. Cover and let stand 8 hours or overnight.
• **Drain** peas, and return to Dutch oven. Add 8 cups water; bring to a boil. Cover, reduce heat, and simmer 30 minutes, stirring occasionally.
• **Add** bacon and next 12 ingredients; return to a boil. Cover, reduce heat, and simmer 30 minutes or until black-eyed peas are tender.
• **Add** sausage, ham, and tomatoes; return to a boil. Cover, reduce heat, and simmer 30 minutes. Remove bacon, if desired. **Yield:** 14 servings.

BAKED PLEATED POTATOES

6 small baking potatoes (about
     1½ pounds)
¼ cup butter or margarine, melted
1 tablespoon dried chives
1 teaspoon dried tarragon
1 teaspoon dried chervil
¾ teaspoon salt
½ teaspoon pepper

• **Wash** potatoes, and pat dry. Cut each potato crosswise into ⅛-inch slices,

cutting to, but not through, bottom of potato. Place on a baking sheet.
• **Combine** butter and remaining 5 ingredients; brush over potato. Bake at 400° for 1 hour or until done. **Yield:** 6 servings.

Sharon Avinger
Lexington, South Carolina

BAKED POTATO FRIES

QUICK!

1 cup Italian-seasoned
     breadcrumbs
1 (28-ounce) package frozen
     dinner fries
2 large eggs, lightly beaten
3 tablespoons butter or margarine,
     melted
1 teaspoon salt

• **Place** breadcrumbs in a shallow dish. Dip fries into egg, and dredge in breadcrumbs. Place fries in a single layer on an ungreased 15- x 10- x 1-inch jellyroll pan; drizzle with butter.
• **Bake** at 400° for 25 minutes or until golden, turning once. Sprinkle with salt, and serve warm. **Yield:** 8 servings.

Jennifer Schair
Woodstock, Georgia

MIXED VEGETABLE FRIES

2 medium-size red potatoes
2 medium turnips
2 large beets
2 large carrots
2 cups all-purpose flour
½ cup cornstarch
1 teaspoon salt
½ teaspoon ground red
     pepper
Vegetable oil

• **Peel** potatoes, turnips, beets, and carrots; cut vegetables into thin strips. Cover with cold water, and let stand 10 minutes. Drain.
• **Cook** vegetables in boiling water to cover 2 minutes; drain and plunge into cold water to stop the cooking process. Drain and pat dry. Set vegetables aside.

• **Combine** flour and next 3 ingredients in a large heavy-duty, zip-top plastic bag. Add vegetables; shake bag to coat.
• **Fry** vegetables, a few at a time, in deep hot oil (380°) in a Dutch oven 4 to 6 minutes or until golden. Drain and serve immediately. **Yield:** 6 servings.

GARLIC ROASTED POTATOES

QUICK!

3 tablespoons butter or margarine,
     melted
3 tablespoons olive oil
3 to 4 cloves garlic, minced
4 medium-size baking potatoes,
     cut into 1-inch pieces
¼ teaspoon salt
¼ teaspoon pepper
⅓ cup grated Parmesan cheese

• **Combine** all ingredients except cheese in a 13- x 9- x 2-inch pan, and toss gently to coat.
• **Bake** at 500° for 25 minutes or until potato is tender, stirring every 10 minutes. Sprinkle with cheese; bake 5 additional minutes. **Yield:** 4 servings.

Ellen W. Benjamin
Stephens City, Virginia

GOLDEN POTATOES

QUICK!

¼ cup grated Parmesan cheese
¼ cup all-purpose flour
1 teaspoon garlic salt
½ teaspoon salt
¼ teaspoon pepper
6 medium-size red potatoes
½ cup butter or margarine

• **Combine** first 5 ingredients in a large heavy-duty, zip-top plastic bag. Cut potatoes lengthwise into fourths; add to bag, and shake gently to coat. Set aside.
• **Place** butter in a 15- x 10- x 1-inch jellyroll pan; place pan in a 425° oven until butter melts. Add potato; return to oven.
• **Bake** 30 minutes, turning once. **Yield:** 4 to 6 servings.

Frances Christopher
Iron Station, North Carolina

QUICK POTATOES

QUICK!

1 tablespoon olive oil
1 large onion, chopped
2 cloves garlic, minced
½ cup chopped red bell pepper
½ teaspoon salt
¼ teaspoon pepper
¼ teaspoon hot sauce
3 cups unpeeled cubed red potato
2 tablespoons butter or margarine

• **Heat** oil in a 10-inch cast-iron skillet. Add onion and garlic; cook over medium heat, stirring constantly, until tender. Stir in bell pepper and next 3 ingredients; cook 2 minutes, stirring constantly. Add potato and butter, stir well.
• **Bake** at 400° for 20 to 30 minutes. **Yield:** 4 servings.

Pam Floyd
Birmingham, Alabama

BUTTERMILK-BASIL MASHED POTATOES

QUICK!

3½ pounds baking potatoes, peeled and cut into 1-inch cubes
1 onion, chopped
3 stalks celery, cut in half
12 cloves garlic, peeled
½ teaspoon salt
¾ cup nonfat cottage cheese
½ cup nonfat buttermilk
2 to 4 tablespoons chopped fresh basil
1 teaspoon salt
¼ teaspoon freshly ground pepper

• **Combine** first 5 ingredients in a Dutch oven; add water to cover. Bring to a boil; reduce heat, and simmer 20 minutes or until potato is tender. Drain; remove and discard celery. Mash potato mixture.
• **Position** knife blade in food processor bowl; add cottage cheese and buttermilk. Process until smooth, stopping once to scrape down sides.
• **Add** cottage cheese mixture to potato mixture; stirring mixture thoroughly until smooth. Stir in basil, 1 teaspoon salt, and pepper.

• **Cook** over low heat until heated. Serve immediately. **Yield:** 8 servings.

Ray Overton
Roswell, Georgia

♥ Per serving: Calories 205
Fat 0.3g Cholesterol 2mg
Sodium 639mg

ROASTED GARLIC MASHED POTATOES

4 heads garlic
1 tablespoon olive oil
4 pounds baking potatoes, peeled and cut into 1-inch pieces
½ cup butter or margarine
1 cup milk
1½ teaspoons salt
½ teaspoon pepper

• **Place** garlic on a square of aluminum foil; drizzle with oil, and wrap in foil.
• **Bake** at 425° for 30 minutes; remove from oven, and set aside.
• **Cook** potato in boiling water to cover 15 to 20 minutes or until tender; drain and transfer to a mixing bowl. Add butter and remaining 3 ingredients; beat at medium speed with an electric mixer until fluffy (do not overbeat).
• **Cut** off pointed ends of garlic; squeeze pulp from garlic cloves, and stir into potato mixture. **Yield:** 8 servings.

Adelyne Smith
Dunnville, Kentucky

WHIPPED CELERY POTATOES

2 pounds Yukon Gold or red potatoes
3½ cups water
1½ teaspoons salt
1 cup butter or margarine, divided
1 cup finely chopped celery
¼ cup finely chopped onion
¼ cup milk
¼ teaspoon salt
⅛ teaspoon pepper
⅛ teaspoon ground nutmeg

• **Combine** first 3 ingredients in a large saucepan; bring to a boil. Cover and

simmer 30 to 35 minutes or until tender; drain potatoes. Cool 5 minutes; peel and place potatoes in a large mixing bowl.
• **Melt** 2 tablespoons butter in a skillet; add celery and onion. Cook, stirring constantly, 3 minutes or until tender.
• **Add** celery mixture to potatoes; beat at low speed with an electric mixer until potatoes are mashed. Add remaining butter, milk, and remaining ingredients; beat at high speed until whipped. Serve immediately. **Yield:** 6 to 8 servings.

Chef David Everett
Dining Room at Ford's Colony
Williamsburg, Virginia

THUNDERBOLT POTATOES
(pictured at right)

QUICK!

1 cup fresh yellow corn, cut from cob (about 2 ears)
2 cloves garlic, minced
2 tablespoons butter, melted
4 large baking potatoes, peeled and quartered (about 2¾ pounds)
½ to ¾ cup warm milk
1 teaspoon salt
⅛ teaspoon pepper
2 teaspoons chili powder
½ teaspoon ground cumin
1 (4.5-ounce) can chopped green chiles, undrained
Garnish: chili powder

• **Cook** corn and garlic in butter in a skillet over medium-high heat, stirring constantly, until tender; set aside.
• **Cook** potato in boiling water to cover 20 minutes or until tender; drain.
• **Combine** potato, milk, and next 4 ingredients in a mixing bowl; beat at medium speed with an electric mixer until smooth. Stir in corn mixture and chiles. Garnish, if desired. **Yield:** 4 to 6 servings.

Thunderbolt Potato Patties: Combine 2 cups leftover Thunderbolt Potatoes, 1 large egg, and 2 tablespoons all-purpose flour. Shape mixture into 8 (3-inch) patties, and dredge in ½ cup cornmeal. Cook patties in ½ cup hot oil in a large skillet until golden, turning once. **Yield:** 8 patties.

Thunderbolt Potatoes;
Thunderbolt Potato Patties

LEFTOVER POTATO PANCAKES

QUICK!

1 (16-ounce) package frozen whole kernel corn, thawed
1 small onion, finely chopped
½ cup chopped green onions
2 teaspoons vegetable oil
2 cups mashed potatoes
½ cup all-purpose flour
2 large eggs, lightly beaten
¾ teaspoon salt
½ teaspoon freshly ground pepper
Vegetable cooking spray

● **Cook** first 3 ingredients in hot oil in a large nonstick skillet over medium-high heat, stirring constantly, until vegetables are crisp-tender. Remove from heat.
● **Combine** mashed potatoes, flour, and eggs, stirring well; stir in corn mixture, salt, and pepper.
● **Coat** a large skillet with cooking spray. Place skillet over medium heat until hot. Drop mixture by rounded tablespoonfuls into skillet; cook 3 minutes on each side or until golden, wiping skillet with a paper towel as necessary. Drain; serve with salsa. **Yield:** 14 (4-inch) pancakes.

Gwen Louer
Roswell, Georgia

SOUTHWESTERN POTATO BOATS

3 baking potatoes (1½ pounds)
1 (14.5-ounce) can chili-style stewed tomatoes, drained
½ cup chopped purple onion
2 tablespoons chopped fresh cilantro
2 tablespoons minced jalapeño pepper
¾ teaspoon salt
¼ teaspoon pepper
1½ teaspoons vegetable oil
1½ teaspoons white vinegar
¼ teaspoon minced garlic
¼ pound bacon, cooked and crumbled
1 (8-ounce) package shredded colby-Monterey Jack cheese blend

● **Pierce** potatoes with a fork, and bake at 350° for 1 hour or until done. Let potatoes cool to touch.
● **Cut** potatoes in half lengthwise, and scoop out pulp, leaving ¼-inch-thick shells. Reserve pulp for another use.
● **Combine** tomatoes and next 8 ingredients; stir in bacon and cheese.
● **Bake** potato shells at 350° for 5 to 8 minutes or until lightly browned; spoon tomato mixture evenly into shells. Bake 10 to 15 additional minutes or until cheese melts. **Yield:** 6 servings.

POTATO AND RUTABAGA GRATIN

1 large rutabaga
4 medium-size red potatoes
¼ cup butter or margarine
¼ cup all-purpose flour
2 cups whipping cream
1 teaspoon salt
¼ teaspoon ground white pepper
¼ teaspoon ground red pepper
Dash of ground nutmeg
½ cup grated Parmesan cheese
Garnishes: fresh sage and rosemary sprigs

● **Peel**, quarter, and thinly slice rutabaga. Peel and thinly slice potatoes.
● **Melt** butter in a heavy saucepan over low heat; add flour, stirring until smooth. Cook 1 minute, stirring constantly. Gradually add whipping cream; cook over medium heat, stirring constantly, until thickened and bubbly. Stir in salt and next 3 ingredients. Set aside.
● **Sprinkle** cheese in a 10-inch cast-iron skillet lined with parchment paper or aluminum foil, and arrange half of rutabaga slices over cheese.
● **Layer** ¾ cup sauce, potato slices, and ¾ cup sauce over rutabaga. Arrange remaining rutabaga slices on top, and add remaining sauce. Cover skillet tightly with aluminum foil.
● **Bake** at 400° for 1 hour; uncover and bake 20 additional minutes. Let stand 15 minutes. Invert onto a serving platter, and garnish, if desired. To serve, cut into wedges. **Yield:** 8 servings.

Steve Oldecker
Brunswick, Georgia

DUAL POTATO GRATIN

Garlic Mashed Potatoes ✳
3 tablespoons butter or margarine
3 large baking potatoes, peeled and cut into ⅛-inch slices
Butter-flavored cooking spray
2 tablespoons grated Parmesan cheese
Garnish: fresh chives

● **Spoon** Garlic Mashed Potatoes evenly into four lightly greased 4-inch gratin dishes, reserving ¾ cup mashed potatoes; set aside.
● **Melt** butter in a large saucepan; add half of potato slices in a single layer, and cook 2 minutes on each side or until tender. Drain on paper towels. Repeat procedure with remaining slices.
● **Layer** potato slices around outside edges of mashed potatoes forming circles. Pipe reserved mashed potatoes in center of each dish or roll mixture into balls, placing in center.
● **Coat** gratins with cooking spray, and sprinkle evenly with Parmesan cheese. Bake at 400° for 10 minutes or until lightly browned. Garnish, if desired. **Yield:** 4 servings.

✳ You can substitute 3 cups leftover mashed potatoes.

Garlic Mashed Potatoes

3 large baking potatoes
1 teaspoon vegetable oil
2 tablespoons butter or margarine
¼ cup sour cream
2 cloves garlic, crushed
½ teaspoon salt
¼ teaspoon pepper

● **Scrub** potatoes, and rub evenly with vegetable oil. Bake at 400° for 1 hour or until done.
● **Cut** potatoes in half; scoop out pulp, discarding skin. Combine potato pulp, butter, and remaining ingredients in a large mixing bowl, and beat at medium speed with an electric mixer until fluffy. **Yield:** 3 cups.

Jean Carriger
Lakeland, Florida

CHEESY SCALLOPED POTATOES

2½ pounds red potatoes
3 tablespoons butter or margarine
⅓ cup chopped green onions
⅓ cup chopped red bell pepper
1 clove garlic, minced
¼ teaspoon ground red pepper
2 cups whipping cream
¾ cup milk
¾ teaspoon salt
¼ teaspoon freshly ground pepper
1 cup (4 ounces) shredded Swiss
    cheese
¼ cup grated Parmesan cheese

● **Cut** potatoes into ⅛-inch-thick slices; set aside.
● **Melt** butter in a Dutch oven over medium-high heat; add green onions and next 3 ingredients. Cook 2 minutes, stirring constantly. Stir in whipping cream and next 3 ingredients.
● **Add** potato slices; bring to a boil over medium heat, and cook 15 minutes or until potato slices are tender, stirring gently. Spoon into a lightly greased 11- x 7- x 1½-inch baking dish; sprinkle with cheeses.
● **Bake** at 350° for 45 minutes or until bubbly and golden. Let stand 15 minutes before serving. **Yield:** 8 servings.

Lee Wells
Knoxville, Tennessee

PEPPERY POTATO CASSEROLE

8 large potatoes, unpeeled (about
    5 pounds)
¼ cup butter or margarine
1 green bell pepper, chopped
1½ tablespoons all-purpose
    flour
1½ cups milk
1 (6-ounce) package process
    cheese spread with garlic flavor
1 (6-ounce) package process
    cheese spread with jalapeño
    pepper
¼ to ½ teaspoon salt
¼ to ½ teaspoon pepper

● **Combine** potatoes and water to cover in a Dutch oven; bring to a boil over medium-high heat. Cover, reduce heat, and simmer 25 minutes or until tender; drain and cool.
● **Melt** butter in Dutch oven over medium-high heat; add chopped pepper, and cook, stirring constantly, 5 minutes or until tender. Remove pepper, reserving drippings in pan; set aside.
● **Add** flour to drippings, stirring until smooth. Cook 1 minute, stirring constantly. Gradually add milk, and cook over medium heat, stirring constantly, until mixture thickens and bubbles.
● **Stir** in cheeses, and cook, stirring constantly, until cheeses melt. Remove mixture from heat.
● **Peel** potatoes, and cut into thin slices. Layer potato in a lightly greased 13- x 9- x 2-inch baking dish, sprinkling each layer with salt, pepper, and chopped green bell pepper.
● **Spoon** cheese mixture over potato. Bake at 375° for 30 minutes or until heated. **Yield:** 8 to 10 servings.

Dianna Jolly
Harrison, Arkansas

HASH BROWN BAKE

3 cups frozen shredded potatoes
⅓ cup butter or margarine,
    melted
1 cup finely chopped cooked
    ham
1 cup (4 ounces) shredded
    Cheddar cheese
¼ cup finely chopped green bell
    pepper
2 large eggs, beaten
½ cup milk
½ teaspoon salt
¼ teaspoon pepper

● **Thaw** potato between layers of paper towels to remove excess moisture. Press potato in bottom and up sides of an ungreased 9-inch pieplate; drizzle with butter.
● **Bake** at 425° for 25 minutes or until lightly browned; cool on a wire rack 10 minutes.
● **Combine** ham, cheese, and green pepper; spoon into potato shell. Combine eggs and remaining 3 ingredients, stirring well; pour over ham mixture.

● **Bake** at 350° for 25 to 30 minutes or until set; let stand 10 minutes before serving. **Yield:** 6 to 8 servings.

Note: Assemble Hash Brown Bake ahead, omitting egg mixture, and store in refrigerator 8 hours. Let stand at room temperature 30 minutes. Combine eggs, milk, salt, and pepper; pour over ham mixture. Bake at 350° for 25 to 30 minutes.

Bernadette Colvin
Houston, Texas

CARROT HASH BROWNS
QUICK!

4 carrots, scraped and shredded
2 medium baking potatoes, peeled
    and shredded
½ small onion, grated
1 teaspoon salt
1 teaspoon pepper
3 tablespoons butter or margarine

● **Combine** first 5 ingredients, stirring mixture well.
● **Melt** butter in a large nonstick skillet over high heat; add carrot mixture, pressing firmly with a spatula or wooden spoon. Cook 5 to 6 minutes or until browned on bottom.
● **Invert** hash browns onto a plate; slide back into skillet. Cook 5 to 6 additional minutes or until browned on bottom.
● **Transfer** to a serving plate carefully, and cut into wedges. Serve immediately. **Yield:** 8 to 10 servings.

CARROT AND SWEET POTATO PUREE

This colorful vegetable casserole offers an excellent reason to try fresh sweet potatoes in the spring. You can make it ahead, too.

6 large sweet potatoes (about
   5¾ pounds)
1½ pounds carrots, scraped and
   cut into 1-inch pieces
½ cup butter or margarine,
   divided
1½ cups water
2 tablespoons sugar
½ teaspoon salt
½ teaspoon freshly ground black
   pepper
½ cup lemon low-fat yogurt
½ cup nonfat sour cream
¾ teaspoon ground nutmeg
¼ teaspoon ground red
   pepper
Garnish: fresh mint leaves

● **Scrub** sweet potatoes, and pat dry. Prick sweet potatoes several times with a fork.
● **Microwave** at HIGH 35 to 40 minutes or until tender, rotating sweet potatoes at 10-minute intervals. Let cool to touch; peel and cut into chunks.
● **Position** knife blade in food processor bowl. Add half of sweet potatoes, and process until smooth. Transfer sweet potato to a large bowl, and repeat procedure. Set aside.
● **Combine** carrot, 1 tablespoon butter, water, and next 3 ingredients in a medium saucepan.
● **Bring** to a boil, and cook 10 to 15 minutes or until carrot is tender and liquid evaporates.
● **Position** knife blade in food processor bowl. Add carrot, remaining butter, yogurt, sour cream, nutmeg, and red pepper; process until smooth. Stir carrot mixture into sweet potato. Reserve 2 cups sweet potato mixture.
● **Spoon** remaining sweet potato mixture into a lightly greased 3-quart shallow casserole; pipe or dollop reserved sweet potato mixture around edges of casserole.
● **Bake** at 350° for 30 minutes or until thoroughly heated. Garnish, if desired. **Yield:** 12 to 14 servings.

Note: To make ahead, assemble casserole; cover and refrigerate. Remove from refrigerator, and let stand 30 minutes. Bake at 350° for 45 minutes or until thoroughly heated.

GRILLED SWEET POTATOES

QUICK!

3 medium sweet potatoes (about
   2¼ pounds)
⅓ cup butter or margarine
¼ cup firmly packed brown sugar
1 tablespoon ground cinnamon

● **Wash** potatoes, and pat dry; cut in half lengthwise. Place each half in center of a 12- x 10-inch piece of aluminum foil; dot evenly with butter.
● **Combine** brown sugar and cinnamon; sprinkle evenly over potato. Wrap well, and place on food rack. Cook, without grill lid, over hot coals (400° to 500°) for 25 to 30 minutes or until done, turning foil packets once. **Yield:** 6 servings.

Bill Duke
Atlanta, Georgia

SWEET POTATO SOUFFLÉ

Attention R.E.M. fans: This home-style casserole is reportedly lead singer Michael Stipe's favorite side dish at Weaver D's.

6 small sweet potatoes (about
   3 pounds)
¾ cup sugar
3 large eggs, lightly beaten
½ cup butter or margarine, melted
3 tablespoons milk
2 teaspoons ground nutmeg
2 teaspoons vanilla extract
¾ teaspoon lemon extract

● **Peel** sweet potatoes, and cut into cubes. Cook sweet potato in boiling water to cover 15 to 20 minutes or until tender; drain and mash.
● **Combine** sweet potato, sugar, and remaining ingredients, stirring until smooth. Spoon mixture into a lightly greased 11- x 7- x 1½-inch baking dish.

● **Bake** at 350° for 30 minutes or until bubbly. **Yield:** 6 to 8 servings.

Dexter Weaver
Weaver D's Delicious Fine Foods
Athens, Georgia

BRANDIED YAMS

5 large sweet potatoes (about
   4¼ pounds)
¼ cup sugar
¼ to ⅓ cup brandy
3 tablespoons butter or margarine,
   melted
1 teaspoon salt
½ teaspoon ground nutmeg
½ teaspoon ground ginger
⅛ teaspoon pepper
1 tablespoon butter or margarine,
   melted
1 tablespoon grated orange rind
Garnish: orange slices

● **Cook** sweet potatoes in boiling water to cover 45 minutes or until tender; cool to touch. Peel and mash.
● **Stir** in sugar and next 6 ingredients; spoon into a greased 11- x 7- x 1½-inch baking dish. Brush with 1 tablespoon butter; sprinkle with orange rind.
● **Bake** at 350° for 25 to 30 minutes. Garnish, if desired. **Yield:** 8 servings.

Phyllis Taylor
Gillham, Arkansas

RUTABAGA WHIP

QUICK!

Mellow, earthy rutabagas join potatoes and become deliciously rich and fluffy. Even those who think they don't like rutabagas will like this.

2 pounds rutabagas, peeled and
   chopped
6 cups water
2 pounds baking potatoes, peeled
   and chopped
¼ cup butter or margarine,
   softened
½ cup whipping cream
1 teaspoon salt
½ teaspoon pepper

- **Combine** rutabagas and water in a Dutch oven. Bring to a boil; cook 15 minutes. Add potato; cook 15 minutes or until vegetables are tender. Drain.
- **Combine** vegetables, butter, and remaining ingredients in a large mixing bowl; beat at medium speed with an electric mixer until fluffy. **Yield:** 6 to 8 servings.

CREAMED SPINACH

QUICK!

¼ cup pine nuts
½ cup butter or margarine
2 cups whipping cream
⅔ cup grated Parmesan cheese
½ teaspoon salt
½ teaspoon freshly ground pepper
½ teaspoon freshly grated nutmeg
2 (10-ounce) packages fresh spinach, washed, trimmed, and shredded
Hot cooked grits or cornbread (optional)

- **Place** pine nuts in a shallow pan; bake at 350° for 5 minutes or until toasted, stirring occasionally. Set aside.
- **Bring** butter and whipping cream to a boil over medium-high heat; reduce heat to medium, and cook 15 minutes or until thickened, stirring often.
- **Stir** in cheese and next 3 ingredients. Add shredded spinach; cook over low heat until wilted, stirring often. Serve over grits or cornbread, if desired; sprinkle with pine nuts. **Yield:** 4 servings.

Ronda Carman
Houston, Texas

SKILLET SPINACH

QUICK!

4 slices bacon
2½ tablespoons balsamic vinegar
1 (10-ounce) package fresh spinach
2 tablespoons chopped pecans, toasted
¼ teaspoon salt
¼ teaspoon pepper
Pinch of sugar (optional)

- **Cook** bacon in a large skillet until crisp; remove bacon, reserving 1 tablespoon drippings in skillet. Crumble bacon, and set aside.
- **Add** vinegar to bacon drippings in skillet, and bring mixture to a boil over medium-high heat, stirring to loosen particles that cling to bottom.
- **Add** spinach to mixture in skillet; cook, stirring constantly, 1 to 2 minutes or until spinach is wilted. Stir in reserved bacon, pecans, salt, pepper, and sugar, if desired. Serve immediately. **Yield:** 2 servings.

Joel Allard
San Antonio, Texas

SPANAKOPITA

2 (10-ounce) packages frozen chopped spinach, thawed and drained
1 (8-ounce) package feta cheese, crumbled
1 tablespoon dried oregano
1 tablespoon dried dillweed
1 (16-ounce) package frozen phyllo pastry, thawed
⅓ cup butter or margarine, melted
Garnishes: crumbled feta cheese, tomato wedges, pepperoncini peppers, kalamata olives

- **Combine** first 4 ingredients in a bowl, stirring well.
- **Unfold** phyllo, and cut into 2 (13- x 9-inch) rectangles, keeping remaining phyllo covered with a slightly damp towel.
- **Place** 1 phyllo sheet in a buttered 13- x 9- x 2-inch baking dish; brush with melted butter. Place 1 phyllo sheet on top, allowing half of sheet to drape over one side of dish; brush portion in dish with melted butter. Repeat procedure with 15 more phyllo sheets, alternating sides of dish after each sheet so that each side of dish is covered.
- **Spread** spinach mixture evenly in dish; top with a phyllo sheet, and brush with melted butter. Fold 1 overhanging sheet on each side toward center; brush with butter. Top with a phyllo sheet; brush with butter. Repeat folding procedure with remaining overhanging phyllo sheets, topping each layer with a phyllo sheet and brushing with butter. Cut into 4 or 8 squares.
- **Bake** at 425° for 20 minutes or until lightly browned. Garnish, if desired. **Yield:** 4 main-dish servings or 8 appetizer servings.

The Cottage Inn
Eureka Springs, Arkansas

FRIED GREEN TOMATOES

4 large green tomatoes (about 2 pounds)
¼ cup sugar
¾ cup all-purpose flour
1 teaspoon salt
⅛ teaspoon pepper
3 tablespoons bacon drippings
6 tablespoons vegetable oil

- **Remove** and discard a thin slice from tops and bottoms of tomatoes; cut tomatoes into ¼-inch-thick slices.
- **Layer** tomato slices in a small deep dish, sprinkling each layer with sugar; let stand 1 hour. Drain tomato slices, reserving sugar liquid.
- **Combine** flour, salt, and pepper in a shallow dish; dredge tomato slices in mixture.
- **Heat** 1 tablespoon bacon drippings and 2 tablespoons oil in a large cast-iron skillet over medium-high heat until hot; add about one-third of tomato slices. Cook 2 to 3 minutes on each side or until golden. Drain on paper towels. Repeat procedure twice with remaining tomato slices, bacon drippings, and oil.
- **Drain** off pan drippings, reserving 1 tablespoon in skillet. Stir reserved sugar liquid until sugar dissolves. Add to drippings in skillet; bring to a boil.
- **Cook** over medium heat, stirring constantly, 1 minute or until slightly thickened. Place fried tomatoes on a serving platter, and drizzle with sugar mixture. Serve immediately. **Yield:** 4 to 6 servings.

Rose W. Roberson
Ocala, Florida

Herbed Tomato Tart

HERBED TOMATO TART
(pictured at left)

QUICK!

1 (17¼-ounce) package frozen
   puff pastry sheets, thawed
4 plum tomatoes, thinly sliced
1 teaspoon salt
1 (8-ounce) package shredded
   mozzarella cheese
1 (4-ounce) package crumbled feta
   cheese
¼ cup chopped onion
1 clove garlic, minced
¼ cup finely chopped mixed fresh
   herbs *
1 tablespoon olive oil

• **Roll** 1 pastry sheet into a 14-inch
square on a lightly floured surface; place
on an ungreased baking sheet. Cut 4 (12-
x 1-inch) strips from remaining pastry
sheet, and place along edges on top of
pastry square, forming a border. Reserve remaining pastry for another use.
• **Bake** at 400° for 10 minutes or until
golden. Transfer to a wire rack to cool.
• **Place** tomato slices in a single layer on
paper towels; sprinkle evenly with salt.
Let stand 20 minutes.
• **Place** baked pastry shell on baking
sheet; sprinkle with mozzarella cheese
and next 3 ingredients. Arrange tomato
slices in a single layer on top. Sprinkle
with herbs; drizzle with oil.
• **Bake** at 400° for 15 minutes or until
cheese melts; serve immediately. **Yield:**
4 servings.

✻ For the mixed fresh herbs, we combined oregano, basil, chives, sage, tarragon, rosemary, thyme, and dill. You
can substitute 1 tablespoon mixed dried
herbs for fresh.

BAKED RANCH TOMATOES

QUICK!

2 tomatoes, cut in half
Vegetable cooking spray
¼ teaspoon dried Italian seasoning
1½ tablespoons Ranch-style
   dressing
Garnish: fresh flat-leaf parsley
   sprigs

• **Place** tomato halves in an 8-inch
square pan. Coat top of halves with
cooking spray.
• **Bake** tomato halves at 350° for 16 to
20 minutes.
• **Sprinkle** with Italian seasoning, and
top evenly with dressing.
• **Broil** 3 inches from heat (with electric
oven door partially opened) 2 to 3 minutes or until tomatoes begin to brown.
Garnish, if desired. **Yield:** 4 servings.

CHILE-CHEESE STUFFED TOMATOES

QUICK!

4 medium tomatoes
½ cup sour cream
2 teaspoons all-purpose flour
1 tablespoon chopped green
   onions
½ cup (2 ounces) shredded
   Cheddar cheese
3 tablespoons canned chopped
   green chiles, drained

• **Cut** tomatoes in half horizontally;
scoop out pulp, leaving shells intact.
(Reserve pulp for another use.) Place
upside down on paper towels to drain.
• **Combine** sour cream and remaining 4
ingredients. Spoon into tomatoes. Place
in a greased 13- x 9- x 2-inch baking pan.
• **Broil** 5½ inches from heat (with electric oven door partially opened) 4 minutes or until heated. **Yield:** 8 servings.

Carol Barclay
Portland, Texas

VEGETABLE STUFFED TOMATOES

6 medium tomatoes
⅔ cup finely chopped zucchini
⅔ cup finely chopped green bell
   pepper
⅔ cup finely chopped onion
2 tablespoons olive oil
1 cup corn cut from cob
1 teaspoon sugar
¼ teaspoon salt
¼ teaspoon pepper
¼ teaspoon hot sauce

• **Cut** tops from tomatoes; chop tops,
and set aside. Scoop out pulp, leaving
shells intact; chop pulp, and set aside.
Place shells upside down on paper towels to drain.
• **Cook** zucchini, green bell pepper, and
onion in oil in a skillet over medium
heat 5 minutes, stirring constantly.
• **Stir** in chopped tomato tops and pulp,
corn, and remaining 4 ingredients.
Cover, reduce heat, and simmer 20 minutes, stirring often.
• **Spoon** into tomato shells, and place in
a shallow baking dish.
• **Bake,** uncovered, at 350° for 20 minutes. **Yield:** 6 servings.

Caroline Wallace Kennedy
Newborn, Georgia

SPINACH-TOPPED TOMATOES

1 (10-ounce) package frozen
   chopped spinach
2 teaspoons chicken-flavored
   bouillon granules
3 large tomatoes, cut in half
   crosswise
1 teaspoon salt
⅓ cup freshly grated Parmesan
   cheese
1 cup cornbread stuffing mix
½ cup butter or margarine, melted
1 large egg, lightly beaten
⅓ cup chopped onion
1 clove garlic, minced
¼ teaspoon pepper
Freshly grated Parmesan cheese

• **Cook** spinach according to package
directions, adding chicken bouillon
granules to cooking water; drain well.
• **Sprinkle** tomato with salt; place, cut
side down, on paper towels, and let
stand 15 minutes.
• **Combine** spinach, ⅓ cup Parmesan
cheese, and next 6 ingredients; set
aside.
• **Place** tomato, cut side up, on a baking
sheet. Top each tomato evenly with
spinach mixture.
• **Bake** at 350° for 15 minutes. Sprinkle
with additional Parmesan cheese; bake
5 additional minutes. **Yield:** 6 servings.

Kathy Zenor-Horine
Louisville, Kentucky

GINGERED ACORN SQUASH WITH SPICED CRANBERRY SAUCE

6 small acorn squash
1 cup water
½ cup butter or margarine
2 cloves garlic, minced
¼ cup whipping cream
1½ tablespoons minced fresh
     ginger
¾ teaspoon salt
¼ teaspoon ground white pepper
Spiced Cranberry Sauce

• **Cut** squash in half crosswise; remove and discard seeds. Place, cut side down, in a 15- x 10- x 1-inch jellyroll pan, and add 1 cup water.
• **Bake** at 350° for 1 hour or until tender; drain. Scoop pulp from bottom halves, leaving ½-inch shells; set shells aside. Scoop all pulp from remaining squash halves; mash all pulp.
• **Melt** butter in a large skillet; add garlic, and cook until tender, stirring often. Stir in squash pulp, whipping cream, and next 3 ingredients; cook over low heat, stirring constantly, until thoroughly heated.
• **Spoon** into squash shells; top and serve with Spiced Cranberry Sauce. **Yield:** 6 servings.

Spiced Cranberry Sauce

QUICK!

1 cup water
1 cup sugar
1 (3-inch) piece fresh ginger,
     peeled
1 firm pear, diced
1 teaspoon grated lemon rind
1 (12-ounce) package fresh or
     frozen cranberries
2 tablespoons fresh lemon
     juice

• **Bring** first 3 ingredients to a boil in a heavy saucepan, stirring constantly; boil 5 minutes.
• **Add** pear and lemon rind; return mixture to a boil, and cook 3 minutes, stirring occasionally. Stir in cranberries. Reduce heat, and simmer, without stirring, 3 to 5 minutes or until cranberry skins pop. Remove from heat; cool. Cover and chill.

• **Discard** ginger; cover and chill sauce up to 2 days. Stir in lemon juice just before serving. **Yield:** 2½ cups.

Sudi Swirles and Jan Hryharrow
Durham, North Carolina

BUTTERNUT SQUASH CASSEROLE

2 cups cooked, mashed butternut
     squash
3 large eggs
¾ cup sugar
⅓ cup butter, softened
⅓ cup milk
1 teaspoon ground ginger
½ teaspoon coconut flavoring
Crunchy Cereal Topping

• **Combine** first 7 ingredients; pour into a greased 8-inch square baking dish.
• **Bake** at 350° for 35 minutes. Sprinkle with topping; bake 10 additional minutes. **Yield:** 6 to 8 servings.

Crunchy Cereal Topping

QUICK!

1½ cups corn flake crumbs
¾ cup firmly packed brown sugar
½ cup chopped pecans
¼ cup butter or margarine, melted

• **Combine** all ingredients in a bowl. **Yield:** 2½ cups.

Fay Redding
Gastonia, North Carolina

HARVEST SQUASH MEDLEY

1 (1½-pound) butternut squash,
     peeled and seeded
2 sweet potatoes (about
     ¾ pound), peeled
3 tablespoons butter or margarine
¼ cup honey
¼ cup orange juice
½ teaspoon ground cinnamon
⅛ teaspoon ground nutmeg
1 tablespoon grated orange rind
2 small cooking apples, peeled,
     cored, and sliced
½ cup chopped walnuts, toasted

• **Cut** squash and sweet potatoes into ¾-inch chunks. Place in a greased 11- x 7- x 1½-inch baking dish; set aside.
• **Combine** butter and next 5 ingredients in a small saucepan. Bring to a boil over medium heat, stirring constantly; pour over squash and sweet potato.
• **Cover** and bake at 350° for 30 minutes. Uncover and stir in apple. Bake, uncovered, at 350° for 30 additional minutes or until tender. Sprinkle with walnuts. **Yield:** 6 to 8 servings.

Valerie Stutsman
Norfolk, Virginia

SAUTÉED CHAYOTE SQUASH WITH CILANTRO

1 (¾-pound) chayote squash, cut
     into wedges
2 tablespoons hot red chili oil
1 teaspoon chopped fresh cilantro
1 clove garlic, pressed
¼ teaspoon salt
1 cup bean sprouts

• **Cook** squash in oil in a skillet over medium-high heat, turning often, 10 minutes or until tender. Add cilantro, garlic, and salt; cook 2 minutes. Add sprouts, and serve immediately. **Yield:** 2 to 3 servings.

Chef Siegfried Eisenberger
Broadmoor Hotel
Colorado Springs, Colorado

ASIAN SPAGHETTI SQUASH

2 (2¼-pound) spaghetti squash
1 clove garlic
2 tablespoons sesame or olive oil
2 tablespoons vegetable oil
2 tablespoons rice wine vinegar
2 tablespoons soy sauce
1 teaspoon sugar
½ to 1 teaspoon dried crushed red
     pepper
½ cup sliced green onions
½ cup grated carrot
½ cup snow pea pods, cut
     lengthwise into thin strips
2 tablespoons sesame seeds,
     toasted

• **Cut** squash in half lengthwise; remove seeds. Place squash, cut side down, in a shallow baking dish or pan. Add water to dish to depth of ½ inch.

• **Bake** at 375° for 45 minutes or until skin is tender and strands may be easily loosened with a fork. Drain and cool slightly.

• **Position** knife blade in food processor bowl; add garlic, and process until finely chopped, scraping down sides, if necessary. Add sesame oil and next 5 ingredients. Process until blended, stopping once to scrape down sides; set garlic mixture aside.

• **Remove** spaghetti-like strands of squash, using a fork; discard shells. Combine squash, green onions, carrot, and snow peas in a large bowl. Add garlic mixture; toss gently. Sprinkle with sesame seeds. Serve immediately. **Yield:** 6 to 8 servings.

CAJUN VEGETABLE SAUTÉ

QUICK!

2 tablespoons olive oil
1 large zucchini, sliced
1 large yellow squash, sliced
1 medium onion, chopped
1 clove garlic, crushed
¼ cup chopped fresh chives
1 teaspoon Creole seasoning
½ teaspoon pepper
¼ teaspoon hot sauce

• **Heat** olive oil in a large skillet until hot; add zucchini and remaining ingredients, and toss gently. Cover, reduce heat, and cook 10 minutes or until crisp-tender. **Yield:** 3 to 4 servings.

Marie Wiker
Gaithersburg, Maryland

DILLED SUMMER SQUASH

2 tablespoons butter or margarine
2 cloves garlic, minced
2 teaspoons chopped fresh dill
6 green onions, cut into 1-inch pieces
2 yellow squash, thinly sliced
2 zucchini, thinly sliced
½ green bell pepper, sliced
⅓ cup water
¼ teaspoon salt
¼ teaspoon pepper

• **Melt** butter in a skillet; add garlic, dill, and green onions. Cook over medium-high heat 1 minute, stirring constantly. Add squash and zucchini; cook 1 minute, stirring constantly. Add bell pepper and remaining ingredients; cook 2 minutes, stirring constantly. Cover, reduce heat, and simmer 3 minutes or until crisp-tender. **Yield:** 4 servings.

Deborah D. Forster
Atascosa, Texas

SQUASH CASSEROLE

2½ pounds yellow squash, sliced *
½ cup butter or margarine
2 large eggs
¼ cup mayonnaise
1 (8-ounce) can sliced water chestnuts, drained
1 (4-ounce) jar diced pimiento, drained
½ cup chopped onion
¼ cup chopped green bell pepper
2 teaspoons sugar
1½ teaspoons salt
10 round buttery crackers, crushed (about ½ cup)
½ cup (2 ounces) shredded sharp Cheddar cheese

• **Cover** and cook squash in a small amount of boiling water 8 to 10 minutes or until tender; drain well, pressing between layers of paper towels to remove excess moisture.

• **Combine** squash and butter in a bowl; mash until butter melts. Stir in eggs and next 7 ingredients; spoon into a lightly greased shallow 2-quart baking dish. Sprinkle squash with crushed crackers.

• **Bake** at 325° for 30 minutes. Sprinkle with cheese; bake 5 additional minutes or until cheese melts. **Yield:** 8 servings.

* You can substitute 2½ pounds zucchini, sliced, for the squash.

Judy Frazer
Sylacauga, Alabama

VEGETABLE BURRITOS

QUICK!

1 pound fresh mushrooms, sliced
1 cup chopped onion
1 cup chopped green bell pepper
2 cloves garlic, crushed
2 teaspoons olive oil
1 (15-ounce) can kidney beans, drained
2 tablespoons finely chopped ripe olives
¼ teaspoon pepper
8 (8-inch) flour tortillas
½ cup nonfat sour cream
1 cup chunky salsa, divided
½ cup (2 ounces) shredded reduced-fat sharp Cheddar cheese
Vegetable cooking spray

• **Cook** first 4 ingredients in olive oil in a large nonstick skillet over medium-high heat, stirring constantly, until tender. Remove from heat; drain. Combine cooked vegetables, kidney beans, olives, and pepper.

• **Spoon** about ½ cup bean mixture evenly down center of each tortilla. Top evenly with sour cream, ½ cup salsa, and cheese; fold opposite sides of tortillas over filling.

• **Coat** a large nonstick skillet or griddle with cooking spray. Heat over medium-high heat until hot. Cook tortillas, seam-side down, 1 minute on each side or until thoroughly heated. Top each tortilla evenly with remaining ½ cup salsa. **Yield:** 8 servings.

Linda Askey
Birmingham, Alabama

❤ Per serving: Calories 259
Fat 6.2g Cholesterol 4mg
Sodium 443mg

MARINATED GRILLED VEGETABLES

Don't let the long ingredient list discourage you from making this delicious recipe. It's simply a variety of vegetables marinated in a vinaigrette dressing and then grilled.

½ cup balsamic vinegar
¼ cup extra-virgin olive oil
2 tablespoons dry white wine
1 tablespoon finely chopped shallot
½ tablespoon minced garlic
½ tablespoon freshly ground black pepper
1 teaspoon kosher salt
4 new potatoes, unpeeled
4 plum tomatoes, cut in half lengthwise
3 small zucchini, cut in half lengthwise
2 ears yellow corn, cut into 3-inch pieces
2 purple onions, cut into ¾-inch slices
2 fresh portobello mushrooms, quartered
1 pound fresh asparagus, trimmed
1 small eggplant, cut lengthwise into 1-inch slices
1 red bell pepper, quartered
1 yellow bell pepper, quartered
1 tablespoon chopped fresh chives
1 tablespoon chopped fresh rosemary
1 tablespoon chopped fresh parsley

• **Combine** first 7 ingredients in a large bowl; set aside.
• **Cook** potatoes in boiling water 5 minutes; drain. Cut potatoes in half.
• **Add** potato, tomato, and next 8 ingredients to vinegar mixture; toss gently to coat. Let stand about 1 hour, tossing mixture occasionally.
• **Remove** vegetables from marinade; reserving marinade.
• **Cook** vegetables, covered with grill lid, over medium-hot coals (350° to 400°) 12 to 14 minutes, turning vegetables once. Remove vegetables from grill as they are done.
• **Drizzle** remaining marinade over cooked vegetables, and arrange on serving plates.

• **Combine** chopped chives, rosemary, and parsley; sprinkle over vegetables. **Yield:** 8 servings.

Chefs' Café
Atlanta, Georgia

♥ Per serving: Calories 218
Fat 7.7g   Cholesterol 0mg
Sodium 312mg

CHINESE VEGETABLE POUCHES

1 tablespoon peanut oil
1 large carrot, scraped and chopped
1 pound cabbage, chopped
2 green onions, chopped
2 tablespoons soy sauce
2 tablespoons dry sherry
½ teaspoon sugar
¼ teaspoon ground ginger
1 clove garlic, pressed
¼ cup chopped roasted cashews
1 tablespoon cornstarch
2 tablespoons water
1 teaspoon hoisin sauce (optional)
1 (16-ounce) package egg roll wrappers (12 wrappers)
12 to 36 fresh chives
3 cups peanut oil
Garnishes: green onion fan, finely chopped carrot

• **Pour** 1 tablespoon peanut oil around top of a preheated wok, coating sides; heat at high (400°) 1 minute. Add carrot, and cook 1 minute, stirring constantly. Add cabbage, and cook, stirring constantly, 5 minutes or until tender. Stir in green onions and next 6 ingredients.
• **Combine** cornstarch, water, and hoisin sauce, if desired, stirring until smooth; add to cabbage mixture. Cook, stirring constantly, 1 minute or until thickened. Let cool.
• **Spoon** evenly into centers of wrappers; moisten edges with water. Bring ends to the middle, pressing together in center. Pull ends up and out to resemble a pouch. Tie chives around centers.
• **Pour** 3 cups peanut oil into a wok; heat to 375°. Fry pouches 4 minutes or until lightly browned, turning, if necessary. Drain on paper towels. Garnish, if desired. **Yield:** 12 pouches.

STEAMED VEGETABLES WITH GARLIC-GINGER BUTTER SAUCE

1 pound small fresh asparagus
3 carrots, scraped and cut into thin strips
3 small round red potatoes, sliced
Garlic-Ginger Butter Sauce
Chopped fresh parsley
Garnish: grated orange rind

• **Snap** off tough ends of asparagus. Remove scales with a vegetable peeler, if desired. Set aside.
• **Arrange** carrot and potato in a steamer basket; place over boiling water. Cover and steam 5 minutes.
• **Add** asparagus; cover and steam 5 minutes or until crisp-tender.
• **Arrange** vegetables on plates; drizzle with Garlic-Ginger Butter Sauce, and sprinkle with parsley. Garnish, if desired. **Yield:** 4 servings.

Garlic-Ginger Butter Sauce

QUICK!

⅓ cup butter or margarine
1 tablespoon brown sugar
½ teaspoon ground ginger
¼ teaspoon grated orange rind
1 clove garlic, minced

• **Combine** all ingredients in a saucepan. Cook over medium heat, stirring until sugar dissolves. **Yield:** ⅓ cup.

CHEESY SUMMER VEGETABLES

QUICK!

1 (10-ounce) package frozen sliced okra
1 (10-ounce) package frozen whole kernel corn
2 (10-ounce) cans diced tomatoes and green chiles, undrained
1 (15-ounce) can black beans, drained and rinsed
½ teaspoon garlic powder
½ teaspoon pepper
1 cup (4 ounces) shredded reduced-fat Cheddar cheese

• **Combine** first 6 ingredients in a large saucepan. Cover and cook over medium heat 8 minutes, stirring occasionally.

• **Sprinkle** with shredded cheese just before serving. Serve with a slotted spoon. **Yield:** 6 servings.

♥ Per 1-cup serving: Calories 177
Fat 4.2g   Cholesterol 12mg
Sodium 540mg

ROASTED VEGETABLES

QUICK!

4   small yellow squash, cut into
      1-inch slices
4   small zucchini, cut into 1-inch
      slices
2   large purple or sweet onions,
      quartered
2   tablespoons olive oil
2   teaspoons dried oregano
½ to ¾   teaspoon salt
½   teaspoon pepper
2   large red bell peppers, cut into
      ½-inch strips
2   large yellow bell peppers, cut
      into ½-inch strips
2   tablespoons balsamic vinegar
¼   cup chopped fresh parsley

• **Toss** first 3 ingredients with olive oil; spread in a large roasting pan, and sprinkle with oregano, salt, and pepper.

• **Bake** at 500° for 10 minutes. Add pepper strips; toss gently. Bake 10 additional minutes or until vegetables are tender and begin to char.

• **Place** in a serving bowl; cool slightly. Add vinegar and parsley; toss gently. **Yield:** 6 to 8 servings.

Ann Beckham
Macon, Georgia

TANGY MIXED VEGETABLES

QUICK!

1   (8-ounce) package sliced fresh
      mushrooms
1   green bell pepper, cut into 1-inch
      pieces
1   medium onion, chopped
1   (8-ounce) can pineapple chunks,
      undrained
4   medium carrots, scraped and
      sliced
½   teaspoon ground ginger
½   teaspoon curry powder
½   teaspoon dried basil
1   (8-ounce) can sliced water
      chestnuts, drained
1   tablespoon brown sugar
¼   teaspoon salt

• **Cook** first 3 ingredients in a large non-stick skillet 5 minutes or until tender, stirring often. Drain and set aside.

• **Drain** pineapple, reserving juice. Pour juice into skillet; set pineapple chunks aside. Add carrot and next 3 ingredients to juice; bring to a boil. Cover, reduce heat, and simmer 10 to 15 minutes or until carrot is tender.

• **Stir** in mushroom mixture, pineapple, water chestnuts, brown sugar, and salt; cook until heated. **Yield:** 4 servings.

Hilda Marshall
Bealeton, Virginia

SKILLET ZUCCHINI COMBO

(pictured on page 379)

QUICK!

3   ears fresh corn
1   onion, quartered and sliced
1   red bell pepper, cut into ½-inch
      squares
1   clove garlic, minced
2   tablespoons vegetable oil
3   medium zucchini, sliced
1   large tomato, peeled and
      chopped
2   jalapeño peppers, seeded and
      minced
1½   teaspoons chopped fresh basil
½   teaspoon dried Italian seasoning
½   teaspoon salt
¼   cup freshly grated Parmesan
      cheese

• **Cut** corn kernels from cobs, and set aside.

• **Cook** onion, bell pepper, and garlic in oil in a large skillet 5 minutes, stirring often.

• **Add** zucchini; cook 7 minutes, stirring often.

• **Add** corn, tomato, and next 4 ingredients; cover and cook over low heat 7 minutes, stirring often. Sprinkle with Parmesan cheese, and serve immediately. **Yield:** 6 side-dish servings or 3 main-dish servings.

Janice Rinks
Bluff City, Tennessee

VEGETARIAN SAUTÉ

QUICK!

1   medium onion, chopped
1   medium-size green bell pepper,
      chopped
1   medium zucchini, chopped
2   cloves garlic, minced
2   tablespoons olive oil
1   (14½-ounce) can chili-style
      stewed tomatoes, undrained
1   (15-ounce) can dark red kidney
      beans, rinsed and drained
½   teaspoon dried oregano
¼   teaspoon salt
¼   teaspoon pepper
½   cup (2 ounces) shredded
      Cheddar cheese

• **Cook** first 4 ingredients in olive oil in a large skillet over medium-high heat 5 minutes or until tender.

• **Stir** in tomatoes and next 4 ingredients; cook until heated. Sprinkle with Cheddar cheese. **Yield:** 4 servings.

Valerie Stutsman
Norfolk, Virginia

FRESH VEGETABLE SKILLET DINNER

2 tablespoons butter or margarine
1 large onion, sliced
2 medium-size yellow squash, sliced (about ½ pound)
1 large red or green bell pepper, sliced
2 large tomatoes, cut into wedges
¼ teaspoon salt
¼ teaspoon freshly ground black pepper
3 cups packed fresh spinach
1 cup (4 ounces) shredded Monterey Jack cheese

• **Melt** butter in a large skillet over medium-high heat; add onion, and cook 5 minutes, stirring often. Add squash and red or green pepper; cook 3 to 5 minutes, stirring often.
• **Add** tomato, salt, and pepper; cover, reduce heat, and simmer 5 to 10 minutes. Place spinach over mixture; cover and cook over low heat 3 additional minutes.
• **Add** shredded cheese; cover and cook 2 minutes or until spinach wilts and cheese melts. Serve immediately. **Yield:** 2 to 3 servings.

Chef Mark Abernathy
Juanita's
Little Rock, Arkansas

MEXICAN VEGETARIAN CASSEROLE

1 (15¼-ounce) can whole kernel corn, drained
1 (15-ounce) can black beans, rinsed and drained
1 (10-ounce) can whole tomatoes and green chiles
1 (8-ounce) carton sour cream
1 (8-ounce) jar picante sauce
2 cups (8 ounces) shredded Cheddar cheese
2 cups cooked rice
¼ teaspoon pepper
1 bunch green onions, chopped
1 (2¼-ounce) can sliced ripe olives
1 (8-ounce) package Monterey Jack cheese, shredded

• **Combine** first 8 ingredients; spoon into a lightly greased 13- x 9- x 2-inch baking dish. Sprinkle with green onions, olives, and Monterey Jack cheese.
• **Bake** at 350° for 50 minutes. **Yield:** 6 servings.

Margaret Monger
Germantown, Tennessee

VEGETABLE TAGINE

1 onion
1 green bell pepper
3 carrots, scraped
2 sweet potatoes
1 eggplant
4 plum tomatoes
3 zucchini
1 tablespoon olive oil
3 cloves garlic, minced
5 (16-ounce) cans fat-free chicken broth
2 tablespoons lemon juice
1 tablespoon honey
½ cup golden raisins
½ teaspoon ground cumin
½ teaspoon ground coriander
½ teaspoon ground turmeric
¼ teaspoon ground cinnamon
1 (15.5-ounce) can chickpeas, rinsed and drained
1 teaspoon salt
1 teaspoon pepper
2 tablespoons sambal oelek *

• **Chop** onion and bell pepper; cut carrots and next 4 ingredients into 2-inch pieces.
• **Cook** onion and bell pepper in oil in a Dutch oven 6 minutes or until tender, stirring often. Add garlic, and cook 1 minute, stirring often; stir in carrot, sweet potato, eggplant, tomato, broth, and next 7 ingredients. Bring to a boil over medium-high heat; cover, reduce heat, and simmer 30 minutes, stirring occasionally.
• **Stir** in zucchini, chickpeas, salt, and pepper; simmer 10 to 15 minutes or until zucchini is tender. Remove 1 cup cooking liquid; stir sambal oelek into liquid, and serve sauce with tagine. Serve over couscous. **Yield:** 4 servings.

✳ Sambal oelek is a hot chile paste. You can substitute any Asian or Mexican chile paste.

Liz Lorber
Atlanta, Georgia

♥ Per serving: Calories 205
Fat 2.8g Cholesterol 0mg
Sodium 421mg

NANNIE'S CORNBREAD DRESSING

2 cups self-rising flour
1 cup self-rising white cornmeal
2 cups buttermilk
3 large eggs
½ cup butter or margarine, melted
Vegetable cooking spray
1 cup chopped celery
1 to 2 medium onions, chopped
1 jalapeño pepper, seeded and chopped
¼ teaspoon pepper
2 to 3 cups chicken broth
Paprika
Garnish: celery leaves

• **Combine** flour and cornmeal in a large bowl; make a well in center of mixture.
• **Combine** buttermilk, eggs, and butter, stirring well; add to dry ingredients, stirring mixture just until moistened.
• **Place** a 9-inch square pan in a 400° oven for 5 minutes or until hot. Remove pan from oven, and carefully coat with cooking spray. Spoon batter into hot pan.
• **Bake** at 400° for 25 minutes or until lightly browned. Cool in pan on a wire rack; crumble into a large bowl.
• **Add** celery, onion, jalapeño pepper, and pepper, stirring well. Stir in enough broth to make a moist, thick mixture.
• **Spoon** cornbread mixture into an 11- x 7- x 1½-inch baking dish coated with cooking spray.
• **Bake** at 350° for 20 minutes or until lightly browned. Sprinkle dressing with paprika, and garnish, if desired. **Yield:** 8 servings.

Carole Miller Radford
Lincolnton, Georgia

GREEN CHILE-CORNBREAD DRESSING

QUICK!

¼ cup butter or margarine
2 cups chopped onion
1 cup sliced celery
1 (14½-ounce) can chicken broth
1 (17-ounce) can whole kernel
    corn, drained
2 (4.5-ounce) cans chopped green
    chiles, drained
3 tablespoons chopped fresh
    parsley
½ teaspoon salt
½ teaspoon poultry seasoning
¼ teaspoon dried oregano
¼ teaspoon pepper
6 cups cornbread crumbs
½ cup chopped pecans, toasted

● **Melt** butter in a large Dutch oven; add onion and celery, and cook over medium-high heat, stirring constantly, until tender.
● **Stir** in broth and next 7 ingredients. Add cornbread crumbs and pecans, tossing until moistened; spoon into a greased 13- x 9- x 2-inch baking dish, and cover with aluminum foil.
● **Bake** at 350° for 30 minutes or until dressing is thoroughly heated. **Yield:** 8 to 10 servings.

Charlotte Pierce Bryant
Greensburg, Kentucky

SAUSAGE-CORNBREAD DRESSING

1 pound ground pork sausage
2 medium onions, chopped
4 stalks celery, chopped
6 cups crumbled cornbread
3 cups white bread cubes,
    toasted
2 teaspoons rubbed sage
¼ teaspoon salt (optional)
1 teaspoon pepper
4 cups turkey broth
2 large eggs, lightly beaten

● **Combine** sausage, onion, and celery in a large skillet; cook over medium heat, stirring until sausage crumbles. Drain well.

● **Combine** cornbread, bread cubes, sage, salt, if desired, and pepper in a large bowl; stir in sausage mixture. Add broth and eggs, stirring well. Spoon mixture into a lightly greased 13- x 9- x 2-inch baking dish.
● **Bake** at 350° for 45 minutes or until lightly browned. **Yield:** 10 to 12 servings (9 cups).

Marjorie Henson
Benton, Kentucky

GRITS DRESSING

3 cups regular grits, uncooked
1 cup all-purpose flour
1 teaspoon baking powder
¼ teaspoon baking soda
2 large eggs
4 cups buttermilk
2 tablespoons vegetable oil
1 large onion, chopped
1 cup chopped celery
2 to 4 tablespoons dried sage,
    crumbled
1 teaspoon baking powder
2 large eggs, lightly beaten
1 (12-ounce) can evaporated milk
2 (14½-ounce) cans chicken
    broth

● **Heat** a well-greased 10-inch cast-iron skillet in a 325° oven 5 minutes or until skillet is hot.
● **Combine** first 4 ingredients in a large bowl; make a well in center of mixture. Combine 2 eggs, buttermilk, and oil; add to grits mixture, stirring just until dry ingredients are moistened.
● **Remove** skillet from oven, and pour batter into skillet. Bake at 325° for 1 hour or until firm in center, but not browned. Cool and crumble.
● **Combine** crumbled grits mixture, onion, and remaining ingredients in a bowl; pour mixture into a greased 13- x 9- x 2-inch baking dish.
● **Bake** at 325° for 50 minutes or until dressing is firm. **Yield:** 10 servings.

APPLE-WALNUT STUFFING

⅓ cup butter or margarine
1 large onion, finely chopped
2 stalks celery, finely chopped
1 cup chopped red cooking apple
1 cup chopped green cooking apple
2 cups white bread cubes, toasted
1 cup chopped walnuts
2 tablespoons dried whole-leaf
    sage
½ teaspoon dried rosemary
½ teaspoon dried thyme
1 large egg, beaten
½ cup milk
½ teaspoon salt
¼ teaspoon pepper

● **Melt** butter in a small skillet over medium-high heat; add onion and celery, and cook, stirring constantly, until tender.
● **Combine** apple, bread cubes, and next 4 ingredients in a large bowl; stir in vegetable mixture, egg, and remaining ingredients. Spoon mixture into a lightly greased 11- x 7- x 1½-inch baking dish.
● **Bake** at 350° for 30 minutes. **Yield:** 6 servings (4½ cups).

Crown Pork Roast with Apple-Walnut Stuffing: Purchase a well-trimmed (12-rib) crown pork roast (about 7 pounds), and season it with salt and pepper. Fold a piece of aluminum foil into an 8-inch square; place on rack in roasting pan. Place roast, bone ends up, on foil-lined rack. Bake at 325° for 1 hour. Cut a piece of foil long enough to fit around ribs. Wrap foil around ribs, and fold over tips of ribs. Spoon Apple-Walnut Stuffing into center of roast, and cover with additional foil. Insert a meat thermometer into roast without touching fat or bone. Bake at 325° for 1½ hours or until thermometer registers 160°. Remove foil from roast, and let stand 15 minutes before serving. **Yield:** 12 servings.

Susie Smith
Springville, Alabama

INDEX

Index 421

Index   423

METRIC EQUIVALENTS

The recipes that appear in this cookbook use the standard United States method for measuring liquid and dry or solid ingredients (teaspoons, tablespoons, and cups). The information on this chart is provided to help cooks outside the U.S. successfully use these recipes. All equivalents are approximate.

METRIC EQUIVALENTS FOR DIFFERENT TYPES OF INGREDIENTS

A standard cup measure of a dry or solid ingredient will vary in weight depending on the type of ingredient.
A standard cup of liquid is the same volume for any type of liquid. Use the following chart when converting standard cup measures to grams (weight) or milliliters (volume).

Standard Cup	Fine Powder (ex. flour)	Grain (ex. rice)	Granular (ex. sugar)	Liquid Solids (ex. butter)	Liquid (ex. milk)
1	140 g	150 g	190 g	200 g	240 ml
¾	105 g	113 g	143 g	150 g	180 ml
⅔	93 g	100 g	125 g	133 g	160 ml
½	70 g	75 g	95 g	100 g	120 ml
⅓	47 g	50 g	63 g	67 g	80 ml
¼	35 g	38 g	48 g	50 g	60 ml
⅛	18 g	19 g	24 g	25 g	30 ml

USEFUL EQUIVALENTS FOR LIQUID INGREDIENTS BY VOLUME

¼ tsp					=	1 ml	
½ tsp					=	2 ml	
1 tsp					=	5 ml	
3 tsp	=	1 tbls		=	½ fl oz =	15 ml	
		2 tbls	=	⅛ cup	= 1 fl oz =	30 ml	
		4 tbls	=	¼ cup	= 2 fl oz =	60 ml	
		5⅓ tbls	=	⅓ cup	= 3 fl oz =	80 ml	
		8 tbls	=	½ cup	= 4 fl oz =	120 ml	
		10⅔ tbls	=	⅔ cup	= 5 fl oz =	160 ml	
		12 tbls	=	¾ cup	= 6 fl oz =	180 ml	
		16 tbls	=	1 cup	= 8 fl oz =	240 ml	
		1 pt	=	2 cups	= 16 fl oz =	480 ml	
		1 qt	=	4 cups	= 32 fl oz =	960 ml	
					33 fl oz =	1000 ml	= 1 l

USEFUL EQUIVALENTS FOR DRY INGREDIENTS BY WEIGHT

(To convert ounces to grams, multiply the number of ounces by 30.)

1 oz	=	1/16 lb	=	30 g
4 oz	=	¼ lb	=	120 g
8 oz	=	½ lb	=	240 g
12 oz	=	¾ lb	=	360 g
16 oz	=	1 lb	=	480 g

USEFUL EQUIVALENTS FOR LENGTH

(To convert inches to centimeters, multiply the number of inches by 2.5.)

1 in					=	2.5 cm	
6 in	=	½ ft			=	15 cm	
12 in	=	1 ft			=	30 cm	
36 in	=	3 ft	=	1 yd	=	90 cm	
40 in					=	100 cm	= 1 m

USEFUL EQUIVALENTS FOR COOKING/OVEN TEMPERATURES

	Fahrenheit	Celcius	Gas Mark
Freeze Water	32° F	0° C	
Room Temperature	68° F	20° C	
Boil Water	212° F	100° C	
Bake	325° F	160° C	3
	350° F	180° C	4
	375° F	190° C	5
	400° F	200° C	6
	425° F	220° C	7
	450° F	230° C	8
Broil			Grill